Named Test Suite (592): We define a test suite, suitably named, that contains a set of tests that we wish to be able to run as a group.

Parameterized Test (607): We pass the information needed to do fixture setup and result verification to a utility method that implements the entire test life cycle.

Prebuilt Fixture (429): We build the Shared Fixture separately from running the tests.

Recorded Test (278): We automate tests by recording interactions with the application and playing them back using a test tool.

Scripted Test (285): We automate the tests by writing test programs by hand.

Setup Decorator (447): We wrap the test suite with a Decorator that sets up the shared test fixture before running the tests and tears it down after all the tests are done.

Shared Fixture (317): We reuse the same instance of the test fixture across many tests.

Standard Fixture (305): We reuse the same design of the test fixture across many tests.

State Verification (462): We inspect the state of the SUT after it has been exercised and compare it to the expected state.

Stored Procedure Test (654): We write Fully Automated Tests for each stored procedure.

Suite Fixture Setup (441): We build/destroy the shared fixture in special methods called by the Test Automation Framework before/after the first/last Test Method is called.

Table Truncation Teardown (661): We truncate the tables modified during the test to tear down the fixture.

Test Automation Framework (298): We use a framework that provides all the mechanisms needed to run the test logic so the test writer needs to provide only the test-specific logic.

Test Discovery (393): The Test Automation Framework discovers all the tests that belong to the test suite automatically.

Test Double (522): We replace a component on which the SUT depends with a "test-specific equivalent."

Test Enumeration (399): The test automater manually writes the code that enumerates all tests that belong to the test suite.

Test Helper (643): We define a helper class to hold any Test Utility Methods we want to reuse in several tests.

Test Hook (709): We modify the SUT to behave differently during the test.

Test Method (348): We encode each test as a single Test Method on some class.

Test Runner (377): We define an application that instantiates a Test Suite Object and executes all the Testcase Objects it contains.

Test Selection (403): The Test Automation Framework selects the Test Methods to be run at runtime based on attributes of the tests.

Test Spy (538): We use a Test Double to capture the indirect output calls made to another component by the SUT for later verification by the test.

Test Stub (529): We replace a real object with a test-specific object that feeds the desired indirect inputs into the SUT.

Test Suite Object (387): We define a collection class that implements the standard test interface and use it to run a set of related Testcase Objects.

Test Utility Method (599): We encapsulate the test logic we want to reuse behind a suitably named utility method.

Test-Specific Subclass (579): We add methods that expose the state or behavior needed by the test to a subclass of the SUT.

Testcase Class (373): We group a set of related Test Methods on a single Testcase Class.

Testcase Class per Class (617): We put all the Test Methods for one SUT class onto a single Testcase Class.

Testcase Class per Feature (624): We group the Test Methods onto Testcase Classes based on which testable feature of the SUT they exercise.

Testcase Class per Fixture (631): We organize Test Methods into Testcase Classes based on commonality of the test fixture.

Testcase Object (382): We create a Command object for each test and call the run method when we wish to execute it.

Testcase Superclass (638): We inherit reusable test-specific logic from an abstract Testcase Superclass.

Transaction Rollback Teardown (668): We roll back the uncommitted test transaction as part of the teardown.

Unfinished Test Assertion (494): We ensure that incomplete tests fail by executing an assertion that is guaranteed to fail.

D1568535

xUnit Test Patterns

The Addison-Wesley Signature Series

The Addison-Wesley Signature Series provides readers with practical and authoritative information on the latest trends in modern technology for computer professionals. The series is based on one simple premise: great books come from great authors. Books in the series are personally chosen by expert advisors, world-class authors in their own right. These experts are proud to put their signatures on the covers, and their signatures ensure that these thought leaders have worked closely with authors to define topic coverage, book scope, critical content, and overall uniqueness. The expert signatures also symbolize a promise to our readers: you are reading a future classic.

THE ADDISON–WESLEY SIGNATURE SERIES
SIGNERS: KENT BECK AND MARTIN FOWLER

Kent Beck has pioneered people-oriented technologies like JUnit, Extreme Programming, and patterns for software development. Kent is interested in helping teams do well by doing good — finding a style of software development that simultaneously satisfies economic, aesthetic, emotional, and practical constraints. His books focus on touching the lives of the creators and users of software.

Martin Fowler has been a pioneer of object technology in enterprise applications. His central concern is how to design software well. He focuses on getting to the heart of how to build enterprise software that will last well into the future. He is interested in looking behind the specifics of technologies to the patterns, practices, and principles that last for many years; these books should be usable a decade from now. Martin's criterion is that these are books he wished he could write.

TITLES IN THE SERIES

Test-Driven Development: By Example
Kent Beck, ISBN 0321146530

User Stories Applied: For Agile Software Development
Mike Cohn, ISBN 0321205685

Implementing Lean Software Development: From Concept to Cash
Mary and Tom Poppendieck, ISBN 0321437381

Refactoring Databases: Evolutionary Database Design
Scott W. Ambler and Pramodkumar J. Sadalage, ISBN 0321293533

Continuous Integration: Improving Software Quality and Reducing Risk
Paul M. Duvall, with Steve Matyas and Andrew Glover, 0321336380

Patterns of Enterprise Application Architecture
Martin Fowler, ISBN 0321127420

Beyond Software Architecture: Creating and Sustaining Winning Solutions
Luke Hohmann, ISBN 0201775948

Enterprise Integration Patterns: Designing, Building, and Deploying Messaging Solutions
Gregor Hohpe and Bobby Woolf, ISBN 0321200683

Refactoring to Patterns
Joshua Kerievsky, ISBN 0321213351

xUnit Test Patterns: Refactoring Test Code
Gerard Meszaros, 0131495054

For more information, check out the series web site at www.awprofessional.com

xUnit Test Patterns

Refactoring Test Code

Gerard Meszaros

✦Addison-Wesley

Upper Saddle River, NJ • Boston • Indianapolis • San Francisco
New York • Toronto • Montreal • London • Munich • Paris • Madrid
Capetown • Sydney • Tokyo • Singapore • Mexico City

Many of the designations used by manufacturers and sellers to distinguish their products are claimed as trademarks. Where those designations appear in this book, and the publisher was aware of a trademark claim, the designations have been printed with initial capital letters or in all capitals.

The author and publisher have taken care in the preparation of this book, but make no expressed or implied warranty of any kind and assume no responsibility for errors or omissions. No liability is assumed for incidental or consequential damages in connection with or arising out of the use of the information or programs contained herein.

The publisher offers excellent discounts on this book when ordered in quantity for bulk purchases or special sales, which may include electronic versions and/or custom covers and content particular to your business, training goals, marketing focus, and branding interests. For more information, please contact:

> U.S. Corporate and Government Sales
> (800) 382-3419
> corpsales@pearsontechgroup.com

For sales outside the United States please contact:

> International Sales
> international@pearsoned.com

 This Book Is Safari Enabled

The Safari® Enabled icon on the cover of your favorite technology book means the book is available through Safari Bookshelf. When you buy this book, you get free access to the online edition for 45 days.

Safari Bookshelf is an electronic reference library that lets you easily search thousands of technical books, find code samples, download chapters, and access technical information whenever and wherever you need it.

To gain 45-day Safari Enabled access to this book:

- Go to http://www.awprofessional.com/safarienabled
- Complete the brief registration form
- Enter the coupon code CCGA-REVE-DPXQ-5DE4-QFWR

If you have difficulty registering on Safari Bookshelf or accessing the online edition, please e-mail customer-service@safaribooksonline.com.

Visit us on the Web: www.awprofessional.com

Library of Congress Cataloging-in-Publication Data

Meszaros, Gerard.

XUnit test patterns : refactoring test code / Gerard Meszaros.
    p. cm.
Includes bibliographical references and index.
ISBN-13: 978-0-13-149505-0 (hardback : alk. paper)
ISBN-10: 0-13-149505-4
1. Software patterns. 2. Computer software—Testing. I. Title.
QA76.76.P37M49 2007
005.1—dc22

                        2006103488

ISBN 13: 978-0-13-149505-0
ISBN 10:   0-13-149505-4
Text printed in the United States on recycled paper at Courier in Westford, Massachusetts.
Second printing, August 2007

This book is dedicated to the memory of Denis Clelland, who recruited me away from Nortel in 1995 to work at ClearStream Consulting and thereby gave me the opportunity to have the experiences that led to this book. Sadly, Denis passed away on April 27, 2006, while I was finalizing the second draft.

Contents

Visual Summary of the Pattern Language

Goals, Principles, and Smells

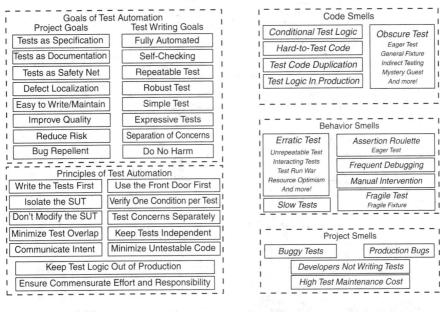

Goals of Test Automation

Project Goals	Test Writing Goals
Tests as Specification	Fully Automated
Tests as Documentation	Self-Checking
Tests as Safety Net	Repeatable Test
Defect Localization	Robust Test
Easy to Write/Maintain	Simple Test
Improve Quality	Expressive Tests
Reduce Risk	Separation of Concerns
Bug Repellent	Do No Harm

Principles of Test Automation

Write the Tests First	Use the Front Door First
Isolate the SUT	Verify One Condition per Test
Don't Modify the SUT	Test Concerns Separately
Minimize Test Overlap	Keep Tests Independent
Communicate Intent	Minimize Untestable Code

Keep Test Logic Out of Production

Ensure Commensurate Effort and Responsibility

Code Smells

Conditional Test Logic

Hard-to-Test Code

Test Code Duplication

Test Logic In Production

Obscure Test
Eager Test
General Fixture
Indirect Testing
Mystery Guest
And more!

Behavior Smells

Erratic Test
Unrepeatable Test
Interacting Tests
Test Run War
Resource Optimism
And more!

Slow Tests

Assertion Roulette
Eager Test

Frequent Debugging

Manual Intervention

Fragile Test
Fragile Fixture

Project Smells

Buggy Tests

Production Bugs

Developers Not Writing Tests

High Test Maintenance Cost

Key to Visual Summary of the Pattern Language

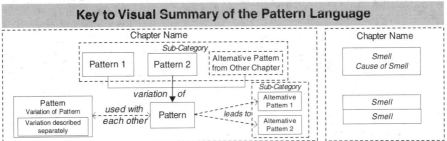

The Patterns

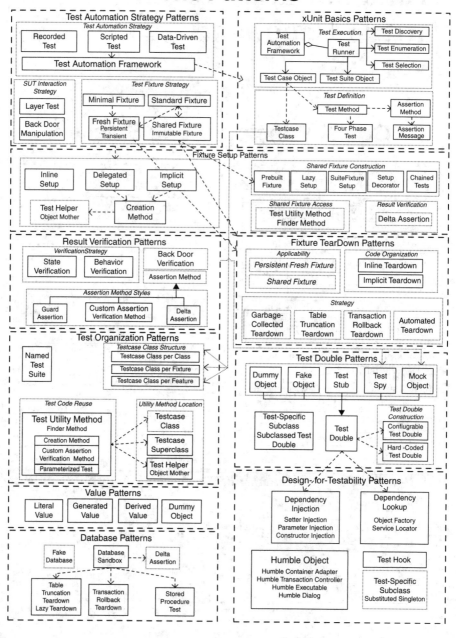

Foreword

If you go to junit.org, you'll see a quote from me: "Never in the field of software development have so many owed so much to so few lines of code." JUnit has been criticized as a minor thing, something any reasonable programmer could produce in a weekend. This is true, but utterly misses the point. The reason JUnit is important, and deserves the Churchillian knock-off, is that the presence of this tiny tool has been essential to a fundamental shift for many programmers: Testing has moved to a front and central part of programming. People have advocated it before, but JUnit made it happen more than anything else.

It's more than just JUnit, of course. Ports of JUnit have been written for lots of programming languages. This loose family of tools, often referred to as xUnit tools, has spread far beyond its java roots. (And of course the roots weren't really in Java—Kent Beck wrote this code for Smalltalk years before.)

xUnit tools, and more importantly their philosophy, offer up huge opportunities to programming teams—the opportunity to write powerful regression test suites that enable teams to make drastic changes to a code-base with far less risk; the opportunity to re-think the design process with Test Driven Development.

But with these opportunities come new problems and new techniques. Like any tool, the xUnit family can be used well or badly. Thoughtful people have figured out various ways to use xUnit, to organize the tests and data effectively. Like the early days of objects, much of the knowledge to really use the tools is hidden in the heads of its skilled users. Without this hidden knowledge you really can't reap the full benefits.

It was nearly twenty years ago when people in the object-oriented community realized this problem for objects and began to formulate an answer. The answer was to describe their hidden knowledge in the form of patterns. Gerard Meszaros was one of the pioneers in doing this. When I first started exploring patterns, Gerard was one of the leaders that I learned from. Like many in the patterns world, Gerard also was an early adopter of eXtreme Programming, and thus worked with xUnit tools from the earliest days. So it's entirely logical that he should have taken on the task of capturing that expert knowledge in the form of patterns.

I've been excited by this project since I first heard about it. (I had to launch a commando raid to steal this book from Bob Martin because I wanted it to grace my series instead.) Like any good patterns book it provides knowledge to new people in the field, and just as important, provides the vocabulary and foundations for experienced practitioners to pass their knowledge on to their colleagues. For many people, the famous Gang of Four book *Design Patterns* unlocked the hidden gems of object-oriented design. This book does the same for xUnit.

Martin Fowler
Series Editor
Chief Scientist, ThoughtWorks

Preface

The Value of Self-Testing Code

In Chapter 4 of *Refactoring* [Ref], Martin Fowler writes:

> *If you look at how most programmers spend their time, you'll find that writing code is actually a small fraction. Some time is spent figuring out what ought to be going on, some time is spent designing, but most time is spent debugging. I'm sure every reader can remember long hours of debugging, often long into the night. Every programmer can tell a story of a bug that took a whole day (or more) to find. Fixing the bug is usually pretty quick, but finding it is a nightmare. And then when you do fix a bug, there's always a chance that anther one will appear and that you might not even notice it until much later. Then you spend ages finding that bug.*

Some software is very difficult to test manually. In these cases, we are often forced into writing test programs.

I recall a project I was working on in 1996. My task was to build an event framework that would let client software register for an event and be notified when some other software raised that event (the Observer [GOF] pattern). I could not think of a way to test this framework without writing some sample client software. I had about 20 different scenarios I needed to test, so I coded up each scenario with the requisite number of observers, events, and event raisers. At first, I logged what was occurring in the console and scanned it manually. This scanning became very tedious very quickly.

Being quite lazy, I naturally looked for an easier way to perform this testing. For each test I populated a Dictionary indexed by the expected event and the expected receiver of it with the name of the receiver as the value. When a particular receiver was notified of the event, it looked in the Dictionary for the entry indexed by itself and the event it had just received. If this entry existed, the receiver removed the entry. If it didn't, the receiver added the entry with an error message saying it was an unexpected event notification.

After running all the tests, the test program merely looked in the Dictionary and printed out its contents if it was not empty. As a result, running all of my tests had a nearly zero cost. The tests either passed quietly or spewed a list of test failures. I had unwittingly discovered the concept of a *Mock Object* (page 544) and a *Test Automation Framework* (page 298) out of necessity!

My First XP Project

In late 1999, I attended the OOPSLA conference, where I picked up a copy of Kent Beck's new book, *eXtreme Programming Explained* [XPE]. I was used to doing iterative and incremental development and already believed in the value of automated unit testing, although I had not tried to apply it universally. I had a lot of respect for Kent, whom I had known since the first PLoP[1] conference in 1994. For all these reasons, I decided that it was worth trying to apply eXtreme Programming on a ClearStream Consulting project. Shortly after OOPSLA, I was fortunate to come across a suitable project for trying out this development approach—namely, an add-on application that interacted with an existing database but had no user interface. The client was open to developing software in a different way.

We started doing eXtreme Programming "by the book" using pretty much all of the practices it recommended, including pair programming, collective ownership, and test-driven development. Of course, we encountered a few challenges in figuring out how to test some aspects of the behavior of the application, but we still managed to write tests for most of the code. Then, as the project progressed, I started to notice a disturbing trend: It was taking longer and longer to implement seemingly similar tasks.

I explained the problem to the developers and asked them to record on each task card how much time had been spent writing new tests, modifying existing tests, and writing the production code. Very quickly, a trend emerged. While the time spent writing new tests and writing the production code seemed to be staying more or less constant, the amount of time spent modifying existing tests was increasing and the developers' estimates were going up as a result. When a developer asked me to pair on a task and we spent 90% of the time modifying existing tests to accommodate a relatively minor change, I knew we had to change something, and soon!

When we analyzed the kinds of compile errors and test failures we were experiencing as we introduced the new functionality, we discovered that many of the tests were affected by changes to methods of the system under test (SUT). This came as no surprise, of course. What *was* surprising was that most of the impact was felt during the fixture setup part of the test and that the changes were not affecting the core logic of the tests.

This revelation was an important discovery because it showed us that we had the knowledge about how to create the objects of the SUT scattered across most of the tests. In other words, the tests knew too much about nonessential

---

[1] The Pattern Languages of Programs conference.

parts of the behavior of the SUT. I say "nonessential" because most of the affected tests did not care about *how* the objects in the fixture were created; they *were* interested in ensuring that those objects were in the correct state. Upon further examination, we found that many of the tests were creating identical or nearly identical objects in their test fixtures.

The obvious solution to this problem was to factor out this logic into a small set of *Test Utility Methods* (page 599). There were several variations:

- When we had a bunch of tests that needed identical objects, we simply created a method that returned that kind of object ready to use. We now call these *Creation Methods* (page 415).

- Some tests needed to specify different values for some attribute of the object. In these cases, we passed that attribute as a parameter to the *Parameterized Creation Method* (see *Creation Method*).

- Some tests wanted to create a malformed object to ensure that the SUT would reject it. Writing a separate *Parameterized Creation Method* for each attribute cluttered the signature of our *Test Helper* (page 643), so we created a valid object and then replaced the value of the *One Bad Attribute* (see *Derived Value on page* 718).

We had discovered what would become[2] our first test automation patterns.

Later, when tests started failing because the database did not like the fact that we were trying to insert another object with the same key that had a unique constraint, we added code to generate the unique key programmatically. We called this variant an *Anonymous Creation Method* (see *Creation Method*) to indicate the presence of this added behavior.

Identifying the problem that we now call a *Fragile Test* (page 239) was an important event on this project, and the subsequent definition of its solution patterns saved this project from possible failure. Without this discovery we would, at best, have abandoned the automated unit tests that we had already built. At worst, the tests would have reduced our productivity so much that we would have been unable to deliver on our commitments to the client. As it turned out, we were able to deliver what we had promised and with very good quality. Yes, the testers[3] still found bugs in our code because we were definitely missing some tests. Introducing the changes needed to fix those bugs, once we had figured

---

[2] Technically, they are not truly patterns until they have been discovered by three independent project teams.

[3] The testing function is sometimes referred to as "Quality Assurance." This usage is, strictly speaking, incorrect.

out what the missing tests needed to look like, was a relatively straightforward process, however.

We were hooked. Automated unit testing and test-driven development really did work, and we have been using them consistently ever since.

As we applied the practices and patterns on subsequent projects, we have run into new problems and challenges. In each case, we have "peeled the onion" to find the root cause and come up with ways to address it. As these techniques have matured, we have added them to our repertoire of techniques for automated unit testing.

We first described some of these patterns in a paper presented at XP2001. In discussions with other participants at that and subsequent conferences, we discovered that many of our peers were using the same or similar techniques. That elevated our methods from "practice" to "pattern" (a recurring solution to a recurring problem in a context). The first paper on test smells [RTC] was presented at the same conference, building on the concept of code smells first described in [Ref].

My Motivation

I am a great believer in the value of automated unit testing. I practiced software development without it for the better part of two decades, and I know that my professional life is much better with it than without it. I believe that the xUnit framework and the automated tests it enables are among the truly great advances in software development. I find it very frustrating when I see companies trying to adopt automated unit testing but being unsuccessful because of a lack of key information and skills.

As a software development consultant with ClearStream Consulting, I see a lot of projects. Sometimes I am called in early on a project to help clients make sure they "do things right." More often than not, however, I am called in when things are already off the rails. As a result, I see a lot of "worst practices" that result in test smells. If I am lucky and I am called early enough, I can help the client recover from the mistakes. If not, the client will likely muddle through less than satisfied with how TDD and automated unit testing worked—and the word goes out that automated unit testing is a waste of time.

In hindsight, most of these mistakes and best practices are easily avoidable given the right knowledge at the right time. But how do you obtain that knowledge without making the mistakes for yourself? At the risk of sounding self-serving, hiring someone who has the knowledge is the most time-efficient way of learning any new practice or technology. According to Gerry Weinberg's

"Law of Raspberry Jam" [SoC],[4] taking a course or reading a book is a much less effective (though less expensive) alternative. I hope that by writing down a lot of these mistakes and suggesting ways to avoid them, I can save you a lot of grief on your project, whether it is fully agile or just more agile than it has been in the past—the "Law of Raspberry Jam" not withstanding.

Who This Book Is For

I have written this book primarily for software developers (programmers, designers, and architects) who want to write better tests and for the managers and coaches who need to understand what the developers are doing and why the developers need to be cut enough slack so they can learn to do it even better! The focus here is on developer tests and customer tests that are automated using xUnit. In addition, some of the higher-level patterns apply to tests that are automated using technologies other than xUnit. Rick Mugridge and Ward Cunningham have written an excellent book on Fit [FitB], and they advocate many of the same practices.

Developers will likely want to read the book from cover to cover, but they should focus on skimming the reference chapters rather than trying to read them word for word. The emphasis should be on getting an overall idea of which patterns exist and how they work. Developers can then return to a particular pattern when the need for it arises. The first few elements (up to and include the "When to Use It" section) of each pattern should provide this overview.

Managers and coaches might prefer to focus on reading Part I, *The Narratives,* and perhaps Part II, *The Test Smells.* They might also need to read Chapter 18, *Test Strategy Patterns,* as these are decisions they need to understand and provide support to the developers as they work their way through these patterns. At a minimum, managers should read Chapter 3, *Goals of Test Automation.*

About the Cover Photo

Every book in the Martin Fowler Signature Series features a picture of a bridge on the cover. One of the thoughts I had when Martin Fowler asked if he could "steal me for his series" was "Which bridge should I put on the cover?" I thought about the ability of testing to avoid catastrophic failures of software

---

[4] The Law of Raspberry Jam: "The wider you spread it, the thinner it gets."

and how that related to bridges. Several famous bridge failures immediately came to mind, including "Galloping Gertie" (the Tacoma Narrows bridge) and the Iron Workers Memorial Bridge in Vancouver (named for the iron workers who died when a part of it collapsed during construction).

After further reflection, it just did not seem right to claim that testing might have prevented these failures, so I chose a bridge with a more personal connection. The picture on the cover shows the New River Gorge bridge in West Virginia. I first passed over and subsequently paddled under this bridge on a whitewater kayaking trip in the late 1980s. The style of the bridge is also relevant to this book's content: The complex arch structure underneath the bridge is largely hidden from those who use it to get to the other side of the gorge. The road deck is completely level and four lanes wide, resulting in a very smooth passage. In fact, at night it is quite possible to remain completely oblivious to the fact that one is thousands of feet above the valley floor. A good test automation infrastructure has the same effect: Writing tests is easy because most of the complexity lies hidden beneath the road bed.

Colophon

This book's manuscript was written using XML, which I published to HTML for previewing on my Web site. I edited the XML using Eclipse and the XML Buddy plug-in. The HTML was generated using a Ruby program that I first obtained from Martin Fowler and which I then evolved quite extensively as I evolved my custom markup language. Code samples were written, compiled, and executed in (mostly) Eclipse and were inserted into the HTML automatically by XML tag handlers (one of the main reasons for using Ruby instead of XSLT). This gave me the ability to "publish early, publish often" to the Web site. I could also generate a single Word or PDF document for reviewers from the source, although this required some manual steps.

Acknowledgments

While this book is largely a solo writing effort, many people have contributed to it in their own ways. Apologies in advance to anyone whom I may have missed.

People who know me well may wonder how I found enough time to write a book like this. When I am not working, I am usually off doing various (some would say "extreme") outdoor sports, such as back-country (extreme) skiing, whitewater (extreme) kayaking, and mountain (extreme) biking. Personally, I do not agree with this application of the "extreme" adjective to my activities any more than I agree with its use for highly iterative and incremental (extreme) programming. Nevertheless, the question of where I found the time to write this book is a valid one. I must give special thanks to my friend Heather Armitage, with whom I engage in most of the above activities. She has driven many long hours on the way to or from these adventures with me hunched over my laptop computer in the passenger seat working on this book. Also, thanks go to Alf Skrastins, who loves to drive all his friends to back-country skiing venues west of Calgary in his Previa. Also, thanks to the operators of the various back-country ski lodges who let me recharge my laptop from their generators so I could work on the book while on vacation—Grania Devine at Selkirk Lodge, Tannis Dakin at Sorcerer Lodge, and Dave Flear and Aaron Cooperman at Sol Mountain Touring. Without their help, this book would have taken much longer to write!

As usual, I'd like to thank all my reviewers, both official and unofficial. Robert C. ("Uncle Bob") Martin reviewed an early draft. The official reviewers of the first "official" draft were Lisa Crispin and Rick Mugridge. Lisa Crispin, Jeremy Miller, Alistair Duguid, Michael Hedgpeth, and Andrew Stopford reviewed the second draft.

Thanks to my "shepherds" from the various PLoP conferences who provided feedback on drafts of these patterns—Michael Stal, Danny Dig, and especially Joe Yoder; they provided expert comments on my experiments with the pattern form. I would also like to thank the members of the PLoP workshop group on Pattern Languages at PLoP 2004 and especially Eugene Wallingford, Ralph Johnson, and Joseph Bergin. Brian Foote and the SAG group at UIUC posted several gigabytes of MP3's of the review sessions in which they discussed the early drafts of the book. Their comments caused me to rewrite from scratch at least one of the narrative chapters.

Many people e-mailed me comments about the material posted on my Web site at http://xunitpatterns.com or posted comments on the Yahoo! group; they provided very timely feedback on the sometimes very draft-like material I had posted there. These folks included Javid Jamae, Philip Nelson, Tomasz Gajewski, John Hurst, Sven Gorts, Bradley T. Landis, Cédric Beust, Joseph Pelrine, Sebastian Bergmann, Kevin Rutherford, Scott W. Ambler, J. B. Rainsberger, Oli Bye, Dale Emery, David Nunn, Alex Chaffee, Burkhardt Hufnagel, Johannes Brodwall, Bret Pettichord, Clint Shank, Sunil Joglekar, Rachel Davies, Nat Pryce, Paul Hodgetts, Owen Rogers, Amir Kolsky, Kevin Lawrence, Alistair Cockburn, Michael Feathers, and Joe Schmetzer. Special thanks go to Neal Norwitz, Markus Gaelli, Stephane Ducasse, and Stefan Reichhart, who provided copious feedback as unofficial reviewers.

Quite a few people sent me e-mails describing their favorite pattern or special feature from their member of the xUnit family. Most of these were variations on patterns I had already documented; I've included them in this book as aliases or implementation variations as appropriate. A few were more esoteric patterns that I had to leave out for space reasons—for that, I apologize.

Many of the ideas described in this book came from projects I worked on with my colleagues from ClearStream Consulting. We all pushed one another to find better ways of doing things back in the early days of eXtreme Programming when few—if any—resources were available. It was this single-minded determination that led to many of the more useful techniques described here. Those colleagues are Jennitta Andrea, Ralph Bohnet, Dave Braat, Russel Bryant, Greg Cook, Geoff Hardy, Shaun Smith, and Thomas (T2) Tannahill. Many of them also provided early reviews of various chapters. Greg also provided many of the code samples in Chapter 25, *Database Patterns*, while Ralph set up my CVS repository and automated build process for the Web site. I would also like to thank my bosses at ClearStream, who let me take time off from consulting engagements to work on the book and for permission to use the code-based exercises from our two-day "Testing for Developers" course as the basis for many of the code samples. Thanks, Denis Clelland and Luke McFarlane!

Several people encouraged me to keep working on the book when the going got tough. They were always willing to take a phone call to discuss some sticky issue I was grappling with. Foremost among these individuals were Joshua Kerievsky and Martin Fowler.

I'd like to especially thank Shaun Smith for helping me get started on this book and for the technical support he provided throughout the early part of writing it. He hosted my Web site, created the first CSS style sheets, taught me Ruby, set up a wiki for discussing the patterns, and even provided some of the early content before personal and work demands forced him to pull out of the writing side of the project. Whenever I say "we" when I talk about experiences, I am probably referring to Shaun and myself, although other coworkers may also share the same opinion.

Introduction

It has been said before but it bears repeating: Writing defect-free software is exceedingly difficult. Proof of correctness of real systems is still well beyond our abilities, and specification of behavior is equally challenging. Predicting future needs is a hit or miss affair—we'd all be getting rich on the stock market instead of building software systems if we were any good at it!

Automated verification of software behavior is one of the biggest advances in development methods in the last few decades. This very developer-friendly practice has huge benefits in terms of increasing productivity, improving quality, and keeping software from becoming brittle. The very fact that so many developers are now doing it of their own free will speaks for its effectiveness.

This chapter introduces the concept of test automation using a variety of tools (including **xUnit**), describes why you would do it, and explains what makes it difficult to do test automation well.

Feedback

Feedback is a very important element in many activities. Feedback tells us whether our actions are having the right effect. The sooner we get feedback, the more quickly we can react. A good example of this kind of feedback is the rumble strips now being ground into many highways between the main driving surface and the shoulders. Yes, driving off the shoulder gives us feedback that we have left the road. But getting feedback *earlier* (when our wheels first enter the shoulder) gives us more time to correct our course and reduces the likelihood that we will drive off the road at all.

Testing is all about getting feedback on software. For this reason, feedback is one of the essential elements of "agile" or "lean" software development. Having feedback loops in the development process is what gives us confidence in the software that we write. It lets us work more quickly and with less paranoia. It lets us focus on the new functionality we are adding by having the tests tell us whenever we break old functionality.

Testing

The traditional definition of "testing" comes from the world of quality assurance. We test software because we are sure it has bugs in it! So we test and we test and we test some more, until we cannot prove there are still bugs in the software. Traditionally, this testing occurs after the software is complete. As a result, it is a way of measuring quality—not a way of building quality into the product. In many organizations, testing is done by someone other than the software developers. The feedback provided by this kind of testing is very valuable, but it comes so late in the development cycle that its value is greatly diminished. It also has the nasty effect of extending the schedule as the problems found are sent back to development for rework, to be followed by another round of testing. So what kind of testing should software developers do to get feedback earlier?

Developer Testing

Rare is the software developer who believes he or she can write code that works "first time, every time." In fact, most of us are pleasantly surprised when something does work the first time. (I hope I am not shattering any illusions for the nondeveloper readers out there!)

So developers do testing, too. We want to prove to ourselves that the software works as we intended it to. Some developers might do their testing the same way as testers do it: by testing the whole system as a single entity. Most developers, however, prefer to test their software unit by unit. The "units" may be larger-grained components or they may be individual classes, methods, or functions. The key thing that distinguishes these tests from the ones that the testers write is that the units being tested are a consequence of the design of the software, rather than being a direct translation of the requirements.[1]

Automated Testing

Automated testing has been around for several decades. When I worked on telephone switching systems at Nortel's R&D subsidiary Bell-Northern Research in the early 1980s, we did automated regression and load testing of

---

[1] A small percentage of the **unit tests** may correspond directly to the **business logic** described in the requirements and the **customer tests**, but a large majority tests the code that surrounds the business logic.

the software/hardware that we were building. This testing was done primarily in the context of the "System Test" organization using specialized hardware and software that were programmed with test scripts. The test machines connected to the switch being tested as though it were a bunch of telephones and other telephone switches; it made telephone calls and exercised the myriad of telephone features. Of course, this automated testing infrastructure was not suitable for **unit testing**, nor was it generally available to the developers because of the huge amounts of hardware involved.

In the last decade, more general-purpose test automation tools have become available for testing applications through their user interfaces. Some of these tools use scripting languages to define the tests; the sexier tools rely on the "robot user" or "record and playback" metaphor for test automation. Unfortunately, many of the early experiences with these latter tools left the testers and test managers less than satisfied. The cause was high test maintenance costs caused by the "fragile test" problem.

The "Fragile Test" Problem

Test automation using commercial "record and playback" or "robot user" tools has gained a bad reputation among early users of these tools. Tests automated using this approach often fail for seemingly trivial reasons. It is important to understand the limitations of this style of test automation to avoid falling victim to the pitfalls commonly associated with it—namely, behavior sensitivity, interface sensitivity, data sensitivity, and context sensitivity.

Behavior Sensitivity

If the behavior of the system is changed (e.g., if the requirements are changed and the system is modified to meet the new requirements), any tests that exercise the modified functionality will most likely fail when replayed.[2] This is a basic reality of testing regardless of the test automation approach used. The real problem is that we often need to use that functionality to maneuver the system into the right state to start a test. As a consequence, behavioral changes have a much larger impact on the testing process than one might expect.

---

[2] A change in behavior could occur because the system is doing something different or because it is doing the same thing with different timing or sequencing.

Interface Sensitivity

Testing the business logic inside the **system under test (SUT)** via the user interface is a bad idea. Even minor changes to the interface can cause tests to fail, even though a human user might say the test should still pass. Such unintended interface sensitivity is partly what gave test automation tools such a bad name in the past decade. Although the problem occurs regardless of which user interface technology is being used, it seems to be worse with some types of interfaces than with others. Graphical user interfaces (GUIs) are a particularly challenging way to interact with the business logic inside the system. The recent shift to Web-based (HTML) user interfaces has made some aspects of test automation easier but has introduced yet another problem because of the executable code needed within the HTML to provide a rich user experience.

Data Sensitivity

All tests assume some starting point, called the **test fixture**; this **test context** is sometimes called the "pre-conditions" or "before picture" of the test. Most commonly, this test fixture is defined in terms of data that is already in the system. If the data changes, the tests may fail unless great effort has been expended to make them insensitive to the data being used.

Context Sensitivity

The behavior of the system may be affected by the state of things outside the system. These external factors could include the states of devices (e.g., printers, servers), other applications, or even the system clock (e.g., the time and/or date of execution of the test). Any tests that are affected by this context will be difficult to repeat deterministically without getting control over the context.

Overcoming the Four Sensitivities

The four sensitivities exist regardless of which technology we use to automate the tests. Of course, some technologies give us ways to work around these sensitivities, while others force us down a particular path. The xUnit family of test automation frameworks gives us a large degree of control; we just have to learn how to use it effectively.

Uses of Automated Tests

Thus far, most of the discussion here has centered on regression testing of applications. This is a very valuable form of feedback when modifying existing applications because it helps us catch defects that we have introduced inadvertently.

Tests as Specification

A completely different use of automated testing is seen in **test-driven development** (TDD), which is one of the core practices of agile methods such as **eXtreme Programming**. This use of automated testing is more about specification of the behavior of the software yet to be written than it is about **regression testing**. The effectiveness of TDD comes from the way it lets us separate our thinking about software into two separate phases: what it should do, and how it should do it.

Hold on a minute! Don't the proponents of agile software development eschew waterfall-style development? Yes, indeed. Agilists prefer to design and build a system feature by feature, with working software being available at every step to prove that each feature works before they move on to develop the next feature. That does not mean we do not do design; it simply means we do "continuous design"! Taking this to the extreme results in "emergent design," where very little design is done upfront. But development does not have to be done that way. We *can* combine high-level design (or architecture) upfront with detailed design on a feature-by-feature basis. Either way, it can be useful to delay thinking about how to achieve the behavior of a specific class or method for a few minutes while we capture what that behavior should be in the form of an executable specification. After all, most of us have trouble concentrating on one thing at a time, let alone several things simultaneously.

Once we have finished writing the tests and verifying that they fail as expected, we can switch our perspective and focus on making them pass. The tests are now acting as a progress measurement. If we implement the functionality incrementally, we can see each test pass one by one as we write more code. As we work, we keep running all of the previously written tests as regression tests to make sure our changes have not had any unexpected side effects. This is where the true value of automated unit testing lies: in its ability to "pin down" the functionality of the SUT so that the functionality is not changed accidentally. That is what allows us to sleep well at night!

Test-Driven Development

Many books have been written recently on the topic of test-driven development, so this one will not devote a lot of space to that topic. This book focuses on what the code in the tests looks like, rather than when we wrote the tests. The closest we will get to talking about how the tests come into being is when we investigate **refactoring** of tests and learn how to refactor tests written using one pattern into tests that use a pattern with different characteristics.

I am trying to stay "development process agnostic" in this book because automated testing can help any team regardless of whether its members are doing TDD, **test-first development**, or **test-last development**. Also, once people learn how to automate tests in a "test last" environment, they are likely to be more inclined to experiment with a "test first" approach. Nevertheless, we do explore some parts of the development process because they affect how easily we can do test automation. There are two key aspects of this investigation: (1) the interplay between *Fully Automated Tests* (see page 26) and our development integration process and tools, and (2) the way in which the development process affects the testability of our designs.

Patterns

In preparing to write this book, I read a lot of conference papers and books on xUnit-based test automation. Not surprisingly, each author seems to have a particular area of interest and favorite techniques. While I do not always agree with their practices, I am always trying to understand *why* these authors do things a particular way and *when* it would be more appropriate to use their techniques than the ones I already use.

This level of understanding is one of the major differences between examples and prose that merely explain the "how to" of a technique and a pattern. A pattern helps readers understand the *why* behind the practice, allowing them to make intelligent choices between the alternative patterns and thereby avoid any unexpected nasty consequences in the future.

Software patterns have been around for a decade, so most readers should at least be aware of the concept. A pattern is a "solution to a recurring problem." Some problems are bigger than others and, therefore, too big to solve with a single pattern. That is where the **pattern language** comes into play; this collection (or grammar) of patterns leads the reader from an overall problem step by step to a detailed solution. In a pattern language, some of the patterns will necessarily be of higher levels of abstraction, while others will focus on lower-level details. To be useful, there must be linkages between the patterns so that we can work our way down from the higher-level "strategy" patterns to the more detailed "design patterns" and the most detailed "coding idioms."

Patterns versus Principles versus Smells

This book includes three kinds of patterns. The most traditional kind of pattern is the "recurring solution to a common problem"; most of the patterns in this book fall into this general category. I do distinguish between three different levels:

- "Strategy"-level patterns have far-reaching consequences. The decision to use a *Shared Fixture* (page 317) rather than a *Fresh Fixture* (page 311) takes us down a very different path and leads to a different set of test design patterns. Each of the strategy patterns has its own write-up in the "Strategy Patterns" chapter in the reference section of the book.

- Test "design"-level patterns are used when developing tests for specific functionality. They focus on how we organize our test logic. An example that should be familiar to most readers is the *Mock Object* pattern (page 544). Each test design pattern has its own write-up and the patterns are grouped into chapters in the reference section of the book based on topics such as *Test Double* patterns.

- Test "coding idioms" describe different ways to code a specific test. Many of these are language specific; examples include using **block closures** for *Expected Exception Tests* (see *Test Method* on page 348) in Smalltalk and anonymous inner classes for Mock Objects in Java. Some, such as *Simple Success Test* (see *Test Method*), are fairly generic in that they have analogs in each language. These idioms are typically listed as implementation variations or examples within the write-up of a "test design pattern."

Often, several alternative patterns *could* be used at each level. Of course, I almost always have a preference for which patterns to use, but one person's "anti-pattern" may be another person's "best practice pattern." As a result, this book includes patterns that I do not necessarily advocate. It describes the advantages and disadvantages of each of those patterns, allowing readers to make informed decisions about their use. I have tried to provide linkages to those alternatives in each of the pattern descriptions as well as in the introductory narratives.

The nice thing about patterns is that they provide enough information to make an intelligent decision between several alternatives. The pattern we choose may be affected by the goals we have for test automation. The goals describe desired outcomes of the test automation efforts. These goals are supported by a number of principles that codify a belief system about what makes automated tests "good." In this book, the goals of test automation are described in Chapter 3, *Goals of Test Automation,* and the principles are described in Chapter 5, *Principles of Test Automation.*

The final kind of pattern is more of an anti-pattern [AP]. These **test smells** describe recurring problems that our patterns help us address in terms of the symptoms we might observe and the root causes of those symptoms. **Code smells** were first popularized in Martin Fowler's book [Ref] and applied to xUnit-based testing as test smells in a paper presented at XP2001 [RTC]. The test smells are cross-referenced with the patterns that can be used to banish them as well as the patterns[3] that are more likely to lead to them.[4] In addition, the test smells are covered in depth in their own section: Part II, *The Test Smells.*

Pattern Form

This book includes my *descriptions* of patterns. The patterns themselves existed before I started cataloging them, by virtue of having been invented independently by at least three different **test automaters**. I took it upon myself to write them down as a way of making the knowledge more easily distributable. But to do so, I had to choose a pattern description form.

Pattern descriptions come in many shapes and sizes. Some have a very rigid structure defined by many headings that help the reader find the various sections. Others read more like literature but may be more difficult to use as a reference. Nevertheless, all patterns have a common core of information, however it is presented.

My Pattern Form

I have really enjoyed reading the works of Martin Fowler, and I attribute much of that enjoyment to the pattern form that he uses. As the saying goes, "Imitation is the sincerest form of flattery": I have copied his format shamelessly with only a few minor modifications.

The template begins with the problem statement, the summary statement, and a sketch. The italicized problem statement summarizes the core of the problem

---

[3] Some might want to call these patterns "anti-patterns." Just because a pattern often has negative consequences, it does not imply that the pattern is *always* bad. For this reason, I prefer not to call these anti-patterns; I just do not use them very often.

[4] In a few cases, there are even a pattern and a smell with similar names.

that the pattern addresses. It is often stated as a question: "How do we . . . ?" The boldface summary statement captures the essence of the pattern in one or two sentences, while the sketch provides a visual representation of the pattern. The untitled section of text immediately after the sketch summarizes why we might want to use the pattern in just a few sentences. It elaborates on the problem statement and includes both the "Problem" and "Context" sections from the traditional pattern template. A reader should be able to get a sense of whether he or she wants to read any further by skimming this section.

The next three sections provide the meat of the pattern. The "How It Works" section describes the essence of how the pattern is structured and what it is about. It also includes information about the "resulting context" when there are several ways to implement some important aspect of the pattern. This section corresponds to the "Solution" or "Therefore" sections of more traditional pattern forms. The "When to Use It" section describes the circumstances in which you should consider using the pattern. This section corresponds to the "Problem," "Forces," "Context," and "Related Patterns" sections of traditional pattern templates. It also includes information about the "Resulting Context," when this information might affect whether you would want to use this pattern. I also include any "test smells" that might suggest that you should use this pattern. The "Implementation Notes" section describes the nuts and bolts of how to implement the pattern. Subheadings within this section indicate key components of the pattern or variations in how the pattern can be implemented.

Most of the concrete patterns include three additional sections. The "Motivating Example" section provides examples of what the test code might have looked like before this pattern was applied. The section titled "Example: {Pattern Name}" shows what the test would look like after the pattern was applied. The "Refactoring Notes" section provides more detailed instructions on how to get from the "Motivating Example" to the "Example: {Pattern Name}."

If the pattern is written up elsewhere, the description may include a section titled "Further Reading." A "Known Uses" section appears when there is something particularly interesting about those applications. Most of these patterns have been seen in many systems, of course, so picking three uses to substantiate them would be arbitrary and meaningless.

Where a number of related techniques exist, they are often presented here as a single pattern with several variations. If the variations are different ways to implement the same fundamental pattern (namely, solving the same problem the same general way), the variations and the differences between them are listed in the "Implementation Notes" section. If the variations are primarily a different reason for using the pattern, the variations are listed in the "When to Use It" section.

Historical Patterns and Smells

I struggled mightily when trying to come up with a concise enough list of patterns and smells while still keeping historical names whenever possible. I often list the historical name as an alias for the pattern or smell. In some cases, it made more sense to consider the historical version of the pattern as a specific variation of a larger pattern. In such a case, I usually include the historical pattern as a named variation in the "Implementation Notes" section.

Many of the historical smells did not pass the "sniff test"—that is, the smell described a root cause rather than a symptom.[5] Where an historical test smell describes a cause and not a symptom, I have chosen to move it into the corresponding symptom-based smell as a special kind of variation titled "Cause." *Mystery Guest* (see *Obscure Test* on page 186) is a good example.

Referring to Patterns and Smells

I also struggled to come up with a good way to refer to patterns and smells, especially the historical ones. I wanted to be able to use both the historical names when appropriate and the new aggregate names, whichever was more appropriate. I also wanted the reader to be able to see which was which. In the online version of this book, hyperlinks were used for this purpose. For the printed version, however, I needed a way to represent this linkage as a page number annotation of the reference without cluttering up the entire text with references. The solution I landed on after several tries includes the page number where the pattern or smell can be found the first time it is referenced in a chapter, pattern, or smell. If the reference is to a pattern *variation* or the *cause* of a smell, I include the aggregate pattern or smell name the first time. Note how this second reference to the *Mystery Guest* cause of *Obscure Test* shows up without the smell name, whereas references to other causes of *Obscure Test* such as *Irrelevant Information* (see *Obscure Test*) include the aggregate smell name but not the page number.

Refactoring

Refactoring is a relatively new concept in software development. While people have always had a need to modify existing code, refactoring is a highly

---

[5] The "sniff test" is based on the diaper story in [Ref] wherein Kent Beck asks Grandma Beck, "How do I know that it is time to change the diaper?" "If it stinks, change it!" was her response. Smells are named based on the "stink," not the cause of the stink.

disciplined approach to changing the design *without* changing the behavior of the code. It goes hand-in-hand with automated testing because it is very difficult to do refactoring without having the safety net of automated tests to prove that you have not broken anything during your redesign.

Many of the modern integrated development environments (IDEs) have built-in support for refactoring. Most of them automate the refactoring steps of at least a few of the refactorings described in Martin Fowler's book [Ref]. Unfortunately, the tools do not tell us when or why we should use refactoring. We will have to get a copy of Martin's book for that! Another piece of mandatory reading on this topic is Joshua Kerievsky's book [RtP].

Refactoring tests differs a bit from refactoring production code because we do not have automated tests for our automated tests! If a test fails after a refactoring of the test, did the failure occur because we made a mistake during the refactoring? Just because a test passes after a test refactoring, can we be sure it will still fail when appropriate? To address this issue, many test refactorings are very conservative, "safe refactorings" that minimize the chance of introducing a change of behavior into the test. We also try to avoid having to do major refactorings of tests by adopting an appropriate test strategy, as described in Chapter 6, *Test Automation Strategy*.

This book focuses more on the target of the refactoring than on the mechanics of this endeavor. A short summary of the refactorings does appear in Appendix A, but the process of refactoring is not the primary focus of this book. The patterns themselves are new enough that we have not yet had time to agree on their names, content, or applicability, let alone reach consensus on the best way to refactor to them. A further complication is that there are potentially many starting points for each refactoring target (pattern), and attempting to provide detailed refactoring instructions would make this already large book much larger.

Assumptions

In writing this book, I assumed that the reader is somewhat familiar with object technology (also known as "object-oriented programming"); object technology seemed to be a prerequisite for automated unit testing to become popular. That does not mean we cannot perform testing in procedural or functional languages, but use of these languages may make it more challenging (or at least different).

Different people have different learning styles. Some need to start with the "big picture" abstractions and work down to "just enough" detail. Others can understand only the details and have no need for the "big picture." Some learn best by hearing or reading words; others need pictures to help them visualize a concept. Still others learn programming concepts best by reading code. I've tried to accommodate all of these learning styles by providing a summary, a detailed description, code samples, and a picture wherever possible. These items should be Skippable Sections [PLOPD3] for those readers who won't benefit from that style of learning.

Terminology

This book brings together terminology from two different domains: software development and software testing. As a consequence, some terminology will inevitably be unfamiliar to some readers. Readers should refer to the glossary when they encounter any terms that they do not understand. I will, however, point out one or two terms here, because becoming familiar with these terms is essential to understanding most of the material in this book.

Testing Terminology

Software developers will probably find the term "system under test" (abbreviated throughout this book as SUT) unfamiliar. It is short for "whatever thing we are testing." When we are writing unit tests, the SUT is whatever class or method(s) we are testing; when we are writing customer tests, the SUT is probably the entire application (or at least a major subsystem of it).

Any part of the application or system we are building that is *not* included in the SUT may still be required to run our test because it is called by the SUT or because it sets up prerequisite data that the SUT will use as we exercise it. The former type of element is called a **depended-on component** (DOC), and both types are part of the test fixture. This is illustrated in Figure I.1.

Language-Specific xUnit Terminology

Although this book includes examples in a variety of languages and xUnit family members, **JUnit** figures prominently in this coverage. JUnit is the language and xUnit framework that most people are at least somewhat familiar with. Many of the translations of JUnit to other languages are relatively faithful ports, with only minor changes in class and method names needed to accommodate the differences in the underlying language. Where this isn't the case, Appendix B, *xUnit Terminology Cross-Reference*, often includes the appropriate mapping.

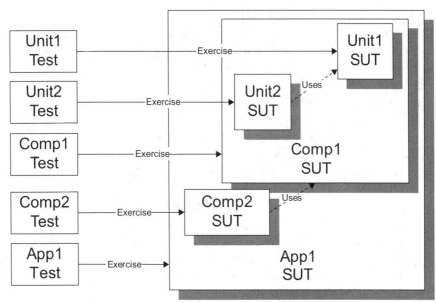

Figure I.1. *A range of tests each with its own SUT. An application, component, or unit is only the SUT with respect to a specific set of tests. The "Unit1 SUT" plays the role of DOC (part of the fixture) to "Unit2 Test" and is part of the "Comp1 SUT" and the "App1 SUT."*

Using Java as the main sample language also means that in some discussions we will refer to the JUnit name of a method and will not list the corresponding method names in each of the xUnit frameworks. For example, a discussion may refer to JUnit's assertTrue method without mentioning that the **NUnit** equivalent is Assert.IsTrue, the **SUnit** equivalent is should:, and the **VbUnit** equivalent is verify. Readers are expected to do the mental swap of method names to the SUnit, VbUnit, **Test::Unit**, and other equivalents with which they may be most familiar. The Intent-Revealing Names [SBPP] of the JUnit methods should be clear enough for the purposes of our discussion.

Code Samples

Sample code is always a problem. Samples of code from real projects are typically much too large to include and are usually covered by nondisclosure agreements that preclude their publication. "Toy programs" do not get much respect because "they aren't real." A book such as this one has little choice except to use "toy programs," but I have tried to make them as representative as possible of real projects.

Almost all of the code samples presented here came from "real" compilable and executable code, so they should not (knock on wood) contain any compile errors unless they were introduced during the editing process. Most of the Ruby examples come from the XML-based publishing system I used to prepare this book, while many of the Java and C# samples came from courseware that we use at ClearStream to teach these concepts to ClearStream's clients.

I have tried to use a variety of languages to illustrate the nearly universal application of the patterns across the members of the xUnit family. In some cases, the specific pattern dictated the use of language because of specific features of either the language or the xUnit family member. In other cases, the language was dictated by the availability of third-party extensions for a specific member of the xUnit family. Otherwise, the default language for examples is Java with some C# because most people have at least reading-level familiarity with them.

Formatting code for a book is a particular challenge due to the recommended line length of just 65 characters. I have taken some liberties in shortening variable and class names simply to reduce the number of lines that wrap. I've also invented some line-wrapping conventions to minimize the vertical size of these samples. You can take solace in the fact that your test code should look a lot "shorter" than mine because you have to wrap many fewer lines!

Diagramming Notation

"A picture is worth a thousand words." Wherever possible, I have tried to include a sketch of each pattern or smell. I've based the sketches loosely on the Unified Modeling Language (UML) but took a few liberties to make them more expressive. For example, I use the aggregation symbol (diamond) and the inheritance symbol (a triangle) of UML class diagrams, but I mix classes and objects on the same diagram along with associations and object interactions. Most of the notation is introduced in the patterns in Chapter 19, *xUnit Basics Patterns*, so you may find it worthwhile to skim this chapter just to look at the pictures.

Although I have tried to make this notation "discoverable" simply through comparing sketches, a few conventions are worth pointing out. Objects have shadows; classes and methods do not. Classes have square corners, in keeping with UML; methods have round corners. Large exclamation marks are **assertions** (potential **test failures**), and a starburst is an error or exception being raised. The fixture is a cloud, reflecting its nebulous nature, and any components the SUT depends on are superimposed on the cloud. Whatever the sketch is trying to illustrate is highlighted with heavier lines and darker shading. As a result, you should be able to compare two sketches of related concepts and quickly determine what is emphasized in each.

Limitations

As you use these patterns, please keep in mind that I could not have seen every test automation problem and every solution to every problem; there may well be other, possibly better, ways to solve some of these problems. These solutions are just the ones that have worked for me and for the people I have been communicating with. Accept everyone's advice with a grain of salt!

My hope is that these patterns will give you a starting point for writing good, robust automated tests. With luck, you will avoid many of the mistakes we made on our first attempts and will go on to invent even better ways of automating tests. I'd love to hear about them!

Refactoring a Test

Why Refactor Tests?

Tests can quickly become a bottleneck in an agile development process. This may not be immediately obvious to those who have never experienced the difference between simple, easily understood tests and complex, obtuse, hard-to-maintain tests. The productivity difference can be staggering!

This section of the book acts as a "motivating example" for the entire book by showing you how much of a difference refactoring tests can make. It walks you through an example starting with a complex test and, step by step, refactors it to a simple, easily understood test. Along the way, I will point out some key smells and the patterns that we can use to remove them. Ideally, this exercise will whet your appetite for more.

A Complex Test

Here is a test that is not atypical of some of the tests I have seen on various projects:

```
public void testAddItemQuantity_severalQuantity_v1(){
    Address billingAddress = null;
    Address shippingAddress = null;
    Customer customer = null;
    Product product = null;
    Invoice invoice = null;
    try {
        //   Set up fixture
        billingAddress = new Address("1222 1st St SW",
            "Calgary", "Alberta", "T2N 2V2","Canada");
        shippingAddress = new Address("1333 1st St SW",
            "Calgary", "Alberta", "T2N 2V2", "Canada");
        customer = new Customer(99, "John", "Doe",
                            new BigDecimal("30"),
                            billingAddress,
                            shippingAddress);
        product = new Product(88, "SomeWidget",
                            new BigDecimal("19.99"));
        invoice = new Invoice(customer);
```

```
      // Exercise SUT
      invoice.addItemQuantity(product, 5);
      // Verify outcome
      List lineItems = invoice.getLineItems();
      if (lineItems.size() == 1) {
         LineItem actItem = (LineItem) lineItems.get(0);
         assertEquals("inv", invoice, actItem.getInv());
         assertEquals("prod", product, actItem.getProd());
         assertEquals("quant", 5, actItem.getQuantity());
         assertEquals("discount", new BigDecimal("30"),
                        actItem.getPercentDiscount());
         assertEquals("unit price",new BigDecimal("19.99"),
                        actItem.getUnitPrice());
         assertEquals("extended", new BigDecimal("69.96"),
                        actItem.getExtendedPrice());
      } else {
         assertTrue("Invoice should have 1 item", false);
      }
   } finally {
      // Teardown
      deleteObject(invoice);
      deleteObject(product);
      deleteObject(customer);
      deleteObject(billingAddress);
      deleteObject(shippingAddress);
   }
}
```

This test is quite long[1] and is much more complicated than it needs to be. This *Obscure Test* (page 186) is difficult to understand because the sheer number of lines in the test makes it hard to see the big picture. It also suffers from a number of other problems that we will address individually.

Cleaning Up the Test

Let's look at each of the various parts of the test.

Cleaning Up the Verification Logic

First, let's focus on the part that verifies the expected outcome. Maybe we can infer from the assertions which test conditions this test is trying to verify.

---

[1] While the need to wrap lines to keep them at 65 characters makes this code look even longer than it really is, it is still unnecessarily long. It contains 25 executable statements including initialized declarations, 6 lines of control statements, 4 in-line comments, and 2 lines to declare the test method—giving a total of 37 lines of unwrapped source code.

```
List lineItems = invoice.getLineItems();
if (lineItems.size() == 1) {
    LineItem actItem = (LineItem) lineItems.get(0);
    assertEquals("inv", invoice, actItem.getInv());
    assertEquals("prod", product, actItem.getProd());
    assertEquals("quant", 5, actItem.getQuantity());
    assertEquals("discount", new BigDecimal("30"),
                    actItem.getPercentDiscount());
    assertEquals("unit price",new BigDecimal("19.99"),
                    actItem.getUnitPrice());
    assertEquals("extended", new BigDecimal("69.96"),
                    actItem.getExtendedPrice());
} else {
    assertTrue("Invoice should have 1 item", false);
}
```

A simple problem to fix is the obtuse assertion on the very last line. Calling assertTrue with an argument of false should always result in a test failure, so why don't we say so directly? Let's change this to a call to fail:

```
List lineItems = invoice.getLineItems();
if (lineItems.size() == 1) {
    LineItem actItem = (LineItem) lineItems.get(0);
    assertEquals("inv", invoice, actItem.getInv());
    assertEquals("prod", product, actItem.getProd());
    assertEquals("quant", 5, actItem.getQuantity());
    assertEquals("discount", new BigDecimal("30"),
                    actItem.getPercentDiscount());
    assertEquals("unit price",new BigDecimal("19.99"),
                    actItem.getUnitPrice());
    assertEquals("extended", new BigDecimal("69.96"),
                    actItem.getExtendedPrice());
} else {
    fail("Invoice should have exactly one line item");
}
```

We can think of this move as an Extract Method [Fowler] refactoring, because we are replacing the *Stated Outcome Assertion* (see *Assertion Method* on page 362) with a hard-coded parameter with a more intent-revealing call to a *Single Outcome Assertion* (see *Assertion Method*) method that encapsulates the call.

Of course, this set of assertions suffers from several more problems. For example, why do we need so many of them? It turns out that many of these assertions are testing fields set by the constructor for the LineItem, which is itself covered by another unit test. So why repeat these assertions here? It will just create more test code to maintain when the logic changes.

One solution is to use a single assertion on an *Expected Object* (see *State Verification* on page 462) instead of one assertion per object field. First, we define an object that looks exactly how we expect the result to look. In this case, we create an expected LineItem with the fields filled in with the expected values, including the unitPrice and extendedPrice initialized from the product.

```
List lineItems = invoice.getLineItems();
if (lineItems.size() == 1) {
   LineItem expected =
       new LineItem(invoice, product, 5,
                   new BigDecimal("30"),
                   new BigDecimal("69.96"));
   LineItem actItem = (LineItem) lineItems.get(0);
   assertEquals("invoice", expected.getInv(),
                          actItem.getInv());
   assertEquals("product", expected.getProd(),
                          actItem.getProd());
   assertEquals("quantity",expected.getQuantity(),
                          actItem.getQuantity());
   assertEquals("discount",
                   expected.getPercentDiscount(),
                   actItem.getPercentDiscount());
   assertEquals("unit pr", new BigDecimal("19.99"),
                          actItem.getUnitPrice());
   assertEquals("extend pr",new BigDecimal("69.96"),
                          actItem.getExtendedPrice());
} else {
   fail("Invoice should have exactly one line item");
}
```

Once we have created our *Expected Object*, we can then assert on it using assertEquals:

```
List lineItems = invoice.getLineItems();
if (lineItems.size() == 1) {
   LineItem expected =
       new LineItem(invoice, product,5,
                   new BigDecimal("30"),
                   new BigDecimal("69.96"));
   LineItem actItem = (LineItem) lineItems.get(0);
   assertEquals("invoice", expected, actItem);
} else {
   fail("Invoice should have exactly one line item");
}
```

Clearly, the Preserve Whole Object [Fowler] refactoring makes the code a lot simpler and more obvious. But wait! Why do we have an if statement in a test? If there are several paths through a test, how do we know which one is actually being executed? It would be a lot better if we could eliminate this *Conditional Test Logic* (page 200). Luckily for us, the pattern *Guard Assertion* (page 490) is designed to handle exactly this case. We simply use a Replace Conditional with Guard Clause [Fowler] refactoring to replace the if ... else fail() ... sequence with an assertion on the same condition. This *Guard Assertion* halts execution if the condition is not met without introducing *Conditional Test Logic*.

```
List lineItems = invoice.getLineItems();
assertEquals("number of items", 1,lineItems.size());
LineItem expected =
    new LineItem(invoice, product, 5,
                new BigDecimal("30"),
                new BigDecimal("69.96"));
LineItem actItem = (LineItem) lineItems.get(0);
assertEquals("invoice", expected, actItem);
```

So far, we have reduced 11 lines of verification code to just 4, and those 4 lines are a lot simpler code to boot.[2] Some people might suggest that this refactoring is good enough. But can't we make this assertion even more obvious? What are we really trying to verify? We are trying to say that there should be only one line item and it should look exactly like our expectedLineItem. We can say this explicitly by using an Extract Method refactoring to define a *Custom Assertion* (page 474).

```
LineItem expected =
    new LineItem(invoice, product, 5,
                new BigDecimal("30"),
                new BigDecimal("69.96"));
assertContainsExactlyOneLineItem(invoice, expected);
```

That is better! Now we have the verification part of the test down to just two lines. Let's review what the whole test looks like:

```
public void testAddItemQuantity_severalQuantity_v6(){
    Address billingAddress = null;
    Address shippingAddress = null;
    Customer customer = null;
    Product product = null;
    Invoice invoice = null;
    try {
        // Set up fixture
        billingAddress = new Address("1222 1st St SW",
                "Calgary", "Alberta", "T2N 2V2", "Canada");
        shippingAddress = new Address("1333 1st St SW",
                "Calgary", "Alberta", "T2N 2V2", "Canada");
        customer = new Customer(99, "John", "Doe",
                        new BigDecimal("30"),
                        billingAddress,
                        shippingAddress);
        product = new Product(88, "SomeWidget",
                        new BigDecimal("19.99"));
        invoice = new Invoice(customer);
        // Exercise SUT
        invoice.addItemQuantity(product, 5);
```

[2] It's a good thing we are not being rewarded for the number of lines of code we write! This is yet another example of why KLOC is such a poor measure of productivity.

```
        // Verify outcome
        LineItem expected =
            new LineItem(invoice, product, 5,
                        new BigDecimal("30"),
                        new BigDecimal("69.96"));
        assertContainsExactlyOneLineItem(invoice, expected);
    } finally {
        // Teardown
        deleteObject(invoice);
        deleteObject(product);
        deleteObject(customer);
        deleteObject(billingAddress);
        deleteObject(shippingAddress);
    }
}
```

Cleaning Up the Fixture Teardown Logic

Now that we have cleaned up the result verification logic, let's turn our attention to the finally block at the end of the test. What is *this* code doing?

```
    } finally {
        // Teardown
        deleteObject(invoice);
        deleteObject(product);
        deleteObject(customer);
        deleteObject(billingAddress);
        deleteObject(shippingAddress);
    }
```

Most modern languages have an equivalent construct to the try/finally block that can be used to ensure that code gets run even when an error or exception occurs. In a *Test Method* (page 348), the finally block ensures that any cleanup code gets run regardless of whether the test passed or failed. A failed assertion throws an exception, which would transfer control back to the *Test Automation Framework's* (page 298) exception-handling code, so we use the finally block to clean up first. This approach means that we avoid having to catch the exception and then rethrow it.

In this test, the finally block calls the deleteObject method on each of the objects created by the test. Unfortunately, this code suffers from a fatal flaw. Have you noticed it yet?

Things could go wrong during the teardown itself. What happens if the first call to deleteObject throws an exception? As coded here, none of the other calls to deleteObject would be executed. The solution is to use a nested try/finally block around this first call, thereby ensuring that the second call to deleteObject always executes. But what if the second call fails? In this case, we would need a total of six nested try/finally blocks to make this maneuver work. That would almost double the length of the test, and we cannot afford to write and maintain so much code in each test.

```
} finally {
    //      Teardown
    try {
        deleteObject(invoice);
    } finally {
        try {
            deleteObject(product);
        } finally {
            try {
                deleteObject(customer);
            } finally {
                try {
                    deleteObject(billingAddress);
                } finally {
                    deleteObject(shippingAddress);
                }
            }
        }
    }
}
```

The problem is that we now have a *Complex Teardown* (see *Obscure Test*). What are the chances of getting this code right? And how do we test the test code? Clearly, our current approach is not going to be very effective.

Of course, we could move this code into the tearDown method. That would have the advantage of removing it from the *Test Method*. Also, because the tearDown method acts as a finally block, we would get rid of the outermost try/finally. Unfortunately, this strategy doesn't address the root of the problem: the need to write detailed teardown code in each test.

We could try to avoid creating the objects in the first place by using a *Shared Fixture* (page 317) that is not torn down between tests. Unfortunately, this approach is likely to lead to a number of test smells, including *Unrepeatable Test* (see *Erratic Test* on page 228) and *Interacting Tests* (see *Erratic Test*), caused by interactions via the shared fixture. Another issue is that the references to objects used from the shared fixture are often *Mystery Guests* (see *Obscure Test*).[3]

The best solution is to use a *Fresh Fixture* (page 311) but to avoid writing teardown code for every test. To do so, we can use an in-memory fixture that is automatically garbage collected. This approach won't work, however, if the objects we create are persistent (e.g., if they are saved in a database). While it is best to construct the system architecture so that most of our tests can

---

[3] The test reader cannot see the objects being used by the test.

be executed without the database, we almost always have some tests that need it. In these cases, we can extend the *Test Automation Framework* to do most of the work for us. We can add a means to register each object we create with the framework so that it can do the deleting for us.

First, we need to register each object as we create it:

```
//    Set up fixture
billingAddress = new Address("1222 1st St SW", "Calgary",
                "Alberta", "T2N 2V2", "Canada");
registerTestObject(billingAddress);
shippingAddress = new Address("1333 1st St SW", "Calgary",
                "Alberta","T2N 2V2", "Canada");
registerTestObject(shippingAddress);
customer = new Customer(99, "John", "Doe",
                        new BigDecimal("30"),
                        billingAddress,
                        shippingAddress);
registerTestObject(shippingAddress);
product = new Product(88, "SomeWidget",
                        new BigDecimal("19.99"));
registerTestObject(shippingAddress);
invoice = new Invoice(customer);
registerTestObject(shippingAddress);
```

Registration consists of adding the object to a collection of test objects:

```
List testObjects;

protected void setUp() throws Exception {
    super.setUp();
    testObjects = new ArrayList();
}

protected void registerTestObject(Object testObject) {
    testObjects.add(testObject);
}
```

In the `tearDown` method, we iterate through the list of test objects and delete each one:

```
public void tearDown() {
    Iterator i = testObjects.iterator();
    while (i.hasNext()) {
        try {
            deleteObject(i.next());
        } catch (RuntimeException e) {
            // Nothing to do; we just want to make sure
            // we continue on to the next object in the list
        }
    }
}
```

Now our test looks like this:

```
public void testAddItemQuantity_severalQuantity_v8(){
    Address billingAddress = null;
    Address shippingAddress = null;
    Customer customer = null;
    Product product = null;
    Invoice invoice = null;
    //   Set up fixture
    billingAddress = new Address("1222 1st St SW", "Calgary",
                        "Alberta", "T2N 2V2", "Canada");
    registerTestObject(billingAddress);
    shippingAddress = new Address("1333 1st St SW", "Calgary",
                        "Alberta","T2N 2V2", "Canada");
    registerTestObject(shippingAddress);
    customer = new Customer(99, "John", "Doe",
                            new BigDecimal("30"),
                            billingAddress,
                            shippingAddress);
    registerTestObject(shippingAddress);
    product = new Product(88, "SomeWidget",
                            new BigDecimal("19.99"));
    registerTestObject(shippingAddress);
    invoice = new Invoice(customer);
    registerTestObject(shippingAddress);
    // Exercise SUT
    invoice.addItemQuantity(product, 5);
    // Verify outcome
    LineItem expected =
        new LineItem(invoice, product, 5,
                    new BigDecimal("30"),
                    new BigDecimal("69.96"));
    assertContainsExactlyOneLineItem(invoice, expected);
}
```

We have been able to remove the try/finally block and, except for the additional calls to registerTestObject, our code is much simpler. But we can still clean this code up a bit more. Why, for example, do we need to declare the variables and initialize them to null, only to reinitialize them later? This action was needed with the original test because they had to be accessible in the finally block; now that we have removed this block, we can combine the declaration with the initialization:

```
public void testAddItemQuantity_severalQuantity_v9(){
    //   Set up fixture
    Address billingAddress = new Address("1222 1st St SW",
                "Calgary", "Alberta", "T2N 2V2", "Canada");
    registerTestObject(billingAddress);
    Address shippingAddress = new Address("1333 1st St SW",
                "Calgary", "Alberta", "T2N 2V2", "Canada");
```

```
        registerTestObject(shippingAddress);
        Customer customer = new Customer(99, "John", "Doe",
                                    new BigDecimal("30"),
                                    billingAddress,
                                    shippingAddress);
        registerTestObject(shippingAddress);
        Product product = new Product(88, "SomeWidget",
                                    new BigDecimal("19.99"));
        registerTestObject(shippingAddress);
        Invoice invoice = new Invoice(customer);
        registerTestObject(shippingAddress);
        // Exercise SUT
        invoice.addItemQuantity(product, 5);
        // Verify outcome
        LineItem expected =
            new LineItem(invoice, product, 5,
                        new BigDecimal("30"),
                        new BigDecimal("69.95"));
        assertContainsExactlyOneLineItem(invoice, expected);
    }
```

Cleaning Up the Fixture Setup

Now that we have cleaned up the assertions and the fixture teardown, let's turn our attention to the fixture setup. One obvious "quick fix" would be to take each of the calls to a constructor, take the subsequent call to registerTestObject, and use an Extract Method refactoring to define a *Creation Method* (page 415). This will make the test a bit simpler to read and write. The use of *Creation Methods* has another advantage: They encapsulate the API of the SUT and reduce the test maintenance effort when the various object constructors change by allowing us to modify only a single place rather than having to change each test.

```
    public void testAddItemQuantity_severalQuantity_v10(){
        //   Set up fixture
        Address billingAddress =
            createAddress( "1222 1st St SW", "Calgary", "Alberta",
                        "T2N 2V2", "Canada");
        Address shippingAddress =
            createAddress( "1333 1st St SW", "Calgary", "Alberta",
                        "T2N 2V2", "Canada");
        Customer customer =
            createCustomer( 99, "John", "Doe", new BigDecimal("30"),
                        billingAddress, shippingAddress);
        Product product =
            createProduct( 88,"SomeWidget",new BigDecimal("19.99"));
        Invoice invoice = createInvoice(customer);
        // Exercise SUT
        invoice.addItemQuantity(product, 5);
```

```
     // Verify outcome
     LineItem expected =
        new LineItem(invoice, product,5, new BigDecimal("30"),
                     new BigDecimal("69.96")));
     assertContainsExactlyOneLineItem(invoice, expected);
}
```

This fixture setup logic still suffers from several problems. The first problem is that it is difficult to tell how the fixture is related to the expected outcome of the test. Do the customer's particulars affect the outcome in some way? Does the customer's address affect the outcome? What is this test really verifying?

The other problem is that this test exhibits *Hard-Coded Test Data* (see *Obscure Test*). Given that our SUT persists all objects we create in a database, the use of *Hard-Coded Test Data* may result in an *Unrepeatable Test*, an *Interacting Test*, or a *Test Run War* (see *Erratic Test*) if any of the fields of the customer, product, or invoice must be unique.

We can solve this problem by generating a unique value for each test and then using that value to seed the attributes of the objects we create for the test. This approach will ensure that the test creates different objects each time the test is run. Because we have already moved the object creation logic into *Creation Methods*, this step is relatively easy; we just put this logic into the *Creation Method* and remove the corresponding parameters. This is another application of the Extract Method refactoring, in which we create a new, parameterless version of the *Creation Method*.

```
   public void testAddItemQuantity_severalQuantity_v11(){
      final int QUANTITY = 5;
      //   Set up fixture
      Address billingAddress = createAnAddress();
      Address shippingAddress = createAnAddress();
      Customer customer = createACustomer(new BigDecimal("30"),
              billingAddress, shippingAddress);
      Product product = createAProduct(new BigDecimal("19.99"));
      Invoice invoice = createInvoice(customer);
      // Exercise SUT
      invoice.addItemQuantity(product, QUANTITY);
      // Verify outcome
      LineItem expected =
         new LineItem(invoice, product, 5, new BigDecimal("30"),
                      new BigDecimal("69.96")));
      assertContainsExactlyOneLineItem(invoice, expected);
   }
   private Product createAProduct(BigDecimal unitPrice) {
      BigDecimal uniqueId = getUniqueNumber();
      String uniqueString = uniqueId.toString();
      return new Product(uniqueId.toBigInteger().intValue(),
                      uniqueString, unitPrice);
   }
```

We call this pattern an *Anonymous Creation Method* (see *Creation Method*) because we are declaring that we don't care about the particulars of the object. If the expected behavior of the SUT depends on a particular value, we can either pass the value as a parameter or imply it in the name of the creation method.

This test looks a lot better now, but we are not done yet. Does the expected outcome depend in any way on the addresses of the customer? If not, we can hide their construction completely by using an Extract Method refactoring (again!) to create a version of the createACustomer method that fabricates them for us.

```
public void testAddItemQuantity_severalQuantity_v12(){
   // Set up fixture
   Customer cust = createACustomer(new BigDecimal("30"));
   Product prod = createAProduct(new BigDecimal("19.99"));
   Invoice invoice = createInvoice(cust);
   // Exercise SUT
   invoice.addItemQuantity(prod, 5);
   // Verify outcome
   LineItem expected = new LineItem(invoice, prod, 5,
         new BigDecimal("30"), new BigDecimal("69.96"));
   assertContainsExactlyOneLineItem(invoice, expected);
}
```

By moving the calls that create the addresses into the method that creates the customer, we have made it clear that the addresses do not affect the logic that we are verifying in this test. The outcome does depend on the customer's discount, however, so we pass the discount percentage to the customer creation method.

We still have one or two things to clean up. For example, the *Hard-Coded Test Data* for the unit price, quantity, and customer's discount is repeated twice in the test. We can clarify the meaning of these numbers by using a Replace Magic Number with Symbolic Constant [Fowler] refactoring to give them role-describing names. Also, the constructor we are using to create the LineItem is not used anywhere in the SUT itself because the LineItem normally calculates the extendedCost when it is constructed. We should turn this test-specific code into a Foreign Method [Fowler] implemented within the test harness. We have already seen examples of how to do so with the Customer and Product: We use a *Parameterized Creation Method* (see *Creation Method*) to return the expected LineItem based on only those values of interest.

```
public void testAddItemQuantity_severalQuantity_v13(){
   final int QUANTITY = 5;
   final BigDecimal UNIT_PRICE = new BigDecimal("19.99");
   final BigDecimal CUST_DISCOUNT_PC = new BigDecimal("30");
```

```
    //   Set up fixture
    Customer customer = createACustomer(CUST_DISCOUNT_PC);
    Product product = createAProduct( UNIT_PRICE);
    Invoice invoice = createInvoice(customer);
    // Exercise SUT
    invoice.addItemQuantity(product, QUANTITY);
    // Verify outcome
    final BigDecimal EXTENDED_PRICE = new BigDecimal("69.96");
    LineItem expected =
        new LineItem(invoice, product, QUANTITY,
                        CUST_DISCOUNT_PC, EXTENDED_PRICE);
    assertContainsExactlyOneLineItem(invoice, expected);
}
```

One final point: Where did the value "69.96" come from? If this value comes from the output of some reference system, we should say so. Because it was just manually calculated and typed into the test, we can show the calculation in the test for the **test reader's** benefit.

The Cleaned-Up Test

Here is the final cleaned-up version of the test:

```
public void testAddItemQuantity_severalQuantity_v14(){
    final int QUANTITY = 5;
    final BigDecimal UNIT_PRICE = new BigDecimal("19.99");
    final BigDecimal CUST_DISCOUNT_PC =  new BigDecimal("30");
    // Set up fixture
    Customer customer = createACustomer(CUST_DISCOUNT_PC);
    Product product = createAProduct( UNIT_PRICE);
    Invoice invoice = createInvoice(customer);
    // Exercise SUT
    invoice.addItemQuantity(product, QUANTITY);
    // Verify outcome
    final BigDecimal BASE_PRICE =
        UNIT_PRICE.multiply(new BigDecimal(QUANTITY));
    final BigDecimal EXTENDED_PRICE =
        BASE_PRICE.subtract(BASE_PRICE.multiply(
            CUST_DISCOUNT_PC.movePointLeft(2)));
    LineItem expected =
        createLineItem(QUANTITY, CUST_DISCOUNT_PC,
                        EXTENDED_PRICE, product, invoice);
    assertContainsExactlyOneLineItem(invoice, expected);
}
```

We have used an Introduce Explaining Variable [Fowler] refactoring to better document the calculation of the BASE_PRICE (price*quantity) and EXTENDED_PRICE (the price with discount). The revised test is now much smaller and clearer than the bulky code we started with. It fulfills the role of *Tests as Documentation* (see page 23) very well. So what did we discover that this test verifies? It confirms that the line items added to an invoice are, indeed, added to the invoice and that the extended cost is based on the product price, the customer's discount, and the quantity ordered.

Writing More Tests

It seemed like we went to a lot of effort to refactor this test to make it clearer. Will we have to spend so much effort on every test?

I should hope not! Much of the effort here related to the discovery of which *Test Utility Methods* (page 599) were required for writing the test. We defined a *Higher-Level Language* (see page 41) for testing our application. Once we have those methods in place, writing other tests becomes much simpler. For example, if we want to write a test that verifies that the extended cost is recalculated when we change the quantity of a LineItem, we can reuse most of the *Test Utility Methods*.

```
public void testAddLineItem_quantityOne(){
    final BigDecimal BASE_PRICE = UNIT_PRICE;
    final BigDecimal EXTENDED_PRICE = BASE_PRICE;
    //    Set up fixture
    Customer customer = createACustomer(NO_CUST_DISCOUNT);
    Invoice invoice = createInvoice(customer);
    //    Exercise SUT
    invoice.addItemQuantity(PRODUCT, QUAN_ONE);
    // Verify outcome
    LineItem expected =
       createLineItem( QUAN_ONE, NO_CUST_DISCOUNT,
                       EXTENDED_PRICE, PRODUCT, invoice);
    assertContainsExactlyOneLineItem( invoice, expected );
}

public void testChangeQuantity_severalQuantity(){
    final int ORIGINAL_QUANTITY = 3;
    final int NEW_QUANTITY = 5;
    final BigDecimal BASE_PRICE =
       UNIT_PRICE.multiply(   new BigDecimal(NEW_QUANTITY));
    final BigDecimal EXTENDED_PRICE =
       BASE_PRICE.subtract(BASE_PRICE.multiply(
                   CUST_DISCOUNT_PC.movePointLeft(2)));
    //    Set up fixture
    Customer customer = createACustomer(CUST_DISCOUNT_PC);
    Invoice invoice = createInvoice(customer);
    Product product = createAProduct( UNIT_PRICE);
    invoice.addItemQuantity(product, ORIGINAL_QUANTITY);
```

```
    // Exercise SUT
    invoice.changeQuantityForProduct(product, NEW_QUANTITY);
    // Verify outcome
    LineItem expected = createLineItem( NEW_QUANTITY,
        CUST_DISCOUNT_PC, EXTENDED_PRICE, PRODUCT, invoice);
    assertContainsExactlyOneLineItem( invoice, expected );
}
```

This test was written in about two minutes and did not require adding any new *Test Utility Methods*. Contrast that with how long it would have taken to write a completely new test in the original style. And the effort saved in writing the tests is just part of the equation—we also need to consider the effort we saved understanding existing tests each time we need to revisit them. Over the course of a development project and the subsequent maintenance activity, this cost savings will really add up.

Further Compaction

Writing these additional tests revealed a few more sources of *Test Code Duplication* (page 213). For example, it seems that we always create both a Customer and an Invoice. Why not combine these two lines? Similarly, we continually define and initialize the QUANTITY and CUSTOMER_DISCOUNT_PC constants inside our test methods. Why can't we do these tasks just once? The Product does not seem to play any roles in these tests; we always create it exactly the same way. Can we factor this responsibility out, too? Certainly! We just apply an Extract Method refactoring to each set of duplicated code to create more powerful *Creation Methods*.

```
public void testAddItemQuantity_severalQuantity_v15(){
    // Set up fixture
    Invoice invoice = createCustomerInvoice(CUST_DISCOUNT_PC);
    // Exercise SUT
    invoice.addItemQuantity(PRODUCT, SEVERAL);
    // Verify outcome
    final BigDecimal BASE_PRICE =
        UNIT_PRICE.multiply(new BigDecimal(SEVERAL));
    final BigDecimal EXTENDED_PRICE =
        BASE_PRICE.subtract(BASE_PRICE.multiply(
            CUST_DISCOUNT_PC.movePointLeft(2)));
    LineItem expected = createLineItem( SEVERAL,
        CUST_DISCOUNT_PC, EXTENDED_PRICE, PRODUCT, invoice);
    assertContainsExactlyOneLineItem(invoice, expected);
}

public void testAddLineItem_quantityOne_v2(){
    final BigDecimal BASE_PRICE = UNIT_PRICE;
    final BigDecimal EXTENDED_PRICE = BASE_PRICE;
```

```
    //   Set up fixture
    Invoice invoice = createCustomerInvoice(NO_CUST_DISCOUNT);
    //   Exercise SUT
    invoice.addItemQuantity(PRODUCT, QUAN_ONE);
    // Verify outcome
    LineItem expected = createLineItem( SEVERAL,
        CUST_DISCOUNT_PC, EXTENDED_PRICE, PRODUCT, invoice);
    assertContainsExactlyOneLineItem( invoice, expected );
}

public void testChangeQuantity_severalQuantity_V2(){
    final int NEW_QUANTITY = SEVERAL + 2;
    final BigDecimal BASE_PRICE =
        UNIT_PRICE.multiply(  new BigDecimal(NEW_QUANTITY));
    final BigDecimal EXTENDED_PRICE =
        BASE_PRICE.subtract(BASE_PRICE.multiply(
                    CUST_DISCOUNT_PC.movePointLeft(2)));
    //   Set up fixture
    Invoice invoice = createCustomerInvoice(CUST_DISCOUNT_PC);
    invoice.addItemQuantity(PRODUCT, SEVERAL);
    // Exercise SUT
    invoice.changeQuantityForProduct(PRODUCT, NEW_QUANTITY);
    // Verify outcome
    LineItem expected = createLineItem( NEW_QUANTITY,
        CUST_DISCOUNT_PC, EXTENDED_PRICE, PRODUCT, invoice);
    assertContainsExactlyOneLineItem( invoice, expected );
}
```

We have now reduced the number of lines of code we need to understand from 35 statements in the original test to just 6 statements.[4] We are left with just a bit more than one sixth of the original code to maintain! We could go further by factoring out the fixture setup into a setUp method, but that effort would be worthwhile only if a lot of tests needed the same Customer/Discount/Invoice configuration. If we wanted to reuse these *Test Utility Methods* from other *Testcase Classes* (page 373), we could use an Extract Superclass [Fowler] refactoring to create a *Testcase Superclass* (page 638), and then use a Pull Up Method [Fowler] refactoring to move the *Test Utility Methods* to it so they can be reused.

---

[4] Ignoring wrapped lines, we have 6 executable statements surrounded by the two lines of method declarations/end.

PART I

The Narratives

Chapter 1

A Brief Tour

About This Chapter

There are a lot of principles, patterns, and smells in this book—and even more patterns that couldn't fit into the book. Do you need to learn them all? Do you need to use them all? Probably not! This chapter provides an abbreviated introduction to the bulk of the material in the entire book. You can use it as a quick tour of the material before diving into particular patterns or smells of interest. You can also use it as a warm-up before exploring the more detailed narrative chapters.

The Simplest Test Automation Strategy That Could Possibly Work

There is a simple test automation strategy that will work for many, many projects. This section describes this minimal test strategy. The principles, patterns, and smells referenced here are the core patterns that will serve us well in the long run. If we learn to apply them effectively, we will probably be successful in our test automation endeavors. If we find that we really cannot make the minimal test strategy work on *our* project by using these patterns, we can fall back to the alternative patterns listed in the full descriptions of these patterns and in the other narratives.

I have laid out this simple strategy in five parts:

- Development Process: How the process we use to develop the code affects our tests.

- Customer Tests: The first tests we should write as the ultimate definition of "what done looks like."

3

- Unit Tests: The tests that help our design emerge incrementally and ensure that *all* our code is tested.

- Design for Testability: The patterns that make our design easier to test, thereby reducing the cost of test automation.

- Test Organization: How we can organize our *Test Methods* (page 348) and *Testcase Classes* (page 373).

Development Process

First things first: When do we write our tests? Writing tests before we write our software has several benefits. In particular, it gives us an agreed-upon definition of what success looks like.[1]

When doing new software development, we strive to do **storytest-driven development** by first automating a suite of **customer tests** that verify the functionality provided by the application. To ensure that all of our software is tested, we augment these tests with a suite of **unit tests** that verify all code paths or, at a minimum, all the code paths that are not covered by the customer tests. We can use code coverage tools to discover which code is not being exercised and then retrofit unit tests to accommodate the untested code.[2]

By organizing the unit tests and customer tests into separate **test suites**, we ensure that we can run just the unit tests or just the customer tests if necessary. The unit tests should always pass before we check them in; this is what we mean by the phrase "keep the bar green." To ensure that the unit tests are run frequently, we can include them in the Smoke Tests [SCM] that are run as part of the Integration Build [SCM]. Although many of the customer tests will fail until the corresponding functionality is built, it is nevertheless useful to run all the passing customer tests as part of the integration build phase—but only if this step does not slow the build down too much. In that case, we can leave them out of the check-in build and simply run them every night.

We can ensure that our software is testable by doing **test-driven development (TDD)**. That is, we write the unit tests before we write the code, and we use the tests to help us define the software's design. This strategy helps concentrate all the **business logic** that needs verification in well-defined objects that can be tested independently of the database. Although we should also have unit tests

---

[1] If our customer cannot define the tests *before* we have built the software, we have every reason to be worried!

[2] We will likely find fewer *Missing Unit Tests* (see *Production Bugs* on page 268) when we practice test-driven development than if we adopt a "test last" policy. Even so, there is still value in running the code coverage tools with TDD.

for the data access layer and the database, we try to keep the dependency on the database to a minimum in the unit tests for the business logic.

Customer Tests

The customer tests should capture the essence of what the customer wants the system to do. Enumerating the tests before we begin their development is an important step whether or not we actually automate the tests, because it helps the development team understand what the customer really wants; these tests define what success looks like. We can automate the tests using *Scripted Tests* (page 285) or *Data-Driven Tests* (page 288) depending on who is preparing the tests; customers can take part in test automation if we use *Data-Driven Tests*. On rare occasions, we might even use *Recorded Tests* (page 278) for regression testing an existing application while we refactor the application to improve its testability. Of course, we usually discard these tests once we have developed other tests that cover the functionality, because *Recorded Tests* tend to be *Fragile Tests* (page 239).

During their development, we strive to make our customer tests representative of how the system is really used. Unfortunately, this goal often conflicts with attempts to keep the tests from becoming too long, because long tests are often *Obscure Tests* (page 186) and tend not to provide very good *Defect Localization* (see page 22) when they fail partway through the test. We can also use well-written *Tests as Documentation* (see page 23) to identify how the system is supposed to work. To keep the tests simple and easy to understand, we can bypass the user interface by performing *Subcutaneous Testing* (see *Layer Test* on page 337) against one or more Service Facades [CJ2EEP]. Service Facades encapsulate all of the business logic behind a simple interface that is also used by the presentation layer.

Every test needs a starting point. As part of our testing plan, we take care that each test sets up this starting point, known as the test fixture, each time the test is run. This *Fresh Fixture* (page 311) helps us avoid *Interacting Tests* (see *Erratic Test* on page 228) by ensuring that tests do not depend on anything they did not set up themselves. We avoid using a *Shared Fixture* (page 317), unless it is an *Immutable Shared Fixture,* to avoid starting down the slippery slope to *Erratic Tests*.

If our application normally interacts with other applications, we may need to isolate it from any applications that we do not have in our development environment by using some form of *Test Double* (page 522) for the objects that act as interfaces to the other applications. If the tests run too slowly because of database access or other slow components, we can replace them with functionally equivalent *Fake Objects* (page 551) to speed up our tests, thereby encouraging developers to run them more regularly. If at all possible, we avoid using *Chained Tests* (page 454)—they are just the test smell *Interacting Tests* in disguise.

Unit Tests

For our unit tests to be effective, each one should be a *Fully Automated Test* (page 26) that does a **round-trip test** against a class through its public interface. We can strive for *Defect Localization* by ensuring that each test is a *Single-Condition Test* (see page 45) that exercises a single method or object in a single scenario. We should also write our tests so that each part of the *Four-Phase Test* (page 358) is easily recognizable, which enables us to use the *Tests as Documentation*.

We use a *Fresh Fixture* strategy so that we do not have to worry about *Interacting Tests* or **fixture teardown**. We begin by creating a *Testcase Class* for each class we are testing (see *Testcase Class per Class* on page 617), with each test being a separate *Test Method* on that class. Each *Test Method* can use *Delegated Setup* (page 411) to build a *Minimal Fixture* (page 302) that makes the tests easily understood by calling well-named *Creation Methods* (page 415) to build the objects required for each test fixture.

To make the tests self-checking (*Self-Checking Test*; see page 26), we express the expected outcome of each test as one or more *Expected Objects* (see *State Verification* on page 462) and compare them with the actual objects returned by the **system under test (SUT)** using the built-in *Equality Assertions* (see *Assertion Method* on page 362) or *Custom Assertions* (page 474) that implement our own **test-specific equality**. If several tests are expected to result in the same outcome, we can factor out the verification logic into an outcome-describing *Verification Method* (see *Custom Assertion*) that the test reader can more easily recognize.

If we have *Untested Code* (see *Production Bugs* on page 268) because we cannot find a way to execute the path through the code, we can use a *Test Stub* (page 529) to gain control of the **indirect inputs** of the SUT. If there are *Untested Requirements* (see *Production Bugs*) because not all of the system's behavior is observable via its public interface, we can use a *Mock Object* (page 544) to intercept and verify the **indirect outputs** of the SUT.

Design for Testability

Automated testing is much simpler if we adopt a Layered Architecture [DDD, PEAA, WWW]. At a minimum, we should separate our business logic from the database and the user interface, thereby enabling us to test it easily using either *Subcutaneous Tests* or *Service Layer Tests* (see *Layer Test*). We can minimize any dependence on a *Database Sandbox* (page 650) by doing most—if not all—of our testing using in-memory objects only. This scheme lets the runtime environment implement *Garbage-Collected Teardown* (page 500) for us automatically, meaning that we can avoid writing potentially complex, error-prone teardown logic (a sure source of *Resource Leakage;* see *Erratic Test*). It also helps us avoid *Slow Tests* (page 253) by reducing disk I/O, which is much slower than memory manipulation.

If we are building a **GUI**, we should try to keep the complex GUI logic out of the visual classes. Using a *Humble Dialog* (see *Humble Object* on page 695) that delegates all decision making to nonvisual classes allows us to write unit tests for the GUI logic (e.g., enabling/disabling buttons) without having to instantiate the graphical objects or the framework on which they depend.

If the application is complex enough or if we are expected to build **components** that will be reused by other projects, we can augment the unit tests with **component tests** that verify the behavior of each component in isolation. We will probably need to use *Test Doubles* to replace any components on which our component depends. To install the *Test Doubles* at runtime, we can use either *Dependency Injection* (page 678), *Dependency Lookup* (page 686), or a *Subclassed Singleton* (see *Test-Specific Subclass* on page 579).

Test Organization

If we end up with too many *Test Methods* on our *Testcase Class*, we can consider splitting the class based on either the methods (or features) verified by the tests or their fixture needs. These patterns are called *Testcase Class per Feature* (page 624) and *Testcase Class per Fixture* (page 631), respectively. *Testcase Class per Fixture* allows us to move all of the fixture setup code into the setUp method, an approach called *Implicit Setup* (page 424). We can then aggregate the *Test Suite Objects* (page 387) for the resulting *Testcase Classes* into a single *Test Suite Object,* resulting in a *Suite of Suites* (see *Test Suite Object*) containing all the tests from the original *Testcase Class*. This *Test Suite Object* can, in turn, be added to the *Test Suite Object* for the containing package or namespace. We can then run all of the tests or just a subset that is relevant to the area of the software in which we are working.

What's Next?

This whirlwind tour of the most important goals, principles, patterns, and smells is just a brief introduction to test automation. Chapters 2 through 14 give a more detailed overview of each area touched upon here. If you have already spotted some patterns or smells you want to learn more about, you can certainly proceed directly to the detailed descriptions in Parts II and III. Otherwise, your next step is to delve into the subsequent narratives, which provide a somewhat more in-depth examination of these patterns and the alternatives to them. First up is Chapter 2, *Test Smells,* which describes some common "test smells" that motivate much of the refactoring we do on our tests.

Chapter 2

Test Smells

About This Chapter

Chapter 1, *A Brief Tour,* provided a very quick introduction to the core patterns and smells covered in this book. This chapter provides a more detailed examination of the "test smells" we are likely to encounter on our projects. We explore the basic concept of test smells first, and then move on to investigate the smells in three broad categories: test code smells, automated test behavior smells, and project smells related to automated testing.

An Introduction to Test Smells

In his book *Refactoring: Improving the Design of Existing Code,* Martin Fowler documented a number of ways that the design of code can be changed without actually changing what the code does. The motivation for this refactoring was the identification of "bad smells" that frequently occur in object-oriented code. These code smells were described in a chapter coauthored by Kent Beck that started with the famous quote from Grandma Beck: "If it stinks, change it." The context of this quote was the question, "How do you know you need to change a baby's diaper?" And so a new term was added to the programmer's lexicon.

The code smells described in *Refactoring* focused on problems commonly found in production code. Many of us had long suspected that there were smells unique to automated test scripts. At XP2001, the paper "Refactoring Test Code" [RTC] confirmed these suspicions by identifying a number of "bad smells" that occur specifically in test code. The authors also recommended a set of refactorings that can be applied to the tests to remove the noxious smells.

This chapter provides an overview of these **test smells.** More detailed examples of each test smell can be found in the reference section.

What's a Test Smell?

A smell is a symptom of a problem. A smell doesn't necessarily tell us what is wrong, because a particular smell may originate from any of several sources. Most of the smells in this book have several different named causes; some causes even appear under several smells. That's because a root cause may reveal itself through several different symptoms (i.e., smells).

Not all problems are considered smells, and some problems may even be the root cause of several smells. The "Occam's razor" test for deciding whether something really is a smell (versus just a problem) is the "sniffability test." That is, the smell must grab us by the nose and say, "Something is wrong here." As discussed in the next section, I have classified the smells based on the kinds of symptoms they exhibit (how they "grab us by the nose").

Based on the "sniffability" criteria, I have demoted some of the test smells listed in prior papers and articles to "cause" status. I have mostly left their names unchanged so that we can still refer to them when talking about a particular side effect of applying a pattern. In this case, it is more appropriate to refer directly to the cause rather than to the more general but sniffable smell.

Kinds of Test Smells

Over the years we have discovered that there are at least two different kinds of smells: **code smells**, which must be recognized when looking at code, and **behavior smells**, which affect the outcome of tests as they execute.

Code smells are coding-level **anti-patterns** that a developer, tester, or coach may notice while reading or writing test code. That is, the code just doesn't look quite right or doesn't communicate its intent very clearly. Code smells must first be recognized before we can take any action, and the need for action may not be equally obvious to everyone. Code smells apply to all kinds of tests, including both *Scripted Tests* (page 285) and *Recorded Tests* (page 278). They become particularly relevant for *Recorded Tests* when we must maintain the recorded code. Unfortunately, most *Recorded Tests* suffer from *Obscure Tests* (page 186), because they are recorded by a tool that doesn't know what is relevant to the human reader.

Behavior smells, by contrast, are much more difficult to ignore because they cause tests to fail (or not compile at all) at the most inopportune times, such as when we are trying to integrate our code into a crucial build; we are forced to unearth the problems before we can "make the bar green." Like code smells, behavior smells are relevant to both *Scripted Tests* and *Recorded Tests*.

Developers typically notice code and behavior smells when they automate, maintain, and run tests. More recently, we have identified a third kind of smell—a smell that is usually noticed by the project manager or the customer, who does not look at the test code or run the tests. These **project smells** are indicators of the overall health of a project.

What to Do about Smells?

Some smells are inevitable simply because they take too much effort to eliminate. The important thing is that we are aware of the smells and know what causes them. We can then make a conscious decision about which ones we must address to keep the project running efficiently.

The decision of which smells must be eliminated comes down to the balance between cost and benefit. Some smells are harder to stamp out than others; some smells cause more grief than others. We need to eradicate those smells that cause us the most grief because they will keep us from being successful. That being said, many smells can be avoided by selecting a sound test automation strategy and by following good test automation coding standards.

While we carefully delineated the various types of smells, it is important to note that very often we will observe symptoms of each kind of smell at the same time. Project smells, for example, are the project-level symptoms of some underlying cause. That cause may show up as a behavior smell but ultimately there is probably an underlying code smell that is the root cause of the problem. The good news: We have three different ways to identify a problem. The bad news: It is easy to focus on the symptom at one level and to try to solve that problem directly without understanding the root cause.

A very effective technique for identifying the root cause is the "Five Why's" [TPS]. First, we ask *why* something is occurring. Once we have identified the factors that led to it, we next ask *why* each of those factors occurred. We repeat this process until no new information is forthcoming. In practice, asking *why* five times is usually enough—hence the name "Five Why's."[1]

In the rest of this chapter, we will look at the test-related smells that we are most likely to encounter on our projects. We will begin with the project smells, and then work our way down to the behavior smells and code smells that cause them.

---

[1] This practice is also called "root cause analysis" or "peeling the onion" in some circles.

A Catalog of Smells

Now that we have a better understanding of test smells and their role in projects that use automated testing, let's look at some smells. Based on the "sniffability" criteria outlined earlier, this section focuses on introducing the smells. Discussions of their causes and the individual smell descriptions appear in Part II of this book.

The Project Smells

Project smells are symptoms that something has gone wrong on the project. Their root cause is likely to be one or more of the code or behavior smells. Because project managers rarely run or write tests, however, project smells are likely to be the first hint they get that something may be less than perfect in test automation land.

Project managers focus most on functionality, quality, resources, and cost. For this reason, the project-level smells tend to cluster around these issues. The most obvious metric a project manager is likely to encounter as a smell is the quality of the software as measured in defects found in formal testing or by users/customers. If the number of *Production Bugs* (page 268) is higher than expected, the project manager must ask, "Why are all of these bugs getting through our safety net of automated tests?"

The project manager may be monitoring the number of times the daily integration build fails as a way of getting an early indication of software quality and adherence to the team's development process. The manager may become worried if the build fails too frequently, and especially if it takes more than a few minutes to fix the build. **Root cause analysis** of the failures may indicate that many of the test failures are not the result of buggy software but rather derive from *Buggy Tests* (page 260). This is an example in which the tests cry "Wolf!" and consume a lot of resources as part of their correction, but do not actually increase the quality of the **production code**.

Buggy Tests are just one contributor to the more general problem of *High Test Maintenance Cost* (page 265), which can severely affect the productivity of the team if not addressed quickly. If the tests need to be modified too often (e.g., every time the SUT is modified) or if the cost of modifying tests is too high due to *Obscure Tests*, the project manager may decide that the effort and expense being directed toward writing the automated tests would be better spent on writing more production code or doing manual testing. At this point, the manager is likely to tell the developers to stop writing tests.[2]

Alternatively, the project manager may decide that the *Production Bugs* are caused by *Developers Not Writing Tests* (page 263). This pronouncement is likely to come during a process **retrospective** or as part of a root cause analysis session. *Developers Not Writing Tests* may be caused by an overly aggressive development schedule, supervisors who tell developers not to "waste time writing tests," or developers who do not have the skills to write tests. Other potential causes might include an imposed design that is not conducive to testing or a test environment that leads to *Fragile Tests* (page 239). Finally, this problem could result from *Lost Tests* (see *Production Bugs*)—tests that exist but are not included in the *AllTests Suite* (see *Named Test Suite* on page 592) used by developers during check-in or by the automated build tool.

The Behavior Smells

Behavior smells are encountered when we compile or run tests. We don't have to be particularly observant to notice them, as these smells will take the form of compile errors or test failures.

The most common behavior smell is *Fragile Tests*. It arises when tests that once passed begin failing for some reason. The *Fragile Test* problem has given test automation a bad name in many circles, especially when commercial "record and playback" test tools fail to deliver on their promise of easy test automation. Once recorded, these tests are very susceptible to breakage. Often the only remedy is to rerecord them because the test recordings are difficult to understand or modify by hand.

The root causes of *Fragile Tests* can be classified into four broad categories:

- *Interface Sensitivity* (see *Fragile Test*) occurs when tests are broken by changes to the test programming API or the user interface used to automate the tests. Commercial *Record and Playback Test* (see *Recorded Test*) tools typically interact with the system via the user interface. Even minor changes to the interface can cause tests to fail, even in circumstances in which a human user would say that the test should still pass.

---

[2] It can be hard enough to get project managers to buy into letting developers write automated tests. It is crucial that we don't squander this opportunity by being sloppy or inefficient. The need for this balancing act is, in a nutshell, why I started writing this book: to help developers succeed and avoid giving the pessimistic project manager an excuse for calling a halt to automated unit testing.

- *Behavior Sensitivity* (see *Fragile Test*) occurs when tests are broken by changes to the behavior of the SUT. This may seem like a "no-brainer" (of course, the tests should break if we change the SUT!) but the issue is that only a few tests should be broken by any one change. If many or most of the tests break, we have a problem.

- *Data Sensitivity* (see *Fragile Test*) occurs when tests are broken by changes to the data already in the SUT. This issue is particularly a problem for applications that use databases. *Data Sensitivity* is a special case of *Context Sensitivity* (see *Fragile Test*) where the context in question is the database.

- *Context Sensitivity* occurs when tests are broken by differences in the environment surrounding the SUT. The most common example is when tests depend on the time or date, but this problem can also arise when tests rely on the state of devices such as servers, printers, or monitors.

Data Sensitivity and *Context Sensitivity* are examples of a special kind of *Fragile Test*, known as a *Fragile Fixture*, in which changes to a commonly used test fixture cause multiple existing tests to fail. This scenario increases the cost of extending the *Standard Fixture* (page 305) to support new tests and, in turn, discourages good test coverage. Although *Fragile Fixture's* root cause is poor test design, the problem actually appears when the fixture is changed rather than when the SUT is changed.

Most agile projects use some form of daily or **continuous integration** that includes two steps: compiling the latest version of the code and running all of the automated tests against the newly compiled build. *Assertion Roulette* (page 224) can make it difficult to determine how and why tests failed during the integration build because the failure log does not include sufficient information to clearly identify which assertion failed. Troubleshooting of the build failures may proceed slowly, because the failure must be reproduced in the development environment before we can speculate on the cause of the failure.

A common cause of grief is tests that fail for no apparent reason. That is, neither the tests nor the production code has been modified, yet the tests suddenly begin failing. When we try to reproduce these results in the development environment, the tests may or may not fail. These *Erratic Tests* (page 228) are both very annoying and time-consuming to fix, because they have numerous possible causes. A few are listed here:

- *Interacting Tests* arise when several tests use a *Shared Fixture* (page 317). They make it hard to run tests individually or to run several test suites as part of a larger *Suite of Suites* (see *Test Suite Object* on page 387). They can also cause cascading failures (where a single test failure leaves the *Shared Fixture* in a state that causes many other tests to fail).

- *Test Run Wars* occur when several *Test Runners* (page 377) run tests against a *Shared Fixture* at the same time. They invariably happen at the worst possible time, such as when you are trying to fix the last few bugs before a release.

- *Unrepeatable Tests* provide a different result between the first and subsequent **test runs**. They may force the test automater to perform a *Manual Intervention* (page 250) between test runs.

Another productivity-sapping smell is *Frequent Debugging* (page 248). Automated unit tests should obviate the need to use a debugger in all but rare cases, because the set of tests that are failing should make it obvious why the failure is occurring. *Frequent Debugging* is a sign that the unit tests are lacking in coverage or are trying to test too much functionality at once.

The real value of having *Fully Automated Tests* (page 26) is being able to run them frequently. Agile developers who are doing test-driven development often run (at least a subset of) the tests every few minutes. This behavior should be encouraged because it shortens the feedback loop, thereby reducing the cost of any defects introduced into the code. When tests require *Manual Intervention* each time they are run, developers tend to run the tests less frequently. This practice increases the cost of finding all defects introduced since the tests were last run, because more changes will have been made to the software since it was last tested.

Another smell that has the same net impact on productivity is *Slow Tests* (page 253). When tests take more than approximately 30 seconds to run, developers stop running them after every individual code change, instead waiting for a "logical time" to run them—for example, before a coffee break, lunch, or a meeting. This delayed feedback results in a loss of "flow" and increases the time between when a defect is introduced and when it is identified by a test. The most frequently used solution to *Slow Tests* is also the most problematic; a *Shared Fixture* can result in many behavior smells and should be the solution of last resort.

The Code Smells

Code smells are the "classic" bad smells that were first described by Martin Fowler in *Refactoring* [Ref]. Indeed, most of the smells identified by Fowler are code smells. These smells must be recognized by test automaters as they maintain test code. Although code smells typically affect maintenance cost of tests, they may also be early warning signs of behavior smells to follow.

When reading tests, a fairly obvious—albeit often overlooked—smell is *Obscure Test*. It can take many forms, but all versions have the same impact: It becomes difficult to tell what the test is trying to do, because the test does not *Communicate Intent* (page 41). This ambiguity increases the cost of test maintenance and can lead to *Buggy Tests* when a **test maintainer** makes the wrong change to the test.

A related smell is *Conditional Test Logic* (page 200). Tests should be simple, linear sequences of statements. When tests have multiple execution paths, we cannot be sure exactly how the test will execute in a specific case.

Hard-Coded Test Data (see *Obscure Test*) can be insidious for several reasons. First, it makes tests more problematic to understand: We need to look at each value and guess whether it is related to any of the other values to understand how the SUT is supposed to behave. Second, it creates challenges when we are testing a SUT that includes a database. *Hard-Coded Test Data* can lead to *Erratic Tests* (if tests happen to use the same database key) or *Fragile Fixtures* (if the values refer to records in the database that have been changed).

Hard-to-Test Code (page 209) may be a contributing factor to a number of other code and behavior smells. This problem is most obvious to the person who is writing a test and cannot find a way to set up the fixture, exercise the SUT, or verify the expected outcome. The test automater may then be forced to test more software (a larger SUT consisting of many classes) than he or she would like. When reading a test, *Hard-to-Test Code* tends to show up as an *Obscure Test* because of the hoops the test automater had to jump through to interact with the SUT.

Test Code Duplication (page 213) is a poor practice because it increases the cost of maintaining tests. We have more test code to maintain and that code is more challenging to maintain because it often coincides with an *Obscure Test*. Duplication often arises when the automated tester clones tests and does not put enough thought into how to reuse test logic intelligently.[3] As testing needs emerge, it is important that the test automater factor out commonly used sequences of statements into *Test Utility Methods* (page 599) that can be reused

---

[3] Note that I said "reuse test logic" and not "reuse Test Methods."

by various *Test Methods* (page 348).[4] This practice reduces the maintenance cost of tests in several ways.

Test Logic in Production (page 217) is undesirable because there is no way to ensure that it will not run accidentally.[5] It also makes the production code larger and more complicated. Finally, this error may cause other software components or libraries to be included in the executable.

What's Next?

In this chapter, we saw a plethora of things that can go wrong when automating tests. Chapter 3, *Goals of Test Automation*, describes the goals we need to keep in mind while automating tests so that we can have an effective test automation experience. That understanding will prepare us to look at the principles that will help us steer clear of many of the problems described in this chapter.

---

[4] It is equally important that we do not reuse *Test Methods*, as that practice results in *Flexible Tests* (see *Conditional Test Logic*).

[5] See the sidebar on Ariane (page 218) for a cautionary tale.

Chapter 3

Goals of Test Automation

About This Chapter

Chapter 2, *Test Smells,* introduced the various "test smells" that can act as symptoms of problems with automated testing. This chapter describes the goals we should be striving to reach to ensure successful automated unit tests and customer tests. It begins with a general discussion of why we automate tests, then turns to a description of the overall goals of test automation, including reducing costs, improving quality, and improving the understanding of code. Each of these areas has more detailed named goals that are discussed briefly here as well. This chapter doesn't describe *how* to achieve these goals; that explanation will come in subsequent chapters where these goals are used as the rationale for many of the principles and patterns.

Why Test?

Much has been written about the need for automated unit and acceptance tests as part of agile software development. Writing good test code is hard, and maintaining obtuse test code is even harder. Because test code is optional (i.e., it is not what the customer is paying for), there is a strong temptation to abandon testing when the tests become difficult or expensive to maintain. Once we have given up on the principle of "keep the bar green to keep the code clean," much of the value of the automated tests is lost.

Over a series of projects, the teams I have worked with have faced a number of challenges to automated testing. The cost of writing and maintaining test suites has been a particular challenge, especially on projects with thousands of tests. Fortunately, as the cliché says, "Necessity is the mother of invention." My teams, and others, have developed a number of solutions to address these challenges. I have since spent a lot of time reflecting on these solutions to ask why they are good

19

solutions. Along the way, I have divided the components of successful solutions into goals (things to achieve) and principles (ways to achieve them). Adherence to these goals and principles will result in automated tests that are easier to write, read, and maintain.

Economics of Test Automation

Of course, there is always a cost incurred in building and maintaining an automated test suite. Ardent test automation advocates will argue that it is worth spending more to have the ability to change the software later. Unfortunately, this "pay me now so you don't have to pay me later" argument doesn't go very far in a tough economic climate.[1]

Our goal should be to make the decision to do test automation a "no-brainer" by ensuring that it does not increase the cost of software development. Thus the additional cost of building and maintaining automated tests must be offset by savings through reduced manual unit testing and debugging/troubleshooting as well as the remediation cost of the defects that would have gone undetected until the formal test phase of the project or early production usage of the application. Figure 3.1 shows how the cost of automation is offset by the savings received from automation.

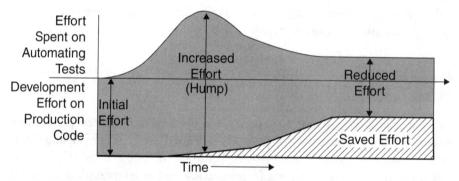

Figure 3.1   *An automated unit test project with a good return on investment. The cost-benefit trade-off when the total cost is reduced by good test practices.*

Initially, the cost of learning the new technology and practices takes additional effort. Once we get over this "hump," however, we should settle down to a steady state where the added cost (the part above the line) is fully offset by the

---

[1] The argument that the quality improvement is worth the extra cost also doesn't go very far in these days of "just good enough" software quality.

savings (the part below the line). If tests are difficult to write, are difficult to understand, and require frequent, expensive maintenance, the total cost of software development (the heights of the vertical arrows) goes up as illustrated in Figure 3.2.

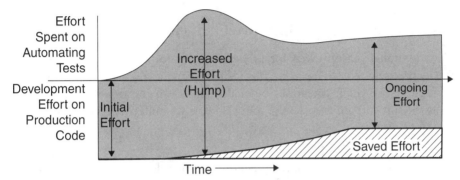

Figure 3.2 *An automated unit test project with a poor return on investment. The cost-benefit trade-off when the total cost is increased by poor test practices.*

Note how the added work above the line in Figure 3.2 is more than that seen in Figure 3.1 and continues to increase over time. Also, the saved effort below the line is reduced. This reflects the increase in overall effort, which exceeds the original effort without test automation.

Goals of Test Automation

We all come to test automation with some notion of why having automated tests would be a "good thing." Here are some high-level objectives that might apply:

- Tests should help us improve quality.

- Tests should help us understand the SUT.

- Tests should reduce (and not introduce) risk.

- Tests should be easy to run.

- Tests should be easy to write and maintain.

- Tests should require minimal maintenance as the system evolves around them.

The first three objectives demonstrate the value provided by the tests, whereas the last three objectives focus on the characteristics of the tests themselves. Most of these objectives can be decomposed into more concrete (and measurable) goals. I have given these short catchy names so that I can refer to them as motivators of specific principles or patterns.

Tests Should Help Us Improve Quality

The traditional reason given for doing testing is for quality assurance (QA). What, precisely, do we mean by this? What is quality? Traditional definitions distinguish two main categories of quality based on the following questions: (1) Is the software built correctly? and (2) Have we built the right software?

Goal: Tests as Specification

Also known as:
*Executable
Specification*

If we are doing test-driven development or test-first development, the tests give us a way to capture what the SUT should be doing before we start building it. They enable us to specify the behavior in various scenarios captured in a form that we can then execute (essentially an "executable specification"). To ensure that we are "building the right software," we must ensure that our tests reflect how the SUT will actually be used. This effort can be facilitated by developing user interface mockups that capture just enough detail about how the application appears and behaves so that we can write our tests.

The very act of thinking through various scenarios in enough detail to turn them into tests helps us identify those areas where the requirements are ambiguous or self-contradictory. Such analysis improves the quality of the specification, which improves the quality of the software so specified.

Goal: Bug Repellent

Yes, tests find bugs—but that really isn't what automated testing is about. Automated testing tries to prevent bugs from being introduced. Think of automated tests as "bug repellent" that keeps nasty little bugs from crawling back into our software after we have made sure it doesn't contain any bugs. Wherever we have regression tests, we won't have bugs because the tests will point the bugs out before we even check in our code. (We *are* running all the tests before every check-in, aren't we?)

Goal: Defect Localization

Mistakes happen! Of course, some mistakes are much more expensive to prevent than to fix. Suppose a bug does slip through somehow and shows up in the Integration Build [SCM]. If our unit tests are fairly small (i.e., we test only a single behavior in each one), we should be able to pinpoint the bug quickly based on which test fails. This specificity is one of the major advantages that unit tests enjoy over customer tests. The customer tests tell us that some behavior expected by the customer isn't working; the unit tests tell us why. We call this phenomenon *Defect Localization*. If a customer test fails but no unit tests fail, it indicates a *Missing Unit Test* (see *Production Bugs* on page 268).

All of these benefits are wonderful—but we cannot achieve them if we don't write tests for all possible scenarios that each unit of software needs to cover. Nor will we realize these benefits if the tests themselves contain bugs. Clearly, it is crucial that we keep the tests as simple as possible so that they can be easily seen to be correct. While writing unit tests for our unit tests is not a practical solution, we can—and should—write unit tests for any *Test Utility Method* (page 599) to which we delegate complex algorithms needed by the test methods.

Tests Should Help Us Understand the SUT

Repelling bugs isn't the only thing the tests can do for us. They can also show the **test reader** how the code is *supposed* to work. **Black box** component tests are—in effect—describing the requirements of that of software component.

Goal: Tests as Documentation

Without automated tests, we would need to pore over the SUT code trying to answer the question, "What should be the result if . . . ?" With automated tests, we simply use the corresponding *Tests as Documentation*; they tell us what the result should be (recall that a *Self-Checking Test* states the expected outcome in one or more assertions). If we want to know *how* the system does something, we can turn on the debugger, run the test, and single-step through the code to see how it works. In this sense, the automated tests act as a form of documentation for the SUT.

Tests Should Reduce (and Not Introduce) Risk

As mentioned earlier, tests should improve the quality of our software by helping us better document the requirements and prevent bugs from creeping in during incremental development. This is certainly one form of risk reduction. Other forms of risk reduction involve verifying the software's behavior in the "impossible" circumstances that cannot be induced when doing traditional customer testing of the entire application as a black box. It is a very useful exercise to review all of the project's risks and brainstorm about which kinds of risks could be at least partially mitigated through the use of *Fully Automated Tests*.

Also known as:
Safety Net

Goal: Tests as Safety Net

When working on legacy code, I always feel nervous. By definition, legacy code doesn't have a suite of automated regression tests. Changing this kind of code is risky because we never know what we might break, and we have no way of knowing whether we *have* broken something! As a consequence, we must work very slowly and carefully, doing a lot of manual analysis before making any changes.

When working with code that has a regression test suite, by contrast, we can work much more quickly. We can adopt a more experimental style of changing the software: "I wonder what would happen if I changed this? Which tests fail? Interesting! So that's what this parameter is for." In this way, the automated tests act as a safety net that allows us to take chances.[2]

The effectiveness of the safety net is determined by how completely our tests verify the behavior of the system. Missing tests are like holes in the safety net. Incomplete assertions are like broken strands. Each gap in the safety net can let bugs of various sizes through.

The effectiveness of the safety net is amplified by the version-control capabilities of modern software development environments. A source code repository [SCM] such as CVS, Subversion, or SourceSafe lets us roll back our changes to a known point if our tests suggest that the current set of changes is affecting the code too extensively. The built-in "undo" or "local history" features of the **IDE** let us turn the clock back 5 seconds, 5 minutes, or even 5 hours.

Also known as:
No Test Risk

Goal: Do No Harm

Naturally, there is a flip side to this discussion: How might automated tests introduce risk? We must be careful not to introduce new kinds of problems into the SUT as a result of doing automated testing. The *Keep Test Logic Out of Production Code* principle directs us to avoid putting test-specific hooks into the SUT. It is certainly desirable to design the system for testability, but any test-specific code should be plugged in by the test and only in the test environment; it should not exist in the SUT when it is in production.

Another form of risk is believing that some code is reliable because it has been thoroughly tested when, in fact, it has not. A common mistake made by developers new to the use of *Test Doubles* (page 522) is replacing too much of

---

[2] Imagine trying to learn to be a trapeze artist in the circus without having that big net that allows you to make mistakes. You would never progress beyond swinging back and forth!

the SUT with a *Test Double*. This leads to another important principle: *Don't Modify the SUT*. That is, we must be clear about which SUT we are testing and avoid replacing the parts we are testing with test-specific logic (Figure 3.3).

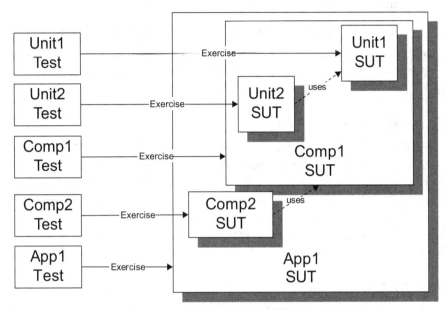

Figure 3.3   *A range of tests, each with its own SUT. An application, component, or unit is only the SUT with respect to a specific set of tests. The "Unit1 SUT" plays the role of DOC (part of the fixture) to the "Unit2 Test" and is part of the "Comp1 SUT."*

Tests Should Be Easy to Run

Most software developers just want to write code; testing is simply a necessary evil in our line of work. Automated tests provide a nice safety net so that we can write code more quickly,[3] but we will run the automated tests frequently only if they are *really easy* to run.

What makes tests easy to run? Four specific goals answer this question:

- They must be *Fully Automated Tests* so they can be run without any effort.

---

[3] "With less paranoia" is probably more accurate!

- They must be *Self-Checking Tests* so they can detect and report any errors without manual inspection.

- They must be *Repeatable Tests* so they can be run multiple times with the same result.

- Ideally, each test should be an *Independent Test* that can be run by itself.

With these four goals satisfied, one click of a button (or keyboard shortcut) is all it should take to get the valuable feedback the tests provide. Let's look at these goals in a bit more detail.

Goal: Fully Automated Test

A test that can be run without any *Manual Intervention* (page 250) is a *Fully Automated Test*. Satisfying this criterion is a prerequisite to meeting many of the other goals. Yes, it is possible to write *Fully Automated Tests* that don't check the results and that can be run only once. The main() program that runs the code and directs print statements to the console is a good example of such a test. I consider these two aspects of test automation to be so important in making tests easy to run that I have made them separate goals: *Self-Checking Test* and *Repeatable Test*.

Goal: Self-Checking Test

A *Self-Checking Test* has encoded within it everything that the test needs to verify that the expected outcome is correct. *Self-Checking Tests* apply the Hollywood principle ("Don't call us; we'll call you") to running tests. That is, the *Test Runner* (page 377) "calls us" only when a test *did not* pass; as a consequence, a clean test run requires zero manual effort. Many members of the xUnit family provide a *Graphical Test Runner* (see *Test Runner*) that uses a **green bar** to signal that everything is "A-okay"; a **red bar** indicates that a test has failed and warrants further investigation.

Goal: Repeatable Test

A *Repeatable Test* can be run many times in a row and will produce exactly the same results without any human intervention between runs. *Unrepeatable Tests* (see *Erratic Test* on page 228) increase the overhead of running tests significantly. This outcome is very undesirable because we want all developers to be able to run the tests very frequently—as often as after every "save." *Unrepeatable Tests* can be run only once before whoever is running the tests must perform a *Manual Intervention*. Just as bad are *Nondeterministic Tests* (see *Erratic Test*) that produce different results at different times; they force us to spend lots of time chasing down failing tests. The power of the red bar diminishes significantly when we see it regularly without good reason. All too soon, we begin ignoring the red bar, assuming that it will go away if we wait long enough. Once this happens, we have lost a lot of the value of our automated tests, because the feedback indicating that we *have* introduced a bug and *should* fix it right away disappears. The longer we wait, the more effort it takes to find the source of the failing test.

Tests that run only in memory and that use only local variables or fields are usually repeatable without us expending any additional effort. *Unrepeatable Tests* usually come about because we are using a *Shared Fixture* (page 317) of some sort (this definition includes any persistence of data implemented within the SUT). In such a case, we must ensure that our tests are "self-cleaning" as well. When cleaning is necessary, the most consistent and foolproof strategy is to use a generic *Automated Teardown* (page 503) mechanism. Although it is possible to write teardown code for each test, this approach can result in *Erratic Tests* when it is not implemented correctly in every test.

Tests Should Be Easy to Write and Maintain

Coding is a fundamentally difficult activity because we must keep a lot of information in our heads as we work. When we are writing tests, we should stay focused on *testing* rather than *coding* of the tests. This means that tests must be simple—simple to read *and* simple to write. They need to be simple to read and understand because testing the automated tests themselves is a complicated endeavor. They can be tested properly only by introducing the very bugs that they are intended to detect into the SUT; this is hard to do in an automated way so it is usually done only once (if at all), when the test is first written. For these reasons, we need to rely on our eyes to catch any problems that creep into the tests, and that means we must keep the tests simple enough to read quickly.

Of course, if we are changing the behavior of part of the system, we should expect a small number of tests to be affected by our modifications. We want to *Minimize Test Overlap* so that only a few tests are affected by any one change. Contrary to popular opinion, having more tests pass through the same code doesn't improve the quality of the code if most of the tests do exactly the same thing.

Tests become complicated for two reasons:

- We try to verify too much functionality in a single test.

- Too large an "expressiveness gap" separates the test scripting language (e.g., Java) and the before/after relationships between domain concepts that we are trying to express in the test.

Goal: Simple Tests

To avoid "biting off more than they can chew," our tests should be small and test one thing at a time. Keeping tests simple is particularly important during test-driven development because code is written to pass one test at a time and we want each test to introduce only one new bit of behavior into the SUT. We should strive to *Verify One Condition per Test* by creating a separate *Test Method* (page 348) for each unique combination of pre-test state and input. Each *Test Method* should drive the SUT through a single code path.[4]

The major exception to the mandate to keep *Test Methods* short occurs with customer tests that express real usage scenarios of the application. Such extended tests offer a useful way to document how a potential user of the software would go about using it; if these interactions involve long sequences of steps, the *Test Methods* should reflect this reality.

Goal: Expressive Tests

The "expressiveness gap" can be addressed by building up a library of *Test Utility Methods* that constitute a domain-specific testing language. Such a collection of methods allows test automaters to express the concepts that they wish to test without having to translate their thoughts into much more detailed code. *Creation Methods* (page 415) and *Custom Assertion* (page 474) are good examples of the building blocks that make up such a *Higher-Level Language*.

The key to solving this dilemma is avoiding duplication within tests. The DRY principle—"Don't repeat yourself"—of the Pragmatic Programmers (http://www.pragmaticprogrammer.com) should be applied to test code in the same way it is applied to production code. There is, however, a counterforce at play. Because the tests should *Communicate Intent,* it is best to keep the core test logic in each *Test Method* so it can be seen in one place. Nevertheless, this idea doesn't preclude moving a lot of supporting code into *Test Utility Methods,* where it needs to be modified in only one place if it is affected by a change in the SUT.

Goal: Separation of Concerns

Separation of Concerns applies in two dimensions: (1) We want to keep test code separate from our production code *(Keep Test Logic Out of Production Code)* and (2) we want each test to focus on a single concern *(Test Concerns Separately)* to avoid *Obscure Tests* (page 186). A good example of what *not* to do is testing the business logic in the same tests as the user interface, because it involves testing

---

[4] There should be at least one *Test Method* for each unique path through the code; often there will be several, one for each **boundary value** of the **equivalence class**.

two concerns at the same time. If either concern is modified (e.g., the user inter-face changes), all the tests would need to be modified as well. Testing one concern at a time may require separating the logic into different components. This is a key aspect of **design for testability,** a consideration that is explored further in Chapter 11, *Using Test Doubles.*

Tests Should Require Minimal Maintenance as the System Evolves Around Them

Change is a fact of life. Indeed, we write automated tests mostly to make change easier, so we should strive to ensure that our tests don't inadvertently make change more difficult.

Suppose we want to change the signature of some method on a class. When we add a new parameter, suddenly 50 tests no longer compile. Does that result en-courage us to make the change? Probably not. To counter this problem, we intro-duce a new method with the parameter and arrange to have the old method call the new method, defaulting the missing parameter to some value. Now all of the tests compile but 30 of them still fail! Are the tests helping us make the change?

Goal: Robust Test

Inevitably, we will want to make many kinds of changes to the code as a project unfolds and its requirements evolve. For this reason, we want to write our tests in such a way that the number of tests affected by any one change is quite small. That means we need to minimize overlap between tests. We also need to ensure that changes to the test environment don't affect our tests; we do this by isolat-ing the SUT from the environment as much as possible. This results in much more *Robust Tests.*

We should strive to *Verify One Condition per Test.* Ideally, only one kind of change should cause a test to require maintenance. System changes that affect fixture setup or teardown code can be encapsulated behind *Test Utility Methods* to further reduce the number of tests directly affected by the change.

What's Next?

This chapter discussed why we have automated tests and specific goals we should try to achieve when writing *Fully Automated Tests.* Before moving on to Chapter 5, *Principles of Test Automation,* we need to take a short side-trip to Chapter 4, *Philosophy of Test Automation,* to understand the different mindsets of various kinds of test automaters.

Chapter 4

Philosophy of Test Automation

About This Chapter

Chapter 3, *Goals of Test Automation,* described many of the goals and benefits of having an effective test automation program in place. This chapter introduces some differences in the way people think about design, construction, and testing that change the way they might naturally apply these patterns. The "big picture" questions include whether we write tests first or last, whether we think of them as tests or examples, whether we build the software from the inside-out or from the outside-in, whether we verify state or behavior, and whether we design the fixture upfront or test by test.

Why Is Philosophy Important?

What's philosophy got to do with test automation? A lot! Our outlook on life (and testing) strongly affects how we go about automating tests. When I was discussing an early draft of this book with Martin Fowler (the series editor), we came to the conclusion that there were philosophical differences between how different people approached xUnit-based test automation. These differences lie at the heart of why, for example, some people use *Mock Objects* (page 544) sparingly and others use them everywhere.

Since that eye-opening discussion, I have been on the lookout for other philosophical differences among test automaters. These alternative viewpoints tend to come up as a result of someone saying, "I never (find a need to) use that pattern" or "I never run into that smell." By questioning these statements, I can learn a lot about the testing philosophy of the speaker. Out of these discussions have come the following philosophical differences:

- "Test after" versus "test first"

- Test-by-test versus test all-at-once

- "Outside-in" versus "inside-out" (applies independently to design and coding)

- Behavior verification versus state verification

- "Fixture designed test-by-test" versus "big fixture design upfront"

Some Philosophical Differences

Test First or Last?

Traditional software development prepares and executes tests after all software is designed and coded. This order of steps holds true for both customer tests and unit tests. In contrast, the agile community has made writing the tests first the standard way of doing things. Why is the order in which testing and development take place important? Anyone who has tried to retrofit *Fully Automated Tests* (page 22) onto a legacy system will tell you how much more difficult it is to write automated tests after the fact. Just having the discipline to write automated unit tests after the software is "already finished" is challenging, whether or not the tests themselves are easy to construct. Even if we **design for testability**, the likelihood that we can write the tests easily and naturally without modifying the production code is low. When tests are written first, however, the design of the system is inherently testable.

Writing the tests first has some other advantages. When tests are written first and we write only enough code to make the tests pass, the production code tends to be more minimalist. Functionality that is optional tends not to be written; no extra effort goes into fancy error-handling code that doesn't work. The tests tend to be more robust because only the necessary methods are provided on each object based on the tests' needs.

Access to the state of the object for the purposes of fixture setup and result verification comes much more naturally if the software is written "test first." For example, we may avoid the test smell *Sensitive Equality* (see *Fragile Test* on page 239) entirely because the correct attributes of objects are used in assertions rather than comparing the string representations of those objects. We may even find that we don't need to implement a String representation at all because we have no real need for it. The ability to substitute dependencies with *Test Doubles* (page 522) for the purpose of verifying the outcome is also greatly enhanced because **substitutable dependency** is designed into the software from the start.

Tests or Examples?

Whenever I mention the concept of writing automated tests for software before the software has been written, some listeners get strange looks on their faces. They ask, "How can you possibly write tests for software that doesn't exist?" In these cases, I follow Brian Marrick's lead by reframing the discussion to talk about "examples" and **example-driven development (EDD)**. It seems that examples are much easier for some people to envision writing before code than are "tests." The fact that the examples are executable and reveal whether the requirements have been satisfied can be left for a later discussion or a discussion with people who have a bit more imagination.

By the time this book is in your hands, a family of EDD frameworks is likely to have emerged. The Ruby-based **RSpec** kicked off the reframing of TDD to EDD, and the Java-based **JBehave** followed shortly thereafter. The basic design of these "unit test frameworks" is the same as xUnit but the terminology has changed to reflect the *Executable Specification* (see *Goals of Test Automation* on page 21) mindset.

Another popular alternative for specifying components that contain **business logic** is to use **Fit** tests. These will invariably be more readable by nontechnical people than something written in a programming language regardless of how "business friendly" we make the programming language syntax!

Test-by-Test or Test All-at-Once?

The test-driven development process encourages us to "write a test" and then "write some code" to pass that test. This process isn't a case of *all* tests being written before *any* code, but rather the writing of tests and code being interleaved in a very fine-grained way. "Test a bit, code a bit, test a bit more"—this is **incremental development** at its finest. Is this approach the only way to do things? Not at all! Some developers prefer to identify all tests needed by the current **feature** before starting any coding. This strategy enables them to "think like a client" or "think like a tester" and lets developers avoid being sucked into "solution mode" too early.

Test-driven purists argue that we can design more incrementally if we build the software one test at a time. "It's easier to stay focused if only a single test is failing," they say. Many **test drivers** report not using the debugger very much because the fine-grained testing and incremental development leave little doubt about why tests are failing; the tests provide *Defect Localization* (see *Goals of Test Automation* on page 22) while the last change we made (which caused the problem) is still fresh in our minds.

This consideration is especially relevant when we are talking about unit tests because we can choose when to enumerate the detailed requirements (tests) of each object or method. A reasonable compromise is to identify all unit tests at the beginning of a **task**—possibly roughing in empty *Test Method* (page 348) skeletons, but coding only a single *Test Method* body at a time. We could also code all *Test Method* bodies and then disable all but one of the tests so that we can focus on building the production code one test at a time.

With customer tests, we probably don't want to feed the tests to the developer one by one within a **user story**. Therefore, it makes sense to prepare all the tests for a single story before we begin development of that story. Some teams prefer to have the customer tests for the story identified—although not necessarily fleshed out—before they are asked to estimate the effort needed to build the story, because the tests help frame the story.

Outside-In or Inside-Out?

Designing the software from the outside inward implies that we think first about black-box customer tests (also known as **storytests**) for the entire system and then think about unit tests for each piece of software we design. Along the way, we may also implement **component tests** for the large-grained **components** we decide to build.

Each of these sets of tests inspires us to "think like the client" well before we start thinking like a software developer. We focus first on the interface provided to the user of the software, whether that user is a person or another piece of software. The tests capture these usage patterns and help us enumerate the various scenarios we need to support. Only when we have identified all the tests are we "finished" with the specification. Some people prefer to *design* outside-in but then *code* inside-out to avoid dealing with the "dependency problem." This tactic requires anticipating the needs of the outer software when writing the tests for the inner software. It also means that we don't actually test the outer software in isolation from the inner software. Figure 4.1 illustrates this concept. The top-to-bottom progression in the diagram implies the order in which we write the software. Tests for the middle and lower classes can take advantage of the already-built classes above them—a strategy that avoids the need for *Test Stubs* (page 529) or *Mock Objects* in many of the tests. We may still need to use *Test Stubs* in those tests where the inner components could potentially return specific values or throw exceptions, but cannot be made to do so on cue. In such a case, a *Saboteur* (see *Test Stub*) comes in very handy.

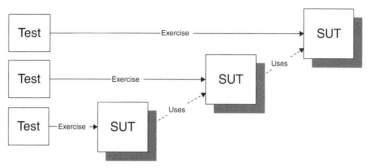

Figure 4.1 *"Inside-out" development of functionality. Development starts with the innermost components and proceeds toward the user interface, building on the previously constructed components.*

Other test drivers prefer to design *and* code from the outside-in. Writing the code outside-in forces us to deal with the "dependency problem." We can use *Test Stubs* to stand in for the software we haven't yet written, so that the outer layer of software can be executed and tested. We can also use *Test Stubs* to inject "impossible" **indirect inputs** (return values, out parameters, or exceptions) into the SUT to verify that it handles these cases correctly.

In Figure 4.2, we have reversed the order in which we build our classes. Because the subordinate classes don't exist yet, we used *Test Doubles* to stand in for them.

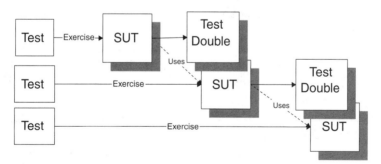

Figure 4.2 *"Outside-in" development of functionality supported by Test Doubles. Development starts at the outside using Test Doubles in place of the depended-on components (DOCs) and proceeds inward as requirements for each DOC are identified.*

Once the subordinate classes *have* been built, we *could* remove the *Test Doubles* from many of the tests. Keeping them provides better *Defect Localization* at the cost of potentially higher test maintenance cost.

State or Behavior Verification?

From writing code outside-in, it is but a small step to verifying behavior rather than just state. The "statist" view suggests that it is sufficient to put the SUT into a specific state, exercise it, and verify that the SUT is in the expected state at the end of the test. The "behaviorist" view says that we should specify not only the start and end states of the SUT, but also the calls the SUT makes to its dependencies. That is, we should specify the details of the calls to the "outgoing interfaces" of the SUT. These **indirect outputs** of the SUT are outputs just like the values returned by functions, except that we must use special measures to trap them because they do not come directly back to the client or test.

The behaviorist school of thought is sometimes called **behavior-driven development**. It is evidenced by the copious use of *Mock Objects* or *Test Spies* (page 538) throughout the tests. Behavior verification does a better job of testing each unit of software in isolation, albeit at a possible cost of more difficult refactoring. Martin Fowler provides a detailed discussion of the statist and behaviorist approaches in [MAS].

Fixture Design Upfront or Test-by-Test?

In the traditional test community, a popular approach is to define a "test bed" consisting of the application and a database already populated with a variety of test data. The content of the database is carefully designed to allow many different test scenarios to be exercised.

When the fixture for xUnit tests is approached in a similar manner, the test automater may define a *Standard Fixture* (page 305) that is then used for all the *Test Methods* of one or more *Testcase Classes* (page 373). This fixture may be set up as a *Fresh Fixture* (page 311) in each *Test Method* using *Delegated Setup* (page 411) or in the setUp method using *Implicit Setup* (page 424). Alternatively, it can be set up as a *Shared Fixture* (page 317) that is reused by many tests. Either way, the test reader may find it difficult to determine which parts of the fixture are truly pre-conditions for a particular *Test Method*.

The more agile approach is to custom design a *Minimal Fixture* (page 302) for each *Test Method*. With this perspective, there is no "big fixture design upfront" activity. This approach is most consistent with using a *Fresh Fixture*.

When Philosophies Differ

We cannot always persuade the people we work with to adopt our philosophy, of course. Even so, understanding that others subscribe to a different philosophy helps us appreciate *why* they do things differently. It's not that these individuals don't share the same goals as ours;[1] it's just that they make the decisions about how to achieve those goals using a different philosophy. Understanding that different philosophies exist and recognizing which ones we subscribe to are good first steps toward finding some common ground between us.

My Philosophy

In case you were wondering what my personal philosophy is, here it is:

- Write the tests first!

- Tests *are* examples!

- I usually write tests one at a time, but sometimes I list all the tests I can think of as skeletons upfront.

- Outside-in development helps clarify which tests are needed for the next layer inward.

- I use primarily *State Verification* (page 462) but will resort to *Behavior Verification* (page 468) when needed to get good code coverage.

- I perform fixture design on a test-by-test basis.

There! Now you know where *I'm* coming from.

What's Next?

This chapter introduced the philosophies that anchor software design, construction, testing, and test automation. Chapter 5, *Principles of Test Automation,* describes key principles that will help us achieve the goals described in Chapter 3, *Goals of Test Automation.* We will then be ready to start looking at the overall test automation strategy and the individual patterns.

---

[1] For example, high-quality software, fit for purpose, on time, under budget.

Chapter 5

Principles of Test Automation

About This Chapter

Chapter 3, *Goals of Test Automation,* described the goals we should strive to achieve to help us be successful at automating our unit tests and customer tests. Chapter 4, *Philosophy of Test Automation,* discussed some of the differences in the way people approach software design, construction, and testing. This provides the background for the principles that experienced test automaters follow while automating their tests. I call them "principles" for two reasons: They are too high level to be patterns and they represent a value system that not everyone will share. A different value system may cause you to choose different patterns than the ones presented in this book. Making this value system explicit will, I hope, accelerate the process of understanding where we disagree and why.

The Principles

When Shaun Smith and I came up with the list in the original Test Automation Manifesto [TAM], we considered what was driving us to write tests the way we did. The Manifesto is a list of the *qualities* we would like to see in a test—not a set of patterns that can be directly applied. However, those principles have led us to identify a number of somewhat more concrete principles, some of which are described in this chapter. What makes these principles different from the goals is that there is more debate about them.

Principles are more "prescriptive" than patterns and higher level in nature. Unlike patterns, they don't have alternatives, but rather are presented in a "do this because" fashion. To distinguish them from patterns, I have given them imperative names rather than the noun-phrase names I use for goals, patterns, and smells.

For the most part, these principles apply equally well to unit tests and story-tests. A possible exception is the principle *Verify One Condition per Test,* which may not be practical for customer tests that exercise more involved chunks of functionality. It is, however, still worth striving to follow these principles and to deviate from them only when you are fully cognizant of the consequences.

Also known as:

Also known as:
Test-Driven
Development,
Test-First
Development

Principle: Write the Tests First

Test-driven development is very much an acquired habit. Once one has "gotten the hang of it," writing code in any other way can seem just as strange as TDD seems to those who have never done it. There are two major arguments in favor of doing TDD:

1. The unit tests save us a lot of debugging effort—effort that often fully offsets the cost of automating the tests.

2. Writing the tests before we write the code forces the code to be designed for testability. We don't need to think about testability as a separate design condition; it just happens because we have written tests.

Principle: Design for Testability

Given the last principle, this principle may seem redundant. For developers who choose to ignore *Write the Tests First*, *Design for Testability* becomes an even more important principle because they won't be able to write automated tests after the fact if the testability wasn't designed in. Anyone who has tried to retrofit automated unit tests onto legacy software can testify to the difficulty this raises. Mike Feathers talks about special techniques for introducing tests in this case in [WEwLC].

Also known as:
Front Door First

Principle: Use the Front Door First

Objects have several kinds of interfaces. There is the "public" interface that clients are expected to use. There may also be a "private" interface that only close friends should use. Many objects also have an "outgoing interface" consisting of the used part of the interfaces of any objects on which they depend.

The types of interfaces we use influence the robustness of our tests. The use of *Back Door Manipulation* (page 327) to set up the fixture or verify the expected outcome or a test can result in *Overcoupled Software* (see *Fragile Test* on page 239) that needs more frequent test maintenance. Overuse of *Behavior Verification* (page 468) and *Mock Objects* (page 544) can result in *Overspecified Software* (see *Fragile Test*) and tests that are more brittle and may discourage developers from doing desirable refactorings.

When all choices are equally effective, we should use round-trip tests to test our SUT. To do so, we test an object through its public interface and use *State Verification* (page 462) to determine whether it behaved correctly. If this is not sufficient to accurately describe the expected behavior, we can make our tests **layer-crossing tests** and use *Behavior Verification* to verify the calls the SUT makes to **depended-on components (DOCs)**. If we must replace a slow or unavailable DOC with a faster *Test Double* (page 522), using a *Fake Object* (page 551) is preferable because it encodes fewer assumptions into the test (the only assumption is that the component that the *Fake Object* replaces is actually needed).

Principle: Communicate Intent

Also known as:
*Higher-Level Language,
Single-Glance Readable*

Fully Automated Tests, especially *Scripted Tests* (page 285), are programs. They need to be syntactically correct to compile and semantically correct to run successfully. They need to implement whatever detailed logic is required to put the SUT into the appropriate starting state and to verify that the expected outcome has occurred. While these characteristics are necessary, they are not sufficient because they neglect the single most important interpreter of the tests: the **test maintainer**.

Tests that contain a lot of code[1] or *Conditional Test Logic* (page 200) are usually *Obscure Tests* (page 186). They are much harder to understand because we need to infer the "big picture" from all the details. This reverse engineering of meaning takes extra time whenever we need to revisit the test either to maintain it or to use the *Tests as Documentation*. It also increases the cost of ownership of the tests and reduces their return on investment.

Tests can be made easier to understand and maintain if we *Communicate Intent*. We can do so by calling *Test Utility Methods* (page 599) with Intent-Revealing Names [SBPP] to set up our test fixture and to verify that the expected outcome has been realized. It should be readily apparent within the *Test Method* (page 348) how the test fixture influences the **expected outcome** of each test—that is, which inputs result in which outputs. A rich library of *Test Utility Methods* also makes tests easier to write because we don't have to code the details into every test.

Principle: Don't Modify the SUT

Effective testing often requires us to replace a part of the application with a *Test Double* or override part of its behavior using a *Test-Specific Subclass* (page 579). This may be because we need to gain control over its **indirect inputs** or because we need to perform *Behavior Verification* by intercepting its **indirect outputs**. It may

---

[1] Anything more than about ten lines is getting to be too much.

also be because parts of the application's behavior have unacceptable side effects or dependencies that are impossible to satisfy in our development or test environment.

Modifying the SUT is a dangerous thing whether we are putting in *Test Hooks* (page 709), overriding behavior in a *Test-Specific Subclass,* or replacing a DOC with a *Test Double.* In any of these circumstances, we may no longer actually be testing the code we plan to put into production.

We need to ensure that we are testing the software in a configuration that is truly representative of how it will be used in production. If we do need to replace something the SUT depends on to get better control of the context surrounding the SUT, we must make sure that we are doing so in a representative way. Otherwise, we may end up replacing part of the SUT that we think we are testing. Suppose, for example, that we are writing tests for objects X, Y, and Z, where object X depends on object Y, which in turn depends on object Z. When writing tests for X, it is reasonable to replace Y and Z with a *Test Double.* When testing Y, we can replace Z with a *Test Double.* When testing Z, however, we cannot replace it with a *Test Double* because Z is what we are testing! This consideration is particularly salient when we have to refactor the code to improve its testability.

When we use a *Test-Specific Subclass* to override part of the behavior of an object to allow testing, we have to be careful that we override only those methods that the test specifically needs to null out or use to inject indirect inputs. If we choose to reuse a *Test-Specific Subclass* created for another test, we must ensure that it does not override any of the behavior that *this* test is verifying.

Another way of looking at this principle is as follows: The term *SUT* is relative to the tests we are writing. In our "X uses Y uses Z" example, the SUT for some component tests might be the aggregate of X, Y, and Z; for unit testing purposes, it might be just X for some tests, just Y for other tests, and just Z for yet other tests. Just about the only time we consider the entire application to be the SUT is when we are doing **user acceptance testing** using the user interface and going all the way back to the database. Even here, we might be testing only one **module** of the entire application (e.g., the "Customer Management Module"). Thus "SUT" rarely equals "application."

Principle: Keep Tests Independent

Also known as:
*Independent
Test*

When doing **manual testing**, it is common practice to have long test procedures that verify many aspects of the SUT's behavior in a single test. This aggregation of tasks is necessary because the steps involved in setting up the starting state of the system for one test may simply repeat the steps used to verify other parts of its behavior. When tests are executed manually, this repetition is not cost-effective. In addition, human testers have the ability to recognize when a test failure should preclude continuing execution of the test, when it should cause certain tests to be skipped, or when the failure is immaterial to subsequent tests (though it may still count as a failed test.)

If tests are interdependent and (even worse) order dependent, we will deprive ourselves of the useful feedback that individual test failures provide. *Interacting Tests* (see *Erratic Test* on page 228) tend to fail in a group. The failure of a test that moved the SUT into the state required by the dependent test will lead to the failure of the dependent test, too. With both tests failing, how can we tell whether the failure reflects a problem in code that both tests rely on in some way or whether it signals a problem in code that only the first test relies on? When both tests fail, we can't tell. And we are talking about only two tests in this case—imagine how much worse matters would be with tens or even hundreds of *Interacting Tests*.

An *Independent Test* can be run by itself. It sets up its own *Fresh Fixture* (page 311) to put the SUT into a state that lets it verify the behavior it is testing. Tests that build a *Fresh Fixture* are much more likely to be independent than tests that use a *Shared Fixture* (page 317). The latter can lead to various kinds of *Erratic Tests,* including *Lonely Tests, Interacting Tests,* and *Test Run Wars.* With independent tests, unit test failures give us *Defect Localization* to help us pinpoint the source of the failure.

Principle: Isolate the SUT

Some pieces of software depend on nothing but the (presumably correct) runtime system or operating system. Most pieces of software build on other pieces of software developed by us or by others. When our software depends on other software that may change over time, our tests may suddenly start failing because the behavior of the other software has changed. This problem, which is called *Context Sensitivity* (see *Fragile Test*), is a form of *Fragile Test.*

When our software depends on other software whose behavior we cannot control, we may find it difficult to verify that our software behaves properly with all possible return values. This is likely to lead to *Untested Code* (see *Production Bugs* on page 268) or *Untested Requirements* (see *Production Bugs*). To avoid this problem, we need to be able to inject all possible reactions of the DOC into our software under the complete control of our tests.

Whatever application, component, class, or method we are testing, we should strive to isolate it as much as possible from all other parts of the software that we choose not to test. This isolation of elements allows us to *Test Concerns Separately* and allows us to *Keep Tests Independent* of one another. It also helps us create a *Robust Test* by reducing the likelihood of *Context Sensitivity* caused by too much coupling between our SUT and the software that surrounds it.

   We can satisfy this principle by designing our software such that each piece of depended-on software can be replaced with a *Test Double* using *Dependency Injection* (page 678) or *Dependency Lookup* (page 686) or overridden with a *Test-Specific Subclass* that gives us control of the indirect inputs of the SUT. This design for testability makes our tests more repeatable and robust.

Principle: Minimize Test Overlap

Most applications have lots of functionality to verify. Proving that all of the functionality works correctly in all possible combinations and interaction scenarios is nearly impossible. Therefore, picking the tests to write is an exercise in risk management.

   We should structure our tests so that as few tests as possible depend on a particular piece of functionality. This may seem counter-intuitive at first because one would think that we would want to improve test coverage by testing the software as often as possible. Unfortunately, tests that verify the same functionality typically fail at the same time. They also tend to need the same maintenance when the functionality of the SUT is modified. Having several tests verify the same functionality is likely to increase test maintenance costs and probably won't improve quality very much.

   We do want to ensure that all test conditions are covered by the tests that we do use. Each test condition should be covered by exactly one test—no more, no less. If it seems to provide value to test the code in several different ways, we may have identified several different test conditions.

Principle: Minimize Untestable Code

Some kinds of code are difficult to test using *Fully Automated Tests*. GUI components, multithreaded code, and *Test Methods* immediately spring to mind as "untestable" code. All of these kinds of code share the same problem: They are embedded in a context that makes it hard to instantiate or interact with them from automated tests.

   Untestable code simply won't have any *Fully Automated Tests* to protect it from those nefarious little bugs that can creep into code when we aren't looking. That makes it more difficult to refactor this code safely and more dangerous to modify existing functionality or introduce new functionality.

   It is highly desirable to minimize the amount of untestable code that we have to maintain. We can refactor the untestable code to improve its testability by moving the logic we want to test out of the class that is causing the lack of testability. For active objects and multithreaded code, we can refactor to *Humble Executable* (see *Humble Object* on page 695). For user interface objects, we can refactor to *Humble Dialog* (see *Humble Object*). Even *Test Methods* can have much of their untestable code extracted into *Test Utility Methods,* which can then be tested.

When we *Minimize Untestable Code,* we improve the overall test coverage of our code. In so doing, we also improve our confidence in the code and extend our ability to refactor at will. The fact that this technique improves the quality of the code is yet another benefit.

Principle: Keep Test Logic Out of Production Code

Also known as:
*No Test Logic
in Production
Code*

When the production code hasn't been designed for testability (whether as a result of test-driven development or otherwise), we may be tempted to put "hooks" into the production code to make it easier to test. These hooks typically take the form of if testing then ... and may either run alternative logic or prevent certain logic from running.

Testing is about verifying the behavior of a system. If the system behaves differently when under test, then how can we be certain that the production code actually works? Even worse, the test hooks could *cause* the software to fail in production!

The production code should not contain any conditional statements of the if testing then sort. Likewise, it should not contain any test logic. A well-designed system (from a testing perspective) is one that allows for the isolation of functionality. Object-oriented systems are particularly amenable to testing because they are composed of discrete objects. Unfortunately, even object-oriented systems can be built in such a way as to be difficult to test, and we may still encounter code with embedded test logic.

Principle: Verify One Condition per Test

Also known as:
*Single-Condition
Test*

Many tests require a starting state other than the default state of the SUT, and many operations of the SUT leave it in a different state from its original state. There is a strong temptation to reuse the end state of one test condition as the starting state of the next test condition by combining the verification of the two test conditions into a single *Test Method* because this makes testing more efficient. This approach is not recommended, however, because when one assertion fails, the rest of the test will not be executed. As a consequence, it becomes more difficult to achieve *Defect Localization.*

Verifying multiple conditions in a single test makes sense when we execute tests manually because of the high overhead of test setup and because the liveware can adapt to test failures. It is too much work to set up the fixture for a large number of manual tests, so human testers naturally tend to write long multiple-condition tests.[2] They also have the intelligence to work around any issues they encounter so that all is not lost if a single step fails. In contrast, with automated tests, a single failed assertion will cause the test to stop running and the rest of the test will provide no data on what works and what doesn't.

Each *Scripted Test* should verify a single test condition. This single-mindedness is possible because the test fixture is set up programmatically rather than by a human. Programs can set up fixtures very quickly and they don't have trouble executing exactly the same sequence of steps hundreds of times! If several tests need the same test fixture, either we can move the *Test Methods* into a single *Testcase Class per Fixture* (page 631) so we can use *Implicit Setup* (page 424) or we can call *Test Utility Methods* to set up the fixture using *Delegated Setup* (page 411).

We design each test to have four distinct phases (see *Four-Phase Test* on page 358) that are executed in sequence: **fixture setup, exercise SUT, result verification,** and **fixture teardown.**

- In the first phase, we set up the test fixture (the "before" picture) that is required for the SUT to exhibit the expected behavior as well as anything we need to put in place to observe the actual outcome (such as using a *Test Double*).

- In the second phase, we interact with the SUT to exercise whatever behavior we are trying to verify. This should be a single, distinct behavior; if we try to exercise several parts of the SUT, we are not writing a *Single-Condition Test*.

- In the third phase, we do whatever is necessary to determine whether the expected outcome has been obtained and fail the test if it has not.

- In the fourth phase, we tear down the test fixture and put the world back into the state in which we found it.

Note that there is a single exercise SUT phase and a single result verification phase. We avoid having a series of such alternating calls (exercise, verify, exercise, verify) because that approach would be trying to verify several distinct conditions—something that is better handled via distinct *Test Methods*.

One possibly contentious aspect of *Verify One Condition per Test* is what we mean by "one condition." Some test drivers insist on one *assertion* per test. This insistence may be based on using a *Testcase Class per Fixture* organization of the *Test Methods* and naming each test based on what the one assertion is

---

[2] Clever testers often use automated test scripts to put the SUT into the correct starting state for their manual tests, thereby avoiding long manual test scripts.

verifying.[3] Having one assertion per test makes such naming very easy but also leads to many more test methods if we have to assert on many output fields. Of course, we can often comply with this interpretation by extracting a *Custom Assertion* (page 474) or *Verification Method* (see *Custom Assertion*) that allows us to reduce the multiple assertion method calls to a single call. Sometimes that approach makes the test more readable. When it doesn't, I wouldn't be too dogmatic about insisting on a single assertion.

Principle: Test Concerns Separately

The behavior of a complex application consists of the aggregate of a large number of smaller behaviors. Sometimes several of these behaviors are provided by the same component. Each of these behaviors is a different concern and may have a significant number of scenarios in which it needs to be verified.

The problem with testing several concerns in a single *Test Method* is that this method will be broken whenever any of the tested concerns is modified. Even worse, it won't be obvious which concern is the one at fault. Identifying the real culprit typically requires *Manual Debugging* (see *Frequent Debugging* on page 248) because of the lack of *Defect Localization*. The net effect is that more tests will fail and each test will take longer to troubleshoot and fix. Refactoring is also made more difficult by testing several concerns in the same test; it will be harder to "tease apart" the eager class into several independent classes, each of which implements a single concern, because the tests will need extensive redesign.

Testing our concerns separately allows a failure to tell us that we have a problem in a specific part of our system rather than simply saying that we have a problem somewhere. This approach to testing also makes it easier to understand the behavior now and to separate the concerns in subsequent refactorings. That is, we should just be able to move a subset of the tests to a different *Testcase Class* (page 373) that verifies the newly created class; it shouldn't be necessary to modify the test much more than changing the class name of the SUT.

Principle: Ensure Commensurate Effort and Responsibility

The amount of effort it takes to write or modify tests should not exceed the effort it takes to implement the corresponding functionality. Likewise, the tools required to write or maintain the test should require no more expertise than the tools used to implement the functionality. For example, if we can configure the

---

[3] For example, `AwaitingApprovalFlight.validApproverRequestShouldBeApproved`.

behavior of a SUT using metadata and we want to write tests that verify that the metadata is set up correctly, we should not have to write code to do so. A *Data-Driven Test* (page 288) would be much more appropriate in these circumstances.

What's Next?

Previous chapters covered the common pitfalls (in the form of test smells) and goals of test automation. This chapter made the value system we use while choosing patterns explicit. In Chapter 6, *Test Automation Strategy*, we will examine the "hard to change" decisions that we should try to get right early in the project.

Chapter 6

Test Automation Strategy

About This Chapter

In previous chapters, we saw some of the problems we might encounter with test automation. In Chapter 5, *Principles of Test Automation,* we learned about some of the principles we can apply to help address those problems. This chapter gets a bit more concrete but still focuses at the 30,000-foot level. In the logical sequence of things, test strategy comes before fixture setup but is a somewhat more advanced topic. If you are new to test automation using xUnit, you may want to skip this chapter and come back after reading more about the basics of xUnit in Chapter 7, *xUnit Basics,* and about fixture setup and teardown in Chapter 8, *Transient Fixture Management,* and subsequent chapters.

What's Strategic?

As the story in the preface amply demonstrates, it is easy to get off on the wrong foot. This is especially true when you lack experience in test automation and when this testing strategy is adopted "bottom up." If we catch the problems early enough, the cost of refactoring the tests to eliminate the problems can be manageable. If, however, the problems are left to fester for too long or the wrong approach is taken to address them, a very large amount of effort can be wasted. This is not to suggest that we should follow a "big design upfront" (BDUF) approach to test automation. BDUF is almost always the wrong answer. Rather, it is helpful to be aware of the strategic decisions necessary and to make them "just in time" rather than "much too late." This chapter gives a "head's up" about some of the strategic issues we want to keep in mind so that we don't get blindsided by them later.

What makes a decision "strategic"? A decision is strategic if it is "hard to change." That is, a strategic decision affects a large number of tests, especially such that many or all the tests would need to be converted to a different approach at the same time. Put another way, any decision that could cost a large amount of effort to change is strategic.

Common strategic decisions include the following considerations:

- Which kinds of tests to automate?

- Which tools to use to automate them?

- How to manage the test fixture?

- How to ensure that the system is easily tested and how the tests interact with the SUT?

Each of these decisions can have far-reaching consequences, so they are best made consciously, at the right time, and based on the best available information.

The strategies and more detailed patterns described in this book are equally applicable regardless of the kind of *Test Automation Framework* (page 298) we choose to use. Most of my experience is with xUnit, so it is the focus of this book. But "don't throw out the baby with the bath water": If you find yourself using a different kind of *Test Automation Framework,* remember that most of what you learn in regard to xUnit may still be applicable.

Which Kinds of Tests Should We Automate?

Roughly speaking, we can divide tests into the following two categories:

- Per-functionality tests (also known as functional tests) verify the behavior of the SUT in response to a particular stimulus.

- Cross-functional tests verify various aspects of the system's behavior that cut across specific functionality.

Figure 6.1 shows these two basic kinds of tests as two columns, each of which is further subdivided into more specific kinds of tests.

Per-Functionality Tests

Per-functionality tests verify the directly observable behavior of a piece of software. The functionality can be business related (e.g., the principal use cases of the system) or related to operational requirements (e.g., system maintenance and specific fault-tolerance scenarios). Most of these requirements can also be expressed as **use cases, features, user stories,** or test scenarios.

Per-functionality tests can be characterized by whether the functionality is business (or user) facing and by the size of the SUT on which they operate.

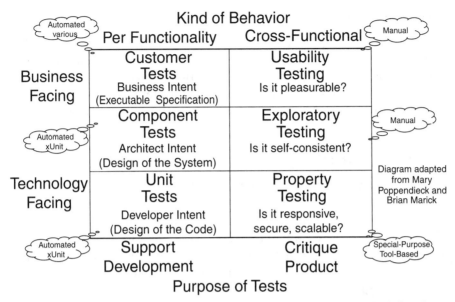

Figure 6.1 *A summary of the kinds of tests we write and why. The left column contains the tests we write that describe the functionality of the product at various levels of granularity; we perform these tests to support development. The right column contains tests that span specific chunks of functionality; we execute these tests to critique the product. The bottom of each cell describes what we are trying to communicate or verify.*

Customer Tests

Customer tests verify the behavior of the entire system or application. They typically correspond to scenarios of one or more use cases, features, or user stories. These tests often go by other names such as functional tests, **acceptance tests,** or end-user tests. Although they may be automated by developers, their key characteristic is that an end user should be able to recognize the behavior specified by the test even if the user cannot read the test representation.

Unit Tests

Unit tests verify the behavior of a single class or method that is a consequence of a design decision. This behavior is typically not directly related to the requirements except when a key chunk of business logic is encapsulated within the class or method in question. These tests are written by developers for their own use; they help developers describe what "done looks like" by summarizing the behavior of the unit in the form of tests.

Component Tests

Component tests verify components consisting of groups of classes that collectively provide some service. They fit somewhere between unit tests and customer tests in terms of the size of the SUT being verified. Although some people call these "integration tests" or "subsystem tests," those terms can mean something entirely different from "tests of a specific larger-grained subcomponent of the overall system."

Fault Insertion Tests

Fault insertion tests typically show up at all three levels of granularity within these functional tests, with different kinds of faults being inserted at each level. From a test automation strategy point of view, fault insertion is just another set of tests at the unit and component test levels. Things get more interesting at the whole-application level, however. Inserting faults here can be hard to automate because it is challenging to automate insertion of the faults without replacing parts of the application.

Cross-Functional Tests

Property Tests

Performance tests verify various "nonfunctional" (also known as "extra-functional" or "cross-functional") requirements of the system. These requirements are different in that they span the various kinds of functionality. They often correspond to the architectural "-ilities." These kinds of tests include

- Response time tests
- Capacity tests
- Stress tests

From a test automation perspective, many of these tests *must* be automated (at least partially) because human testers would have a hard time creating enough load to verify the behavior under stress. While we can run the same test many times in a row in xUnit, the xUnit framework is not particularly well suited to automating performance tests.

One advantage of agile methods is that we can start running these kinds of tests quite early in the project—as soon as the key components of the architecture have been roughed in and the skeleton of the functionality is executable. The same tests can then be run continuously throughout the project as new features are added to the system skeleton.

Usability Tests

Usability tests verify "fitness for purpose" by confirming that real users can use the software application to achieve the stated goals. These tests are very difficult to automate because they require subjective assessment by people regarding how easy it is to use the SUT. For this reason, usability tests are rarely automated and will not be discussed further in this book.

Exploratory Testing

Exploratory testing is a way to determine whether the product is self-consistent. The testers use the product, observe how it behaves, form hypotheses, design tests to verify those hypotheses, and exercise the product with them. By its very nature, exploratory testing cannot be automated, although automated tests can be used to set up the SUT in preparation for doing exploratory testing.

Which Tools Do We Use to Automate Which Tests?

Choosing the right tool for the job is as important as having good skills with the tools selected for use. A wide array of tools are available in the marketplace, and it is easy to be seduced by the features of a particular tool. The choice of tool is a strategic decision: Once we have invested a lot of time and effort in learning a tool and automating many tests using that tool, it becomes much more difficult to change to a different tool.

There are two fundamentally different approaches to automating tests (Figure 6.2). The *Recorded Test* (page 278) approach involves the use of tools that monitor our interactions with the SUT while we test it manually. This information is then saved to a file or database and becomes the script for replaying this test against another (or even the same) version of the SUT. The main problem with *Recorded Tests* is the level of granularity they record. Most commercial tools record actions at the user interface (UI) element level, which results in *Fragile Tests* (page 239).

The second approach to automating tests, *Hand-Scripted Tests* (see *Scripted Test* on page 285), involves the hand-coding of test programs ("scripts") that exercise the system. While xUnit is probably the most commonly used *Test Automation Framework* for preparing *Hand-Scripted Tests*, they may be prepared in other ways, including "batch" files, macro languages, and commercial or open-source test tools. Some of the better-known open-source tools for preparing *Scripted Tests* are **Watir** (test scripts coded in Ruby and run inside Internet Explorer), **Canoo WebTest** (tests scripted in XML and run using the WebTest tool), and the ever-popular **Fit** (and its wiki-based sibling **FitNesse**). Some of these tools even provide a test capture capability, thereby blurring the lines between *Scripted Tests* and *Recorded Tests*.

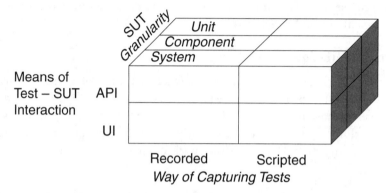

Figure 6.2 *A summary of the three dimensions of test automation choices. The left side shows the two ways of interacting with the SUT. The bottom edge enumerates how we create the test scripts. The front-to-back dimension categorizes the different sizes of SUT we may choose to test.*

Choosing which test automation tools to use is a large part of the test strategy decision. A full survey of the different kinds of tools available is beyond the scope of this book, but a somewhat more detailed treatment of the topic is available in [ARTRP]. The following sections summarize the information here to provide an overview of the strengths and weaknesses of each approach.

Test Automation Ways and Means

Figure 6.3 depicts the decision-making possibilities as a matrix. In theory, there are 2 × 2 × 3 possible combinations in this matrix, but it is possible to understand the primary differences between the approaches by looking at the front face of the cube. Some of the four quadrants are applicable to all levels of granularity; others are primarily used for automating customer tests.

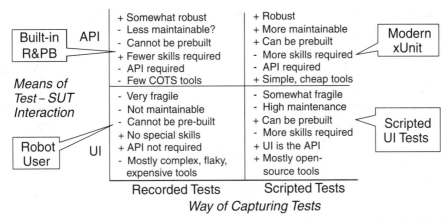

Figure 6.3 *The choices on the front face of the cube. A more detailed look at the front face of the cube in Figure 6.2 along with the advantages (+) and disadvantages of each (–).*

Upper-Right Quadrant: Modern xUnit

The upper-right quadrant of the front face of the cube is dominated by the xUnit family of testing frameworks. These frameworks involve hand-scripting tests that exercise the system at all three levels of granularity (system, component, and unit) via internal interfaces. A good example is unit tests automated using JUnit or NUnit.

Lower-Right Quadrant: Scripted UI Tests

This quadrant represents a variation on the "modern xUnit" approach, with the most common examples being the use of **HttpUnit**, **JFCUnit**, **Watir**, or similar tools to hand-script tests using the UI. It is also possible to hand-script tests using commercial *Recorded Test* tools such as **QTP**. These approaches all reside within the lower-right quadrant at various levels of SUT granularity. For example, when used for customer tests, these tools would perform at the system test level of granularity. They could also be used to test just the UI component of the system (or possibly even some UI units such as custom widgets), although this effort would require stubbing out the actual system behind the UI.

Lower-Left Quadrant: Robot User

The "robot user" quadrant focuses on recording tests that interact with the system via the UI. Most commercial test automation tools follow this approach. It applies primarily at the "whole system" granularity but, like scripted UI Tests, could be applied to the UI components or units if the rest of the system can be stubbed out.

Upper-Left Quadrant: Internal Recording

For completeness, the upper-left quadrant involves creating *Recorded Tests* via an API somewhere behind the UI by recording all inputs and responses as the SUT is exercised. It may even involve inserting observation points between the SUT (at whatever granularity we are testing) and any DOCs. During test playback, the test APIs inject the inputs recorded earlier and compare the results with what was recorded

This quadrant is not well populated with commercial tools[1] but is a feasible option when building a *Recorded Test* mechanism into the application itself.

Introducing xUnit

The xUnit family of *Test Automation Frameworks* is designed for use in automating programmer tests. Its design is intended to meet the following goals:

- Make it easy for developers to write tests without needing to learn a new programming language. xUnit is available in most languages in use today.

- Make it easy to test individual classes and objects without needing to have the rest of the application available. xUnit is designed to allow us to test the software from the inside; we just have to design for testability to take advantage of this capability.

- Make it easy to run one test or many tests with a single action. xUnit includes the concept of a test suite and *Suite of Suites* (see *Test Suite Object* on page 387) to support this kind of test execution.

- Minimize the cost of running the tests so programmers aren't discouraged from running the existing tests. For this reason, each test should be a *Self-Checking Test* (page 26) that implements the **Hollywood principle**.[2]

---

[1] Most of the tools in this quadrant focus on recording regression tests by inserting observation points into a component-based application and recording the (remote) method calls and responses between the components. This approach is becoming more popular with the advent of service-oriented architecture (SOA).

[2] The name is derived from what directors in Hollywood tell aspiring applicants at mass casting calls: "Don't call us; we'll call you (if we want you)."

The xUnit family has been extraordinarily successful at meeting its goals. I cannot imagine that Erich Gamma and Kent Beck could have possibly anticipated just how big an impact that first version of JUnit would have on software development![3] The same characteristics that make xUnit particularly well suited to automating programmer tests, however, may make it less suitable for writing some other kinds of tests. In particular, the "stop on first failure" behavior of assertions in xUnit has often been criticized (or overridden) by people who want to use xUnit for automating multistep customer tests so that they can see the whole score (what worked and what didn't) rather than merely the first deviation from the expected results. This disagreement points out several things:

- "Stop on first failure" is a tool philosophy, not a characteristic of unit tests. It so happens that most test automaters prefer to have their unit tests stop on first failure, and most recognize that customer tests must necessarily be longer than unit tests.

- It *is possible* to change the fundamental behavior of xUnit to satisfy specific needs; this flexibility is just one advantage of open-source tools.

- Seeing a need to change the fundamental behavior of xUnit should probably be interpreted as a trigger for *considering* whether some other tool might *possibly* be a better fit.

For example, the Fit framework has been designed specifically for the purpose of running customer tests. It overcomes the limitations of xUnit that lead to the "stop on first failure" behavior by communicating the pass/fail status of each step of a test using color coding. Another option for Java developers is TestNG, which provides capabilities for explicitly sequencing *Chained Tests* (page 454).

Having said this, choosing a different tool doesn't eliminate the need to make many of the strategic decisions unless the tool constrains that decision making in some way. For example, we still need to set up the test fixture for a Fit test. Some patterns—such as *Chained Tests*, where one test sets up the fixture for a subsequent test—are difficult to automate and may therefore be less attractive in Fit than in xUnit. And isn't it ironic that the very flexibility of xUnit is what allows test automaters to get themselves into so much trouble by creating *Obscure Tests* (page 186) that result in *High Test Maintenance Cost* (page 265)?

---

[3] Technically, SUnit came first but it took JUnit and the "Test Infected" article [TI] to really get things rolling.

The xUnit Sweet Spot

The xUnit family works best when we can organize our tests as a large set of small tests, each of which requires a small test fixture that is relatively easy to set up. This allows us to create a separate test for each test scenario of each object. The test fixture should be managed using a *Fresh Fixture* (page 311) strategy by setting up a new *Minimal Fixture* (page 302) for each test.

xUnit works best when we write tests against software APIs and then test single classes or small groups of classes in isolation. This approach allows us to build small test fixtures that can be instantiated quickly.

When doing customer tests, xUnit works best if we define a *Higher-Level Language* (page 41) with which to describe our tests. This choice moves the level of abstraction higher, away from the nitty-gritty of the technology and closer to the business concepts that customers understand. From here, it is a very small step to convert these tests to *Data-Driven Tests* (page 288) implemented in xUnit or Fit.

Note that many of the higher-level patterns and principles described in this book apply equally well to both Fit tests and xUnit tests. I have also found them to be useful when working with commercial GUI-based testing tools, which typically use a "record and playback" metaphor. The fixture management patterns are particularly salient in this arena, as are reusable "test components" that may be strung together to form a variety of test scripts. This is entirely analogous to the xUnit practice of single-purpose *Test Methods* (page 348) calling reusable *Test Utility Methods* (page 599) to reduce their coupling to the SUT's API.

Which Test Fixture Strategy Do We Use?

The test fixture management strategy is strategic because it has a large impact on the execution time and robustness of the tests. The effects of picking the wrong strategy won't be felt immediately because it takes at least a few hundred tests before the *Slow Tests* (page 253) smell becomes evident and probably several months of development before the *High Test Maintenance Cost* smell starts to emerge. Once these smells appear, however, the need to change the test automation strategy will become apparent—and its cost will be significant because of the number of tests affected.

What Is a Fixture?

Every test consists of four parts, as described in *Four-Phase Test* (page 358). In the first phase, we create the SUT and everything it depends on and put them into the state required to exercise the SUT. In xUnit, we call everything we need in place to exercise the SUT the **test fixture,** and we call the part of the test logic that we execute to set it up the **fixture setup** phase of the test.

At this point, a word of caution is in order. The term "fixture" means many things to many people:

- Some variants of xUnit keep the concept of the fixture separate from the *Testcase Class* (page 373) that creates it. JUnit and its direct ports fall into this category.

- Other members of the xUnit family assume that an instance of the *Testcase Class* "is a" fixture. NUnit is a good example.

- A third camp uses an entirely different name for the fixture. For example, **RSpec** captures the pre-conditions of the test in a test context class that holds the *Test Methods* (same idea as NUnit but with different terminology).

- The term "fixture" is used to mean entirely different things in other kinds of test automation. In Fit, for example, it means the custom-built parts of the *Data-Driven Test* Interpreter [GOF] that we use to define our *Higher-Level Language.*

The "class 'is a' fixture" approach assumes the *Testcase Class per Fixture* (page 631) approach to organizing the tests. When we choose a different way of organizing the tests, such as *Testcase Class per Class* (page 617) or *Testcase Class per Feature* (page 624), this merging of the concepts of test fixture and *Testcase Class* can be confusing. Throughout this book, I use "test fixture"—or just "fixture"—to mean "the pre-conditions of the test" and *Testcase Class* to mean "the class that contains the *Test Methods* and any code needed to set up the test fixture."

The most common way to set up the fixture is to use **front door** fixture setup by calling the appropriate methods on the SUT to construct the objects. When the state of the SUT is stored in other objects or components, we can do *Back Door Setup* (see *Back Door Manipulation* on page 327) by inserting the necessary records directly into the other component on which the behavior of the SUT depends. We use *Back Door Setup* most often with databases or when we need to use a *Mock Object* (page 544) or *Test Double* (page 522); these concepts are covered in more detail in Chapter 13, *Testing with Databases,* and Chapter 11, *Using Test Doubles.*

Major Fixture Strategies

There are probably many ways to classify just about anything. For the purposes of this discussion, we will classify our test fixture strategies based on what kinds of test development work we need to do for each one.

The first and simplest fixture management strategy requires us to worry only how we will organize the code to build the fixture for each test. That is, do we put this code in our *Test Methods*, factor it into *Test Utility Methods* that we call from our *Test Methods*, or put it into a setUp method in our *Testcase Class*? This strategy involves the use of *Transient Fresh Fixtures* (see *Fresh Fixture*). These fixtures live only in memory and very conveniently disappear as soon as we are done with them.

A second strategy involves the use of *Fresh Fixtures* that, for one reason or another, persist beyond the single *Test Method* that uses it. To keep them from turning into *Shared Fixtures* (page 317), these *Persistent Fresh Fixtures* (see *Fresh Fixture*) require explicit code to tear them down at the end of each test. This requirement brings into play the fixture teardown patterns.

A third strategy involves persistent fixtures that are deliberately reused across many tests. This *Shared Fixture* strategy is often used to improve the execution speed of tests that use a *Persistent Fresh Fixture* but comes with a fair amount of baggage. These tests require the use of one of the fixture construction and teardown triggering patterns. They also involve tests that interact with one another, whether by design or by consequence, which often leads to *Erratic Tests* (page 228) and *High Test Maintenance Costs*.

Table 6.1 summarizes the fixture management overhead associated with each of the three styles of fixtures.

Table 6.1 *A Summary of the Fixture Setup and Teardown Requirements of the Various Test Fixture Strategies*

	Set Up Code	Tear Down Code	Setup/Teardown Triggering
Transient Fresh Fixture	Yes		
Persistent Fresh Fixture	Yes	Yes	
Shared Fixture	Yes	Yes	Yes

Note: The Shared Fixture row assumes we are building a new *Shared Fixture* each test run rather than using a *Prebuilt Fixture* (page 429).

Figure 6.4 illustrates the interaction between our goals, freshness of fixtures or fixture reuse, and fixture persistence. It also illustrates a few variations of the *Shared Fixture*.

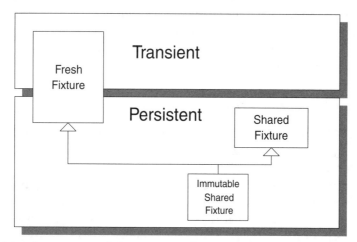

Figure 6.4 *A summary of the main test fixture strategies. Fresh Fixtures can be either transient or persistent; Shared Fixtures must be persistent. An Immutable Shared Fixture (see Shared Fixture) must not be modified by any test. As a consequence, most tests augment the Shared Fixture with a Fresh Fixture that they can modify.*

The relationship between persistence and freshness is reasonably obvious for two of these combinations. The persistent *Fresh Fixture* is discussed in more detail later in this chapter. The transient *Shared Fixture* is inherently transient—how we hold references to these fixtures is what makes them persist. Other than this distinction, transient *Shared Fixtures* can be treated exactly like persistent *Shared Fixtures*.

Transient Fresh Fixtures

In this approach, each test creates a temporary *Fresh Fixture* as it runs. Any objects or records it requires are created by the test itself (though not necessarily inside the *Test Method*). Because the test fixture visibility is restricted to the one test alone, we ensure that each test is completely independent because it cannot depend, either accidentally or on purpose, on the output of any other tests that use the same fixture.

We call this approach *Fresh Fixture* because each test starts with a clean slate and builds from there. It does not "inherit" or "reuse" any part of the fixture from other tests or from a *Prebuilt Fixture* (page 429). Every object or record used by the SUT is "fresh," "brand new," and not "previously enjoyed."

The main disadvantage of using the *Fresh Fixture* approach is the additional CPU cycles it takes to create all the objects for each test. As a consequence, the tests may run more slowly than under a *Shared Fixture* approach, especially if we use a *Persistent Fresh Fixture*.

Persistent Fresh Fixtures

A *Persistent Fresh Fixture* sounds a bit oxymoronic. We want the fixture to be fresh, yet it persists beyond the lifetime of a single test! What kind of strategy is that? Some might say "stupid," but sometimes one has to do this.

We are "forced" into this strategy when we are testing components that are tightly coupled to a database or other persistence mechanism. The obvious solution is that we should not let the coupling be so tight, but rather make the database a **substitutable dependency** of the component we are testing. This step may not be practical when testing **legacy software**, however—yet we may still want to partake of the benefits of a *Fresh Fixture*. Hence the existence of the *Persistent Fresh Fixture* strategy. The key difference between this strategy and the *Transient Fresh Fixture* is the need for code to tear down the fixture after each test. *Persistent Fresh Fixtures* can result in *Slow Tests* if the persistence of the fixture is caused by the use of a database, file system, or other high-latency dependency.

We can at least partially address the resulting *Slow Tests* by applying one or more of the following patterns:

1. Construct a *Minimal Fixture* (the smallest fixture possible).

2. Speed up the construction by using a *Test Double* to replace the provider of any data that takes too long to set up.

3. If the tests still are not fast enough, minimize the size of the part of the fixture we need to destroy and reconstruct each time by using an *Immutable Shared Fixture* for any objects that are referenced but not modified.

The project teams with which I have worked have found that, on average, our tests run 50 times faster (yes, they take 2% as long) when we use *Dependency Injection* (page 678) or *Dependency Lookup* (page 686) to replace the entire database with a *Fake Database* (see *Fake Object* on page 551) that uses a set of hash tables instead of tables. Each test may require many, many database operations to set up and tear down the fixture required by a single query in the SUT.

There is a lot to be said for minimizing the size and complexity of the test fixture. A *Minimal Fixture* (see *Minimal Fixture*) is much easier to understand and helps highlight the cause–effect relationship between the fixture and the expected outcome. In this regard, it is a major enabler of *Tests as Documentation* (page 23). In some cases, we can make the test fixture much smaller by using *Entity Chain Snipping* (see *Test Stub* on page 529) to eliminate the need to instantiate those objects on which our test depends only indirectly. This tactic will certainly speed up the instantiation of our test fixture.

Shared Fixture Strategies

Sometimes we cannot—or choose not to—use a *Fresh Fixture* strategy. In these cases, we can use a *Shared Fixture*. In this approach, many tests reuse the same *instance* of a test fixture.

The major advantage of *Shared Fixtures* is that we save a lot of execution time in setting up and tearing down the fixture. The main disadvantage is conveyed by one of its aliases, Stale Fixture, and by the test smell that describes its most common side effects, *Interacting Tests* (see *Erratic Test*). Although *Shared Fixtures* do have other benefits, most can be realized by applying other patterns to *Fresh Fixtures*; *Standard Fixture* (page 305) avoids the fixture design and coding effort for every test without actually sharing the fixture.

Now, if *Shared Fixtures* are so bad, why even discuss them? Because everyone seems to go down this road at least once in his or her career—so we might as well share the best available information about them should you venture down that path. Mind you, this discussion isn't meant to encourage anyone to go down this path unnecessarily because it is paved with broken glass, infested with poisonous snakes, and . . . well, you get my drift.

Given that we have decided to use a *Shared Fixture* (we did investigate *every* possible alternative, didn't we?), what are our options? We can make the following adjustments (Figure 6.5):

- How far and wide we share a fixture (e.g., a *Testcase Class*, all tests in a test suite, all test run by a particular user)

- How often we recreate the fixture

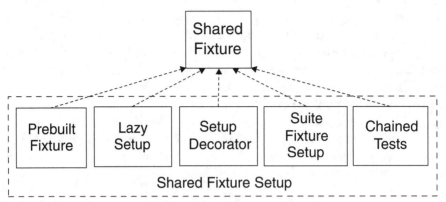

Figure 6.5   *The various ways we can manage a Shared Fixture. The strategies are ordered by the length of the fixture's lifetime, with the longestlasting fixture appearing on the left.*

The more tests that share a fixture, the more likely that one of them will make a mess of things and spoil everything for all the tests that follow it. The less often we reconstruct the fixture, the longer the effects of a messed-up fixture will persist. For example, a *Prebuilt Fixture* can be set up outside the test run, thereby avoiding the entire cost of setting up the fixture as part of the test run; unfortunately, it can also result in *Unrepeatable Tests* (see *Erratic Test*) if tests don't clean up after themselves properly. This strategy is most commonly used with a *Database Sandbox* (page 650) that is initialized using a database script; once the fixture is corrupted, it must be reinitialized by rerunning the script. If the *Shared Fixture* is accessible to more than one *Test Runner* (page 377), we may end up in a *Test Run War* (see *Erratic Test*), in which tests fail randomly as they try to use the same fixture resource at the same time as some other test.

We can avoid both *Unrepeatable Tests* and *Test Run Wars* by setting up the fixture each time the test suite is run. xUnit provides several ways to do so, including *Lazy Setup* (page 435), *Suite Fixture Setup* (page 441), and *Setup Decorator* (page 447). The concept of "lazy initialization" should be familiar to most object-oriented developers; here we just apply the concept to the construction of the test fixture. The latter two choices provide a way to tear down the test fixture when the test run is finished because they call a setUp method and a corresponding tearDown at the appropriate times; *Lazy Setup* does not give us a way to do this.

Chained Tests represent another option for setting up a *Shared Fixture*, one that involves running the tests in a predefined order and letting each test use the previous test's results as its test fixture. Unfortunately, once one test fails, many of the tests that follow will provide erratic results because their pre-conditions have not been satisfied. This problem *can* be made easier to diagnose by having each test use *Guard Assertions* (page 490) to verify that its pre-conditions have been met.[4]

As mentioned earlier, an *Immutable Shared Fixture* is a strategy for speeding up tests that use a *Fresh Fixture*. We can also use an *Immutable Shared Fixture* to make tests based on a *Shared Fixture* less erratic by restricting changes to a smaller, mutable part of a *Shared Fixture*.

How Do We Ensure Testability?

The last strategic concern touched on in this chapter is ensuring testability. The discussion here isn't intended to be a complete treatment of the topic—it is too large to cover in a single chapter on test strategy. Nevertheless, we shouldn't sweep this issue under the carpet either, because it definitely has a major impact on test automation. But first, I must climb onto my soapbox for a short digression into the development process.

Test Last—at Your Peril

Anyone who has tried to retrofit unit tests onto an existing application has probably experienced a lot of pain! This is the hardest kind of test automation we can do as well as the least productive. A lot of the benefit of automated tests is derived during the "debugging phase" of software development, when such tests can reduce the amount of time spent working with debugging tools. Tackling a test retrofit on legacy software as your first attempt at automated unit testing is the last thing you want to try, as it is sure to discourage even the most determined developers and project managers.

Design for Testability—Upfront

BDUF[5] design for testability is hard because it is difficult to know what the tests will need in the way of control points and observation points on the SUT. We can easily build software that is difficult to test. We can also spend a lot of time *designing in* testability mechanisms that are either insufficient or unnecessary. Either way, we will have spent a lot of effort with nothing to show for it.

---

[4] Unfortunately, this may result in slower tests when the fixture is in a database. Nevertheless, it will still be many times faster than if each test had to insert all the records it needed.

[5] "Big Design Upfront" (also known as "waterfall design") is the opposite of **emergent design** ("just-in-time design").

Test-Driven Testability

The nice thing about building our software driven by tests is that we don't have to think very much about *design for testability;* we just write the tests and that forces us to *build for testability.* The act of writing the test defines the control points and observation points that the SUT needs to provide. Once we have passed the tests, we know we have a testable design.

Now that I've done my bit promoting TDD as a "design for testability" process, let's get on with our discussion of the mechanics of actually making our software testable.

Control Points and Observation Points

A test interacts with the software[6] through one or more interfaces or **interaction points**. From the test's point of view, these interfaces can act as either **control points** or **observation points** (Figure 6.6).

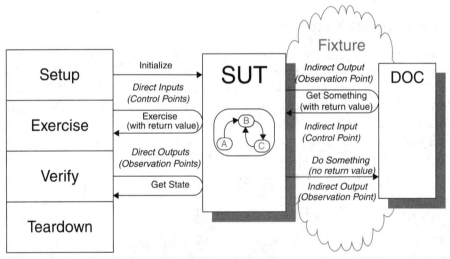

Figure 6.6 *Control points and observation points. The test interacts with the SUT through interaction points. Direct interaction points are synchronous method calls made by the test; indirect interaction points require some form of Back Door Manipulation. Control points have arrows pointing toward the SUT; observation points have arrows pointing away from the SUT.*

---

[6] I am deliberately not saying "SUT" here because it interacts with more than just the SUT.

A control point is how the test asks the software to do something for it. This could be for the purpose of putting the software into a specific state as part of setting up or tearing down the test fixture, or it could be to exercise the SUT. Some control points are provided strictly for the tests; they should not be used by the production code because they bypass input validation or short-circuit the normal life cycle of the SUT or some object on which it depends.

An observation point is how the test finds out about the SUT's behavior during the result verification phase of the test. Observation points can be used to retrieve the post-test state of the SUT or a DOC. They can also be used to spy on the interactions between the SUT and any components with which it is expected to interact while it is being exercised. Verifying these indirect outputs is an example of *Back Door Verification* (see *Back Door Manipulation*).

Both control points and observation points can be provided by the SUT as synchronous method calls; we call this "going in the front door." Some interaction points may be via a "back door" to the SUT; we call this *Back Door Manipulation*. In the diagrams that follow, control points are represented by the arrowheads that point to the SUT, whether from the test or from a DOC. Observation points are represented by the arrows whose heads point back to the test itself. These arrows typically start at the SUT or DOC[7] or start at the test and interact with either the SUT or DOC before returning to the test.[8]

Interaction Styles and Testability Patterns

When testing a particular piece of software, our tests can take one of two basic forms.

A **round-trip test** interacts with the SUT in question only through its public interface—that is, its "front door" (Figure 6.7). Both the control points and the observation points in a typical round-trip test are simple method calls. The nice thing about this approach is that it does not violate encapsulation. The test needs to know only the public interface of the software; it doesn't need to know anything about how it is built.

The main alternative is the **layer-crossing test** (Figure 6.8), in which we exercise the SUT through the API and keep an eye on what comes out the back door using some form of *Test Double* such as a *Test Spy* (page 538) or *Mock Object*. This can be a very powerful testing technique for verifying certain kinds of mostly architectural requirements. Unfortunately, this approach can also result in *Overspecified Software* (see *Fragile Test*) if it is overused because changes in how the software implements its responsibilities can cause tests to fail.

---

[7] An asynchronous observation point.

[8] A synchronous observation point.

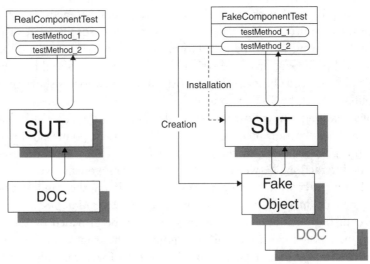

Figure 6.7   *A round-trip test interacts with the SUT only via the front door. The test on the right replaces a DOC with a Fake Object to improve its repeatability or performance.*

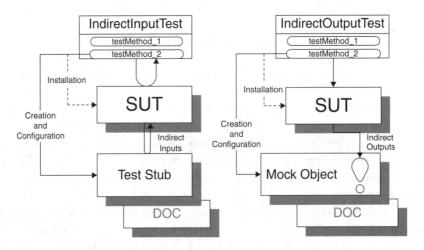

Figure 6.8   *A layer-crossing test can interact with the SUT via a "back door." The test on the left controls the SUT's indirect inputs using a Test Stub. The test on the right verifies its indirect outputs using a Mock Object.*

In Figure 6.8, the test on the right uses a *Mock Object* that stands in for the DOC as the observation point. The test on the left uses a *Test Stub* that stands in for the DOC as a control point. Testing in this style implies a Layered Architecture [DDD, PEAA, WWW], which in turn opens the door to using *Layer Tests* (page 337) to test each layer of the architecture independently (Figure 6.9). An even more general concept is the use of *Component Tests* (see *Layer Test*) to test each component within a layer independently.

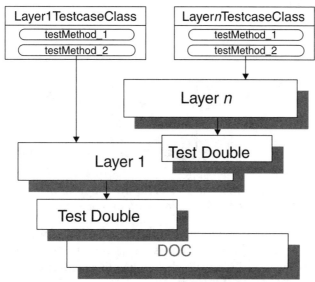

Figure 6.9 *A pair of Layer Tests each testing a different layer of the system. Each layer of a layered architecture can be tested independently using a distinct set of Layer Tests. This ensures good separation of concerns, and the tests reinforce the layered architecture.*

Whenever we want to write layer-crossing tests, we need to ensure that we have built in a substitutable dependency mechanism for any components on which the SUT depends but that we want to test independently. The leading contenders include any of the variations of *Dependency Injection* (Figure 6.10) or some form of *Dependency Lookup* such as *Object Factory* or *Service Locator*. These dependency substitution mechanisms can be hand-coded or we can use an inversion of control (IOC) framework if one is available in our programming environment. The fallback plan is to use a *Test-Specific Subclass* (page 579) of the SUT or the DOC in question. This subclass can be used to override the dependency access or construction mechanism within the SUT or to replace the behavior of the DOC with test-specific behavior.

The "solution of last resort" is the *Test Hook* (page 709).[9] These constructs do have utility as temporary measures that allow us to automate tests to act as a *Safety Net* (page 24) while refactoring to retrofit testability. We definitely shouldn't make a habit of using them, however, as continued use of *Test Hooks* will result in *Test Logic in Production* (page 217).

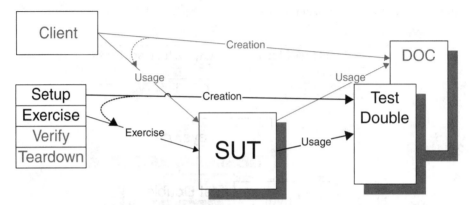

Figure 6.10   *A Test Double being "injected" into a SUT by a test. A test can use Dependency Injection to replace a DOC with an appropriate Test Double. The DOC is passed to the SUT by the test as or after it has been created.*

A third kind of test worth mentioning is the **asynchronous test,** in which the test interacts with the SUT through real messaging. Because the responses to these requests also come asynchronously, these tests must include some kind of inter-process synchronization such as calls to wait. Unfortunately, the need to wait for message responses that might never arrive can cause these tests to take much, much longer to execute. This style of testing should be avoided at all costs in unit and component tests.

Fortunately, the *Humble Executable* pattern (see *Humble Object* on page 695) can remove the need to conduct unit tests this way (Figure 6.11). It involves putting the logic that handles the incoming message into a separate class or component, which can then be tested synchronously using either a round-trip or layer-crossing style.

A related issue is the testing of business logic through a UI. In general, such *Indirect Testing* (see *Obscure Test*) is a bad idea because changes to the UI code will break tests that are trying to verify the business logic behind it. Because the UI tends to change frequently, especially on agile projects, this strategy will greatly increase test maintenance costs. Another reason this is a bad idea is that

---

[9] These typically take the form of if (testing) then ... else ... endif.

UIs are inherently asynchronous. Tests that exercise the system through the UI have to be asynchronous tests along with all the issues that come with them.

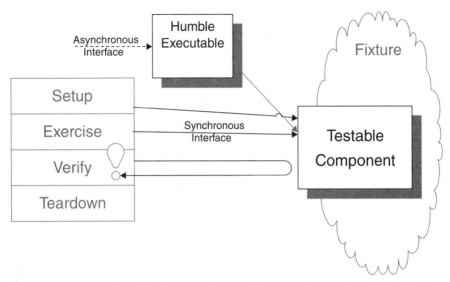

Figure 6.11 *A Humble Executable making testing easier. The Humble Executable pattern can improve the repeatability and speed of verifying logic that would otherwise have to be verified via asynchronous tests.*

Divide and Test

We can turn almost any *Hard-to-Test Code* (page 209) into easily tested code through refactoring as long as we have enough tests in place to ensure that we do not introduce bugs during this refactoring.

We can avoid using the UI for customer tests by writing those tests as *Subcutaneous Tests* (see *Layer Test*). These tests bypass the UI layer of the system and exercise the business logic via a Service Facade [CJ2EEP] that exposes the necessary synchronous interaction points to the test. The UI relies on the same facade, enabling us to verify that the business logic works correctly even before we hook up the UI logic. The layered architecture also enables us to test the UI logic before the business logic is finished; we can replace the Service Facade with a *Test Double* that provides completely deterministic behavior that our tests can depend on.[10]

---

[10] This *Test Double* can be either hard-coded or file driven. Either way, it should be independent of the real implementation so that the UI tests need to know only which data to use to evoke specific behaviors from the Service Facade, not the logic behind it.

When conducting unit testing of nontrivial UIs,[11] we can use a *Humble Dialog* (see *Humble Object*) to move the logic that makes decisions about the UI out of the visual layer, which is difficult to test synchronously, and into a layer of supporting objects, which can be verified with standard unit-testing techniques (Figure 6.12). This approach allows the presentation logic behavior to be tested as thoroughly as the business logic behavior.

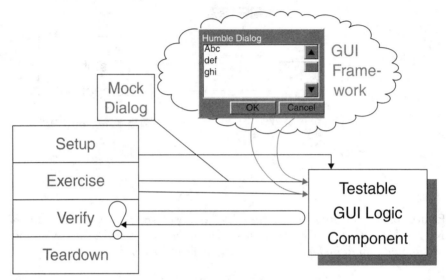

Figure 6.12 *A Humble Dialog reducing the dependency of the test on the UI framework. The logic that controls the state of UI components can be very difficult to test. Extracting it into a testable component leaves behind a Humble Dialog that requires very little testing.*

From a test automation *strategy* perspective, the key thing is to make the decision about which test–SUT interaction styles should be used and which ones should be avoided, and to ensure that the software is designed to support that decision.

---

[11] Any UI that contains state information or supports conditional display or enabling of elements should be considered nontrivial.

What's Next?

This concludes our introduction to the hard-to-change decisions we must make as we settle upon our test automation strategy. Given that you are still reading, I will assume that you have decided xUnit is an appropriate tool for doing your test automation. The following chapters introduce the detailed patterns for implementing our chosen fixture strategy, whether it involves a *Fresh Fixture* or a *Shared Fixture*. First, we will explore the simplest case, a *Transient Fresh Fixture*, in Chapter 8, *Transient Fixture Management*. We will then investigate the use of persistent fixtures in Chapter 9, *Persistent Fixture Management*. But first, we must establish the basic xUnit terminology and notation that is used throughout this book in Chapter 7, *xUnit Basics*.

Chapter 7

xUnit Basics

About This Chapter

Chapter 6, *Test Automation Strategy,* introduced the "hard to change" decisions that we need to get right early in the project. The current chapter serves two purposes. First, it introduces the xUnit terminology and diagramming notation used throughout this book. Second, it explains how the xUnit framework operates beneath the covers and why it was built that way. This knowledge can help the builder of a new *Test Automation Framework* (page 298) understand how to port xUnit. It can also help test automaters understand how to use certain features of xUnit.

An Introduction to xUnit

The term **xUnit** is how we refer to any member of the family of *Test Automation Frameworks* used for automating *Hand-Scripted Tests* (see *Scripted Test* on page 285) that share the common set of features described here. Most programming languages in widespread use today have at least one implementation of xUnit; *Hand-Scripted Tests* are usually automated using the same programming language as is used for building the SUT. Although this is not necessarily the case, this strategy is usually much easier because our tests have easy access to the SUT API. By using a programming language with which the developers are familiar, less effort is required to learn how to automate *Fully Automated Tests* (page 26).[1]

---

[1] See the sidebar "Testing Stored Procs with JUnit" (page 657) for an example of using a testing framework in one language to test an SUT in another language.

Common Features

Given that most members of the xUnit family are implemented using an object-oriented programming language (OOPL), they are described here first and then places where the non-OOPL members of the family differ are noted.

All members of the xUnit family implement a basic set of features. They all provide a way to perform the following tasks:

- Specify a test as a *Test Method* (page 348)

- Specify the expected results within the test method in the form of calls to *Assertion Methods* (page 362)

- Aggregate the tests into test suites that can be run as a single operation

- Run one or more tests to get a report on the results of the test run

Because many members of the xUnit family support *Test Method Discovery* (see *Test Discovery* on page 393), we do not have to use *Test Enumeration* (page 399) in these members to manually add each *Test Method* we want to run to a test suite. Some members also support some form of *Test Selection* (page 403) to run subsets of test methods based on some criteria.

The Bare Minimum

Here is the bare minimum we need to understand about how xUnit operates (Figure 7.1):

- How we define tests using *Test Methods* on *Testcase Classes* (page 373)

- How we can build up arbitrary *Suites of Suites* (see *Test Suite Object* on page 387)[2]

- How we run the tests

- How we interpret the test results

Defining Tests

Each test is represented by a *Test Method* that implements a single *Four-Phase Test* (page 358) by following these steps:

---

[2] Even those xUnit variants that don't have an explicit Suite class or method still build *Test Suite Objects* behind the scene.

- Setting up the test fixture using either *In-line Setup* (page 408), *Delegated Setup* (page 411), or *Implicit Setup* (page 424)

- Exercising the SUT by interacting with methods in its public or private interface

- Verifying that the expected outcome has occurred using calls to *Assertion Methods*

- Tearing down the test fixture using either *Garbage-Collected Teardown* (page 500), *In-line Teardown* (page 509), *Implicit Teardown* (page 516), or *Automated Teardown* (page 503)

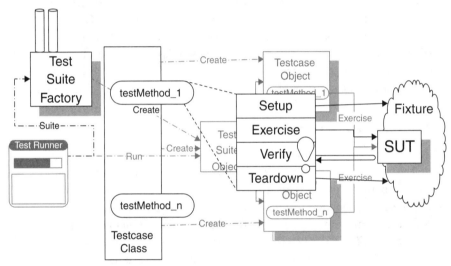

Figure 7.1 *The static test structure as seen by a test automater. The test automater sees only the static structure as he or she reads or writes tests. The test automater writes one Test Method with four distinct phases for each test in the Testcase Class. The Test Suite Factory (see Test Enumeration) is used only for Test Enumeration. The runtime structure (shown grayed out) is left to the test automater's imagination.*

The most common types of tests are the *Simple Success Test* (see *Test Method*), which verifies that the SUT has behaved correctly with valid inputs, and the *Expected Exception Test* (see *Test Method*), which verifies that the SUT raises an exception when used incorrectly. A special type of test, the *Constructor Test* (see *Test Method*), verifies that the object constructor logic builds new objects correctly. Both "simple success" and "expected exception" forms of the *Constructor Test* may be needed. The *Test Methods* that contain our test logic need to live somewhere, so we define them as methods of a *Testcase Class*.[3] We then pass the name of this *Testcase Class* (or the module or assembly in which it resides) to the *Test Runner* (page 377) to run our tests. This may be done explicitly—such as when invoking the *Test Runner* on a command line—or implicitly by the integrated development environment (IDE) that we are using.

What's a Fixture?

The **test fixture** is everything we need to have in place to exercise the SUT. Typically, it includes at least an instance of the class whose method we are testing. It may also include other objects on which the SUT depends. Note that some members of the xUnit family call the *Testcase Class* the test fixture—a preference that likely reflects an assumption that all *Test Methods* on the *Testcase Class* should use the same fixture. This unfortunate name collision makes discussing test fixtures particularly problematic. In this book, I have used different names for the *Testcase Class* and the test fixture it creates. I trust that the reader will translate this terminology to the terminology of his or her particular member of the xUnit family.

Defining Suites of Tests

Most *Test Runners* "auto-magically" construct a test suite containing all of the *Test Methods* in the *Testcase Class*. Often, this is all we need. Sometimes we want to run all the tests for an entire application; at other times we want to run just those tests that focus on a specific subset of the functionality. Some members of the xUnit family and some third-party tools implement *Testcase Class Discovery* (see *Test Discovery*) in which the *Test Runner* finds the test suites by searching either the file system or an executable for test suites.

If we do not have this capability, we need to use *Test Suite Enumeration* (see *Test Enumeration*), in which we define the overall test suite for the entire system or application as an aggregate of several smaller test suites. To do so, we must define a special *Test Suite Factory* class whose suite method returns a *Test Suite Object* containing the collection of *Test Methods* and other *Test Suite Objects* to run.

This collection of test suites into increasingly larger *Suites of Suites* is commonly used as a way to include the unit test suite for a class into the test suite for the package or module, which is in turn included in the test suite for the entire system. Such a hierarchical organization supports the running of test suites with varying degrees of completeness and provides a practical way for developers to run that subset of the tests that is most relevant to the software of

---

[3] This scheme is called a test fixture in some variants of xUnit, probably because the creators assumed we would have a single *Testcase Class per Fixture* (page 631).

interest. It also allows them to run all the tests that exist with a single command before they commit their changes into the source code repository [SCM].

Running Tests

Tests are run by using a *Test Runner*. Several different kinds of *Test Runners* are available for most members of the xUnit family.

A *Graphical Test Runner* (see *Test Runner*) provides a visual way for the user to specify, invoke, and observe the results of running a test suite. Some *Graphical Test Runners* allow the user to specify a test by typing in the name of a *Test Suite Factory*; others provide a graphical *Test Tree Explorer* (see *Test Runner*) that can be used to select a specific *Test Method* to execute from within a tree of test suites, where the *Test Methods* serve as the tree's leaves. Many *Graphical Test Runners* are integrated into an IDE to make running tests as easy as selecting the Run As Test command from a context menu.

A *Command-Line Test Runner* (see *Test Runner*) can be used to execute tests when running the test suite from the command line, as in Figure 7.2. The name of the *Test Suite Factory* that should be used to create the test suite is included as a command-line parameter. *Command-Line Test Runners* are most commonly used when invoking the *Test Runner* from Integration Build [SCM] scripts or sometimes from within an IDE.

```
>ruby testrunner.rb c:/examples/tests/SmellHandlerTest.rb
Loaded suite SmellHandlerTest
Started
.....
Finished in 0.016 seconds.
5 tests, 6 assertions, 0 failures, 0 errors
>Exit code: 0
```

Figure 7.2 *Using a Command-Line Test Runner to run tests from the command line.*

Test Results

Naturally, the main reason for running automated tests is to determine the results. For the results to be meaningful, we need a standard way to describe them. In general, members of the xUnit family follow the Hollywood principle ("Don't call us; we'll call you"). In other words, "No news is good news"; the tests will "call you" when a problem occurs. Thus we can focus on the test failures rather than inspecting a bunch of passing tests as they roll by.

Test results are classified into one of three categories, each of which is treated slightly differently. When a test runs without any errors or failures, it is considered to be successful. In general, xUnit does not do anything special for successful tests—there should be no need to examine any output when a *Self-Checking Test* (page 26) passes.

A test is considered to have failed when an **assertion** fails. That is, the test asserts that something should be true by calling an *Assertion Method,* but that assertion turns out not to be the case. When it fails, an *Assertion Method* throws an assertion failure exception (or whatever facsimile the programming language supports). The *Test Automation Framework* increments a counter for each failure and adds the failure details to a list of failures; this list can be examined more closely later, after the test run is complete. The failure of a single test, while significant, does not prevent the remaining tests from being run; this is in keeping with the principle *Keep Tests Independent* (see page 42).

A test is considered to have an error when either the SUT or the test itself fails in an unexpected way. Depending on the language being used, this problem could consist of an uncaught exception, a raised error, or something else. As with assertion failures, the *Test Automation Framework* increments a counter for each error and adds the error details to a list of errors, which can then be examined after the test run is complete.

For each test error or test failure, xUnit records information that can be examined to help understand exactly what went wrong. As a minimum, the name of the *Test Method* and *Testcase Class* are recorded, along with the nature of the problem (whether it was a failed assertion or a software error). In most *Graphical Test Runners* that are integrated with an IDE, one merely has to (double-) click on the appropriate line in the traceback to see the source code that emitted the failure or caused the error.

Because the name **test error** sounds more drastic than a **test failure,** some test automaters try to catch all errors raised by the SUT and turn them into test failures. This is simply unnecessary. Ironically, in most cases it is easier to determine the cause of a test error than the cause of a test failure: The stack trace for a test error will typically pinpoint the problem code within the SUT, whereas the stack track for a test failure merely shows the location in the test where the failed assertion was made. It is, however, worthwhile using *Guard Assertions* (page 490) to avoid executing code within the *Test Method* that would result in a test error being raised from within the *Test Method*[4] itself; this is just a normal part of verifying the expected outcome of exercising the SUT and does not remove useful diagnostic tracebacks.

---

[4] For example, before executing an assertion on the contents of a field of an object returned by the SUT, it is worthwhile to assertNotNull on the object reference so as to avoid a "null reference" error.

Under the xUnit Covers

The description thus far has focused on *Test Methods* and *Testcase Classes* with the odd mention of test suites. This simplified "compile time" view is enough for most people to get started writing automated unit tests in xUnit. It is *possible* to use xUnit without any further understanding of how the *Test Automation Framework* operates—but the lack of more extensive knowledge is likely to lead to confusion when building and reusing test fixtures. Thus it is better to understand how xUnit actually runs the *Test Methods*. In most[5] members of the xUnit family, each *Test Method* is represented at runtime by a *Testcase Object* (page 382) because it is a lot easier to manipulate tests if they are "first-class" objects (Figure 7.3). The *Testcase Objects* are aggregated into *Test Suite Objects*, which can then be used to run many tests with a single user action.

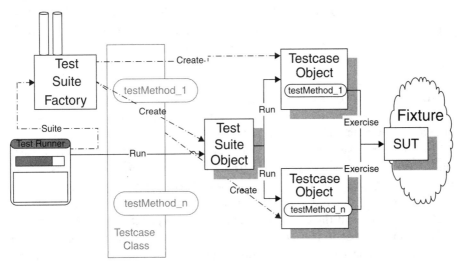

Figure 7.3 *The runtime test structure as seen by the Test Automation Framework. At runtime, the Test Runner asks the Testcase Class or a Test Suite Factory to instantiate one Testcase Object for each Test Method, with the objects being wrapped up in a single Test Suite Object. The Test Runner tells this Composite [GOF] object to run its tests and collect the results. Each Testcase Object runs one Test Method.*

---

[5] NUnit is a known exception and others may exist. See the sidebar "There's Always an Exception" (page 384) for more information.

Test Commands

The *Test Runner* cannot possibly know how to call each *Test Method* individually. To avoid the need for this, most members of the xUnit family convert each *Test Method* into a Command [GOF] object with a run method. To create these *Testcase Objects*, the *Test Runner* calls the suite method of the *Testcase Class* to get a *Test Suite Object*. It then calls the run method via the standard test interface. The run method of a *Testcase Object* executes the specific *Test Method* for which it was instantiated and reports whether it passed or failed. The run method of a *Test Suite Object* iterates over all the members of the collection of tests, keeping track of how many tests were run and which ones failed.

Test Suite Objects

A *Test Suite Object* is a Composite object that implements the same standard test interface that all *Testcase Objects* implement. That interface (implicit in languages lacking a type or interface construct) requires provision of a run method. The expectation is that when run is invoked, all of the tests *contained* in the receiver will be run. In the case of a *Testcase Object*, it is itself a "test" and will run the corresponding *Test Method*. In the case of a *Test Suite Object*, that means invoking run on all of the *Testcase Objects* it contains. The value of using a Composite Command is that it turns the processes of running one test and running many tests into exactly the same process.

To this point, we have assumed that we already have the *Test Suite Object* instantiated. But where did it come from? By convention, each *Testcase Class* acts as a *Test Suite Factory*. The *Test Suite Factory* provides a **class method** called suite that returns a *Test Suite Object* containing one *Testcase Object* for each *Test Method* in the class. In languages that support some form of reflection, xUnit may use *Test Method Discovery* to discover the test methods and automatically construct the *Test Suite Object* containing them. Other members of the xUnit family require test automaters to implement the suite method themselves; this kind of *Test Enumeration* takes more effort and is more likely to lead to *Lost Tests* (see *Production Bugs* on page 268).

xUnit in the Procedural World

Test Automation Frameworks and test-driven development became popular only after object-oriented programming became commonplace. Most members of the xUnit family are implemented in object-oriented programming languages that support the concept of a *Testcase Object*. Although the lack of objects should not keep us from testing procedural code, it does make writing *Self-Checking Tests* more labor-intensive and building generic, reusable *Test Runners* more difficult.

In the absence of objects or classes, we must treat *Test Methods* as global (public static) procedures. These methods are typically stored in files or modules (or whatever modularity mechanism the language supports). If the language supports the concept of **procedure variables** (also known as **function pointers**), we can define a generic *Test Suite Procedure* (see *Test Suite Object*) that takes an array of *Test Methods* (commonly called "test procedures") as an argument. Typically, the *Test Methods* must be aggregated into the arrays using *Test Enumeration* because very few non-object-oriented programming languages support reflection.

If the language does not support any way of treating *Test Methods* as data, we must define the test suites by writing *Test Suite Procedures* that make explicit calls to *Test Methods* and/or other *Test Suite Procedures*. Test runs may be initiated by defining a main method on the module.

A final option is to encode the tests as data in a file and use a single *Data-Driven Test* (page 288) interpreter to execute them. The main disadvantage of this approach is that it restricts the kinds of tests that can be run to those implemented by the *Data-Driven Test* interpreter, which must itself be written anew for each SUT. This strategy does have the advantage of moving the coding of the actual tests out of the developer arena and into the end-user or tester arena, which makes it particularly appropriate for customer tests.

What's Next?

In this chapter we established the basic terminology for talking about how xUnit tests are put together. Now we turn our attention to a new task—constructing our first test fixture in Chapter 8, *Transient Fixture Management*.

Chapter 8

Transient Fixture Management

About This Chapter

Chapter 6, *Test Automation Strategy,* looked at the strategic decisions that we need to make. That included the definition of the term "fixture" and the selection of a test fixture strategy. Chapter 7, *xUnit Basics,* established our basic xUnit terminology and diagramming notation. This chapter builds on both of these earlier chapters by focusing on the *mechanics* of implementing the chosen fixture strategy.

There are several different ways to set up a *Fresh Fixture* (page 311), and our decision will affect how much effort it takes to write the tests, how much effort

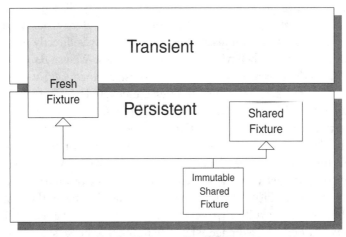

Figure 8.1 *Transient Fresh Fixture. Fresh Fixtures come in two flavors: Transient and Persistent. Both require fixture setup; the latter also requires fixture teardown.*

85

it takes to maintain our tests, and whether we achieve *Tests as Documentation* (see page 23). *Persistent Fresh Fixtures* (see *Fresh Fixture*) are set up the same way as *Transient Fresh Fixtures* (see *Fresh Fixture*), albeit with some additional factors to consider related to fixture teardown (Figure 8.1). *Shared Fixtures* (page 317) introduce another set of considerations. *Persistent Fresh Fixtures* and *Shared Fixtures* are discussed in detail in Chapter 9.

Test Fixture Terminology

Before we can talk about setting up a fixture, we need to agree what a fixture is.

What Is a Fixture?

Every test consists of four parts, as described in *Four-Phase Test* (page 358). The first part is where we create the SUT and everything it depends on and where we put those elements into the state required to exercise the SUT. In xUnit, we call everything we need in place to exercise the SUT the **test fixture** and the part of the test logic that we execute to set it up the **fixture setup**.

The most common way to set up the fixture is using front door fixture set-up—that is, to call the appropriate methods on the SUT to put it into the starting state. This may require constructing other objects and passing them to the SUT as arguments of method calls. When the state of the SUT is stored in other objects or components, we can do *Back Door Setup* (see *Back Door Manipulation* on page 327)—that is, we can insert the necessary records directly into the other component on which the behavior of the SUT depends. We use *Back Door Setup* most often with databases or when we need to use a *Mock Object* (page 544) or *Test Double* (page 522). These possibilities are covered in Chapter 13, *Testing with Databases,* and Chapter 11, *Using Test Doubles,* respectively.

It is worth noting that the term "fixture" is used to mean different things in different kinds of test automation. The xUnit variants for the Microsoft languages call the *Testcase Class* (page 373) the test fixture. Most other variants of xUnit distinguish between the *Testcase Class* and the test fixture (or test context) it sets up. In Fit [FitB], the term "fixture" is used to mean the custom-built parts of the *Data-Driven Test* (page 288) interpreter that we use to define our *Higher-Level Language* (see page 41). Whenever this book says "test fixture" without further qualifying this term, it refers to the stuff we set up before exercising the SUT. To refer to the class that hosts the *Test Methods* (page 348), whether it be in Java or C#, Ruby or VB, this book uses *Testcase Class*.

What Is a Fresh Fixture?

In a *Fresh Fixture* strategy, we set up a brand-new fixture for every test we run (Figure 8.2). That is, each *Testcase Object* (page 382) builds its own fixture before exercising the SUT and does so every time it is rerun. That is what makes the fixture "fresh." As a result, we completely avoid the problems associated with *Interacting Tests* (see *Erratic Test* on page 228).

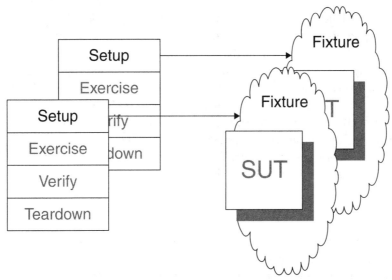

Figure 8.2 *A pair of Fresh Fixtures, each with its creator. A Fresh Fixture is built specifically for a single test, used once, and then retired.*

What Is a Transient Fresh Fixture?

When our fixture is an in-memory fixture referenced only by local variables or instance variables,[1] the fixture just "disappears" after every test courtesy of *Garbage-Collected Teardown* (page 500). When fixtures are persistent, this is not the case. Thus we have some decisions to make about how we implement the *Fresh Fixture* strategy. In particular, we have two different ways to keep them "fresh." The obvious option is tear down the fixture after each test. The less obvious option is to leave the old fixture around and then build a new fixture in such a way that it does not collide with the old fixture.

---

[1] See the sidebar "There's Always an Exception" (page 384).

Most *Fresh Fixtures* we build are transient, so we will cover that case first. We will then come back to managing *Persistent Fresh Fixtures* in Chapter 9.

Building Fresh Fixtures

Whether we are building a *Transient Fresh Fixture* or a *Persistent Fresh Fixture*, the choices we have for how to construct it are pretty much the same. The fixture setup logic includes the code needed to instantiate the SUT,[2] the code to put the SUT into the appropriate starting state, and the code to create and initialize the state of anything the SUT depends on or that will be passed to it as an argument. The most obvious way to set up a *Fresh Fixture* is through *In-line Setup* (page 408), in which all fixture setup logic is contained within the *Test Method*. This type of fixture can also be constructed by using *Delegated Setup* (page 411), which involves calling *Test Utility Methods* (page 599). Finally, we can use *Implicit Setup* (page 424), in which the *Test Automation Framework* (page 298) calls a special setUp method we provide on our *Testcase Class*. We can also use a combination of these three approaches. Let's look at each possibility individually.

In-line Fixture Setup

In *In-line Setup*, the test handles all of the fixture setup within the body of the *Test Method*. We construct objects, call methods on them, construct the SUT, and call methods on it to put into a specific state. We perform all of these tasks from within our *Test Method*. Think of *In-line Setup* as the do-it-yourself approach to fixture creation.

```
public void testStatus_initial() {
    // In-line setup
    Airport departureAirport = new Airport("Calgary", "YYC");
    Airport destinationAirport = new Airport("Toronto", "YYZ");
    Flight flight = new Flight( flightNumber,
                                departureAirport,
                                destinationAirport);
    // Exercise SUT and verify outcome
    assertEquals(FlightState.PROPOSED, flight.getStatus());
    // tearDown:
    //      Garbage-collected
}
```

---

[2] This discussion assumes that the SUT is an object and not just static methods on a class.

The main drawback of *In-line Setup* is that it tends to lead to *Test Code Duplication* (page 213) because each *Test Method* needs to construct the SUT. Many of the *Test Methods* also need to perform similar fixture setup. This *Test Code Duplication* leads, in turn, to *High Test Maintenance Cost* (page 265) caused by *Fragile Tests* (page 239). If the work to create the fixture is complex, it can also lead to *Obscure Tests* (page 186). A related problem is that *In-line Setup* tends to encourage *Hard-Coded Test Data* (see *Obscure Test*) within each *Test Method* because creating a local variable with an Intent-Revealing Name [SBPP] may seem like too much work for the benefit yielded.

We can prevent these test smells by moving the code that sets up the fixture out of the *Test Method*. The location where we move it determines which of the alternative fixture setup strategies we have used.

Delegated Fixture Setup

A quick and easy way to reduce *Test Code Duplication* and the resulting *Obscure Tests* is to refactor our *Test Methods* to use *Delegated Setup*. We can use an Extract Method [Fowler] refactoring to move a sequence of statements used in several *Test Methods* into a *Test Utility Method* that we then call from those *Test Methods*. This is a very simple and safe refactoring, especially when we let the IDE do all the heavy lifting for us. When the extracted method contains logic to create an object on which our test depends, we call it a *Creation Method* (page 415). *Creation Methods*[3] with Intent-Revealing Names make the test's pre-conditions readily apparent to the reader while avoiding unnecessary *Test Code Duplication*. They allow both the test reader and the test automater to focus on *what* is being created without being distracted by *how* it is created. The *Creation Methods* act as reusable building blocks for test fixture construction.

```
public void testGetStatus_inital() {
    // Setup
    Flight flight = createAnonymousFlight();
    // Exercise SUT and verify outcome
    assertEquals(FlightState.PROPOSED, flight.getStatus());
    // Teardown
    //     Garbage-collected
}
```

One goal of these *Creation Methods* is to eliminate the need for every test to know the details of how the objects it requires are created. This streamlining goes a long way toward preventing *Fragile Tests* caused by changes to

---

[3] When referenced via a *Test Helper* (page 643) class, they are often called the *Object Mother* pattern (see *Test Helper* on page 643).

constructor method signatures or semantics. When a test does not care about the specific identity of the objects it is creating, we can use *Anonymous Creation Methods* (see *Creation Method*). These methods generate any unique keys required by the object being created. By using a *Distinct Generated Value* (see *Generated Value* on page 723), we can guarantee that no other test instance that requires a similar object will accidentally use the same object as this test. This safeguard prevents many forms of the behavior smell *Erratic Test*, including *Unrepeatable Tests, Interacting Tests,* and *Test Run Wars,* even if we happen to be using a persistent object repository that supports *Shared Fixtures.*

When a test does care about the attributes of the object being created, we use a *Parameterized Anonymous Creation Method* (see *Creation Method*). This method is passed any attributes that the test cares about (i.e., attributes that are important to the test outcome), leaving all other attributes to be defaulted by the implementation of the *Creation Method*. My motto is this:

> *When it is not important for something to be seen in the test method, it is important that it **not** be seen in the test method!*

Delegated Setup is often used when we write input validation tests for SUT methods that are expected to validate the attributes of an object argument. In such a case, we need to write a separate test for each invalid attribute that should be detected. Building all of these slightly invalid objects would be a lot of work using *In-line Setup*. We can reduce the effort and the amount of *Test Code Duplication* dramatically by using the pattern *One Bad Attribute* (see *Derived Value* on page 718). That is, we first call a *Creation Method* to create a valid object, and then we replace one attribute with an invalid value that should be rejected by the SUT. Similarly, we might create an object in the correct state by using a *Named State Reaching Method* (see *Creation Method*).

Some people prefer to *Reuse Tests for Fixture Setup* (see *Creation Method*) as an alternative to using *Chained Tests* (page 454). That is, they call other tests directly within the setup portion of their test. This approach is not an unreasonable one as long as the test reader can readily identify what the other test is setting up for the current test. Unfortunately, very few tests are named in such a way as to convey this intention. For this reason, if we value *Tests as Documentation*, we will want to consider wrapping the called test with a *Creation Method* that has an Intent-Revealing Name so that test reader can get a sense of what the fixture looks like.

The *Creation Methods* can be kept as private methods on the *Testcase Class*, pulled up to a *Testcase Superclass* (page 638), or moved to a *Test Helper* (page 643). The "mother of all creation methods" is *Object Mother* (see *Test*

Helper). This strategy-level pattern describes a family of approaches that center on the use of *Creation Methods* on one or more *Test Helpers* and may include *Automated Teardown* (page 503) as well.

Implicit Fixture Setup

Most members of the xUnit family provide a convenient hook for calling code that needs to be run before every *Test Method*. Some members call a method with a specific name (e.g., setUp). Others call a method that has a specific **annotation** (e.g., "@before" in JUnit) or **method attribute** (e.g., "[Setup]" in NUnit). To avoid repeating these alternative ways every time we need to refer to this mechanism, this book simply calls it the setUp method regardless of how we indicate this fact to the *Test Automation Framework*. The setUp method is optional or an empty default implementation is provided by the framework, so we do not *have* to provide one in each *Testcase Class*.

In *Implicit Setup*, we take advantage of this framework "hook" by putting all of the fixture creation logic into the setUp method. Because every *Test Method* on the *Testcase Class* shares this fixture setup logic, all *Test Methods* need to be able to use the fixture it creates. This tactic certainly addresses the *Test Code Duplication* problem but it does have several consequences. What does the following test actually verify?

```
Airport departureAirport;
Airport destinationAirport;
Flight flight;

public void testGetStatus_inital() {
    // Implicit setup
    // Exercise SUT and verify outcome
    assertEquals(FlightState.PROPOSED, flight.getStatus());
}
```

The first consequence is that this approach can make the tests more difficult to understand because we cannot see how the pre-conditions of the test (the test fixture) correlate with the expected outcome within the *Test Method;* we have to look in the setUp method to see this relationship.

```
public void setUp() throws Exception{
    super.setUp();
    departureAirport = new Airport("Calgary", "YYC");
    destinationAirport = new Airport("Toronto", "YYZ");
    BigDecimal flightNumber = new BigDecimal("999");
    flight = new Flight( flightNumber , departureAirport,
                        destinationAirport);
}
```

We can mitigate this problem by naming our *Testcase Class* based on the test fixture created in the setUp method. Of course, this makes sense only if all of the *Test Methods* really need the same fixture—it is an example of *Testcase Class per Fixture* (page 631). As mentioned earlier, several members of the xUnit family (VbUnit and NUnit, to name two) use the term "test fixture" to describe what this book calls the *Testcase Class*. This nomenclature is probably based on the assumption that we are using a *Testcase Class per Fixture* strategy.

Another consequence of using *Implicit Setup* is that we cannot use local variables to hold references to the objects in our fixture. Instead, we are forced to use instance variables to refer to any objects that are constructed in the setUp method and that are needed either when exercising the SUT, when verifying the expected outcome, or when tearing down the fixture. These instance variables act as global variables between the parts of the test. As long as we stick to instance variables rather than class variables, however, the test fixture will be newly constructed for each test case in the *Testcase Class*. Most members of xUnit provide isolation between the fixture created for each *Test Method* but at least one (NUnit) does not; see the sidebar "There's Always an Exception" (page 384) for more information. In any event, we should definitely give the variables Intent-Revealing Names so that we do not need to keep referring back to the setUp method to understand what they hold.

Misuse of the SetUp Method

When you have a new hammer, everything looks like a nail!

Like any feature of any system, the setUp method can be abused. We should not feel obligated to use it just because it is provided. It is one of several code reuse mechanisms that are available for our application. When object-oriented languages were first introduced, programmers were enamored with inheritance and tried to apply it in all possible reuse scenarios. Over time, we learned when inheritance was appropriate and when we should resort to other mechanisms such as delegation. The setUp method is xUnit's inheritance.

The setUp method is most prone to misuse when it is applied to build a *General Fixture* (see *Obscure Test*) with multiple distinct parts, each of which is dedicated to a different *Test Method*. This can lead to *Slow Tests* (page 253) if we are building a *Persistent Fresh Fixture*. More importantly, it can lead to *Obscure Tests* by hiding the cause–effect relationship between the fixture and the expected outcome of exercising the SUT.

If we do not adopt the practice of grouping the *Test Methods* into *Testcase Classes* based on identical fixtures but we do use the setUp method, we should build only the lowest common denominator part of the fixture in the setUp method. That is, only the setup logic that will not cause problems in any of the tests should be placed in the setUp method. Even the fixture setup code that does not cause problems for any of the *Test Methods* can still cause other problems if we use the setUp method to build a *General Fixture* instead of a *Minimal Fixture* (page 302). A *General Fixture* is a common cause of *Slow Tests* because each test spends much more time than necessary building the test fixture. It also tends to produce *Obscure Tests* because the test reader cannot easily see which part of the fixture a particular *Test Method* depends on. A *General Fixture* often evolves into a *Fragile Fixture* (see *Fragile Test*) as the relationship between its various elements and the tests that use them is forgotten over time. Changes made to the fixture to support a newly added test may then cause existing tests to fail.

Note that if we use a class variable to hold the object, we may have crossed the line into the world of *Persistent Fresh Fixtures*. Use of *Lazy Setup* (page 435) to populate the variable, by contrast, carries us into the world of *Shared Fixtures* because later tests within the test suite may reuse the object(s) created in earlier tests and thus may become dependent on the changes the other test (should have) made to it.

Hybrid Fixture Setup

This chapter has presented the three styles of fixture construction as strict alternatives to one another. In practice, there is value in combining them. Test automaters often call some *Creation Methods* from within the *Test Method* but then do some additional setup on an in-line basis. The readability of the setUp method can also be improved if it calls *Creation Methods* to construct the fixture. An additional benefit is that the *Creation Methods* can be unit-tested much more easily than either in-line fixture construction logic or the setUp method. These methods can also be located on a class outside the *Testcase Class* hierarchy such as a *Test Helper*.

Tearing Down Transient Fresh Fixtures

One really nice thing about *Transient Fresh Fixtures* is that fixture teardown requires very little effort. Most members of the xUnit family are implemented in languages that support **garbage collection**. As long as our references to the fixture are held in variables that go out of scope, we can count on *Garbage-Collected Teardown* to do all the work for us. See the sidebar "There's Always an Exception" on page 384 for a description of why the same is not true in NUnit.

If we are using one of the few members of the xUnit family that does not support garbage collection, we may have to treat all *Fresh Fixtures* as persistent.

What's Next?

This chapter introduced techniques for setting up and tearing down an in-memory *Fresh Fixture*. With some planning and a bit of luck, they are all you should need for the majority of your tests. Managing *Fresh Fixtures* is more complicated when the fixture is persisted either by the SUT or by the test itself. Chapter 9, *Persistent Fixture Management*, introduces additional techniques needed for managing persistent fixtures, including *Persistent Fresh Fixtures* and *Shared Fixtures*.

Chapter 9

Persistent Fixture Management

About This Chapter

In Chapter 8, *Transient Fixture Management*, we saw how we can go about building in-memory *Fresh Fixtures* (page 311). We noted in that chapter that managing *Fresh Fixtures* is more complicated when the fixture is persisted either by the SUT or by the test itself. This chapter introduces the additional patterns required to manage persistent fixtures, including both *Persistent Fresh Fixtures* (see *Fresh Fixture*) and *Shared Fixtures* (page 317).

Managing Persistent Fresh Fixtures

The term *Persistent Fresh Fixture* might sound like an oxymoron but it is actually not as large a contradiction as it might first seem. The *Fresh Fixture* strategy means that each run of each *Test Method* (page 348) uses a newly created fixture. The name speaks to its intent: We do not reuse the fixture! It does not need to imply that the fixture is transient—only that it is not reused (Figure 9.1). *Persistent Fresh Fixtures* present several challenges not encountered with *Transient Fresh Fixtures*. In this chapter, we focus on the challenge posed by *Unrepeatable Tests* (see *Erratic Test* on page 228) caused by leftover *Persistent Fresh Fixtures* and *Slow Tests* (page 253) caused by *Shared Fixtures* (page 317).

What Makes Fixtures Persistent?

A fixture, fresh or otherwise, can become persistent for one of two reasons. The first reason is that the SUT is a stateful object and "remembers" how it was used in the past. This scenario most often occurs when the SUT includes a database,

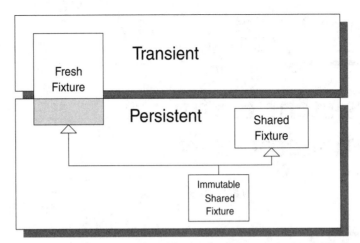

Figure 9.1 *A Fresh Fixture can be either transient or persistent. We can apply a Fresh Fixture strategy even if the test fixture is naturally persistent but we must have a way to tear it down after each test.*

but it can occur simply because the SUT uses class variables to hold some of its data. The second reason is that the *Testcase Class* (page 373) holds a reference to an otherwise *Transient Fresh Fixture* in a way that makes it survive across *Test Method* invocations.

Some members of the xUnit family provide a mechanism to reload all classes at the beginning of each test run. This behavior may appear as an option—a check box labeled "Reload Classes"—or it may be automatic. Such a feature keeps the fixture from becoming persistent when it is referenced from a class variable; it does not prevent the *Fresh Fixture* from becoming persistent if either the SUT or the test puts the fixture into the file system or a database.

Issues Caused by Persistent Fresh Fixtures

When fixtures are persistent, we may find that subsequent runs of the same *Test Method* try to recreate a fixture that already exists. This behavior may cause conflicts between the preexisting and newly created resources. Although violating unique key constraints in the database is the most common example of this problem, the conflict could be as simple as trying to create a file with the same name as one that already exists. One way to avoid these *Unrepeatable Tests* is to tear down the fixture at the end of each test; another is to use *Distinct Generated Values* (see *Generated Value* on page 723) for any identifiers that might cause conflicts.

Tearing Down Persistent Fresh Fixtures

Unlike fixture setup code, which should help us understand the pre-conditions of the test, fixture teardown code is purely a matter of good housekeeping. It does not help us understand the behavior of the SUT but it has the potential to obscure the intent of the test or at least make it more difficult to understand. Therefore, the best kind of teardown code is the nonexistent kind. We should avoid writing teardown code whenever we can, which is why *Garbage-Collected Teardown* (page 500) is so preferable. Unfortunately, we cannot take advantage of *Garbage-Collected Teardown* if our *Fresh Fixture* is persistent.

Hand-Coded Teardown

One way to ensure that the fixture is destroyed after we are done with it is to include test-specific teardown code within our *Test Methods*. This teardown mechanism might seem simple, but it is actually more complex than immediately meets the eye. Consider the following example:

```
public void testGetFlightsByOriginAirport_NoFlights()
        throws Exception {
    // Fixture Setup
    BigDecimal outboundAirport = createTestAirport("1OF");
    // Exercise System
    List flightsAtDestination1 =
            facade.getFlightsByOriginAirport(outboundAirport);
    // Verify Outcome
    assertEquals(0,flightsAtDestination1.size());
    facade.removeAirport(outboundAirport);
}
```

This *Naive In-line Teardown* (see *In-line Teardown* on page 509) will tear down the fixture when the test passes—but it won't tear down the fixture if the test fails or ends with an error. This is because the calls to the *Assertion Methods* (page 362) throw an exception; therefore, we may never make it to the teardown code. To ensure that the *In-line Teardown* code always executes, we must surround everything in the *Test Method* that *might* raise an exception with a try/catch control structure. Here's the same test suitably modified:

```
public void testGetFlightsByOriginAirport_NoFlights_td()
        throws Exception {
    // Fixture Setup
    BigDecimal outboundAirport = createTestAirport("1OF");
    try {
        // Exercise System
        List flightsAtDestination1 =
                facade.getFlightsByOriginAirport(outboundAirport);
```

```
        // Verify Outcome
        assertEquals(0,flightsAtDestination1.size());
    } finally {
        facade.removeAirport(outboundAirport);
    }
}
```

Unfortunately, the mechanism to ensure that the teardown code always runs introduces a fair bit of complication into the *Test Method*. Matters become even more complicated when we must tear down several resources: Even if our attempt to clean up one resource fails, we want to ensure that the other resources are still cleaned up. We can address part of this problem by using Extract Method [Fowler] refactoring to move the teardown code into a *Test Utility Method* (page 599) that we call from inside the error-handling construct. Although this *Delegated Teardown* (see *In-line Teardown*) hides the complexity of dealing with teardown errors, we still need to ensure that the method gets called even when test errors or test failures occur.

Most members of the xUnit family solve this problem by supporting *Implicit Teardown* (page 516). The *Test Automation Framework* (page 298) calls a special tearDown method after each *Test Method* regardless of whether the test passed or failed. This approach avoids placing the error-handling code within the *Test Method* but imposes two requirements on our tests. First, the fixture must be accessible from the tearDown method, so we must use instance variables (preferred), class variables, or global variables to hold the fixture. Second, we must ensure that the tearDown method works properly with each of the *Test Methods* regardless of which fixture it sets up.[1]

Matching Setup with Teardown Code Organization

Given the three ways of organizing our setup code—*In-line Setup* (page 408), *Delegated Setup* (page 411), and *Implicit Setup* (page 424)—and the three ways of organizing our teardown code—*In-line Teardown*, *Delegated Teardown*, and *Implicit Teardown*—nine different combinations are available to us. Choosing the right one turns out to be an easy decision because it is not important for the teardown code to be visible to the test reader. We simply choose the most appropriate setup code organization and either the equivalent or more hidden version of teardown (Table 9.1). For example, it is appropriate to use *Implicit Teardown* even with *In-line Setup* or *Delegated Setup*; it is almost never a good

---

[1] This is less of an issue with *Testcase Class per Fixture* (page 631) because the fixture should always be the same. With other *Testcase Class* organizations, we may need to include *Teardown Guard Clauses* (see *In-line Teardown*) within the tearDown method to ensure that it doesn't produce errors when it runs.

idea to use *In-line Teardown* with anything other than *In-line Setup,* and even then it should probably be avoided!

Table 9.1 *The Compatibility of Various Fixture Setup and Teardown Strategies for Persistent Test Fixtures*

	Teardown Mechanism		
Setup Mechanism	In-line Teardown	Delegated Teardown	Implicit Teardown
In-line Setup	Not recommended	Acceptable	Recommended
Delegated Setup	Not recommended	Acceptable	Recommended
Implicit Setup	Not recommended	Not recommended	Recommended

Automated Teardown

Hand-coded teardown is associated with two problems: Extra work is required to write the tests, and the teardown code is hard to get right and even harder to test. When the teardown goes wrong, it may lead to *Erratic Tests* caused by *Resource Leakage* because the test that fails as a result is often different from the one that didn't clean up properly.

In languages that support garbage collection, tearing down a *Transient Fresh Fixture* should be pretty much automatic. As long as our fixtures are referenced only by instance variables that go out of scope when our *Testcase Object* (page 382) is destroyed, garbage collection will clean them up. Garbage collection won't work, however, if we use class variables or if our fixtures include persistent objects such as files or database rows. In those cases, we need to perform our own cleanup.

Not surprisingly, this situation may inspire the lazy but creative programmer to come up with a way to automate the teardown logic. The important thing to note is that teardown code doesn't help us understand the test so it is *better* for it to remain hidden.[2] We can eliminate the need to write hand-crafted teardown code for each *Test Method* or *Testcase Class* by building an *Automated Teardown* (page 503) mechanism. It consists of three parts:

1. A well-tested mechanism to iterate over a list of objects that need to be deleted and catch/report any errors it encounters while ensuring that all the deletions are attempted.

2. A dispatching mechanism that invokes the deletion code appropriate to the kind of object to be deleted. This mechanism is often implemented as a Command [GOF] object that wraps each object to be

---

[2] Unlike setup code, which is often very important for understanding the test.

deleted, but could be as simple as calling a delete method on the object itself or using a switch statement based on the object's class.

3. A registration mechanism to add newly created objects (suitably wrapped if necessary) to the list of objects to be deleted.

Once we have built our *Automated Teardown* mechanism, we can simply invoke the registration method from our *Creation Methods* (page 415) and the cleanup method from the tearDown method. The latter operation can be specified in a *Testcase Superclass* (page 638) that all of our *Testcase Classes* inherit from. We can even extend this mechanism to delete objects created by the SUT as it is exercised. To do so, we use an observable *Object Factory* (see *Dependency Lookup* on page 686) inside the SUT and have our *Testcase Superclass* register itself as an Observer [GOF] of object creation.

Database Teardown

When our persistent *Fresh Fixture* has been built entirely in a relational database, we can take advantage of certain features of the database to implement its teardown. *Table Truncation Teardown* (page 661) is a brute-force way to blow away the entire contents of a table with a single database command. Of course, it is appropriate only when each *Test Runner* (page 377) has its own *Database Sandbox* (page 650). A somewhat less drastic approach is to use *Transaction Rollback Teardown* (page 668) to undo all changes made within the context of the current test. This mechanism relies on the SUT having been designed using the *Humble Transaction Controller* pattern (see *Humble Object* on page 695) so that we can invoke the business logic from the test without having the SUT commit the transaction automatically. Both of these database-specific teardown patterns are most commonly implemented using *Implicit Teardown* to keep the teardown logic out of the *Test Methods*.

Avoiding the Need for Teardown

So far, we have looked at ways to *do* fixture teardown. Now, let us look at ways to *avoid* fixture teardown.

Avoiding Fixture Collisions

We need to do fixture teardown for three reasons:

1. The accumulation of leftover fixture objects can cause tests to run slowly.

2. The leftover fixture objects can cause the SUT to behave differently or our assertions to report incorrect results.

3. The leftover fixture objects can prevent us from creating the *Fresh Fixture* required by our test.

The issue that is easiest to address is the first one: We can schedule a periodic cleansing of the persistence mechanism back to a known, minimalist state. Unfortunately, this tactic is useful only if we can get the tests to run correctly in the presence of accumulated test detritus.

The second issue can be addressed by using *Delta Assertions* (page 485) rather than "absolute" assertions. *Delta Assertions* work by taking a snapshot of the fixture before the test is run and verifying that the expected differences have appeared after we exercise the SUT.

The third issue can be addressed by ensuring that each test generates a different set of fixture objects each time it is run. Thus any objects that the test needs to create must be given totally unique identifiers—that is, unique filenames, unique keys, and so on. To do so, we can build a simple unique ID generator and create a new ID at the beginning of each test. We can then use that unique ID as part of the identity of each newly created fixture object. If the fixture is shared beyond a single *Test Runner*, we may need to include something about the user in the unique identifiers we create; the currently logged-in user ID is usually sufficient. Using *Distinct Generated Values* as keys offers another benefit: It allows us to implement a *Database Partitioning Scheme* (see *Database Sandbox*) in which we can use absolute assertions despite the presence of leftover fixture objects.

Avoiding Fixture Persistence

We seem to be going to a lot of trouble to undo the side effects caused by a persistent *Fresh Fixture*. Wouldn't it be nice if we could avoid all of this work? The good news is that we can. The bad news is that we need to make our *Fresh Fixture* nonpersistent to do so. When the SUT is to blame for the persistence of the fixture, one possibility is to replace the persistence mechanism with a *Test Double* (page 522) that the test can wipe out at will. A good example of this approach is the use of a *Fake Database* (see *Fake Object* on page 551). When the test is to blame for fixture persistence, the solution is even easier: Just use a less persistent fixture reference mechanism.

Dealing with Slow Tests

A major drawback of using a *Persistent Fresh Fixture* is speed or, more precisely, the lack thereof. File systems and databases are much slower than the processors used in modern computers. As a consequence, tests that interact with databases tend to run much more slowly than tests that run entirely in memory. Part of this difference arises because the SUT is accessing the fixture from disk—but this issue turns out to be only a small part of the reason for the slowdown. Setting up the *Fresh Fixture* at the beginning of each test and tearing it down at the end of each test typically takes many more disk accesses than those used by the SUT to access the fixture. As a result, tests that access the database often take 50 to 100 times[3] longer to run than tests that run entirely in memory, all other things being equal.

The typical reaction to slow tests caused by *Persistent Fresh Fixtures* is to eliminate the fixture setup and teardown overhead by reusing the fixture across many tests. Assuming we have five disk accesses to set up and tear down the fixture for every disk access performed by the SUT, the *absolute best*[4] we can do by switching to a *Shared Fixture* is somewhere around ten times as slow. Of course, this outcome is still too slow in most situations and it comes with a hefty price: The tests are no longer independent. That means we will likely have *Interacting Tests* (see *Erratic Test*), *Lonely Tests* (see *Erratic Test*), and *Unrepeatable Tests* on top of our *Slow Tests*!

A much better solution is to eliminate the need to have a disk-based database under the application. With a small amount of effort, we should be able to replace the disk-based database with an *In-Memory Database* (see *Fake Object*) or a *Fake Database*. This decision is best made early in the project while the effort is still low. Yes, there are some challenges, such as dealing with stored procedures, but they are all surmountable.

This tactic isn't the only way to deal with *Slow Tests*, of course. The sidebar "Faster Tests Without Shared Fixtures" (page 319) explores some other strategies.

---

[3] This is two orders of magnitude!

[4] Your mileage may vary.

Managing Shared Fixtures

Managing *Shared Fixtures* has a lot in common with managing *Persistent Fresh Fixtures,* except that we deliberately choose not to tear the fixture down after every test so that we can reuse it in subsequent tests (Figure 9.2). This implies two things. First, we must be able to access the fixture in the other tests. Second, we must have a way of triggering both the construction and the teardown of the fixture.

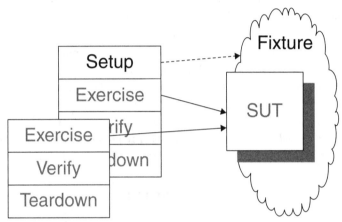

Figure 9.2 *A Shared Fixture with two Test Methods that share it. A Shared Fixture is set up once and used by two or more tests that may interact, either deliberately or accidentally, as a result. Note the lack of a fixture setup phase for the second test.*

Accessing Shared Fixtures

Regardless of how and when we choose to build the *Shared Fixture,* the tests need a way to find the test fixture they are to reuse. The choices available to us depend on the nature of the fixture. When the fixture is stored in a database (the most common usage of a *Shared Fixture*), tests may access it directly without making direct references to the fixture objects as long as they know about the database. There may be a temptation to use *Hard-Coded Values* (see *Literal Value* on page 714) in database lookups to access the fixture objects. This is almost always a bad idea, however, because it leads to a close coupling between tests and the fixture implementation and because it has poor documentation value (*Obscure Test;* page 186). To avoid these potential problems, we can use *Finder Methods* (see *Test Utility Method*) with Intent-Revealing Names [SBPP] to access the fixture. These *Finder Methods* may have names that are very similar to those of *Creation Methods,* but they return references to existing fixture objects rather than building brand new ones.

We have a range of possible solutions when the fixture is stored in memory. If all tests that need to share the fixture are in the same *Testcase Class*, we can use a **fixture holding class variable** to hold the reference to the fixture. As long as we give the variable an Intent-Revealing Name, the test reader should be able to understand the pre-conditions of the test. Another alternative is to use a *Finder Method.*

If we need to share the fixture across many *Testcase Classes*, we must use a more sophisticated technique. We could, of course, let one class declare the fixture holding class variable and have the other tests access the fixture via that variable. Unfortunately, this approach may create unnecessary coupling between the tests. Another alternative is to move the declaration to a well-known object—namely, a *Test Fixture Registry* (see *Test Helper* on page 643). This Registry [PEAA] object could be something like a test database or it could merely be a class. It can expose various parts of a fixture via discrete fixture holding class variables or via *Finder Methods*. When the *Test Fixture Registry* has only *Finder Methods* that know how to access the objects but don't hold references to them, we call it a *Test Helper.*

Triggering Shared Fixture Construction

For a test fixture to be shared, it must be built before any *Test Method* needs it. This construction could take place as late as right before the *Test Method's* logic is run, just before the entire test suite is run, or at some earlier time (Figure 9.3). This leads us to the basic patterns of *Shared Fixture* creation.

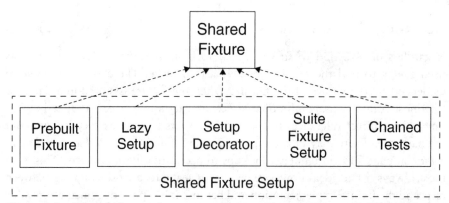

Figure 9.3   *The plethora of ways to manage a Shared Fixture. A Shared Fixture can be set up at a variety of times; the decision is based on how many tests need to reuse the fixture and how many times they need to do so.*

If we are happy with the idea of creating the test fixture the first time any test needs it, we can use *Lazy Setup* (page 435) in the setUp method of the corresponding *Testcase Class* to create it as part of running the first test. Subsequent tests will then see that the fixture already exists and reuse it. Because there is no obvious signal that the last test in a test suite (or *Suite of Suites;* see *Test Suite Object* on page 387) has been run, we won't know when to tear down the fixture after each test run. This *can* lead to *Unrepeatable Tests* because the fixture may survive across test runs (depending on how the various tests access it).

If we need to share the fixture more broadly, we could include a *Fixture Setup Testcase* at the beginning of the test suite. This is a special case of *Chained Tests* and suffers from the same problem as *Lazy Setup*—specifically, we don't know when it is time to tear down the fixture. It also depends on the ordering of tests within a suite, so it works best with *Test Enumeration* (page 399).

If we need to be able to tear down the test fixture after running a test suite, we must use a fixture management mechanism that tells us when the last test has been run. Several members of the xUnit family support the concept of a setUp method that runs just once for the test suite created from a single *Testcase Class*. This *Suite Fixture Setup* (page 441) method has a corresponding tearDown method that is called when the last *Test Method* has finished running.[5] We can then guarantee that a new fixture is built for each test run. The fixture is not left over to cause problems with subsequent test runs, which prevents *Unrepeatable Tests*; it does not prevent *Interacting Tests* within the test run, however. This capability could be added as an extension to any member of the xUnit family. When it isn't supported or when we need to share the fixture beyond a single *Testcase Class*, we can resort to using a *Setup Decorator* (page 447) to bracket the running of a test suite with the execution of the fixture setUp and tearDown logic. The biggest drawback of *Setup Decorator* is that tests that depend on the decorator cannot be run by themselves; they are *Lonely Tests*.

The final option is to build the fixture well before the tests are run—that is, to employ a *Prebuilt Fixture* (page 429). This approach offers the most options regarding how the test fixture is actually constructed because the fixture setup need not be executable from within xUnit. For example, it could be set up manually, by using database scripts, by copying a "golden" database, or by running a data generation program. The major disadvantage with a *Prebuilt Fixture* is that if any tests are *Unrepeatable Tests*, we will need to perform a *Manual Intervention* (page 250) before each test run. As a result, a *Prebuilt Fixture* is often used in combination with a *Fresh Fixture* to construct an *Immutable Shared Fixture* (see *Shared Fixture*).

---

[5] Think of it as a built-in decorator for a single *Testcase Class*.

What's Next?

Now that we've determined how we will set up and tear down our fixtures, we are ready to turn our attention to exercising the SUT and verifying that the expected outcome has occurred using calls to *Assertion Methods*. This process is described in more detail in Chapter 10, *Result Verification*.

Chapter 10

Result Verification

About This Chapter

Chapter 8, *Transient Fixture Management,* and Chapter 9, *Persistent Fixture Management,* described how to set up the test fixture and how to tear it down after exercising the SUT. This chapter introduces a variety of options for verifying that the SUT has behaved correctly, including exercising the SUT and comparing the actual outcome with the expected outcome.

Making Tests Self-Checking

One of the key characteristics of tests automated using xUnit is that they can be (and should be) *Self-Checking Tests* (see *Goals of Test Automation* on page 21). This characteristic makes them cost-effective enough to be run very frequently. Most members of the xUnit family come with a collection of built-in *Assertion Methods* (page 362) and some documentation that tells us which one to use when. On the surface this sounds pretty simple—but there's a lot more to writing good tests than just calling the built-in *Assertion Methods*. We also need to learn key techniques for making tests easy to understand and for avoiding and removing *Test Code Duplication* (page 213).

A key challenge in coding the assertions is getting access to the information we want to compare with the expected results. This is where observation points come into play; they provide a window into the state or behavior of the SUT so that we can pass it to the *Assertion Methods*. Observation points for information accessible via synchronous method calls are relatively straightforward; observation points for other kinds of information can be quite challenging, which is precisely what makes automated unit testing so interesting.

Assertions are usually—but not always—called from within the *Test Method* (page 348) body right after the SUT has been exercised. Some test automaters put assertions after the fixture setup phase of the test to ensure that the fixture is set up correctly. This practice almost always contributes to *Obscure Tests* (page 186), so I would rather write unit tests for the *Test Utility Methods* (page 599).[1] Some styles of testing do require us to set up our expectations *before* we exercise the SUT; this topic is discussed in more detail in Chapter 11, *Using Test Doubles*. We'll see several examples of calling *Assertion Methods* from within *Test Utility Methods* in this chapter.

One possible—though rarely used—place to put calls to *Assertion Methods* is in the tearDown method used in *Implicit Teardown* (page 516). Because this method is run for every test, whether that test passed or failed (as long as the setUp method succeeded), one *can* put assertions here. This scheme involves the same trade-off as using *Implicit Setup* (page 424) for building our test fixture; it's less visible but done automatically. See the sidebar "Using Delta Assertions to Detect Data Leakage" (page 487) for an example of putting assertions in the tearDown method used by *Implicit Teardown* of a superclass to detect when tests leave leftover test objects in the database.

Verify State or Behavior?

Ultimately, test automation is about verifying the behavior of the SUT. Some aspects of the SUT's behavior can be verified directly; the value returned by a function is a good example. Other aspects of the behavior are more easily verified indirectly by looking at the state of some object. We can verify the actual behavior of the SUT in our tests in two ways:

1. We can verify the states of various objects affected by the SUT by extracting each state using an observation point and using assertions to compare it to the expected state.

2. We can verify the behavior of the SUT directly by using observation points inserted between the SUT and its depended-on component (DOC) to monitor its interactions (in the form of the method calls it makes) and comparing those method calls with what we expected.

State Verification (page 462) is done using assertions and is the simpler of the two approaches. *Behavior Verification* (page 468) is more complicated and builds on the assertion techniques we use for verifying state.

---

[1] The one exception is when we *must* use a *Shared Fixture* (page 317); it may be worthwhile to use a *Guard Assertion* (page 490) to document what the test requires from it and to produce a test failure if the fixture is corrupted. We could also do so from within the *Finder Methods* (see *Test Utility Method*) that we use to retrieve the objects in the *Shared Fixture* (page 317) we will use in our tests.

State Verification

The "normal" way to verify the expected outcome has occurred is called *State Verification* (Figure 10.1). First we exercise the SUT; then we examine the post-exercise state of the SUT using assertions. We may also examine anything returned by the SUT as a result of the method call we made to exercise it. What is most notable is what we do not do: We do not instrument the SUT in any way to detect how it interacts with other components of the system. That is, we inspect only direct outputs and we use only direct method calls as our observation points.

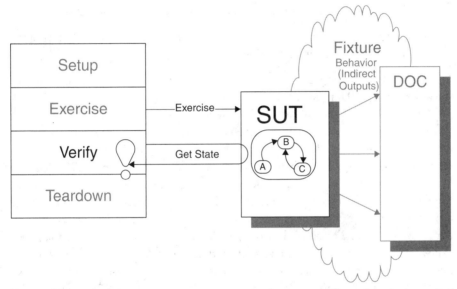

Figure 10.1 *State Verification. In State Verification, we assert that the SUT and any objects it returns are in the expected state after we have exercised the SUT. We "pay no attention to the man behind the curtain."*

State Verification can be done in two slightly different ways. *Procedural State Verification* (see *State Verification*) involves writing a sequence of assertions that pick apart the end state of the SUT and verify that it is as expected. *Expected Object* (see *State Verification*) is a way of describing the expected state in such a way that it can be compared with a single *Assertion Method* call; this approach minimizes *Test Code Duplication* and increases test clarity (more on this later in this chapter). With both strategies, we can use either "built-in" assertions or *Custom Assertions* (page 474).

Using Built-in Assertions

We use the assertions provided by our testing framework to specify what *should be* and depend on them to tell us when it isn't so! But simply using the built-in assertions is only a small part of the story.

The simplest form of result verification is the assertion in which we specify what should be true. Most members of the xUnit family support a range of different *Assertion Methods,* including the following:

- *Stated Outcome Assertions* (see *Assertion Method*) such as assertTrue (aBooleanExpression)

- Simple *Equality Assertions* such as assertEquals(expected, actual)

- *Fuzzy Equality Assertions* such as assertEquals(expected, actual, tolerance), which are used for comparing floats

Of course, the test programming language has some influence on the nature of the assertions. In JUnit, SUnit, CppUnit, NUnit, and CsUnit, most of the *Equality Assertions* take a pair of Objects as their parameters. Some languages support "overloading" of method parameter types so we can have different implementations of an assertion for different types of objects. Some languages—C, for example—don't support objects, so we cannot compare objects, only values.

There are several issues to consider when using *Assertion Methods.* Naturally, the first priority is the verification of all things that should be true. The better our assertions, the finer our *Safety Net* (see page 24) and the higher our confidence in our code. The second priority is the documentation value of the assertions. Each test should make it very clear that "When the system is in state S1 and I do X, the result should be R and the system should be in state S2." We put the system into state S1 in our fixture setup logic. "I do X" corresponds to the exercise SUT phase of the test. "The result is R" and "the system is in state S2" are implemented using assertions. Thus we want to write our assertions in such a way that they succinctly describe "R" and "S2."

Another thing to consider is that when the test fails, we want the failure message to tell us enough to enable us to identify the problem.[2] Therefore, we should almost always include an *Assertion Message* (page 370) as the optional message parameter (assuming our xUnit family member has one!). This tactic avoids the possibility of us playing *Assertion Roulette* (page 224), in which we cannot even tell which assertion is failing without running the test interactively;

---

[2] In his book [TDD-APG], Dave Astels claims he never/rarely used the Eclipse Debugger while writing the code samples because the assertions always told him enough about what was wrong. This is what we strive for!

it makes Integration Build [SCM] failures much easier to reproduce and fix. It also makes troubleshooting broken tests easier by telling us what *should have* happened; the actual outcome tells us what *did* happen!

When we use a *Stated Outcome Assertion* (such as JUnit's assertTrue), the failure messages tend to be unhelpful (e.g., "Assertion failed"). We can make the assertion output much more specific by using an *Argument-Describing Message* (see *Assertion Message*) constructed by incorporating useful bits of data into the message. A good start is to include each of the values in the expression passed as the *Assertion Method's* arguments.

Delta Assertions

When using a *Shared Fixture* (page 317), we may find that we have *Interacting Tests* (see *Erratic Test* on page 228) because each test adds more objects/rows into the database and we can never be certain exactly what should be there after the SUT has been exercised. One way to deal with this uncertainty is to use *Delta Assertions* (page 485) to verify only the newly added objects/rows. In this approach, we take some sort of "snapshot" of the relevant tables/classes at the beginning of the test; we then remove these tables/classes from the collection of actual objects/rows produced at the end of the test before comparing them to the *Expected Objects*. Although this tactic can introduce significant extra complexity into the tests, the added complexity can be refactored into *Custom Assertions* and/or *Verification Methods* (see *Custom Assertion*). The "before" snapshot may be taken on an in-line basis within the *Test Method* or in the setUp method if all setup occurs before the *Test Method* is invoked [e.g., *Implicit Setup*, a *Shared Fixture,* or a *Prebuilt Fixture* (page 429)].

External Result Verification

Thus far we have described only conventional "in-memory" verification of the expected results. In fact, another approach is possible—one that involves storing the expected and actual results in files and using an external comparison program to report on any differences. This is, in effect, a form of *Custom Assertion* that uses a "deep compare" on two file references. The comparison program often needs to be told which parts of the files to ignore (or these parts need to be stripped out first), effectively making this a *Fuzzy Equality Assertion*.

External result verification is particularly appropriate for automating acceptance tests for regression-testing an application that hasn't changed very much. The major disadvantage of this approach is that we almost always end up with a *Mystery Guest* (see *Obscure Test*) from the test reader's perspective because the expected results are not visible inside the test. One way to avoid this problem is to have the test write the contents of the expected file, thereby making the contents visible to the test reader. This step is practical only if the amount of data is quite small—another argument in favor of a *Minimal Fixture* (page 302).

Verifying Behavior

Verifying behavior is more complicated than verifying state because behavior is dynamic. We have to catch the SUT "in the act" as it generates indirect outputs to the objects it depends on (Figure 10.2). Two basic styles of behavior verification are worth discussing: *Procedural Behavior Verification* and *Expected Behavior*. Both require a mechanism to access the outgoing method calls of the SUT (its indirect outputs). This and other uses of *Test Doubles* (page 522) are described in more detail in Chapter 11, *Using Test Doubles*.

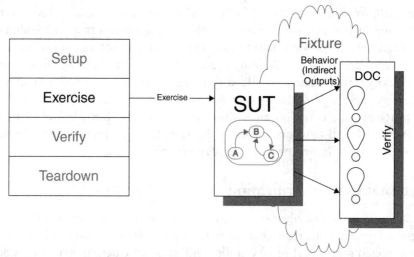

Figure 10.2 *Behavior Verification. In Behavior Verification, we focus our assertions on the indirect outputs (outgoing interfaces) of the SUT. This typically involves replacing the DOC with something that facilitates observing and verifying the outgoing calls.*

Procedural Behavior Verification

In *Procedural Behavior Verification,* we capture the behavior of the SUT as it executes and save that data for later retrieval. The test then compares each output of the SUT (one by one) with the corresponding expected output. Thus, in *Procedural Behavior Verification,* the test executes a procedure (a set of steps) to verify the behavior.

```
public void testRemoveFlightLogging_recordingTestStub()
        throws Exception {
    // fixture setup
    FlightDto expectedFlightDto = createAnUnregFlight();
    FlightManagementFacade facade =
        new FlightManagementFacadeImpl();
    //    Test Double setup
    AuditLogSpy logSpy = new AuditLogSpy();
    facade.setAuditLog(logSpy);
    // exercise
    facade.removeFlight(expectedFlightDto.getFlightNumber());
    // verify
    assertEquals("number of calls", 1,
                logSpy.getNumberOfCalls());
    assertEquals("action code",
                Helper.REMOVE_FLIGHT_ACTION_CODE,
                logSpy.getActionCode());
    assertEquals("date", helper.getTodaysDateWithoutTime(),
                logSpy.getDate());
    assertEquals("user", Helper.TEST_USER_NAME,
                logSpy.getUser());
    assertEquals("detail",
                expectedFlightDto.getFlightNumber(),
                logSpy.getDetail());
}
```

The key challenge in *Procedural Behavior Verification* is capturing the behavior as it occurs and saving it until the test is ready to use this information. This task is accomplished by configuring the SUT to use a *Test Spy* (page 538) or a *Self Shunt* (see *Hard-Coded Test Double* on page 568)[3] instead of the depended-on class. After the SUT has been exercised, the test retrieves the recording of the behavior and verifies it using assertions.

Expected Behavior Specification

If we can build an *Expected Object* and compare it with the actual object returned by the SUT for verifying state, can we do something similar for verifying

---

[3] A *Test Spy* built into the *Testcase Class* (page 373).

behavior? Yes, we can and do. *Expected Behavior* is often used in conjunction with layer-crossing tests to verify the indirect outputs of an object or component. We configure a *Mock Object* (page 544) with the method calls we expect the SUT to make to it and install this object before exercising the SUT.

```
public void testRemoveFlight_JMock() throws Exception {
    // fixture setup
    FlightDto expectedFlightDto = createAnonRegFlight();
    FlightManagementFacade facade =
            new FlightManagementFacadeImpl();
    // mock configuration
    Mock mockLog = mock(AuditLog.class);
    mockLog.expects(once()).method("logMessage")
            .with(eq(helper.getTodaysDateWithoutTime()),
                  eq(Helper.TEST_USER_NAME),
                  eq(Helper.REMOVE_FLIGHT_ACTION_CODE),
                  eq(expectedFlightDto.getFlightNumber()));
    // mock installation
    facade.setAuditLog((AuditLog) mockLog.proxy());
    // exercise
    facade.removeFlight(expectedFlightDto.getFlightNumber());
    // verify
    // verify() method called automatically by JMock
}
```

Reducing Test Code Duplication

One of the most common test smells is *Test Code Duplication*. With every test we write, there is a good chance we have introduced some duplication, but especially if we used "cut and paste" to create a new test from an existing test. Some will argue that duplication in test code is not nearly as bad as duplication in production code. *Test Code Duplication is* bad if it leads to some other smell such as *Fragile Test* (page 239), *Fragile Fixture* (see *Fragile Test*), or *High Test Maintenance Cost* (page 265) because too many tests are too closely coupled to the *Standard Fixture* (page 305) or the API of the SUT. In addition, *Test Code Duplication* may sometimes be a symptom of another problem—namely, the intent of the tests being obscured by too much code (i.e., an *Obscure Test*).

In result verification logic, *Test Code Duplication* usually shows up as a set of repeated assertions. Several techniques are available to reduce the number of assertions in such cases:

- *Expected Objects*
- *Custom Assertions*
- *Verification Methods*

Expected Objects

Often, we will find ourselves doing a series of assertions on different fields of the same object. If we begin repeating this group of assertions (whether multiple times in a single test or in multiple tests), we should look for a way to reduce the *Test Code Duplication*. The next listing shows one *Test Method* that compares several attributes of a single object. Many other *Test Methods* probably require the same sequence of assertions.

```
public void testInvoice_addLineItem7() {
    LineItem expItem = new LineItem(inv, product, QUANTITY);
    // Exercise
    inv.addItemQuantity(product, QUANTITY);
    // Verify
    List lineItems = inv.getLineItems();
    LineItem actual = (LineItem)lineItems.get(0);
    assertEquals(expItem.getInv(), actual.getInv());
    assertEquals(expItem.getProd(), actual.getProd());
    assertEquals(expItem.getQuantity(), actual.getQuantity());
}
```

The most obvious alternative is to use a single *Equality Assertion* to compare two whole objects to each other rather than using many *Equality Assertion* calls to compare them field by field. If the values are stored in individual variables, we may need to create a new object of the appropriate class and initialize its fields with those values. This technique works as long as we have an equals method that compares only those fields and we have the ability to create the *Expected Object* at will.

```
public void testInvoice_addLineItem8() {
    LineItem expItem = new LineItem(inv, product, QUANTITY);
    // Exercise
    inv.addItemQuantity(product, QUANTITY);
    // Verify
    List lineItems = inv.getLineItems();
    LineItem actual = (LineItem)lineItems.get(0);
    assertEquals("Item", expItem, actual);
}
```

But what if we don't want to compare all the fields in an object or the equals method looks for identity rather than equality? What if we want **test-specific** equality? What if we cannot create an instance of the *Expected Object* because no constructor exists? In this scenario, we have two options: We can implement a *Custom Assertion* that defines equality the way we want it or we can implement our test-specific equality in the equals method of the class of the *Expected Object* we pass to the *Assertion Method*. This class doesn't need to be the same class as that of the actual object; it just needs to implement equals to compare itself with an instance of the actual object's class. Therefore, it can be a simple Data Transfer Object [CJ2EEP] or it can be a *Test-Specific Subclass* (page 579) of the real (production) class with just the equals method overridden.

Some test automaters don't think we should ever rely on the equals method of the SUT when making assertions because it *could* change, thereby causing tests that depend on this method to fail (or to miss important differences). I prefer to be pragmatic about this decision. If it seems reasonable to use the equals definition supplied by the SUT, then I do so. If I need something else, I define a *Custom Assertion* or a test-specific *Expected Object* class. I also ask myself how hard it would be to change my strategy if the equals method should later change. For example, in statically typed languages that support parameter type overloading (such as Java), we can add a *Custom Assertion* that uses different parameter types to override the default implementation when specific types are used. This code can often be retrofitted quite easily if a change to equals causes problems at a later date.

Custom Assertions

A *Custom Assertion* is a domain-specific assertion we write ourselves. *Custom Assertions* hide the procedure for verifying the results behind a declarative name, making our result verification logic more intent-revealing. They also prevent *Obscure Tests* by eliminating of a lot of potentially distracting code. Another benefit of moving the code into a *Custom Assertion* is that the assertion logic can now be unit-tested by writing *Custom Assertion Tests* (see *Custom Assertion*). The assertions are no longer *Untestable Test Code* (see *Hard-to-Test Code* on page 209)!

```
static void assertLineItemsEqual(
                String  msg, LineItem exp, LineItem act) {
    assertEquals (msg+" Inv",  exp.getInv(), act.getInv());
    assertEquals (msg+" Prod", exp.getProd(), act.getProd());
    assertEquals (msg+" Quan", exp.getQuantity(), act.getQuantity());
}
```

There are two ways to create *Custom Assertions*: (1) by refactoring existing complex test code to reduce *Test Code Duplication* and (2) by coding calls to nonexistent *Assertion Methods* as we write tests and then filling in the method bodies with the appropriate logic once we land on the suite of *Custom Assertions* needed by a set of *Test Methods*. The latter technique is a good way of reminding ourselves what we expect the outcome of exercising the SUT to be, even though we haven't yet written the code to verify it. Either way, the definition of a set of *Custom Assertions* is the first step toward creating a *Higher-Level Language* (see page 41) for specifying our tests.

When refactoring to *Custom Assertions,* we simply use Extract Method [Fowler] on the repeated assertions and give the new method an Intent-Revealing Name [SBPP]. We pass in the objects used by the existing verification logic as arguments and include an *Assertion Message* to differentiate between calls to the same assertion method.

Outcome-Describing Verification Method

Another technique that is born from ruthless refactoring of test code is the "outcome-describing" *Verification Method.* Suppose we find that a group of tests all have identical exercise SUT and verify outcome sections. Only the setup portion is different for each test. If we do an Extract Method refactoring on the common code and give it a meaningful name, we need less code, achieve more understandable tests, and produce testable verification logic all at the same time! If this isn't a worthwhile reason for refactoring code, then I don't know what else could be.

```
void assertInvoiceContainsOnlyThisLineItem(
                            Invoice inv,
                            LineItem expItem) {
    List lineItems = inv.getLineItems();
    assertEquals("number of items", lineItems.size(), 1);
    LineItem actual = (LineItem)lineItems.get(0);
    assertLineItemsEqual("",expItem, actual);
}
```

The major difference between a *Verification Method* and a *Custom Assertion* is that the latter only makes assertions, while the former also interacts with the SUT (typically for the purpose of exercising it). Another difference is that *Custom Assertions* typically have a standard *Equality Assertion* signature: assertSomething(message, expected, actual). In contrast, *Verification Methods* may have completely arbitrary parameters because they require additional parameters to pass into the SUT. They are, in essence, halfway between a *Custom Assertion* and a *Parameterized Test* (page 607).

Parameterized and Data-Driven Tests

We can go even further in factoring out the commonality between tests. If the logic to set up the test fixture is the same but uses different data, we can extract the common fixture setup, exercise SUT, and verify outcome phases of the test into a new *Parameterized Test* method. This *Parameterized Test* is not called automatically by the *Test Automation Framework* (page 298) because it requires arguments; instead, we define very simple *Test Methods* for each test, which then call the *Parameterized Test* and pass in the data required to make this test unique. This data may include that required for fixture setup, exercising the SUT, and the corresponding expected result. In the following tests, the method generateAndVerifyHtml is the *Parameterized Test*.

```
def test_extref
    sourceXml = "<extref id='abc' />"
    expectedHtml = "<a href='abc.html'>abc</a>"
    generateAndVerifyHtml(sourceXml,expectedHtml,"<extref>")
end

def test_testterm_normal
    sourceXml = "<testterm id='abc'/>"
    expectedHtml = "<a href='abc.html'>abc</a>"
    generateAndVerifyHtml(sourceXml,expectedHtml,"<testterm>")
end

def test_testterm_plural
    sourceXml = "<testterms id='abc'/>"
    expectedHtml = "<a href='abc.html'>abcs</a>"
    generateAndVerifyHtml(sourceXml,expectedHtml,"<plural>")
end
```

In a *Data-Driven Test* (page 288), the test case is completely generic *and* directly executable by the framework; it reads the arguments from a test data file as it executes. Think of a *Data-Driven Test* as a *Parameterized Test* turned inside out: A *Test Method* passes test-specific data to a *Parameterized Test*; a *Data-Driven Test* is the *Test Method* and reads the test-specific data from a file. The contents of the file are a *Higher-Level Language* for testing; the *Data-Driven Test* method is the Interpreter [GOF] of that language. This scheme is the xUnit equivalent of a Fit test. A simple example of a *Data-Driven Test* method is shown in this code sample written in Ruby:

```
def test_crossref
    executeDataDrivenTest "CrossrefHandlerTest.txt"
end

def executeDataDrivenTest filename
    dataFile = File.open(filename)
```

```
dataFile.each_line do | line |
  desc, action, part2 = line.split(",")
    sourceXml, expectedHtml, leftOver = part2.split(",")
    if "crossref"==action.strip
       generateAndVerifyHtml sourceXml, expectedHtml, desc
    else # new "verbs" go before here as elsif's
       report_error( "unknown action" + action.strip )
    end
  end
end
```

Here is the comma-delimited data file that the *Data-Driven Test* method reads:

```
ID,    Action,    SourceXml,         ExpectedHtml
Extref,crossref,<extref id='abc'/>,<a href='abc.html'>abc</a>
TTerm,crossref,<testterm id='abc'/>,<a href='abc.html'>abc</a>
TTerms,crossref,<testterms id='abc'/>,<a href='abc.html'>abcs</a>
```

Avoiding Conditional Test Logic

Another thing we want to avoid in our tests is conditional logic. *Conditional Test Logic* (page 200) is bad because the same test may execute differently in different circumstances. *Conditional Test Logic* reduces our trust in the tests because the code in our *Test Methods* is *Untestable Test Code*. Why is this important? Because the only way we can verify our *Test Method* is to manually edit the SUT so that it produces the error we want to be detected. If the *Test Method* has many paths through it, we need to make sure each path is coded correctly. Isn't it so much simpler just to have only one possible execution path through the test? Let us look at some reasons why we might include conditional logic in our tests:

- We don't want to execute certain assertions because their execution doesn't make sense given what we have already discovered at this point in the test (typically a failure condition).

- We have to allow for various situations in the actual results that we are comparing to the expected results.

- We are trying to reuse a *Test Method* in several different circumstances (essentially merging several tests into a single *Test Method*).

The problem with using *Conditional Test Logic* in the first two cases is that it makes the code hard to read and may mask cases of reusing test methods via *Flexible Tests* (see *Conditional Test Logic*). The last "reason" is just a bad idea, plain and simple. There are much better ways of reusing test logic than trying to reuse the *Test Method* itself. We have already seen some of these reuse techniques elsewhere in this chapter (in *Reducing Test Code Duplication*), and we will see other ways elsewhere in this book. Just say "no"!

The good news is that it is relatively straightforward to remove all legitimate uses of *Conditional Test Logic* from our tests.

Eliminating "if" Statements

What should we do when we don't want to execute an assertion because we know it will result in a test error and we would prefer to have a more meaningful test failure message? The normal reaction is to place the assertion inside an "if" statement, as shown in the following listing. Unfortunately, this approach results in *Conditional Test Logic,* which we would dearly like to avoid because we want exactly the same code to run each time we run the test.

```
List lineItems = invoice.getLineItems();
if (lineItems.size() == 1) {
   LineItem expected =
      new LineItem(invoice, product,5,
                    new BigDecimal("30"),
                    new BigDecimal("69.96"));
   LineItem actItem = (LineItem) lineItems.get(0);
   assertEquals("invoice", expected, actItem);
} else {
   fail("Invoice should have exactly one line item");
}
```

The preferred solution is to use a *Guard Assertion* (page 490) as shown in this revised version of the test code:

```
List lineItems = invoice.getLineItems();
assertEquals("number of items", lineItems.size(), 1);
LineItem expected =
   new LineItem(invoice, product, 5,
                 new BigDecimal("30"),
                 new BigDecimal("69.96"));
LineItem actItem = (LineItem) lineItems.get(0);
assertEquals("invoice", expected, actItem);
```

The nice thing about *Guard Assertions* is that they keep us from hitting the assertion that would cause a test error but without introducing *Conditional Test Logic.* Once we get used to them, these assertions are fairly obvious and intuitive to read. We may even find ourselves wanting to assert the pre-conditions of our methods in our production code!

Eliminating Loops

Conditional Test Logic may also appear as loops that verify the content of a collection returned by the SUT matches what we expected. Putting loops directly into the *Test Method* creates three problems:

- It introduces *Untestable Test Code* because the looping code, which is part of the test, cannot be tested with *Fully Automated Tests* (see page 26).

- It leads to *Obscure Tests* because all that looping code obscures the real intent: Does or doesn't the collection match?

- It can lead to the project-level smell *Developers Not Writing Tests* (page 263) because the complexity of writing the loops may discourage the developer from writing the *Self-Checking Test*.

A better solution is to delegate this logic to a *Test Utility Method* with an Intent-Revealing Name, which can be both tested and reused.

Other Techniques

This section outlines some other techniques for writing easy-to-understand tests.

Working Backward, Outside-In

A useful little trick for writing very intent-revealing code is to work backward. This is an application of Stephen Covey's idea, "Start with the end in mind." To do so, we write the last line of the function or test first. For a function, its whole reason for existence is to return a value; for a procedure, it is to produce one or more side effects by modifying something. For a test, the raison d' tre is to verify that the expected outcome has occurred (by making assertions).

Working backward means we write these assertions first. We assert on the values of suitably named local variables to ensure that the assertion is intent-revealing. The rest of writing the test simply consists of filling in whatever is needed to execute those assertions: We declare variables to hold the assertion arguments and initialize them with the appropriate content. Because at least one argument should have been retrieved from the SUT, we must, of course, invoke the SUT. To do so, we may need some variables to use as SUT arguments. Declaring and initializing a variable after it has been used forces us to understand the variable better when we introduce it. This scheme also results in better variable names and avoids meaningless names like invoice1 and invoice2.

Working "outside-in" (or "top-down" as it is sometimes called) means staying at a consistent level of abstraction. The *Test Method* should focus on what we need to have in place to induce the relevant behavior in the SUT. The mechanics of how we reach that place should be delegated to a "lower layer" of test software. In practice, we code this behavior as calls to *Test Utility Methods*, which allows us to stay focused on the requirements of the SUT as we write each *Test Method*. We don't need to worry about *how* we will create that object or verify that outcome; we merely need to describe what that object or outcome *should be*. The utility method we just used but haven't yet defined acts as a placeholder for the unfinished test automation logic.[4] We can move on to writing the other tests we need for this SUT while they are still fresh in our minds. Later, we can switch to our "toolsmith" hat and implement the *Test Utility Methods*.

Using Test-Driven Development to Write Test Utility Methods

Once we are finished writing the *Test Method(s)* that used the *Test Utility Method*, we can start the process of writing the *Test Utility Method* itself. Along the way, we can take advantage of test-driven development by writing *Test Utility Tests* (see *Test Utility Method*). It doesn't take very long to write these unit tests that verify the behavior of our *Test Utility Methods* and we will have much more confidence in them.

We start with the simple case (say, asserting the equality of two identical collections that hold the same item) and work up to the most complicated case that the *Test Methods actually require* (say, two collections that contain the same two items but in different order). TDD helps us find the minimal implementation of the *Test Utility Method*, which may be much simpler than a complete generic solution. There is no point in writing generic logic that handles cases that aren't actually needed but it may be worthwhile to include a *Guard Assertion* or two inside the *Custom Assertion* to fail tests in cases it doesn't support.

Where to Put Reusable Verification Logic?

Suppose we have decided to use Extract Method refactorings to create some reusable *Custom Assertions* or we have decided to write our tests in an intent-revealing way using *Verification Methods*. Where should we put these bits of reusable test

---

[4] We should always give this method an Intent-Revealing Name and stub it out with a call to the `fail` assertion to remind ourselves that we still need to write the method's body.

logic? The most obvious place is in the *Testcase Class* (page 373) itself. We can allow this logic to be reused more broadly by using a Pull-Up Method [Fowler] refactoring to move them up to a *Testcase Superclass* (page 638) or a Move Method [Fowler] refactoring to move them into a *Test Helper* (page 643). This issue is discussed in more detail in Chapter 12, *Organizing Our Tests*.

What's Next?

This discussion of techniques for verifying the expected outcome concludes our introduction to the basic techniques of automating tests using xUnit. Chapter 11, *Using Test Doubles,* introduces some advanced techniques involving the use of *Test Doubles.*

Chapter 11

Using Test Doubles

About This Chapter

The last few chapters concluding with Chapter 10, *Result Verification,* introduced the basic mechanisms of running tests using the xUnit family of *Test Automation Frameworks* (page 298). For the most part we assumed that the SUT was designed such that it could be tested easily in isolation of other pieces of software. When a class does *not* depend on any other classes, testing it is relatively straightforward and the techniques described in this chapter are unnecessary. When a class *does* depend on other classes, we have two choices: We can test it together with all the other classes it depends on or we can try to isolate it from the other classes so that we can test it by itself. This chapter introduces techniques for isolating the SUT from the other software components on which it depends.

What Are Indirect Inputs and Outputs?

The problem with testing classes in groups or clusters is that it becomes very hard to cover all the paths through the code. The depended-on component (DOC) may return values or throw exceptions that affect the behavior of the SUT, but it may prove difficult or impossible to cause certain cases to occur. The indirect inputs received from the DOC may be unpredictable (such as the system clock or calendar). In other cases, the DOC may not be available in the test environment or may not even exist. How can we test dependent classes in these circumstances?

In other cases, we need to verify that certain side effects of executing the SUT have, indeed, occurred. If it is too difficult to monitor these indirect outputs of the SUT (or if it is too expensive to retrieve them), the effectiveness of our automated testing may be compromised.

As you will no doubt have guessed from the title of this chapter, the solution to these problems is often the use of a *Test Double* (page 522). We will start by looking at how we can use *Test Doubles* to test indirect inputs and outputs. We will then describe a few other uses of these helpful mechanisms.

Why Do We Care about Indirect Inputs?

Calls to DOCs often return objects or values, update their arguments or even throw exceptions. Many of the execution paths within the SUT are intended to deal with these return values and to handle the possible exceptions. Leaving these paths un-tested leads to *Untested Code* (see *Production Bugs* on page 268). These paths can be the most challenging to test effectively but are also among the most likely to lead to catastrophic failures if exercised for the very first time in production.

   We certainly would rather not have the exception-handling code execute for the first time in production. What if it was coded incorrectly? Clearly, it would be high-ly desirable to have automated tests for such code. The testing challenge is to some-how cause the DOC to throw an exception so that the error path can be tested. The exception we expect the DOC to throw is a good example of an **indirect input test condition** (Figure 11.1). Our means of injecting this input is a **control point**.

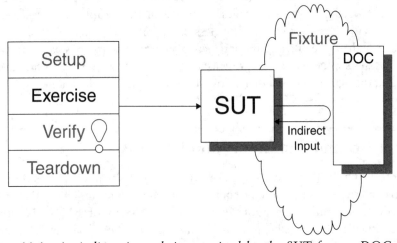

Figure 11.1 *An indirect input being received by the SUT from a DOC. Not all inputs of the SUT come from the test. Some indirect inputs come from other components called by the SUT in the form of return values, updated parameters, or exceptions thrown.*

Why Do We Care about Indirect Outputs?

The concept of encapsulation often directs us to not care about how some-thing is implemented. After all, that is the whole purpose of encapsulation—to alleviate the need for clients of our interface to care about our implementation.

When testing, we try to verify the implementation precisely so our clients do not have to care about it.

Consider for a moment a component that has a method in its API that returns nothing—or at least nothing that can be used to determine whether it has performed its function correctly. In this situation, we have no choice but to test through the back door. A good example of this is a message logging system. Calls to the API of a logger rarely return anything that indicates it did its job correctly. The only way to determine whether the message logging system is working as expected is to interact with it through some other interface—one that allows us to retrieve the logged messages.

A client of the logger may specify that the logger be called when certain conditions are met. These calls will not be visible on the client's interface but would typically be a requirement that the client needs to satisfy and, therefore, would be something we want to test. The circumstances that should result in a messaging being logged are **indirect output** test conditions (Figure 11.2) for which we need to write tests so that we can avoid having *Untested Requirements* (see *Production Bugs*). Our means of seeing this output is an **observation point**.

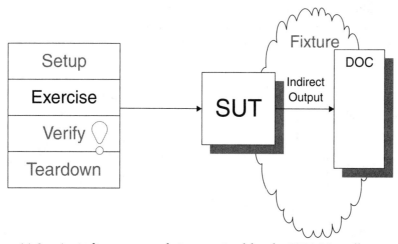

Figure 11.2 *An indirect output being received by the SUT. Not all outputs of the SUT are directly visible to the test. Some indirect outputs are sent to other components in the form of method calls or messages.*

In other cases, the SUT does produce visible behavior that can be verified through the front door but also has some expected side effects. Both outputs need to be verified in our tests. Sometimes this testing is simply a matter of adding assertions for the indirect outputs to the existing tests to verify the *Untested Requirement*.

How Do We Control Indirect Inputs?

Testing with indirect inputs is a bit simpler than testing with indirect outputs because the techniques used to test outputs build on those used to test inputs. Let's delve into indirect inputs first.

To test the SUT with *indirect* inputs, we must be able to control th e DOC well enough to cause it to return every possible kind of return value. That implies the availability of a suitable control point.

Examples of the kinds of indirect inputs we want to be able to induce via this control point include

- Return values of methods/functions

- Values of updatable arguments

- Exceptions that could be thrown

Often, the test can interact with the DOC to set up how it will respond to requests. For example, if a component provides access to data in a database, then we can use *Back Door Setup* (see *Back Door Manipulation* on page 327) to insert specific values into a database that cause the component to respond in the desired ways (e.g., no items found, one item found, many items found). (See Figure 11.3.) In this specific case, we can use the database itself as a control point.

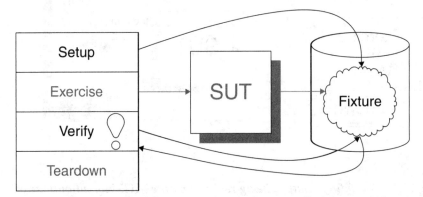

Figure 11.3   *Using Back Door Manipulation to indirectly control and observe the SUT. When the SUT stores its state in another component, we may be able to manipulate that state by having the test interact directly with the other component via a "back door."*

In most cases, however, this approach is neither practical nor even possible. We might *not* be able to use the real component for the following reasons:

- The real component cannot be manipulated to produce the desired indirect input. Only a true software error within the real component would result in the desired input to the SUT.

- The real component could be manipulated to make the input occur but doing so would not be cost-effective.

- The real component could be manipulated to make the input occur but doing so could have unacceptable side effects.

- The real component is not yet available for use.

If we cannot use the real component as a control point, then we have to replace it with one that we *can* control. This replacement can be done in a number of different ways, which are the focus of the section *Installing the Test Double* later in this chapter. The most common approach is to configure a *Test Stub* (page 529) with a set of values to return from its functions and then to install this *Test Stub* into the SUT. During execution of the SUT, the *Test Stub* receives the calls and returns the previously configured responses (Figure 11.4). It has become our control point.

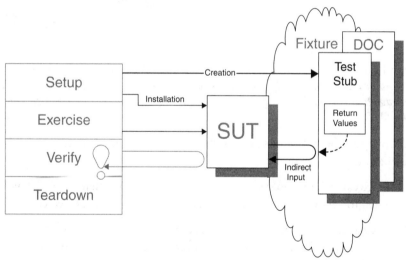

Figure 11.4 *Using a Test Stub as a control point for indirect inputs. One way to use a control point to inject indirect inputs into the SUT is to install a Test Stub in place of the DOC. Before exercising the SUT, we tell the Test Stub what it should return to the SUT when it is called. This strategy allows us to force the SUT through all its code paths.*

How Do We Verify Indirect Outputs?

In normal usage, as the SUT is exercised, it interacts naturally with the component(s) upon which it depends. To test the *indirect* outputs, we must be able to observe the calls that the SUT makes to the API of the DOC (Figure 11.5). Furthermore, if we need the test to progress beyond that point, we need to be able to control the values returned (as was discussed in the discussion of indirect inputs).

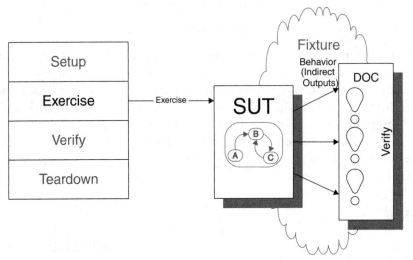

Figure 11.5   *Using Behavior Verification to verify the indirect outputs of the SUT. When we care about exactly what calls our SUT makes to other components, we may have to do Behavior Verification rather than simply verifying the post-test state of the SUT.*

In many cases, the test can use the DOC as an observation point to find out how it has been used. For example:

- We can ask the file system for the contents of a file that the SUT has written to verify that it exists and was written with the expected contents.

- We can ask the database for the contents of a table or specific record to verify that the SUT wrote the expected records to the database.

- We can interact directly with the e-mail sending component to ask whether the SUT had asked it to send a particular e-mail.

These are all examples of *Back Door Verification* (see *Back Door Manipulation* on page 327). Some DOCs allow us to configure their behavior in such a way that we can use them to keep the test informed of how they are being used:

- We can ask the file system to notify the test whenever a file is created or modified so we can verify its contents.

- We can use a database trigger to notify the test when a record is written or deleted.

- We can configure the e-mail sending component to deliver all outgoing e-mail to the test.

Sometimes, as we have seen with indirect inputs, it is not practical to use the real component as an observation point. When all else fails, we may need to replace the real component with a test-specific alternative. For example, we might need to do this for the following reasons:

- The calls to (or the internal state of) the DOC cannot be queried.

- The real component can be queried but doing so is cost-prohibitive.

- The real component can be queried but doing so has unacceptable side effects.

- The real component is not yet available for use.

The replacement of the real component can be done in a number of different ways, as will be discussed in *Installing the Test Double*.

Two basic styles of indirect output verification are available. *Procedural Behavior Verification* (see *Behavior Verification*) captures the calls to a DOC (or their results) during SUT execution and then compares them with the expected calls after the SUT has finished executing. This verification involves replacing a **substitutable dependency** with a *Test Spy* (page 538). During execution of the SUT, the *Test Spy* receives the calls and records them. After the *Test Method* (page 348) has finished exercising the SUT, it retrieves the actual calls from the *Test Spy* and uses *Assertion Methods* (page 362) to compare them with the expected calls (Figure 11.6).

Expected Behavior (see Behavior Verification) involves building a "behavior specification" during the fixture setup phase of the test and then comparing the actual behavior with this *Expected Behavior*. It is typically done by loading a *Mock Object* (page 544) with a set of expected procedure call descriptions and installing this object into the SUT (Figure 11.7). During execution of the SUT, the *Mock Object* receives the calls and compares them to the previously defined expected calls (the "behavior specification"). As the test proceeds, if the *Mock Object* receives an unexpected call, it fails the test immediately. The test failure traceback will show the exact location in the SUT where the problem occurred because the *Assertion Methods* are called from the *Mock Object,* which is in turn called by the SUT. We can also see exactly where in the *Test Method* the SUT was being exercised.

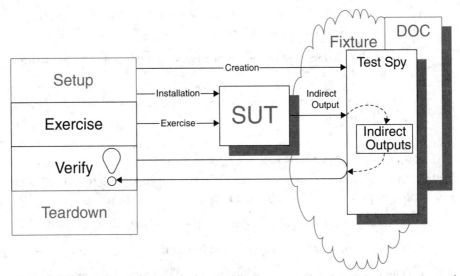

Figure 11.6   *Using a Test Spy as an observation point for indirect outputs of the SUT. One way to implement Behavior Verification is to install a Test Spy in place of the target of the indirect outputs. After exercising the SUT, the test asks the Test Spy for information about how it was used and compares that information to the expected behavior using assertions.*

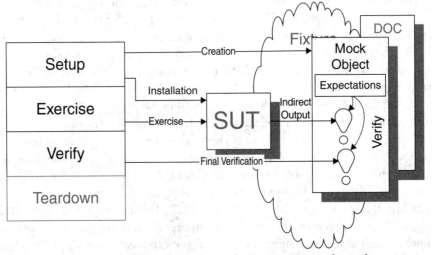

Figure 11.7   *Using a Mock Object as an observation point for indirect outputs of the SUT. Another way to implement Behavior Verification is to install a Mock Object in place of the target of the indirect outputs. As the SUT makes calls to the DOC, the Mock Object uses assertions to compare the actual calls and arguments with the expected calls and arguments.*

When we use a *Test Spy* or a *Mock Object*, we may also have to employ it as a control point for any indirect inputs on which the SUT depends after the *Test Spy* or *Mock Object* has been called to allow test execution to continue.

Testing with Doubles

By now you are probably wondering about how to replace those inflexible and uncooperative real components with something that makes it easier to control the indirect inputs and to verify the indirect outputs.

As we have seen, to test the indirect inputs, we must be able to control the DOC well enough to cause it to return every possible kind of return value (valid, invalid, and exception). To test indirect outputs, we must be able to track the calls the SUT makes to other components. A *Test Double* is a type of object that is much more cooperative and lets us write tests the way we want to.

Types of Test Doubles

A *Test Double* is any object or component that we install in place of the real component for the express purpose of running a test. Depending on the reason why we are using it, a *Test Double* can behave in one of four ways (summarized in Figure 11.8):

- A *Dummy Object* (page 728) is a placeholder object that is passed to the SUT as an argument (or an attribute of an argument) but is never actually used.

- A *Test Stub* is an object that replaces a real component on which the SUT depends so that the test can control the indirect inputs of the SUT. It allows the test to force the SUT down paths it might not otherwise exercise. A *Test Spy*, which is a more capable version of a *Test Stub*, can be used to verify the indirect outputs of the SUT by giving the test a way to inspect them after exercising the SUT.

- A *Mock Object* is an object that replaces a real component on which the SUT depends so that the test can verify its indirect outputs.

- A *Fake Object* (page 551) (or just "Fake" for short) is an object that replaces the functionality of the real DOC with an alternative implementation of the same functionality.

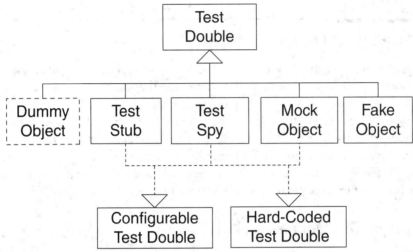

Figure 11.8 *Several kinds of Test Doubles exist. Dummy Objects are really an alternative to the value patterns. Test Stubs are used to verify indirect inputs; Test Spies and Mock Objects are used to verify indirect outputs. Fake objects emulate the behavior of the real depended-on component, but with test-friendly characteristics.*

Dummy Objects

Dummy Objects are a degenerate form of *Test Double*. They exist solely so that they can be passed around from method to method; they are never used. That is, *Dummy Objects* are not expected to do anything except exist. Often, we can get away with using "null" (or "nil" or "nothing"); at other times, we may be forced to create a real object because the code expects something non-null. In dynamically typed languages, almost any real object will do; in statically typed languages, we must make sure that the *Dummy Object* is "type-compatible" with the parameter it is being passed as or the variable to which it is being assigned.

   In the following example, we pass an instance of DummyCustomer to the Invoice constructor to satisfy a mandatory argument. We do not expect the DummyCustomer to be used by the code we are testing here.

```
public void testInvoice_addLineItem_DO() {
    final int QUANTITY = 1;
    Product product = new Product("Dummy Product Name",
                                   getUniqueNumber());
    Invoice inv = new Invoice( new DummyCustomer() );
    LineItem expItem = new LineItem(inv, product, QUANTITY);
    // Exercise
    inv.addItemQuantity(product, QUANTITY);
    // Verify
    List lineItems = inv.getLineItems();
    assertEquals("number of items", lineItems.size(), 1);
    LineItem actual = (LineItem)lineItems.get(0);
    assertLineItemsEqual("", expItem, actual);
}
```

Note that a *Dummy Object* is not the same as a Null Object [PLOPD3]. A *Dummy Object* is *not* used by the SUT, so its behavior is irrelevant. By contrast, a Null Object is used by the SUT but is designed to do nothing. That's a small but very important distinction!

Dummy Objects are in a different league than the other *Test Doubles;* they are really an alternative to the attribute value patterns such as *Literal Value* (page 714), *Generated Value* (page 723), and *Derived Value* (page 718). Therefore, we don't need to "configure" them or "install" them. In fact, almost nothing we say about the other *Test Doubles* applies to *Dummy Objects,* so we won't mention them again in this chapter.

Test Stubs

A *Test Stub* is an object that acts as a control point to deliver indirect inputs to the SUT when the *Test Stub*'s methods are called. Its use allows us to exercise *Untested Code* paths in the SUT that might otherwise be impossible to traverse during testing. A *Responder* (see *Test Stub*) is a basic *Test Stub* that is used to inject valid and invalid indirect inputs into the SUT via normal returns from method calls. A *Saboteur* (see *Test Stub*) is a special *Test Stub* that raises exceptions or errors to inject abnormal indirect inputs into the SUT. Because procedural programming languages do not support objects, they force us to use *Procedural Test Stubs* (see *Test Stub*).

In the following example, the *Saboteur*—implemented as an anonymous inner class in Java—throws an exception when the SUT calls the getTime method to allow us to verify that the SUT behaves correctly in this case:

```
public void testDisplayCurrentTime_exception()
        throws Exception {
    // Fixture setup
```

```
//   Define and instantiate Test Stub
TimeProvider testStub = new TimeProvider()
   { // Anonymous inner Test Stub
      public Calendar getTime() throws TimeProviderEx {
         throw new TimeProviderEx("Sample");
      }
   };
//   Instantiate SUT
TimeDisplay sut = new TimeDisplay();
sut.setTimeProvider(testStub);
// Exercise SUT
String result = sut.getCurrentTimeAsHtmlFragment();
// Verify direct output
String expectedTimeString =
      "<span class=\"error\">Invalid Time</span>";
assertEquals("Exception", expectedTimeString, result);
}
```

In procedural programming languages, a *Procedural Test Stub* is either (1) a *Test Stub* implemented as a stand-in for an as-yet-unwritten procedure or (2) an alternative implementation of a procedure linked into the program instead of the real implementation of the procedure. Traditionally, *Procedural Test Stubs* are introduced to allow debugging to proceed while we are waiting for other code to be ready. They are rarely "swapped in" at runtime—this is hard to do in most procedural languages. If we do not mind introducing *Test Logic in Production* (page 217) code, we can implement a *Procedural Test Stub* using *Test Hooks* (page 709) such as if testing then ... else in the SUT. This is illustrated in the following listing:

```
public Calendar getTime() throws TimeProviderEx {
   Calendar theTime = new GregorianCalendar();
   if (TESTING) {
      theTime.set(Calendar.HOUR_OF_DAY, 0);
      theTime.set(Calendar.MINUTE, 0);}
   else {
      // just return the calendar
   }
   return theTime;
};
```

The key exception occurs in languages that support **procedure variables**.[1] These variables allow us to implement dynamic binding as long as the client code accesses the procedure to be replaced via a procedure variable.

---

[1] Also called **function pointers**.

Test Spies

A *Test Spy* is an object that can act as an observation point for the indirect outputs of the SUT. To the capabilities of a *Test Stub,* it adds the ability to quietly record all calls made to its methods by the SUT. The verification part of the test performs *Procedural Behavior Verification* on those calls by using a series of assertions to compare the actual calls received by the *Test Spy* with the expected calls.

The following example uses the *Retrieval Interface* (see *Test Spy*) on the *Test Spy* to verify that the correct information was passed as arguments in the call to the logMessage method by the SUT (the removeFlight method of the facade).

```
public void testRemoveFlightLogging_recordingTestStub()
        throws Exception {
    // Fixture setup
    FlightDto expectedFlightDto = createAnUnregFlight();
    FlightManagementFacade facade =
        new FlightManagementFacadeImpl();
    //    Test Double setup
    AuditLogSpy logSpy = new AuditLogSpy();
    facade.setAuditLog(logSpy);
    // Exercise
    facade.removeFlight(expectedFlightDto.getFlightNumber());
    // Verify state
    assertFalse("flight still exists after being removed",
            facade.flightExists( expectedFlightDto.
                                    getFlightNumber()));
    // Verify indirect outputs using retrieval interface of spy
    assertEquals("number of calls", 1,
            logSpy.getNumberOfCalls());
    assertEquals("action code",
            Helper.REMOVE_FLIGHT_ACTION_CODE,
            logSpy.getActionCode());
    assertEquals("date", helper.getTodaysDateWithoutTime(),
            logSpy.getDate());
    assertEquals("user", Helper.TEST_USER_NAME,
            logSpy.getUser());
    assertEquals("detail",
            expectedFlightDto.getFlightNumber(),
            logSpy.getDetail());
}
```

Mock Objects

A *Mock Object* is also an object that can act as an observation point for the indirect outputs of the SUT. Like a *Test Stub*, it may need to return information in response to method calls. Also like a *Test Spy*, a *Mock Object* pays attention to how it was called by the SUT. It differs from a *Test Spy*, however, in that the

Mock Object compares actual calls received with the previously defined expectations using assertions and fails the test on behalf of the *Test Method*. As a consequence, we can reuse the logic employed to verify the indirect outputs of the SUT across all tests that use the same *Mock Object*. *Mock Objects* come in two basic flavors:

- A strict *Mock Object* fails the test if the correct calls are received in a different order than was specified.

- A lenient[2] *Mock Object* tolerates out-of-order calls. Some lenient *Mock Objects* tolerate or even ignore unexpected calls or missed calls. That is, the *Mock Object* may verify only those actual calls that correspond to expected ones.

The following test configures a *Mock Object* with the arguments of the expected call to logMessage. When the SUT (the removeFlight method) calls logMessage, the *Mock Object* asserts that each of the actual arguments equals the expected argument. If it discovers that any wrong arguments were passed, the test fails.

```
public void testRemoveFlight_Mock() throws Exception {
    // Fixture setup
    FlightDto expectedFlightDto = createAnonRegFlight();
    // Mock configuration
    ConfigurableMockAuditLog mockLog =
        new ConfigurableMockAuditLog();
    mockLog.setExpectedLogMessage(
                        helper.getTodaysDateWithoutTime(),
                        Helper.TEST_USER_NAME,
                        Helper.REMOVE_FLIGHT_ACTION_CODE,
                        expectedFlightDto.getFlightNumber());
    mockLog.setExpectedNumberCalls(1);
    // Mock installation
    FlightManagementFacade facade =
            new FlightManagementFacadeImpl();
    facade.setAuditLog(mockLog);
    // Exercise
    facade.removeFlight(expectedFlightDto.getFlightNumber());
    // Verify
    assertFalse("flight still exists after being removed",
                facade.flightExists( expectedFlightDto.
                                        getFlightNumber()));
    mockLog.verify();
}
```

---

[2] Lenient *Mock Objects* are sometimes called "nice," but "lenient" is a more precise adjective.

Like *Test Stubs, Mock Objects* often support configuration with any indirect inputs required to allow the SUT to advance to the point where it would generate the indirect outputs they are verifying.

Fake Objects

A *Fake Object* is quite different from a *Test Stub* or a *Mock Object* in that it is neither directly controlled nor observed by the test. The *Fake Object* is used to replace the functionality of the real DOC in a test for reasons other than verification of indirect inputs and outputs. Typically, a *Fake Object* implements the same functionality or a subset of the functionality of the real DOC, albeit in a much simpler way. The most common reasons for using a *Fake Object* are that the real DOC has not yet been built, is too slow, or is not available in the test environment.

The sidebar "Faster Tests without Shared Fixtures" (page 319) describes how my team encapsulated all database access behind a persistence layer interface and then replaced the persistence layer component with one that used in-memory hash tables instead of a real database, thereby making our tests run 50 times faster. To do so, we used a *Fake Database* (see *Fake Object*) that was something like this one:

```
public class InMemoryDatabase implements FlightDao{
    private List airports = new Vector();
    public Airport createAirport(String airportCode,
                    String name, String nearbyCity)
        throws DataException, InvalidArgumentException {
    assertParamtersAreValid( airportCode, name, nearbyCity);
    assertAirportDoesntExist( airportCode);
    Airport result = new Airport(getNextAirportId(),
        airportCode, name, createCity(nearbyCity));
    airports.add(result);
    return result;
    }
    public Airport getAirportByPrimaryKey(BigDecimal airportId)
            throws DataException, InvalidArgumentException {
    assertAirportNotNull(airportId);

    Airport result = null;
    Iterator i = airports.iterator();
    while (i.hasNext()) {
       Airport airport = (Airport) i.next();
       if (airport.getId().equals(airportId)) {
          return airport;
       }
    }
    throw new DataException("Airport not found:"+airportId);
    }
```

Providing the Test Double

There are two approaches to providing a *Test Double*: a *Hand-Built Test Double* (see *Configurable Test Double* on page 558), which is coded by the test automater, or a *Dynamically Generated Test Double* (see *Configurable Test Double*), which is generated at runtime using a framework or toolkit provided by some other developer.[3] All generated *Test Doubles* must be, by their very nature, *Configurable Test Doubles;* these components are covered in more detail in the next section. *Hand-Built Test Doubles,* by contrast, tend to be *Hard-Coded Test Doubles* (page 568) but can also be made configurable with some additional effort. The following code sample illustrates a hand-coded *Inner Test Double* (see *Hard-Coded Test Double*) that uses Java's **anonymous inner class** construct:

```
public void testDisplayCurrentTime_AtMidnight_PS()
      throws Exception {
  // Fixture setup
  //     Define and instantiate Test Stub
  TimeProvider testStub = new PseudoTimeProvider()
  { // Anonymous inner stub
    public Calendar getTime(String timeZone) {
      Calendar myTime = new GregorianCalendar();
      myTime.set(Calendar.MINUTE, 0);
      myTime.set(Calendar.HOUR_OF_DAY, 0);
      return myTime;
    }
  };
  //    Instantiate SUT
  TimeDisplay sut = new TimeDisplay();
  //    Inject Test Stub into SUT
  sut.setTimeProvider(testStub);
  // Exercise SUT
  String result = sut.getCurrentTimeAsHtmlFragment();
  // Verify direct output
  String expectedTimeString =
        "<span class=\"tinyBoldText\">Midnight</span>";
  assertEquals("Midnight", expectedTimeString, result);
}
```

We can greatly simplify the development of *Hand-Built Test Doubles* in statically typed languages such as Java and C# by providing a set of base classes called *Pseudo-Objects* (see *Hard-Coded Test Double*) from which to create subclasses. *Pseudo-Objects* can reduce the number of methods we need to implement

---

[3] **JMock** and its ports to other languages are good examples of such toolkits. Other toolkits, such as **EasyMock**, implement *Statically Generated Test Doubles* (see *Configurable Test Double*) by generating code that is then compiled just like a *Hand-Built Test Double*.

in each *Test Stub*, *Test Spy*, or *Mock Object* to just the ones we *expect* to be called. They are especially helpful when we are using *Inner Test Doubles* or *Self Shunts* (see *Hard-Coded Test Double*). The class definition for the *Pseudo-Object* used in the previous example looks like this:

```
/**
 * Base class for hand-coded Test Stubs and Mock Objects
 */
public class PseudoTimeProvider implements ComplexTimeProvider {

    public Calendar getTime() throws TimeProviderEx {
        throw new PseudoClassException();
    }

    public Calendar getTimeDifference(Calendar baseTime,
                                      Calendar otherTime)
            throws TimeProviderEx {
        throw new PseudoClassException();
    }

    public Calendar getTime( String timeZone )
            throws TimeProviderEx {
        throw new PseudoClassException();
    }
}
```

Configuring the Test Double

Some *Test Doubles* (specifically, *Test Stubs* and *Mock Objects*) need to be told which values to return and/or which values to expect. A *Hard-Coded Test Double* receives these instructions at design time from the test automater; a *Configurable Test Double* is told this information at runtime by the test (Figure 11.9). A *Test Stub* or *Test Spy* needs to be configured only with the values that will be returned by the methods that the SUT is expected to invoke. A *Mock Object* also needs to be configured with the names and arguments of all methods we expect the SUT to invoke on it. In all cases, the test automater ultimately decides with which values to configure the *Test Double*. Not surprisingly, the primary considerations when making this decision are the understandability of the test and the potential reusability of the *Test Double* code.

   Fake Objects do not need to be "configured" at runtime because they are just used by the SUT; later outputs depend on the earlier calls by the SUT. Similarly, *Dummy Objects* do not need to be "configured" because they should never be executed.[4] *Procedural Test Stubs* are typically built as *Hard-Coded Test Doubles*. That is, they are hard-coded to return a particular value when the function is called—thus they are the simplest form of *Test Double*.

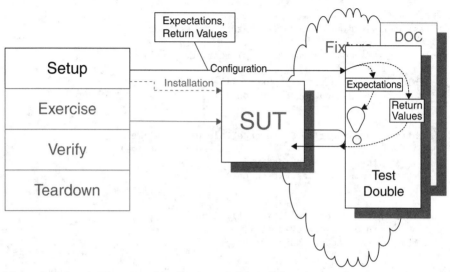

Figure 11.9 *A Test Double being configured by the test. We can avoid a proliferation of Hard-Coded Test Doubles classes by passing return values or expectation to the Configurable Test Double at runtime.*

A *Configurable Test Double* can provide either a *Configuration Interface (see Configurable Test Double)* or a *Configuration Mode (see Configurable Test Double)* that the test can use to configure the *Test Double* with the values to return or expect. As a consequence, *Configurable Test Doubles* are reusable across many tests. Use of these *Configurable Test Doubles* also makes tests more understandable because the values used by the *Test Double* are visible within the test, thus avoiding the smell of a *Mystery Guest (see Obscure Test on page 186)*.

So where should this configuration take place? The installation of the *Test Double* should be treated just like any other part of fixture setup. Alternatives such as *In-line Setup* (page 408), *Implicit Setup* (page 424), and *Delegated Setup* (page 411) are all available.

---

[4] A *Dummy Object* can be used as an observation point to verify that it was *never* used by ensuring that the *Dummy Object* throws an exception if any of its methods are called.

Installing the Test Double

Before we exercise the SUT, we need to "install" any *Test Doubles* on which our test depends. The term "install" here serves as a generic way to describe the process of telling the SUT to use our *Test Double*, regardless of the exact details regarding how we do it. The normal sequence is to instantiate the *Test Double*, configure it if it is a *Configurable Test Double*, and then tell the SUT to use the *Test Double* either before or as we exercise the SUT. There are several distinct ways to "install" the *Test Double*, and the choice between them may be as much a matter of style as of necessity if we are designing the SUT for testability. Our choices may be much more constrained, however, when we try to retrofit our tests to an existing design.

The basic choices boil down to *Dependency Injection* (page 678), in which the client software tells the SUT which DOC to use; *Dependency Lookup* (page 686), in which the SUT delegates the construction or retrieval of the DOC to another object; and *Test Hook,* in which the DOC or the calls to it within the SUT are modified.

If an **inversion of control** framework is available in our language, our tests can substitute dependencies without much additional work on our part. This removes the need for building in the *Dependency Injection* or *Dependency Lookup* mechanism.

Dependency Injection

Dependency Injection is a class of design decoupling in which the client tells the SUT which DOC to use at runtime (Figure 11.10). The test-driven development (TDD) movement has greatly increased its popularity because *Dependency Injection* makes for more easily tested designs. This pattern also makes it possible to reuse the SUT more broadly because it removes knowledge of the dependency from the SUT; often the SUT will be aware of only a generic **interface** that the DOC must implement. *Dependency Injection* comes in several specific flavors, with the choice between them being largely a matter of taste:

- *Setter Injection* (see *Dependency Injection*): The SUT accesses the DOC through a public attribute (i.e., a variable or property). The test explicitly sets the attribute after instantiating the SUT to installing the *Test Double*. The SUT may have previously initialized the attribute with the real DOC in its constructor (in which case the test is replacing it) or the SUT may use Lazy Initialization [SBPP] to initialize the attribute (in which case the SUT will not bother to install the real DOC).

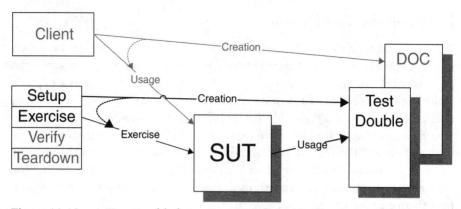

Figure 11.10 *A Test Double being "injected" into the SUT by a test. Using Test Doubles requires a means to replace the DOC. Using Dependency Injection involves having the caller supply the dependency to the SUT before or as it is used.*

- *Constructor Injection* (see *Dependency Injection*): The SUT accesses the DOC through a private attribute. The test passes the *Test Double* to the SUT via a constructor that takes the DOC to be used as an explicit argument and initializes the attribute from it. This may be the primary constructor used by production code clients or it may be an alternative constructor. In the latter case, the primary constructor should call this constructor, passing the default DOC to it as an argument.

- *Parameter Injection* (see *Dependency Injection*): The SUT receives the DOC as a method parameter. The test passes in a *Test Double,* whereas the production code passes in the real object.[5] This approach works well when the API of the SUT takes as a parameter the object we need to replace. Although *Mock Object* aficionados might argue that designing APIs in this way improves the design of the SUT, it is not always possible or practical to pass everything required to each method.

Dependency Lookup

When software is not designed for testability or when *Dependency Injection* is not appropriate, we may find it convenient to use *Dependency Lookup*. This pattern also removes the knowledge of exactly which DOC should be used from

[5] This approach was advocated in the original paper on Mock Objects [ET]. In this paper, *Mock Objects* passed as parameters to methods are called "Smart Handlers."

the SUT, but it does so by having the SUT ask another piece of software to create or find the DOC on its behalf (Figure 11.11). This opens the door to changing the DOC at runtime without modifying the SUT's code. We do have to modify the behavior of the intermediary somehow, and this is where the specific variants of *Dependency Lookup* differ from one another:

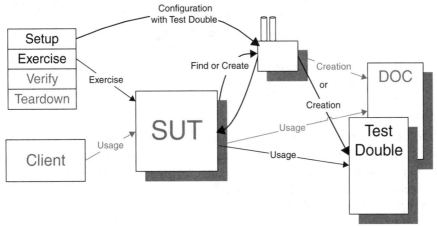

Figure 11.11 *A Service Locator being "configured" by a test to return a Test Double to the SUT. Using Test Doubles requires a means to replace the DOC. Using Dependency Lookup involves having the SUT ask a well-known object to provide a reference to the DOC; the test can provide the Service Locator with a Test Double to return.*

- *Object Factory* (see *Dependency Lookup*): The SUT creates the DOC by calling a Factory Method [GOF] on a well-known object instead of using an object constructor to create the DOC directly. The test explicitly tells the *Object Factory* to create a *Test Double* instead of a normal DOC whenever this method is called .

- *Service Locator* (see *Dependency Lookup*): The SUT retrieves a previously created service object by asking a well-known Registry [PEAA] object for it. The test configures the *Service Locator* to return the *Test Double* when the SUT requests the DOC.

The line between these two patterns can become quite blurry when we use Lazy Initialization to create the object being returned by a *Service Locator*. Should it be called an *Object Factory* instead? Does it really matter which label we apply? Probably not—hence the generic name of *Dependency Lookup*.

Retrofitting Testability Using a Test-Specific Subclass

Even when none of these mechanisms is built into the SUT, we may be able to retrofit them relatively easily by using a *Test-Specific Subclass*.

The use of Singletons [GOF] specifically to act as an *Object Factory* or *Service Locator* is common. If the Singleton has hard-coded behavior, we may have to turn it into a *Substitutable Singleton* (see *Test-Specific Subclass* on page 579) to enable overriding the normally returned DOC with our *Test Double*. The use of Singletons can be avoided through the use of an **IOC** tool or a manually coded *Dependency Injection* mechanism. Both of these choices are preferable because they make the test's dependency on a *Test Double* more obvious. Singletons used for other purposes almost always cause headaches when we are writing tests and should be avoided if possible.

Our test can instantiate a *Test-Specific Subclass* of the SUT to add a *Dependency Injection* mechanism or to replace other methods of the SUT with test-specific behavior; see Figure 11.12. We can override any logic used to access a DOC, thereby making it possible to return a *Test Double* instead of the normal DOC without modifying the production code. We can also replace the implementations of any methods being called from the method we are testing with *Test Stub*-like behavior, thereby turning the SUT into its own *Subclassed Test Double* (see *Test-Specific Subclass*). This is one way to inject indirect inputs into the SUT.

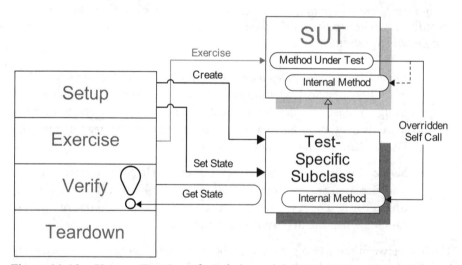

Figure 11.12   *Using a Test-Specific Subclass of the SUT. When all else fails, we can always try subclassing the SUT to change or expose functionality we need to enable testing*

The main prerequisite of using a *Test-Specific Subclass* of the SUT is that the SUT must use Self-Calls [WWW] to nonprivate methods that implement any functionality we need to override from the test. Small, single-purpose methods rule! The main drawback of this approach is that it is possible to accidentally override parts of the behavior we are intending to test.

We can also subclass the DOC to insert test-specific behavior, effectively turning it into a *Subclassed Test Double* (Figure 11.13). This strategy is somewhat safer than subclassing the SUT because it avoids the possibility of accidentally overriding those parts of the SUT that we are testing. The trick, however, is to get the SUT to use the *Test-Specific Subclass* instead of the DOC. In practice, this implies that we must use one of the *Dependency Injection* or *Dependency Lookup* techniques, unless the DOC is a Singleton. When the SUT uses a Singleton by calling a static soleInstance method on a hard-coded class name, the test can cause the soleInstance method to return an instance of a *Test Double* by subclassing the Singleton class and initializing the real Singleton's soleInstance class variable to hold an instance of the *Test Double*. The returned *Test Double* may need to be a *Subclassed Test Double* if the type of the variable used to hold the Singleton's sole instance is hard-coded as the Singleton's class. Although we often use this technique to get a *Service Locator* to return a different service, but we can also use a *Subclassed Test Double* directly without an intermediary *Service Locator*.

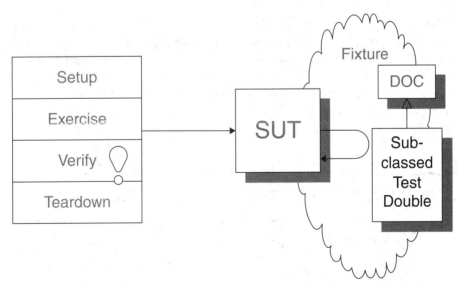

Figure 11.13 *Using A Test Double subclassed from the DOC. One way to build a Test Double is to subclass the real class and override the implementation of any methods we need to control the indirect inputs or verify indirect outputs.*

Other Ways of Retrofitting Testability

All is not lost when none of the techniques described thus far can be used to introduce testability. We still have a few tricks left up our sleeves.

Test Hooks are the "elephant in the room" that no one wants to talk about because they may lead to *Test Logic in Production*. *Test Hooks,* however, are a perfectly legitimate way to get legacy code under test when it is too hard or dangerous to introduce one of the techniques described earlier. They are best used as a "transition" strategy to allow *Scripted Tests* (page 285) or *Recorded Tests* (page 278) to be automated to provide a *Safety Net* (see page 24) while large-scale refactoring is undertaken to improve testability. Ideally, once the code has been made more testable, better tests can be prepared using the techniques described earlier and the *Test Hooks* can be removed.

Michael Feathers [WEwLC] has described several other techniques to replace dependencies with test-specific code under the general heading of finding "object seams." For example, we can replace a depended-on library with a library designed specifically for testing. A seemingly hard-coded dependency can be broken this way. Most of these techniques are less applicable when we need to dynamically replace dependencies within individual tests than either *Dependency Injection* or *Dependency Lookup* because they require changes to the environment. Object seams are, however, an excellent way to place legacy code under test so that it can be refactored to introduce either of the previously mentioned dependency-breaking techniques.

We can use aspect-oriented programming (AOP) to install the *Test Double* behavior by defining a test point-cut that matches the place where the SUT calls the DOC and we would rather have it call the *Test Double*. Although we need an AOP-enabled development environment to do this, we do not need to deploy the AOP-generated code into a production environment. As a consequence, this technique may be used even in AOP-hostile environments.

Other Uses of Test Doubles

So far, we have covered the testing of indirect inputs and indirect outputs. Now let's look at some other uses of *Test Doubles*.

Endoscopic Testing

Tim Mackinnon et al. introduced the concept of **endoscopic testing** [ET] in their initial *Mock Objects* paper. Endoscopic testing focuses on testing the SUT from the inside by passing in a *Mock Object* as an argument to the method under test. This allows verification of certain internal behaviors of the SUT that may not always be visible from the outside.

The classic example that Mackinnon and colleagues cite is the use of a mock collection class preloaded with all of the expected members of the collection. When the **SUT** tries to add an unexpected member, the mock collection's assertion fails. The full stack trace of the internal call stack then becomes visible in the xUnit failure report. If our IDE supports breaking on specified exceptions, we can also inspect the local variables at the point of failure.

Need-Driven Development

A refinement of endoscopic testing is "need-driven development" [MRNO], in which the dependencies of the SUT are defined as the tests are written. This "outside-in" approach to writing and testing software combines the conceptual elegance of the traditional "top-down" approach to writing code with modern TDD techniques supported by *Mock Objects*. It allows us to build *and test* the software *layer by layer*, starting at the outermost layer *before* we have implemented the lower layers.

Need-driven development combines the benefits of test-driven development (specifying all software with tests before we build them) with a highly incremental approach to design that removes the need for any speculation about how a depended-on class *might* be used.

Speeding Up Fixture Setup

Another application of *Test Doubles* is to reduce the runtime cost of *Fresh Fixture* (page 311) setup. When the SUT needs to interact with other objects that are difficult to create because they have many dependencies, a single *Test Double* can be created instead of the complex network of objects. When applied to networks of entity objects, this technique is called *Entity Chain Snipping* (see *Test Stub*).

Speeding Up Test Execution

Test Doubles may also be used to speed up tests by replacing slow components with faster ones. Replacing a relational database with an in-memory *Fake Object*, for example, can reduce test execution times by an order of magnitude! The extra effort required to code the *Fake Database* is more than offset by the reduced waiting time and the quality improvement due to the more timely feedback that comes from running the tests more frequently. Refer to the sidebar "Faster Tests without Shared Fixtures" on page 319 for a more detailed discussion of this issue.

Other Considerations

Because many of our tests will involve replacing a real DOC with a *Test Double*, how do we know that the production code will work properly when it uses the real DOC? Of course, we would expect our customer tests to verify behavior with the real DOCs in place (except, possibly, when the real DOCs are interfaces to other systems that need to be stubbed out during single-system testing). We should write a special form of *Constructor Test* (see *Test Method*)—a "substitutable initialization test"—to verify that the real DOC is installed properly. The trigger for writing this test is performing the first test that replaces the DOC with a *Test Double*—that point is often when the *Test Double* installation mechanism is introduced.

Finally, we want to be careful that we don't fall into the "new hammer trap."[6] Overuse of *Test Doubles* (and especially *Mock Objects* or *Test Stubs*) can lead to *Overspecified Software* (see *Fragile Test* on page 239) by encoding implementation-specific information about the design in our tests. The design may be then much more difficult to change if many tests are affected by the change simply because they use a *Test Double* that has been affected by the design change.

---

[6] "When you have a new hammer, everything looks like a nail."

What's Next?

In this chapter, we examined techniques for testing software with indirect inputs and indirect outputs. In particular, we explored the concept of *Test Doubles* and various techniques for installing them. In Chapter 12, *Organizing Our Tests*, we will turn our attention to strategies for organizing the test code into *Test Methods* and *Test Utility Methods* (page 599) implemented on *Testcase Classes* (page 373) and *Test Helpers* (page 643).

Chapter 12

Organizing Our Tests

About This Chapter

In the chapters concluding with Chapter 11, *Using Test Doubles,* we looked at various techniques for interacting with the SUT for the purpose of verifying its behavior. In this chapter, we turn our attention to the question of how to organize the test code to make it easy to find and understand.

The basic unit of test code organization is the *Test Method* (page 348). Deciding what to put in the *Test Method* and where to put it is central to the topic of test organization. When we have only a few tests, how we organize them isn't terribly important. By contrast, when we have hundreds of tests, test organization becomes a critical factor in keeping our tests easy to understand and find.

This chapter begins by discussing what we should and should not include in a *Test Method.* Next, it explores how we can decide on which *Testcase Classes* (page 373) to put our *Test Methods.* Test naming depends heavily on how we have organized our tests, so we will talk about this issue next. We will then consider how to organize the *Testcase Classes* into test suites and where to put test code. The final topic is test code reuse—specifically, where to put reusable test code.

Basic xUnit Mechanisms

The xUnit family of *Test Automation Frameworks* (page 298) provides a number of features to help us organize our tests. The basic question, "Where do I code my tests?", is answered by putting our test code into a *Test Method* on a *Testcase Class.* We then use either *Test Discovery* (page 393) or *Test Enumeration* (page 399) to create a *Test Suite Object* (page 387) containing all the tests from the *Testcase Class.* The *Test Runner* (page 377) invokes a method on the *Test Suite Object* to run all the *Test Methods.*

Right-Sizing Test Methods

A **test condition** is something we need to prove the SUT really does; it can be described in terms of what the starting state of the SUT is, how we exercise the SUT, how we expect the SUT to respond, and what the ending state of the SUT is expected to be. A *Test Method* is a sequence of statements in our test scripting language that exercises one or more test conditions (Figure 12.1). What should we include in a single *Test Method*?

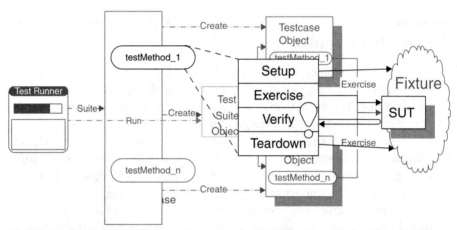

Figure 12.1   *The four phases of a typical test. Each Test Method implements a Four-Phase Test (page 358) that ideally verifies a single test condition. Not all phases of the Four-Phase Test need be in the Test Method.*

Many xUnit purists prefer to *Verify One Condition per Test* (see page 45) because it gives them good *Defect Localization* (see page 22). That is, when a test fails, they know exactly what is wrong in the SUT because each test verifies exactly one test condition. This is very much in contrast with manual testing, where one tends to build long, involved multiple-condition tests because of the overhead involved in setting up each test's pre-conditions. When creating xUnit-based automated tests, we have many ways of dealing with this frequently re-peated fixture setup (as described in Chapter 8, *Transient Fixture Management*), so we tend to *Verify One Condition per Test*. We call a test that verifies too many test conditions an *Eager Test* (see *Assertion Roulette* on page 224) and consider it a code smell.

A test that verifies a single test condition executes a single code path through the SUT and it should execute exactly the same path each time it runs; that is what makes it a *Repeatable Test* (see page 26). Yes, that means we need as many test methods as we have paths through the code—but how else can we expect to achieve full code coverage? What makes this pattern manageable is that we *Isolate the SUT* (see page 43) when we write unit tests for each class so we only have to focus on paths through a single object. Also, because each test should verify only a single path through the code, each test method should consist of strictly sequential statements that describe what should happen on that one path.[1] Another reason we *Verify One Condition per Test* (see page 45) is to *Minimize Test Overlap* (see page 44) so that we have fewer tests to modify if we later modify the behavior of the SUT.

Brian Marrick has developed an interesting compromise that I call "While We're at It,"[2] which leverages the test fixture we already have set up to run some additional checks and assertions. Marrick clearly marks these elements with comments to indicate that if changes to the SUT obsolete that part of the test, they can be easily deleted. This strategy minimizes the effort needed to maintain the extra test code.

Test Methods and Testcase Classes

A *Test Method* needs to live on a *Testcase Class*. Should we put all our *Test Methods* onto a single *Testcase Class* for the application? Or should we create a *Testcase Class* for each *Test Method*? Of course, the right answer lies somewhere between these two extremes, and it will change over the life of our project.

Testcase Class per Class

When we write our first few *Test Methods*, we can put them all onto a single *Testcase Class*. As the number of *Test Methods* increases, we will likely want to split the *Testcase Class* so that one *Testcase Class per Class* (page 617) is tested, which reduces the number of *Test Methods* per class (Figure 12.2). As those *Testcase Classes* get too big, we usually split the classes further. In that case, we need to decide which *Test Methods* to include in each *Testcase Class*.

---

[1] A *Test Method* that contains *Conditional Test Logic* (page 200) is a sign of a test trying to accommodate different circumstances because it does not have control of all indirect inputs of the SUT or because it is trying to verify complex expected states on an in-line basis within the *Test Method*.

[2] He calls it "Just for Laughs" but I don't find that name very intent-revealing.

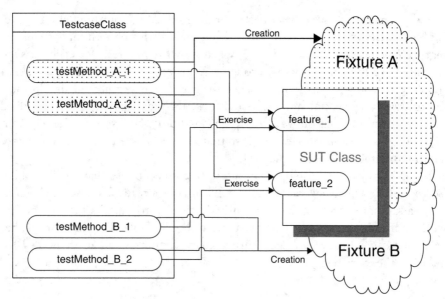

Figure 12.2 *A production class with a single Testcase Class. With the Testcase Class per Class pattern, a single Testcase Class holds all the Test Methods for all the behavior of our SUT class. Each Test Method may need to create a different fixture either in-line or by delegating that task to a Creation Method (page 415).*

Testcase Class per Feature

One school of thought is to put all *Test Methods* that verify a particular feature of the SUT—where a "feature" is defined as one or more methods and attributes that collectively implement some capability of the SUT—into a single *Testcase Class* (Figure 12.3). This makes it easy to see all test conditions for that feature. (Use of appropriate *Test Naming Conventions* helps achieve this clarity.) It can, however, result in similar fixture setup code being required in each *Testcase Class*.

Testcase Class per Fixture

The opposing view is that one should group all *Test Methods* that require the same test fixture (same pre-conditions) into one *Testcase Class per Fixture* (page 631; see Figure 12.4). This facilitates putting the test fixture setup code into the setUp method (*Implicit Setup; see* page 424) but can result in scattering of the test conditions for each feature across many *Testcase Classes*.

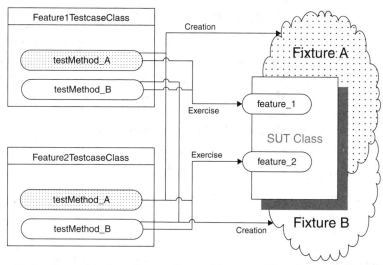

Figure 12.3 *A production class with one Testcase Class for each feature. With the Testcase Class per Feature pattern, we have one Testcase Class for each major capability or feature supported by our SUT class. The Test Methods on that test class exercise various aspects of that feature after building whatever test fixture they require.*

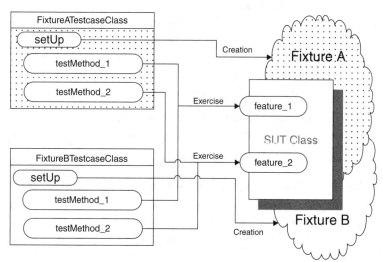

Figure 12.4 *A production class with one Testcase Class for each fixture. With the Testcase Class per Fixture pattern, we have one Testcase Class for each possible test fixture (test pre-condition) of our SUT class. The Test Methods on that test class exercise various features from the common starting point.*

Choosing a Test Method Organization Strategy

Clearly, there is no single "best practice" we can always follow; the best practice is the one that is most appropriate for the particular circumstance. *Testcase Class per Fixture* is commonly used when we are writing unit tests for stateful objects and each method needs to be tested in each state of the object. *Testcase Class per Feature* (page 624) is more appropriate when we are writing customer tests against a Service Facade [CJ2EEP]; it enables us to keep all the tests for a customer-recognizable feature together. This pattern is also more commonly used when we rely on a *Prebuilt Fixture* (page 429) because fixture setup logic is not required in each test. When each test needs a slightly different fixture, the right answer may be to select the *Testcase Class per Feature* pattern and use a *Delegated Setup* (page 411) to facilitate setting up the fixtures.

Test Naming Conventions

The names we give to our *Testcase Classes* and *Test Methods* are crucial in making our tests easy to find and understand. We can make the test coverage more obvious by naming each *Test Method* systematically based on which test condition it verifies. Regardless of which test method organization scheme we use, we would like the combination of the names of the test package, the *Testcase Class*, and the *Test Method* to convey at least the following information:

- The name of the SUT class

- The name of the method or feature being exercised

- The important characteristics of any input values related to the exercising of the SUT

- Anything relevant about the state of the SUT or its dependencies

These items are the "input" part of the test condition. Obviously, this is a lot to communicate in just two names but the reward is high if we can achieve it: We can tell exactly what test conditions we have tests for merely by looking at the names of the classes and methods in an outline view of our IDE. Figure 12.5 provides an example.

Figure 12.5 *A production class with one Testcase Class for each test fixture. When we use the Testcase Class per Fixture pattern, the class name can describe the fixture, leaving the method name available for describing the inputs and expected outputs.*

Figure 12.5 also shows how useful it is to include the "expectations" side of the test condition:

- The outputs (responses) expected when exercising the SUT

- The expected post-exercise state of the SUT and its dependencies

This information can be included in the name of the *Test Method* prefixed by "should." If this nomenclature makes the names too long,[3] we can always access the expected outcome by looking at the body of the *Test Method*.

---

[3] Many xUnit variants "encourage" us to start all our *Test Method* names with "test" so that these methods can be automatically detected and added to the *Test Suite Object*. This constrains our naming somewhat compared to variants that indicate test methods via **method attributes** or **annotations**.

Organizing Test Suites

The *Testcase Class* acts as a *Test Suite Factory* (see *Test Enumeration*) when it returns a *Test Suite Object* containing a collection of *Testcase Objects* (page 382), each representing a *Test Method* (Figure 12.6). This is the default organization mechanism provided by xUnit. Most *Test Runners* allow any class to act as a *Test Suite Factory* by implementing a Factory Method [GOF], which is typically called suite.

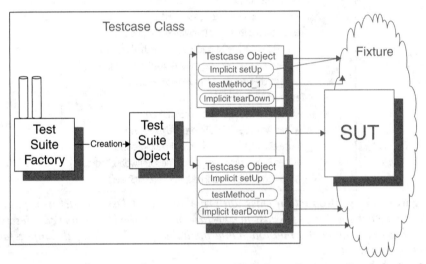

Figure 12.6   *A Testcase Class acting as a Test Suite Factory. By default, the Testcase Class acts as a Test Suite Factory to produce the Test Suite Object that the Test Runner requires to execute our tests. We can also enumerate a specific set of tests we want to run by providing a Test Suite Factory that returns a Test Suite Object containing only the desired tests.*

Running Groups of Tests

We often want to run groups of tests (i.e., a test suite) but we don't want this decision to constrain how we organize them. A popular convention is to create a special *Test Suite Factory* called AllTests for each package of tests. We don't need to stop there, however: We can create *Named Test Suites* (page 592) for *any* collection of tests we want to run together. A good example is a *Subset Suite* (see *Named Test Suite*) that allows us to run just those tests that need software deployed to the Web server (or not deployed to the Web server!). We usually have at least a *Subset Suite* for all the unit tests and another *Subset Suite* for just the customer tests (they often take a long time to execute). Some variants of xUnit support *Test Selection* (page 403), which we can use instead of defining *Subset Suites*.

Such runtime groupings of tests often reflect the environment in which they need to run. For example, we might have one *Subset Suite* that includes all tests that can be run without the database and another *Subset Suite* that includes all tests that depend on the database. Likewise, we might have separate *Subset Suites* for tests that do, and do not, rely on the Web server. If our test package includes these various kinds of test suites, we can define AllTests as a *Suite of Suites* (see *Test Suite Object*) composed of these *Subset Suites*. Then any test that is added to one of the *Subset Suites* will also be run in AllTests without incurring extra test maintenance effort.

Running a Single Test

Suppose a *Test Method* fails in our *Testcase Class*. We decide to put a breakpoint on a particular method—but that method is called in every test. Our first reaction might be to just muddle through by clicking "Go" each time the breakpoint is hit until we are being called from the test of interest. One possibility is to disable (by commenting out) the other *Test Methods* so they are not run. Another option is to rename the other *Test Methods* so that the xUnit *Test Discovery* mechanism will not recognize them as tests. In variants of xUnit that use method attributes or annotations, we can add the "Ignore" attribute to a test method instead. Each of these approaches introduces the potential problem of a *Lost Test* (see *Production Bugs* on page 268), although the "Ignore" approach does remind us that some tests are being ignored. In members of the xUnit family that provide a *Test Tree Explorer* (see *Test Runner*), we can simply select a single test to be run from the hierarchy view of the test suite, as shown in Figure 12.7.

When none of these options is available, we can use a *Test Suite Factory* to run a single test. Wait a minute! Aren't test suites all about running groups of tests that live in different *Testcase Classes*? Well, yes, but that doesn't mean we can't use them for other purposes. We can define a *Single Test Suite*[4] (see *Named Test Suite*) that runs a particular test. To do so, we call the constructor of the *Testcase Class* with the specific *Test Method's* name as an argument.

---

[4] I usually call it MyTest.

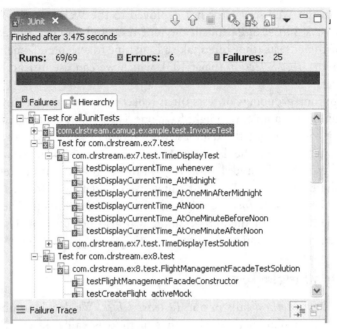

Figure 12.7   *A Test Tree Explorer showing the structure of the tests in our suite. We can use the Test Tree Explorer to drill down into the runtime structure of the test suite and run individual tests or subsuites.*

Test Code Reuse

Test Code Duplication (page 213) can significantly increase the cost of writing and maintaining tests. Luckily, a number of techniques for reusing test logic are available to us. The most important consideration is that any reuse not compromise the value of the *Tests as Documentation* (see page 23). I don't recommend reuse of the actual *Test Method* in different circumstances (e.g., with different fixtures), as this kind of reuse is typically a sign of a *Flexible Test* (see *Conditional Test Logic* on page 200) that tests different things in different circumstances. Most test code reuse is achieved either through *Implicit Setup* or *Test Utility Methods* (page 599). The major exception is the reuse of *Test Doubles* (page 522) by many tests; we can treat these *Test Double* classes as a special kind of *Test Helper* (page 643) when thinking about where to put them.

Test Utility Method Locations

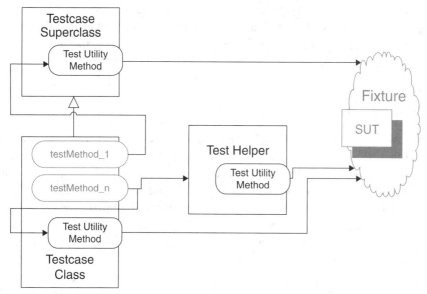

Figure 12.8 *The various places we can put Test Utility Methods. The primary decision-making criterion is the desired scope of reusability of the Test Methods.*

Many variants of xUnit provide a special *Testcase Superclass* (page 638)—typically called "TestCase"—from which all *Testcase Classes* should (and, in some cases, must) inherit either directly or indirectly (Figure 12.8). If we have useful utility methods on our *Testcase Class* that we want to reuse in other *Testcase Classes*, we may find it helpful to create one or more *Testcase Superclasses* from which to inherit instead of "TestCase." If we take this step, we need to be careful if those methods need to see types or classes that reside in various packages within the SUT—our root *Testcase Superclass* should not depend on those types or classes directly, as that is likely to result in a cyclical dependency graph. We may be able to create a *Testcase Superclass* for each test package to keep our test class dependencies noncyclic. The alternative is to create a *Test Helper* for each domain package and put the various *Test Helpers* in the appropriate test packages. This way, a *Testcase Class* is not forced to choose a single *Testcase Superclass*; it can merely "use" the appropriate *Test Helpers*.

TestCase Inheritance and Reuse

The most commonly used reason for inheriting methods from a *Testcase Superclass* is to access *Test Utility Methods*. Another use is when testing frameworks and their plug-ins; it can be useful to create a conformance test that specifies the general behavior of the plug-in via a Template Method [GOF] that calls methods provided by a subclass specific to the kind of plug-in being tested to check specific details of the plug-in. This scenario is rare enough that I won't describe it further here; please refer to [FaT] for a more complete description.

Test File Organization

Now we face a new question: Where should we put our *Testcase Classes*? Obviously, these classes should be stored in the source code repository [SCM] along with the production code. Beyond that criterion, we have quite a range of choices. The test packaging strategy we choose will very much depend on our environment—many IDEs include constraints that make certain strategies unworkable. The key issue is to *Keep Test Logic Out of Production Code* (see page 45) and yet to be able to find the corresponding test for each piece of code or functionality.

Built-in Self-Test

With a **built-in self-test,** the tests are included with the production code and can be run at any time. No provision is made for keeping them separate. Many organizations want to *Keep Test Logic Out of Production Code* so built-in self-tests may not be a good option for them. This consideration is particularly important in memory-constrained environments where we don't want test code taking up valuable space.

Some development environments encourage us to keep the tests and the production code together. For example, SAP's **ABAP Unit** supports the keyword "For Testing," which tells the system to disable the tests when the code is transported into the production environment.

Test Packages

If we decide to put the *Testcase Classes* into separate test packages, we can organize them in several ways. We can keep the tests separate by putting them into one or more test packages while keeping them in the same source tree, or we can put the tests into the same logical package but physically store them in a parallel source tree. The latter approach is frequently used in Java because it avoids the problem of tests not being able to see "package-protected" methods on the SUT.[5] Some IDEs may reject using this approach by insisting that a package be wholly contained within a single folder or project. When we use test packages under each production code package, we may need to use a build-time **test stripper** to exclude them from production builds.

Test Dependencies

However we decide to store and manage the source code, we need to ensure that we eliminate any *Test Dependency in Production* (see *Test Logic in Production* on page 217) because even a test stripper cannot remove the tests if production code needs them to be present to run. This requirement makes paying attention to our class dependencies important. We also don't want to have any *Test Logic in Production* because it means we aren't testing the same code that we will eventually run in production. This issue is discussed in more detail in Chapter 6, *Test Automation Strategy*.

What's Next?

Now that we've looked at how to organize our test code, we should become familiar with a few more testing patterns. These patterns are introduced in Chapter 13, *Testing with Databases*.

---

[5] Java offers another way to get around the visibility issue: We can define our own test Security Manager to allow tests to access all methods on the SUT, not just the "package-protected" ones. This approach solves the problem in a general way but requires a good understanding of Java class loaders. Other languages may not have the equivalent functionality (or problem!).

Chapter 13

Testing with Databases

About This Chapter

In Chapter 12, *Organizing Our Tests*, we looked at techniques for organizing our test code. In this chapter, we explore the issues that arise when our application includes a database. Applications with databases present some special challenges when writing automated tests. Databases are much slower than the processors used in modern computers. As a result, tests that interact with databases tend to run much, much more slowly than tests that can run entirely in memory.

Even ignoring the potential for Slow Tests (page 253), databases are a ripe source for many test smells in our automated test suites. Some of these smells are a direct consequence of the persistent nature of the database, while others result from our choice to share the fixture instance between tests. These smells were introduced in Chapter 9, *Persistent Fixture Management*. This chapter expands on them and provides a more focused treatment of testing with databases.

Testing with Databases

Here is my first, and most critical, piece of advice on this subject:

> *When there is any way to test without a database, test without the database!*

This seems like pretty strong advice but it is phrased this way for a reason. Databases introduce all sorts of complications into our applications and especially into our tests. Tests that require a database run, on average, two orders of magnitude slower than the same tests that run without a database.

Why Test with Databases?

Many applications include a database to persist objects or data into longer-term storage. The database is a necessary part of the application, so verifying that the database is used properly is a necessary part of building the application. Therefore, the use of a *Database Sandbox* (page 650) to isolate developers and testers from production (and each other) is a fundamental practice on almost every project (Figure 13.1).

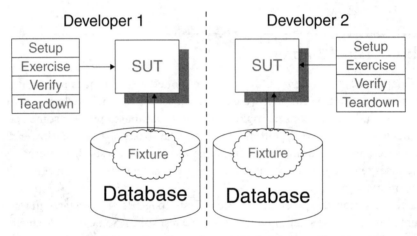

Figure 13.1   *A Database Sandbox for each developer. Sharing a Database Sandbox among developers is false economy. Would you make a plumber and an electrician work in the same wall at the same time?*

Issues with Databases

A database introduces a number of issues that complicate test automation. Many of these issues relate to the fact that the fixture is persistent. These issues were introduced in Chapter 9, *Persistent Fixture Management*, and are summarized briefly here.

Persistent Fixtures

Applications with databases present some special challenges when we are writing automated tests. Databases are much slower than the processors used in modern computers. As a consequence, tests that interact with a database tend to run much more slowly than tests that can run entirely in memory. But even ignoring the *Slow Tests* issue, databases are a prime source of test smells in our automated test suites. Commonly encountered smells include *Erratic*

Tests (page 228) and *Obscure Tests* (page 186). Because the data in a database may potentially persist long after we run our test, we must pay special attention to this data to avoid creating tests that can be run only once or tests that interact with one another. These *Unrepeatable Tests* (see *Erratic Test*) and *Interacting Tests* (see *Erratic Test*) are a direct consequence of the persistence of the test fixture and can result in more expensive maintenance of our tests as the application evolves.

Shared Fixtures

Persistence of the fixture is one thing; choosing to share it is another. Deliberate sharing of the fixture can result in *Lonely Tests* (see *Erratic Test*) if some tests depend on other tests to set up the fixture for them—a situation called *Chained Tests* (page 454). If we haven't provided each developer with his or her own *Database Sandbox,* we might spark a *Test Run War* (see *Erratic Test*) between developers. This problem arises when the tests being run from two or more *Test Runners* (page 377) interact by virtue of their accessing the same fixture objects in the shared database instance. Each of these behavior smells is a direct consequence of the decision to share the test fixture. The degree of persistence and the scope of fixture sharing directly affect the presence or absence of these smells.

General Fixtures

Another problem with tests that rely on databases is that databases tend to evolve into a large *General Fixture* (see *Obscure Test*) that many tests use for different purposes. This outcome is particularly likely when we use a *Prebuilt Fixture* (page 429) to avoid setting up the fixture in each test. It can also result from the decision to use a *Standard Fixture* (page 305) when we employ a *Fresh Fixture* (page 311) strategy. This approach makes it difficult to determine exactly what each test is specifying. In effect, the database appears as a *Mystery Guest* (see *Obscure Test*) in all of the tests.

Testing without Databases

Modern layered software architecture [DDD, PEAA, WWW] opens up the possibility of testing the **business logic** without using the database at all. We can test the business logic layer in isolation from the other layers of the system by using *Layer Tests* (page 337) and replacing the **data access layer** with a *Test Double* (page 522); see Figure 13.2.

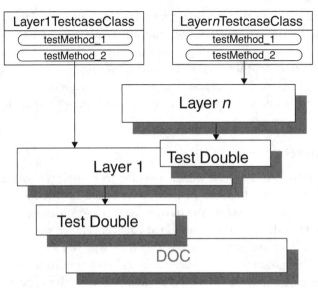

Figure 13.2   *A pair of Layer Tests, each of which tests a different layer of the system. Layer Tests allow us to build each layer independently of the other layers. They are especially useful when the persistence layer can be replaced by a Test Double that reduces the Context Sensitivity (see Fragile Test on page 239) of the tests.*

If our architecture is not sufficiently layered to allow for *Layer Tests*, we may still be able to test without a real database by using either a *Fake Database* (see *Fake Object* on page 551) or an *In-Memory Database* (see *Fake Object*). An *In-Memory Database* is a database but stores its tables in memory; this structure makes it run much faster than a disk-based database. A *Fake Database* isn't really a database at all; it is a data access layer that merely pretends to be one. As a rule, it is easier to ensure independence of tests by using a *Fake Database* because we typically create a new one as part of our fixture setup logic, thereby implementing a *Transient Fresh Fixture* (see *Fresh Fixture*) strategy. Nevertheless, both of these strategies allow our tests to run at in-memory speeds, thereby avoiding *Slow Tests*. We don't introduce too much knowledge of the SUT's structure as long as we continue to write our tests as round-trip tests.

Replacing the database with a *Test Double* works well as long as we use the database only as a data repository. Things get more interesting if we use any vendor-specific functionality, such as sequence number generation or stored procedures. Replacing the database then becomes a bit more challenging because it requires more attention to creating a **design for testability**. The general strategy is to encapsulate all database interaction within the data access layer. Where the data access layer provides data access functionality, we can simply delegate these duties to the "database object." We must provide test-specific implementations for any parts of the data access layer interface that implement the vendor-specific functionality—a task for which a *Test Stub* (page 529) fits the bill nicely.

If we are taking advantage of vendor-specific database features such as sequence number generation, we will need to provide this functionality when executing the tests in memory. Typically, we will not need to substitute a *Test Double* for any functionality-related object because the functionality happens behind the scenes within the database. We can add this functionality into the in-memory version of the application using a Strategy [GOF] object, which by default is initialized to a null object [PLOPD3]. When run in production, the null object does nothing; when run in memory, the strategy object provides the missing functionality. As an added benefit, we will find it easier to change to a different database vendor once we have taken this step because the hooks to provide this functionality already exist.[1]

Replacing the database (or the data access layer) via an automated test implies that we have a way to instruct the SUT to use the replacement object. This is commonly done in one of two ways: through direct *Dependency Injection* (page 678) or by ensuring that the business logic layer uses *Dependency Lookup* (page 686) to find the data access layer.

Testing the Database

Assuming we have found ways to test most of our software without using a database, then what? Does the need to test the database disappear? Of course not! We should ensure that the database functions correctly, just like any other software we write. We can, however, focus our testing of the database logic so as to reduce the number and kinds of tests we need to write. Because tests that involve the database will run much more slowly than our in-memory tests, we want to keep the number of these tests to the bare minimum.

What kinds of database tests will we require? The answer to this question depends on how our application uses the database. If we have stored procedures, we should write unit tests to verify their logic. If a data access layer hides the database from the business logic, we should write tests for the data access functionality.

---

[1] Just one more example of how design for testability improves the design of our applications.

Testing Stored Procedures

We can write tests for stored procedures in one of two ways. A *Remote Stored Procedure Test* (see *Stored Procedure Test* on page 654) is written in the same programming language and framework as we write all of our other unit tests. It accesses the stored procedure via the same invocation mechanism as used within the application logic (i.e., by some sort of Remote Proxy [GOF], Facade [GOF], or Command object [GOF]). Alternatively, we can write *In-Database Stored Procedure Tests* (see *Stored Procedure Test*) in the same language as the stored procedure itself; these tests will run inside the database (Figure 13.3). xUnit family members are available for several of the most common stored procedure languages; **utPLSQL** is just one example.

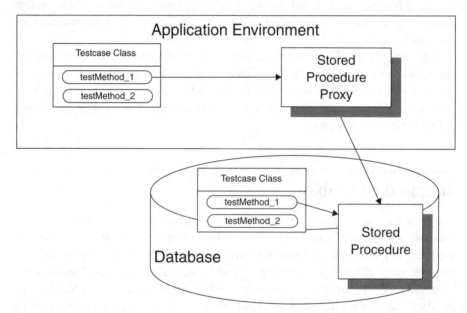

Figure 13.3 *Testing a stored procedure using Self-Checking Tests (see page 26). There is great value in having automated regression test for stored procedures, but we must take care to make them repeatable and robust.*

Testing the Data Access Layer

We also want to write some unit tests for the data access layer. For the most part, these data access layer tests can be round-trip tests. Nevertheless, it is useful to have a few layer-crossing tests to ensure that we are putting information into the correct columns. This can be done using xUnit framework extensions for database testing (e.g., DbUnit for Java) to insert data directly into the database (for "Read" tests) or to verify the post-test contents of the database (for "Create/Update/Delete" tests).

A useful trick for keeping our fixture from becoming persistent during data access layer testing is to use *Transaction Rollback Teardown* (page 668). To do so, we rely on the *Humble Transaction Controller* (see *Humble Object* on page 695) **DFT** pattern when constructing our data access layer. That is, the code that reads or writes the database should never commit a transaction; this allows the code to be exercised by a test that rolls back the transaction to prevent any of the changes made by the SUT from being applied.

Another way to tear down any changes made to the database during the fixture setup and exercise SUT phases of the test is *Table Truncation Teardown* (page 661). This "brute force" technique for deleting data works only when each developer has his or her own *Database Sandbox* and we want to clear out *all* the data in one or more tables.

Ensuring Developer Independence

Testing the database means we need to have the real database available for running these tests. During this testing process, every developer needs to have his or her *own Database Sandbox*. Trying to share a single sandbox among several or all developers is a false economy; the developers will simply end up tripping over one another and wasting a lot of time.[2] I have heard many different excuses for not giving each developer his or her own sandbox, but frankly none of them holds water. The most legitimate concern relates to the cost of a database license for each developer—but even this obstacle can be surmounted by choosing one of the "virtual sandbox" variations. If the database technology supports it, we can use a *DB Schema per TestRunner* (see *Database Sandbox*); otherwise, we have to use a *Database Partitioning Scheme* (see *Database Sandbox*).

Testing with Databases (Again!)

Suppose we have done a good job layering our system and achieved our goal of running most of our tests without accessing the real database. Now what kinds of tests should we run against the *real* database? The answer is simple: "As few as possible, but no fewer!" In practice, we want to run at least a representative sample of our customer tests against the database to ensure that the SUT behaves

---

[2] Can you image asking a team of carpenters to share a single hammer?

the same way with a database as without one. These tests need not access the business logic via the user interface unless some particular user interface functionality depends on the database; *Subcutaneous Tests* (see *Layer Test*) should be adequate in most circumstances.

What's Next?

In this chapter, we looked at special techniques for testing with databases. This discussion has merely scratched the surface of the interactions between agile software development and databases.[3] Chapter 14, *A Roadmap to Effective Test Automation*, summarizes the material we have covered thus far and makes some suggestions about how a project team should come up to speed on developer test automation.

---

[3] For a more complete treatment of the topic, refer to [RDb].

Chapter 14

A Roadmap to Effective Test Automation

About This Chapter

Chapter 13, *Testing with Databases*, introduced a set of patterns specific to testing applications that have a database. These patterns built on the techniques described in Chapter 6, *Test Automation Strategy*; Chapter 9, *Persistent Fixture Management*; and Chapter 11, *Using Test Doubles*. This was a lot of material to become familiar with before we could test effectively with and without databases!

This raises an important point: We don't become experts in test automation overnight—these skills take time to develop. It also takes time to learn the various tools and patterns at our disposal. This chapter provides something of a roadmap for how to learn the patterns and acquire the skills. It introduces the concept of "test automation maturity," which is loosely based on the SEI's Capability Maturity Model (CMM).

Test Automation Difficulty

Some kinds of tests are harder to write than others. This difficulty arises partly because the techniques are more involved and partly because they are less well known and the tools to do this kind of test automation are less readily available. The following common kinds of tests are listed in approximate order of difficulty, from easiest to most difficult:

1. Simple **entity objects** (Domain Model [PEAA])

    - Simple business classes with *no* dependencies

    - Complex business classes *with* dependencies

2. Stateless **service objects**

    •   Individual components via component tests

    •   The entire business logic layer via *Layer Tests* (page 337)

3. Stateful **service objects**

    •   Customer tests via a Service Facade [CJ2EEP] using *Subcutaneous Tests* (see *Layer Test*)

    •   Stateful components via component tests

4. "Hard-to-test" code

    •   User interface logic exposed via *Humble Dialog* (see *Humble Object* on page 695)

    •   Database logic

    •   Multi-threaded software

5. Object-oriented legacy software (software built without any tests)

6. Non-object-oriented legacy software

As we move down this list, the software becomes increasingly more challenging to test. The irony is that many teams "get their feet wet" by trying to retrofit tests onto an existing application. This puts them in one of the last two categories in this list, which is precisely where the most experience is required. Unfortunately, many teams fail to test the legacy software successfully, which may then prejudice them against trying automated testing, with or without test-driven development. If you find yourself trying to learn test automation by retrofitting tests onto legacy software, I have two pieces of advice for you: First, hire someone who has done it before to help you through this process. Second, read Michael Feathers' excellent book [WEwLC]; he covers many techniques specifically applicable to retrofitting tests.

Roadmap to Highly Maintainable Automated Tests

Given that some kinds of tests are much harder to write than others, it makes sense to focus on learning to write the easier tests first before we move on to the more difficult kinds of tests. When teaching automated testing to developers, I introduce the techniques in the following sequence. This roadmap is based on Maslow's hierarchy of needs [HoN], which says that we strive to meet the higher-level needs only after we have satisfied the lower-level needs.

1. Exercise the **happy path** code

    *   Set up a simple pre-test state of the SUT

    *   Exercise the SUT by calling the method being tested

2. Verify direct outputs of the happy path

    *   Call *Assertion Methods* (page 362) on the SUT's responses

    *   Call *Assertion Methods* on the post-test state

3. Verify alternative paths

    *   Vary the SUT method arguments

    *   Vary the pre-test state of the SUT

    *   Control indirect inputs of the SUT via a *Test Stub* (page 529)

4. Verify indirect output behavior

    *   Use *Mock Objects* (page 544) or *Test Spies* (page 538) to intercept and verify outgoing method calls

5. Optimize test execution and maintainability

    *   Make the tests run faster

    *   Make the tests easy to understand and maintain

    *   Design the SUT for testability

    *   Reduce the risk of missed bugs

This ordering of needs isn't meant to imply that this is the order in which we might think about implementing any specific test.[1] Rather, it is likely to be the order in which a project team might reasonably expect to learn about the techniques of test automation.

Let's look at each of these points in more detail.

Exercise the Happy Path Code

To run the happy path through the SUT, we must automate one *Simple Success Test* (see *Test Method* on page 348) as a simple round-trip test through the SUT's API. To get this test to pass, we might simply hard-code some of the logic in the

---

[1] Although it can also be used that way, I find it better to write the assertions first and then work back from there.

SUT, especially where it might call other components to retrieve information it needs to make decisions that would drive the test down the happy path. Before exercising the SUT, we need to set up the test fixture by initializing the SUT to the pre-test state. As long as the SUT executes without raising any errors, we consider the test as having passed; at this level of maturity we don't check the actual results against the expected results.

Verify Direct Outputs of the Happy Path

Once the happy path is executing successfully, we can add result verification logic to turn our test into a *Self-Checking Test* (see page 26). This involves adding calls to *Assertion Methods* to compare the expected results with what actually occurred. We can easily make this change for any objects or values returned to the test by the SUT (e.g., "return values," "out parameters"). We can also call other methods on the SUT or use public fields to access the post-test state of the SUT; we can then call *Assertion Methods* on these values as well.

Verify Alternative Paths

At this point the happy path through the code is reasonably well tested. The alternative paths through the code are still *Untested Code* (see *Production Bugs* on page 268) so the next step is to write tests for these paths (whether we have already written the production code or we are striving to automate the tests that would drive us to implement them). The question to ask here is "What causes the alternative paths to be exercised?" The most common causes are as follows:

- Different values passed in by the client as arguments

- Different prior state of the SUT itself

- Different results of invoking methods on components on which the SUT depends

The first case can be tested by varying the logic in our tests that calls the SUT methods we are exercising and passing in different values as arguments. The second case involves initializing the SUT with a different starting state. Neither of these cases requires any "rocket science." The third case, however, is where things get interesting.

Controlling Indirect Inputs

Because the responses from other components are supposed to cause the SUT to exercise the alternative paths through the code, we need to get control over these indirect inputs. We can do so by using a *Test Stub* that returns the value that should drive the SUT into the desired code path. As part of fixture setup, we must force the SUT to use the stub instead of the real component. The *Test Stub* can be built two ways: as a *Hard-Coded Test Stub* (see *Test Stub*), which contains hand-written code that returns the specific values, or as a *Configurable Test Stub* (see *Test Stub*), which is configured by the test to return the desired values. In both cases, the SUT must use the *Test Stub* instead of the real component.

Many of these alternative paths result in "successful" outputs from the SUT; these tests are considered *Simple Success Tests* and use a style of *Test Stub* called a *Responder* (see *Test Stub*). Other paths are expected to raise errors or exceptions; they are considered *Expected Exception Tests* (see *Test Method*) and use a style of stub called a *Saboteur* (see *Test Stub*).

Making Tests Repeatable and Robust

The act of replacing a real depended-on component (DOC) with a *Test Stub* has a very desirable side effect: It makes our tests both more robust and more repeatable.[2] By using a *Test Stub*, we replace a possibly nondeterministic component with one that is completely deterministic and under test control. This is a good example of the *Isolate the SUT* principle (see page 43).

Verify Indirect Output Behavior

Thus far we have focused on getting control of the indirect inputs of the SUT and verifying readily visible direct outputs by inspecting the post-state test of the SUT. This kind of result verification is known as *State Verification* (page 462). Sometimes, however, we cannot confirm that the SUT has *behaved* correctly simply by looking at the post-test state. That is, we may still have some *Untested Requirements* (see *Production Bugs*) that can only be verified by doing *Behavior Verification* (page 468).

We can build on what we already know how to do by using one of the close relatives of the *Test Stub* to intercept the outgoing method calls from our SUT. A *Test Spy* "remembers" how it was called so that the test can later retrieve the usage information and use *Assertion Method* calls to compare it to the expected usage. A *Mock Object* can be loaded with expectations during fixture setup, which it subsequently compares with the actual calls as they occur while the SUT is being exercised.

---

[2] See *Robust* Test (see page 29) and *Repeatable* Test (see page 26) for a more detailed description.

Optimize Test Execution and Maintenance

At this point we should have automated tests for all the paths through our code. We may, however, have less than optimal tests:

- We may have *Slow Tests* (page 253).

- The tests may contain *Test Code Duplication* (page 213) that makes them hard to understand.

- We may have *Obscure Tests* (page 186) that are hard to understand and maintain.

- We may have *Buggy Tests* (page 260) that are caused by unreliable *Test Utility Methods* (page 599) or *Conditional Test Logic* (page 200).

Make the Tests Run Faster

Slow Tests is often the first behavior smell we need to address. To make tests run faster, we can reuse the test fixture across many tests—for example, by using some form of *Shared Fixture* (page 317). Unfortunately, this tactic typically produces its own share of problems. Replacing a DOC with a *Fake Object* (page 551) that is functionally equivalent but executes much faster is almost always a better solution. Use of a *Fake Object* builds on the techniques we learned for verifying indirect inputs and outputs.

Make the Tests Easy to Understand and Maintain

We can make *Obscure Tests* easier to understand and remove a lot of *Test Code Duplication* by refactoring our *Test Methods* to call *Test Utility Methods* that contain any frequently used logic instead of doing everything on an in-line basis. *Creation Methods* (page 415), *Custom Assertions* (page 474), *Finder Methods* (see *Test Utility Method*), and *Parameterized Tests* (page 607) are all examples of this approach.

If our *Testcase Classes* (page 373) are getting too big to understand, we can reorganize these classes around fixtures or features. We can also better communicate our intent by using a systematic way of naming *Testcase Classes* and *Test Methods* that exposes the test conditions we are verifying in them.

Reduce the Risk of Missed Bugs

If we are having problems with *Buggy Tests* or *Production Bugs*, we can reduce the risk of **false negatives** (tests that pass when they shouldn't) by encapsulating complex test logic. When doing so, we should use intent-revealing names for our

Test Utility Methods. We should verify the behavior of nontrivial *Test Utility Methods* using *Test Utility Tests* (see *Test Utility Method*).

What's Next?

This chapter concludes Part I, *The Narratives.* Chapters 1–14 have provided an overview of the goals, principles, philosophies, patterns, smells, and coding idioms related to writing effective automated tests. Part II, *The Test Smells*, and Part III, *The Patterns*, contain detailed descriptions of each of the smells and patterns introduced in these narrative chapters, complete with code samples.

PART II

The Test Smells

Chapter 15

Code Smells

Smells in This Chapter

Obscure Test

It is difficult to understand the test at a glance.

Automated tests should serve at least two purposes. First, they should act as documentation of how the system under test (SUT) *should* behave; we call this *Tests as Documentation* (see page 23). Second, they should be a self-verifying executable specification. These two goals are often contradictory because the level of detail needed for tests to be executable may make the test so verbose as to be difficult to understand.

Symptoms

We are having trouble understanding what behavior a test is verifying.

Impact

The first issue with an *Obscure Test* is that it makes the test harder to understand and therefore maintain. It will almost certainly preclude achieving *Tests as Documentation,* which in turn can lead to *High Test Maintenance Cost* (page 265).

The second issue with an *Obscure Test* is that it may allow bugs to slip through because of test coding errors hidden in the *Obscure Test*. This can result in *Buggy Tests* (page 260). Furthermore, a failure of one assertion in an *Eager Test* may hide many more errors that simply aren't run, leading to a loss of test debugging data.

Causes

Paradoxically, an *Obscure Test* can be caused by either *too much* information in the *Test Method* (page 348) or *too little* information. *Mystery Guest* is an example of too little information; *Eager Test* and *Irrelevant Information* are examples of too much information.

The root cause of an *Obscure Test* is typically a lack of attention to keeping the test code clean and simple. Test code is just as important as the production code, and it needs to be refactored just as often. A major contributor to an *Obscure Test* is a "just do it in-line" mentality when writing tests. Putting code in-line results in large, complex *Test Methods* because some things just take a lot of code to do.

The first few causes of *Obscure Test* discussed here relate to having the wrong information in the test:

- *Eager Test:* The test verifies too much functionality in a single *Test Method*.

- *Mystery Guest:* The test reader is not able to see the cause and effect between fixture and verification logic because part of it is done outside the *Test Method*.

The general problem of *Verbose Tests*—tests that use too much code to say what they need to say—can be further broken down into a number of root causes:

- *General Fixture:* The test builds or references a larger fixture than is needed to verify the functionality in question.

- *Irrelevant Information:* The test exposes a lot of irrelevant details about the fixture that distract the test reader from what really affects the behavior of the SUT.

- *Hard-Coded Test Data:* Data values in the fixture, assertions, or arguments of the SUT are hard-coded in the *Test Method*, obscuring cause–effect relationships between inputs and expected outputs.

- *Indirect Testing:* The *Test Method* interacts with the SUT indirectly via another object, thereby making the interactions more complex.

Cause: Eager Test

The test verifies too much functionality in a single *Test Method*.

Symptoms

The test goes on and on verifying this, that, and "everything but the kitchen sink." It is hard to tell which part is fixture setup and which part is exercising the SUT.

```
public void testFlightMileage_asKm2() throws Exception {
    // set up fixture
    // exercise constructor
    Flight newFlight = new Flight(validFlightNumber);
    // verify constructed object
    assertEquals(validFlightNumber, newFlight.number);
    assertEquals("", newFlight.airlineCode);
    assertNull(newFlight.airline);
    // set up mileage
    newFlight.setMileage(1122);
    // exercise mileage translator
    int actualKilometres = newFlight.getMileageAsKm();
    // verify results
    int expectedKilometres = 1810;
```

```
        assertEquals( expectedKilometres, actualKilometres);
        // now try it with a canceled flight
        newFlight.cancel();
        try {
            newFlight.getMileageAsKm();
            fail("Expected exception");
        } catch (InvalidRequestException e) {
            assertEquals( "Cannot get cancelled flight mileage",
                            e.getMessage());
        }
    }
```

Root Cause

When executing tests manually, it makes sense to chain a number of logically distinct test conditions into a single test case to reduce the setup overhead of each test. This works because we have **liveware** (an intelligent human being) executing the tests, and this person can decide at any point whether it makes sense to keep going or whether the failure of a step is severe enough to abandon the execution of the test.

Possible Solution

When the tests are automated, it is better to have a suite of independent *Single-Condition Tests* (see page 45) as these provide much better *Defect Localization* (see page 22).

Cause: Mystery Guest

The test reader is not able to see the cause and effect between fixture and verification logic because part of it is done outside the *Test Method*.

Symptoms

Tests invariably require passing data to the SUT. The data used in the fixture setup and exercise SUT phases of the *Four-Phase Test* (page 358) define the pre-conditions of the SUT and influence how it should behave. The post-conditions (the expected outcomes) are reflected in the data passed as arguments to the *Assertion Methods* (page 362) in the verify outcome phase of the test.

When either the fixture setup or the result verification part of a test depends on information that is not visible within the test and the test reader finds it difficult to understand the behavior that is being verified without first finding and inspecting the external information, we have a *Mystery Guest* on our hands. Here's an example where we cannot tell what the fixture looks like, making it difficult to relate the expected outcome to the pre-conditions of the test:

```
public void testGetFlightsByFromAirport_OneOutboundFlight_mg()
                throws Exception {
    loadAirportsAndFlightsFromFile("test-flights.csv");
    // Exercise System
    List flightsAtOrigin = facade.getFlightsByOriginAirportCode( "YYC");
    // Verify Outcome
    assertEquals( 1, flightsAtOrigin.size());
    FlightDto firstFlight = (FlightDto) flightsAtOrigin.get(0);
    assertEquals( "Calgary", firstFlight.getOriginCity());
}
```

Impact

The *Mystery Guest* makes it hard to see the cause–effect relationship between the test fixture (the pre-conditions of the test) and the expected outcome of the test. As a consequence, the tests don't fulfill the role of *Tests as Documentation*. Even worse, someone may modify or delete the external resource without realizing the impact this action will have when the tests are run. This behavior smell has its own name: *Resource Optimism* (see *Erratic Test* on page 228)!

If the *Mystery Guest* is a *Shared Fixture* (page 317), it may also lead to *Erratic Tests* if other tests modify it.

Root Cause

A test depends on mysterious external resources, making it difficult to understand the behavior that it is verifying. *Mystery Guests* may take many forms:

- A filename of an existing external file is passed to a method of the SUT; the *contents* of the file should determine the behavior of the SUT.

- The contents of a database record identified by a literal key are read into an object that is then used by the test or passed to the SUT.

- The contents of a file are read and used in calls to *Assertion Methods* to verify the expected outcome.

- A *Setup Decorator* (page 447) is used to create a *Shared Fixture,* and objects in this fixture are then referenced via variables within the result verification logic.

- A *General Fixture* is set up using *Implicit Setup* (page 424), and the *Test Methods* then access them via instance variables or class variables.

All of these scenarios share a common outcome: It is hard to see the cause–effect relationship between the test fixture and the expected outcome of the test because the relevant data are not visible in the tests. If the contents of the data are not clearly described by the names we give to the variables and files that contain them, we have a *Mystery Guest.*

Possible Solution

Using a *Fresh Fixture* (page 311) built using *In-line Setup* (page 408) is the obvious solution for a *Mystery Guest.* When applied to the file example, this would involve creating the contents of the file as a string within our test so that the contents are visible and then writing them out to the file system [Setup External Resource (page 772) refactoring] or putting it into a file system *Test Stub* (page 529) as part of the fixture setup.[1] To avoid *Irrelevant Information*, we may want to hide the details of the construction behind one or more evocatively named *Creation Methods* (page 415) that append to the file's contents.

If we must use a *Shared Fixture* or *Implicit Setup,* we should consider using evocatively named *Finder Methods* (see *Test Utility Method* on page 599) to access the objects in the fixture. If we must use external resources such as files, we should put them into a special folder or directory and give them names that make it obvious what kind of data they hold.

Cause: General Fixture

The test builds or references a larger fixture than is needed to verify the functionality in question.

Symptoms

There seems to be a lot of test fixture being built—much more than would appear to be necessary for any particular test. It is hard to understand the cause–effect relationship between the fixture, the part of the SUT being exercised, and the expected outcome of a test.

Consider the following set of tests:

```
public void testGetFlightsByFromAirport_OneOutboundFlight()
            throws Exception {
    setupStandardAirportsAndFlights();
    FlightDto outboundFlight = findOneOutboundFlight();
    // Exercise System
    List flightsAtOrigin = facade.getFlightsByOriginAirport(
                outboundFlight.getOriginAirportId());
    // Verify Outcome
```

---

[1] See In-line Resource (page 736) refactoring for details.

```
    assertOnly1FlightInDtoList( "Flights at origin",
                               outboundFlight,
                               flightsAtOrigin);
  }

  public void testGetFlightsByFromAirport_TwoOutboundFlights()
          throws Exception {
    setupStandardAirportsAndFlights();
    FlightDto[] outboundFlights =
            findTwoOutboundFlightsFromOneAirport();
    // Exercise System
    List flightsAtOrigin = facade.getFlightsByOriginAirport(
                outboundFlights[0].getOriginAirportId());
    // Verify Outcome
    assertExactly2FlightsInDtoList( "Flights at origin",
                                    outboundFlights,
                                    flightsAtOrigin);
  }
```

From reading the exercise SUT and verifing outcome parts of the tests, it would appear that they need very different fixtures. Even though these tests are using a *Fresh Fixture* setup strategy, they are using the same fixture setup logic by calling the setupStandardAirportsAndFlights method. The name of the method is a clue to this classic but easily recognized example of a *General Fixture*. A more difficult case to diagnose would be if each test created the *Standard Fixture* (page 305) in-line or if each test created a somewhat different fixture but each fixture contained much more than was needed by each individual test.

We may also be experiencing *Slow Tests* (page 253) or a *Fragile Fixture* (see *Fragile Test* on page 239).

Root Cause

The most common cause of this problem is a test that uses a fixture that is designed to support many tests. Examples include the use of *Implicit Setup* or a *Shared Fixture* across many tests with different fixture requirements. This problem results in the fixture becoming large and difficult to understand. The fixture may also grow larger over time. The root cause is that both approaches rely on a *Standard Fixture* that must meet the requirements of all tests that use it. The more diverse the needs of those tests, the more likely we are to create a *General Fixture*.

Impact

When the test fixture is designed to support many different tests, it can be very difficult to understand how each test uses the fixture. This complexity reduces the likelihood of using *Tests as Documentation* and can result in a *Fragile Fixture* as people alter the fixture so that it can handle new tests. It can also result in *Slow*

Obscure
Test

Tests because a larger fixture takes more time to build, especially if a file system or database is involved.

Possible Solution

We need to move to a *Minimal Fixture* (page 302) to address this problem. To do so, we can use a *Fresh Fixture* for each test. If we must use a *Shared Fixture,* we should consider applying the *Make Resource Unique* (page 737) refactoring to create a virtual *Database Sandbox* (page 650) for each test.[2]

Cause: Irrelevant Information

The test exposes a lot of irrelevant details about the fixture that distract the test reader from what really affects the behavior of the SUT.

Symptoms

As test readers, we find it hard to determine which of the values passed to objects actually affect the expected outcome:

```
public void testAddItemQuantity_severalQuantity_v10(){
    //   Set Up Fixture
    Address billingAddress =
       createAddress( "1222 1st St SW", "Calgary", "Alberta",
                       "T2N 2V2", "Canada");
    Address shippingAddress =
       createAddress( "1333 1st St SW", "Calgary", "Alberta",
                       "T2N 2V2", "Canada");
    Customer customer =
       createCustomer( 99, "John", "Doe", new BigDecimal("30"),
                        billingAddress, shippingAddress);
    Product product =
       createProduct( 88,"SomeWidget",new BigDecimal("19.99"));
    Invoice invoice = createInvoice(customer);
    // Exercise SUT
    invoice.addItemQuantity(product, 5);
    // Verify Outcome
    LineItem expected =
       new LineItem(invoice, product,5, new BigDecimal("30"),
                 new BigDecimal("69.96"));
    assertContainsExactlyOneLineItem(invoice, expected);
}
```

---

[2] Switching to an *Immutable Shared Fixture* (see *Shared Fixture*) does not fully address the core of this problem because it does not help us determine which parts of the fixture are needed by each test; only the parts that are modified are so identified!

Fixture setup logic may seem very long and complicated as it weaves together many interrelated objects. This makes it hard to determine what the test is verifying because the reader doesn't understand the pre-conditions of the test:

```
public void testGetFlightsByOriginAirport_TwoOutboundFlights()
      throws Exception {
  FlightDto expectedCalgaryToSanFran = new FlightDto();
  expectedCalgaryToSanFran.setOriginAirportId(calgaryAirportId);
  expectedCalgaryToSanFran.setOriginCity(CALGARY_CITY);
  expectedCalgaryToSanFran.setDestinationAirportId(sanFranAirportId);
  expectedCalgaryToSanFran.setDestinationCity(SAN_FRAN_CITY);
  expectedCalgaryToSanFran.setFlightNumber(
     facade.createFlight(calgaryAirportId,sanFranAirportId));
  FlightDto expectedCalgaryToVan = new FlightDto();
  expectedCalgaryToVan.setOriginAirportId(calgaryAirportId);
  expectedCalgaryToVan.setOriginCity(CALGARY_CITY);
  expectedCalgaryToVan.
        setDestinationAirportId(vancouverAirportId);
  expectedCalgaryToVan.setDestinationCity(VANCOUVER_CITY);
  expectedCalgaryToVan.setFlightNumber(facade.createFlight(
     calgaryAirportId, vancouverAirportId));
```

The code that verifies the expected outcome of a test can also be too complicated to understand:

```
  List lineItems = inv.getLineItems();
  assertEquals("number of items", lineItems.size(), 2);
  //   verify first item
  LineItem actual = (LineItem)lineItems.get(0);
  assertEquals(expItem1.getInv(), actual.getInv());
  assertEquals(expItem1.getProd(), actual.getProd());
  assertEquals(expItem1.getQuantity(), actual.getQuantity());
  //   verify second item
  actual = (LineItem)lineItems.get(1);
  assertEquals(expItem2.getInv(), actual.getInv());
  assertEquals(expItem2.getProd(), actual.getProd());
  assertEquals(expItem2.getQuantity(), actual.getQuantity());
}
```

Root Cause

A test contains a lot of data, either as *Literal Values* (page 714) or as variables. *Irrelevant Information* often occurs in conjunction with *Hard-Coded Test Data* or a *General Fixture* but can also arise because we make visible all data the test needs to *execute* rather than focusing on the data the test needs to be *understood*. When writing tests, the path of least resistance is to use whatever methods are available (on the SUT and other objects) and to fill in all parameters with values, whether or not they are relevant to the test.

Obscure Test

Another possible cause is when we include all the code needed to verify the outcome using *Procedural State Verification* (see *State Verification* on page 462) rather than using a much more compact "declarative" style to specify the expected outcome.

Impact

It is hard to achieve *Tests as Documentation* if the tests contain many seemingly random bits of *Obscure Test* that don't clearly link the pre-conditions with the post-conditions. Likewise, wading through many steps of fixture setup or result verification logic can result in *High Test Maintenance Cost* and can increase the likelihood of *Production Bugs* (page 268) or *Buggy Tests*.

Possible Solution

The best way to get rid of *Irrelevant Information* in fixture setup logic is to replace direct calls to the constructor or *Factory Methods* [GOF] with calls to *Parameterized Creation Methods* (see *Creation Method*) that take only the *relevant* information as parameters. Fixture values that do not matter to the test (i.e., those that do not affect the expected outcome) should be defaulted within *Creation Methods* or replaced by *Dummy Objects* (page 728). In this way we say to the test reader, "The values you don't see don't affect the expected outcome." We can replace fixture values that appear in both the fixture setup and outcome verification parts of the test with suitably initialized named constants as long as we are using a *Fresh Fixture* approach to fixture setup.

To hide *Irrelevant Information* in result verification logic, we can use assertions on entire *Expected Objects* (see *State Verification*), rather than asserting on individual fields, and we can create *Custom Assertions* (page 474) that hide complex procedural verification logic.

Cause: Hard-Coded Test Data

Data values in the fixture, assertions, or arguments of the SUT are hard-coded in the *Test Method,* obscuring cause–effect relationships between inputs and expected outputs.

Symptoms

As test readers, we find it difficult to determine how various hard-coded (i.e., literal) values in the test are related to one another and which values should affect the behavior of the SUT. We may also encounter behavior smells such as *Erratic Tests.*

```
public void testAddItemQuantity_severalQuantity_v12(){
    //  Set Up Fixture
    Customer cust = createACustomer(new BigDecimal("30"));
    Product prod = createAProduct(new BigDecimal("19.99"));
    Invoice invoice = createInvoice(cust);
    // Exercise SUT
    invoice.addItemQuantity(prod, 5);
    // Verify Outcome
    LineItem expected = new LineItem(invoice, prod, 5,
            new BigDecimal("30"), new BigDecimal("69.96"));
    assertContainsExactlyOneLineItem(invoice, expected);
}
```

This specific example isn't so bad because there aren't very many literal values. If we aren't good at doing math in our heads, however, we might miss the relationship between the unit price ($19.99), the item quantity (5), the discount (30%), and the total price ($69.96).

Root Cause

Hard-Coded Test Data occurs when a test contains a lot of seemingly unrelated *Literal Values*. Tests invariably require passing data to the SUT. The data used in the fixture setup and exercise SUT phases of the *Four-Phase Test* define the pre-conditions of the SUT and influence how it should behave. The post-conditions (the expected outcomes) are reflected in the data passed as arguments to the *Assertion Methods* in the verify outcome phase of the test. When writing tests, the path of least resistance is to use whatever methods are available (on the SUT and other objects) and to fill in all parameters with values, whether or not they are relevant to the test.

When we use "cut-and-paste" reuse of test logic, we find ourselves replicating the literal values to the derivative tests.

Impact

It is hard to achieve *Tests as Documentation* if the tests contain many seemingly random bits of *Obscure Test* that don't clearly link the pre-conditions with the post-conditions. A few literal parameters might not seem like a bad thing—after all, they don't require us to make *that* much more effort to understand a test. As the number of literal values grows, however, it can become *much* more difficult to understand a test. This is especially true when the signal-to-noise ratio drops dramatically because the majority of the values are irrelevant to the test.

The second major impact occurs when collisions between tests occur *because* the tests are using the same values. This situation happens only when we use a *Shared Fixture* because a *Fresh Fixture* strategy shouldn't litter the scene with any objects with which a subsequent test can collide.

Possible Solution

The best way to get rid of the *Obscure Test* smell is to replace the literal constants with something else. Fixture values that determine which scenario is being executed (e.g., type codes) are probably the only ones that are reasonable to leave as literals—but even these values can be converted to named constants.

Fixture values that do not matter to the test (i.e., those that do not affect the expected outcome) should be defaulted within *Creation Methods*. In this way we say to the test reader, "The values you don't see don't affect the expected outcome." We can replace fixture values that appear in both the fixture setup and outcome verification parts of the test with suitably initialized named constants as long as we are using a *Fresh Fixture* approach to fixture setup.

Values in the result verification logic that are based on values used in the fixture or that are used as arguments of the SUT should be replaced with *Derived Values* (page 718) to make those calculations obvious to the test reader.

If we are using any variant of *Shared Fixture*, we should try to use *Distinct Generated Values* (see *Generated Value* on page 723) to ensure that each time a test is run, it uses a different value. This consideration is especially important for fields that serve as unique keys in databases. A common way of encapsulating this logic is to use *Anonymous Creation Methods* (see *Creation Method*).

Cause: Indirect Testing

The *Test Method* interacts with the SUT indirectly via another object, thereby making the interactions more complex.

Symptoms

A test interacts primarily with objects other than the one whose behavior it purports to verify. The test must construct and interact with objects that contain references to the SUT rather than with the SUT itself. Testing business logic through the presentation layer is a common example of *Indirect Testing*.

```
private final int LEGAL_CONN_MINS_SAME = 30;
public void testAnalyze_sameAirline_LessThanConnectionLimit()
throws Exception {
    // setup
    FlightConnection illegalConn =
        createSameAirlineConn( LEGAL_CONN_MINS_SAME - 1);
    // exercise
    FlightConnectionAnalyzerImpl sut =
        new FlightConnectionAnalyzerImpl();
```

```
    String actualHtml =
        sut.getFlightConnectionAsHtmlFragment(
                illegalConn.getInboundFlightNumber(),
                illegalConn.getOutboundFlightNumber());
    // verification
    StringBuffer expected = new StringBuffer();
    expected.append("<span class="boldRedText">");
    expected.append("Connection time between flight ");
    expected.append(illegalConn.getInboundFlightNumber());
    expected.append(" and flight ");
    expected.append(illegalConn.getOutboundFlightNumber());
    expected.append(" is ");
    expected.append(illegalConn.getActualConnectionTime());
    expected.append(" minutes.</span>");
    assertEquals("html", expected.toString(), actualHtml);
}
```

Impact

It may not be possible to test "anything that could possibly break" in the SUT via the intermediate object. Indeed, such tests are unlikely to be very clear or understandable. They certainly will not result in *Tests as Documentation*.

Indirect Testing may result in *Fragile Tests* because changes in the intermediate objects may require modification of the tests even when the SUT is *not* modified.

Root Cause

The SUT may be "private" to the class being used to access it from the test. It may not be possible to create the SUT directly because the constructors themselves are private. This problem is just one sign that the software is not designed for testability.

It may be that the actual outcome of exercising the SUT cannot be observed directly. In such a case, the expected outcome of the test must be verified through an intermediate object.

Possible Solution

It may be necessary to improve the design-for-testability of the SUT to remove this smell. We might be able to expose the SUT directly to the test by using an Extract Testable Component refactoring (a variant of the Sprout Class [WEwLC] refactoring). This approach may result in an untestable *Humble Object* (page 695) and an easily tested object that contains most or all of the actual logic.

```
public void testAnalyze_sameAirline_EqualsConnectionLimit()
throws Exception {
    // setup
    Mock flightMgntStub = mock(FlightManagementFacade.class);
```

```
    Flight firstFlight = createFlight();
    Flight secondFlight = createConnectingFlight(
                      firstFlight, LEGAL_CONN_MINS_SAME);
    flightMgntStub.expects(once()).method("getFlight")
                    .with(eq(firstFlight.getFlightNumber()))
                    .will(returnValue(firstFlight));
    flightMgntStub.expects(once()).method("getFlight")
                    .with(eq(secondFlight.getFlightNumber()))
                    .will(returnValue(secondFlight));
    // exercise
    FlightConnAnalyzer theConnectionAnalyzer =
          new FlightConnAnalyzer();
    theConnectionAnalyzer.facade =
          (FlightManagementFacade)flightMgntStub.proxy();
    FlightConnection actualConnection =
          theConnectionAnalyzer.getConn(
                        firstFlight.getFlightNumber(),
                        secondFlight.getFlightNumber());
    // verification
    assertNotNull("actual connection", actualConnection);
    assertTrue("IsLegal", actualConnection.isLegal());
}
```

Sometimes we may be forced to interact with the SUT indirectly because we cannot refactor the code to expose the logic we are trying to test. In these cases, we should encapsulate the complex logic forced by *Indirect Testing* behind suitably named *Test Utility Methods*. Similarly, fixture setup can be hidden behind *Creation Methods* and result verification can be hidden by *Verification Methods* (see *Custom Assertion*). Both are examples of *SUT API Encapsulation* (see *Test Utility Method*).

```
public void testAnalyze_sameAirline_LessThanConnLimit()
throws Exception {
   // setup
   FlightConnection illegalConn =
         createSameAirlineConn( LEGAL_CONN_MINS_SAME - 1);
   FlightConnectionAnalyzerImpl sut =
         new FlightConnectionAnalyzerImpl();
   // exercise SUT
   String actualHtml =
         sut.getFlightConnectionAsHtmlFragment(
                   illegalConn.getInboundFlightNumber(),
                   illegalConn.getOutboundFlightNumber());
   // verification
   assertConnectionIsIllegal(illegalConn, actualHtml);
}
```

The following *Custom Assertion* hides the ugliness of extracting the business result from the presentation noise. It was created by doing a simple Extract Method [Fowler] refactoring on the test. Of course, this example would be more robust if it searched inside the HTML for key strings rather than building up the entire expected string and comparing it all at once. Other *Presentation Layer Tests* (see *Layer Test* on page 337) might then verify that the presentation logic is formatting the HTML string properly.

```
private void assertConnectionIsIllegal( FlightConnection conn,
                                        String actualHtml) {
    // set up expected value
    StringBuffer expected = new StringBuffer();
    expected.append("<span class="boldRedText">");
    expected.append("Connection time between flight ");
    expected.append(conn.getInboundFlightNumber());
    expected.append(" and flight ");
    expected.append(conn.getOutboundFlightNumber());
    expected.append(" is ");
    expected.append(conn.getActualConnectionTime());
    expected.append(" minutes.</span>");
    // verification
    assertEquals("html", expected.toString(), actualHtml);
}
```

Solution Patterns

A good test strategy helps keep the test code understandable. Nevertheless, just as "no battle plan survives the first contact with the enemy," no test infrastructure can anticipate all needs of all tests. We should expect the test infrastructure to evolve as the software matures and our test automation skills improve.

We can reuse test logic for several scenarios by having several tests call *Test Utility Methods* or by asking a common *Parameterized Test* (page 607) to pass in the already built test fixture or *Expected Objects*.

Writing tests in an "outside-in" way can minimize the likelihood of producing an *Obscure Test* that might then need to be refactored. This approach starts by outlining the *Four-Phase Test* using calls to nonexistent *Test Utility Methods*. Once we are satisfied with these tests, we can write the utility methods needed to run them. By writing the tests first, we gain a better understanding of what the utility methods need to do for us to make writing the tests as simple as possible. The "test-infected" will, of course, write *Test Utility Tests* (see *Test Utility Method*) before writing the *Test Utility Methods*.

Conditional Test Logic

A test contains code that may or may not be executed.

A *Fully Automated Test* (see page 26) is just code that verifies the behavior of other code. But if this code is complicated, how do we verify that *it* works properly? We could write tests for our tests—but when would this recursion stop? The simple answer is that *Test Methods* (page 348) must be simple enough to not need tests.

Conditional Test Logic is one factor that makes tests more complicated than they really should be.

Symptoms

As a code smell, *Conditional Test Logic* may not produce any behavioral symptoms but its presence should be reasonably obvious to the test reader. View any control structures within a *Test Method* with extreme suspicion! The test reader may also wonder which code path is the one that is being executed. The following is an example of *Conditional Test Logic* that involves both looping and if statements:

```
//   verify Vancouver is in the list
actual = null;
i = flightsFromCalgary.iterator();
while (i.hasNext()) {
   FlightDto flightDto = (FlightDto) i.next();
   if (flightDto.getFlightNumber().equals(
         expectedCalgaryToVan.getFlightNumber()))
   {
      actual = flightDto;
      assertEquals("Flight from Calgary to Vancouver",
                  expectedCalgaryToVan,
                  flightDto);
      break;
   }
 }
}
```

This code begs the question, "What is this test code doing and how do we know that it is doing it correctly?" One behavioral symptom may be the presence of the related project-level smell *High Test Maintenance Cost* (page 265), which may be caused by the complexity introduced by the *Conditional Test Logic*.

Impact

Conditional Test Logic makes it difficult to know *exactly* what a test is going to do when it really matters. Code that has only a single execution path always executes in exactly the same way. Code that has multiple execution paths presents much greater challenges and does not inspire as much confidence about its outcome.

To increase our confidence in production code, we can write *Self-Checking Tests* (see page 26) that exercise the code. How can we increase our confidence in the test code if it executes differently each time we run it? It is hard to know (or prove) that the test is verifying the behavior we want it to verify. A test that has branches or loops, or that uses different values each time it is run, can be very difficult to debug simply because it isn't completely deterministic.

A related issue is that *Conditional Test Logic* makes writing the test correctly a more difficult task. Because the test itself cannot be tested easily, how do we know that it will actually detect the bugs it is intended to catch? [This is a general problem with *Obscure Tests* (page 186); they are more likely to result in *Buggy Tests* (page 260) than simple code.]

Causes

Test automaters may introduce *Conditional Test Logic* for several reasons:

- They may use if statements to steer execution to a fail statement or to avoid executing certain pieces of test code when the SUT fails to return valid data.

- They may use loops to verify the contents of collections of objects (*Conditional Verification Logic*). This may also result in an *Obscure Test*.

- They may use *Conditional Test Logic* to verify complex objects or polymorphic data structures (another form of *Conditional Verification Logic*). This is just a Foreign Method [Fowler] implementation of the equals method.

- They may use *Conditional Test Logic* to initialize the test fixture or *Expected Object* (see *State Verification* on page 462) so they can reuse a single test to verify several different cases (*Flexible Test*).

- They may use if statements to avoid tearing down nonexistent fixture objects (*Complex Teardown*).

Some of these causes are worth examining in more detail.

Cause: Flexible Test

The test code verifies different functionality depending on when or where it is run.

Symptoms

The test contains conditional logic that does different things depending on the current environment. Most commonly this functionality takes the form of *Conditional Test Logic* to build different versions of the expected results based on some factor external to the test.

Consider the following test, which gets the current time so that it can determine what the output of the SUT should be:

```
public void testDisplayCurrentTime_whenever() {
    // fixture setup
    TimeDisplay sut = new TimeDisplay();
    // exercise SUT
    String result = sut.getCurrentTimeAsHtmlFragment();
    // verify outcome
    Calendar time = new DefaultTimeProvider().getTime();
    StringBuffer expectedTime = new StringBuffer();
    expectedTime.append("<span class=\"tinyBoldText\">");

    if ((time.get(Calendar.HOUR_OF_DAY) == 0)
        && (time.get(Calendar.MINUTE) <= 1)) {
      expectedTime.append( "Midnight");
    } else if ((time.get(Calendar.HOUR_OF_DAY) == 12)
                && (time.get(Calendar.MINUTE) == 0)) { // noon
      expectedTime.append("Noon");
    } else {
      SimpleDateFormat fr = new SimpleDateFormat("h:mm a");
      expectedTime.append(fr.format(time.getTime()));
    }
    expectedTime.append("</span>");

    assertEquals( expectedTime, result);
  }
```

Root Cause

A *Flexible Test* is caused by a lack of control of the environment. The test automater probably wasn't able to decouple the SUT from its dependencies and decided to adapt the test logic based on the state of the environment.

Impact

The first issue is that using a *Flexible Test* makes the test harder to understand and therefore to maintain. The second issue is that we don't know which test scenarios are actually being exercised and whether all scenarios are, in fact, exercised regularly. For example, in our sample test, is the midnight scenario ever exercised? How often? Probably rarely, if ever, because the test would have to be run at exactly midnight—an unlikely event, even if we timed the nightly build such that it ran over midnight.

Possible Solution

A *Flexible Test* is best addressed by decoupling the SUT from whatever dependencies prompted the test automater to make the test flexible. This involves refactoring the SUT to support **substitutable dependency**. We can then replace the dependency with a *Test Double* (page 522), such as a *Test Stub* (page 529) or *Mock Object* (page 544), and write separate tests for each circumstance previously covered by the *Flexible Test*.

Cause: Conditional Verification Logic

Conditional Test Logic (page 200) may also create problems when it is used to verify the expected outcome. This issue usually arises when the tester tries to prevent the execution of assertions if the SUT fails to return the right objects or uses loops to verify the contents of collections returned by the SUT.

```
//   verify Vancouver is in the list
actual = null;
i = flightsFromCalgary.iterator();
while (i.hasNext()) {
   FlightDto flightDto = (FlightDto) i.next();
   if (flightDto.getFlightNumber().equals(
         expectedCalgaryToVan.getFlightNumber()))
   {
      actual = flightDto;
      assertEquals("Flight from Calgary to Vancouver",
               expectedCalgaryToVan,
               flightDto);
      break;
   }
}
```

Possible Solution

We can replace the if statements that steer execution to a call to fail with a *Guard Assertion* (page 490) that causes the test to fail before we reach the code we don't want to execute. This works well unless the test is an *Expected Exception Test* (see *Test Method.*) In the latter case, we should use the standard *Expected Exception Test* coding idiom for the xUnit family member and language.

We can replace *Conditional Test Logic* for verification of complex objects with an *Equality Assertion* (see *Assertion Method* on page 362) on an *Expected Object*. If the production code's equals method is too strict, we can use a *Custom Assertion* (page 474) to define **test-specific equality**.

We should move any loops in the verification logic to a *Custom Assertion*. We can then verify this assertion's behavior by using *Custom Assertion Tests* (see *Custom Assertion*).

We can reuse test logic in several tests by calling a *Test Utility Method* (page 599) or a common *Parameterized Test* (page 607) that passes in the already built test fixture and *Expected Objects*.

Cause: Production Logic in Test

Symptoms

Some forms of *Conditional Test Logic* are found in the result verification section of our tests. Let us look more closely inside the loops of this test:

```
public void testCombinationsOfInputValues() {
    // Set up fixture
    Calculator sut = new Calculator();
    int expected;   // TBD inside loops

    for (int i = 0; i < 10; i++) {
        for (int j = 0; j < 10; j++) {
            // Exercise SUT
            int actual = sut.calculate( i, j );

            // Verify result
            if (i==3 & j==4)  // special case
                expected = 8;
            else
                expected = i+j;

            assertEquals(message(i,j), expected, actual);
        }
    }
}

private String message(int i, int j) {
    return "Cell( " + String.valueOf(i)+ ","
                    + String.valueOf(j) + ")";
}
```

The nested loops in this *Loop-Driven Test* (see *Parameterized Test*) exercise the SUT with various combinations of values of i and j as inputs. Here we will focus on the *Conditional Test Logic* inside the loop.

Root Cause

This *Production Logic in Test* is a direct result of wanting to verify multiple test conditions in a single *Test Method*. Given that multiple input values are passed to the SUT, we should also have multiple expected results. It is hard to enumerate the expected result for each set of inputs if we pass in many combinations of several input arguments to the SUT in nested loops. A common solution to this problem is to use a *Calculated Value* (see *Derived Value* on page 718) based on the inputs. The potential downfall (as we see here) is that we find ourselves replicating the expected SUT logic inside our test to calculate the expected values for assertions.

Possible Solution

If at all possible, it is better to enumerate the sets of precalculated values with which to test the SUT. The following example tests the same logic using a (smaller) set of enumerated values:

```
public void testMultipleValueSets() {
    // Set Up Fixture
    Calculator sut = new Calculator();
    TestValues[] testValues = {
                new TestValues(1,2,3),
                new TestValues(2,3,5),
                new TestValues(3,4,8), // special case!
                new TestValues(4,5,9)
                        };

    for (int i = 0; i < testValues.length; i++) {
        TestValues values = testValues[i];
        // Exercise SUT
        int actual = sut.calculate( values.a, values.b);
        // Verify Result
        assertEquals(message(i), values.expectedSum, actual);
    }
}

private String message(int i) {
    return "Row "+ String.valueOf(i);
}
```

Cause: Complex Teardown

Symptoms

Complex fixture teardown code is more likely to leave the test environment corrupted if it does not clean up after itself correctly. It is hard to verify that teardown code has been written correctly, and such code can easily result in "data leaks" that may later cause this or other tests to fail for no apparent reason. Consider this example:

```
public void testGetFlightsByOrigin_NoInboundFlight_SMRTD()
        throws Exception {
  // Set Up Fixture
  BigDecimal outboundAirport = createTestAirport("1OF");
  BigDecimal inboundAirport = null;
  FlightDto expFlightDto = null;
  try {
    inboundAirport = createTestAirport("1IF");
    expFlightDto =
          createTestFlight(outboundAirport, inboundAirport);
    // Exercise System
    List flightsAtDestination1 =
          facade.getFlightsByOriginAirport(inboundAirport);
    // Verify Outcome
    assertEquals(0,flightsAtDestination1.size());
  } finally {
    try {
      facade.removeFlight(expFlightDto.getFlightNumber());
    } finally {
      try {
        facade.removeAirport(inboundAirport);
      } finally {
        facade.removeAirport(outboundAirport);
      }
    }
  }
}
```

Root Cause

Teardown is typically required only when we use persistent resources that are beyond the reach of our **garbage collection** system. *Complex Teardown* occurs when many such resources are used in the same *Test Method*.

Possible Solution

To avoid complex teardown logic, we should use *Implicit Teardown* (page 516), which will make the code both reusable and testable, or *Automated Teardown* (page 503), which can be verified with automated unit tests. We can also eliminate the need to tear down any fixture objects by using a *Fresh Fixture* (page 311) strategy and by avoiding the use of any persistent objects in our tests by using some sort of *Test Double*.

Cause: Multiple Test Conditions

Symptoms

A test tries to apply the same test logic to many sets of input values, each with its own corresponding expected result. In the following example, the test iterates over a collection of test values and applies the test logic to each set:

```
public void testMultipleValueSets() {
   // Set Up Fixture
   Calculator sut = new Calculator();
   TestValues[] testValues = {
                  new TestValues(1,2,3),
                  new TestValues(2,3,5),
                  new TestValues(3,4,8), // special case!
                  new TestValues(4,5,9)
                              };

   for (int i = 0; i < testValues.length; i++) {
      TestValues values = testValues[i];
      // Exercise SUT
      int actual = sut.calculate( values.a, values.b);
      // Verify Outcome
      assertEquals(message(i), values.expectedSum, actual);
   }
}

private String message(int i) {
   return "Row "+ String.valueOf(i);
}
```

Root Cause

The test automater is trying to test many test conditions using the same test logic in a single *Test Method*. In the preceding example, it is fairly simple *Conditional Test Logic*. Matters could be a lot worse if the code contained multiple nested loops and maybe even if statements to calculate different cases of the expected values.

Possible Solution

Of all sources of *Conditional Test Logic*, *Multiple Test Conditions* is probably the most innocuous. Other than scaring the test reader, the main impact of such a test is that it stops executing at the first failure and doesn't provide *Defect Localization* (see page 22) when a bug is introduced into the code. The readability issue can easily be addressed by using an Extract Method [Fowler] refactoring to create a *Parameterized Test* call from within the loop. The lack of *Defect Localization* can be addressed by calling the *Parameterized Test* from a separate *Test Method* for each test condition. For large sets of values, a *Data-Driven Test* (page 288) might be a better solution.

Hard-to-Test Code

Code is difficult to test.

Automated testing is a powerful tool that helps us develop software quickly even when we have a large code base to maintain. Of course, it provides these benefits only if most of our code is protected by *Fully Automated Tests* (see page 26). The effort of writing these tests must be added to the effort of writing the product code they verify. Not surprisingly, we would prefer to make it easy to write the automated tests.[3]

Hard-to-Test Code is one factor that makes it difficult to write complete, correct automated tests in a cost-efficient manner.

Symptoms

Some kinds of code are inherently difficult to test—GUI components, multi-threaded code, and test code, for example. It may be difficult to get at the code to be tested because it is not visible to a test. It may be problematic to compile a test because the code is too highly coupled to other classes. It may be hard to create an instance of the object because the constructors don't exist, are private, or take too many other objects as parameters.

Impact

Whenever we have *Hard-to-Test Code*, we cannot easily verify the quality of that code in an automated way. While manual quality assessment is often possible, it doesn't scale very well because the effort to perform this assessment after each code change usually means it doesn't get done. Nor is this strategy readily repeated without a large test documentation cost.

Solution Patterns

A better solution is to make the code more amenable to testing. This topic is big enough that it warrants a whole chapter of its own, but this section covers a few of the highlights.

---

[3] We would also like to recoup this cost by reducing effort somewhere else. The best way to achieve this is to avoid *Frequent Debugging* (page 248) by writing the tests first and achieving *Defect Localization* (see page 22).

Causes

There are a number of reasons for *Hard-to-Test Code*; the most common causes are discussed here.

Cause: Highly Coupled Code

Symptoms

A class cannot be tested without also testing several other classes.

Impact

Code that is highly coupled to other code is very difficult to unit test because it won't execute in isolation.

Root Cause

Highly Coupled Code can be caused by many factors, including poor design, lack of object-oriented design experience, and lack of a reward structure that encourages decoupling.

Possible Solution

The key to testing overly coupled code is to break the coupling. This happens naturally when we are doing test-driven development.

A technique that we often use to decouple code for the purpose of testing is a *Test Double* (page 522) or, more specifically, a *Test Stub* (page 529) or *Mock Object* (page 544). This topic is covered in much more detail in Chapter 11, *Using Test Doubles*.

Retrofitting tests onto existing code is a more challenging task, especially when we are dealing with a legacy code base. This is a big enough topic that Michael Feathers wrote a whole book on techniques for doing this, titled *Working Effectively with Legacy Code* [WEwLC].

Cause: Asynchronous Code

Symptoms

A class cannot be tested via direct method calls. The test must start an executable (such as a thread, process, or application) and wait until its start-up has finished before interacting with the executable.

Impact

Code that has an asynchronous interface is hard to test because the tests of these elements must coordinate their execution with that of the SUT. This requirement can add a lot of complexity to the tests and causes them to take much, much longer to run. The latter issue is a major concern with unit tests, which must run very quickly to ensure that developers will run them frequently.

Root Cause

The code that implements the algorithm we wish to test is highly coupled to the active object in which it normally executes.

Possible Solution

The key to testing asynchronous code is to separate the logic from the asynchronous access mechanism. The design-for-testability pattern *Humble Object* (page 695; including *Humble Dialog* and *Humble Executable*) is a good example of a way to restructure otherwise asynchronous code so it can be tested in a synchronous manner.

Cause: Untestable Test Code

Symptoms

The body of a *Test Method* (page 348) is obscure enough (*Obscure Test;* see page 186) or contains enough *Conditional Test Logic* (page 200) that we wonder whether the test is correct.

Impact

Any *Conditional Test Logic* within a *Test Method* has a higher probability of producing *Buggy Tests* (page 260) and will likely result in *High Test Maintenance Cost* (page 265). Too much code in the test method body can make the test hard to understand and hard to construct correctly.

Root Cause

The code within the body of the *Test Method* is inherently hard to test using a *Self-Checking Test* (see page 26). To do so, we would have to replace the SUT with a *Test Double* that injects the target error and then run the test method inside another *Expected Exception Test* (see *Test Method*) method—much too much trouble to bother with in all but the most unusual circumstances.

Possible Solution

We can remove the need to test the body of a *Test Method* by making it extremely simple and relocating any *Conditional Test Logic* from it into *Test Utility Methods* (page 599), for which we can easily write *Self-Checking Tests*.

Test Code Duplication

The same test code is repeated many times.

Many of the tests in a suite need to do similar things. For example, tests often exercise scenarios that are variations on the same theme. Tests may require similar fixture setup or result verification logic. In some cases, even the exercise SUT phase of many tests involves repeating the same nontrivial logic.

The need for tests to do similar things often results in *Test Code Duplication*.

Symptoms

Several tests may contain a common subset of essentially the same statements, as in the following example:

```
public void testInvoice_addOneLineItem_quantity1_b() {
    // Exercise
    inv.addItemQuantity(product, QUANTITY);
    // Verify
    List lineItems = inv.getLineItems();
    assertEquals("number of items", lineItems.size(), 1);
    // Verify only item
    LineItem expItem = new LineItem(inv, product, QUANTITY);
    LineItem actual = (LineItem)lineItems.get(0);
    assertEquals(expItem.getInv(), actual.getInv());
    assertEquals(expItem.getProd(), actual.getProd());
    assertEquals(expItem.getQuantity(), actual.getQuantity());
}


public void testRemoveLineItemsForProduct_oneOfTwo() {
    // Set up
    Invoice inv = createAnonInvoice();
    inv.addItemQuantity(product, QUANTITY);
    inv.addItemQuantity(anotherProduct, QUANTITY);
    LineItem expItem = new LineItem(inv, product, QUANTITY);
    // Exercise
    inv.removeLineItemForProduct(anotherProduct);
    // Verify
    List lineItems = inv.getLineItems();
    assertEquals("number of items", lineItems.size(), 1);
    LineItem actual = (LineItem)lineItems.get(0);
    assertEquals(expItem.getInv(), actual.getInv());
    assertEquals(expItem.getProd(), actual.getProd());
    assertEquals(expItem.getQuantity(), actual.getQuantity());
}
```

A single test may also contain repeated groups of similar statements:

```
public void testInvoice_addTwoLineItems_sameProduct() {
    Invoice inv = createAnonInvoice();
    LineItem expItem1 = new LineItem(inv, product, QUANTITY1);
    LineItem expItem2 = new LineItem(inv, product, QUANTITY2);
    // Exercise
    inv.addItemQuantity(product, QUANTITY1);
    inv.addItemQuantity(product, QUANTITY2);
    // Verify
    List lineItems = inv.getLineItems();
    assertEquals("number of items", lineItems.size(), 2);
    //    Verify first item
    LineItem actual = (LineItem)lineItems.get(0);
    assertEquals(expItem1.getInv(), actual.getInv());
    assertEquals(expItem1.getProd(), actual.getProd());
    assertEquals(expItem1.getQuantity(), actual.getQuantity());
    //    Verify second item
    actual = (LineItem)lineItems.get(1);
    assertEquals(expItem2.getInv(), actual.getInv());
    assertEquals(expItem2.getProd(), actual.getProd());
    assertEquals(expItem2.getQuantity(), actual.getQuantity());
}
```

Both of the preceding examples exhibit *Test Code Duplication* that is easily noticed. By comparison, it is more challenging to identify duplication when it occurs across *Test Methods* (page 348) that reside in different *Testcase Classes* (page 373).

Impact

"Cut and paste" often results in many copies of the same code. This code must be maintained every time the SUT is modified in a way that affects the semantics (e.g., number of arguments, argument attributes, returned object attributes, calling sequences) of its methods. This necessity can greatly increase the cost to introduce new functionality (*High Test Maintenance Cost; see page* 265) because of the effort involved in updating all tests that contain copies of the affected code.

Causes

Cause: Cut-and-Paste Code Reuse

"Cut and paste" is a powerful tool for writing code fast but it results in many copies of the same code, each of which must be maintained in parallel.

Root Cause

Cut-and-Paste Code Reuse is often the default way to reuse logic. Developers who focus on details of "how" to do something will often repeat the same code many times because they cannot (or do not take the time to) focus on the big picture (the intent) of the test.

A contributing factor may be a lack of refactoring skills or refactoring experience that keeps developers from extracting the big picture from the detailed code they have written. Of course, time pressure may also be the culprit that keeps the refactoring from occurring. As a result, test code grows more complicated over time rather than becoming simpler.

Possible Solution

Once *Test Code Duplication* has occurred, the best solution is to use an Extract Method [Fowler] refactoring to create a *Test Utility Method* (page 599) from one of the examples and then to generalize that method to handle each of the copies. When the *Test Code Duplication* consists of fixture setup logic, we end up with *Creation Methods* (page 415) or *Finder Methods* (see *Test Utility Method*). When the logic carries out result verification, we end up with *Custom Assertions* (page 474) or *Verification Methods* (see *Custom Assertion*).

We can use an Introduce Parameter [JBrains] refactoring to convert any literal constants inside the extracted method into parameters that can be passed in to customize the method's behavior for each test that calls it.

More simply, we can avoid most *Test Code Duplication* by writing the *Test Methods* in an "outside-in" manner, focusing on their intent. Whenever we need to do something that involves several lines of code, we simply call a nonexistent *Test Utility Method* to do it. We write all our tests this way and then fill in implementations of the *Test Utility Methods* to get the tests to compile and run. (Modern IDEs facilitate this process by providing automatic method skeleton generation at a click of the mouse.)

Cause: Reinventing the Wheel

While *Cut-and-Paste Code Reuse* deliberately makes copies of existing code to reduce the effort of writing tests, it is also possible to accidentally write the same sequence of statements in different tests.

Root Cause

This problem is primarily caused by a lack of awareness of which *Test Utility Methods* are available. It can also be caused by a predisposition to write one's own code rather than reuse code written by others.

**Test Code
Duplication**

Possible Solution

The technical solution is largely the same as for *Cut-and-Paste Code Reuse* but the process solution is somewhat different. The test automater must look around more places to discover which *Test Utility Methods* are available before reinventing the wheel (i.e., writing new code).

Further Reading

Test Code Duplication was first described in a paper at XP2001 called "Refactoring Test Code" [RTC].

Test Logic in Production

**The code that is put into production contains logic that should be exercised
only during tests.**

The SUT may contain logic that cannot be run in a test environment. Tests may
require the SUT to behave in specific ways to allow full test coverage.

Symptoms

The logic in the SUT is there solely to support testing. This logic may be "extra
stuff" that the tests require to gain access to the SUT's internal state for fixture
setup or result verification purposes. It may also consist of changes that the logic
of the system undergoes when it detects that it is being tested.

Impact

We would prefer not to end up with *Test Logic in Production*, as it can make
the SUT more complex and opens the door to additional kinds of bugs that
we would like to avoid. A system that behaves one way in the test lab and an
entirely different way in production is a recipe for disaster!

Causes

Cause: Test Hook

Conditional logic within the SUT determines whether the "real" code or test-
specific logic is run.

Symptoms

With this code smell, either there may be no behavioral symptoms or something
may go wrong in production. We may see snippets of code in the SUT that look
something like this:

```
if (testing) {
   return hardCodedCannedData;
} else { // the real logic ...
   return gatheredData;
}
```

Ariane

The maiden flight of the Ariane 5 rocket was a complete disaster: The rocket blew up only 37 seconds after takeoff. The culprit was a seemingly innocuous bit of code that was used only while the rocket was on the ground but unfortunately was left running for the first 40 seconds of flight. When it tried to assign a 64-bit number representing the sideways velocity of the rocket to a 16-bit field, the navigation computer decided that the rocket was going the wrong way! It tried to correct the course, but the sudden change in direction tore the booster rocket apart. While this is not quite an example of *Test Logic in Production* (page 217), it certainly does illustrate the risks associated with this type of error.

Could this disaster have been prevented by use of automated tests? While it is difficult to say with certainty, and one could certainly claim that any number of process changes could have detected this problem before it occurred, it is conceivable that automated tests could have averted this catastrophe.

In particular, a test should have addressed the boundary condition—namely, what happens when a number exceeds the maximum value storable. Such a test would have prevented an exception from occurring for the first time ever in production.

In addition, the presence of the tests from the Ariane 4 version of the rocket would have documented the maximum down-range velocity. It is quite possible that these tests would have been updated when the Ariane 5 software was being developed and that the new tests would have failed because of the new rocket's higher speed.

For a slightly more detailed (and very interesting) description of "the little bug that could," visit http://www.around.com/ariane.html.

Impact

Code that was not designed to work in production and that has not been verified to work properly in the production environment could accidentally be run in production and create serious problems.

The Ariane 5 rocket blew up 37 seconds after takeoff on its maiden flight because a piece of code that was used only while the rocket was on the ground was left running for the first 40 seconds of flight. This code tried to assign a 64-bit number representing the sideways velocity of the rocket to a 16-bit field—an operation that convinced the rocket's navigation computer that it was going the wrong way. (See the sidebar on Ariane on page 218 for more details.) While we believe the *Test Hook* would never be exercised in production, do we really want to take this kind of chance?

Root Cause

In some cases, the *Test Logic in Production* is introduced to make the behavior of the SUT more deterministic by returning known (hard-coded) values. In other cases, the *Test Logic in Production* may have been introduced to avoid executing code that cannot be run in a test environment. Unfortunately, this approach can result in failure to execute that code in the production environment if something is misconfigured.

In some cases, tests may require that the SUT execute additional code that would otherwise be executed by a depended-on component. For example, code run from a trigger in a database will not run if the database is replaced by a *Fake Database* (see *Fake Object* on page 551); thus the test needs to ensure that the equivalent logic is executed from somewhere within the SUT.

Possible Solution

Instead of adding test logic into the production code directly, we can move logic into a substitutable dependency. We can put code that should be run in only production into a Strategy [GOF] object that is installed by default and replaced by a Null Object [PLOPD3] when running our tests. In contrast, code that should be run only during tests can be put into a Strategy [GOF] object that is configured as a Null Object by default. Then, when we want the SUT to execute extra code during testing, we can replace this Strategy object with a test-specific version. To ensure this mechanism is configured properly, we should have a *Constructor Test* (see *Test Method* on page 348) to verify that any variables holding references to Strategy objects are initialized correctly when they are not overridden by the test.

It may also be possible to override specific methods of the SUT in a *Test-Specific Subclass* (page 579) if the production logic we want to circumvent is localized in overridable methods. This ability is enabled by Self-Calls [WWW].

Cause: For Tests Only

Code exists in the SUT strictly for use by tests.

Symptoms

Some of the methods of the SUT are used only by tests. Some of the attributes are public when they really should be private.

Test
Logic in
Production

Impact

Software that is added to the SUT *For Tests Only* makes the SUT more complex. It can confuse potential clients of the software's interface by introducing additional methods that should not be used by any code other than the tests. These methods may have been tested only in very specific circumstances, so they might not work in the typical usage patterns used by real client software.

Root Cause

The test automater may need to add methods to a class that expose information needed by the test or methods that provide greater control over initialization (such as for the installation of a *Test Double*; see page 522). Test-driven development will lead to the creation of these additional methods even though they aren't really needed by clients. When retrofitting tests onto legacy code, the test automater may need access to information or functionality that is not already exposed.

For Tests Only can also result when a SUT is used asymmetrically in real life. Automated tests (especially round-trip tests) typically use software in a more symmetric fashion and hence may need methods that the real software clients do not need.

Possible Solution

We can assure that tests have access to private information by creating a *Test-Specific Subclass* of the SUT, which then provides methods to expose the needed attributes or initialization logic. A test needs to be able to create instances of the subclass instead of the SUT class for this approach to work.

If for some reason the extra methods cannot be moved to a *Test-Specific Subclass*, they should be clearly labeled *For Tests Only*. This can be done by adopting a naming convention such as starting the names with "FTO_".

Cause: Test Dependency in Production

Production executables depend on test executables.

Symptoms

We cannot build only the production code; some test code must be included in the build to allow the production code to compile. Alternatively, we might notice that we cannot run the production code if the test executables are not present.

Impact

Even if the production modules do not contain any test code, problems can arise if any of these modules depends on a test module. At minimum, this dependency increases the size of the executable even if none of the test code is actually used in production scenarios. It also opens the door to accidental execution of test code during production.

Root Cause

Test Dependency in Production is usually caused by a lack of attention to inter-module dependencies. It may also arise when a **built-in self-test** requires access to parts of the test automation infrastructure, such as *Test Utility Methods* (page 599) or the *Test Automation Framework* (page 298), to report test results.

Possible Solution

We must manage our dependencies carefully to ensure that no production code depends on test code even for innocuous things such as type definitions.

Anything required by both test and production code should live in a production module or class that is accessible to both.

Cause: Equality Pollution

Another cause of *Test Logic in Production* is the implementation of **test-specific equality** in the equals method of the SUT.

Symptoms

Equality Pollution can be difficult to spot once it has occurred—what is notable is that the SUT doesn't actually need the equals method to be implemented. In other cases, behavioral symptoms may appear, such as test failure when the equals method is modified to support the specific needs of a test or when the definition of equals changes within the SUT as part of a new feature or user story.

Impact

We may write unnecessary equals methods simply to satisfy tests. We may also change the definition of equals so that it no longer satisfies the business requirements.

Equality Pollution may make it difficult to introduce the equals logic prescribed by some new requirement if it already exists to support test-specific equality for another test.

Test Logic in Production

Root Cause

Equality Pollution is caused by a lack of awareness of the concept of test-specific equality. Some early versions of dynamic *Mock Object* (page 544) generation tools forced us to use the SUT's definition of equals, which led to *Equality Pollution*.

Possible Solution

When a test requires test-specific equality, we should use a *Custom Assertion* (page 474) instead of modifying the equals method just so that we can use a built-in *Equality Assertion* (see *Assertion Method* on page 362).

When using dynamic *Mock Object* generation tools, we should use a Comparator [WWW] rather than relying on the equals method supplied by the SUT. We can also implement the equals method on a *Test-Specific Subclass* of an *Expected Object* (see *State Verification* on page 462) to avoid adding it to a production class directly.

Further Reading

For Tests Only and *Equality Pollution* were first introduced in a paper at XP2001 called "Refactoring Test Code" [RTC].

Chapter 16

Behavior Smells

Smells in This Chapter

Assertion Roulette

**It is hard to tell which of several assertions within the same
test method caused a test failure.**

Symptoms

A test fails. Upon examining the output of the *Test Runner* (page 377), we cannot
determine exactly which assertion failed.

Impact

When a test fails during an automated Integration Build [SCM], it may be hard
to tell exactly which assertion failed. If the problem cannot be reproduced on
a developer's machine (as may be the case if the problem is caused by environ-
mental issues or *Resource Optimism; see Erratic Test* on page 228) fixing the
problem may be difficult and time-consuming.

Causes

Cause: Eager Test

A single test verifies too much functionality.

Symptoms

A test exercises several methods of the SUT or calls the same method several
times interspersed with fixture setup logic and assertions.

```
public void testFlightMileage_asKm2() throws Exception {
    // set up fixture
    // exercise constructor
    Flight newFlight = new Flight(validFlightNumber);
    // verify constructed object
    assertEquals(validFlightNumber, newFlight.number);
    assertEquals("", newFlight.airlineCode);
    assertNull(newFlight.airline);
    // set up mileage
    newFlight.setMileage(1122);
    // exercise mileage translator
    int actualKilometres = newFlight.getMileageAsKm();
    // verify results
    int expectedKilometres = 1810;
    assertEquals( expectedKilometres, actualKilometres);
```

```
   // now try it with a canceled flight
   newFlight.cancel();
   try {
      newFlight.getMileageAsKm();
      fail("Expected exception");
   } catch (InvalidRequestException e) {
      assertEquals( "Cannot get cancelled flight mileage",
                    e.getMessage());
   }
}
```

Another possible symptom is that the test automater wants to modify the *Test Automation Framework* (page 298) to keep going after an assertion has failed so that the rest of the assertions can be executed.

Root Cause

An *Eager Test* is often caused by trying to minimize the number of unit tests (whether consciously or unconsciously) by verifying many test conditions in a single *Test Method* (page 348). While this is a good practice for manually executed tests that have "liveware" interpreting the results and adjusting the tests in real time, it just doesn't work very well for *Fully Automated Tests* (see page 26).

Another common cause of *Eager Tests* is using xUnit to automate customer tests that require many steps, thereby verifying many aspects of the SUT in each test. These tests are necessarily longer than unit tests but care should be taken to keep them as short as possible (but no shorter!).

Possible Solution

For unit tests, we break up the test into a suite of *Single-Condition Tests* (see page 45) by teasing apart the *Eager Test*. It may be possible to do so by using one or more Extract Method [Fowler] refactorings to pull out independent pieces into their own *Test Methods*. Sometimes it is easier to clone the test once for each test condition and then clean up each *Test Method* by removing any code that is not required for that particular test conditions. Any code required to set up the fixture or put the SUT into the correct starting state can be extracted into a *Creation Method* (page 415). A good IDE or compiler will then help us determine which variables are no longer being used.

If we are automating customer tests using xUnit, and this effort has resulted in many steps in each test because the work flows require complex fixture setup, we could consider using some other way to set up the fixture for the latter parts of the test. If we can use *Back Door Setup* (see *Back Door Manipulation* on page 327) to create the fixture for the last part of the test independently of the first part, we can break one test into two, thereby improving our *Defect Local-ization* (see *Goals of Test Automation*). We should repeat this process as many times as it takes to make the tests short enough to be readable at a single glance and to *Communicate Intent* (see page 41) clearly.

Cause: Missing Assertion Message

Symptoms

A test fails. Upon examining the output of the *Test Runner*, we cannot deter-mine exactly which assertion failed.

Root Cause

This problem is caused by the use of *Assertion Method* (page 362) calls with identical or missing *Assertion Messages* (page 370). It is most commonly encountered when running tests using a *Command-Line Test Runner* (see *Test Runner*) or a *Test Runner* that is not integrated with the program text editor or development environment.

In the following test, we have a number of *Equality Assertions* (see *Assertion Method*):

```
public void testInvoice_addLineItem7() {
    LineItem expItem = new LineItem(inv, product, QUANTITY);
    // Exercise
    inv.addItemQuantity(product, QUANTITY);
    // Verify
    List lineItems = inv.getLineItems();
    LineItem actual = (LineItem)lineItems.get(0);
    assertEquals(expItem.getInv(), actual.getInv());
    assertEquals(expItem.getProd(), actual.getProd());
    assertEquals(expItem.getQuantity(), actual.getQuantity());
}
```

When an assertion fails, will we know which one it was? An *Equality Assertion* typically prints out both the expected and the actual values—but it may prove difficult to tell which assertion failed if the expected values are similar or print out cryptically. A good rule of thumb is to include at least a minimal *Assertion Message* whenever we have more than one call to the same kind of *Assertion Method*.

Possible Solution

If the problem occurred while we were running a test using a *Graphical Test Runner* (see *Test Runner*) with IDE integration, we should be able to click on the appropriate line in the stack traceback to have the IDE highlight the failed assertion. Failing this, we can turn on the debugger and single-step through the test to see which assertion statement fails.

If the problem occurred while we were running a test using a *Command-Line Test Runner,* we can try running the test from a *Graphical Test Runner* with IDE integration to determine the offending assertion. If that doesn't work, we may have to resort to using line numbers (if available) or apply a process of elimination to deduce which of the assertions it couldn't be to narrow down the possibilities. Of course, we could just bite the bullet and add a unique *Assertion Message* (even just a number!) to each call to an *Assertion Method.*

**Assertion
Roulette**

Further Reading

Assertion Roulette and *Eager Test* were first described in a paper presented at XP2001 called "Refactoring Test Code" [RTC].

Erratic Test

Erratic Test

**One or more tests behave erratically; sometimes they pass
and sometimes they fail.**

Symptoms

We have one or more tests that run but give different results depending on when they are run and who is running them. In some cases, the *Erratic Test* will consistently give the same results when run by one developer but fail when run by someone else or in a different environment. In other cases, the *Erratic Test* will give different results when run from the same *Test Runner* (page 377).

Impact

We may be tempted to remove the failing test from the suite to "keep the bar green" but this would result in an (intentional) *Lost Test* (see *Production Bugs* on page 268). If we choose to keep the *Erratic Test* in the test suite despite the failures, the known failure may obscure other problems, such as another issue detected by the same tests. Just having a test fail can cause us to miss additional failures because it is much easier to see the change from a **green bar** to a **red bar** than to notice that two tests are failing instead of just the one we expected.

Troubleshooting Advice

Erratic Tests can be challenging to troubleshoot because so many potential causes exist. If the cause cannot be easily determined, it may be necessary to collect data systematically over a period of time. Where (in which environments) did the tests pass, and where did they fail? Were all the tests being run or just a subset of them? Did any change in behavior occur when the test suite was run several times in a row? Did any change in behavior occur when it was run from several *Test Runners* at the same time?

Once we have some data, it should be easier to match up the observed symptoms with those listed for each of the potential causes and to narrow the list of possibilities to a handful of candidates. Then we can collect some more data focusing on differences in symptoms between the possible causes. Figure 16.1 summarizes the process for determining which cause of an *Erratic Test* we are dealing with.

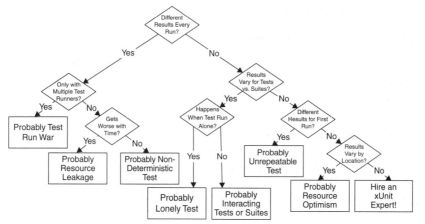

Figure 16.1 *Troubleshooting an Erratic Test.*

Causes

Tests may behave erratically for a number of reasons. The underlying cause can usually be determined through some persistent sleuthing by paying attention to patterns regarding how and when the tests fail. Some of the causes are common enough to warrant giving them names and specific advice for rectifying them.

Cause: Interacting Tests

Tests depend on other tests in some way. Note that *Interacting Test Suites* and *Lonely Test* are specific variations of *Interacting Tests*.

Symptoms

A test that works by itself suddenly fails in the following circumstances:

- Another test is added to (or removed from) the suite.

- Another test in the suite fails (or starts to pass).

- The test (or another test) is renamed or moved in the source file.

- A new version of the *Test Runner* is installed.

Root Cause

Interacting Tests usually arise when tests use a *Shared Fixture* (page 317), with one test depending in some way on the outcome of another test. The cause of *Interacting Tests* can be described from two perspectives:

- The *mechanism* of interaction

- The *reason* for interaction

The mechanism for interaction could be something blatantly obvious—for example, testing an SUT that includes a database—or it could be more subtle. Anything that outlives the lifetime of the test can lead to interactions; static variables can be depended on to cause *Interacting Tests* and, therefore, should be avoided in both the SUT and the *Test Automation Framework* (page 298)! See the sidebar "There's Always an Exception" on page 384 for an example of the latter problem. Singletons [GOF] and Registries [PEAA] are good examples of things to avoid in the SUT if at all possible. If we must use them, it is best to include a mechanism to reinitialize their static variables at the beginning of each test.

Tests may interact for a number of reasons, either by design or by accident:

- Depending on the fixture constructed by the fixture setup phase of another test

- Depending on the changes made to the SUT during the exercise SUT phase of another test

- A collision caused by some mutually exclusive action (which may be either of the problems mentioned above) between two tests run in the same test run

The dependencies may suddenly cease to be satisfied if the depended-on test

- Is removed from the suite,

- Is modified to no longer change the state of the SUT,

- Fails in its attempt to change the state of the SUT, or

- Is run after the test in question (because it was renamed or moved to a different *Testcase Class;* see page 373).

Similarly, collisions may start occurring when the colliding test is

- Added to the suite,

- Passes for the first time, or

- Runs before the dependent test.

In many of these cases, multiple tests will fail. Some of the tests may fail for a good reason—namely, the SUT is not doing what it is supposed to do. Dependent tests may fail for the wrong reason—because they were coded to depend on other tests' success. As a result, they may be giving a "false-positive" (false-failure) indication.

In general, depending on the order of test execution is not a wise approach because of the problems described above. Most variants of the xUnit framework do not make any guarantees about the order of test execution within a test suite. (**TestNG,** however, promotes interdependencies between tests by providing features to manage the dependencies.)

Possible Solution

Using a *Fresh Fixture* (page 311) is the preferred solution for *Interacting Tests*; it is almost guaranteed to solve the problem. If we must use a *Shared Fixture,* we should consider using an *Immutable Shared Fixture* (see *Shared Fixture*) to prevent the tests from interacting with one another through changes in the fixture by creating from scratch those parts of the fixture that they intend to modify.

If an unsatisfied dependency arises because another test does not create the expected objects or database data, we should consider using *Lazy Setup* (page 435) to create the objects or data in both tests. This approach ensures that the *first* test to execute creates the objects or data for *both* tests. We can put the fixture setup code into a *Creation Method* (page 415) to avoid *Test Code Duplication* (page 213). If the tests are on different *Testcase Classes,* we can move the fixture setup code to a *Test Helper* (page 643).

Sometimes the collision may be caused by objects or database data that are created in our test but not cleaned up afterward. In such a case, we should consider implementing *Automated Fixture Teardown* (see *Automated Teardown* on page 503) to remove them safely and efficiently.

A quick way to find out whether any tests depend on one another is to run the tests in a different order than the normal order. Running the entire test suite in reverse order, for example, would do the trick nicely. Doing so regularly would help avoid accidental introduction of *Interacting Tests*.

Cause: Interacting Test Suites

In this special case of *Interacting Tests,* the tests are in different test suites.

Symptoms

A test passes when it is run in its own test suite but fails when it is run within a *Suite of Suites* (see *Test Suite Object* on page 387).

```
Suite1.run()--> Green
Suite2.run()--> Green
Suite(Suite1,Suite2).run()--> Test C in Suite2 fails
```

Erratic Test

Root Cause

Interacting Test Suites usually occur when tests in separate test suites try to create the same resource. When they are run in the same suite, the first one succeeds but the second one fails while trying to create the resource.

The nature of the problem may be obvious just by looking at the test failure or by reading the failed *Test Method* (page 348). If it is not, we can try removing other tests from the (nonfailing) test suite, one by one. When the failure stops occurring, we simply examine the last test we removed for behaviors that might cause the interactions with the other (failing) test. In particular, we need to look at anything that might involve a *Shared Fixture,* including all places where class variables are initialized. These locations may be within the *Test Method* itself, within a setUp method, or in any *Test Utility Methods* (page 599) that are called.

Warning: There may be more than one pair of tests interacting in the same test suite! The interaction may also be caused by the *Suite Fixture Setup* (page 441) or *Setup Decorator* (page 447) of several *Testcase Classes* clashing rather than by a conflict between the actual *Test Methods!*

Variants of xUnit that use *Testcase Class Discovery* (see *Test Discovery* on page 393), such as NUnit, may appear to not use test suites. In reality, they do—they just don't expect the test automaters to use a *Test Suite Factory* (see *Test Enumeration* on page 399) to identify the *Test Suite Object* to the *Test Runner.*

Possible Solution

We could, of course, eliminate this problem entirely by using a *Fresh Fixture.* If this solution isn't within our scope, we could try using an *Immutable Shared Fixture* to prevent the tests' interaction.

If the problem is caused by leftover objects or database rows created by one test that conflict with the fixture being created by a later test, we should consider using *Automated Teardown* to eliminate the need to write error-prone cleanup code.

Cause: Lonely Test

A *Lonely Test* is a special case of *Interacting Tests.* In this case, a test can be run as part of a suite but cannot be run by itself because it depends on something in a *Shared Fixture* that was created by another test (e.g., *Chained Tests;* see page 454) or by suite-level fixture setup logic (e.g., a *Setup Decorator*).

We can address this problem by converting the test to use a *Fresh Fixture* or by adding *Lazy Setup* logic to the *Lonely Test* to allow it to run by itself.

Cause: Resource Leakage

Tests or the SUT consume finite resources.

Symptoms

Tests run more and more slowly or start to fail suddenly. Reinitializing the *Test Runner*, SUT, or *Database Sandbox* (page 650) clears up the problem—only to have it reappear over time.

Root Cause

Tests or the SUT consume finite resources by allocating those resources and failing to free them afterward. This practice may make the tests run more slowly. Over time, all the resources are used up and tests that depend on them start to fail.

This problem can be caused by one of two types of bugs:

- The SUT fails to clean up the resources properly. The sooner we detect this behavior, the sooner we can track it down and fix it.

- The tests themselves cause the resource leakage by allocating resources as part of fixture setup and failing to clean them up during fixture teardown.

Possible Solution

If the problem lies in the SUT, then the tests have done their job and we can fix the bug. If the tests are causing the *resource leakage*, then we must eliminate the source of the leaks. If the leaks are caused by failure to clean up properly when tests fail, we may need to ensure that all tests do *Guaranteed In-line Teardown* (see *In-line Teardown* on page 509) or convert them to use *Automated Teardown*.

In general, it is a good idea to set the size of all resource pools to 1. This choice will cause the tests to fail much sooner, allowing us to more quickly determine which tests are causing the leak(s).

Cause: Resource Optimism

A test that depends on external resources has nondeterministic results depending on when or where it is run.

Symptoms

A test passes when it is run in one environment and fails when it is run in another environment.

Root Cause

A resource that is available in one environment is not available in another environment.

Possible Solution

If possible, we should convert the test to use a *Fresh Fixture* by creating the resource as part of the test's fixture setup phase. This approach ensures that the resource exists wherever it is run. It may necessitate the use of relative addressing of files to ensure that the specific location in the file system exists regardless of where the SUT is executed.

If an external resource *must* be used, the resources should be stored in the source code repository [SCM] so that all *Test Runners* run in the same environment.

Cause: Unrepeatable Test

A test behaves differently the first time it is run compared with how it behaves on subsequent test runs. In effect, it is interacting with itself across test runs.

Symptoms

Either a test passes the first time it is run and fails on all subsequent runs, or it fails the first time and passes on all subsequent runs. Here's an example of what "Pass-Fail-Fail" might look like:

```
Suite.run()--> Green
Suite.run()--> Test C fails
Suite.run()--> Test C fails
User resets something
Suite.run()--> Green
Suite.run()--> Test C fails
```

Here's an example of what "Fail-Pass-Pass" might look like:

```
Suite.run()--> Test C fails
Suite.run()--> Green
Suite.run()--> Green
User resets something
Suite.run()--> Test C fails
Suite.run()--> Green
```

Be forewarned that if our test suite contains several *Unrepeatable Tests*, we may see results that look more like this:

```
Suite.run()--> Test C fails
Suite.run()--> Test X fails
Suite.run()--> Test X fails
```

```
User resets something
Suite.run()--> Test C fails
Suite.run()--> Test X fails
```

Test C exhibits the "Fail-Pass-Pass" behavior, while test X exhibits the "Pass-Fail-Fail" behavior at the same time. It is easy to miss this problem because we see a red bar in each case; we notice the difference only if we look closely to see which tests fail each time we run them.

Root Cause

The most common cause of an *Unrepeatable Test* is the use—either deliberate or accidental—of a *Shared Fixture*. A test may be modifying the test fixture such that, during a subsequent run of the test suite, the fixture is in a different state. Although this problem most commonly occurs with a *Prebuilt Fixture* (see *Shared Fixture*), the only true prerequisite is that the fixture outlasts the test run.

The use of a *Database Sandbox* may isolate our tests from other developers' tests but it won't prevent the tests we run from colliding with themselves or with other tests we run from the same *Test Runner*.

The use of *Lazy Setup* to initialize a **fixture holding class variable** can result in the test fixture not being reinitialized on subsequent runs of the same test suite. In effect, we are sharing the test fixture between all runs started from the same *Test Runner*.

Possible Solution

Because a persistent *Shared Fixture* is a prerequisite for an *Unrepeatable Test*, we can eliminate the problem by using a *Fresh Fixture* for each test. To fully isolate the tests, we must make sure that no shared resource, such as a *Database Sandbox,* outlasts the lifetimes of the individual tests. One option is to replace a database with a *Fake Database* (see *Fake Object* on page 551). If we must work with a persistent data store, we should use *Distinct Generated Values* (see *Generated Value* on page 723) for all database keys to ensure that we create different objects for each test and test run. The other alternative is to implement *Automated Teardown* to remove all newly created objects and rows safely and efficiently.

Cause: Test Run War

Test failures occur at random when several people are running tests simultaneously.

Erratic Test

Symptoms

We are running tests that depend on some shared external resource such as a database. From the perspective of a single person running tests, we might see something like this:

```
Suite.run() --> Test 3 fails
Suite.run() --> Test 2 fails
Suite.run() --> All tests pass
Suite.run() --> Test 1 fails
```

Upon describing our problem to our teammates, we discover that they are having the same problem at the same time. When only one of us runs tests, all of the tests pass.

Impact

A *Test Run War* can be very frustrating because the probability of it occurring increases the closer we get to a code cutoff deadline. This isn't just Murphy's law kicking in: It really does happen more often at this point! We tend to commit smaller changes at more frequent intervals as the deadline approaches (think "last-minute bug fixing"!). This, in turn, increases the likelihood that someone else will be running the test suite at the same time, which itself increases the likelihood of test collisions between test runs occurring at the same time.

Root Cause

A *Test Run War* can happen only when we have a globally *Shared Fixture* that various tests access and sometimes modify. This shared fixture could be a file that must be opened or read by either a test or the SUT, or it could consist of the records in a test database.

Database contention can be caused by the following activities:

- Trying to update or delete a record while another test is also updating the same record

- Trying to update or delete a record while another test has a read lock (pessimistic locking) on the same record

File contention can be caused by an attempt to access a file that has already been opened by another instance of the test running from a different *Test Runner*.

Possible Solution

Using a *Fresh Fixture* is the preferred solution for a *Test Run War*. An even simpler solution is to give each *Test Runner* his or her own *Database Sandbox*. This

Erratic Test

should *not* involve making any changes to the tests but will completely eliminate the possibility of a *Test Run War*. It will not, however, eliminate other sources of *Erratic Tests* because the tests can still interact through the *Shared Fixture* (the *Database Sandbox*). Another option is to switch to an *Immutable Shared Fixture* by having each test create new objects whenever it plans to change those objects. This approach *does* require changes to the *Test Methods*.

If the problem is caused by leftover objects or database rows created by one test that pollutes the fixture of a later test, another solution is using *Automated Teardown* to clean up after each test safely and efficiently. This measure, by itself, is unlikely to completely eliminate a *Test Run War* but it might reduce its frequency.

Cause: Nondeterministic Test

Test failures occur at random, even when only a single *Test Runner* is running tests.

Symptoms

We are running tests and the results vary each time we run them, as shown here:

```
Suite.run() --> Test 3 fails
Suite.run() --> Test 3 crashes
Suite.run() --> All tests pass
Suite.run() --> Test 3 fails
```

After comparing notes with our teammates, we rule out a *Test Run War* either because we are the only person running tests or because the test fixture is not shared between users or computers.

As with an *Unrepeatable Test*, having multiple *Nondeterministic Tests* in the same test suite can make it more difficult to detect the failure/error pattern: It looks like different tests are failing rather than a single test producing different results.

Impact

Debugging *Nondeterministic Tests* can be very time-consuming and frustrating because the code executes differently each time. Reproducing the failure can be problematic, and characterizing exactly what causes the failure may require many attempts. (Once the cause has been characterized, it is often a straightforward process to replace the random value with a value known to cause the problem.)

Root Cause

Nondeterministic Tests are caused by using different values each time a test is run. Sometimes, of course, it *is* a good idea to use different values each time the same test is run. For example, *Distinct Generated Values* may legitimately be used as unique keys for objects stored in a database. Use of generated values as input to an algorithm where the behavior of the SUT is expected to differ for different values can cause *Nondeterministic Tests*, however, as in the following examples:

- Integer values where negative (or even zero) values are treated differently by the system, or where there is a maximum allowable value. If we generate a value at random, the test could fail in some test runs and pass on others.

- String values where the length of a string has minimum or maximum allowed values. This problem often occurs accidentally when we generate a random or unique numeric value and then convert it to a string representation without using an explicit format that guarantees the length is constant.

It might seem like a good idea to use random values because they would improve our test coverage. Unfortunately, this tactic decreases our *understanding* of the test coverage and the repeatability of our tests (which violates the *Repeatable Test* principle; see page 26).

Another potential cause of *Nondeterministic Tests* is the use of *Conditional Test Logic* (page 200) in our tests. Its inclusion can result in different code paths being executed on different test runs, which in turn makes our tests nondeterministic. A common "reason" cited for doing so is the *Flexible Test* (see *Conditional Test Logic*). Anything that makes the tests less than completely deterministic is a bad idea!

Possible Solution

The first step is to make our tests repeatable by ensuring that they execute in a completely linear fashion by removing any *Conditional Test Logic*. Then we can go about replacing any random values with deterministic values. If this results in poor test coverage, we can add more tests for the interesting cases we aren't covering. A good way to determine the best set of input values is to use the **boundary values** of the **equivalence classes**. If their use results in a lot of *Test Code Duplication*, we can extract a *Parameterized Test* (page 607) or put the input values and the expected results into a file read by a *Data-Driven Test* (page 288).

Erratic Test

Fragile Test

A test fails to compile or run when the SUT is changed in ways that do not affect the part the test is exercising.

Symptoms

We have one or more tests that used to run and pass but now either fail to compile and run or fail when they are run. When we have changed the behavior of the SUT in question, such a change in test results is expected. When we don't think the change should have affected the tests that are failing or we haven't changed any production code or tests, we have a case of *Fragile Tests*.

Past efforts at automated testing have often run afoul of the "four sensitivities" of automated tests. These sensitivities are what cause *Fully Automated Tests* (see page 26) that previously passed to suddenly start failing. The root cause for tests failing can be loosely classified into one of these four sensitivities. Although each sensitivity may be caused by a variety of specific test coding behaviors, it is useful to understand the sensitivities in their own right.

Impact

Fragile Tests increase the cost of test maintenance by forcing us to visit many more tests each time we modify the functionality of the system or the fixture. They are particularly deadly when projects rely on highly incremental delivery, as in agile development (such as **eXtreme Programming**).

Troubleshooting Advice

We need to look for patterns in how the tests fail. We ask ourselves, "What do all of the broken tests have in common?" The answer to this question should help us understand how the tests are coupled to the SUT. Then we look for ways to minimize this coupling.

Figure 16.2 summarizes the process for determining which sensitivity we are dealing with.

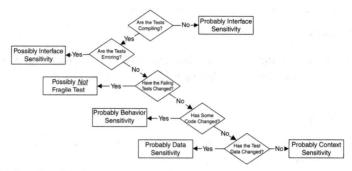

Fragile Test

Figure 16.2   *Troubleshooting a Fragile Test.*

The general sequence is to first ask ourselves whether the tests are failing to compile; if so, *Interface Sensitivity* is likely to blame. With dynamic languages we may see type incompatibility test errors at runtime—another sign of *Interface Sensitivity*.

   If the tests are running but the SUT is providing incorrect results, we must ask ourselves whether we have changed the code. If so, we can try backing out of the latest code changes to see if that fixes the problem. If that tactic stops the failing tests,[1] then we had *Behavior Sensitivity*.

   If the tests still fail with the latest code changes backed out, then something else must have changed and we must be dealing with either *Data Sensitivity* or *Context Sensitivity*. The former occurs only when we use a *Shared Fixture* (page 317) or we have modified fixture setup code; otherwise, we must have a case of *Context Sensitivity*.

   While this sequence of asking questions isn't foolproof, it will give the right answer probably nine times out of ten. *Caveat emptor!*

Causes

Fragile Tests may be the result of several different root causes. They may be a sign of *Indirect Testing* (see *Obscure Test* on page 186)—that is, using the objects we modified to access other objects—or they may be a sign that we have *Eager Tests* (see *Assertion Roulette* on page 224) that are verifying too much functionality. *Fragile Tests* may also be symptoms of overcoupled software that is hard to test in small pieces (*Hard-to-Test Code*; see page 209) or our lack of experience with unit testing using *Test Doubles* (page 522) to test pieces in isolation (*Overspecified Software*).

---

[1] Other tests may fail because we have removed the code that made them pass—but at least we have established which part of the code they depend on.

Regardless of their root cause, *Fragile Tests* usually show up as one of the four sensitivities. Let's start by looking at them in a bit more detail; we'll then examine some more detailed examples of how specific causes change test output.

Cause: Interface Sensitivity

Interface Sensitivity occurs when a test fails to compile or run because some part of the interface of the SUT that the test uses has changed.

Symptoms

In statically typed languages, *Interface Sensitivity* usually shows up as a failure to compile. In dynamically typed languages, it shows up only when we run the tests. A test written in a dynamically typed language may experience a test error when it invokes an **application programming interface (API)** that has been modified (via a method name change or method signature change). Alternatively, the test may fail to find a user interface element it needs to interact with the SUT via a user interface. *Recorded Tests* (page 278) that interact with the SUT through a user interface[2] are particularly prone to this problem.

Possible Solution

The cause of the failures is usually reasonably apparent. The point at which the test fails (to compile or execute) will usually point out the location of the problem. It is rare for the test to continue to run beyond the point of change—after all, it is the change itself that causes the test error.

When the interface is used only internally (within the organization or application) and by automated tests, *SUT API Encapsulation* (see *Test Utility Method* on page 599) is the best solution for *Interface Sensitivity*. It reduces the cost and impact of changes to the API and, therefore, does not discourage necessary changes from being made. A common way to implement *SUT API Encapsulation* is through the definition of a *Higher-Level Language* (see page 41) that is used to express the tests. The verbs in the test language are translated into the appropriate method calls by the encapsulation layer, which is then the only software that needs to be modified when the interface is altered in somewhat backward-compatible ways. The "test language" can be implemented in the form of *Test Utility Methods* such as *Creation Methods* (page 415) and *Verification Methods* (see *Custom Assertion* on page 474) that hide the API of the SUT from the test.

---

[2] Often called "screen scraping."

The only other way to avoid *Interface Sensitivity* is to put the interface under strict change control. When the clients of the interface are external and anonymous (such as the clients of Windows DLLs), this tactic may be the only viable alternative. In these cases, a protocol usually applies to making changes to interfaces. That is, all changes must be backward compatible; before older versions of methods can be removed, they must be deprecated, and deprecated methods must exist for a minimum number of releases or elapsed time.

Fragile Test

Cause: Behavior Sensitivity

Behavior Sensitivity occurs when changes to the SUT cause other tests to fail.

Symptoms

A test that once passed suddenly starts failing when a new feature is added to the SUT or a bug is fixed.

Root Cause

Tests may fail because the functionality they are verifying has been modified. This outcome does not necessarily signal a case of *Behavior Sensitivity* because it is the whole reason for having regression tests. It *is* a case of *Behavior Sensitivity* in any of the following circumstances:

- The functionality the regression tests use to set up the pre-test state of the SUT has been modified.

- The functionality the regression tests use to verify the post-test state of the SUT has been modified.

- The code the regression tests use to tear down the fixture has been changed.

If the code that changed is not part of the SUT we are verifying, then we are dealing with *Context Sensitivity*. That is, we may be testing too large a SUT. In such a case, what we really need to do is to separate the SUT into the part we are verifying and the components on which that part depends.

Possible Solution

Any newly incorrect assumptions about the behavior of the SUT used during fixture setup may be encapsulated behind *Creation Methods*. Similarly, assumptions about the details of post-test state of the SUT can be encapsulated in *Custom Assertions* or *Verification Methods*. While these measures won't eliminate the need to update test code when the assumptions change, they certainly do reduce the amount of test code that needs to be changed.

Cause: Data Sensitivity

Data Sensitivity occurs when a test fails because the data being used to test the SUT has been modified. This sensitivity most commonly arises when the contents of the test database change.

Symptoms

A test that once passed suddenly starts failing in any of the following circumstances:

- Data is added to the database that holds the pre-test state of the SUT.

- Records in the database are modified or deleted.

- The code that sets up a *Standard Fixture* (page 305) is modified.

- A *Shared Fixture* is modified before the first test that uses it.

In all of these cases, we must be using a *Standard Fixture,* which may be either a *Fresh Fixture* (page 311) or a *Shared Fixture* such as a *Prebuilt Fixture* (see *Shared Fixture*).

Root Cause

Tests may fail because the result verification logic in the test looks for data that no longer exists in the database or uses search criteria that accidentally include newly added records. Another potential cause of failure is that the SUT is being exercised with inputs that reference missing or modified data and, therefore, the SUT behaves differently.

In all cases, the tests make assumptions about which data exist in the database—and those assumptions are violated.

Possible Solution

In those cases where the failures occur during the exercise SUT phase of the test, we need to look at the pre-conditions of the logic we are exercising and make sure they have not been affected by recent changes to the database.

In most cases, the failures occur during result verification. We need to examine the result verification logic to ensure that it does not make any unreasonable assumptions about which data exists. If it does, we can modify the verification logic.

Fragile Test

Why Do We Need 100 Customers?

A software development coworker of mine was working on a project as an analyst. One day, the manager she was working for came into her office and asked, "Why have you requested 100 unique customers be created in the test database instance?"

As a systems analyst, my coworker was responsible for helping the business analysts define the requirements and the acceptance tests for a large, complex project. She wanted to automate the tests but had to overcome several hurdles. One of the biggest hurdles was the fact that the SUT got much of its data from an upstream system—it was too complex to try to generate this data manually.

The systems analyst came up with a way to generate XML from tests captured in spreadsheets. For the fixture setup part of the tests, she transformed the XML into QaRun (a *Record and Playback Test* tool—*see Recorded Test* on page 278) scripts that would load the data into the upstream system via the user interface. Because it took a while to run these scripts and for the data to make its way downstream to the SUT, the systems analyst had to run these scripts ahead of time. This meant that a *Fresh Fixture* (page 311) strategy was unachievable; a *Prebuilt Fixture* (page 429) was the best she could do. In an attempt to avoid the *Interacting Tests* (see *Erratic Test* on page 228) that were sure to result from a *Shared Fixture* (page 317), the systems analyst decided to implement a virtual *Database Sandbox* (page 650) using a *Database Partitioning Scheme* based on a unique customer number for each test. This way, any side effects of one test couldn't affect any other tests.

Given that she had about 100 tests to automate, the systems analyst needed about 100 test customers defined in the database. And that's what she told her manager.

The failure can show up in the result verification logic even if the problem is that the inputs of the SUT refer to nonexistent or modified data. This may require examining the "after" state of the SUT (which differs from the expected post-test state) and tracing it back to discover *why* it does not match our expectations. This should expose the mismatch between SUT inputs and the data that existed before the test started executing.

The best solution to *Data Sensitivity* is to make the tests independent of the existing contents of the database—that is, to use a *Fresh Fixture*. If this is not possible, we can try using some sort of *Database Partitioning Scheme* (see *Database Sandbox* on page 650) to ensure that the data modified for one test does not overlap with the data used by other tests. (See the sidebar "Why Do We Need 100 Customers?" on page 244 for an example.)

Another solution is to verify that the right changes have been made to the data. *Delta Assertions* (page 485) compare before and after "snapshots" of the data, thereby ignoring data that hasn't changed. They eliminate the need to hard-code knowledge about the entire fixture into the result verification phase of the test.

Fragile Test

Cause: Context Sensitivity

Context Sensitivity occurs when a test fails because the state or behavior of the context in which the SUT executes has changed in some way.

Symptoms

A test that once passed suddenly starts failing for mysterious reasons. Unlike with an *Erratic Test* (page 228), the test produces consistent results when run repeatedly over a short period of time. What is different is that it consistently fails regardless of how it is run.

Root Cause

Tests may fail for two reasons:

- The functionality they are verifying depends in some way on the time or date.

- The behavior of some other code or system(s) on which the SUT depends has changed.

A major source of *Context Sensitivity* is confusion about which SUT we are intending to verify. Recall that the SUT is whatever piece of software we are *intending* to verify. When unit testing, it should be a very small part of the overall system or application. Failure to isolate the specific unit (e.g., class or method) is bound to lead to *Context Sensitivity* because we end up testing too much software all at once. Indirect inputs that should be controlled by the test are then left to chance. If someone then modifies a depended-on component (DOC), our tests fail.

To eliminate *Context Sensitivity,* we must track down which indirect input to the SUT has changed and why. If the system contains any date- or time-related logic, we should examine this logic to see whether the length of the month or other similar factors could be the cause of the problem.

If the SUT depends on input from any other systems, we should examine these inputs to see if anything has changed recently. Logs of previous interactions with these other systems are very useful for comparison with logs of the failure scenarios.

If the problem comes and goes, we should look for patterns related to when it passes and when it fails. See *Erratic Test* for a more detailed discussion of possible causes of *Context Sensitivity*.

Fragile Test

Possible Solution

We need to control all the inputs of the SUT if our tests are to be deterministic. If we depend on inputs from other systems, we may need to control these inputs by using a *Test Stub* (page 529) that is configured and installed by the test. If the system contains any time- or date-specific logic, we need to be able to control the system clock as part of our testing. This may necessitate stubbing out the system clock with a *Virtual Clock* [VCTP] that gives the test a way to set the starting time or date and possibly to simulate the passage of time.

Also known as:
Overcoupled
Test

Cause: Overspecified Software

A test says too much about how the software should be structured or behave. This form of *Behavior Sensitivity* (see *Fragile Test* on page 239) is associated with the style of testing called *Behavior Verification* (page 468). It is characterized by extensive use of *Mock Objects* (page 544) to build layer-crossing tests. The main issue is that the tests describe *how* the software should do something, not *what* it should achieve. That is, the tests will pass only if the software is implemented in a particular way. This problem can be avoided by applying the principle *Use the Front Door First* (see page 40) whenever possible to avoid encoding too much knowledge about the implementation of the SUT into the tests.

Cause: Sensitive Equality

Objects to be verified are converted to strings and compared with an expected string. This is an example of *Behavior Sensitivity* in that the test is sensitive to behavior that it is not in the business of verifying. We could also think of it as a case of *Interface Sensitivity* where the *semantics* of the interface have changed. Either way, the problem arises from the way the test was coded; using the string representations of objects for verifying them against expected values is just asking for trouble.

Cause: Fragile Fixture

When a *Standard Fixture* is modified to accommodate a new test, several other tests fail. This is an alias for either *Data Sensitivity* or *Context Sensitivity* depending on the nature of the fixture in question.

Further Reading

Sensitive Equality and *Fragile Fixture* were first described in [RTC], which was the first paper published on test smells and refactoring test code. The four sensitivities were first described in [ARTRP], which also described several ways to avoid *Fragile Tests* in *Recorded Tests*.

Frequent Debugging

Manual debugging is required to determine the cause of most test failures.

Symptoms

A test run results in a test failure or a test error. The output of the *Test Runner* (page 377) is insufficient for us to determine the problem. Thus we have to use an interactive debugger (or sprinkle print statements throughout the code) to determine where things are going wrong.

If this case is an exception, we needn't worry about it. If most test failures require this kind of debugging, however, we have a case of *Frequent Debugging*.

Causes

Frequent Debugging is caused by a lack of *Defect Localization* (see page 22) in our suite of automated tests. The failed tests should tell us what went wrong either through their individual failure messages (see *Assertion Message* on page 370) or through the pattern of test failures. If they don't:

- We may be missing the detailed unit tests that would point out a logic error inside an individual class.

- We may be missing the component tests for a cluster of classes (i.e., a component) that would point out an integration error between the individual classes. This can happen when we use *Mock Objects* (page 544) extensively to replace depended-on objects but the unit tests of the depended-on objects don't match the way the *Mock Objects* are programmed to behave.

I've encountered this problem most frequently when I wrote higher-level (functional or component) tests but failed to write all the unit tests for the individual methods. (Some people would call this approach **storytest-driven development** to distinguish it from unit test-driven development, in which every little bit of code is pulled into existence by a failing unit test.)

Frequent Debugging can also be caused by *Infrequently Run Tests* (see *Production Bugs* on page 268). If we run our tests after every little change we make to the software, we can easily remember what we changed since the last time we ran the tests. Thus, when a test fails, we don't have to spend a lot of time troubleshooting the software to discover where the bug is—we know where it is because we remember putting it there!

Impact

Manual debugging is a slow, tedious process. It is easy to overlook subtle indications of a *bug* and spend many hours tracking down a single logic error. *Frequent Debugging* reduces productivity and makes development schedules much less predictable because a single manual debugging session could extend the time required to develop the software by half a day or more.

Solution Patterns

If we are missing the customer tests for a piece of functionality and manual user testing has revealed a problem not exposed by any automated tests, we probably have a case of *Untested Requirements* (see *Production Bugs*). We can ask ourselves, "What kind of automated test would have prevented the manual debugging session?" Better yet, once we have identified the problem, we can write a test that exposes it. Then we can use the failing test to do **test-driven bug fixing**. If we suspect this to be a widespread problem, we can create a development task to identify and write any additional tests that would be required to fill the gap we just exposed.

Doing true test-driven development is the best way to avoid the circumstances that lead to *Frequent Debugging*. We should start as close as possible to the skin of the application and do storytest-driven development—that is, we should write unit tests for individual classes as well as component tests for the collections of related classes to ensure we have good *Defect Localization*.

Manual Intervention

**A test requires a person to perform some manual action
each time it is run.**

Symptoms

The person running the test must do something manually either before the test
is run or partway through the test run; otherwise, the test fails. The *Test Runner*
may need to verify the results of the test manually.

Impact

Automated tests are all about getting early feedback on problems introduced
into the software. If the cost of getting that feedback is too high—that is, if it
takes the form of *Manual Intervention*—we likely won't run the tests very often
and we won't get the feedback very often. If we don't get that feedback very
often, we'll probably introduce lots of problems between test runs, which will
ultimately lead to *Frequent Debugging* (page 248) and *High Test Maintenance
Cost* (page 265).

   Manual Intervention also makes it impractical to have a fully automated
Integration Build [SCM] and regression test process.

Causes

The causes of *Manual Intervention* are as varied as the kinds of things our software does or encounters. The following are some general categories of the kinds
of issues that require *Manual Intervention*. This list is by no means exhaustive,
though.

Cause: Manual Fixture Setup

Symptoms

A person has to set up the test environment manually before the automated tests
can be run. This activity may take the form of configuring servers, starting server
processes, or running scripts to set up a *Prebuilt Fixture* (page 429).

Root Cause

This problem is typically caused by a lack of attention to automating the fixture
setup phase of the test. It may also be caused by excessive coupling between

components in the SUT that prevents us from testing a majority of the code in the system inside the development environment.

Possible Solution

We need to make sure that we are writing *Fully Automated Tests*. This may require opening up test-specific APIs to allow tests to set up the fixture. Where the issue is related to an inability to run the software in the development environment, we may need to refactor the software to decouple the SUT from the steps that would otherwise need to be done manually.

Cause: Manual Result Verification

Symptoms

We can run the tests but they almost always pass—even when we know that the SUT is not returning the correct results.

Root Cause

If the tests we write are not *Self-Checking Tests* (see page 26), we can be given a false sense of security because tests will fail only if an error/exception is thrown.

Possible Solution

We can ensure that our tests are all self-checking by including result verification logic such as calls to *Assertion Methods* (page 362) within the *Test Methods* (page 348).

Cause: Manual Event Injection

Symptoms

A person must intervene during test execution to perform some manual action before the test can proceed.

Root Cause

Many events in a SUT are hard to generate under program control. Examples include unplugging network cables, bringing down database connections, and clicking buttons on a user interface.

Impact

If a person needs to do something manually, it both increases the effort to run the test and ensures that the test cannot be run unattended. This torpedoes any attempt to do a fully automated build-and-test cycle.

Possible Solution

The best solution is to find ways to test the software that do not require a real person to do the manual actions. If the events are reported to the SUT through asynchronous events, we can have the *Test Method* invoke the SUT directly, passing it a simulated event object. If the SUT experiences the situation as a synchronous response from some other part of the system, we can get control of the indirect inputs by replacing some part of the SUT with a *Test Stub* (page 529) that simulates the circumstances to which we want to expose the SUT.

Further Reading

Refer to Chapter 11, *Using Test Doubles,* for a much more detailed description of how to get control of the indirect inputs of the SUT.

Manual Intervention

Slow Tests

The tests take too long to run.

Symptoms

The tests take long enough to run that developers don't run them every time they make a change to the SUT. Instead, the developers wait until the next coffee break or another interruption before running them. Or, whenever they run the tests, they walk around and chat with other team members (or play Doom or surf the Internet or . . .).

Impact

Slow Tests obviously have a direct cost: They reduce the productivity of the person running the test. When we are **test driving** the code, we'll waste precious seconds every time we run our tests; when it is time to run all the tests before we commit our changes, we'll have an even more significant wait time.

Slow Tests also have many indirect costs:

- The bottleneck created by holding the "integration token" longer because we need to wait for the tests to run after merging all our changes.

- The time during which other people are distracted by the person waiting for his or her test run to finish.

- The time spent in debuggers finding a problem that was inserted sometime after the last time we ran the test. The longer it has been since the test was run, the less likely we are to remember exactly what we did to break the test. This cost is a result of the breakdown of the rapid feedback that automated unit tests provide.

A common reaction to *Slow Tests* is to immediately go for a *Shared Fixture* (page 317). Unfortunately, this approach almost always results in other problems, including *Erratic Tests* (page 228). A better solution is to use a *Fake Object* (page 551) to replace slow components (such as the database) with faster ones. However, if all else fails and we must use some kind of *Shared Fixture*, we should make it immutable if at all possible.

Troubleshooting Advice

Slow Tests can be caused either by the way the SUT is built and tested or by the way the tests are designed. Sometimes the problem is obvious—we can just watch the green bar grow as we run the tests. There may be notable pauses in the execution; we may see explicit delays coded in a *Test Method* (page 348). If the cause is not obvious, however, we can run different subsets (or subsuites) of tests to see which ones run quickly and which ones take a long time to run.

A profiling tool can come in handy to see where we are spending the extra time in test execution. Of course, xUnit gives us a simple means to build our own mini-profiler: We can edit the setUp and tearDown methods of our *Testcase Superclass* (page 638). We then write out the start/end times or test duration into a log file, along with the name of the *Testcase Class* (page 373) and *Test Method*. Finally, we import this file into a spreadsheet, sort by duration, and voila—we have found the culprits. The tests with the longest execution times are the ones on which it will be most worthwhile to focus our efforts.

Causes

The specific cause of the *Slow Tests* could lie either in how we built the SUT or in how we coded the tests themselves. Sometimes, the way the SUT was built forces us to write our tests in a way that makes them slow. This is particularly a problem with legacy code or code that was built with a "test last" perspective.

Cause: Slow Component Usage

A component of the SUT has high latency.

Root Cause

The most common cause of Slow Tests is interacting with a database in many of the tests. Tests that have to write to a database to set up the fixture and read a database to verify the outcome (a form of *Back Door Manipulation*; see page 327) take about 50 times longer to run than the same tests that run against in-memory data structures. This is an example of the more general problem of using slow components.

Possible Solution

We can make our tests run much faster by replacing the slow components with a *Test Double* (page 522) that provides near-instantaneous responses. When the slow component is the database, the use of a *Fake Database* (see *Fake Object*) can make the tests run on average 50 times faster! See the sidebar "Faster Tests Without Shared Fixtures" on page 319 for other ways to skin this cat.

Cause: General Fixture

Symptoms

Tests are consistently slow because each test builds the same over-engineered fixture.

Root Cause

Each test constructs a large *General Fixture* each time a *Fresh Fixture* (page 311) is built. Because a *General Fixture* contains many more objects than a *Minimal Fixture* (page 302), it naturally takes longer to construct. *Fresh Fixture* involves setting up a brand-new instance of the fixture for each *Testcase Object* (page 382), so multiply "longer" by the number of tests to get an idea of the magnitude of the slowdown!

Possible Solution

Our first inclination is often to implement the *General Fixture* as a *Shared Fixture* to avoid rebuilding it for each test. Unless we can make this *Shared Fixture* immutable, however, this approach is likely to lead to *Erratic Tests* and should be avoided. A better solution is to reduce the amount of fixture setup performed by each test.

Cause: Asynchronous Test

Symptoms

A few tests take inordinately long to run; those tests contain explicit delays.

Root Cause

Delays included within a *Test Method* slow down test execution considerably. This slow execution may be necessary when the software we are testing spawns threads or processes (*Asynchronous Code; see Hard-to-Test Code* on page 209) and the test needs to wait for them to launch, run, and verify whatever side effects they were expected to have. Because of the variability in how long it takes for these threads or processes to be started, the test usually needs to include a long delay "just in case"—that is, to ensure it passes consistently. Here's an example of a test with delays:

```
public class RequestHandlerThreadTest extends TestCase {
    private static final int TWO_SECONDS = 3000;

    public void testWasInitialized_Async() = throws InterruptedException {
        // Setup
        RequestHandlerThread sut = new RequestHandlerThread();
        // Exercise
        sut.start();
        //    Verify
        Thread.sleep(TWO_SECONDS);
        assertTrue(sut.initializedSuccessfully());
    }

    public void testHandleOneRequest_Async()
            throws InterruptedException {
        // Setup
        RequestHandlerThread sut = new RequestHandlerThread();
        sut.start();
        // Exercise
        enqueRequest(makeSimpleRequest());
        // Verify
        Thread.sleep(TWO_SECONDS);
        assertEquals(1, sut.getNumberOfRequestsCompleted());
        assertResponseEquals(makeSimpleResponse(), getResponse());
    }
}
```

Impact

A two-second delay might not seem like a big deal. But consider what happens when we have a dozen such tests: It would take almost half a minute to run these tests. In contrast, we can run several hundred normal tests each second.

Possible Solution

The best way to address this problem is to avoid asynchronicity in tests by testing the logic synchronously. This may require us to do an Extract Testable Component (page 767) refactoring to implement a *Humble Executable* (see *Humble Object* on page 695).

Cause: Too Many Tests

Symptoms

There are so many tests that they are bound to take a long time to run regardless of how fast they execute.

Root Cause

The obvious cause of this problem is having so many tests. Perhaps we have such a large system that the large number of tests really is necessary, or perhaps we have too much overlap between tests.

The less obvious cause is that we are running too many of the tests too frequently!

Possible Solution

We don't have to run *all the tests all the time!* The key is to ensure that all tests are run regularly. If the entire suite is taking too long to run, consider creating a *Subset Suite* (see *Named Test Suite* on page 592) with a suitable cross section of tests; run this subsuite before every commit operation. The rest of the tests can be run regularly, albeit less often, by scheduling them to run overnight or at some other convenient time. Some people call this technique a "build pipeline." For more on this and other ideas, see the sidebar "Faster Tests Without Shared Fixtures" on page 319.

If the system is large in size, it is a good idea to break it into a number of fairly independent subsystems or components. This allows teams working on each component to work independently and to run only those tests specific to their own component. Some of those tests should act as proxies for how the other components would use the component; they must be kept up-to-date if the interface contract changes. Hmmm, *Tests as Documentation* (see page 23); I like it! Some end-to-end tests that exercise all the components together (likely a form of storytests) would be essential, but they don't need to be included in the pre-commit suite.

Chapter 17

Project Smells

Smells in This Chapter

Buggy Tests

Buggy Tests

Bugs are regularly found in the automated tests.

Fully Automated Tests (see page 26) are supposed to act as a "safety net" for teams doing iterative development. But how can we be sure the safety net actually works?

   Buggy Tests is a project-level indication that all is not well with our automated tests.

Symptoms

A build fails, and a failed test is to blame. Upon closer inspection, we discover that the code being testing works correctly, but the test indicated it was broken.

   We encountered *Production Bugs* (page 268) despite having tests that verify the specific scenario in which the bug was found. Root-cause analysis indicates the test contains a bug that precluded catching the error in the production code.

Impact

Tests that give misleading results are dangerous! Tests that pass when they shouldn't (a **false negative,** as in "nothing wrong here") give a false sense of security. Tests that fail when they shouldn't (a **false positive**) discredit the tests. They are like the little boy who cried, "Wolf!"; after a few occurrences, we tend to ignore them.

Causes

Buggy Tests can have many causes. Most of these problems also show up as code or behavior smells. As project managers, we are unlikely to see these underlying smells until we specifically look for them.

Cause: Fragile Test

Buggy Tests may just be project-level symptoms of a *Fragile Test* (page 239). For false-positive test failures, a good place to start is the "four sensitivities": *Interface Sensitivity* (see *Fragile Test*), *Behavior Sensitivity* (see *Fragile Test*), *Data Sensitivity* (see *Fragile Test*), and *Context Sensitivity* (see *Fragile Test*). Each of these sensitivities *could* be the change that caused the test to fail. Removing the sensitivities by using *Test Doubles* (page 522) and refactoring can be challenging but ultimately it will make the tests much more dependable and cost-effective.

Cause: Obscure Test

A common cause of false-negative test results (tests that pass when they shouldn't) is an *Obscure Test* (page 186), which is difficult to get right—especially when we are modifying existing tests that were broken by a change we made. Because automated tests are hard to test, we don't often verify that a modified test still catches all the bugs it was initially designed to trap. As long as we see a green bar, we think we are "good to go." In reality, we may have created a test that never fails.

Obscure Tests are best addressed through refactoring of tests to focus on the reader of the tests. The real goal is *Tests as Documentation* (see page 23)—anything less will increase the likelihood of *Buggy Tests*.

Cause: Hard-to-Test Code

Another common cause of *Buggy Tests*, especially with "legacy software" (i.e., any software that doesn't have a complete suite of automated tests), is that the design of the software is not conducive to automated testing. This *Hard-to-Test Code* (page 209) may force us to use *Indirect Testing* (see *Obscure Test*), which in turn may result in a *Fragile Test*.

The only way *Hard-to-Test Code* will become easy to test is if we refactor the code to improve its testability. (This transformation is described in Chapter 6, *Test Automation Strategy,* and Chapter 11, *Using Test Doubles.*) If this is not an option, we may be able to reduce the amount of test code affected by a change by applying *SUT API Encapsulation* (see *Test Utility Method* on page 599).

Troubleshooting Advice

When we have *Buggy Tests,* it is important to ask lots of questions. We must ask the "five why's" [TPS] to get to the bottom of the problem—that is, we must determine exactly which code and/or behavior smells are causing the *Buggy Tests* and find the root cause of each smell.

Solution Patterns

The solution depends very much on why the *Buggy Tests* occurred. Refer to the underlying behavior and code smells for possible solutions.

As with all "project smells," we should look for project-level causes. These include not giving developers enough time to perform the following activities:

- Learn to write the tests properly

- Refactor the legacy code to make test automation easier and more robust

- Write the tests first

Failure to address these project-level causes guarantees that the problems will recur in the near future.

Buggy Tests

Developers Not Writing Tests

Developers aren't writing automated tests.

Symptoms

We hear that our developers aren't writing tests. Or maybe we have observed *Production Bugs* (page 268) and asked, "Why are so many bugs getting through?", only to be told, "Because we aren't writing tests to cover that part of the software."

Impact

If the team isn't writing automated tests for every piece of software "that could possibly break," it is mortgaging its future. The current pace of software development will not be sustainable over the long haul because the system will be in **test debt**. It will take longer and longer to add new functionality, and refactoring the code to improve its design will be fraught with peril (so it will happen less and less frequently). This problem marks the beginning of a trip down the proverbial "slippery slope" to traditional paranoid, non-agile development. If that is where we aspire to be, we should stay the course. Otherwise, it is time to take action.

Causes

Cause: Not Enough Time

Developers may have trouble writing tests in the time they are given to do the development. This problem could be caused by an overly aggressive development schedule or supervisors/team leaders who instruct developers, "Don't waste time writing tests." Alternatively, developers may not have the skills needed to write tests efficiently and may not be allocated the time required to work their way up the learning curve.

If time is what the developers need, managers need to adjust the project schedule to give them that time. This extension need be only a temporary adjustment while the developers learn the skills and test automation infrastructure that will enable them to write the tests more quickly. In my experience, once developers have internalized the process, they can write the tests and the code in the same amount of time it once took them to write and debug just the code. The time spent writing the tests is more than compensated for by the time not spent in the debugger.

Cause: Hard-to-Test Code

A common cause of *Developers Not Writing Tests*, especially with "legacy software" (i.e., any software that doesn't have a complete suite of automated tests), is that the design of the software is not conducive to automated testing. This situation is described in more detail in its own smell, *Hard-to-Test Code* (page 209).

Cause: Wrong Test Automation Strategy

Another cause of *Developers Not Writing Tests* may be a test environment or test automation strategy that leads to *Fragile Tests* (page 239) or *Obscure Tests* (page 186) that take too long to write. We need to ask the "five why's" [TPS] to find the root causes. Then we can address those causes and get the ship back on course.

Troubleshooting Advice

Project-level smells such as *Developers Not Writing Tests* are more likely to be detected by a project manager, scrum master, or team leader than by a developer. As managers, we may not know how to fix the problem, but our awareness and recognition of it is what matters. This unique perspective allows managers to ask the development team questions about why they aren't writing tests, in which circumstances, and how long it takes to write tests when they do so. Then managers can encourage and empower the developers to come up with ways of addressing the root causes so that they write all the necessary tests.

Of course, managers must give the developers their full support in carrying out whatever improvement plan they come up with. That support must include enough time to learn the requisite skills and build or set up the necessary test infrastructure. And managers shouldn't expect things to turn around overnight. They might set a process improvement goal for each iteration, such as "20% reduction in code not tested" or "20% improvement in code coverage." These goals should be reasonable and at a high-enough level that they encourage the right behavior, as opposed to just making the numbers look good. (A goal of 205 more tests written, for example, could be achieved without increasing the test coverage one iota simply by splitting tests into smaller pieces or cloning tests.)

High Test Maintenance Cost

Too much effort is spent maintaining existing tests.

Test code needs to be maintained along with the production code it verifies. As an application evolves, we will likely have to revisit our tests on a regular basis whenever we change the SUT classes to add new functionality or whenever we refactor the tests to simplify those classes. *High Test Maintenance Cost* occurs when the tests become overly difficult to understand and maintain.

Symptoms

Development of new functionality slows down. Every time we add some new functionality, we need to make extensive changes to the existing tests. Developers or test automaters may tell the project manager or coach that they need a "test refactoring/cleanup iteration."

If we have been tracking the amount of time we spend writing the new tests and modifying existing tests separately from the time we spend implementing the code to make the tests pass, we notice that most of the time is spent modifying the existing tests.

Most test maintainability issues are accompanied by other smells, such as the following:

- A *Fragile Test* (page 239) indicates that tests are too closely coupled to the SUT.

- A *Fragile Fixture* (see *Fragile Test*) signals that too many tests depend on the same fixture design (*Standard Fixture* on page 305), which leads to *High Test Maintenance Cost*.

- An *Erratic Test* (page 228) may be a sign that a *Shared Fixture* (page 317) is causing our problem.

Impact

Team productivity drops significantly because the tests take so much effort to maintain. Developers may be agitating to "cut and run" (remove the affected tests from the test suites). While writing the production code is mandatory, maintaining the tests is completely optional (at least to the uninformed). If nothing is done about this problem, the entire test automation effort may be wasted when the team or management decides that test automation just "doesn't work" and abandons the tests.

Causes

The root cause of *High Test Maintenance Cost* is failing to pay attention to the principles described in Chapter 5, *Principles of Test Automation*. A more immediate cause is often too much *Test Code Duplication* (page 213) and tests that are too closely coupled to the API of the SUT.

Cause: Fragile Test

Tests that fail because minor changes were made to the SUT are called *Fragile Tests*. They result in *High Test Maintenance Cost* because they need to be revisited and "giggled" after all manner of minor changes that really shouldn't affect them.

The root cause of this failure can be any of the "four sensitivities": *Interface Sensitivity* (see *Fragile Test*), *Behavior Sensitivity* (see *Fragile Test*), *Data Sensitivity* (see *Fragile Test*), and *Context Sensitivity* (see *Fragile Test*). We can reduce the *High Test Maintenance Cost* by protecting the tests against as many of these sensitivities as possible through the use of *Test Doubles* (page 522) and by refactoring the system into smaller components and classes that can be tested individually.

Cause: Obscure Test

Obscure Tests (page 186) are a major contributor to *High Test Maintenance Cost* because they take longer to understand each time they are visited. When they need to be modified, they take more effort to adjust and are much less likely to "work the first time," resulting in more debugging of tests. *Obscure Tests* are also more likely to end up not catching conditions they were intended to detect, which can lead to *Buggy Tests* (page 260).

Obscure Tests are best addressed by refactoring tests to focus on the reader of the tests. The real goal is *Tests as Documentation* (see page 23)—anything less will increase the likelihood of *High Test Maintenance Cost*.

Cause: Hard-to-Test Code

"Legacy software" (i.e., any software that doesn't have a complete suite of automated tests) can be hard to test because we typically write the tests "last" (after the software already exists). If the design of the software is not conducive to automated testing, we may be forced to use *Indirect Testing* (see *Obscure Test*) via awkward interfaces that involve a lot of accidental complexity; that effort may result in *Fragile Tests*.

It will take both time and effort to refactor the code to improve its testability. Nevertheless, that time and effort are well spent if they eliminate the *High Test Maintenance Cost*. If refactoring is not an option, we may be able to reduce the amount of test code affected by a change by doing *SUT API Encapsulation* (see *Test Utility Method* on page 599) using *Test Utility Methods*. For example, *Creation Methods* (page 415) encapsulate the constructors, thereby rendering the tests less susceptible to changes in constructor signatures or semantics.

Troubleshooting Advice

High Test
Maintenance
Cost

As a project-level smell, *High Test Maintenance Cost* is as likely to be detected by a project manager, scrum master, or team leader as by a developer. While managers may not have the technical depth needed to troubleshoot and fix the problem, the fact that they become aware of it is what is important. This awareness allows the manager to question the development team about how long it is taking to maintain tests, how often test maintenance occurs, and why it is necessary. Then the manager can challenge the developers to find a better way—one that won't result in such *High Test Maintenance Costs*!

Of course, the developers will need the manager's support to carry out whatever improvement plan they come up with. That support must include time to conduct the investigations (**spikes**), learning/training time, and time to do the actual work. Managers can make time for this activity by having "test refactoring stories," adjusting the velocity to reduce the new functionality committed to the customer, or other means. Regardless of how managers carve out this time, they must remember that if they don't give the development team the resources needed to fix the problem now, the problem will simply get worse and become even more challenging to fix in the future when the team has twice as many tests.

Production Bugs

We find too many bugs during formal tests or in production.

Symptoms

We have put a lot of effort into writing automated tests, yet the number of bugs showing up in formal (i.e., system) testing or production remains too high.

Impact

It takes longer to troubleshoot and fix bugs found in formal testing than those found in development, and even longer to troubleshoot and fix bugs found in production. We may be forced to delay shipping the product or putting the application into production to allow time for the bug fixes and retesting. This time and effort translate directly into monetary costs and consume resources that might otherwise be used to add more functionality to the product or to build other products. The delay may also damage the organization's credibility in the eyes of its customers. Poor quality has an indirect cost as well, in that it lowers the value of the product or service we are supplying.

Causes

Bugs may slip through to production for several reasons, including *Infrequently Run Tests* or *Untested Code*. The latter problem may result from *Missing Unit Tests* or *Lost Tests*.

By specifying that "enough tests" be run, we mean the test coverage should be adequate, rather than that some specific number of tests must be carried out. Changes to *Untested Code* are more likely to result in *Production Bugs* because there are no automated tests to tell the developers when they have introduced problems. *Untested Requirements* aren't being verified every time the tests are run, so we don't know for sure what is working. Both of these problems are related to *Developers Not Writing Tests* (page 263).

Cause: Infrequently Run Tests

Symptoms

We hear that our developers aren't running the tests very often. When we ask some questions, we discover that running the tests takes too long (*Slow Tests;* see page 253) or produces too many extraneous failures (*Buggy Tests;* see page 260).

We see test failures in the daily Integration Build [SCM]. When we dig deeper, we find that developers often commit their code without running the tests on their own machines.

Root Cause

Once they've seen the benefits of working with the safety net of automated tests, most developers will continue using these tests unless something gets in the way. The most common impediments are *Slow Tests* that slow down the pre-integration regression testing or *Unrepeatable Tests* (see *Erratic Test* on page 228) that force developers to restart their test environment or do *Manual Intervention* (page 250) before running the tests.

Possible Solution

If the root cause is *Unrepeatable Tests*, we can try switching to a *Fresh Fixture* (page 311) strategy to make the tests more deterministic. If the cause is *Slow Tests*, we must put more effort into speeding up the test run.

Cause: Lost Test

Symptoms

The number of tests being executed in a test suite has declined (or has not increased as much as expected). We may notice this directly if we are paying attention to test counts. Alternatively, we may find a bug that should have been caused by a test that we know exists but, upon poking around, we discover that the test has been disabled.

Root Cause

Lost Tests can be caused by either a *Test Method* (page 348) or a *Testcase Class* (page 373) that has been disabled or has never been added to the *AllTests Suite* (see *Named Test Suite* on page 592).

Tests can be accidentally left out (i.e., never run) of test suite in the following circumstances:

- We forget to add the [test] attribute to the *Test Method*, or we accidentally use a method name that doesn't match the naming convention used by the *Test Discovery* (page 393) mechanism.

- We forget to add a call to `suite.addTest` to add the *Test Method* to the *Test Suite Object* (page 387) when we are automating tests in a *Test Automation Framework* (page 298) that supports only *Test Enumeration* (page 399).

- We forget to add a call to the *Test Method* explicitly in the *Test Suite Procedure* (see *Test Suite Object*) in procedural-language variations of xUnit.

- We forget to add the test suite to the *Suite of Suites* (see *Test Suite Object*) or forget to add the [Test Fixture] attribute to the *Testcase Class*.

Tests that ran in the past may have been disabled in any of the following ways:

Production Bugs

- We renamed the *Test Method* to not match the pattern that causes *Test Discovery* to include the test in the test suite (e.g., the method name starts with "test . . .").

- We added an [Ignore] attribute in variants of xUnit that use method attributes to indicate *Test Methods*.

- We commented out (or deleted) the code that adds the test (or suite) to the suite explicitly.

Typically, a *Lost Test* occurs when a test is failing and someone disables it to avoid having to wade through the failing tests when running other tests. It may also occur accidentally, of course.

Possible Solution

There are a number of ways to avoid introducing *Lost Tests*.

We can use a *Single Test Suite* (see *Named Test Suite*) to run a single *Test Method* instead of disabling the failing or slow test. We can use the *Test Tree Explorer* (see *Test Runner* on page 377) to drill down and run a single test from within a test suite. Both of these techniques are made difficult by *Chained Tests* (page 454)—a deliberate form of *Interacting Tests* (see *Erratic Test*)—so this is just one more reason to avoid them.

If our variant of xUnit supports it, we can use the provided mechanism to ignore[1] a test. It will typically remind us of the number of tests not being run so we don't forget to re-enable them. We can also configure our **continuous integration** tool to fail the build if the number of tests "ignored" exceeds a certain threshold.

We can compare the number of tests we have after check-in with the number of tests that existed in the code branch immediately before we started integration. We simply verify that this count has increased by the number of tests we have added.

---

[1] For example, NUnit lets us put the attribute [Ignore] on a *Test Method* to keep it from being run.

We can implement or take advantage of *Test Discovery* if our programming language supports reflection.

We can use a different strategy for finding the tests to run in the Integration Build. Some build tools (such as Ant) let us find all files that match a name pattern (e.g., those ending in "Test"). We won't lose entire test suites if we use this capability to pick up all the tests.

Cause: Missing Unit Test

Symptoms

All the unit tests pass but a customer test continues to fail. At some point, the customer test passed—but no unit tests were written to verify the behavior of the individual classes. Then, a subsequent code change modified the behavior of one of the classes, which broke its functionality.

Root Cause

Missing Unit Tests often happen when a team focuses on writing the customer tests but fails to do test-driven development using unit tests. The team members may have built enough functionality to pass the customer tests, but a subsequent refactoring broke it. Unit tests would likely have prevented the code change from reaching the Integration Build.

Missing Unit Tests can also arise during test-driven development when developers get ahead of themselves and write some code without having a failing test to guide them.

Possible Solution

The trite answer is to write more unit tests. Of course, this is easier said than done, and it isn't always effective. Doing true test-driven development is the best way to avoid having *Missing Unit Tests* without writing unnecessary tests merely to get the test count up.

Cause: Untested Code

Symptoms

We may just "know" that some piece of code in the SUT is not being exercised by any tests. Perhaps we have never seen that code execute, or perhaps we used code coverage tools to prove this fact beyond a doubt. In the following example, how can we test that when timeProvider throws an exception, this exception is handled correctly?

```
public String getCurrentTimeAsHtmlFragment()
    throws TimeProviderEx {
  Calendar currentTime;
  try {
     currentTime = getTimeProvider().getTime();
  } catch (Exception e) {
     return e.getMessage();
  }
  // etc.
```

**Production
Bugs**

Root Cause

The most common cause of *Untested Code* is that the SUT includes code paths
that react to particular ways that a depended-on component (DOC) behaves
and we haven't found a way to exercise those paths. Typically, the DOC is
being called synchronously and either returns certain values or throws exceptions. During normal testing, only a subset of the possible **equivalence classes**
of indirect inputs are actually encountered.

Another common cause of *Untested Code* is incompleteness of the test suite
caused by incomplete characterization of the functionality exposed via the
SUT's interface.

Possible Solution

If the *Untested Code* is caused by an inability to control the indirect inputs of
the SUT, the most common solution is to use a *Test Stub* (page 529) to feed the
various kinds of indirect inputs into the SUT to cover all the code paths. Otherwise, it may be sufficient to configure the DOC to cause it to return the various
indirect inputs required to fully test the SUT.

Cause: Untested Requirement

Symptoms

We may just "know" that some piece of functionality is not being tested. Alternatively, we may be trying to test a piece of software but cannot see any visible
functionality that can be tested via the public interface of the software. All the
tests we have written pass, however.

When doing test-driven development, we know we need to add some
code to handle a requirement. However, we cannot find a way to express the
need for code to log the action in a *Fully Automated Test* (see page 26) such
as this:

```
public void testRemoveFlight() throws Exception {
    // set up
    FlightDto expectedFlightDto = createARegisteredFlight();
    FlightManagementFacade facade =
            new FlightManagementFacadeImpl();
    // exercise
    facade.removeFlight(expectedFlightDto.getFlightNumber());
    // verify
    assertFalse("flight should not exist after being removed",
                facade.flightExists( expectedFlightDto.
                                        getFlightNumber()));
}
```

Note that this test does not verify that the correct logging action has been done. It will pass regardless of whether the logging was implemented correctly—or even at all. Here's the code that this test is verifying, complete with the indirect output of the SUT that has not been implemented correctly:

```
public void removeFlight(BigDecimal flightNumber)
        throws FlightBookingException {
    System.out.println("        removeFlight("+flightNumber+")");
    dataAccess.removeFlight(flightNumber);
    logMessage("CreateFlight", flightNumber); // Bug!
}
```

If we plan to depend on the information captured by logMessage when maintaining the application in production, how can we ensure that it is correct? Clearly, it is desirable to have automated tests verify this functionality.

Impact

Part of the required behavior of the SUT could be accidentally disabled without causing any tests to fail. Buggy software could be delivered to the customer. The fear of introducing bugs could discourage ruthless refactoring or deletion of code suspected to be unneeded (i.e., dead code).

Root Cause

The most common cause of *Untested Requirements* is that the SUT includes behavior that is not visible through its public interface. It may have expected "side effects" that cannot be observed directly by the test (such as writing out a file or record or calling a method on another object or component)—in other words, it may have indirect outputs.

When the SUT is an entire application, the *Untested Requirement* may be a result of not having a full suite of customer tests that verify all aspects of the visible behavior of the SUT.

Possible Solution

If the problem is missing customer tests, we need to write at least enough customer tests to ensure that all components are integrated properly. This may
require improving the design-for-testability of the application by separating the
presentation layer from the business logic layer.

When we have indirect outputs that we need to verify, we can do *Behavior
Verification* (page 468) through the use of *Mock Objects* (page 544). Testing of
indirect outputs is covered in Chapter 11, *Using Test Doubles*.

**Production
Bugs**

Cause: Neverfail Test

Symptoms

We may just "know" that some piece of functionality is not working, even
though the tests for that functionality pass. When doing test-driven development, we have added a test for functionality we have not yet written but we
cannot get the test to fail.

Impact

If a test won't fail even when the code to implement the functionality doesn't
exist, how useful is it for *Defect Localization* (see page 22)? Not very!

Root Cause

This problem can be caused by improperly coded assertions such as `assertTrue-
(aVariable, true)` instead of `assertEquals(aVariable, true)` or just `assertTrue(aVariable)`.
Another cause is more sinister: When we have asynchronous tests, failures thrown
in the other thread or process may not be seen or reported by the *Test Runner*.

Possible Solution

We can implement cross-thread failure detection mechanisms to ensure that
asynchronous tests do, indeed, fail. An even better solution is to refactor the
code to support a *Humble Executable* (see *Humble Object* on page 695).

PART III

The Patterns

Chapter 18

Test Strategy Patterns

Patterns in This Chapter

**Recorded
Test**

Recorded Test

How do we prepare automated tests for our software?

**We automate tests by recording interactions with the application and
playing them back using a test tool.**

Also known as:
*Record and
Playback Test,
Robot User
Test, Capture/
Playback Test*

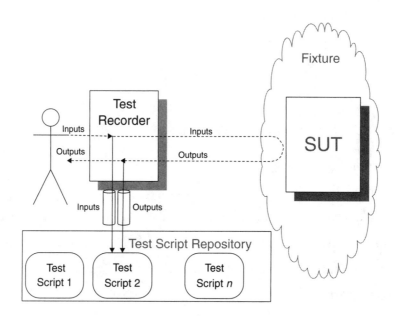

Automated tests serve several purposes. They can be used for regression testing
software after it has been changed. They can help document the behavior of the
software. They can specify the behavior of the software before it has been written. How we prepare the automated test scripts affects which purposes they can
be used for, how robust they are to changes in the SUT, and how much skill and
effort it takes to prepare them.

Recorded Tests allow us to rapidly create regression tests after the SUT has
been built and before it is changed.

How It Works

We use a tool that monitors our interactions with the SUT as we work with
it. This tool keeps track of most of what the SUT communicates to us and our
responses to the SUT. When the recording session is done, we can save the session to a file for later playback. When we are ready to run the test, we start up

the "playback" part of the tool and point it at the recorded session. It starts up the SUT and feeds it our recorded inputs in response to the SUT's outputs. It may also compare the SUT's outputs with the SUT's responses during the recording session. A mismatch may be cause for failing the test.

Some *Recorded Test* tools allow us to adjust the sensitivity of the comparisons that the tool makes between what the SUT said during the recording session and what it said during the playback. Most *Recorded Test* tools interact with the SUT through the user interface.

When to Use It

Once an application is up and running and we don't expect a lot of changes to it, we can use *Recorded Tests* to do regression testing. We could also use *Recorded Tests* when an existing application needs to be refactored (in anticipation of modifying the functionality) and we do not have *Scripted Tests* (page 285) available to use as regression tests. It is typically much quicker to produce a set of *Recorded Tests* than to prepare *Scripted Tests* for the same functionality. In theory, the test recording can be done by anyone who knows how to operate the application; very little technical expertise should be required. In practice, many of the commercial tools have a steep learning curve. Also, some technical expertise may be required to add "checkpoints," to adjust the sensitivity of the playback tool, or to adjust the test script if the recording tool became confused and recorded the wrong information.

Most *Recorded Test* tools interact with the SUT through the user interface. This approach makes them particularly prone to fragility if the user interface of the SUT is evolving (*Interface Sensitivity; see Fragile Test* on page 239). Even small changes such as changing the internal name of a button or field may be enough to cause the playback tool to stumble. The tools also tend to record information at a very low and detailed level, making the tests hard to understand (*Obscure Test;* page 186); as a result, they are also difficult to repair by hand if they are broken by changes to the SUT. For these reasons, we should plan on rerecording the tests fairly regularly if the SUT will continue to evolve.

If we want to use the *Tests as Documentation* (see page 23) or if we want to use the tests to drive new development, we should consider using *Scripted Tests.* These goals are difficult to address with commercial *Recorded Test* tools because most do not let us define a *Higher-Level Language* (see page 41) for the test recording. This issue *can* be addressed by building the *Recorded Test* capability into the application itself or by using *Refactored Recorded Test.*

Recorded Test

Variation: Refactored Recorded Test

A hybrid of the two strategies is to use the "record, refactor, playback"[1] sequence to extract a set of "action components" or "verbs" from the newly *Recorded Tests* and then rewire the test cases to call these "action components" instead of having detailed in-line code. Most commercial capture/replay tools provide the means to turn *Literal Values* (page 714) into parameters that can be passed into the "action component" by the main test case. When a screen changes, we simply rerecord the "action component"; all the test cases continue to function by automatically using the new "action component" definition. This strategy is effectively the same as using *Test Utility Methods* (page 599) to interact with the SUT in unit tests. It opens the door to using the *Refactored Recorded Test* components as a *Higher-Level Language* in *Scripted Tests*. Tools such as Mercury Interactive's **BPT**[2] use this paradigm for scripting tests in a top-down manner; once the high-level scripts are developed and the components required for the test steps are specified, more technical people can either record or hand-code the individual components.

Implementation Notes

We have two basic choices when using a *Recorded Test* strategy: We can either acquire third-party tools that record the communication that occurs while we interact with the application or we can build a "record and playback" mechanism right into our application.

Variation: External Test Recording

Many test recording tools are available commercially, each of which has its own strengths and weaknesses. The best choice will depend on the nature of the user interface of the application, our budget, the complexity of the functionality to be verified, and possibly other factors.

If we want to use the tests to drive development, we need to pick a tool that uses a test-recording file format that is editable by hand and easily understood. We'll need to handcraft the contents—this situation is really an example of a *Scripted Test* even if we are using a "record and playback" tool to execute the tests.

---

[1] The name "record, refactor, playback" was coined by Adam Geras.
[2] BPT is short for "Business Process Testing."

Variation: Built-In Test Recording

It is also possible to build a *Recorded Test* capability into the SUT. In such a case, the test scripting "language" can be defined at a fairly high level—high enough to make it possible to hand-script the tests even before the system is built. In fact, it has been reported that the VBA macro capability of Microsoft's Excel spreadsheet started out as a mechanism for automated testing of Excel.

Example: Built-In Test Recording

On the surface, it doesn't seem to make sense to provide a code sample for a *Recorded Test* because this pattern deals with how the test is produced, not how it is represented. When the test is played back, it is in effect a *Data-Driven Test* (page 288). Likewise, we don't often refactor *to* a *Recorded Test* because it is often the first test automation strategy attempted on a project. Nevertheless, we might introduce a *Recorded Test* after attempting *Scripted Tests* if we discover that we have too many *Missing Tests* (page 268) because the cost of manual automation is too high. In that case, we would not be trying to turn existing *Scripted Tests* into *Recorded Tests*; we would just record new tests.

Here's an example of a test recorded by the application itself. This test was used to regression-test a safety-critical application after it was ported from C on OS2 to C++ on Windows. Note how the recorded information forms a domain-specific *Higher-Level Language* that is quite readable by a user.

```
<interaction-log>
   <commands>
      <!-- more commands omitted -->
      <command seqno="2" id="Supply Create">
         <field name="engineno" type="input">
            <used-value>5566</used-value>
            <expected></expected>
            <actual status="ok"/>
         </field>
         <field name="direction" type="selection">
            <used-value>SOUTH</used-value>
            <expected>
               <value>SOUTH</value>
               <value>NORTH</value>
            </expected>
            <actual>
               <value status="ok">SOUTH</value>
               <value status="ok">NORTH</value>
            </actual>
         </field>
      </command>
      <!-- more commands omitted -->
   </commands>
</interaction-log>
```

Recorded Test

This sample depicts the output of having played back the tests. The actual elements were inserted by the built-in playback mechanism. The status attributes indicate whether these elements match the expected values. We applied a style sheet to these files to format them much like a Fit test with color-coded results. The business users on the project then handled the recording, replaying, and result analysis.

This recording was made by inserting hooks in the presentation layer of the software to record the lists of choices offered the user and the user's responses. An example of one of these hooks follows:

```
if (playback_is_on()) {
  choice = get_choice_for_playback(dialog_id, choices_list);
} else {
  choice  = display_dialog(choices_list, row, col, title, key);
}

if (recording_is_on())  {
   record_choice(dialog_id, choices_list, choice, key);
}
```

The method get_choice_for_playback retrieves the contents of the used-value element instead of asking the user to pick from the list of choices. The method record_choice generates the actual element and makes the "assertions" against the expected elements, recording the result in the status attribute of each element. Note that recording_is_on() returns true whenever we are in playback mode so that the test results can be recorded.

Example: Commercial Record and Playback Test Tool

Almost every commercial testing tool uses a "record and playback" metaphor. Each tool also defines its own *Recorded Test* file format, most of which are very verbose. The following is a "short" excerpt from a test recorded using Mercury Interactive's QuickTest Professional [**QTP**] tool. It is shown in "Expert View," which exposes what is really recorded: a VbScript program! The example includes comments (preceded by "@@") that were inserted manually to clarify what this test is doing; these comments would be lost if the test were rerecorded after a change to the application caused the test to no longer run.

```
@@
@@ GoToPageMaintainTaxonomy()
@@
Browser("Inf").Page("Inf").WebButton("Login").Click
Browser("Inf").Page("Inf_2").Check CheckPoint("Inf_2")
Browser("Inf").Page("Inf_2"").Link("TAXONOMY LINKING").Click
Browser("Inf").Page("Inf_3").Check CheckPoint("Inf_3")
Browser("Inf").Page("Inf_3").Link("MAINTAIN TAXONOMY").Click
Browser("Inf").Page("Inf_4").Check CheckPoint("Inf_4")
@@
```

```
@@ AddTerm("A","Top Level", "Top Level Definition")
@@
Browser("Inf").Page("Inf_4").Link("Add").Click
wait 4
Browser("Inf_2").Page("Inf").Check CheckPoint("Inf_5")
Browser("Inf_2").Page("Inf").WebEdit("childCodeSuffix").Set "A"
Browser("Inf_2").Page("Inf").
   WebEdit("taxonomyDto.descript").Set "Top Level"
Browser("Inf_2").Page("Inf").
   WebEdit("taxonomyDto.definiti").Set "Top Level Definition"
Browser("Inf_2").Page("Inf").WebButton("Save").Click
wait 4
Browser("Inf").Page("Inf_5").Check CheckPoint("Inf_5_2")
@@
@@ SelectTerm("[A]-Top Level")
@@
Browser("Inf").Page("Inf_5").
   WebList("selectedTaxonomyCode").Select "[A]-Top Level"
@@
@@ AddTerm("B","Second Top Level", "Second Top Level Definition")
@@
Browser("Inf").Page("Inf_5").Link("Add").Click
wait 4
Browser("Inf_2").Page("Inf_2").Check CheckPoint("Inf_2_2")
   infofile_;_Inform_Alberta_21.inf_;_hightlight id_;
      _Browser("Inf_2").Page("Inf_2")_;_
@@
@@ and it goes on, and on, and on ....
```

Note how the test describes all inputs and outputs in terms of the user interface of the application. It suffers from two main issues: *Obscure Tests* (caused by the detailed nature of the recorded information) and *Interface Sensitivity* (resulting in *Fragile Tests*).

Refactoring Notes

We can make this test more useful as documentation, reduce or avoid *High Test Maintenance Cost* (page 265), and support composition of other tests from a *Higher-Level Language* by using a series of Extract Method [Fowler] refactorings.

Example: Refactored Commercial Recorded Test

The following example shows the same test refactored to *Communicate Intent* (see page 41):

```
GoToPage_MaintainTaxonomy()
AddTerm("A","Top Level", "Top Level Definition")
SelectTerm("[A]-Top Level")
AddTerm("B","Second Top Level", "Second Top Level Definition")
```

Recorded
Test

Note how much more intent revealing this test has become. The *Test Utility Methods* we extracted look like this:

```
Method GoToPage_MaintainTaxonomy()
    Browser("Inf").Page("Inf").WebButton("Login").Click
    Browser("Inf").Page("Inf_2").Check CheckPoint("Inf_2")
    Browser("Inf").Page("Inf_2").Link("TAXONOMY LINKING").Click
    Browser("Inf").Page("Inf_3").Check CheckPoint("Inf_3")
    Browser("Inf").Page("Inf_3").Link("MAINTAIN TAXONOMY").Click
    Browser("Inf").Page("Inf_4").Check CheckPoint("Inf_4")
End

Method AddTerm( code, name, description)
    Browser("Inf").Page("Inf_4").Link("Add").Click
    wait 4
    Browser("Inf_2").Page("Inf").Check CheckPoint("Inf_5")
    Browser("Inf_2").Page("Inf").
      WebEdit("childCodeSuffix").Set code
    Browser("Inf_2").Page("Inf").
      WebEdit("taxonomyDto.descript").Set name
    Browser("Inf_2").Page("Inf").
      WebEdit("taxonomyDto.definiti").Set description
    Browser("Inf_2").Page("Inf").WebButton("Save").Click
    wait 4
    Browser("Inf").Page("Inf_5").Check CheckPoint("Inf_5_2")
end

Method SelectTerm( path )
    Browser("Inf").Page("Inf_5").
      WebList("selectedTaxonomyCode").Select path
    Browser("Inf").Page("Inf_5").Link("Add").Click
    wait 4
end
```

This example is one I hacked together to illustrate the similarities to what we do in xUnit. Don't try running this example at home—it is probably not syntactically correct.

Further Reading

The paper "Agile Regression Testing Using Record and Playback" [ARTRP] describes our experiences building a *Recorded Test* mechanism into an application to facilitate porting it to another platform.

Scripted Test

How do we prepare automated tests for our software?

We automate the tests by writing test programs by hand.

Also known as:
*Hand-Written
Test, Hand-
Scripted Test,
Programmatic
Test, Automated
Unit Test*

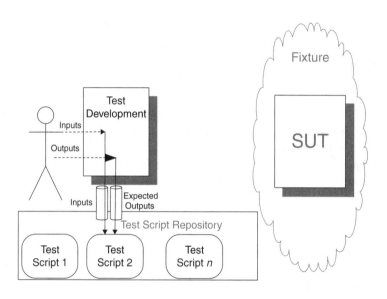

Automated tests serve several purposes. They can be used for regression testing software after it has been changed. They can help document the behavior of the software. They can specify the behavior of the software before it has been written. How we prepare the automated test scripts affects which purpose they can be used for, how robust they are to changes in the SUT, and how much skill and effort it takes to prepare them.

Scripted Tests allow us to prepare our tests before the software is developed so they can help drive the design.

How It Works

We automate our tests by writing test programs that interact with the SUT for the purpose of exercising its functionality. Unlike *Recorded Tests* (page 278), these tests can be either customer tests or unit tests. These test programs are often called "test scripts" to distinguish them from the production code they test.

Scripted
Test

When to Use It

We almost always use *Scripted Tests* when preparing unit tests for our software. This is because it is easier to access the individual units directly from software written in the same programming language. It also allows us to exercise all the code paths, including the "pathological" cases.

Customer tests are a slightly more complicated picture; we should use a *Scripted Test* whenever we use automated **storytests** to drive the development of software. *Recorded Tests* don't serve this need very well because it is difficult to record tests without having an application from which to record them. Preparing *Scripted Tests* takes programming experience as well as experience in testing techniques. It is unlikely that most business users on a project would be interested in learning how to prepare *Scripted Tests*. An alternative to scripting tests in a programming language is to define a *Higher-Level Language* (see page 41) for testing the SUT and then to implement the language as a *Data-Driven Test* (page 288) Interpreter [GOF]. An open-source framework for defining *Data-Driven Tests* is **Fit** and its wiki-based cousin, **FitNesse. Canoo WebTest** is another tool that supports this style of testing.

In case of an existing legacy application,[3] we can consider using *Recorded Tests* as a way of quickly creating a suite of regression tests that will protect us while we refactor the code to introduce testability. We can then prepare *Scripted Tests* for our now testable application.

Implementation Notes

Traditionally, *Scripted Tests* were written as "test programs," often using a special test scripting language. Nowadays, we prefer to write *Scripted Tests* using a *Test Automation Framework* (page 298) such as xUnit in the same language as the SUT. In this case, each test program is typically captured in the form of a *Test Method* (page 348) on a *Testcase Class* (page 373). To minimize *Manual Intervention* (page 250), each test method should implement a *Self-Checking Test* (see page 26) that is also a *Repeatable Test* (see page 26).

---

[3] Among **test drivers**, a legacy application is any system that lacks a safety net of automated tests.

Example: Scripted Test

The following is an example of a *Scripted Test* written in JUnit:

```java
public void testAddLineItem_quantityOne(){
    final BigDecimal BASE_PRICE = UNIT_PRICE;
    final BigDecimal EXTENDED_PRICE = BASE_PRICE;
    //    Set Up Fixture
    Customer customer = createACustomer(NO_CUST_DISCOUNT);
    Invoice invoice = createInvoice(customer);
    //    Exercise SUT
    invoice.addItemQuantity(PRODUCT, QUAN_ONE);
    // Verify Outcome
    LineItem expected =
        createLineItem( QUAN_ONE, NO_CUST_DISCOUNT,
                        EXTENDED_PRICE, PRODUCT, invoice);
    assertContainsExactlyOneLineItem( invoice, expected );
}

public void testChangeQuantity_severalQuantity(){
    final int ORIGINAL_QUANTITY = 3;
    final int NEW_QUANTITY = 5;
    final BigDecimal BASE_PRICE =
        UNIT_PRICE.multiply(   new BigDecimal(NEW_QUANTITY));
    final BigDecimal EXTENDED_PRICE =
        BASE_PRICE.subtract(BASE_PRICE.multiply(
                    CUST_DISCOUNT_PC.movePointLeft(2)));
    //    Set Up Fixture
    Customer customer = createACustomer(CUST_DISCOUNT_PC);
    Invoice invoice = createInvoice(customer);
    Product product = createAProduct( UNIT_PRICE);
    invoice.addItemQuantity(product, ORIGINAL_QUANTITY);
    // Exercise SUT
    invoice.changeQuantityForProduct(product, NEW_QUANTITY);
    // Verify Outcome
    LineItem expected = createLineItem( NEW_QUANTITY,
        CUST_DISCOUNT_PC, EXTENDED_PRICE, PRODUCT, invoice);
    assertContainsExactlyOneLineItem( invoice, expected );
}
```

About the Name

Automated test programs are traditionally called "test scripts," probably due to the heritage of such test programs—originally they were implemented in interpreted test scripting languages such as Tcl. The downside of calling them *Scripted Tests* is that this nomenclature opens the door to confusion with the kind of script a person would follow during manual testing as opposed to unscripted testing such as **exploratory testing**.

Further Reading

Many books have been written about the process of writing *Scripted Tests* and using them to drive the design of the SUT. A good place to start would be [TDD-BE] or [TDD-APG].

Data-Driven Test

How do we prepare automated tests for our software?
How do we reduce Test Code Duplication?

We store all the information needed for each test in a data file and write an interpreter that reads the file and executes the tests.

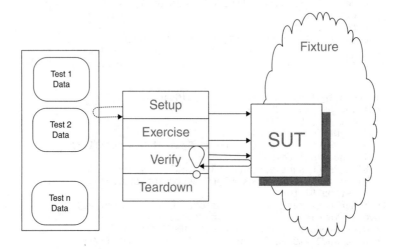

Testing can be very repetitious not only because we must run the same test over and over again, but also because many of the tests differ only slightly. For example, we might want to run essentially the same test with slightly different system inputs and verify that the actual output varies accordingly. Each of these tests would consist of exactly the same steps. While having so many tests is an excellent way to ensure good coverage of functionality, it is not so good for test maintainability because any change made to the algorithm of one of these tests must be propagated to all of the similar tests.

A *Data-Driven Test* is one way to get excellent coverage while minimizing the amount of test code we need to write and maintain.

How It Works

We write a *Data-Driven Test* interpreter that contains all the common logic from the tests. We put the data that varies from test to test into the Data-Driven Test file that the interpreter reads to execute the tests. For each test it performs the same sequence of actions to implement the *Four-Phase Test* (page 358). First, the interpreter retrieves the test data from the file and sets up the test fixture using the data from the file. Second, it exercises the SUT with whatever arguments the file specifies. Third, it compares the actual results produced by the SUT (e.g., returned values, post-test state) with the expected results from the file. If the results don't match, it marks the test as failed; if the SUT throws an exception, it catches the exception and marks the test accordingly and continues. Fourth, the interpreter does any **fixture teardown** that is necessary and then moves on to the next test in the file.

A test that might otherwise require a series of complex steps can be reduced to a single line of data in the *Data-Driven Test* file. Fit is a popular example of a framework for writing *Data-Driven Tests*.

When to Use It

A *Data-Driven Test* is an alternative strategy to a *Recorded Test* (page 278) and a *Scripted Test* (page 285). It can also be used as part of a *Scripted Test* strategy, however, and *Recorded Tests* are, in fact, *Data-Driven Tests* when they are played back. A *Data-Driven Test* is an ideal strategy for getting business people involved in writing automated tests. By keeping the format of the data file simple, we make it possible for the business person to populate the file with data and execute the tests without having to ask a technical person to write test code for each test.

We can consider using a *Data-Driven Test* as part of a *Scripted Test* strategy whenever we have a lot of different data values with which we wish to exercise the SUT where the same sequence of steps must be executed for each data value. Usually, we discover this similarity over time and refactor first to a *Parameterized Test* (page 607) and then to a *Data-Driven Test*. We may also want to arrange a standard set of steps in different sequences with different data values much like in an *Incremental Tabular Test* (see *Parameterized Test*). This approach gives us the best coverage with the least amount of test code to maintain and makes it very easy to add more tests as they are needed.

Another consideration when deciding whether to use *Data-Driven Tests* is whether the behavior we are testing is hard-coded or driven by configuration data. If we automate tests for data-driven behavior using *Scripted Tests*, we must update the test programs whenever the configuration data changes. This behavior is just plain unnatural because it implies that we must commit changes to our source code repository [SCM] whenever we change the data in our configuration database.[4] By making the tests data-driven, changes to the configuration data or

---

[4] Of course, we should be managing our test data in a version-controlled Repository, too—but that topic could fill another book; see [RDb] for details.

Data-Driven Test

meta-objects are then driven by changes to the *Data-Driven Tests*—a much more natural relationship.

Implementation Notes

Our implementation options depend on whether we are using a *Data-Driven Test* as a distinct test strategy or as part of an xUnit-based strategy. Using a *Data-Driven Test* as a stand-alone test strategy typically involves using open-source tools such as Fit or commercial *Recorded Test* tools such as QTP. Using a *Data-Driven Test* as part of a *Scripted Test* strategy may involve implementing a *Data-Driven Test* interpreter within xUnit.

Regardless of which strategy we elect to follow, we should use the appropriate *Test Automation Framework* (page 298) if one is available. By doing so, we effectively convert our tests into two parts: the *Data-Driven Test* interpreter and the *Data-Driven Test* files. Both of these assets should be kept under version control so that we can see how they have evolved over time and to allow us to back out any misguided changes. It is particularly important to store the *Data-Driven Test* files in some kind of Repository, even though this concept may be foreign to business users. We can make this operation transparent by providing the users with a *Data-Driven Test* file-authoring tool such as FitNesse, or we can set up a "user-friendly" Repository such as a document management system that just happens to support version control as well.

It is also important to run these tests as part of the **continuous integration** process to confirm that tests that once passed do not suddenly begin to fail. Failing to do so can result in bugs creeping into the software undetected and significant troubleshooting effort once the bugs are detected. Including the customer tests in the continuous integration process requires some way to keep track of which customer tests were already passing, because we don't insist that all customer tests pass before any code is committed. One option is to keep two sets of input files, migrating tests that pass from the "still red" file into the "all green" file that is used for regression testing as part of the automatic build process.

Variation: Data-Driven Test Framework (Fit)

We should consider using a prebuilt *Data-Driven Test* framework when we are using *Data-Driven Tests* as a test strategy. Fit is a framework originally conceived by Ward Cunningham as a way of involving business users in the automation of tests. Although Fit is typically used to automate customer tests, it can also be used for unit tests if the number of tests warrants building the necessary fixtures. Fit consists of two parts: the framework and a user-created fixture. The Fit

Framework is a generic *Data-Driven Test* interpreter that reads the input file and finds all tables in it. It looks in the top-left cell of each table for a fixture classname and then searches our test executable for that class. When it finds a class, it creates an instance of the class and passes control to that instance as it reads each row and column of the table. We can override methods defined by the framework to specify what should happen for each cell in the table. A Fit fixture, then, is an adapter that Fit calls to interpret a table of data and invoke methods on the SUT.

The Fit table can also contain expected results from the SUT. Fit compares the specified values with the actual values returned by the SUT. Unlike *Assertion Methods* (page 362) in xUnit, however, Fit does not abandon a test at the first value that does not match the expected value. Instead, it colors in each cell in the table, with green cells indicating actual values that matched the expected values and red cells indicating wrong or unexpected values.

Using Fit offers several advantages:

- There is much less code to write than when we build our own test Interpreter [GOF].

- The output makes sense to a business person, not just a technical person.

- The tests don't stop at the first failed assertion. Fit has a way of communicating multiple failures/errors in a way that allows us to see the failure patterns very easily.

- There are a plethora of fixture types available to subclass or use as is.

So why wouldn't we use Fit for all our unit testing instead of xUnit? The main disadvantages of using Fit are described here:

- The test scenarios need to be very well understood before we can build the Fit fixture. We then need to translate each test's logic into a tabular representation; this isn't always a good fit, especially for developers who are used to thinking procedurally. While it may be appropriate to have testers who can write the Fit fixtures for customer tests, this approach wouldn't be appropriate for true unit tests unless we had close to a 1:1 tester-to-developer ratio.

- The tests need to employ the same SUT interaction logic in each test.[5] To run several different styles of tests, we would probably have to build one or more different fixtures for each style of test. Building a new fixture is typically more complex than writing a few *Test Methods* (page 348).

---

[5] The tabular data must be injected into the **SUT** during the **fixture setup** or **exercise SUT** phases or retrieved from the **SUT** during the **result verification** phase.

Although many different fixture types are available to subclass or use as is, their use in this way is yet another thing that developers would be required to learn to do their jobs. Even then, not all unit tests are amenable to automation using Fit.

- Fit tests aren't normally integrated into developers' regression tests that are run via xUnit. Instead, these tests must be run separately—which introduces the possibility that they will not be run at each check-in. Some teams include Fit tests as part of their continuous integration build process to partially mitigate this issue. Other teams have reported great success having a second "customer" build service or server that runs all the customer tests.

Each of these issues is potentially surmountable, of course. In general, xUnit is a more appropriate framework for unit testing than Fit; the reverse is true for customer tests.

Variation: Naive xUnit Test Interpreter

When we have a small number of *Data-Driven Tests* that we wish to run as part of an xUnit-based *Scripted Test* strategy, the simplest implementation is to write a *Test Method* containing a loop that reads one set of input data values from the file along with the expected results. This is the equivalent of converting a single *Parameterized Test* and all its callers into a *Tabular Test* (see *Parameterized Test*). As with a *Tabular Test*, this approach to building the *Data-Driven Test* interpreter will result in a single *Testcase Object* (page 382) with many assertions. This has several ramifications:

- The entire set of *Data-Driven Tests* will count as a single test. Hence, converting a set of *Parameterized Tests* into a single *Data-Driven Test* will reduce the count of tests executed.

- We will stop executing the *Data-Driven Test* on the first failure or error. As a consequence, we will lose a lot of our *Defect Localization* (see page 22). Some variants of xUnit do allow us to specify that failed assertions shouldn't abort execution of the Test Method.

- We need to make sure our assertion failures tell us which subtest we were executing when the failure occurred.

We could address the last two issues by including a try/catch statement inside the loop but surrounding the test logic and then continuing the code's execution. Nevertheless, we still need to find a way to report the test results in a meaningful way (e.g., "Failed subtests 1, 3, and 6 with . . .").

To make it easier to extend the *Data-Driven Test* interpreter to handle several different kinds of tests in the same data file, we can include a "verb" or "action word" as part of each entry in the data file. The interpreter can then dispatch to a different *Parameterized Test* based on the action word.

Variation: Test Suite Object Generator

We can avoid the "stop on first failure" problem associated with a *Naive xUnit Test Interpreter* by having the suite method on the *Test Suite Factory* (see *Test Enumeration* on page 399) fabricate the same *Test Suite Object* (page 387) structure as the built-in mechanism for *Test Discovery* (page 393). To do so, we build a *Testcase Object* for each entry in the *Data-Driven Test* file and initialize each object with the test data for the particular test.[6] That object knows how to execute the *Parameterized Test* with the data loaded into it when the test suite was built. This ensures that the *Data-Driven Test* continues executing even after the first *Testcase Object* encounters an assertion failure. We can then let the *Test Runner* (page 377) count the tests, errors, and failures in the normal way.

Variation: Test Suite Object Simulator

An alternative to building the *Test Suite Object* is to create a *Testcase Object* that behaves like one. This object reads the *Data-Driven Test* file and iterates over all the tests when asked to run. It must catch any exceptions thrown by the *Parameterized Test* and continue executing the subsequent tests. When finished, the *Testcase Object* must report the correct number of tests, failures, and errors back to the *Test Runner*. It also needs to implement any other methods on the standard test interface on which the *Test Runner* depends, such as returning the number of tests in the "suite," returning the name and status of each test in the suite (for the *Graphical Test Tree Explorer,* see *Test Runner*), and so forth.

Motivating Example

Let's assume we have a set of tests as follows:
```
def test_extref
    sourceXml = "<extref id='abc' />"
    expectedHtml = "<a href='abc.html'>abc</a>"
    generateAndVerifyHtml(sourceXml,expectedHtml,"<extref>")
```

---

[6] This is very similar to how **xUnit's** built-in *Test Method Discovery* (see *Test Discovery*) mechanism works, except that we are passing in the test data in addition to the *Test Method* name.

```
        end

        def test_testterm_normal
            sourceXml = "<testterm id='abc'/>"
            expectedHtml = "<a href='abc.html'>abc</a>"
            generateAndVerifyHtml(sourceXml,expectedHtml,"<testterm>")
        end

        def test_testterm_plural
            sourceXml = "<testterms id='abc'/>"
            expectedHtml = "<a href='abc.html'>abcs</a>"
            generateAndVerifyHtml(sourceXml,expectedHtml,"<plural>")
        end
```

The succinctness of these tests is made possible by defining the *Parameterized Test* as follows:

```
        def generateAndVerifyHtml( sourceXml, expectedHtml,
                                   message, &block)
            mockFile = MockFile.new
            sourceXml.delete!("\t")
            @handler = setupHandler(sourceXml, mockFile )
            block.call unless block == nil
            @handler.printBodyContents
            actual_html = mockFile.output
            assert_equal_html( expectedHtml,
                               actual_html,
                               message + "html output")
            actual_html
        end
```

The main problem with these tests is that they are still written in code when, in fact, the only difference between them is the data used as input.

Refactoring Notes

The solution, of course, is to extract the common logic of the *Parameterized Tests* into a *Data-Driven Test* interpreter and to collect all sets of parameters into a single data file that can be edited by anyone. We need to write a "main" test that knows which file to read the test data from and a bit of logic to read and parse the test file. This logic can call our existing *Parameterized Test* logic and let xUnit keep track of the test execution statistics for us.

Example: xUnit Data-Driven Test with XML Data File

In this example, we will use XML as our file representation. Each test consists of a test element with three main parts:

- An action that tells the *Data-Driven Test* interpreter which test logic to run (e.g., `crossref`)

- The input to be passed to the SUT—in this case, the `sourceXml` element

- The HTML we expect the SUT to produce (in the `expectedHtml` element)

These three components are wrapped up in a `testsuite` element.

```
<testsuite id="CrossRefHandlerTest">
   <test id="extref">
      <action>crossref</action>
      <sourceXml>
         <extref id='abc'/>
      </sourceXml>
      <expectedHtml>
         <a href='abc.html'>abc</a>
      </expectedHtml>
   </test>
   <test id="TestTerm">
      <action>crossref</action>
      <sourceXml>
         <testterm id='abc'/>
      </sourceXml>
      <expectedHtml>
         <a href='abc.html'>abc</a>
      </expectedHtml>
   </test>
   <test id="TestTerm Plural">
      <action>crossref</action>
      <sourceXml>
         <testterms id='abc'/>
      </sourceXml>
      <expectedHtml>
         <a href='abc.html'>abcs</a>
      </expectedHtml>
   </test>
</testsuite>
```

This XML file could be edited by anyone with an XML editor without any concern for introducing test logic errors. All the logic for verifying the expected outcome is encapsulated by the *Data-Driven Test* interpreter in much the same way as it would be by a *Parameterized Test*. For viewing purposes we could hide the XML structure from the user by defining a style sheet. In addition, many XML editors will turn the XML into a form-based input to simplify editing.

To avoid dealing with the complexities of manipulating XML, the interpreter can also use a CSV file as input.

Example: xUnit Data-Driven Test with CSV Input File

The test in the previous example would look like this as a CSV file:

```
ID,    Action,    SourceXml,        ExpectedHtml
Extref,crossref,<extref id='abc'/>,<a href='abc.html'>abc</a>
TTerm,crossref,<testterm id='abc'/>,<a href='abc.html'>abc</a>
TTerms,crossref,<testterms id='abc'/>,<a href='abc.html'>abcs</a>
```

The interpreter is relatively simple and is built on the logic we had already developed for our *Parameterized Test*. This version reads the CSV file and uses Ruby's split function to parse each line.

```
def test_crossref
   executeDataDrivenTest "CrossrefHandlerTest.txt"
end

def executeDataDrivenTest filename
   dataFile = File.open(filename)
   dataFile.each_line do | line |
     desc, action, part2 = line.split(",")
      sourceXml, expectedHtml, leftOver = part2.split(",")
       if "crossref"==action.strip
         generateAndVerifyHtml sourceXml, expectedHtml, desc
      else # new "verbs" go before here as elsif's
          report_error( "unknown action" + action.strip )
      end
    end
  end
```

Unless we changed the implementation of generateAndVerifyHtml to catch assertion failures and increment a failure counter, this *Data-Driven Test* will stop executing at the first failed assertion. While this behavior would be acceptable for regression testing, it would not provide very good *Defect Localization*.

Example: Data-Driven Test Using Fit Framework

If we wanted to have even more control over what the user can do, we could create a Fit "column fixture" with the columns "id," "action," "source XML," and "expected Html()" and let the user edit an HTML Web page instead (Figure 18.1).

com.xunitpatterns.fit.CrossrefHandlerFixture			
id	action	source XML	expected Html()
extref	crossref	<extref id='abc' />	<a href='abc.html'>?abc?</a>
TestTerm	crossref	<testterm id='abcd' />	<a href='abc.html'>?abc?</a>
TestTerm Plural	crossref	<testterm id='abc' suffix="s"/>	<a href='abc.html'>?abcs?</a>

Figure 18.1 *A Data-Driven test built using the Fit framework.*

When using Fit, the test interpreter is the Fit framework extended by the Fit fixture class specific to the test:

```
public class CrossrefHandlerFixture extends ColumnFixture {
   // Input columns
   public String id;
   public String action;
   public String sourceXML;

   // Output columns
   public String expectedHtml() {
      return generateHtml(sourceXML);
   }
}
```

The methods of this fixture class are called by the Fit framework for each cell in each line in the Fit table based on the column headers. Simple names are interpreted as the **instance variable** of the fixture (e.g., "id," "source XML"). Column names ending in "()" signify a function that Fit calls and then compares its result with the contents of the cell.

The resulting output is shown in Figure 18.2. This colored-in table allows us to get an overview of the results of running one file of tests at a single glance.

com.xunitpatterns.fit.CrossrefHandlerFixture			
id	action	source XML	expected Html()
extref	crossref	<extref id='abc' />	<a href='abc.html'>?abc?</a>
TestTerm	crossref	<testterm id='abcd' />	<a href='abc.html'>?abc?</a>
TestTerm Plural	crossref	<testterm id='abc' suffix="s"/>	<a href='abc.html'>?abcs?</a> expected <a href='abc.html'>?abc?</a> actual

Figure 18.2 *The results of executing the Fit test.*

Test Automation Framework

How do we make it easy to write and run tests written by different people?

We use a framework that provides all the mechanisms needed to run the test logic so the test writer needs to provide only the test-specific logic.

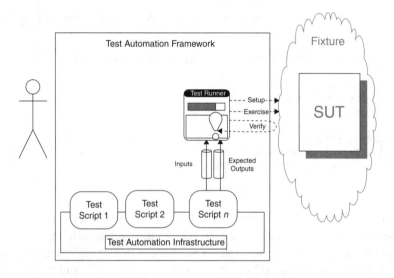

Writing and running automated tests involves several steps, but many of these steps are the same for every test. If every test had to include an implementation of these steps, writing automated tests would be very tedious, time-consuming, prone to errors, and expensive.

Using a *Test Automation Framework* is a way to minimize the effort of writing *Fully Automated Tests* (see page 26).

How It Works

We build a framework that implements all the mechanisms required to run suites of tests and record the results. These mechanisms include the ability to find individual tests, assemble them into a test suite, execute each test in turn, verify expected outcomes, collect and report any test failures or errors, and clean up when failures or errors do occur. The framework provides a way to plug in and run the test-specific behavior that test automaters write.

Why We Do This

Building *Fully Automated Tests* that are repeatable and robust is a much more complicated process than just writing a test script that invokes the SUT. We need to handle success cases and error cases, both expected and unexpected. We need to set up and tear down **test fixtures**. We need to specify which test(s) to run. We also need to report on the results after we have run a suite of tests.

The amount of effort required to build *Fully Automated Tests* can act as a serious deterrent to automation of tests. We can reduce the cost of getting started significantly by providing a framework that implements the most common functionality—the only entry cost is then incurred while learning to use the framework. This cost, in turn, can be reduced if the framework implements a common protocol such as xUnit that makes it easier for us to learn a second or third framework once we have experience with the first.

Using a framework also helps isolate the implementation of the logic required to run the tests from the logic of the tests. This approach can help reduce *Test Code Duplication* (page 213) and minimize the occurrence of *Obscure Tests* (page 186). It also ensures that test written by different **test automaters** can be run easily in a single **test run** with a single report on the **test results**.

Implementation Notes

Many kinds of *Test Automation Frameworks* are available, from both commercial vendors and open-source resources. They can be classified into two main categories: "robot user" test tools and *Scripted Tests* (page 285). The latter category can be further subdivided into the xUnit and *Data-Driven Tests* (page 288) families of *Test Automation Frameworks*.

Variation: Robot User Test Frameworks

A large number of third-party test automation tools are designed to test applications via the user interface. Most of them use the "record and playback" test metaphor. This metaphor leads to some very seductive marketing materials, because it makes test automation seem as simple as running some tests manually while recording the test session. Such a robot user test tool consists of two major parts: the "test recorder," which monitors and records the interactions between the user and the SUT, and the "test runner," which executes the *Recorded Tests* (page 278). Most of these test automation tools are also frameworks that support a number of "widget recognizer" plug-ins. Most commercial tools come with a gaggle of built-in widget recognizers.

Test Automation Framework

Variation: The xUnit Family of Test Automation Frameworks

Most unit-testing tools belong to the xUnit family of testing frameworks designed for automating *Hand-Scripted Tests* (see *Scripted Test*). xUnit has been ported to (or developed from scratch for) most current programming languages. The xUnit family of unit-testing frameworks consists of several major components. The most visible is the *Test Runner* (page 377), which can be invoked either from the command line or as a *Graphical Test Runner* (see *Test Runner*). It builds the *Testcase Objects* (page 382), collects them into *Test Suite Objects* (page 387), and invokes each of the *Test Methods* (page 348). The other major component of the xUnit frameworks is the library of built-in *Assertion Methods* (page 362) that are used within the *Test Methods* to specify the expected outcome of each test.

Variation: Data-Driven Test Frameworks

A *Data-Driven Test* framework provides a way to plug in interpreters that know how to execute a specific kind of test step. This flexibility, in effect, extends the format of the input file with new "verbs" and objects. Such a framework also provides a test runner that reads in the file, passes control to the plug-ins when their corresponding data formats are encountered, and keeps track of statistics for the test run. The most notable member of the *Data-Driven Test Frameworks* family is Fit, which enables test automaters to write tests in tabular form and to "plug in" fixture classes that know how to interpret specific formats of tables.

Example: Test Automation Framework

The *Test Automation Framework* looks somewhat different for each of the possible ways to automate tests. To see these variations, refer to *Recorded Test*, *Scripted Test,* and *Data-Driven Test* for examples of the respective *Test Automation Frameworks*.

Further Reading

Some of the more popular examples of *Test Automation Frameworks* for xUnit are JUnit (Java), **SUnit** (Smalltalk), **CppUnit** (C++), **NUnit** (all .NET languages), **runit** (Ruby), **PyUnit** (Python), and **VbUnit** (Visual Basic). A more complete and up-to-date list can be found at http://xprogramming.com, along with a list of the available extensions (e.g., HttpUnit, Cactus).

Other open-source *Test Automation Frameworks* include Fit, Canoo Web-Test, and **Watir**. Commercial *Test Automation Frameworks* include QTP, BPT, and **eCATT,** among many others.

In *Test-Driven Development—By Example* [TDD-BE], Kent Beck illustrates **TDD** by building a *Test Automation Framework* in Python. In an approach he likens to "doing brain surgery on yourself," he uses the emerging *Test Automation Framework* to run the tests he writes for each new capability. This application is a very good example of both TDD and bootstrapping.

Minimal Fixture

Which fixture strategy should we use?

We use the smallest and simplest fixture possible for each test.

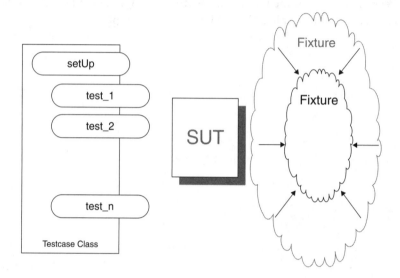

Every test needs some kind of test fixture. A key part of understanding a test is understanding the test fixture and recognizing how it influences the expected outcome of the test. Tests are much easier to understand if the fixture is small and simple.

Why We Do This

A *Minimal Fixture* is important for achieving *Tests as Documentation* (see page 23) and for avoiding *Slow Tests* (page 253). A test that uses a Minimal Fixture will always be easier to understand than one that uses a fixture containing unnecessary or irrelevant information. This is true whether we are using a *Fresh Fixture* (page 311) or a *Shared Fixture* (page 317), although the effort to build a *Minimal Fixture* is typically higher with a *Shared Fixture* because it must be designed to handle several tests. Defining a *Minimal Fixture* is much easier for a *Fresh Fixture* because it need serve only a single test.

Implementation Notes

We design a fixture that includes only those objects that are absolutely necessary to express the behavior that the test verifies. Another way to phrase this is "If the object is not important to understand the test, it is important not to include it in the fixture."

To build a *Minimal Fixture*, we ruthlessly remove anything from the fixture that does not help the test communicate how the SUT should behave. Two forms of "minimization" can be considered:

- We can eliminate objects entirely. That is, we don't even build the objects as part of the fixture. If the object isn't necessary to prove something about how the SUT behaves, we don't include it at all.

- We can hide unnecessary attributes of the object when they don't contribute to the understanding of the expected behavior.

A simple way to find out whether an object is necessary as part of the fixture is to remove it. If the test fails as a result, the object was probably necessary *in some way*. Of course, it may have been necessary only as an argument to some method we are not interested in or as an attribute that is never used (even though the object to which the attribute belongs is required for some reason). Including these kinds of objects as part of fixture setup definitely contributes to *Obscure Tests* (page 186). We can eliminate these unnecessary objects in one of two ways: (1) by hiding them or (2) by eliminating the need for them by passing in *Dummy Objects* (page 728) or using *Entity Chain Snipping* (see *Test Stub* on page 529). If the SUT actually accesses the object as it is executing the logic under test, however, we may be forced to include the object as part of the test fixture.

Having determined that the object is *necessary* for the *execution* of the test, we must now ask whether the object is *helpful in understanding* the test. If we were to initialize it "off-stage," would that make it harder to understand the test? Would the object lead to an *Obscure Test* by acting as a *Mystery Guest* (see *Obscure Test*)? If so, we want to keep the object visible. **Boundary values** are a good example of a case in which we do want to keep the objects and attributes that take on the boundary values visible.

If we have established that the object or attribute isn't necessary for understanding the test, we should make every effort to eliminate it from the *Test Method* (page 348), albeit not necessarily from the test fixture. *Creation Methods* (page 415) are a common way of achieving this goal. We can hide the attributes of objects that don't affect the outcome of the test but that are needed for construction of the object by using *Creation Methods* to fill in all the "don't care" attributes with meaningful default values. We can also hide the creation of necessary depended-on objects within the *Creation Methods*. A good example of this occurs when we write tests that require badly formed objects as input (for testing the SUT with invalid inputs). In this case we don't want to confuse the issue by showing all valid attributes of the object being passed to the SUT; there could be many of these extraneous attributes. Instead, we want to focus on the *invalid* attribute. To do so, we can use the *One Bad Attribute* pattern (see *Derived Value* on page 718) to build malformed objects with a minimum of code by calling a *Creation Method* to construct a valid object and then replacing a single attribute with the invalid value that we want to verify the SUT will handle correctly.

Standard Fixture

Which fixture strategy should we use?

We reuse the design of the text fixture across the many tests.

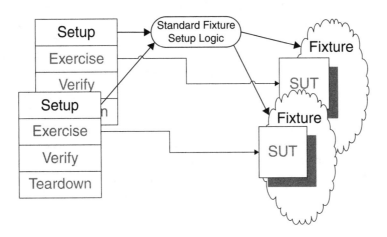

To execute an automated test, we require a text fixture that is well understood and completely deterministic. Designing a custom test fixture for each test requires extra effort. A *Standard Fixture* offers a way to reuse the same fixture *design* in several tests without necessarily sharing the same fixture *instance*.

How It Works

A *Standard Fixture* is more about attitude than about technology. It requires us to decide early on in the testing process that we will design a *Standard Fixture* that can be used by several or many tests rather than mining a common fixture from tests that were designed independently. In a sense, a *Standard Fixture* is the result of "Big Design Upfront" of the test fixture for a whole suite of tests. We then define our specific tests using this common test fixture design.

The choice of a *Standard Fixture* is independent of the choice between a *Fresh Fixture* (page 311) and a *Shared Fixture* (page 317). A *Shared Fixture* is, by definition, a *Standard Fixture*. The reverse is not true, however, because a *Standard Fixture* focuses on reuse of the fixture's *design*—not the time when the fixture is built or its visibility. Having chosen to use a *Standard Fixture*, we still need to decide whether each test will build its own instance of the *Standard*

**Standard
Fixture**

Fixture (a *Fresh Fixture*) or whether we will build it once as a *Shared Fixture* and reuse it across many tests.

When to Use It

When I was reviewing an early draft of this book with Series Editor Martin Fowler, he asked me, "Do people actually do this?" This question exemplifies the philosophical divide of fixture design. Coming from an agile background, Martin lets each test **pull** a fixture into existence. If several tests happen to need the same fixture, then it makes sense to factor it out into the setUp method and split the class into one *Testcase Class per Fixture* (page 631). It doesn't even occur to Martin to design a *Standard Fixture* that all tests can use. So who uses them?

   Standard Fixtures are something of a tradition in the testing (quality assessment) community. It is very commonplace to define a large *Standard Fixture* that is then used as a test bed for testing activities. This approach makes a lot of sense in the context of manual execution of many **customer tests** because it eliminates the need for each tester to spend a lot of time setting up the test environment for each customer test and it allows several testers to work in the same test environment at the same time. Some test automaters also use *Standard Fixtures* when defining their automated customer tests. This strategy is especially prevalent when test automaters use a *Shared Fixture,* for obvious reasons.

   In the xUnit community, use of a *Standard Fixture* simply to avoid designing a *Minimal Fixture* (page 302) for each test is considered undesirable and has been given the name *General Fixture* (see *Obscure Test* on page 186). A more accepted example is the use of *Implicit Setup* (page 424) in conjunction with *Testcase Class per Fixture* because only a few *Test Methods* (page 348) share the design of the fixture and they do so *because* they need the same design. As we make a *Standard Fixture* more reusable across many tests with disparate needs, it tends to grow larger and more complex. This trend can lead to a *Fragile Fixture* (see *Fragile Test* on page 239) as the needs of new tests introduce changes that break existing clients of the *Standard Fixture.* Depending on how we go about building the *Standard Fixture,* we may also find ourselves entertaining a *Mystery Guest* (see *Obscure Test*) if the cause–effect relationships between the fixture and outcome are not easy to discern either because the fixture setup is hidden from the test or because it is not clear which characteristics of the referenced part of the *Standard Fixture* serve as pre-conditions for the test.

   A *Standard Fixture* will also take longer to build than a *Minimal Fixture* because there is more fixture to construct. When we are building a *Fresh Fixture* for each *Testcase Object* (page 382), this effort can lead to *Slow Tests* (page 253), especially if the fixture setup involves a database. (See the sidebar "Unit Test Rulz"

> **Unit Test Rulz**
>
> Michael Feathers of Object Mentor writes:
>
> *I've used these rules with a large number of teams. They encourage good design and rapid feedback and they seem to help teams avoid a lot of trouble.*
>
> *A test is not a unit test if:*
> - *It talks to the database.*
> - *It communicates across the network.*
> - *It touches the file system.*
> - *It can't run correctly at the same time as any of your other unit tests.*
> - *You have to do special things to your environment (such as editing config files) to run it.*
>
> *Tests that do these things aren't bad. Often they are worth writing, and they can be written in a unit test harness. However, it is important to be able to separate them from true unit tests so that we can keep a set of tests that we can run fast whenever we make our changes.*
>
> http://www.objectmentor.com

for an opinion about what kinds of behavior are acceptable for a unit test.) For these reasons, we may be better off using a *Minimal Fixture* to avoid the extra fixture setup overhead associated with creating objects that are only needed in other tests.

Implementation Notes

As mentioned earlier, we can use a *Standard Fixture* as either a *Fresh Fixture* or a *Shared Fixture,* and we can set it up using either *Implicit Setup* or *Delegated Setup* (page 411).[7] When using it as a *Fresh Fixture,* we can define a *Test Utility Method* (page 599) (function or procedure) that builds the *Standard Fixture*; we can then call the *Test Utility Method* from each test that needs this particular design of fixture. Alternatively, we can take advantage of xUnit support for *Implicit Setup* by putting all of the fixture construction logic in the setUp method.

---

[7] Doing it with *In-line Setup* (page 408) would be silly—we would have to copy the code to construct the Standard Fixture to every *Test Method*.

Standard Fixture

When building a *Standard Fixture* for use as a *Shared Fixture*, we can employ any of the *Shared Fixture* setup patterns including *Suite Fixture Setup* (page 441), *Lazy Setup* (page 435), and *Setup Decorator* (page 447).

Motivating Example

As mentioned earlier, we are most likely to end up using a *Standard Fixture* because we started that way—and we probably started that way as the result of the background of one of the project participants. We probably would not refactor our tests to use a *Standard Fixture* when those tests are already written to use a *Minimal Fixture* unless we were refactoring to create a *Testcase Class per Fixture*. For the sake of illustration, let's assume that we did want to get to "here" from "there." The following example uses *Creation Methods* (page 415) to build a custom *Fresh Fixture* for each test:

```
public void testGetFlightsByFromAirport_OneOutboundFlight_c()
        throws Exception {
   FlightDto outboundFlight = createOneOutboundFlightDto();
   // Exercise System
   List flightsAtOrigin =
        facade.getFlightsByOriginAirport(
                         outboundFlight.getOriginAirportId());
   // Verify Outcome
   assertOnly1FlightInDtoList( "Flights at origin",
                              outboundFlight,
                              flightsAtOrigin);
}

public void testGetFlightsByFromAirport_TwoOutboundFlights_c()
        throws Exception {
   FlightDto[] outboundFlights =
       createTwoOutboundFlightsFromOneAirport();
   // Exercise System
   List flightsAtOrigin = facade.getFlightsByOriginAirport(
                   outboundFlights[0].getOriginAirportId());
   // Verify Outcome
   assertExactly2FlightsInDtoList( "Flights at origin",
                              outboundFlights,
                              flightsAtOrigin);
}
```

To keep this test short, we have used *Delegated Setup* to populate the SUT with the *Minimal Fixture* needed for each test. We could have included the fixture setup code in-line in each method, but that choice would take us down the road toward an *Obscure Test*.

Refactoring Notes

Technically speaking, converting a pile of tests to a *Standard Fixture* isn't really a "refactoring" because we actually change the behavior of these tests. The biggest challenge is designing the reusable *Standard Fixture* in such a way that each *Test Method* can find some part of the fixture that serves its needs. This means synthesizing all of the individual purpose-built *Minimal Fixtures* into a single "jack of all trades" fixture. Not surprisingly, this reworking of the code can be a nontrivial exercise when we have a lot of tests.

The easy and mechanical part of the refactoring is to convert the logic in each test that constructs the fixture into calls to *Finder Methods* (see *Test Utility Method*) that retrieve the appropriate part of the *Standard Fixture*. This transformation is most easily done as a series of steps. First, we extract the in-line fixture construction logic in each *Test Method* into one or more *Creation Methods* with *Intent-Revealing Names* [SBPP]. Next, we do a global replace on the "create" part of each call to "find." Finally, we generate (either manually or using our IDE's "quick fix" capability) the *Finder Methods* needed to get the calls to compile. Inside each *Finder Methods* we add in code to return the relevant part of the *Standard Fixture*.

Example: Standard Fixture

Here's the example given earlier converted to use a *Standard Fixture*:

```
public void testGetFlightsByFromAirport_OneOutboundFlight()
        throws Exception {
  setupStandardAirportsAndFlights();
  FlightDto outboundFlight = findOneOutboundFlight();
  // Exercise System
  List flightsAtOrigin = facade.getFlightsByOriginAirport(
              outboundFlight.getOriginAirportId());
  // Verify Outcome
  assertOnly1FlightInDtoList( "Flights at origin",
                              outboundFlight,
                              flightsAtOrigin);
}

public void testGetFlightsByFromAirport_TwoOutboundFlights()
        throws Exception {
  setupStandardAirportsAndFlights();
  FlightDto[] outboundFlights =
            findTwoOutboundFlightsFromOneAirport();
  // Exercise System
  List flightsAtOrigin = facade.getFlightsByOriginAirport(
              outboundFlights[0].getOriginAirportId());
  // Verify Outcome
```

**Standard
Fixture**

```
assertExactly2FlightsInDtoList( "Flights at origin",
                                outboundFlights,
                                flightsAtOrigin);
}
```

To make the use of a *Standard Fixture* really obvious, this example shows a *Fresh Fixture* that is created explicitly in each test by calling the same *Creation Method* to set up the *Standard Fixture* (i.e., using *Delegated Setup*). We could have achieved the same effect by putting the fixture construction logic into the setUp method, thus using *Implicit Setup*. The resulting test would look identical to one that uses a *Shared Fixture*.

Fresh Fixture

Which fixture strategy should we use?

Each test constructs its own brand-new test fixture for its own private use.

Also known as:
*Fresh Context,
Private Fixture*

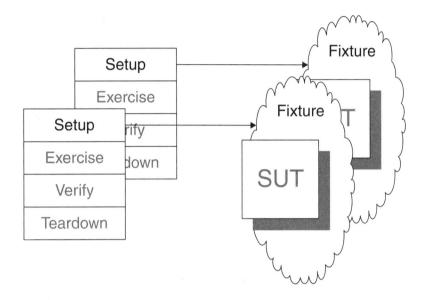

Every test needs a test fixture. It defines the state of the test environment before the test. The choice of whether to build the fixture from scratch each time the test is run or to reuse a fixture built earlier is a key test automation decision.

When each test creates a *Fresh Fixture*, *Erratic Tests* (page 228) are less likely and the testing effort is more likely to result in *Tests as Documentation* (see page 23).

How It Works

We design and build the test fixture such that only a single run of a single test will use it. We construct the fixture as part of running the test and tear down the fixture when the test has finished. We do not reuse any fixture left over by other tests or other test runs. This way, we start and end every test with a "clean slate."

**Fresh
Fixture**

When to Use It

We should use a *Fresh Fixture* whenever we want to avoid any interdependencies between tests that can result in *Erratic Tests* such as *Lonely Tests* (see *Erratic Test*) or *Interacting Tests* (see *Erratic Test*). If we cannot use a *Fresh Fixture* because it slows the tests down too much, we should consider using an *Immutable Shared Fixture* (see *Shared Fixture* on page 317) before resorting to a *Shared Fixture*. Note that using a *Database Partitioning Scheme* (see *Database Sandbox* on page 650) to create a private *Database Sandbox* for the test that no other tests will touch does not result in a *Fresh Fixture* because subsequent test runs could use the same fixture.

Implementation Notes

A fixture is considered a *Fresh Fixture* if we *intend* to use it a single time. Whether the *Fresh Fixture* is transient or persistent depends on the nature of the SUT and how the tests are written (Figure 18.3). While the intent is the same, the implementation considerations are somewhat different when the *Fresh Fixture* is persistent. Fixture setup is largely unaffected, so it is discussed as a feature common to all such fixtures. Fixture teardown is specific to the particular variation.

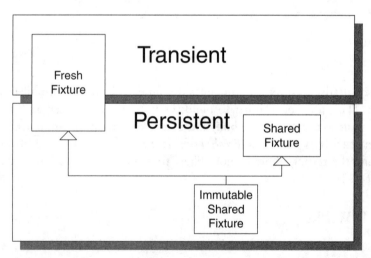

Figure 18.3 *Test fixture strategies. A fixture can be either Fresh, Shared, or a combination of the two (the immutable Shared Fixture) based on whether some, or all, of it persists between tests.*

Why Does a Fixture Persist?

The fixture we construct may hang around after the *Test Method* (page 348) has finished executing for one of two reasons. First, if the fixture primarily consists of the state of some other objects or components on which the SUT depends, its persistence is determined by whether those other objects are themselves persistent. A database is one such beast. That's because as soon as some code persists the fixture objects into a database, the objects "hang around" long after our test is done. Their existence in the database opens the door to collisions between multiple runs of our own test (*Unrepeatable Test; see Erratic Test*). Other tests may also be able to access those objects, which can result in other forms of *Erratic Tests* such as *Interacting Tests* and *Test Run Wars*. If we must use a database or other form of object persistence, we should take extra steps to keep the fixture private. In addition, we should tear down the fixture after each *Test Method*.

The second reason that a fixture might persist lies within the control of our tests—namely, which kind of variable we choose to hold the reference to the fixture. Local variables naturally go out of scope when the *Test Method* finishes executing; therefore any fixture held in a local variable will be destroyed by garbage collection. **Instance variables** go out of scope when the *Testcase Object* is destroyed[8] and require explicit teardown only if the xUnit framework doesn't recreate the *Testcase Object*s during each test run. By contrast, **class variables** usually result in persistent fixtures that can outlive a single test method or even a test run and should therefore be avoided when using a *Fresh Fixture*.

In practice, our fixture will not normally be persistent in unit tests[9] unless we have tightly coupled our application logic to the database. A fixture is more likely to be persistent when we are writing **customer tests** or possibly **component tests**.

Fresh Fixture Setup

Construction of the fixture is largely unaffected by whether it is persistent or transient. The primary consideration is the location of the code to set up the fixture. We can use *In-line Setup* (page 408) if the fixture setup is relatively simple. For more complex fixtures, we generally prefer using *Delegated Setup* (page 411) when our

---

[8] Most members of the **xUnit** family create a separate *Testcase Object* (page 382) for each *Test Method*. A few do not, however. This difference can trip up unwary **test automaters** when they first start using these members of the family because **instance variables** may unexpectedly act like **class variables**. For a detailed description of this issue, see the sidebar "There's Always an Exception" (page 384).

[9] The sidebar "Unit Test Rulz" (page 307) explains what constitutes a **unit test**.

Test Methods are organized using *Testcase Class per Class* (page 617) or *Testcase Class per Feature* (page 624). We can use *Implicit Setup* (page 424) to build the fixture if we have used the *Testcase Class per Fixture* (page 631) organization.

Variation: Transient Fresh Fixture

If we need to refer to the fixture from several places in the test, we should use only local variables or instance variables to refer to the fixture. In most cases we can depend on *Garbage-Collected Teardown* (page 500) to destroy the fixture without any effort on our part.

Note that a *Standard Fixture* (page 305) can also be a *Fresh Fixture* if the fixture is built from scratch before each *Test Method* is run. This approach reuses the *design* of the fixture rather than the *instance*. It is commonly encountered when we use *Implicit Setup* but we are not using *Testcase Class per Fixture* to organize our *Test Methods*.

Variation: Persistent Fresh Fixture

If we do end up using a *Persistent Fresh Fixture*, either we need to tear down the fixture or we need to take special measures to avoid the need for its teardown. We can tear down the fixture using *In-line Teardown* (page 509), *Implicit Teardown* (page 516), *Delegated Teardown* (see *In-line Teardown*), or *Automated Teardown* (page 503) to leave the test environment in the same state as when we entered it.

To avoid fixture teardown, we can use a *Distinct Generated Value* (see *Generated Value* on page 723) for each fixture object that must be unique. This strategy can become the basis of a *Database Partitioning Scheme* that seeks to isolate the tests and test runners from one another. It would prevent *Resource Leakage* (see *Erratic Test*) in case our teardown process fails. We can also combine this approach with one of the teardown patterns to be doubly sure that no *Unrepeatable Tests* or *Interacting Tests* exist.

Not surprisingly, this additional work has some drawbacks: It makes tests more complicated to write and it often leads to *Slow Tests* (page 253). A natural reaction is to take advantage of the persistence of the fixture by reusing it across many tests, thereby avoiding the overhead of setting it up and tearing it down. Unfortunately, this choice has many undesirable ramifications because it violates one of our major principles: *Keep Tests Independent* (see page 42). The resulting *Shared Fixture* invariably leads to *Interacting Tests* and *Unrepeatable Tests*, if not immediately, then at some point down the road. We should not venture down this road without fully understanding the consequences!

Motivating Example

Here's an example of a *Shared Fixture*:

```
static Flight flight;
public void setUp() {
    if (flight == null) {   // Lazy SetUp
        Airport departAirport = new Airport("Calgary", "YYC");
        Airport destAirport = new Airport("Toronto", "YYZ");
        flight = new Flight( flightNumber,
                             departAirport,
                             destAirport);
    }
}

public void testGetStatus_inital_S() {
    // implicit setup
    // exercise SUT and verify outcome
    assertEquals(FlightState.PROPOSED, flight.getStatus());
    // teardown
}
public void testGetStatus_cancelled() {
    // implicit setup partially overridden
    flight.cancel();
    // exercise SUT and verify outcome
    assertEquals(FlightState.CANCELLED, flight.getStatus());
    // teardown
}
```

Based on the code that actually sets up the fixture as shown here, it is a normal *Shared Fixture*, but we could have just as easily used a *Prebuilt Fixture* (page 429) for this motivating example. Either way, these tests *could* start interacting at any time.

Refactoring Notes

Suppose we are using a *Shared Fixture* (same design, single copy) and decide to refactor it to use a *Fresh Fixture*. We can start by refactoring the test to use a fresh *Standard Fixture* (same design, many copies). Then we can decide whether we want to further evolve the test so that it builds a *Minimal Fixture* (page 302) by pruning the fixture setup logic to the bare minimum using a Minimize Data (page 738) refactoring. This point would also be good time to group *Test Methods* that need the same type of test fixture into a *Testcase Class per Fixture* and use *Implicit Setup*; this use of a *Standard Fixture* would reduce the number of *Minimal Fixtures* we need to design and build.

Example: Fresh Fixture

Here's the same test converted to a *Fresh Fixture* to avoid any possibility of *Interacting Tests*:

```
public void testGetStatus_inital() {
    // setup
    Flight flight = createAnonymousFlight();
    // exercise SUT and verify outcome
    assertEquals(FlightState.PROPOSED, flight.getStatus());
    // teardown
    //     garbage-collected
}

public void testGetStatus_cancelled2() {
    // setup
    Flight flight = createAnonymousCancelledFlight();
    // exercise SUT and verify outcome
    assertEquals(FlightState.CANCELLED, flight.getStatus());
    // teardown
    //     garbage-collected
}
```

Note the use of *Anonymous Creation Methods* (see *Creation Method* on page 415) to construct the appropriate state Flight object in each test.

Shared Fixture

How can we avoid Slow Tests?
Which fixture strategy should we use?

We reuse the same instance of the test fixture across many tests.

Also known as:
Shared Context,
Leftover Fixture,
Reused Fixture,
Stale Fixture

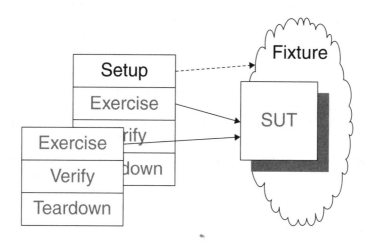

To execute an automated test, we require a text fixture that is well understood and completely deterministic. Setting up a *Fresh Fixture* (page 311) can be time-consuming, especially when we are dealing with complex system state stored in a test database.

We can make our tests run faster by reusing the same fixture for several or many tests.

How It Works

The basic concept is pretty simple: We create a *Standard Fixture* (page 305) fixture that outlasts the lifetime of a single *Testcase Object* (page 382). This approach allows multiple tests to reuse the same test fixture without destroying that fixture and recreating it between tests. A *Shared Fixture* can be either a *Prebuilt Fixture* that is reused by one or more tests in many test runs or a fixture that is created by one test and reused by another test within the same test run. In either case, the key consideration is that many tests do not create their own fixtures but rather reuse a fixture "left over" from some other activity. The tests run faster because they have less fixture setup to perform, which *may* result in the test automater having to do less work to define the fixture for each test.

Shared
Fixture

When to Use It

Regardless of why we use them, *Shared Fixtures* come with some baggage that we should understand before we head down this path. The major issue with a *Shared Fixture* is that it can lead to interactions between tests, possibly resulting in *Erratic Tests* (page 228) if some tests depend on the outcomes of other tests. Another potential problem is that a fixture designed to serve many tests is bound to be much more complicated than the *Minimal Fixture* (page 302) needed for a single test. This greater complexity will typically take more effort to design and can lead to a *Fragile Fixture* (see *Fragile Test* on page 239) later on down the road when we need to modify the fixture.

A *Shared Fixture* will often result in an *Obscure Test* (page 186) because the fixture is not constructed inside the test. This potential disadvantage can be mitigated by using *Finder Methods* (see *Test Utility Method* on page 599) with Intent-Revealing Names [SBPP] to access the relevant parts of the fixture.

There are some valid reasons for using a *Shared Fixture* and some misguided ones. Many of the variations have been devised primarily to mitigate the negative consequences of using a *Shared Fixture*. So, what are *good* reasons for using a *Shared Fixture*?

Variation: Slow Tests

We can use a *Shared Fixture* when we cannot afford to build a new *Fresh Fixture* for each test. Typically, this scenario will occur when it takes too much processing to build a new fixture for each test, which often leads to *Slow Tests* (page 253). It most commonly occurs when we are testing with real test databases due to the high cost of creating each of the records. This growth in overhead tends to be exacerbated when we use the API of the SUT to create the reference data, because the SUT often does a lot of input validation, which may involve reading some of the just-written records.

A better solution is to make the tests run faster by not interacting with the database at all. For a more complete list of options, see the solutions to *Slow Tests* and the sidebar "Faster Tests Without Shared Fixtures" (page 319).

Faster Tests Without Shared Fixtures

The first reaction to *Slow Tests* (page 253) is often to switch to a *Shared Fixture* (page 317) approach. Several other solutions are available, however. This sidebar describes some experiences on several projects.

Fake Database

On one of our early XP projects, we wrote a lot of tests that accessed the database. At first we used a *Shared Fixture*. When we encountered *Interacting Tests* (see *Erratic Test* on page 228) and later *Test Run Wars* (see *Erratic Test*), however, we changed to a *Fresh Fixture* (page 311) approach. Because these tests needed a fair bit of reference data, they were taking a long time to run. On average, for every read or write the SUT did to or from the database, each test did several more. It was taking 15 minutes to run the full test suite of several hundred tests, which greatly impeded our ability to integrate our work quickly and often.

At the time, we were using a **data access layer** to keep the SQL out of our code. We soon discovered that it allowed us to replace the real database with a functionally equivalent *Fake Database* (see *Fake Object* on page 551). We started out by using simple HashTables to store the objects against a key. This approach allowed us to run many of our simpler tests "in memory" rather than against the database. And that bought us a significant drop in test execution time.

Our persistence framework supported an object query interface. We were able to build an interpreter of the object queries that ran against our HashTable database implementation and that allowed the majority of our tests to work entirely in memory. On average, our tests ran about 50 times faster in memory than with the database. For example, a test suite that took 10 minutes to run with the database took 10 seconds to run in memory.

This approach was so successful that we have reused the same testing infrastructure on many of our subsequent projects. Using the faked-out persistence framework also means we don't have to bother with building a "real database" until our object models stabilize, which can be several months into the project.

Incremental Speedups

Ted O'Grady and Joseph King are agile team leads on a large (50-plus developers, subject matter experts, and testers) eXtreme Programming project. Like many project teams building database-centric applications,

Continued...

**Shared
Fixture**

they suffered from *Slow Tests*. But they found a way around this problem: As of late 2005, their check-in test suite ran in less than 8 minutes compared to 8 hours for a full test run against the database. That is a pretty impressive speed difference. Here is their story:

> Currently we have about 6,700 tests that we run on a regular basis. We've actually tried a few things to speed up the tests and they've evolved over time.
>
> In January 2004, we were running our tests directly against a database via Toplink.
>
> In June 2004, we modified the application so we could run tests against an in-memory, in-process Java database (HSQL). This cut the time to run in half.
>
> In August 2004, we created a test-only framework that allowed Toplink to work without a database at all. That cut the time to run all the tests by a factor of 10.
>
> In July 2005, we built a shared "check-in" test execution server that allowed us to run tests remotely. This didn't save any time at first but it has proven to be quite useful nonetheless.
>
> In July 2005, we also started using a clustering framework that allowed us to run tests distributed across a network. This cut the time to run the tests in half.
>
> In August 2005, we removed the GUI and Master Data (reference data crud) tests from the "check-in suite" and ran them only from Cruise Control. This cut the time to run by approximately 15% to 20%.
>
> Since May 2004, we have also had Cruise Control run all the tests against the database at regular intervals. The time it takes Cruise Control to complete [the build and run the tests] has grown with the number of tests from an hour to nearly 8 hours now.
>
> When a threshold has been met that prevents the developers from (a) running [the tests] frequently when developing and (b) creating long check-in queues as people wait for the token to check in, we have adapted by experimenting with new techniques. As a rule we try to keep the running of the tests under 5 minutes, with anything over 8 minutes being a trigger to try something new.
>
> We have resisted thus far the temptation to run only a subset of the tests and instead focused on ways to speed up running all the tests—although as you can see, we have begun removing the tests

developers must run continuously (e.g., Master Data and GUI test suites are not required to check in, as they are run by Cruise Control and are areas that change infrequently).

Two of the most interesting solutions recently (aside from the in-memory framework) are the test server and the clustering framework.

The test server (named the "check-in" box here) is actually quite useful and has proven to be reliable and robust. We bought an Opteron box that is roughly twice as fast as the development boxes (really, the fastest box we could find). The server has an account set up for each development machine in the pit. Using the UNIX tool rsynch, the Eclipse workspace is synchronized with the user's corresponding server account file system. A series of shell scripts then recreates the database on the server for the remote account and runs all the development tests. When the tests have completed, a list of times to run each test is dumped to the console, along with a MyTestSuite.java class containing all the test failures, which the developer can use to run locally to fix any tests that have broken. The biggest advantage the remote server has provided is that it makes running a large number of tests feel fast again, because the developer can continue working while he or she waits for the results of the test server to come back.

The clustering framework (based on Condor) was quite fast but had the defect that it had to ship the entire workspace (11MB) to all the nodes on the network (×20), which had a significant cost, especially when a dozen pairs are using it. In comparison, the test server uses rsynch, which copies only the files that are new or different in the developer's workspace. The clustering framework also proved to be less reliable than the server solution, frequently not returning any status of the test run. There were also some tests that would not run reliably on the framework. Since it gave us roughly the same performance as the "check-in" test server, we have put this solution on the back burner.

Further Reading

A more detailed description of the first experience can be found at http://FasterTestsPaper.gerardmeszaros.com.

**Shared
Fixture**

Variation: Incremental Tests

We may also use *Shared Fixtures* when we have a long, complex sequence of actions, each of which depends on the previous actions. In customer tests, this may show up as a work flow; in unit tests, it may be a sequence of method calls on the same object. This case might be tested using a single *Eager Test* (see *Assertion Roulette* on page 224). The alternative is to put each distinct action into a separate *Test Method* (page 348) that builds upon the actions of a previous test operating on a *Shared Fixture*. This approach, which is an example of *Chained Tests* (page 454), is how testers in the "testing" (i.e., QA) community often operate: They set up a fixture and then run a sequence of tests, each of which builds upon the fixture. The testers do have one significant advantage over our *Fully Automated Tests* (see page 26): When a test partway through the chain fails, they are available to make decisions about how to recover or whether it is worth proceeding at all. In contrast, our automated tests just keep running, and many of them will generate test failures or errors because they did not find the fixture as expected and, therefore, the SUT behaved (probably correctly) differently. The resulting test results can obscure the real cause of the failure in a sea of red. With some experience it is often possible to recognize the failure pattern and deduce the root cause.[10]

This troubleshooting can be made simpler by starting each *Test Method* with one or more *Guard Assertions* (page 490) that document the assumptions the *Test Method* makes about the state of the fixture. When these assertions fail, they tell us to look elsewhere—either at tests that failed earlier in the **test suite** or at the order in which the tests were run.

Implementation Notes

A key implementation question with *Shared Fixtures* is, How do tests know about the objects in the *Shared Fixture* so they can (re)use them? Because the point of a *Shared Fixture* is to save execution time and effort by having multiple tests use the same instance of the test fixture, we'll need to keep a reference to the fixture we create. That way, we can find the fixture if it already exists and we can inform other tests that it now exists once we have constructed it. We have more choices available to us with *Per-Run Fixtures* because we can "remember" the fixture we set up in code more easily than a *Prebuilt Fixture* (page 429) set up by a different program. Although we *could* just hard-code the identifiers (e.g., database keys) of the fixture objects into all our tests, that technique would result in a *Fragile Fixture*. To avoid this problem, we need to keep a reference to the fixture when we create it and we need to make it possible for all tests to access that reference.

---

[10] It may not be as simple as looking at the first test that failed.

Variation: Per-Run Fixture

The simplest form of *Shared Fixture* is the *Per-Run Fixture*, in which we set up the fixture at the beginning of a test run and allow it to be shared by the tests within the run. Ideally, the fixture won't outlive the test run and we don't have to worry about interactions between test runs such as *Unrepeatable Tests* (a cause of *Erratic Tests*). If the fixture *is* persistent, such as when it is stored in a database, we may need to do explicit fixture teardown.

If a *Per-Run Fixture* is shared only within a single *Testcase Class* (page 373), the simplest solution is to use a class variable for each fixture object we need to hold a reference to and then use either *Lazy Setup* (page 435) or *Suite Fixture Setup* (page 441) to initialize the objects just before we run the first test in the suite. If we want to share the test fixture between many *Testcase Classes,* we'll need to use a *Setup Decorator* (page 447) to hold the setUp and tearDown methods and a *Test Fixture Registry* (see *Test Helper* on page 643) (which could just be the test database) to access the fixture.

Variation: Immutable Shared Fixture

The problem with *Shared Fixtures* is that they lead to *Erratic Tests* if tests modify the *Shared Fixture* (page 317). *Shared Fixtures* violate the *Independent Test* principle (see page 42). We can avoid this problem by making the *Shared Fixture* immutable; that is, we partition the fixture needed by tests into two logical parts. The first part is the stuff every test needs to have present but is never modified by any tests—that is, the *Immutable Shared Fixture.* The second part is the objects that *any* test needs to modify or delete; these objects should be built by each test as *Fresh Fixtures.*

The most difficult part of applying an *Immutable Shared Fixture* is deciding what constitutes a change to an object. The key guideline is this: If any test perceives something done by another test as a change to an object in the *Immutable Shared Fixture*, then that change shouldn't be allowed in any test with which it shares the fixture. Most commonly, the *Immutable Shared Fixture* consists of reference data that is needed by the actual per-test fixtures. The per-test fixtures can then be built as *Fresh Fixtures* on top of the *Immutable Shared Fixture.*

Motivating Example

The following example shows a *Testcase Class* setting up the test fixture via *Implicit Setup* (page 424). Each *Test Method* uses an instance variable to access the contents of the fixture.

```
public void testGetFlightsByFromAirport_OneOutboundFlight()
        throws Exception {
  setupStandardAirportsAndFlights();
  FlightDto outboundFlight = findOneOutboundFlight();
  // Exercise System
  List flightsAtOrigin = facade.getFlightsByOriginAirport(
              outboundFlight.getOriginAirportId());
  // Verify Outcome
  assertOnly1FlightInDtoList( "Flights at origin",
                               outboundFlight,
                               flightsAtOrigin);
}

public void testGetFlightsByFromAirport_TwoOutboundFlights()
        throws Exception {
  setupStandardAirportsAndFlights();
  FlightDto[] outboundFlights =
          findTwoOutboundFlightsFromOneAirport();
  // Exercise System
  List flightsAtOrigin = facade.getFlightsByOriginAirport(
          outboundFlights[0].getOriginAirportId());
  // Verify Outcome
  assertExactly2FlightsInDtoList( "Flights at origin",
                                   outboundFlights,
                                   flightsAtOrigin);
}
```

Note that the setUp method is run once for each *Test Method*. If the fixture setup is fairly complex and involves accessing a database, this approach could result in *Slow Tests*.

Refactoring Notes

To convert a *Testcase Class* from a *Standard Fixture* to a *Shared Fixture*, we simply convert the instance variables into class variables to make the fixture outlast the creating *Testcase Object*. We then need to initialize the class variables just once to avoid recreating them for each *Test Method*; *Lazy Setup* is an easy way to accomplish this task. Of course, other ways to set up the *Shared Fixture* are also possible, such as *Setup Decorator* or *Suite Fixture Setup*.

Example: Shared Fixture

This example shows the fixture converted to a *Shared Fixture* set up using *Lazy Setup*.

```
protected void setUp() throws Exception {
  if (sharedFixtureInitialized) {
    return;
```

```
      }
      facade = new FlightMgmtFacadeImpl();
      setupStandardAirportsAndFlights();
      sharedFixtureInitialized = true;
   }

   protected void tearDown() throws Exception {
      // We cannot delete any objects because we don't know
      // whether this is the last test
   }
```

The Lazy Initialization [SBPP] logic in the setUp method ensures that the *Shared Fixture* is created whenever the class variable is uninitialized. The *Test Methods* have also been modified to use a *Finder Method* to access the contents of the fixture:

```
public void testGetFlightsByFromAirport_OneOutboundFlight()
         throws Exception {
   FlightDto outboundFlight = findOneOutboundFlight();
   // Exercise System
   List flightsAtOrigin = facade.getFlightsByOriginAirport(
                        outboundFlight.getOriginAirportId());
   // Verify Outcome
   assertOnly1FlightInDtoList( "Flights at origin",
                               outboundFlight,
                               flightsAtOrigin);
}

public void testGetFlightsByFromAirport_TwoOutboundFlights()
         throws Exception {
   FlightDto[] outboundFlights =
      findTwoOutboundFlightsFromOneAirport();
   // Exercise System
   List flightsAtOrigin = facade.getFlightsByOriginAirport(
                        outboundFlights[0].getOriginAirportId());
   // Verify Outcome
   assertExactly2FlightsInDtoList( "Flights at origin",
                               outboundFlights,
                               flightsAtOrigin);
}
```

The details of how the *Test Utility Methods* such as setupStandardAirportsAndFlights are implemented are not shown here, because they are not important for understanding this example. It should be enough to understand that these methods create the airports and flights and store references to them in static variables so that all *Test Methods* can access the same fixture either directly or via *Test Utility Methods*.

Example: Immutable Shared Fixture

Here's an example of *Shared Fixture* "pollution":

```
public void testCancel_proposed_p()throws Exception {
   // shared fixture
   BigDecimal proposedFlightId = findProposedFlight();
   //      exercise SUT
   facade.cancelFlight(proposedFlightId);
   // verify outcome
   try{
      assertEquals(FlightState.CANCELLED,
                     facade.findFlightById(proposedFlightId));
   } finally {
      // teardown
      // try to undo the damage; hope this works!
      facade.overrideStatus( proposedFlightId,
                               FlightState.PROPOSED);
   }
}
```

We can avoid this problem by making the *Shared Fixture* immutable; that is, we partition the fixture needed by tests into two logical parts. The first part is the stuff every test needs to have present but is never modified by any tests—that is, the *Immutable Shared Fixture*. The second part is the objects that *any* test needs to modify or delete; these objects should be built by each test as *Fresh Fixtures*.

Here's the same test modified to use an *Immutable Shared Fixture*. We simply created our own mutableFlight within the test.

```
public void testCancel_proposed() throws Exception {
   // fixture setup
   BigDecimal mutableFlightId =
      createFlightBetweenInsigificantAirports();
   // exercise SUT
   facade.cancelFlight(mutableFlightId);
   // verify outcome
   assertEquals( FlightState.CANCELLED,
                  facade.findFlightById(mutableFlightId));
   // teardown
   //   None required because we let the SUT create
   //   new IDs for each flight. We might need to clean out
   //   the database eventually.
}
```

Note that we don't need any fixture teardown logic in this version of the test because the SUT uses a *Distinct Generated Value* (see *Generated Value* on page 723)—that is, we do not supply a flight number. We also use the predefined dummyAirport1 and dummyAirport2 to avoid changing the number of flights for airports used by other tests. Therefore, the mutable flights can accumulate in the database trouble-free.

Back Door Manipulation

*How can we verify logic independently when we cannot use
a round-trip test?*

**We set up the test fixture or verify the outcome by going through a back door
(such as direct database access).**

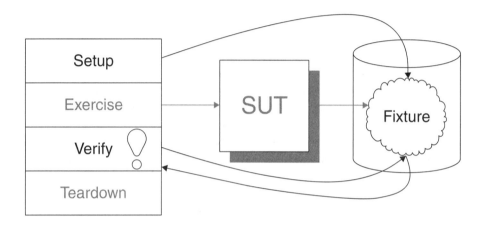

Every test requires a starting point (the test fixture) and an expected finishing
point (the expected results). The "normal" approach is to set up the fixture and
verify the outcome by using the API of the SUT itself. In some circumstances this
is either not possible or not desirable.

In some situations we can use *Back Door Manipulation* to set up the fixture
and/or verify the SUT's state.

How It Works

The state of the SUT comes in many flavors. It can be stored in memory, on disk
as files, in a database, or in other applications with which the SUT interacts.
Whatever form it takes, the pre-conditions of a test typically require that the
state of the SUT is not just known but is a specific state. Likewise, at the end of
the test we often want to do *State Verification* (page 462) of the SUT's state.

If we have access to the state of the SUT from outside the SUT, the test can
set up the pre-test state of the SUT by bypassing the normal API of the SUT
and interacting directly with whatever is holding that state via a "back door."
When exercising of the SUT has been completed, the test can similarly access

**Back Door
Manipulation**

the post-test state of the SUT via a back door to compare it with expected outcome. For customer tests, the back door is most commonly a test database, but it could also be some other component on which the SUT depends, including a Registry [PEAA] object or even the file system. For unit tests, the back door is some other class or object or an alternative interface of the SUT (or a *Test-Specific Subclass;* page 579) that exposes the state in a way "normal" clients wouldn't use. We can also replace a **depended-on component (DOC)** with a suitably configured *Test Double* (page 522) instead of using the real thing if that makes the job easier.

When to Use It

We might choose to use *Back Door Manipulation* for several reasons which we'll examine in more detail shortly. A prerequisite for using this technique is that some sort of back door to the state of the system must exist. The main drawback of *Back Door Manipulation* is that our tests—or the *Test Utility Methods* (page 599) they call—become much more closely coupled to the design decisions we make about how to represent the state of the SUT. If we need to change those decisions, we may encounter *Fragile Tests* (page 239). We need to decide whether this price is acceptable on a case-by-case basis. We can greatly reduce the impact of the close coupling by encapsulating all *Back Door Manipulation* in *Test Utility Methods*.

Using *Back Door Manipulation* can also lead to *Obscure Tests* (page 186) by hiding the relationship of the test outcome to the test fixture. We can avoid this problem by including the test data being passed to the *Back Door Manipulation* mechanism within the *Testcase Class* (page 373), or at least mitigate it by using *Finder Methods* (see *Test Utility Method*) to refer to the objects in the fixture via intent-revealing names.

A common application of *Back Door Manipulation* involves testing basic CRUD (Create, Read, Update, Delete) operations on the SUT's state. In such a case, we want to verify that the information persisted and can be recovered in the same form. It is difficult to write round-trip tests for "Read" without also testing "Create"; likewise, it is difficult to test "Update" or "Delete" without testing both "Create" and "Read." We can certainly test these operations by using round-trip tests, but this kind of testing won't detect certain types of systemic problems, such as putting information into the wrong database column. One solution is to conduct **layer-crossing tests** that use *Back Door Manipulation* to set up or verify the contents of the database directly. For a "Read" test, the test sets up the contents of the database using *Back Door Setup* and then asks the SUT to read the data. For a "Write" test, the test asks the system to write certain objects and then uses *Back Door Verification* on the contents of the database.

Variation: Back Door Setup

One reason for doing *Back Door Manipulation* is to make tests run faster. If a system does a lot of processing before putting data into its data store, the time it takes for a test to set up the fixture via the SUT's API could be quite significant. One way to make the tests run faster is to determine what those data stores should look like and then create a means to set them up via the back door rather than through the API. Unfortunately, this technique introduces its own problem: Because *Back Door Setup* bypasses enforcement of the object creation business rules, we may find ourselves creating fixtures that are not realistic and possibly even invalid. This problem may creep in over time as the business rules are modified in response to changing business needs. At the same time, this approach may allow us to create test scenarios that the SUT will not let us set up through its API.

When we share a database between our SUT and another application, we need to verify that we are using the database correctly and that we can handle all possible data configurations the other applications might create. *Back Door Setup* is a good way to establish these configurations—and it may be the only way if the SUT either doesn't write those tables or writes only specific (and valid) data configurations. *Back Door Setup* lets us create those "impossible" configurations easily so we can verify how the SUT behaves in these situations.

Variation: Back Door Verification

Back Door Verification involves sneaking in to do *State Verification* of the SUT's post-exercise state via a back door; it is mostly applicable to customer tests (or **functional tests,** as they are sometimes called). The back door is typically an alternative way to examine the objects in the database, usually through a standard API such as SQL or via data exports that can then be examined with a file comparison utility program.

As mentioned earlier, *Back Door Manipulation* can make tests run faster. If the only way to get at the SUT's state is to invoke an expensive operation (such as a complex report) or an operation that further modifies the SUT's state, we may be better off using *Back Door Manipulation*.

Another reason for doing *Back Door Manipulation* is that other systems expect the SUT to store its state in a specific way, which they can then access directly. This is a form of indirect output. In this situation, standard round-trip tests cannot prove that the SUT's behavior is correct because they cannot detect a systematic problem if the "Write" and "Read" operations make the same mistake, such as putting information into the wrong database column. The solution is a layer-crossing test that looks at the contents of the database directly to verify that the information is stored correctly. For a "Write" test, the test asks the system to write certain objects and then inspects the contents of the database via the back door.

Variation: Back Door Teardown

We can also use *Back Door Manipulation* to tear down a *Fresh Fixture* (page 311) that is stored in a test database. This ability is especially beneficial if we can use bulk database commands to wipe clean whole tables, as in *Table Truncation Teardown* (page 661) or *Transaction Rollback Teardown* (page 668).

Implementation Notes

How we implement *Back Door Manipulation* depends on where the fixture lives and how easily we can access the state of the SUT. It also depends on why we are doing *Back Door Manipulation*. This section lists the most common implementations, but feel free to use your imagination and come up with other ways to use this pattern.

Variation: Database Population Script

When the SUT stores its state in a database that it accesses as it runs, the easiest way to do *Back Door Manipulation* is to load data directly into that database before invoking the SUT. This approach is most commonly required when we are writing customer tests, but it may also be required for unit tests if the classes we are testing interact directly with the database. We must first determine the pre-conditions of the test and, from that information, identify the data that the test requires for its fixture. We then define a database script that inserts the corresponding records directly into the database bypassing the SUT logic. We use this *Database Population Script* whenever we want to set up the test fixture—a decision that depends on which test fixture strategy we have chosen. (See Chapter 6, *Test Automation Strategy,* for more on that topic.)

When deciding to use a *Database Population Script*, we will need to maintain both the *Database Population Script* and the files it takes as input whenever we modify either the structure of the SUT's data stores or the semantics of the data in them. This requirement can increase the maintenance cost of the tests.

Variation: Data Loader

A *Data Loader* is a special program that loads data into the SUT's data store. It differs from a *Database Population Script* in that the *Data Loader* is written in a programming language rather than a database language. This gives us a bit more flexibility and allows us to use the *Data Loader* even when the system state is stored somewhere other than a relational database.

If the data store is external to the SUT, such as in a relational database, the *Data Loader* can be "just another application" that writes to that data store. It would use the database in much the same way as the SUT but would get its inputs from a file rather than from wherever the SUT normally gets its inputs (e.g., other "upstream" programs). When we are using an object relational mapping (ORM) tool to access the database from our SUT, a simple way to build the *Data Loader* is to use the same domain objects and mappings in our *Data Loader*. We just create the desired objects in memory and commit the ORM's unit of work to save them into the database.

If the SUT stores data in internal data structures (e.g., in memory), the *Data Loader* may need to be an interface provided by the SUT itself. The following characteristics differentiate it from the normal functionality provided by the SUT:

- It is used only by the tests.

- It reads the data from a file rather than wherever the SUT normally gets the data.

- It bypasses a lot of the "edit checks" (input validation) normally done by the SUT.

The input files may be simple flat files containing comma- or tab-delimited text, or they could be structured using XML. DbUnit is an extension of JUnit that implements *Data Loader* for fixture setup.

Variation: Database Extraction Script

When the SUT stores its state in a database that it accesses as it runs, we can take advantage of this structure to do *Back Door Verification*. We simply use a database script to extract data from the test database and verify that it contains the right data either by comparing it to previously prepared "extract" files or by ensuring that specific queries return the right number of records.

Variation: Data Retriever

A *Data Retriever* is the analog of a *Data Loader* that retrieves the state from the SUT when doing *Back Door Verification*. Like a trusty dog, it "fetches" the data so that we can compare it with our expected results within our tests. DbUnit is an extension of JUnit that implements *Data Retriever* to support result verification.

**Back Door
Manipulation**

Variation: Test Double as Back Door

So far, all of the implementation techniques described here have involved interacting with a DOC of the SUT to set up or tear down the fixture or to verify the expected outcome. Probably the most common form of *Back Door Manipulation* involves *replacing* the DOC with a *Test Double*. One option is to use a *Fake Object* (page 551) that we have preloaded with some data as though the SUT had already been interacting with it; this strategy allows us to avoid using the SUT to set up the SUT's state. The other option is to use some kind of *Configurable Test Double* (page 558), such as a *Mock Object* (page 544) or a *Test Stub* (page 529). Either way, we can completely avoid *Obscure Tests* by making the state of the *Test Double* visible within the *Test Method* (page 348).

When we want to perform *Behavior Verification* (page 468) of the calls made by the SUT to one or more DOCs, we can use a layer-crossing test that replaces the DOC with a *Test Spy* (page 538) or a *Mock Object*. When we want to verify that the SUT behaves a specific way when it receives indirect inputs from a DOC (or when in some specific external state), we can replace the DOC with a *Test Stub*.

Motivating Example

The following round-trip test verifies the basic functionality of removing a flight by interacting with the SUT only via the front door. But it does not verify the indirect outputs of the SUT—namely, that the SUT is expected to call a logger to log each time a flight is removed along with the day/time when the request was made and the user ID of the requester. In many systems, this would be an example of "layer-crossing behavior": The logger is part of a generic infrastructure layer, while the SUT is an application-specific behavior.

```
public void testRemoveFlight() throws Exception {
    // setup
    FlightDto expectedFlightDto = createARegisteredFlight();
    FlightManagementFacade facade = new FlightManagementFacadeImpl();
    // exercise
    facade.removeFlight(expectedFlightDto.getFlightNumber());
    // verify
    assertFalse("flight should not exist after being removed",
            facade.flightExists( expectedFlightDto.
                                    getFlightNumber()));
}
```

Refactoring Notes

We can convert this test to use *Back Door Verification* by adding result verification code to access and verify the logger's state. We can do so either by reading that state from the logger's database or by replacing the logger with a *Test Spy* that saves the state for easy access by the tests.

Example: Back Door Result Verification Using a Test Spy

Here's the same test converted to use a *Test Spy* to access the post-test state of the logger:

```
public void testRemoveFlightLogging_recordingTestStub()
        throws Exception {
  // fixture setup
  FlightDto expectedFlightDto = createAnUnregFlight();
  FlightManagementFacade facade =
        new FlightManagementFacadeImpl();
  //    Test Double setup
  AuditLogSpy logSpy = new AuditLogSpy();
  facade.setAuditLog(logSpy);
  // exercise
  facade.removeFlight(expectedFlightDto.getFlightNumber());
  // verify
  assertEquals("number of calls", 1,
              logSpy.getNumberOfCalls());
  assertEquals("action code",
              Helper.REMOVE_FLIGHT_ACTION_CODE,
              logSpy.getActionCode());
  assertEquals("date", helper.getTodaysDateWithoutTime(),
              logSpy.getDate());
  assertEquals("user", Helper.TEST_USER_NAME,
              logSpy.getUser());
  assertEquals("detail",
              expectedFlightDto.getFlightNumber(),
              logSpy.getDetail());
}
```

This approach would be the better way to verify the logging if the logger's database contained so many entries that it wasn't practical to verify the new entries using *Delta Assertions* (page 485).

Example: Back Door Fixture Setup

The next example shows how we can set up a fixture using the database as a back door to the SUT. The test inserts a record into the EmailSubscription table and then asks the SUT to find it. It then makes assertions on various fields of the object returned by the SUT to verify that the record was read correctly.

**Back Door
Manipulation**

```
static final String      TABLE_NAME = "EmailSubscription";
static final BigDecimal RECORD_ID  = new BigDecimal("111");

static final String LOGIN_ID = "Bob";
static final String EMAIL_ID = "bob@foo.com";

public void setUp() throws Exception {
   String xmlString =
         "<?xml version='1.0' encoding='UTF-8'?>" +
         "<dataset>" +
         "     <" + TABLE_NAME +
         "         EmailSubscriptionId='" + RECORD_ID +  "'" +
         "         UserLoginId='" + LOGIN_ID + "'" +
         "         EmailAddress='" + EMAIL_ID + "'" +
         "         RecordVersionNum='62' " +
         "         CreateByUserId='MappingTest' " +
         "         CreateDateTime='2004-03-01 00:00:00.0'  " +
         "         LastModByUserId='MappingTest' " +
         "         LastModDateTime='2004-03-01 00:00:00.0'/>" +
         "</dataset>";
   insertRowsIntoDatabase(xmlString);
}

public void testRead_Login() throws Exception {
   // exercise
   EmailSubscription subs =
         EmailSubscription.findInstanceWithId(RECORD_ID);
   // verify
   assertNotNull("Email Subscription", subs);
   assertEquals("User Name", LOGIN_ID, subs.getUserName());
}

public void testRead_Email() throws Exception {
   // exercise
   EmailSubscription subs =
         EmailSubscription.findInstanceWithId(RECORD_ID);
   // verify
   assertNotNull("Email Subscription", subs);
   assertEquals("Email Address",
               EMAIL_ID,
               subs.getEmailAddress());
}
```

The XML document used to populate the database is built within the *Testcase
Class* so as to avoid the *Mystery Guest* (see *Obscure Test*) that would have been
created if we had used an external file for loading the database [the discussion of
the In-line Resource (page 736) refactoring explains this approach]. To make the
test clearer, we call intent-revealing methods that hide the details of how we use
DbUnit to load the database and clean it out at the end of the test using *Table
Truncation Teardown*. Here are the bodies of the *Test Utility Methods* used in
this example:

```
private void insertRowsIntoDatabase(String xmlString)
        throws Exception {
    IDataSet dataSet = new FlatXmlDataSet(new StringReader(xmlString));
    DatabaseOperation.CLEAN_INSERT.
        execute( getDbConnection(), dataSet);
}

public void tearDown() throws Exception{
    emptyTable(TABLE_NAME);
}

public void emptyTable(String tableName) throws Exception {
    IDataSet dataSet = new DefaultDataSet(new DefaultTable(tableName));
    DatabaseOperation.DELETE_ALL.
        execute(getDbConnection(), dataSet);
}
```

Of course, the implementations of these methods are specific to DbUnit; we must change them if we use some other member of the xUnit family.

Some other observations on these tests: To avoid an *Eager Test* (see *Assertion Roulette* on page 224), the assertion on each field appears in a separate test. This structure could result in *Slow Tests* (page 253) because these tests interact with a database. We could use *Lazy Setup* (page 435) or *Suite Fixture Setup* (page 441) to avoid setting up the fixture more than once as long as the resulting *Shared Fixture* (page 317) was not modified by any of the tests. (I chose not to further complicate this example by taking this tack.)

Further Reading

See the sidebar "Database as SUT API?" on page 336 for an example of when the back door is really a front door.

Back Door Manipulation

Database as SUT API?

A common technique for setting up test fixtures is *Back Door Setup* (see *Back Door Manipulation* on page 327); for verifying test outcomes, *Back Door Verification* (see *Back Door Manipulation*) is a popular option. But when is a test that interacts directly with the database behind a SUT not considered to be going through the back door?

On a recent project, some friends were struggling with this very question, though at first they didn't realize it. One of their analysts (who was also a power user) seemed overly focused on the database schema. At first, they put this narrow focus down to the analyst's Powerbuilder background and tried to break him of the habit. That didn't work. The analyst just dug in his heels. The developers tried explaining that on agile projects it was important not to try to define the whole data schema at the beginning of the project; instead, the schema evolved as the requirements were implemented.

Of course, the analyst complained every time they modified the database schema because the changes broke all his queries. As the project unfolded, the other team members slowly started to understand that the analyst really did need a stable database against which to run queries. It was his way to verify the correctness of the data generated by the system.

Once they recognized this requirement, the developers were able to treat the query schema as a formal interface provided by the system. Customer tests were written against this interface and developers had to ensure that those tests still passed whenever they changed the database. To minimize the impact of database refactorings, they defined a set of query views that implemented this interface. This approach allowed them to refactor the database as needed.

When might you find yourself in this situation? Any time your customer applies reporting tools (such as Crystal Reports) to *your* database, an argument can be made as to whether part of the requirements is a stable reporting interface. Similarly, if the customer uses scripts (such as DTS or SQL) to load data into the database, there may be a requirement for a stable data loading interface.

Layer Test

*How can we verify logic independently when it is part of
a layered architecture?*

We write separate tests for each layer of the layered architecture.

Also known as:
*Single
Layer Test,
Testing by
Layers,
Layered Test*

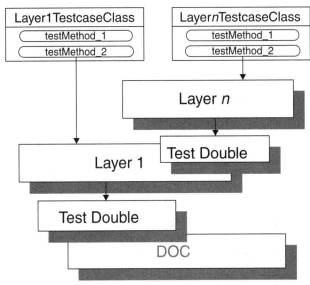

It is difficult to obtain good test coverage when testing an entire application in a top-to-bottom fashion; we are bound to end up doing *Indirect Testing* (see *Obscure Test* on page 186) on some parts of the application. Many applications use a Layered Architecture [DDD, PEAA, WWW] to separate the major technical concerns. Most applications have some kind of presentation (user interface) layer, a business logic layer or **domain layer,** and a persistence layer. Some layered architectures have even more layers.

An application with a layered architecture can be tested more effectively by testing each layer in isolation.

How It Works

We design the SUT using a layered architecture that separates the presentation logic from the business logic and from any persistence mechanism or interfaces to other systems.[11] We put all business logic into a Service Layer [PEAA] that exposes the application functionality to the presentation layer as an **API**. We treat each layer of the architecture as a separate SUT. We write component tests for each layer independent of the other layers of the architecture. That is, for layer n of the architecture, the tests will take the place of layer n+1; we may optionally replace layer n-1 with a *Test Double* (page 522).

When to Use It

We can use a *Layer Test* whenever we have a layered architecture and we want to provide good test coverage of the logic in each layer. It can be much simpler to test each layer independently than it is to test all the layers at once. This is especially true when we want to do defensive coding for return values of calls across the layer boundary. In software that is working correctly, these errors "should never happen"; in real life, they do. To make sure our code handles these errors, we can inject these "never happen" scenarios as indirect inputs to our layer.

Layer Tests are very useful when we want to divide up the project team into subteams based on the technology in which the team members specialize. Each layer of an architecture tends to require different knowledge and often uses different technologies; therefore, the layer boundaries serve as natural team boundaries. *Layer Tests* can be a good way to nail down and document the semantics of the layer interfaces.

Even when we choose to use a *Layer Test* strategy, it is a good idea to include a few "top-to-bottom" tests just to verify that the various layers are integrated correctly. These tests need to cover only one or two basic scenarios; we don't need to test every business test condition because all of them have already been tested in the *Layer Tests* for at least one of the layers.

Most of the variations on this pattern reflect which layer is being tested independently of the other layers.

Variation: Presentation Layer Test

One could write a whole book just on patterns of presentation layer testing. The specific patterns depend on the nature of the presentation layer technology (e.g., graphical user interface, traditional Web interface, "smart" Web interface, Web services). Regardless of the technology, the key is to test the presentation logic separately from the business logic so that we don't have to worry about changes

---

[11] Not all presentation logic relates to the user interface; this logic can also appear in a messaging interface used by another application.

in the underlying logic affecting our presentation layer tests. (They are hard enough to automate well as it is!)

Another consideration is to design the presentation layer so that its logic can be tested independently of the presentation framework. *Humble Dialog* (see *Humble Object* on page 695) is the key **design-for-testability** pattern to apply here. In effect, we are defining sublayers within the presentation layer; the layer containing the *Humble Dialogs* is the "presentation graphic layer" and the layer we have made testable is the "presentation behavior layer." This separation of layers allows us to verify that buttons are activated, menu items are grayed out, and so on, without instantiating any of the real graphical objects.

Variation: Service Layer Test

The Service Layer is where most of our unit tests and component tests are traditionally concentrated. Testing the business logic using customer tests is a bit more challenging because testing the Service Layer via the presentation layer often involves *Indirect Testing* and *Sensitive Equality* (see *Fragile Test* on page 239), either of which can lead to *Fragile Tests* and *High Test Maintenance Cost* (page 265). Testing the Service Layer directly helps avoid these problems.

To avoid *Slow Tests* (page 253), we usually replace the persistence layer with a *Fake Database* (see *Fake Object* on page 551) and then run the tests. In fact, most of the impetus behind a layered architecture is to isolate this code from the other, harder-to-test layers. Alistair Cockburn puts an interesting spin on this idea in his description of a Hexagonal Architecture at http://alistair.cockburn.us [WWW].

The Service Layer may come in handy for other uses. It can be used to run the application in "headless" mode (without a presentation layer attached), such as when using macros to automate frequently done tasks in Microsoft Excel.

Variation: Persistence Layer Test

The persistence layer also needs to be tested. Round-trip tests will often suffice if the application is the only one that uses the data store. But these tests won't catch one kind of programming error: when we accidentally put information into the wrong columns. As long as the data type of the interchanged columns is compatible and we make the same error when reading the data, our round-trip tests will pass! This kind of bug won't affect the operation of our application but it might make support more difficult and it *will* cause problems in interactions with other applications.

When other applications also use the data store, it is highly advisable to implement at least a few layer-crossing tests that verify information is put into the correct columns of tables. We can use *Back Door Manipulation* (page 327) to either set up the database contents or to verify the post-test database contents.

Variation: Subcutaneous Test

A *Subcutaneous Test* is a degenerate form of *Layer Test* that bypasses the presentation layer of the system to interact directly with the Service Layer. In most cases, the Service Layer is not isolated from the layer(s) below; therefore, we test everything except the presentation. Use of a *Subcutaneous Test* does not require as strict a separation of concerns as does a *Service Layer Test,* which makes *Subcutaneous Test* easier to use when we are retrofitting tests onto an application that wasn't designed for testability. We should use a *Subcutaneous Test* whenever we are writing customer tests for an application and we want to ensure our tests are robust. A *Subcutaneous Test* is much less likely to be broken by changes to the application[12] because it does not interact with the application via the presentation layer; as a consequence, a whole category of changes won't affect it.

Variation: Component Test

A *Component Test* is the most general form of *Layer Test,* in that we can think of the layers being made up of individual components that act as "micro-layers." *Component Tests* are a good way to specify or document the behavior of individual components when we are doing component-based development and some of the components must be modified or built from scratch.

Implementation Notes

We can write our *Layer Tests* as either round-trip tests or layer-crossing tests. Each has advantages. In practice, we typically mix both styles of tests. The round-trip tests are easier to write (assuming we already have a suitable *Fake Object* available to use for layer n-1). We need to use layer-crossing tests, however, when we are verifying the error-handling logic in layer n.

Round-Trip Tests

A good starting point for *Layer Tests* is the round-trip test, as it should be sufficient for most *Simple Success Tests* (see *Test Method* on page 348). These tests can be written such that they do not care whether we have fully isolated the layer of interest from the layers below. We can either leave the real components in place so that they are exercised indirectly, or we can replace them

---

[12] Less likely than a test that exercises the logic via the presentation layer, that is.

with *Fake Objects*. The latter option is particularly useful when by a database or asynchronous mechanisms in the layer below lead to *Slow Tests*.

Controlling Indirect Inputs

We can replace a lower layer of the system with a *Test Stub* (page 529) that returns "canned" results based on what the client layer passes in a request (e.g., Customer 0001 is a valid customer, 0002 is a dormant customer, 0003 has three accounts). This technique allows us to test the client logic with well-understood indirect inputs from the layer below. It is particularly useful when we are automating *Expected Exception Tests* (see *Test Method*) or when we are exercising behavior that depends on data that arrives from an upstream system.[13] The alternative is to use *Back Door Manipulation* to set up the indirect inputs.

Verifying Indirect Outputs

When we want to verify the indirect outputs of the layer of interest, we can use a *Mock Object* (page 544) or *Test Spy* (page 538) to replace the components in the layer below the SUT. We can then compare the actual calls made to the DOC with the expected calls. The alternative is to use *Back Door Manipulation* to verify the indirect outputs of the SUT after they have occurred.

Motivating Example

When trying to test all layers of the application at the same time, we must verify the correctness of the business logic through the presentation layer. The following test is a very simple example of testing some trivial business logic through a trivial user interface:

```
private final int LEGAL_CONN_MINS_SAME = 30;
public void testAnalyze_sameAirline_LessThanConnectionLimit()
throws Exception {
    // setup
    FlightConnection illegalConn =
        createSameAirlineConn( LEGAL_CONN_MINS_SAME - 1);
    // exercise
    FlightConnectionAnalyzerImpl sut =
        new FlightConnectionAnalyzerImpl();
    String actualHtml =
        sut.getFlightConnectionAsHtmlFragment(
                illegalConn.getInboundFlightNumber(),
                illegalConn.getOutboundFlightNumber());
```

---

[13] Typically this data goes directly into a shared database or is injected via a "data pump."

```
    // verification
    StringBuffer expected = new StringBuffer();
    expected.append("<span class="boldRedText">");
    expected.append("Connection time between flight ");
    expected.append(illegalConn.getInboundFlightNumber());
    expected.append(" and flight ");
    expected.append(illegalConn.getOutboundFlightNumber());
    expected.append(" is ");
    expected.append(illegalConn.getActualConnectionTime());
    expected.append(" minutes.</span>");
    assertEquals("html", expected.toString(), actualHtml);
}
```

This test contains knowledge about the business layer functionality (what makes a connection illegal) and presentation layer functionality (how an illegal connection is presented). It also depends on the database because the FlightConnections are retrieved from another component. If any of these areas change, this test must be revisited as well.

Refactoring Notes

We can split this test into two separate tests: one to test the business logic (What constitutes an illegal connection?) and one to test the presentation layer (Given an illegal connection, how should it be displayed to the user?). We would typically do so by duplicating the entire *Testcase Class* (page 373), stripping out the presentation layer logic verification from the business layer *Test Methods,* and stubbing out the business layer object(s) in the presentation layer *Test Methods.*

Along the way, we will probably find that we can reduce the number of tests in at least one of the *Testcase Classes* because few test conditions exist for that layer. In this example, we started out with four tests (the combinations of same/different airlines and time periods), each of which tested both the business and presentation layers; we ended up with four tests in the business layer (the original combinations but tested directly) and two tests in the presentation layer (formatting of legal and illegal connections).[14] Therefore, only the latter two tests need to be concerned with the details of the string formatting and, when a test fails, we know which layer holds the bug.

We can take our refactoring even further by using a *Replace Dependency with Test Double* (page 739) refactoring to turn this *Subcutaneous Test* into a true *Service Layer Test.*

---

[14] I'm glossing over the various error-handling tests to simplify this discussion, but note that a Layer Test also makes it easier to exercise the error-handling logic.

Example: Presentation Layer Test

The following example shows the earlier test refactored to verify the behavior of the presentation layer when an illegal connection is requested. It stubs out the FlightConnAnalyzer and configures it with the illegal connection to return to the HtmlFacade when it is called. This technique gives us complete control over the indirect input of the SUT.

```java
public void testGetFlightConnAsHtml_illegalConnection()
throws Exception {
   // setup
   FlightConnection illegalConn = createIllegalConnection();
   Mock analyzerStub = mock(IFlightConnAnalyzer.class);
   analyzerStub.expects(once()).method("analyze")
         .will(returnValue(illegalConn));
   HTMLFacade htmlFacade =
         new HTMLFacade( (IFlightConnAnalyzer)analyzerStub.proxy());
   // exercise
   String actualHtmlString =
         htmlFacade.getFlightConnectionAsHtmlFragment(
                     illegalConn.getInboundFlightNumber(),
                     illegalConn.getOutboundFlightNumber());
   // verify
   StringBuffer expected = new StringBuffer();
   expected.append("<span class=\"boldRedText\">");
   expected.append("Connection time between flight ");
   expected.append(illegalConn.getInboundFlightNumber());
   expected.append(" and flight ");
   expected.append(illegalConn.getOutboundFlightNumber());
   expected.append(" is ");
   expected.append(illegalConn.getActualConnectionTime());
   expected.append(" minutes.</span>");
   assertEquals("returned HTML",
               expected.toString(),
               actualHtmlString);
}
```

We must compare the string representations of the HTML to determine whether the code has generated the correct response. Fortunately, we need only two such tests to verify the basic behavior of this component.

Example: Subcutaneous Test

Here's the original test converted into a *Subcutaneous Test* that bypasses the presentation layer to verify that the connection information is calculated correctly. Note the lack of any string manipulation in this test.

```
private final int LEGAL_CONN_MINS_SAME = 30;
public void testAnalyze_sameAirline_LessThanConnectionLimit()
throws Exception {
  // setup
  FlightConnection expectedConnection =
        createSameAirlineConn( LEGAL_CONN_MINS_SAME -1);
  // exercise
  IFlightConnAnalyzer theConnectionAnalyzer =
        new FlightConnAnalyzer();
  FlightConnection actualConnection =
        theConnectionAnalyzer.getConn(
                expectedConnection.getInboundFlightNumber(),
                expectedConnection.getOutboundFlightNumber());
  // verification
  assertNotNull("actual connection", actualConnection);
  assertFalse("IsLegal", actualConnection.isLegal());
}
```

While we have bypassed the presentation layer, we have not attempted to isolate
the Service Layer from the layers below. This omission could result in *Slow Tests*
or *Erratic Tests* (page 228).

Example: Business Layer Test

The next example shows the same test converted into a *Service Layer Test* that
is fully isolated from the layers below it. We have used JMock to replace these
components with *Mock Objects* that verify the correct flights are being looked
up and that inject the corresponding flight constructed into the SUT.

```
public void testAnalyze_sameAirline_EqualsConnectionLimit()
throws Exception {
  // setup
  Mock flightMgntStub = mock(FlightManagementFacade.class);
  Flight firstFlight = createFlight();
  Flight secondFlight = createConnectingFlight(
                        firstFlight, LEGAL_CONN_MINS_SAME);
  flightMgntStub.expects(once()).method("getFlight")
                .with(eq(firstFlight.getFlightNumber()))
                .will(returnValue(firstFlight));
  flightMgntStub.expects(once()).method("getFlight")
                .with(eq(secondFlight.getFlightNumber()))
                .will(returnValue(secondFlight));
  // exercise
  FlightConnAnalyzer theConnectionAnalyzer = new FlightConnAnalyzer();
  theConnectionAnalyzer.facade =
        (FlightManagementFacade)flightMgntStub.proxy();
  FlightConnection actualConnection =
        theConnectionAnalyzer.getConn(
                        firstFlight.getFlightNumber(),
                        secondFlight.getFlightNumber());
```

```
    // verification
    assertNotNull("actual connection", actualConnection);
    assertTrue("IsLegal", actualConnection.isLegal());
}
```

This test runs very quickly because the Service Layer is fully isolated from any underlying layers. It is also likely to be much more robust because it tests much less code.

Chapter 19

xUnit Basics Patterns

Patterns in This Chapter

Test Method

Where do we put our test code?

We encode each test as a single Test Method on some class.

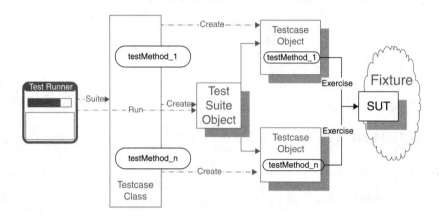

Fully Automated Tests (see page 26) consist of test logic. That logic has to live somewhere before we can compile and execute it.

How It Works

We define each **test** as a method, procedure, or function that implements the *four phases* (see *Four-Phase Test* on page 358) necessary to realize a *Fully Automated Test*. Most notably, the *Test Method* must include assertions if it is to be a *Self-Checking Test* (see page 26).

We organize the test logic following one of the standard *Test Method* templates to make the type of test easily recognizable by test readers. In a *Simple Success Test,* we have a purely linear flow of control from fixture setup through exercising the SUT to result verification. In an *Expected Exception Test,* language-based structures direct us to error-handling code. If we reach that code, we pass the test; if we don't, we fail it. In a *Constructor Test,* we simply instantiate an object and make assertions against its attributes.

Why We Do This

We have to encode the test logic somewhere. In the procedural world, we would encode each test as a test case procedure located in a file or module. In object-oriented programming languages, the preferred option is to encode them as methods on a suitable *Testcase Class* (page 373) and then to turn these *Test Methods* into *Testcase Objects* (page 382) at runtime using either *Test Discovery* (page 393) or *Test Enumeration* (page 399).

We follow the standard test templates to keep our *Test Methods* as simple as possible. This greatly increases their utility as system documentation (see page 23) by making it easier to find the description of the basic behavior of the SUT. It is a lot easier to recognize which tests describe this basic behavior if only *Expected Exception Tests* contain error-handling language constructs such as try/catch.

Implementation Notes

We still need a way to run all the *Test Methods* tests on the *Testcase Class*. One solution is to define a static method on the *Testcase Class* that calls each of the test methods. Of course, we would also have to deal with counting the tests and determining how many passed and how many failed. Because this functionality is needed for a test suite anyway, a simple solution is to instantiate a *Test Suite Object* (page 387) to hold each *Test Method*.[1] This approach is easy to implement if we create an instance of the *Testcase Class* for each *Test Method* using either *Test Discovery* or *Test Enumeration*.

In statically typed languages such as Java and C#, we may have to include a throws clause as part of the *Test Method* declaration so the compiler won't complain about the fact that we are not handling the checked exceptions that the SUT has declared it may throw. In effect, we tell the compiler that "The *Test Runner* (page 377) will deal with the exceptions."

Of course, different kinds of functionality need different kinds of *Test Methods*. Nevertheless, almost all tests can be boiled down to one of three basic types.

Variation: Simple Success Test

Most software has an obvious success scenario (or "happy path"). A *Simple Success Test* verifies the success scenario in a simple and easily recognized way.

---

[1] See the sidebar "There's Always an Exception" (page 384) for an explanation of when this *isn't* the case.

We create an instance of the SUT and call the method(s) that we want to test. We then assert that the expected outcome has occurred. In other words, we follow the normal steps of a *Four-Phase Test*. What we don't do is catch any exceptions that *could* happen. Instead, we let the *Test Automation Framework* (page 298) catch and report them. Doing otherwise would result in *Obscure Tests* (page 186) and would mislead the test reader by making it appear as if exceptions were expected. See *Tests as Documentation* for the rationale behind this approach.

Another benefit of avoiding try/catch-style code is that when errors do occur, it is a lot easier to track them down because the *Test Automation Framework* reports the location where the actual error occurred deep in the SUT rather than the place in our test where we called an *Assertion Method* (page 362) such as fail or assertTrue. These kinds of errors turn out to be much easier to troubleshoot than assertion failures.

Variation: Expected Exception Test

Writing software that passes the *Simple Success Test* is pretty straightforward. Most of the defects in software appear in the various alternative paths—especially the ones that relate to error scenarios, because these scenarios are often *Untested Requirements* (see *Production Bugs* on page 268) or *Untested Code* (see *Production Bugs*). An *Expected Exception Test* helps us verify that the error scenarios have been coded correctly. We set up the test fixture and exercise the SUT in each way that should result in an error. We ensure that the expected error has occurred by using whatever language construct we have available to catch the error. If the error is raised, flow will pass to the error-handling block. This diversion may be enough to let the test pass, but if the type or message contents of the exception or error is important (such as when the error message will be shown to a user), we can use an *Equality Assertion* (see *Assertion Method*) to verify it. If the error is not raised, we call fail to report that the SUT failed to raise an error as expected.

We should write an *Expected Exception Test* for each kind of exception that the SUT is *expected* to raise. It may raise the error because the client (i.e., our test) has asked it to do something invalid, or it may translate or pass through an error raised by some other component it uses. We should not write an *Expected Exception Test* for exceptions that the SUT might raise but that we cannot force to occur on cue, because these kinds of errors should show up as test failures in the *Simple Success Tests*. If we want to verify that these kinds of errors *are* handled properly, we must find a way to force them to occur. The most common way to do so is to use a *Test Stub* (page 529) to control the indirect input of the SUT and raise the appropriate errors in the *Test Stub*.

Test Method

Exception tests are very interesting to write about because of the different ways the xUnit frameworks express them. JUnit 3.x provides a special Expected-Exception class to inherit from. This class forces us to create a *Testcase Class* for each *Test Method* (page 348), however, so it really doesn't save any effort over coding a try/catch block and does result in a large number of very small *Testcase Classes*. Later versions of JUnit and NUnit (for .NET) provide a special ExpectedException **method attribute** (called an **annotation** in Java) to tell the *Test Automation Framework* to fail the test if that exception *isn't* raised. This method attribute allows us to include message text if we want to specify exactly which text to expect in addition to the type of the exception.

Languages that support **blocks,** such as Smalltalk and Ruby, can provide special assertions to which we pass the block of code to be executed as well as the expected exception/error object. The *Assertion Method* implements the error-handling logic required to determine whether the error has, in fact, occurred. This makes our *Test Methods* much simpler, even though we may need to examine the names of the assertions more closely to see which type of test we have.

Variation: Constructor Test

We would have a lot of *Test Code Duplication* (page 213) if every test we wrote had to verify that the objects it creates in its fixture setup phase are correctly instantiated. We avoid this step by testing the constructor(s) separately from other *Test Methods* whenever the constructor contains anything more complex than a simple field assignment from the constructor parameters. These *Constructor Tests* provide better *Defect Localization* (see page 22) than including constructor logic verification in other tests. We may need to write one or more tests for each constructor signature. Most *Constructor Tests* will follow a *Simple Success Test* template; however, we can use an *Expected Exception Test* to verify that the constructor correctly reports invalid arguments by raising an exception.

We should verify each attribute of the object or data structure regardless of whether we expect it to be initialized. For attributes that should be initialized, we can use an *Equality Assertion* to specify the correct value. For attributes that should not be initialized, we can use a *Stated Outcome Assertion* (see *Assertion Method*) appropriate to the type of the attribute [e.g., assertNull(anObjectReference) for object variables or pointers]. Note that if we are organizing our tests with one *Testcase Class per Fixture* (page 631), we can put each assertion into a separate *Test Method* to give optimal *Defect Localization*.

Variation: Dependency Initialization Test

When we have an object with a **substitutable dependency,** we need to make sure that the attribute that holds the reference to the depended-on component (DOC) is initialized to the real DOC when the software is run in production. A *Dependency Initialization Test* is a *Constructor Test* that asserts that this attribute is initialized correctly. It is often done in a different *Test Method* from the normal *Constructor Tests* to improve its visibility.

Example: Simple Success Test

The following example illustrates a test where the novice test automater has included code to catch exceptions that he or she knows might occur (or that the test automater might have encountered while debugging the code).

```
public void testFlightMileage_asKm() throws Exception {
    // set up fixture
    Flight newFlight = new Flight(validFlightNumber);
    try {
        // exercise SUT
        newFlight.setMileage(1122);
        // verify results
        int actualKilometres = newFlight.getMileageAsKm();
        int expectedKilometres = 1810;
        // verify results
        assertEquals( expectedKilometres, actualKilometres);
    } catch (InvalidArgumentException e) {
        fail(e.getMessage());
    } catch (ArrayStoreException e) {
        fail(e.getMessage());
    }
}
```

The majority of the code is unnecessary and just obscures the intent of the test. Luckily for us, all of this exception handling can be avoided. xUnit has built-in support for catching *unexpected* exceptions. We can rip out all the exception-handling code and let the *Test Automation Framework* catch any *unexpected* exception that might be thrown. Unexpected exceptions are counted as test errors because the test terminates in a way we didn't anticipate. This is useful information and is not considered to be any more severe than a test failure.

```
public void testFlightMileage_asKm() throws Exception {
    // set up fixture
    Flight newFlight = new Flight(validFlightNumber);
    newFlight.setMileage(1122);
    // exercise mileage translator
    int actualKilometres = newFlight.getMileageAsKm();
```

```
      // verify results
      int expectedKilometres = 1810;
      assertEquals( expectedKilometres, actualKilometres);
   }
```

This example is in Java (a statically typed language), so we had to declare that the SUT may throw an exception as part of the *Test Method* signature.

Example: Expected Exception Test Using try/catch

The following example is a partially complete test to verify an exception case. The novice test automater has set up the right test condition to cause the SUT to raise an error.

```
   public void testSetMileage_invalidInput() throws Exception {
      // set up fixture
      Flight newFlight = new Flight(validFlightNumber);
      // exercise SUT
      newFlight.setMileage(-1122);  // invalid
      // how do we verify an exception was thrown?
   }
```

Because the *Test Automation Framework* will catch the exception and fail the test, the *Test Runner* will not exhibit the green bar even though the SUT's behavior is correct. We can introduce an error-handling block around the exercise phase of the test and use it to invert the pass/fail criteria (pass when the exception is thrown; fail when it is not). Here's how to verify that the SUT fails as expected in JUnit 3.x:

```
   public void testSetMileage_invalidInput() throws Exception {
      // set up fixture
      Flight newFlight = new Flight(validFlightNumber);
      try {
         // exercise SUT
         newFlight.setMileage(-1122);
         fail("Should have thrown InvalidInputException");
      } catch( InvalidArgumentException e) {
         // verify results
         assertEquals( "Flight mileage must be positive",
                       e.getMessage());
      }
   }
```

This style of try/catch can be used only in languages that allow us to specify exactly which exception to catch. It won't work if we want to catch a generic exception or the same exception that the *Assertion Method* fail throws, because these exceptions will send us into the catch clause. In these cases we need to use the same style of *Expected Exception Test* as used in tests of *Custom Assertions* (page 474).

```
public void testSetMileage_invalidInput2() throws Exception {
    // set up fixture
    Flight newFlight = new Flight(validFlightNumber);
    try {
        // exercise SUT
        newFlight.setMileage(-1122);
        // cannot fail() here if SUT throws same kind of exception
    } catch( AssertionFailedError e) {
        // verify results
        assertEquals( "Flight mileage must be positive",
                      e.getMessage());
        return;
    }
    fail("Should have thrown InvalidInputException");
}
```

Test Method

Example: Expected Exception Test Using Method Attributes

NUnit provides a method attribute that lets us write an *Expected Exception Test* without forcing us to code a try/catch block explicitly.

```
[Test]
[ExpectedException(typeof( InvalidArgumentException),
                          "Flight mileage must be > zero")]
public void testSetMileage_invalidInput_AttributeWithMessage()
{
    // set up fixture
    Flight newFlight = new Flight(validFlightNumber);
    // exercise SUT
    newFlight.setMileage(-1122);
}
```

This approach does make the test much more compact but doesn't provide a way to specify anything but the type of the exception or the message it contains. If we want to make any assertions on other contents of the exception (to avoid *Sensitive Equality; see Fragile Test* on page 239), we'll need to use try/catch.

Example: Expected Exception Test Using Block Closure

Smalltalk's SUnit provides another mechanism to achieve the same thing:

```
testSetMileageWithInvalidInput
    self
        should: [Flight new mileage: -1122]
        raise: RuntimeError new 'Should have raised error'
```

Because Smalltalk supports block closures, we pass the block of code to be executed to the method should:raise: along with the expected Exception object. Ruby's Test::Unit uses the same approach:

```
def testSetMileage_invalidInput
   flight = Flight.new();
   assert_raises( RuntimeError, "Should have raised error") do
      flight.setMileage(-1122)
   end
end
```

The code between the do/end pair is a closure that is executed by the assert_raises method. If it doesn't raise an instance of the first argument (the class RuntimeError), the test fails and presents the error message supplied.

Example: Constructor Test

In this example, we need to build a flight to test the conversion of the flight distance from miles to kilometers. First, we'll make sure the flight is constructed properly.

```
public void testFlightMileage_asKm2() throws Exception {
   // set up fixture
   // exercise constructor
   Flight newFlight = new Flight(validFlightNumber);
   // verify constructed object
   assertEquals(validFlightNumber, newFlight.number);
   assertEquals("", newFlight.airlineCode);
   assertNull(newFlight.airline);
   // set up mileage
   newFlight.setMileage(1122);
   // exercise mileage translator
   int actualKilometres = newFlight.getMileageAsKm();
   // verify results
   int expectedKilometres = 1810;
   assertEquals( expectedKilometres, actualKilometres);
   // now try it with a canceled flight
   newFlight.cancel();
   try {
      newFlight.getMileageAsKm();
      fail("Expected exception");
   } catch (InvalidRequestException e) {
      assertEquals( "Cannot get cancelled flight mileage",
                    e.getMessage());
   }
}
```

This test is not a *Single-Condition Test* (see page 45) because it examines both object construction and distance conversion behavior. If object construction fails, we won't know which issue was the cause of the failure until we start debugging the test.

Test Method

It would be better to separate this *Eager Test* (see *Assertion Roulette* on page 224) into two tests, each of which is a *Single-Condition Test*. This is most easily done by cloning the *Test Method*, renaming each copy to reflect what it would do if it were a *Single-Condition Test*, and then removing any code that doesn't satisfy that goal.

Here's an example of a simple *Constructor Test*:

```
public void testFlightConstructor_OK() throws Exception {
   // set up fixture
   // exercise SUT
   Flight newFlight = new Flight(validFlightNumber);
   // verify results
   assertEquals( validFlightNumber, newFlight.number );
   assertEquals( "", newFlight.airlineCode );
   assertNull( newFlight.airline );
}
```

While we are at it, we might as well specify what should occur if an invalid argument is passed to the constructor by using the *Expected Exception Test* template for our *Constructor Test*:

```
public void testFlightConstructor_badInput() {
   // set up fixture
   BigDecimal invalidFlightNumber = new BigDecimal(-1023);
   // exercise SUT
   try {
      Flight newFlight = new Flight(invalidFlightNumber);
      fail("Didn't catch negative flight number!");
   } catch (InvalidArgumentException e) {
      // verify results
      assertEquals( "Flight numbers must be positive",
                    e.getMessage());
   }
}
```

Now that we know that our constructor logic is well tested, we are ready to write our *Simple Success Test* for our mileage translation functionality. Note how much simpler it has become because we can focus on verifying the business logic:

```
public void testFlightMileage_asKm() throws Exception {
   // set up fixture
   Flight newFlight = new Flight(validFlightNumber);
   newFlight.setMileage(1122);
   // exercise mileage translator
   int actualKilometres = newFlight.getMileageAsKm();
   // verify results
   int expectedKilometres = 1810;
   assertEquals( expectedKilometres, actualKilometres);
}
```

So what happens if the constructor logic *is* defective? This test will likely fail because its output depends on the value passed to the constructor. The constructor test will also fail. That failure will tell us to look at the constructor logic first. Once that problem is fixed, this test will likely pass. If it doesn't, then we can focus on fixing the `getMileageAsKm` method logic. This is a good example of *Defect Localization*.

Test Method

Four-Phase Test

How do we structure our test logic to make what we are testing obvious?

We structure each test with four distinct parts executed in sequence.

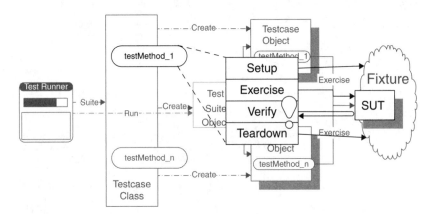

How It Works

We design each test to have four distinct phases that are executed in sequence: fixture setup, exercise SUT, result verification, and fixture teardown.

- In the first phase, we set up the test fixture (the "before" picture) that is required for the SUT to exhibit the expected behavior as well as anything you need to put in place to be able to observe the actual outcome (such as using a *Test Double;* see page 522).

- In the second phase, we interact with the SUT.

- In the third phase, we do whatever is necessary to determine whether the expected outcome has been obtained.

- In the fourth phase, we tear down the test fixture to put the world back into the state in which we found it.

Why We Do This

The test reader must be able to quickly determine what behavior the test is verifying. It can be very confusing when various behaviors of the SUT are being invoked—some to set up the pre-test state (fixture) of the SUT, others to exercise the SUT, and yet others to verify the post-test state of the SUT. Clearly identifying the four phases makes the intent of the test much easier to see.

The fixture setup phase of the test establishes the SUT's state prior to the test, which is an important input to the test. The exercise SUT phase is where we actually run the software we are testing. When reading the test, we need to see which software is being run. The result verification phase of the test is where we specify the expected outcome. The final phase, fixture teardown, is all about housekeeping. We wouldn't want to obscure the important test logic with it because it is completely irrelevant from the perspective of *Tests as Documentation* (see page 23).

We should avoid the temptation to test as much functionality as possible in a single *Test Method* (page 348) because that can result in *Obscure Tests* (page 186). In fact, it is preferable to have many small *Single-Condition Tests* (see page 45). Using comments to mark the phases of a *Four-Phase Test* is a good source of self-discipline, in that it makes it very obvious when our tests are not *Single-Condition Tests*. It will be self-evident if we have multiple exercise SUT phases separated by result verification phases or if we have interspersed fixture setup and exercise SUT phases. Sure, the tests may work—but they will provide less *Defect Localization* (see page 22) than if we have a bunch of independent *Single-Condition Tests*.

Implementation Notes

We have several options for implementing the *Four-Phase Test*. In the simplest case, each test is completely free-standing. All four phases of the test are contained within the body of the *Test Method*. This structure implies we are using *In-line Setup* (page 408) and either *Garbage-Collected Teardown* (page 500) or *In-line Teardown* (page 509). It is the most appropriate choice when we are using *Testcase Class per Class* (page 617) or *Testcase Class per Feature* (page 624) to organize our *Test Methods*.

The other choice is to take advantage of the *Test Automation Framework's* (page 298) support for *Implicit Setup* (page 424) and *Implicit Teardown* (page 516). We factor out the common fixture setup and fixture teardown logic into setUp and tearDown methods on the *Testcase Class* (page 373). This leaves only the exercise SUT and result verification phases in the *Test Method*. This approach is an appropriate choice when we are using *Testcase Class per Fixture* (page 631). We can also use this approach to set up common parts of the fixture when using *Testcase Class per Class* (page 617) or *Testcase Class per Feature* or to tear down the fixture when using *Automated Teardown* (page 503).

Example: Four-Phase Test (In-line)

Here is an example of a test that is clearly a *Four-Phase Test*:

**Four-Phase
Test**

```
public void testGetFlightsByOriginAirport_NoFlights_inline()
        throws Exception {
   // Fixture setup
   NonTxFlightMngtFacade facade =new NonTxFlightMngtFacade();
   BigDecimal airportId = facade.createTestAirport("1OF");
   try {
      // Exercise system
      List flightsAtDestination1 =
                   facade.getFlightsByOriginAirport(airportId);
      // Verify outcome
      assertEquals( 0, flightsAtDestination1.size() );
   } finally {
      // Fixture teardown
      facade.removeAirport( airportId );
   }
}
```

All four phases of the *Four-Phase Test* are included as in-line code. Because the calls to *Assertion Methods* (page 362) raise exceptions, we need to surround the fixture teardown part of the *Test Method* with a try/finally construct to ensure that it is run in all cases.

Example: Four-Phase Test (Implicit Setup/Teardown)

Here is the same *Four-Phase Test* with the fixture setup and fixture teardown logic moved out of the *Test Method*:

```
NonTxFlightMngtFacade facade = new NonTxFlightMngtFacade();
private BigDecimal airportId;

protected void setUp() throws Exception {
   // Fixture setup
   super.setUp();
   airportId = facade.createTestAirport("1OF");
}

public void testGetFlightsByOriginAirport_NoFlights_implicit()
        throws Exception {
   // Exercise SUT
   List flightsAtDestination1 =
        facade.getFlightsByOriginAirport(airportId);
   // Verify outcome
   assertEquals( 0, flightsAtDestination1.size() );
}

protected void tearDown() throws Exception {
```

```
    // Fixture teardown
    facade.removeAirport(airportId);
    super.tearDown();
}
```

Because the tearDown method is called automatically even after test failures, we don't need the try/finally construct inside the *Test Method*. The downside, however, is that references to our fixture must be held in instance variables rather than local variables.

Assertion Method

How do we make tests self-checking?

We call a utility method to evaluate whether an expected outcome has been achieved.

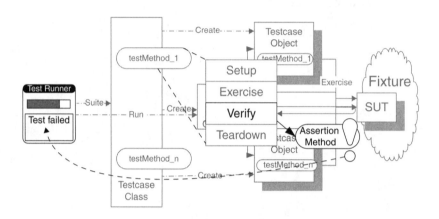

A key part of writing *Fully Automated Tests* (see page 26) is to make them *Self-Checking Tests* (see page 26) to avoid having to inspect the outcome of each test for correctness each time it is run. This strategy involves finding a way to express the expected outcome so that it can be verified automatically by the test itself.

Assertion Methods give us a way to express the expected outcome in a way that is both executable by the computer and useful to the human reader, who can then use the *Tests as Documentation* (see page 23).

How It Works

We encode the expected outcome of the test as a series of assertions that state what should be true for the test to pass. The assertions are realized as calls to *Assertion Methods* that encapsulate the mechanism that causes the test to fail. The *Assertion Methods* may be provided by the *Test Automation Framework* (page 298) or by the test automater as *Custom Assertions* (page 474).

Why We Do This

Encoding the expected outcome using *Conditional Test Logic* (page 200) is very verbose and makes tests hard to read and understand. It is also much more likely to lead to *Test Code Duplication* (page 213) and *Buggy Tests* (page 260). *Assertion Methods* help us avoid these issues by moving that complexity into reusable *Test Utility Methods* (page 599); these methods can then be verified as working correctly using *Test Utility Tests* (see *Test Utility Method*).

Implementation Notes

Although all members of the xUnit family provide *Assertion Methods,* they do so with a fair degree of variability. The key implementation considerations are as follows:

- How to call the *Assertion Methods*

- How to choose the best *Assertion Method* to call

- What information to include in the *Assertion Message* (page 370)

Calling Built-in Assertion Methods

The way the *Assertion Methods* are called from within the *Test Method* (page 348) varies from language to language and from framework to framework. The language features determine what is possible and preferable, while the framework builders chose which options to use. The names these developers chose for the *Assertion Methods* were influenced by how they chose to access them. Here are the most common options for accessing the *Assertion Methods*:

- The *Assertion Methods* are inherited from a *Testcase Superclass* (page 638) provided by the framework. Such methods may be invoked as though they were provided locally on the *Testcase Class* (page 373). The original version of Java's JUnit, for example, used this approach by providing a *Testcase Superclass* that inherits from the class Assert, which contains the actual *Assertion Methods.*

- The *Assertion Methods* are provided via a globally accessible class or module. They are invoked using the class or module name to fully qualify the *Assertion Method* name. NUnit, for example, uses this approach [e.g., Assert.isTrue(x);]. JUnit does allow assertions to be invoked as static methods on the Assert class [e.g., Assert.assertTrue(x)] but this is not usually necessary because they are inherited via the *Testcase Superclass*.

Assertion Method

- The *Assertion Methods* are provided as "mix-ins" or macros. Ruby's Test:: Unit, for example, provides the *Assertion Methods* in a module called Assert that can be included in *any* class,[2] thereby allowing the *Assertion Methods* to be used as though defined within the *Testcase Class* [e.g., assert_equal(a,b)]. CppUnit, by contrast, defines the *Assertion Methods* as macros, which are expanded before the compiler sees the code.

Assertion Messages

Assertion Methods typically take an optional *Assertion Message* as a text parameter that is included in the output when the assertion fails. This structure allows the test automater to explain to the test maintainer exactly which *Assertion Method* failed and to better explain what should have occurred. The error detected by the test will be much easier to debug if the *Assertion Method* provides more information about why it failed. Choosing the right *Assertion Method* goes a long way toward achieving this goal because many of the built-in *Assertion Methods* provide useful diagnostic information about the values of the arguments. This is especially true for *Equality Assertions*.

One of the biggest differences between members of the xUnit family is where the optional *Assertion Message* appears in the argument list. Most members tack it on to the end as an optional argument. JUnit, however, makes the *Assertion Message* the first argument when it is present.

Choosing the Right Assertion

We have two goals for the calls to *Assertion Methods* in our *Test Methods*:

- Fail the test when something other than the expected outcome occurs

- Document how the SUT is *supposed* to behave (i.e., *Tests as Documentation*)

To achieve these goals we must strive to use the most appropriate *Assertion Method*. While the syntax and naming conventions vary from one member of the xUnit family to the next, most provide a basic set of assertions that fall into the following categories:

---

[2] This approach is particularly useful when we are building *Mock Objects* (page 544) because these objects are outside the *Testcase Class* but need to invoke *Assertion Methods*.

- *Single-Outcome Assertions* such as `fail`; these take no arguments because they always behave the same way.

- *Stated Outcome Assertions* such as `assertNotNull(anObjectReference)` and `assertTrue(aBooleanExpression)`; these compare a single argument to an outcome implied by the method name.

- *Expected Exception Assertions* such as `assert_raises(expectedError) { codeToExecute }`; these evaluate a block of code and a single expected exception argument.

- *Equality Assertions* such as `assertEqual(expected, actual)`; these compare two objects or values for equality.

- *Fuzzy Equality Assertions* such as `assertEqual(expected, actual, tolerance)`; these determine whether two values are "close enough" to each other by using a "tolerance" or "comparison mask."

Variation: Equality Assertion

Equality Assertions are the most common examples of *Assertion Methods*. They are used to compare the actual outcome with an expected outcome that is expressed in the form of a constant *Literal Value* (page 714) or an *Expected Object* (see *State Verification* on page 462). By convention, the expected value is specified first and the actual value follows it. The diagnostic message that is generated by the *Test Automation Framework* makes sense only when they are provided in this order. The equality of the two objects is usually determined by invoking the `equals` method on the *expected* object. If the SUT's definition of `equals` is not what we want to use in our tests, either we can make *Equality Assertions* on individual fields of the object or we can implement our **test-specific equality** on a *Test-Specific Subclass* (page 579) of the *Expected Object*.

Variation: Fuzzy Equality Assertion

When we cannot guarantee an exact match due to variations in precision or expected variations in value, it may be appropriate to use a *Fuzzy Equality Assertion*. Typically, these assertions look just like *Equality Assertions* with the addition of an extra "tolerance" or "comparison map" parameter that specifies how close the actual argument must be to the expected one. The most common example of a *Fuzzy Equality Assertion* is the comparison of floating-point numbers where the limitations of arithmetic precision need to be accounted for by providing a tolerance (the maximum acceptable distance between the two values).

We use the same approach when comparing XML documents where direct string comparisons may result in failure owing to certain fields having unpredictable content. In this case, the "fuzz" specification is a "comparison schema" that specifies which fields need to match or which fields should be ignored. This kind of *Equality Assertion* is very similar to asserting that a string conforms to a regular expression or other form of pattern matching.

Assertion Method

Variation: Stated Outcome Assertion

Stated Outcome Assertions are a way of saying exactly what the outcome should be without passing an expected value as an argument. The outcome must be common enough to warrant a special *Assertion Method*. The most common examples are as follows:

- assertTrue(aBooleanExpression), which fails if the expression evaluates to FALSE

- assertNotNull(anObjectReference), which fails if the objectReference doesn't refer to a valid object

Stated Outcome Assertions are often used as *Guard Assertions* (page 490) to avoid *Conditional Test Logic*.

Variation: Expected Exception Assertion

In languages that support **block closures,** we can use a variation of a *Stated Outcome Assertion* that takes an additional parameter specifying the kind of exception we expect. We can use this *Expected Exception Assertion* to say, "Run this block and verify that the following exception is thrown." This format is more compact than using a try/catch construct. Some typical examples follow:

- should: [aBlockToExecute] raise: expectedException in Smalltalk's SUnit

- assert_raises(expectedError) { codeToExecute } in Ruby's Test::Unit

Variation: Single-Outcome Assertion

A *Single-Outcome Assertion* always behaves the same way. The most commonly used *Single-Outcome Assertion* is fail, which causes a test to be treated as a failure. It is typically used in two circumstances:

- As an *Unfinished Test Assertion* (page 494) when a test is first identified and implemented as a nearly empty *Test Method*. By including a call to fail, we can have the *Test Runner* (page 377) remind us that we still have a test to finish writing.

- As part of a try/catch (or equivalent) block in an *Expected Exception Test* (see *Test Method*) by including a call to fail in the try block immediately after the call that is expected to throw an exception. If we don't want to assert something about the exception that was caught, we can avoid an empty catch block by using the *Single-Outcome Assertion* success to document that this is the expected outcome.

One circumstance in which we really should *not* use *Single-Outcome Assertions* is in *Conditional Test Logic*. There is almost never a good reason to include conditional logic in a *Test Method,* as there is usually a more declarative way to handle this situation using other styles of *Assertion Methods.* For example, use of *Guard Assertions* results in tests that are more easily understood and less likely to yield incorrect results.

Motivating Example

The following example illustrates the kind of code that would be required for each item we wanted to verify if we did not have *Assertion Methods.* All we really want to do is this:

```
if (x.equals(y)) {
    throw new AssertionFailedError(
            "expected: <" + x.toString() +
            "> but found: <" + y.toString() + ">");
} else  { // Okay, continue
    // ...
}
```

Unfortunately, this code will cause a NullPointerException if x is null, and it would be hard to distinguish this exception from an error in the SUT. Thus we need to put some guard clauses around this functionality so that we always throw an AssertionFailedException:

```
if (x == null) { // cannot do null.equals(null)
    if (y == null ) {  // they are both null so equal
        return;
    } else {
        throw new AssertionFailedError(
            "expected null but found: <" + y.toString() +">");
    }
} else if (!x.equals(y)) { // comparable but not equal!
    throw new AssertionFailedError(
            "expected: <" + x.toString() +
            "> but found: <" + y.toString() + ">");

} // equal
```

Yikes! That got pretty messy. And we'll have to do the same thing for every attribute we want to verify? This is not good. There must be a better way.

Refactoring Notes

Assertion Method

Luckily for us, the inventors of xUnit recognized this problem and did the requisite Extract Method [Fowler] refactoring to create a library of *Assertion Methods* that we can call instead. We simply replace the mess of in-line if statements and thrown exceptions with a call to the appropriate *Assertion Method*. The next example is the code for the JUnit assertEquals method. Although the intent of this example is the same as the code we wrote earlier, it has been rewritten in terms of guard clauses that identify when things are equal.

```
/**
 * Asserts that two objects are equal. If they are not,
 * an AssertionFailedError is thrown with the given message.
 */
static public void assertEquals(String message,
                                Object expected,
                                Object actual) {
    if (expected == null && actual == null)
        return;
    if (expected != null && expected.equals(actual))
        return;
    failNotEquals(message, expected, actual);
}
```

The method failNotEquals is a *Test Utility Method* that fails the test and provides a diagnostic assertion message.

Example: Equality Assertion

Here is the same assertion logic recoded to take advantage of JUnit's *Equality Assertion*:

```
assertEquals( x, y );
```

Here is the same assertion coded in C#. Note the classname qualifier and the resulting difference in the method name:

```
Assert.AreEqual( x, y );
```

Example: Fuzzy Equality Assertion

To compare two floating-point numbers (which are rarely ever really equal), we specify the acceptable differences using a *Fuzzy Equality Assertion*:

```
assertEquals( 3.1415, diameter/2/radius, 0.001);
assertEquals( expectedXml, actualXml, elementsToCompare );
```

Example: Stated Outcome Assertion

To insist that a particular outcome has occurred, we use a *Stated Outcome Assertion:*

```
assertNotNull( a );
assertTrue( b > c );
assertNonZero( b );
```

Example: Expected Exception Assertion

Here is an example of how we verify that the correct exception was raised when we have blocks. In Smalltalk's SUnit, it looks like this:

```
self
    should: [Flight new mileage: -1122]
    raise: RuntimeError new 'Should have raised error'
```

The should: indicates the block of code to run (surrounded by square brackets), while the raise: specifies the expected exception object. In Ruby, it looks like this:

```
assert_raises( RuntimeError,
            "Should have raised error")
            {flight.setMileage(-1122) }
```

The Ruby language syntax also lets us use this "control structure"-style syntax by delimiting the block using do/end instead of curly braces:

```
assert_raises( RuntimeError, "Should have raised error") do
    flight.setMileage(-1122)
end
```

Example: Single-Outcome Assertion

To fail the test, use the *Single Outcome Assertion:*

```
fail( "Expected an exception" );
unfinishedTest();
```

Assertion Message

How do we structure our test logic to know which assertion failed?

**We include a descriptive string argument in each call to an
Assertion Method.**

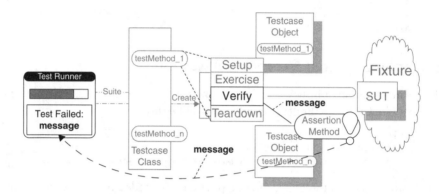

We make tests *Self-Checking* (see page 26) by including calls to *Assertion Methods* (page 362) that specify the expected outcome. When a test fails, the *Test Runner* (page 377) writes an entry to the test result log.

A well-crafted *Assertion Message* makes it very easy to determine which assertion failed and exactly what the symptoms were when the failure happened.

How It Works

Every *Assertion Method* takes an optional string parameter that is included in the failure log. When the condition being asserted is not true, the *Assertion Message* is output to the *Test Runner's* log along with whatever output the assertion method normally generates.

When to Use It

There are two schools of thought on this subject. **Test drivers** who belong to the "single assertion per Test Method" school believe that they don't need to include *Assertion Messages* because only one assertion can possibly fail and, therefore, they always know exactly which assertion happened. They count on the *Assertion Method* to include the arguments (e.g., expected "x" but was "y") but they don't need to include a message.

Conversely, people who find themselves coding several or many assertion method calls in their tests should strongly consider including a message that at least distinguishes *which* assertion failed. This information is especially important if the tests are frequently run using a *Command-Line Test Runner* (see *Test Runner*), which rarely provides failure location information.

Implementation Notes

It is easy to state that we need a message for each assertion method call—but what should we say in the message? It is useful to take a moment as we write each assertion and ask ourselves what the person reading the failure log would hope to get out of it.

Variation: Assertion-Identifying Message

When we include several assertions of the same type in the same *Test Method* (page 348), we make it more difficult to determine exactly which one failed the test. By including some unique text in each *Assertion Message*, we can make it very easy to determine which assertion method call failed. A common practice is to use the name of the variable or attribute being asserted on as the message. This technique is very simple and requires very little thought. Another option is to number the assertions. This information would certainly be unique but understanding it may be less intuitive as we would have to look at the code to determine which assertion was failing.

Variation: Expectation-Describing Message

When a test fails, we know what has *actually* happened. The big question is, "What *should* have happened?" There are several ways of documenting the expected behavior for the test reader. For example, we could place comments in the test code. A better solution is to include a description of the expectation in the *Assertion Message*. While this is done automatically for an *Equality Assertion* (see *Assertion Method*), we need to provide this information ourselves for any *Stated Outcome Assertions* (see *Assertion Method*).

Variation: Argument-Describing Message

Some types of *Assertion Methods* provide less helpful failure messages than others. Among the worst are *Stated Outcome Assertions* such as assertTrue (aBooleanExpression). When they fail, all we know is that the stated outcome did not occur. In these cases we can include the expression that was being evaluated (including the actual values) as part of the *Assertion Message* text. The test maintainer can then examine the failure log and determine what was being evaluated and why it caused the test to fail.

Motivating Example

Assertion Message

```
assertTrue( a > b  );
assertTrue( b > c );
```

This code emits a failure message—something like "Assertion Failed." From this output, we cannot even tell which of the two *Assertion Messages* failed. Not very useful, is it?

Refactoring Notes

Fixing this problem is a simple matter of adding one more parameter to each *Assertion Method* call. In this case, we want to communicate that we are expecting "a" to be greater than "b." Of course, it would also be useful to be able to see what the values of "a" and "b" actually were. We can add both pieces of information into the *Assertion Message* through some judicious string concatenation.

Example: Expectation-Describing Message

Here is the same test with the *Argument-Describing Message* added:

```
assertTrue( "Expected a > b but a was '" + a.toString() +
            "' and b was '" + b.toString() + "'",
         a.gt(b) );
assertTrue( "Expected b > c but b was '" + b.toString() +
            "' and c was '" + c.toString + "'",
         b > c );
```

This will now result in a useful failure message:

Assertion Failed. Expected a > b but a was '17' and b was '19'.

Of course, this output would be even more meaningful if the variables had Intent-Revealing Names [SBPP]!

Testcase Class

Where do we put our test code?

We group a set of related Test Methods on a single Testcase Class.

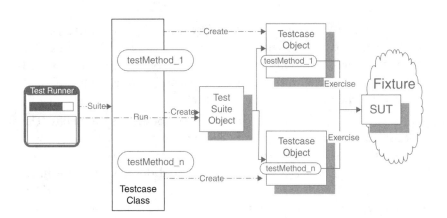

We put our test logic into *Test Methods* (page 348) but those *Test Methods* need to be associated with a class. A *Testcase Class* gives us a place to host those methods that we can later turn into *Testcase Objects* (page 382).

How It Works

We collect all *Test Methods* that are related in some way onto a special kind of class, the Testcase Class. At runtime, the *Testcase Class* acts as a *Test Suite Factory* (see *Test Enumeration* on page 399) that creates a *Testcase Object* for each *Test Method*. It adds all of these objects to a *Test Suite Object* (page 387) that the *Test Runner* (page 377) will use to run them all.

Why We Do This

In object-oriented languages, we prefer to put our *Test Methods* onto a class rather than having them as global functions or procedures (even if that is allowed). By making them instance methods of a *Testcase Class*, we can create a *Testcase Object* for each test by instantiating the Testcase Class once for each *Test Method*. This strategy allows us to manipulate the *Test Methods* at runtime.

Testcase
Class

Class–Instance Duality

Back in high school physics, we learned about the "wave–particle duality" of light. Sometimes light acts like a particle (e.g., going through a small aperture), and sometimes it acts like a wave (e.g., rainbows). The behavior of *Testcase Classes* (page 373) sometimes reminds me of this concept. Let me explain why.

Developers new to xUnit often ask, "Why is the class we subclass called TestCase when we have several *Test Methods* on it? Shouldn't it be called TestSuite?" These questions make a lot of sense when we are focused primarily on the view of the class when we are *writing* the test code as opposed to when we are running the code.

When we are writing test code, we concentrate on the *Test Methods*. The *Testcase Class* is primarily just a place to put the methods. About the only time we think of objects is when we use *Implicit Setup* (page 424) and need to create fields (instance variables) to hold them between the invocation of the setUp method and when they are used in the *Test Method*. When developers new to xUnit test automation are writing their first tests, they tend to code by example. Following an existing example is a good way to get something working quickly but it doesn't necessarily help the developer understand what is really going on.

At runtime, the xUnit framework typically creates one instance of the *Testcase Class* for each *Test Method*. The *Testcase Class* acts as a *Test Suite Factory* (see *Test Enumeration* on page 399) that builds a *Test Suite Object* (page 387) containing all the instances of itself, one instance for each *Test Method*. Now, it's not very often that a static method on a class returns an instance of another class containing many instances of itself. If this behavior wasn't odd enough, the fact that xUnit reports the test failures using the *Test Method* name can be enough to obscure from many test automaters the existence of "objects inside."

When we examine the object relationships at runtime, things become a bit clearer. The *Test Suite Object* returned by the *Test Suite Factory* contains one or more *Testcase Objects* (page 382). So far, so good. Each of these objects is an instance of our *Testcase Class*. Each instance is configured to run one of the *Test Methods*. More importantly, each will run a different *Test Method*. (How this happens is described in more detail in *Test Discovery* on page 393.) So each instance of our *Testcase Class* is, indeed, a test case. The *Test Methods* are just how we tell each instance what it should test.

> **Further Reading**
> Martin Fowler has a great piece on his blog about this issue called "JUnit
> New Instance" [JNI].

We could, of course, implement each *Test Method* on a separate class—but that
creates additional overhead and clutters the class namespace. It also makes it
harder (although not impossible) to reuse functionality between tests.

Implementation Notes

Most of the complexity of writing tests involves how to write the *Test Methods:*
what to include in-line and what to factor out into *Test Utility Methods* (page 599),
how to *Isolate the SUT* (see page 43), and so on.

The real magic associated with the *Testcase Class* occurs at runtime and
is described in *Testcase Object* and *Test Runner*. As far as we are concerned,
all we have to do is write some *Test Methods* that contain our test logic
and let the *Test Runner* work its magic. We can avoid *Test Code Duplication* (page 213) by using an Extract Method [Fowler] refactoring to factor
out common code into *Test Utility Methods*. These methods can be left on the
Testcase Class or they can be moved to an *Abstract Testcase* superclass (see *Testcase Superclass* on page 638), a *Test Helper* class (page 643), or a *Test Helper
Mixin* (see *Testcase Superclass*).

Example: Testcase Class

Here is an example of a simple *Testcase Class*:

```
public class TestScheduleFlight extends TestCase {

   public void testUnscheduled_shouldEndUpInScheduled() throws Exception {
      Flight flight = FlightTestHelper.
            getAnonymousFlightInUnscheduledState();
      flight.schedule();
      assertTrue( "isScheduled()", flight.isScheduled());
   }

   public void testScheduledState_shouldThrowInvalidRequestEx()
            throws Exception {
      Flight flight = FlightTestHelper.
            getAnonymousFlightInScheduledState();
      try {
         flight.schedule();
         fail("not allowed in scheduled state");
```

Testcase Class

```
      } catch (InvalidRequestException e) {
        assertEquals("InvalidRequestException.getRequest()",
                     "schedule",
                     e.getRequest());
        assertTrue( "isScheduled()", flight.isScheduled());
      }
    }

    public void testAwaitingApproval_shouldThrowInvalidRequestEx()
            throws Exception {
      Flight flight = FlightTestHelper.
          getAnonymousFlightInAwaitingApprovalState();
      try {
        flight.schedule();
        fail("not allowed in schedule state");
      } catch (InvalidRequestException e) {
        assertEquals("InvalidRequestException.getRequest()",
                     "schedule",
                     e.getRequest());
        assertTrue( "isAwaitingApproval()",
                    flight.isAwaitingApproval());
      }
    }
  }
```

Further Reading

In some variants of xUnit (most notably VbUnit and NUnit), the *Testcase Class* is called a test fixture. This usage should not be confused with the test fixture (or test context) that consists of everything we need to have in place before we can start exercising the SUT.[3] Neither should it be confused with the fixture term as used by the Fit framework, which is the Adapter [GOF] that interacts with the Fit table and thereby implements a *Data-Driven Test* (page 288) Interpreter [GOF].

---

[3] These are the pre-conditions of the test.

Test Runner

How do we run the tests?

We define an application that instantiates a Test Suite Object and executes all the Testcase Objects it contains.

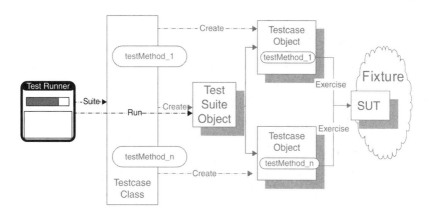

Assuming we have defined our *Test Methods* (page 348) on one or more *Testcase Classes* (page 373), how do we actually cause the *Test Automation Frameworks* (page 298) to run our tests?

How It Works

Each member of the xUnit family of *Test Automation Frameworks* provides some form of command-line or graphical application that can be used to run our automated tests and report on the results. The *Test Runner* uses *Test Enumeration* (page 399), *Test Discovery* (page 393), or *Test Selection* (page 403) to obtain a Composite [GOF] test object. The latter may either be a single *Testcase Object* (page 382), a *Test Suite Object* (page 387), or a Composite test suite (a *Suite of Suites; see Test Suite Object*). Because all of these objects implement the same interface, the *Test Runner* need not care whether it is dealing with a single test or a multilevel suite. The *Test Runner* keeps track of, and reports on, how many tests it has run, how many tests had failed assertions, and how many tests raised errors or exceptions.

Test Runner

Why We Do This

We wouldn't want each test automater to have to provide a special means of running his or her own test suites. That requirement would just get in the way of our ability to simultaneously run all the tests automated by different people. By providing a standard *Test Runner,* we encourage developers to make it easy to run tests written by different people. We can also provide different ways of running the same tests.

Implementation Notes

Several styles of *Test Runners* are available. The most common variations are running tests from within an IDE and running tests from the command line. All of these schemes depend on the fact that all *Testcase Objects* implement a standard interface.

Standard Test Interface

Statically typed languages (such as Java and C#) typically include an interface type (fully abstract class) that defines the interface that all *Testcase Objects* and *Test Suite Objects* must implement. Some languages (such as C# and Java 5.0) "mix" in the implementation by using class attributes or annotations on the *Testcase Class.* In dynamically typed languages, this interface may not exist explicitly. Instead, each implementation class simply implements the standard interface methods. Typically, the standard test interface includes methods on it to count the available tests and to run the tests. Where the framework supports Test Enumeration, each *Testcase Class* and test suite class must also implement the *Test Suite Factory* method (see *Test Enumeration* on page 399), which is typically called suite.

Variation: Graphical Test Runner

A *Graphical Test Runner* is typically a desktop application or part of an IDE (either built-in or a plug-in) for running tests. At least one, **IeUnit,** runs inside a Web browser rather than an IDE. The most common feature of the *Graphical Test Runner* is some sort of real-time progress indicator. This monitor typically includes a running count of test failures and errors and often includes a colored progress bar that starts off green and turns red as soon as an error or failure is encountered. Some members of the xUnit family include a graphical *Test Tree Explorer* as a means to drill down and run a single test from within a *Suite of Suites.*

Here is the *Graphical Test Runner* from the JUnit plug-in for Eclipse:

The red bar near the top indicates that at least one test has failed. The upper text pane shows a list of test failures and test errors. The lower pane shows the traceback from the failed test selected in the upper pane.

Variation: Command-Line Test Runner

Command-Line Test Runners are designed to be used from an operating system command line or from batch files or shell scripts. They are very handy when working remotely via remote shells or when running the tests from a build script such as "make," **Ant,** or a **continuous integration** tool such as "Cruise Control."

The following example shows how to run an **runit** (one of the xUnit implementations for the Ruby programming language) test from the command line:

```
>ruby testrunner.rb c:/examples/tests/SmellHandlerTest.rb
Loaded suite SmellHandlerTest
Started
.....
Finished in 0.016 seconds.
5 tests, 6 assertions, 0 failures, 0 errors
>Exit code: 0
```

Test Runner

The first line is the invocation at the command prompt. In this example we are running the tests defined in a single *Testcase Class*, SmellHandlerTest. The next two lines are the initial feedback as the tests begin. The series of dots indicates the tests' progress, one per test completed. This particular *Command-Line Test Runner* replaces the dot with an "E" or an "F" if the test produces an error or fails. The last three lines are summary statistics that provide an overview of what happened. Typically, the exit code is set to the total number of failed/error tests so that a non-zero exit code can be interpreted easily as a build failure when run from an automated build tool.

Variation: File System Test Runner

Some *Command-Line Test Runners* provide the option of searching a specified directory for all files that are tests and running them all at once. This automated *Testcase Class Discovery* (see *Test Discovery*) avoids the need to build the *Suite of Suites* in code (*Test Enumeration*) and helps avoid *Lost Tests* (see *Production Bugs* on page 268).

In addition, some external tools will search the file system for files matching specific patterns and then invoke an arbitrary command against the matched files. These files can be passed to the *Test Runner* from a build tool.

Variation: Test Tree Explorer

Members of the xUnit family that turn each *Test Method* into a *Testcase Object* can manipulate the tests easily. Many of them provide a graphical representation of the *Suite of Suites* and allow the user to select an entire *Test Suite Object* or a single *Testcase Object* to run. This eliminates the need to create a *Single Test Suite* (see *Named Test Suite* on page 592) class to run a single test.

Here is the *Test Tree Explorer* of JUnit plug-in for Eclipse shown "popped out" over other Eclipse views:

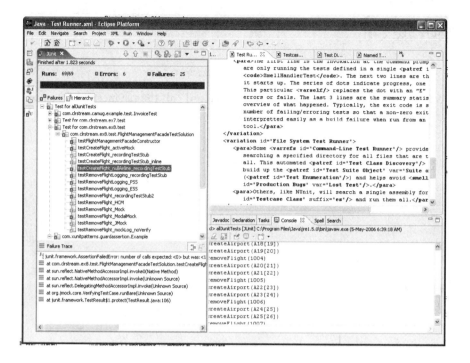

The left pane of the IDE is the JUnit view within Eclipse. The progress bar appears at the top of the view, the upper pane is the *Test Tree Explorer,* and the lower pane is the traceback for the currently selected test failure. Note that some *Test Suite Objects* in the *Test Tree Explorer* are "open," revealing their contents; others are closed down. The colored annotation next to each *Testcase Object* shows its status; the annotations for each *Test Suite Object* indicate whether any contained *Testcase Objects* failed or produced an error. The *Test Suite Object* called "Test for com.clrstream.ex8.test" is a *Suite of Suites* for the package "com.clrstream.ex8.test"; "Test for allJUnitTests" is the topmost *Suite of Suites* for running all the tests.

Testcase Object

How do we run the tests?

**We create a Command object for each test and call the run method when we
wish to execute it.**

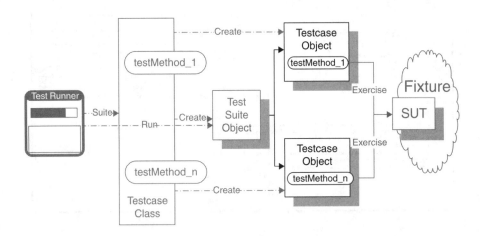

The *Test Runner* (page 377) needs a way to find and invoke the appropriate *Test
Methods* (page 348) and to present the results to the user. Many *Graphical Test
Runners* (see *Test Runner*) let the user drill down into the tree of tests and pick
individual tests to run. This capability requires that the *Test Runner* be able to
inspect and manipulate the tests at runtime.

How It Works

We instantiate a Command [GOF] object to represent each *Test Method* that
should execute. We use the *Testcase Class* (page 373) as a *Test Suite Factory*
to create a *Test Suite Object* (page 387) to hold all the *Testcase Objects* for a
particular *Testcase Class*. We can use either *Test Discovery* (page 393) or *Test
Enumeration* to create the *Testcase Objects*.

Why We Do This

Treating tests as first-class objects opens up many new possibilities that are not available to us if we treat the tests as simple procedures. It is a lot easier for the *Test Runner* of the *Test Automation Framework* (page 298) to manipulate tests when they are objects. We can hold them in collections (*Test Suite Objects*), iterate over them, invoke them, and so on.

Most members of the xUnit family create a separate *Testcase Object* for each test to isolate the tests from one another as prescribed by *Independent Test* (see page 42). Unfortunately, there is always an exception (see the sidebar "There's Always an Exception" on page 384), and users of the affected *Test Automation Frameworks* need to be a bit more cautious.

Testcase Object

Implementation Notes

Each *Testcase Object* implements a standard test interface so that the *Test Runner* does not need to know the specific interface for each test. This scheme allows each *Testcase Object* to act as a Command object [GOF]. This allows us to build collections of these *Testcase Objects*, which we can then iterate across to do counting, running, displaying, and other operations.

In most programming languages, we need to create a class to define the behavior of the *Testcase Objects*. We could create a separate *Testcase Class* for each *Testcase Object*. It is more convenient to host many *Test Methods* on a single *Testcase Class,* however, as this strategy results in fewer classes to manage and facilitates reuse of *Test Utility Methods* (page 599). This approach requires that each *Testcase Object* of the *Testcase Class* have a way to determine which *Test Method* it should invoke. Pluggable Behavior [SBPP] is the most common way to do this. The constructor of the *Testcase Class* takes the name of the method to be invoked as a parameter and stores this name in an instance variable. When the *Test Runner* invokes the run method on the *Testcase Object*, it uses **reflection** to find and invoke the method whose name is in the instance variable.

Testcase Object

There's Always an Exception

Whether we are learning to conjugate verbs in a new language or looking for patterns in how software is built, *there's always an exception!*

One of the most notable exceptions in the xUnit family relates to the use of a *Testcase Object* (page 382) to represent each Test Method (page 348) at runtime. This key design feature of xUnit offers a way to achieve an *Independent Test* (see page 42). The only members of the xUnit family that don't follow this scheme are TestNG and NUnit (version 2.x). For the reasons described below, the builders of NUnit 2.0 chose to stray from the well-worn path of one Testcase Object per Test Method and create only a single instance of the Testcase Class (page 373). This instance, which they call the *test fixture*, is then reused for each Test Method. One of the authors of NUnit 2.0, James Newkirk, writes:

> I think one of the biggest screw-ups that was made when we wrote NUnit V2.0 was to not create a new instance of the test fixture class for each contained test method. I say "we" but I think this one was my fault. I did not quite understand the reasoning in JUnit for creating a new instance of the test fixture for each test method. I look back now and see that reusing the instance for each test method allows someone to store a member variable from one test and use it in another. This can introduce execution-order dependencies, which for this type of testing is an anti-pattern. It is much better to fully isolate each test method from the others. This requires that a new object be created for each test method.

Unfortunately, this has some very interesting—and undesirable—consequences when one is familiar with the "JUnit New Instance Behavior" of a separate *Testcase Object* per method. Because the object is reused, any objects it refers to via an instance variable are available to all subsequent tests. This results in an implicit *Shared Fixture* (page 317) along with all the forms of *Erratic Tests* (page 228) that go with it. James goes on to say:

> Since it would be difficult to change the way that NUnit works now, and too many people would complain, I now make all of the member variables in test fixture classes static. It's almost like truth in advertising. The result is that there is only one instance of this variable, no matter how many test fixture objects are created. If the variable is static, then someone who may not be familiar with

> *how NUnit executes would not assume that a new one is created
> before each test is executed. This is the closest I can get to how
> JUnit works without changing the way that NUnit executes test
> methods.*

Martin Fowler felt this exception was important enough that he wrote
an article about why JUnit's approach is correct. See http://martinfowler.
com/bliki/JunitNewInstance.html.

Example: Testcase Object

The main evidence of the existence of *Testcase Objects* appears in the *Test Tree
Explorer* (see *Test Runner*) when we "drill down" into the *Test Suite Object* to
expose the *Testcase Objects* it contains. Let's look at an example from the JUnit
Graphical Test Runner that is built into Eclipse. Here's the list of objects created
from the sample code from the write-up of *Testcase Class:*

```
TestSuite("...flightstate.featuretests.AllTests")
   TestSuite("...flightstate.featuretests.TestApproveFlight")
      TestApproveFlight("testScheduledState_shouldThrowIn..ReEx")
      TestApproveFlight("testUnsheduled_shouldEndUpInAwai..oval")
      TestApproveFlight("testAwaitingApproval_shouldThrow..stEx")
      TestApproveFlight("testWithNullArgument_shouldThrow..ntEx")
      TestApproveFlight("testWithInvalidApprover_shouldTh..ntEx")
   TestSuite("...flightstate.featuretests.TestDescheduleFlight")
      TestDescheduleFlight("testScheduled_shouldEndUpInSc..tate")
      TestDescheduleFlight("testUnscheduled_shouldThrowIn..stEx")
      TestDescheduleFlight("testAwaitingApproval_shouldTh..stEx")
   TestSuite("...flightstate.featuretests.TestRequestApproval")
      TestRequestApproval("testScheduledState_shouldThrow..stEx")
      TestRequestApproval("testUnsheduledState_shouldEndU..oval")
      TestRequestApproval("testAwaitingApprovalState_shou..stEx")
   TestSuite("...flightstate.featuretests.TestScheduleFlight")
      TestScheduleFlight("testUnscheduled_shouldEndUpInSc..uled")
      TestScheduleFlight("testScheduledState_shouldThrowI..stEx")
      TestScheduleFlight("testAwaitingApproval_shouldThro..stEx")
```

The name outside the parentheses is the name of the class; the string inside the
parentheses is the name of the object created from that class. By convention, the
name of the *Test Method*[4] to be run is used as the name of the *Testcase Object*,
and the name of a *Test Suite Object* is whatever string was passed to the *Test
Suite Object* constructor. In this example we've used the full package and classname of the *Testcase Class.*

---

[4] I replaced part of the name with ".." to keep each line within the page width limit.

This is what this scheme might look like when viewed in a *Test Tree Explorer*:

Testcase Object

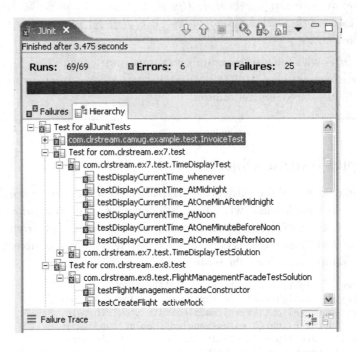

Test Suite Object

How do we run the tests when we have many tests to run?

We define a collection class that implements the standard test interface and use it to run a set of related Testcase Objects.

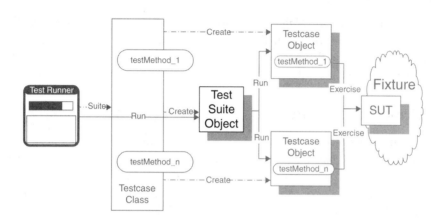

Given that we have created *Test Methods* (page 348) containing our test logic and placed them on a *Testcase Class* (page 373) so we can construct a *Testcase Object* (page 382) for each test, it would be nice to be able to run these tests as a single user operation.

How It Works

We define a Composite [GOF] *Testcase Object* called a *Test Suite Object* to hold the collection of individual *Testcase Objects* to execute. When we want to run all tests in the test suite at once, the *Test Runner* (page 377) asks the *Test Suite Object* to run all its tests.

Why We Do This

Treating test suites as first-class objects makes it easier for the *Test Runner* of the *Test Automation Framework* (page 298) to manipulate tests in the test suite. With or without a *Test Suite Object*, the *Test Runner* would have to hold some kind of collection of *Testcase Objects* (so that we could iterate over them, count them, and so on). When we make the collection "smart," it becomes a simple matter to add other uses such as the *Suite of Suites*.

Variation: Testcase Class Suite

To run all the *Test Methods* in a single *Testcase Class,* we simply build a *Test Suite* Object for the *Testcase Class* and add one *Testcase Object* for each *Test Method*. This allows us to run all the *Test Methods* in the *Testcase Class* simply by passing the name of the *Testcase Class* to the *Test Runner*.

Variation: Suite of Suites

We can build up larger *Named Test Suites* (page 592) by organizing smaller test suites into a tree structure. The Composite pattern makes this organization invisible to the *Test Runner,* allowing it to treat a *Suite of Suites* exactly the same way it treats a simple *Testcase Class Suite* or a single *Testcase Object*.

Implementation Notes

As a Composite object, each *Test Suite Object* implements the same interface as a simple *Testcase Object*. Thus neither the *Test Runner* nor the *Test Suite Object* needs to be aware of whether it is holding a reference to a single test or an entire suite. This makes it easier to implement any operations that involve iterating across all the tests such as counting, running, and displaying.

Before we can do anything with our *Test Suite Object*, we must construct it. We can choose from several options to do so:

- *Test Discovery* (page 393): We can let the *Test Automation Framework* discover our *Testcase Classes* and *Test Methods* for us.

- *Test Enumeration* (page 399): We can write code that enumerates which *Test Methods* we want to include in a *Test Suite Object*. This usually involves creating a *Test Suite Factory* (see *Test Enumeration*).

- *Test Selection* (page 403): We can specify which subset of the *Testcase Objects* we want to include from an existing *Test Suite Object*.

Variation: Test Suite Procedure

Sometimes we have to write code in programming or scripting languages that do not support objects. Given that we have written a number of *Test Methods,* we need to give the *Test Runner* some way to find the tests. A *Test Suite Procedure* allows us to enumerate all the tests we want to run by invoking each test in turn. The calls to each test are hard-coded within the body of the *Test Suite Object*. Of course, a *Test Suite Procedure* may call several other *Test Suite Procedures* to realize a *Suite of Suites*.

The major disadvantage of this approach is that it forces us into *Test Enumeration,* which increases both the effort required to write tests and the likelihood of *Lost Tests* (see *Production Bugs* on page 268). Because we do not treat our code as "data," we lose the ability to manipulate the code at runtime. As a consequence, it is more difficult to build a *Graphical Test Runner* (see *Test Runner*) with a hierarchy (tree) view of our *Suite of Suites.*

Test Suite Object

Example: Test Suite Object

Most members of the xUnit family implement *Test Discovery,* so there isn't much of an example of *Test Suite Object* to see. The main evidence of the existence of *Test Suite Objects* appears in the *Test Tree Explorer* (see *Test Runner*) when we "drill down" into the *Test Suite Object* to expose the *Testcase Objects* it contains. Here's an example from the JUnit *Graphical Test Runner* built into Eclipse:

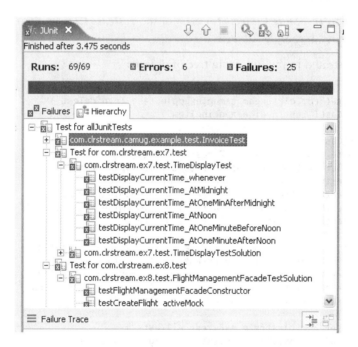

Example: Suite of Suites Built Using Test Enumeration

Here is an example of using *Test Enumeration* to construct a *Suite of Suites:*

```
public class AllTests {

    public static Test suite() {
```

```
            TestSuite suite = new TestSuite("Test for allJunitTests");
            suite.addTestSuite(
                    com.clrstream.camug.example.test.InvoiceTest.class);
            suite.addTest(com.clrstream.ex7.test.AllTests.suite());
            suite.addTest(com.clrstream.ex8.test.AllTests.suite());
            suite.addTestSuite(com.xunitpatterns.guardassertion.Example.class);
            return suite;
        }
    }
```

Test Suite Object

The first and last lines add the *Test Suite Objects* created from a single *Testcase Class*. Each of the middle two lines calls the *Test Suite Factory* for another *Suite of Suites*. The *Test Suite Object* we return is likely at least three levels deep:

1. The *Test Suite Object* we instantiated and populated before returning

2. The AllTests *Test Suite Objects* returned by the two calls to factory methods

3. The *Test Suite Objects* for each of the *Testcase Classes* aggregated into those *Test Suite Objects*

This is illustrated in the following tree of objects:

```
TestSuite("Test for allJunitTests");
    TestSuite("com.clrstream.camug.example.test.InvoiceTest")
        TestCase("testInvoice_addLineItem")
        ...
        TestCase("testRemoveLineItemsForProduct_oneOfTwo")
    TestSuite("com.clrstream.ex7.test.AllTests")
        TestSuite("com.clrstream.ex7.test.TimeDisplayTest")
            TestCase("testDisplayCurrentTime_AtMidnight")
            TestCase("testDisplayCurrentTime_AtOneMinAfterMidnight")
            TestCase("testDisplayCurrentTime_AtOneMinuteBeforeNoon")
            TestCase("testDisplayCurrentTime_AtNoon")
            ...
        TestSuite("com.clrstream.ex7.test.TimeDisplaySolutionTest")
            TestCase("testDisplayCurrentTime_AtMidnight")
            TestCase("testDisplayCurrentTime_AtOneMinAfterMidnight")
            TestCase("testDisplayCurrentTime_AtOneMinuteBeforeNoon")
            TestCase("testDisplayCurrentTime_AtNoon")
            ...
    TestSuite("com.clrstream.ex8.test.AllTests")
        TestSuite("com.clrstream.ex8.FlightMgntFacadeTest")
            TestCase("testAddFlight")
            TestCase("testAddFlightLogging")
            TestCase("testRemoveFlight")
            TestCase("testRemoveFlightLogging")
            ...
    TestSuite("com.xunitpatterns.guardassertion.Example")
            TestCase("testWithConditionals")
            TestCase("testWithoutConditionals")
            ...
```

Note that this class doesn't subclass any other class. It does need to import TestSuite and the classes it is using as *Test Suite Factories*.

Example: Test Suite Procedure

In the early days of agile software development, before any agile project management tools were available, I built a set of Excel spreadsheets for managing tasks and user stories. To make life simpler, I automated frequently performed tasks such as sorting all stories by release and iteration, sorting tasks by iteration and status, and so on. Eventually, I got bold enough to write a macro (a program, really) that would sum up the estimated and actual effort of all tasks for each story. At this point, the code was becoming somewhat complex and was more challenging to maintain. In particular, if one of the named ranges used by the sorting macros was accidentally deleted, the macro would produce an error.

Unfortunately, there was no xUnit framework for VBA at the time, so all of this work was done without *Tests as Safety Net* (see page 24). Here is the main program of the reporting macro. All output was written to a new sheet in the workbook.

```
'Main Macro

Sub summarizeActivities()
    Call VerifyVersionCompatability
    Call initialize
    Call SortByActivity

    For row = firstTaskDataRow To lastTaskDataRow
        If numberOfNumberlessTasks < MaxNumberlessTasks Then
            thisActivity =
                ActiveSheet.Cells(row, TaskActivityColumn).Value

            If thisActivity <> currentActivity Then
                Call finalizeCurrentActivityTotals
                currentActivity = thisActivity
                Call initializeCurrentActivityTotals
            End If

            Call accumulateActivityTotals(row)
        Else
            lastTaskDataRow = row    ' end the For loop right away
        End If
    Next row
    Call cleanUp
End Sub
```

Without any tests or *Test Automation Framework*, I had to do what I could to
introduce some kind of regression testing. In this case, it was enough of a challenge
(and a win) just to be able to exercise all the macros. If they ran to completion, it
was a much better indication that I hadn't broken anything major than not running
the macros at all. Because VBA is based on Visual Basic 5, it has no classes. Thus
we have no *Testcase Class* and no runtime *Testcase Objects*. The following is an
example of the various *Test Suite Procedures* and the *Test Methods* my tests called:

Test Suite Object

```
Sub TestAll()
    Call TestAllStoryMacros
    Call TestAllTaskMacros
    Call TestReportingMacros
    Call TestToolbarMenus  'All The Same
End Sub

Sub TestAllStoryMacros()
    Call TestActivitySorting
    Call TestStoryHiding
    Call ReportSuccess("All Story Macros")
End Sub

Sub TestActivitySorting()
    Call SortStoriesbyAreaAndNumber
    Call SortActivitiesByIteration
    Call SortActivitiesByIterationAndOrder
    Call SortActivitiesByNumber
    Call SortActivitiesByPercentDone
End Sub

Sub TestReportingMacros()
    Call summarizeActivities
End Sub
```

The first *Test Suite Procedure* is a *Suite of Suites;* the second *Test Suite Procedure*
is the equivalent of a single *Test Suite Object*. The third Sub is the *Test Method* for
exercising all of the sorting macros. The last Sub exercises the summarizeActivities
macro using a *Prebuilt Fixture* (page 429). [5]

---

[5] For those who might be wondering what happened to the verify outcome phase of the
test, there isn't one in this test. It is neither a *Self-Checking Test* nor a *Single-Condition
Test*. Shame on me!

Test Discovery

How does the Test Runner know which tests to run?

The Test Automation Framework discovers all tests that belong to the test suite automatically.

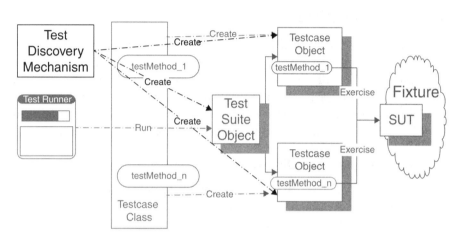

Given that we have written a number of *Test Methods* (page 348) on one or more *Testcase Classes* (page 373), we need to give the *Test Runner* (page 377) some way to find the tests. *Test Discovery* eliminates most of the hassles associated with *Test Enumeration* (page 399).

How It Works

The *Test Automation Framework* (page 298) uses runtime reflection (or compile-time knowledge) to discover all *Test Methods* that belong to the test suite and/or all *Test Suite Objects* (page 387) that belong to a *Suite of Suites* (see *Test Suite Object*). It then builds up the *Test Suite Objects* containing the corresponding *Testcase Objects* (page 382) and other *Test Suite Objects* in preparation for running all the tests.

When to Use It

We should use *Test Discovery* whenever our *Test Automation Framework* supports it. This pattern reduces the effort required to automate tests and greatly reduces the possibility of *Lost Tests* (see *Production Bugs* on page 268). The only times to consider using *Test Enumeration* are (1) when our framework does not support *Test Discovery* and (2) when we wish to define a *Named Test Suite* (page 592) that consists of a subset of tests[6] chosen from other test suites and the *Test Automation Framework* does not support *Test Selection* (page 403). It is not uncommon to combine *Test Suite Enumeration* (see *Test Enumeration*) with *Test Method Discovery*; the reverse is less common.

Implementation Notes

Building the *Suite of Suites* to be executed by the *Test Runner* involves two steps. First, we must find all *Test Methods* to be included in each *Test Suite Object*. Second, we must find all *Test Suite Objects* to be included in the test run, albeit not necessarily in this order. Each of these steps may be done manually via *Test Method Enumeration* (see *Test Enumeration*) and *Test Suite Enumeration* or automatically via *Test Method Discovery* and *Testcase Class Discovery*.

Variation: Testcase Class Discovery

Testcase Class Discovery is the process by which the *Test Automation Framework* discovers the *Testcase Classes* on which it should do *Test Method Discovery*. One solution involves tagging each *Testcase Class* by subclassing a *Testcase Superclass* (page 638) or implementing a Marker Interface [PJV1]. Another alternative, used in the .NET languages and newer versions of JUnit, is to use a class attribute (e.g., `"[Test Fixture]"`) or annotation (e.g., `"@Testcase"`) to identify each *Testcase Class*. Yet another solution is to put all *Testcase Classes* into a common directory and point the *Test Runner* or some other program at this directory. A fourth solution is to follow a *Testcase Class* naming convention and use an external program to find all files matching this naming pattern. Whichever way we choose to perform this task, once a *Testcase Class* has been discovered we can proceed to either *Test Method Discovery* or *Test Method Enumeration*.

Variation: Test Method Discovery

Test Method Discovery involves providing a way for the *Test Automation Framework* to discover the *Test Methods* in our *Testcase Classes*. There are two basic ways to indicate that a method of a *Testcase Class* is a *Test Method*. The more traditional approach is to use a *Test Method* naming convention such as "starts with 'test'." The *Test Automation Framework* then iterates over all methods of the *Testcase Class*, selects those that start with the string "test" (e.g., testCounters),

---

[6] A Smoke Test [SCM] suite is a good example.

and calls the one-argument constructor to create the *Testcase Object* for that *Test Method*. The other alternative, which is used in the .NET languages and newer versions of JUnit, is to use a method attribute (e.g., "[Test]") or annotation (e.g., "@Test") to identify each *Test Method*.

Motivating Example

The following example illustrates the kind of code that would be required for each *Test Method* to do *Test Method Enumeration* if we did not have *Test Discovery* available:

```
public:
   static CppUnit::Test *suite()
   {
      CppUnit::TestSuite *suite =
            new CppUnit::TestSuite( "ComplexNumberTest" );
      suite>addTest(
         new CppUnit::TestCaller<ComplexNumberTest>(
                  "testEquality",
                  &ComplexNumberTest::testEquality ) );
      suite>addTest(
         new CppUnit::TestCaller<ComplexNumberTest>(
                  "testAddition",
                  &ComplexNumberTest::testAddition ) );
      return suite;
   }
```

This example is from the tutorial for an earlier version of CppUnit. Newer versions no longer require this approach.

Refactoring Notes

Luckily for the users of existing xUnit family members, the inventors of xUnit realized the importance of *Test Discovery*. Therefore all we have to do is follow their advice on how to identify our test methods. If the developers of our xUnit version used a naming convention, we may have to do a Rename Method [Fowler] refactoring to get xUnit to discover our *Test Method*. If they implemented method attributes, we just add the appropriate attribute to our *Test Methods*.

Example: Test Method Discovery (Using Method Naming and Compiler Macro)

When the programming language is capable of managing the tests as objects and invoking the methods but cannot easily find all methods to use as tests, we may need to give it a small push as encouragement to do so. Newer versions of CppUnit provide a macro that finds all *Test Methods* at compile time and generates the code to build the test suite as illustrated in the previous example. The following code snippet triggers the *Test Method Discovery*:

```
CPPUNIT_TEST_SUITE_REGISTRATION( FlightManagementFacadeTest );
```

This macro uses a method naming convention to determine which methods ("member functions") it should turn into *Testcase Objects* by wrapping each with a TestCaller, much like in the manual example we saw earlier.

Example: Test Method Discovery (Using Method Naming)

The following examples are more notable for the code that is missing than for the code that is present. Note that there is *no* code to add the *Test Methods* to the *Test Suite Object*.

In this Java example, the framework automatically runs all test methods that start with "test" and have no arguments (a total of two):

```
public class TimeDisplayTest extends TestCase {
    public void testDisplayCurrentTime_AtMidnight()
            throws Exception {
        // Set up SUT
        TimeDisplay theTimeDisplay = new TimeDisplay();
        // Exercise SUT
        String actualTimeString =
            theTimeDisplay.getCurrentTimeAsHtmlFragment();
        // Verify outcome
        String expectedTimeString =
            "<span class=\"tinyBoldText\">Midnight</span>";
        assertEquals( "Midnight",
                      expectedTimeString,
                      actualTimeString);
    }

    public void testDisplayCurrentTime_AtOneMinuteAfterMidnight()
            throws Exception {
        // Set up SUT
        TimeDisplay actualTimeDisplay = new TimeDisplay();
        // Exercise SUT
        String actualTimeString =
            actualTimeDisplay.getCurrentTimeAsHtmlFragment();
        // Verify outcome
        String expectedTimeString =
            "<span class=\"tinyBoldText\">12:01 AM</span>";
        assertEquals( "12:01 AM",
                      expectedTimeString,
                      actualTimeString);
    }
}
```

Example: Test Method Discovery (Using Method Attributes)

In this C# example, the tests are labeled with the method attribute [Test]. Both
CsUnit and NUnit use this way of identifying *Test Methods*.

```
[Test]
public void testFlightMileage_asKm()
{
    // set up fixture
    Flight newFlight = new Flight(validFlightNumber);
    newFlight.setMileage(1122);
    // exercise mileage translator
    int actualKilometres = newFlight.getMileageAsKm();
    int expectedKilometres = 1810;
    // verify results
    Assert.AreEqual( expectedKilometres, actualKilometres);
}

[Test]
[ExpectedException(typeof(InvalidArgumentException))]
public void testSetMileage_invalidInput_attribute()
{
    // set up fixture
    Flight newFlight = new Flight(validFlightNumber);
    // exercise SUT
    newFlight.setMileage(-1122);
}
```

Example: Testcase Class Discovery (Using Class Attributes)

Here is an example of using a class attribute to identify a *Testcase Class* (called
a "Test Fixture" in NUnit) to the *Test Runner*:

```
[TestFixture]
public class SampleTestcase
{

}
```

Example: Testcase Class Discovery (Using Common Location and Testcase Superclass)

The following Ruby example finds all files with the .rb extension in the "tests"
directory and requires them from this file. This causes Test::Unit to look for all tests
in each file because the *Testcase Class* in each file extends Test::Unit::TestCase.

```
Dir['tests/*.rb'].each do |each|
    require each
end
```

The Dir['tests/*.rb'] returns a collection of files over which the each method iterates with the block containing "require each" to implement *Testcase Class Discovery*. The Ruby interpreter and Test::Unit finish the job by doing *Test Method Discovery* on each required class.

**Test
Discovery**

Test Enumeration

How does the Test Runner know which tests to run?

The test automater manually writes the code that enumerates all tests that belong to the test suite.

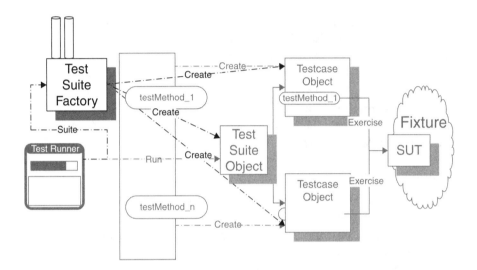

Given that we have written a number of *Test Methods* (page 348) on one or more *Testcase Classes* (page 373), we need to give the *Test Runner* (page 377) some way to find the tests. *Test Enumeration* is the way we do so when we lack support for *Test Discovery* (page 393).

How It Works

The test automater manually writes the code that enumerates all *Test Methods* that belong to the test suite and/or all *Test Suite Objects* (page 387) that belong to a *Suite of Suites* (see *Test Suite Object*). This is typically done by implementing the method suite either on a *Testcase Class* for *Test Method Enumeration* or on a *Test Suite Factory* for *Test Suite Enumeration*.

When to Use It

We need to use *Test Enumeration* if our *Test Automation Framework* (page 298) does not support *Test Discovery*. We can also choose to use *Test Enumeration* when we wish to define a *Named Test Suite* (page 592) that consists of a subset of tests[7] chosen from other test suites and the framework does not support *Test Selection* (page 403).

Many members of the xUnit family support *Test Discovery* at the *Test Method* level but force us to use *Test Enumeration* at the *Testcase Class* level.

Implementation Notes

Building the *Suite of Suites* to be executed by the *Test Runner* involves two steps. First, we must find all *Test Methods* to be included in each *Test Suite Object*. Second, we must find all *Test Suite Objects* to be included in the test run, albeit not necessarily in this order. Each of these steps may be done manually via *Test Method Enumeration* and *Test Suite Enumeration* or automatically via *Test Method Discovery* (see *Test Discovery*) and *Testcase Class Discovery* (see *Test Discovery*). When done manually, we typically use a "Test Suite Factory" that returns the *Test Suite Object*.

Variation: Test Suite Enumeration

Many members of the xUnit family require that we provide a *Test Suite Factory* that builds the top-level *Suite of Suites* (often called "AllTests") as means to specify which *Test Suite Objects* we would like to include in a test run. We do so by providing a class method on a factory class; this Factory Method [GOF] is called suite in most members of the xUnit family. Inside the suite method we use calls to methods such as addTest to add each nested *Test Suite Object* to the suite we are building.

Although this approach is fairly flexible, it can result in *Lost Tests* (see *Production Bugs* on page 268). The alternative is to let the development tools build the *AllTests Suite* (see *Named Test Suite*) automatically or to use a *Test Runner* that finds all test suites in a file system directory automatically. For example, NUnit provides a built-in mechanism that implements *Testcase Class Discovery* at the assembly level. We can also use third-party tools such as Ant to find all *Testcase Class* files in a directory structure.

Even in statically typed languages such as Java, the *Test Suite Factory* (see *Test Enumeration* on page 399) does not need to subclass a specific class or implement a specific interface. Instead, the only dependencies are on the generic *Test Suite Object* class it returns and the *Testcase Classes* or *Test Suite Factories* it asks for the nested suites.

---

[7] A Smoke Test [SCM] suite is a good example.

Variation: Test Method Enumeration

Many members of the xUnit family now support *Test Method Discovery*. If we happen to be using a version that does not, we need to find all *Test Methods* in a *Testcase Class*, turn them into *Testcase Objects* (page 382), and put them into a *Test Suite Object*. We implement *Test Method Enumeration* by providing a class method, typically called suite, on the *Testcase Class* itself.

Test Enumeration

    The capability to construct an object that calls an arbitrary method is often inherited from the *Test Automation Framework* via a *Testcase Superclass* (page 638) or mixed in via a class attribute or Include directive. In some members of the xUnit family, this Pluggable Behavior [SBPP] capability is provided by a separate class (see the CppUnit example below).

Variation: Direct Test Method Invocation

In the pure procedural world where we cannot treat a *Test Method* as an object or data item, we have no choice but to hand-code a *Test Suite Procedure* (see *Test Suite Object*) for each test suite. This procedure then calls each *Test Method* (or other *Test Suite Procedures*) one by one.

Example: Test Method Enumeration in CppUnit

Early versions of most xUnit family members required that the test automater add each *Test Method* manually. Those versions that cannot use reflection still have this requirement. Here is an example from an older version of CppUnit that uses this approach:

```
public:
   static CppUnit::Test *suite()
   {
     CppUnit::TestSuite *suite =
            new CppUnit::TestSuite( "ComplexNumberTest" );
     suite>addTest(
         new CppUnit::TestCaller<ComplexNumberTest>(
                    "testEquality",
                    &ComplexNumberTest::testEquality ) );
     suite>addTest(
         new CppUnit::TestCaller<ComplexNumberTest>(
                    "testAddition",
                    &ComplexNumberTest::testAddition ) );
     return suite;
   }
```

This example also illustrates how CppUnit wraps each *Test Method* with an instance of a class (TestCaller) to turn it into a *Testcase Object*.

Example: Test Method Invocation (Hard-Coded)

The following example is from a test suite for a program written in VBA (Visual Basic for Applications, the macro language used in Microsoft Office products), which lacks support for objects:

Test Enumeration

```
Sub TestAllStoryMacros()
    Call TestActivitySorting
    Call TestStoryHiding
    Call ReportSuccess("All Story Macros")
End Sub
```

Example: Test Suite Enumeration

We can use *Test Suite Enumeration* when the *Test Automation Framework* does not support *Test Discovery* or when we want to define a *Named Test Suite* that includes only a subset of the tests.

The main drawback of using *Test Suite Enumeration* for running all tests is the potential for *Lost Tests* if we forget to include a new test suite in the *AllTests Suite*. This risk can be reduced by paying attention to the number of tests that were run when we first checked out the code and ensuring that the number run just before check-in goes up by the number of new tests we added.

```
public class AllTests {

    public static Test suite() {
        TestSuite suite = new TestSuite("Test for allJunitTests");
        //$JUnit-BEGIN$
        suite.addTestSuite(
                com.clrstream.camug.example.test.InvoiceTest.class);
        suite.addTest(com.clrstream.ex7.test.AllTests.suite());
        suite.addTest(com.clrstream.ex8.test.AllTests.suite());
        suite.addTestSuite(
                com.xunitpatterns.guardassertion.Example.class);
        //$JUnit-END$
        return suite;
    }
}
```

In this example, we take advantage of the IDE's ability to (re)generate the AllTests suite for us. (Eclipse will regenerate the code between the two marker comments whenever we request it to do so.) We still need to remember to regenerate the suite occasionally, but this approach goes a long way toward avoiding *Lost Tests* in the absence of *Test Discovery*.

Test Selection

How does the Test Runner know which tests to run?

The Test Automation Framework selects the Test Methods to be run at runtime based on attributes of the tests.

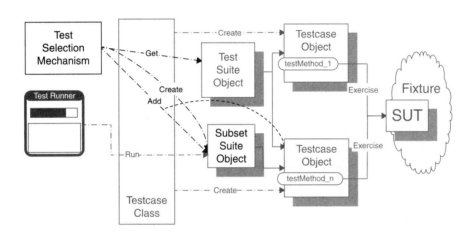

Given that we have written a number of *Test Methods* (page 348) on one or more *Testcase Classes* (page 373), we need to give the *Test Runner* (page 377) some way to find those tests. *Test Selection* is a way to pick subsets of tests dynamically.

How It Works

The test automater specifies the subset of tests to be run when invoking the *Test Runner* by providing test selection criteria. These selection criteria may be based on implicit or explicit attributes of the *Testcase Classes* or *Test Methods*.

When to Use It

We should use *Test Selection* when we wish to run a subset of tests chosen from other test suites and we do not want to maintain a separate structure built using *Test Enumeration* (page 399). A Smoke Test [SCM] suite is a common usage; see *Named Test Suite* (page 592) for other uses.

**Test
Selection**

Implementation Notes

Test Selection can be implemented either by creating a *Subset Suite* (see *Named Test Suite*) from an existing *Test Suite Object* (page 387) or by skipping some of the tests within the *Test Suite Object* as we execute the *Testcase Objects* (page 382) it contains.

As with *Test Discovery* (page 393) and *Test Enumeration*, *Test Selection* can be applied at two different levels: selecting *Testcase Classes* or selecting *Test Methods*. *Test Selection* can be built into the *Test Automation Framework* (page 298) or it can be implemented more crudely as part of the build task.

Variation: Testcase Class Selection

We can select the *Testcase Classes* to be examined for *Test Methods* in several ways. The crudest way to do *Testcase Class Selection* is simply to place the *Testcase Classes* into test packages based on some criteria. Unfortunately, this strategy works only for a single test classification scheme and is likely to reduce the value of *Tests as Documentation* (see page 23). A somewhat more flexible approach is to use a naming convention such as "contains 'WebServer'" to select only those classes that verify the behavior of certain parts of the system. This, too, is somewhat constrained in its utility.

The most flexible way to implement *Test Selection* is within the *Test Automation Framework*. We can use class attributes (.NET) or annotations (Java) to indicate characteristics of the *Testcase Class*. The same technique can also be applied at the *Test Method* level.

Variation: Test Method Selection

When implemented as part of the *Test Automation Framework*, *Test Method Selection* can be done by specifying the "category" (or categories) to which a *Test Method* belongs. This usually requires language support for method attributes (.NET) or annotations (Java). It could also be based on a method name scheme, although this approach is not as flexible and would require tighter coupling to the *Test Runner*.

Example: Testcase Class Selection Using Class Attributes

The following example of *Testcase Class Selection* is from NUnit. The class attribute `Category("FastSuite")` indicates that all tests in this *Testcase Class* should be included (or excluded) when the category "FastSuite" is specified in the *Test Runner*.

```
[TestFixture]
[Category("FastSuite")]
public class CategorizedTests
{
   [Test]
   public void testFlightConstructor_OK()
   // Methods omitted
}
```

Example: Test Method Selection Using Method Attributes

This example of *Test Method Selection* is from NUnit. The method attribute
Category("SmokeTest") indicates that this *Test Method* should be included (or
excluded) when the category "SmokeTest" is specified in the *Test Runner*.

```
[Test]
[Category("SmokeTests")]
public void testFlightMileage_asKm()
{
   // set up fixture
   Flight newFlight = new Flight(validFlightNumber);
   newFlight.setMileage(1122);
   // exercise mileage translator
   int actualKilometres = newFlight.getMileageAsKm();
   int expectedKilometres = 1810;
   // verify results
   Assert.AreEqual( expectedKilometres, actualKilometres);
}
```

Chapter 20

Fixture Setup Patterns

Patterns in This Chapter

In-line Setup

How do we construct the Fresh Fixture?

Each Test Method creates its own Fresh Fixture by calling the appropriate constructor methods to build exactly the test fixture it requires.

In-line Setup

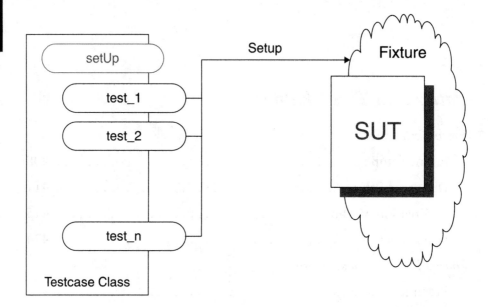

To execute an automated test, we require a text fixture that is well understood and completely deterministic. We can use the *Fresh Fixture* (page 311) approach to build a *Minimal Fixture* (page 302) for the use of this one test. Setting up the test fixture on an in-line basis in each test is the most obvious way to build it.

How It Works

Each *Test Method* (page 348) sets up its own test fixture by directly calling whatever SUT code is required to construct exactly the test fixture it requires. We put the code that creates the fixture, the first phase of the *Four-Phase Test* (page 358), at the top of each *Test Method*.

When to Use It

We can use *In-line Setup* when the fixture setup logic is very simple and straightforward. As soon as the fixture setup gets at all complex, we should consider using *Delegated Setup* (page 411) or *Implicit Setup* (page 424) for part or all of the fixture setup.

We can also use *In-line Setup* when we are writing a first draft of tests and haven't yet figured out which part of the fixture setup will be repeated from test to test. This is an example of applying the "Red–Green–Refactor" process pattern to the tests themselves. Nevertheless, we need to be careful when we refactor the tests to ensure that we don't break the tests in ways that are undetectable.

A third occasion to use *In-line Setup* is when refactoring obtuse fixture setup code. A first step may be to use In-line Method [Fowler] refactorings on all *Creation Methods* (page 415) and the setUp method. Then we can try using a series of Extract Method [Fowler] refactorings to define a new set of *Creation Methods* that are more intent-revealing and reusable.

In-line Setup

Implementation Notes

In practice, most fixture setup logic will include a mix of styles, such as *In-line Setup* building on top of *Implicit Setup* or *Delegated Setup* interspersed with *In-line Setup*.

Example: In-line Setup

Here's an example of simple in-line setup. Everything each *Test Method* needs for exercising the SUT is included in-line.

```
public void testStatus_initial() {
   // in-line setup
   Airport departureAirport = new Airport("Calgary", "YYC");
   Airport destinationAirport = new Airport("Toronto", "YYZ");
   Flight flight = new Flight( flightNumber,
                               departureAirport,
                               destinationAirport);
   // exercise SUT and verify outcome
   assertEquals(FlightState.PROPOSED, flight.getStatus());
   // tearDown:
     //    garbage-collected
}

public void testStatus_cancelled() {
   // in-line setup
   Airport departureAirport = new Airport("Calgary", "YYC");
   Airport destinationAirport = new Airport("Toronto", "YYZ");
```

```
        Flight flight = new Flight( flightNumber,
                                    departureAirport,
                                    destinationAirport);
        flight.cancel(); // still part of setup
        // exercise SUT and verify outcome
        assertEquals(FlightState.CANCELLED, flight.getStatus());
        // tearDown:
          //    garbage-collected
    }
```

Refactoring Notes

In-line Setup is normally the starting point for refactoring, not the end goal. Sometimes, however, we find ourselves with tests that are too hard to understand because of all the stuff happening behind the scenes, which is a form of *Mystery Guest* (see *Obscure Test* on page 186). At other times, we may find ourselves modifying the previously setup fixture in many of the tests.

Both of these situations are indications it may be time to refactor our test class into multiple classes based on the fixture they build. First, we use an In-line Method refactoring on the code to produce an *In-line Setup*. Next, we reorganize the tests using an Extract Class [Fowler] refactoring. Finally, we use a series of Extract Method refactorings to define a more understandable set of fixture setup methods.

Delegated Setup

How do we construct the Fresh Fixture?

Each Test Method creates its own Fresh Fixture by calling Creation Methods from within the Test Methods.

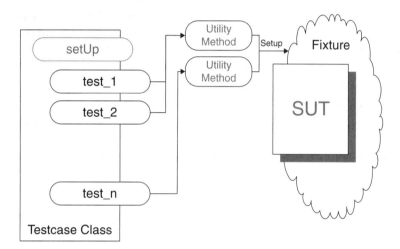

To execute an automated test, we require a text fixture that is well understood and completely deterministic. We are using a *Fresh Fixture* (page 311) approach to build a *Minimal Fixture* (page 302) for the use of this one test and we'd like to avoid *Test Code Duplication* (page 213).

Delegated Setup lets us reuse the code to set up the fixture without compromising our goal of *Tests as Documentation* (see page 23).

How It Works

Each *Test Method* (page 348) sets up its own test fixture by calling one or more *Creation Methods* (page 415) to construct exactly the test fixture it requires. To ensure *Tests as Documentation*, we build a *Minimal Fixture* using *Creation Methods* that build fully formed objects that are ready for use by the test. We strive to ensure that the method calls will convey the "big picture" to the test reader by passing in only those values that affect the behavior of the SUT.

When to Use It

We can use a *Delegated Setup* when we want to avoid the *Test Code Duplication* caused by having to set up similar fixtures for several tests and we want to keep the nature of the fixture visible within the *Test Methods*. A reasonable goal is to encapsulate the *essential but irrelevant* steps of setting up the fixture and leave only the steps and values essential to understanding the test within the *Test Method*. This scheme helps us achieve *Tests as Documentation* by ensuring that excess *In-line Setup* (page 408) code does not obscure the intent of the test. It also avoids the *Mystery Guest* problem (see *Obscure Test* on page 186) by leaving the Intent-Revealing Name [SBPP] of the *Creation Method* call within the *Test Method*.

Delegated Setup

Furthermore, *Delegated Setup* allows us to use whatever organization scheme we want for our *Test Methods*. In particular, we are not forced to put *Test Methods* that require the same test fixture into the same *Testcase Class* (page 373) just to reuse the setUp method as we would have to when using *Implicit Setup* (page 424). Furthermore, *Delegated Setup* helps prevent *Fragile Tests* (page 239) by moving much of the nonessential interaction with the SUT out of the very numerous *Test Methods* and into a much smaller number of *Creation Method* bodies, where it is easier to maintain.

Implementation Notes

With modern refactoring tools, we can often create the first cut of a *Creation Method* by performing a simple Extract Method [Fowler] refactoring. As we are writing a set of tests using "clone and twiddle," we must watch for any *Test Code Duplication* in the fixture setup logic within our tests. For each object that needs to be verified in the verification logic, we extract a *Creation Method* that takes only those attributes as parameters that affect the outcome of the test.

Initially, we can leave the *Creation Method* on our *Testcase Class*. If we need to share them with another class, however, we can move the *Creation Methods* to an *Abstract Testcase* class (see *Testcase Superclass* on page 638) or a *Test Helper* (page 643) class.

Motivating Example

Suppose we are testing the state model of the Flight class. In each test, we need to have a flight in the right state. Because a flight needs to connect at least two airports, we need to create airports before we can create a flight. Of course, airports are typically associated with cities or states/provinces. To keep the example manageable, let's assume that our airports require only a city name and an airport code.

```
public void testStatus_initial() {
    // in-line setup
    Airport departureAirport = new Airport("Calgary", "YYC");
    Airport destinationAirport = new Airport("Toronto", "YYZ");
    Flight flight = new Flight(flightNumber,
                               departureAirport,
                               destinationAirport);
    // exercise SUT and verify outcome
    assertEquals(FlightState.PROPOSED, flight.getStatus());
    // teardown
      //    garbage-collected
}

public void testStatus_cancelled() {
    // in-line setup
    Airport departureAirport = new Airport("Calgary", "YYC");
    Airport destinationAirport = new Airport("Toronto", "YYZ");
    Flight flight = new Flight( flightNumber,
                                departureAirport,
                                destinationAirport);
    flight.cancel(); // still part of setup
    // Exercise SUT and verify outcome
    assertEquals(FlightState.CANCELLED, flight.getStatus());
    // teardown
      //    garbage-collected
}
```

**Delegated
Setup**

These tests contain a fair amount of *Test Code Duplication*.

Refactoring Notes

We can refactor the fixture setup logic by using an Extract Method refactoring to remove any frequently repeated code sequences into utility methods with Intent-Revealing Names. We leave the calls to the methods in the test, however, so that the reader can see what is being done. The method calls that remain within the test will convey the "big picture" to the test reader. The utility method bodies contain the irrelevant mechanics of carrying out the intent. If we need to share the *Delegated Setups* with another *Testcase Class*, we can use either a Pull Up Method [Fowler] refactoring to move them to a *Testcase Superclass* or a Move Method [Fowler] refactoring to move them to a *Test Helper* class.

Example: Delegated Setup

In this version of the test, we use a method that hides the fact that we need two airports instead of creating the two airports needed by the flight within each *Test Method*. We could produce this version of the tests either through refactoring or by writing the test in this intent-revealing style right off the bat.

```
public void testGetStatus_initial() {
    // setup
    Flight flight = createAnonymousFlight();
    // exercise SUT and verify outcome
    assertEquals(FlightState.PROPOSED, flight.getStatus());
    // teardown
    //       garbage-collected
}

public void testGetStatus_cancelled2() {
    // setup
    Flight flight = createAnonymousCancelledFlight();
    // exercise SUT and verify outcome
    assertEquals(FlightState.CANCELLED, flight.getStatus());
    // teardown
    //       garbage-collected
}
```

Delegated Setup

The simplicity of these tests was made possible by the following *Creation Methods*, which hide the "necessary but irrelevant" steps from the test reader:

```
private int uniqueFlightNumber = 2000;

public Flight createAnonymousFlight(){
    Airport departureAirport = new Airport("Calgary", "YYC");
    Airport destinationAirport = new Airport("Toronto", "YYZ");
    Flight flight =
        new Flight( new BigDecimal(uniqueFlightNumber++),
                    departureAirport,
                    destinationAirport);
    return flight;
}
public Flight createAnonymousCancelledFlight(){
    Flight flight = createAnonymousFlight();
    flight.cancel();
    return flight;
}
```

Creation Method

How do we construct the Fresh Fixture?

We set up the test fixture by calling methods that hide the mechanics of building ready-to-use objects behind Intent-Revealing Names.

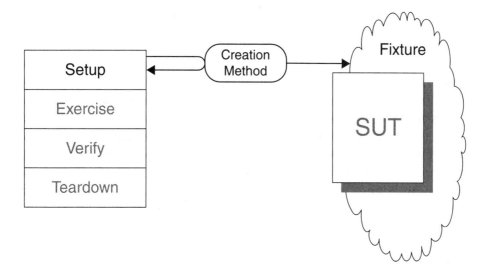

Fixture setup usually involves the creation of a number of objects. In many cases, the details of those objects (i.e., the attribute values) are unimportant but must be specified to satisfy each object's constructor method. Including all of this unnecessary complexity within the fixture setup part of the test can lead to *Obscure Tests* (page 186) and certainly doesn't help us achieve *Tests as Documentation* (see page 23)!

How can a properly initialized object be created without having to clutter the test with *In-line Setup* (page 408)? The answer, of course, is to encapsulate this complexity. *Delegated Setup* (page 411) moves the mechanics of the fixture setup into other methods but leaves overall control and coordination within the test itself. But what to delegate to? A *Creation Method* is one way we can encapsulate the mechanics of object creation so that irrelevant details do not distract the reader.

How It Works

As we write tests, we don't bother asking whether a desired utility function exists; we just use it! (It helps to pretend that we have a loyal helper sitting next to us who will quickly fill in the bodies of any functions we call that do not exist as yet.) We write our tests in terms of these magic functions with Intent-Revealing Names [SBPP], passing as parameters only those things that will be verified in the assertions or that should affect the outcome of the test.

Once we've written the test in this very intent-revealing style, we must implement all of the magic functions that we've been calling. The functions that create objects are our *Creation Methods;* they encapsulate the complexity of object creation. The simple ones call the appropriate constructor, passing it suitable default values for anything needed but not supplied as a parameter. If any of the constructor arguments are other objects, the *Creation Method* will first create those depended-on objects before calling the constructor.

The *Creation Method* may be placed in all the same places where we put *Test Utility Methods* (page 599). As usual, the decision is based on the expected scope of reuse and the *Creation Method's* dependencies on the API of the SUT. A related pattern is *Object Mother* (see *Test Helper* on page 643), which is a combination of *Creation Method, Test Helper,* and optionally *Automated Teardown* (page 503).

When to Use It

We should use a *Creation Method* whenever constructing a *Fresh Fixture* (page 311) requires significant complexity and we value *Tests as Documentation*. Another key indicator for using *Creation Method* is that we are building the system in a highly incremental way and we expect the API of the system (and especially the object constructors) to change frequently. Encapsulating knowledge of how to create a fixture object is a special case of *SUT API Encapsulation* (see *Test Utility Method*), and it helps us avoid both *Fragile Tests* (page 239) and *Obscure Tests*.

The main drawback of a *Creation Method* is that it creates another API for test automaters to learn. This isn't much of a problem for the initial test developers because they are typically involved in building this API but it can create "one more thing" for new additions to the team to learn. Even so, this API should be pretty easy to understand because it is just a set of Factory Methods [GOF] organized in some way.

If we are using a *Prebuilt Fixture* (page 429), we should use *Finder Methods* (see *Test Utility Method*) to locate the prebuilt objects. At the same time, we may still use *Creation Methods* to lay mutable objects that we plan to modify on top of an *Immutable Shared Fixture* (see *Shared Fixture* on page 317).

Several variations of *Creation Method* are worth exploring.

Variation: Parameterized Creation Method

While it is possible (and often very desirable) for *Creation Methods* to take no parameters whatsoever, many tests will require some customization of the created object. A *Parameterized Creation Method* allows the test to pass in some attributes to be used in the creation of the object. In such a case, we should pass only those attributes that are expected to affect (or those we want to demonstrate do not affect) the test's outcome; otherwise, we could be headed down the slippery slope to *Obscure Tests*.

Variation: Anonymous Creation Method

An *Anonymous Creation Method* automatically creates a *Distinct Generated Value* (see *Generated Value* on page 723) as the unique identifier for the object it is creating even though the arguments it receives may not be unique. This behavior is invaluable for avoiding *Unrepeatable Tests* (see *Erratic Test* on page 228) because it ensures that every object we create is unique, even across multiple test runs. If the test cares about some attributes of the object to be created, it can pass them as parameters of the *Creation Method*; this behavior turns the *Anonymous Creation Method* into a *Parameterized Anonymous Creation Method*.

Variation: Parameterized Anonymous Creation Method

A *Parameterized Anonymous Creation Method* is a combination of several other variations of *Creation Method* in that we pass in some attributes to be used in the creation of the object but let the *Creation Method* create the unique identifier for it. A *Creation Method* could also take zero parameters if the test doesn't care about any of the attributes.

Variation: Named State Reaching Method

Some SUTs are essentially stateless, meaning we can call any method at any time. By contrast, when the SUT is state-rich and the validity or behavior of methods is affected by the state of the SUT, it is important to test each method from each possible starting state. We could chain a bunch of such tests together in a single *Test Method* (page 348), but that approach would create an *Eager Test* (see *Assertion Roulette* on page 224). It is better to use a series of *Single-Condition Tests* (see page 45) for this purpose. Unfortunately, that leaves us with the problem of how to set up the starting state in each test without a lot of *Test Code Duplication* (page 213).

One obvious solution is to put all tests that depend on the same starting state into the same *Testcase Class* (page 373) and to create the SUT in the appropriate state in the setUp method using *Implicit Setup* (page 424) (called *Testcase Class per Fixture*; see page 631). The alternative is to use *Delegated Setup* by calling a *Named State Reaching Method*; this approach allows us to choose some other way to organize our *Testcase Classes*.

Either way, the code that sets up the SUT will be easier to understand if it is short and sweet. That's where a *Named State Reaching Method* comes in handy. By encapsulating the logic required to create the test objects in the correct state in a single place (whether on the *Testcase Class* or a *Test Helper*), we reduce the amount of code we must update if we need to change how we put the test object into that state.

Creation Method

Variation: Attachment Method

Suppose we already have a test object and we want to modify it in some way. We find ourselves performing this task in enough tests to want to code this modification once and only once. The solution in this case is an *Attachment Method*. The main difference between this variation and the original *Creation Method* pattern is that we pass in the object to be modified (one that was probably returned by another *Creation Method*) and the object we want to set one of its attributes to; the *Attachment Method* does the rest of the work for us.

Implementation Notes

Most *Creation Methods* are created by doing an Extract Method [Fowler] refactoring on parts of an existing test. When we write tests in an "outside-in" manner, we assume that the *Creation Methods* already exist and fill in the method bodies later. In effect, we define a *Higher-Level Language* (see page 41) for defining our fixtures. Nevertheless, there is another, completely different way to define *Creation Methods*.

Variation: Reuse Test for Fixture Setup

We *can* set up the fixture by calling another *Test Method* to do the fixture setup for us. This assumes that we have some way of accessing the fixture that the other test created, either through a Registry [PEAA] object or through instance variables of the *Testcase Object* (page 382).

It may be appropriate to implement a *Creation Method* in this way when we already have tests that depend on other tests to set up their test fixture but we want to reduce the likelihood that a change in the test execution order of *Chained Tests* (page 454) will cause tests to fail. Mind you, the tests will run more slowly because each test will call all the preceding tests it depends on each time each test is run rather than each test being run only once per test run. Of course, each test needs to call only the specific tests it actually depends on, not all tests in the test suite. This slowdown won't be very noticeable if we have replaced any slow components, such as a database, with a *Fake Object* (page 551).

Wrapping the *Test Method* in a *Creation Method* is a better option than calling the *Test Method* directly from the client *Test Method* because most *Test Methods* are named based on which test condition(s) they verify, not what (fixture) they leave behind. The *Creation Method* lets us put a nice Intent-Revealing Name between the client *Test Method* and the implementing *Test Method*. It also solves the *Lonely Test* (see *Erratic Test*) problem because the other test is run explicitly from within the calling test rather than just assuming that it was already run. This scheme makes the test less fragile and easier to understand but it won't solve the *Interacting Tests* (see *Erratic Test*) problem: If the test we call fails and leaves the test fixture in a different state than we expected, our test will likely fail as well, even if the functionality we are testing is still working.

Motivating Example

In the following example, the testPurchase test requires a Customer to fill the role of the buyer. The first and last names of the buyer have no bearing on the act of purchasing, but are required parameters of the Customer constructor; we do care that the Customer's credit rating is good ("G") and that he or she is currently active.

```
public void testPurchase_firstPurchase_ICC() {
    Customer buyer =
        new Customer(17, "FirstName", "LastName", "G","ACTIVE");
    // ...
}
public void testPurchase_subsequentPurchase_ICC() {
    Customer buyer =
        new Customer(18, "FirstName", "LastName", "G","ACTIVE");
    // ...
}
```

The use of constructors in tests can be problematic, especially when we are building an application incrementally. Every change to the parameters of the constructor will force us to revisit a lot of tests or jump through hoops to keep the constructor signatures backward compatible for the sake of the tests.

Refactoring Notes

We can use an Extract Method refactoring to remove the direct call to the constructor. We can give the new *Creation Method* an appropriate Intent-Revealing Name such as createCustomer based on the style of *Creation Method* we have created.

Example: Anonymous Creation Method

In the following example, instead of making that direct call to the Customer constructor, we now use the Customer *Creation Method*. Notice that the coupling between the fixture setup code and the constructor has been removed. If another parameter such as phone number is added to the Customer constructor, only the Customer *Creation Method* must be updated to provide a default value; the fixture setup code remains insulated from the change thanks to encapsulation.

```
public void testPurchase_firstPurchase_ACM() {
   Customer buyer = createAnonymousCustomer();
   // ...
}
public void testPurchase_subsequentPurchase_ACM() {
   Customer buyer = createAnonymousCustomer();
   // ...
}
```

We call this pattern an *Anonymous Creation Method* because the identity of the customer does not matter. The *Anonymous Creation Method* might look something like this:

```
public Customer createAnonymousCustomer() {
   int uniqueid = getUniqueCustomerId();
   return new Customer(uniqueid,
                       "FirstName" + uniqueid,
                       "LastName" + uniqueid,
                       "G", "ACTIVE");
}
```

Note the use of a *Distinct Generated Value* to ensure that each anonymous Customer is slightly different to avoid accidentally creating an identical Customer.

Example: Parameterized Creation Method

If we wanted to supply some of the Customer's attributes as parameters, we could define a *Parameterized Creation Method*:

```
public void testPurchase_firstPurchase_PCM() {
   Customer buyer =
         createCreditworthyCustomer("FirstName", "LastName");
```

```
        // ...
    }
    public void testPurchase_subsequentPurchase_PCM() {
        Customer buyer = createCreditworthyCustomer("FirstName", "LastName");
        // ...
    }
```

Here's the corresponding *Parameterized Creation Method* definition:

```
public Customer createCreditworthyCustomer(
                    String firstName, String lastName) {
    int uniqueid = getUniqueCustomerId();
    Customer customer =
        new Customer(uniqueid,firstName,lastName,"G","ACTIVE");
    customer.setCredit(CreditRating.EXCELLENT);
    customer.approveCredit();
    return customer;
}
```

Creation
Method

Example: Attachment Method

Here's an example of a test that uses an *Attachment Method* to associate two customers to verify that both get the best discount either of them has earned or negotiated:

```
public void testPurchase_relatedCustomerDiscount_AM() {
    Customer buyer = createCreditworthyCustomer("Related", "Buyer");
    Customer discountHolder =
            createCreditworthyCustomer("Discount", "Holder");
    createRelationshipBetweenCustomers( buyer, discountHolder);
    // ...
}
```

Behind the scenes, the *Attachment Method* does whatever it takes to establish the relationship:

```
private void createRelationshipBetweenCustomers(
                            Customer buyer,
                            Customer discountHolder) {
    buyer.addToRelatedCustomersList( discountHolder );
    discountHolder.addToRelatedCustomersList( buyer );
}
```

Although this example is relatively simple, the call to this method is still easier to understand than reading both the method calls of which it consists.

Example: Test Reused for Fixture Setup

We *can* reuse other tests to set up the fixture for our test. Here is an example of how *not* to do it:

```
private Customer buyer;
private AccountManager sut =  new AccountManager();
private Account account;

public void testCustomerConstructor_SRT() {
   // Exercise
   buyer = new Customer(17, "First", "Last", "G", "ACTIVE");
   // Verify
   assertEquals( "First", buyer.firstName(), "first");
   // ...
}
public void testPurchase_SRT() {
   testCustomerConstructor_SRT();  // Leaves in field "buyer"
   account = sut.createAccountForCustomer( buyer );
   assertEquals( buyer.name, account.customerName, "cust");
   // ...
}
```

The problem here is twofold. First, the name of the *Test Method* we are calling describes what it verifies (e.g., a name) and not what it leaves behind (i.e., a `Customer` in the `buyer` field. Second, the test does not *return* a `Customer`; it leaves the `Customer` in an instance variable. This scheme works only because the *Test Method* we want to reuse is on the same *Testcase Class*; if it were on an unrelated class, we would have to do a few backflips to access the `buyer`. A better way to accomplish this goal is to encapsulate this call behind a *Creation Method*:

```
private Customer buyer;
private AccountManager sut =  new AccountManager();
private Account account;

public void testCustomerConstructor_RTCM() {
   // Exercise
   buyer = new Customer(17, "First", "Last", "G", "ACTIVE");
   // Verify
   assertEquals( "First", buyer.firstName(), "first");
   // ...
}
public void testPurchase_RTCM() {
   buyer = createCreditworthyCustomer();
   account = sut.createAccountForCustomer( buyer );
   assertEquals( buyer.name, account.customerName, "cust");
   // ...
}
public Customer createCreditworthyCustomer() {
   testCustomerConstructor_RTCM();
```

```
        return buyer;
        // ...
    }
```

Notice how much more readable this test has become? We can see where the buyer came from! This was easy to do because both *Test Methods* were on the same class. If they were on different classes, our *Creation Method* would have to create an instance of the other *Testcase Class* before it could run the test. Then it would have to find a way to access the buyer instance variable so that it could return it to the calling *Test Method*.

**Creation
Method**

Implicit Setup

How do we construct the Fresh Fixture?

We build the test fixture common to several tests in the setUp method.

Implicit Setup

Also known as:
*Hooked Setup,
Framework-
Invoked Setup,
Shared Setup
Method*

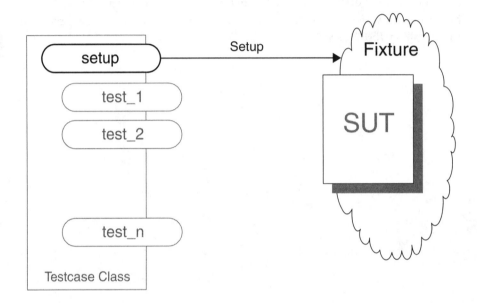

To execute an automated test, we require a text fixture that is well understood and completely deterministic. We are using a *Fresh Fixture* (page 311) approach to build the *Minimal Fixture* (page 302) for the use of this one test.

Implicit Setup is a way to reuse the fixture setup code for all *Test Methods* (page 348) in a *Testcase Class* (page 373).

How It Works

All tests in a *Testcase Class* create identical *Fresh Fixtures* by doing test fixture setup in a special setUp method on the *Testcase Class*. The setUp method is called automatically by the *Test Automation Framework* (page 298) before it calls each *Test Method*. This allows the fixture setup code placed in the setUp method to be reused without reusing the same *instance* of the test fixture. This approach is called "implicit" setup because the calls to the fixture setup logic are not explicit within the *Test Method*, unlike with *In-line Setup* (page 408) and *Delegated Setup* (page 411).

When to Use It

We can use *Implicit Setup* when several *Test Methods* on the same *Testcase Class* need an identical *Fresh Fixture*. If all *Test Methods* need the exact same fixture, then the entire *Minimal Fixture* needed by each test can be set up in the setUp method. This form of *Test Method* organization is known as *Testcase Class per Fixture* (page 631).

When the *Test Methods* need different fixtures because we are using a *Testcase Class per Feature* (page 624) or *Testcase Class per Class* (page 617) scheme, it is more difficult to use *Implicit Setup* and still build a *Minimal Fixture*. We can use the setUp method only to set up the part of the fixture that does not cause any problems for the other tests. A reasonable compromise is to use *Implicit Setup* to set up the parts of the fixture that are *essential but irrelevant* and leave the setup of critical (and different from test to test) parts of the fixture to the individual *Test Methods*. Examples of "essential but irrelevant" fixture setup include initializing variables with "don't care" values and initializing hidden "plumbing" such as database connections. Fixture setup logic that directly affects the state of the SUT should be left to the individual *Test Methods* unless every *Test Method* requires the same starting state.

Implicit
Setup

The obvious alternatives for creating a *Fresh Fixture* are *In-line Setup,* in which we include all setup logic within each *Test Method* without factoring out any common code, and *Delegated Setup,* in which we move all common fixture setup code into a set of *Creation Methods* (page 415) that we can call from within the setup part of each *Test Method.*

Implicit Setup removes a lot of *Test Code Duplication* (page 213) and helps prevent *Fragile Tests* (page 239) by moving much of the nonessential interaction with the SUT out of the very numerous tests and into a much smaller number of places where it is easier to maintain. It can, however, lead to *Obscure Tests* (page 186) when a *Mystery Guest* makes the test fixture used by each test less obvious. It can also lead to a *Fragile Fixture* (see *Fragile Test*) if all tests in the class do not really need identical test fixtures.

Implementation Notes

The main implementation considerations for *Implicit Setup* are as follows:

- How do we cause the fixture setUp method to be called?

- How do we tear the fixture down?

- How do the *Test Methods* access the fixture?

Calling the Setup Code

A setUp method is the most common way to handle *Implicit Setup*; it consists of having the *Test Automation Framework* call the setUp method before each *Test Method*. Strictly speaking, the setUp method is not the only form of *implicit* fixture setup. *Suite Fixture Setup* (page 441), for example, is used to set up and tear down a *Shared Fixture* (page 317) that is reused by the *Test Methods* on a single *Testcase Class*. In addition, *Setup Decorator* (page 447) moves the setUp method to a Decorator [GOF] object installed between the *Test Suite Object* (page 387) and the *Test Runner* (page 377). Both are forms of *Implicit Setup* because the setUp logic is not explicit within the *Test Method*.

Tearing Down the Fixture

The fixture teardown counterpart of *Implicit Setup* is *Implicit Teardown* (page 516). Anything that we set up in the setUp method that is not automatically cleaned up by *Automated Teardown* (page 503) or garbage collection should be torn down in the corresponding tearDown method.

Accessing the Fixture

The *Test Methods* need to be able to access the test fixture built in the setUp method. When they were used in the same method, local variables were sufficient. To communicate between the setUp method and the *Test Method*, however, the local variables must be changed into instance variables. We must be careful not to make them class variables as this will result in the potential for a *Shared Fixture*. (See the sidebar "There's Always an Exception" on page 384 for a description of when instance variations do not provide this level of isolation.)

Motivating Example

In the following example, each test needs to create a flight between a pair of airports.

```
public void testStatus_initial() {
   // in-line setup
   Airport departureAirport = new Airport("Calgary", "YYC");
   Airport destinationAirport = new Airport("Toronto", "YYZ");
   Flight flight = new Flight( flightNumber,
                               departureAirport,
                               destinationAirport);
   // exercise SUT and verify outcome
   assertEquals(FlightState.PROPOSED, flight.getStatus());
   // teardown
     //    garbage-collected
```

```
    }

    public void testStatus_cancelled() {
        // in-line setup
        Airport departureAirport = new Airport("Calgary", "YYC");
        Airport destinationAirport = new Airport("Toronto", "YYZ");
        Flight flight = new Flight( flightNumber,
                                    departureAirport,
                                    destinationAirport);
        flight.cancel(); // still part of setup
        // exercise SUT and verify outcome
        assertEquals(FlightState.CANCELLED, flight.getStatus());
        // teardown
          //    garbage-collected
    }
```

**Implicit
Setup**

Refactoring Notes

These tests contain a fair amount of *Test Code Duplication*. We can remove this duplication by refactoring this *Testcase Class* to use *Implicit Setup*. There are two refactoring cases to consider.

First, when we discover that all tests are doing similar work to set up their test fixtures but are not sharing a setUp method, we can do an Extract Method [Fowler] refactoring of the fixture setup logic in one of the tests to create our setUp method. We will also need to convert any local variables to instance variables (fields) that hold the references to the resulting fixture until the *Test Method* can access it.

Second, when we discover that a *Testcase Class* already uses the setUp method to build the fixture and has tests that need a different fixture, we can use an Extract Class [Fowler] refactoring to move all *Test Methods* that need a different setup method to a different class. We need to ensure any instance variables that are used to convey knowledge of the fixture from the setup method to the *Test Methods* are transferred along with the setUp method. Sometimes it is simpler to clone the *Testcase Class* and delete each test from one or the other copy of the class; we can then delete from each class any instance variables that are no longer being used.

Example: Implicit Setup

In this modified example, we have moved all common fixture setup code to the setUp method of our *Testcase Class*. This avoids the need to repeat this code in each test and makes each test much shorter—which is a good thing.

```
    Airport departureAirport;
    Airport destinationAirport;
```

```
Flight flight;

public void setUp() throws Exception{
    super.setUp();
    departureAirport = new Airport("Calgary", "YYC");
    destinationAirport = new Airport("Toronto", "YYZ");
    BigDecimal flightNumber = new BigDecimal("999");
    flight = new Flight( flightNumber , departureAirport,
                              destinationAirport);
}
```

Implicit Setup

```
public void testGetStatus_initial() {
    // implicit setup
    // exercise SUT and verify outcome
    assertEquals(FlightState.PROPOSED, flight.getStatus());
}

public void testGetStatus_cancelled() {
    // implicit setup partially overridden
    flight.cancel();
    // exercise SUT and verify outcome
    assertEquals(FlightState.CANCELLED, flight.getStatus());
}
```

This approach has several disadvantages, which arise because we are not organizing our *Test Methods* around a *Testcase Class per Fixture*. (We are using *Testcase Class per Feature* here.) All the *Test Methods* on the *Testcase Class* must be able to make do with the same fixture (at least as a starting point), as evidenced by the partially overridden fixture setup in the second test in the example. The fixture is also not very obvious in these tests. Where does the flight come from? Is there anything special about it? We cannot even rename the instance variable to communicate the nature of the flight better because we are using it to hold flights with different characteristics in each test.

Prebuilt Fixture

How do we cause the Shared Fixture to be built before the first test method that needs it?

We build the Shared Fixture separately from running the tests.

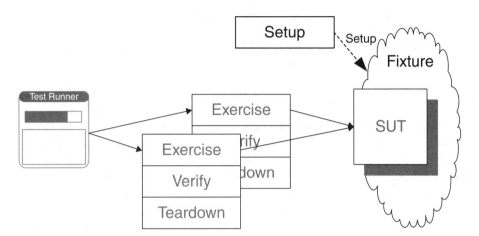

Prebuilt
Fixture

Also known as:
*Prebuilt
Context, Test
Bed*

When we choose to use a *Shared Fixture* (page 317), whether it be for reasons of convenience or out of necessity, we need to create the *Shared Fixture* before we use it.

How It Works

We create the fixture sometime before running the test suite. We can create the fixture a number of different ways that we'll discuss later. The most important point is that we don't need to build the fixture *each* time the test suite is run because the fixture outlives both the mechanism used to build it and any one test run that uses it.

When to Use It

We can reduce the overhead of creating a *Shared Fixture* each time a test suite is run by creating the fixture only occasionally. This pattern is especially appropriate when the cost of constructing the *Shared Fixture* is extremely high or cannot be automated easily.

**Prebuilt
Fixture**

Because of the *Manual Intervention* (page 250) required to (re)build the fixture before the tests are run, we'll probably end up using the same fixture several times, which can lead to *Erratic Tests* (page 228) caused by shared fixture pollution. We may be able to avoid these problems by treating the *Prebuilt Fixture* as an *Immutable Shared Fixture* (see *Shared Fixture*) and building a *Fresh Fixture* (page 311) for anything we plan to modify.

The alternatives to a *Prebuilt Fixture* are a *Shared Fixture* that is built once per test run and a *Fresh Fixture*. *Shared Fixtures* can be constructed using *Suite Fixture Setup* (page 441), *Lazy Setup* (page 435), or *Setup Decorator* (page 447). *Fresh Fixtures* can be constructed using *In-line Setup* (page 408), *Implicit Setup* (page 424), or *Delegated Setup* (page 411).

Variation: Global Fixture

A *Global Fixture* is a special case of *Prebuilt Fixture* where we shared the fixture between multiple test automaters. The key difference is that the fixture is globally visible and not "private" to a particular user. This pattern is most commonly employed when we are using a single shared *Database Sandbox* (page 650) without using some form of *Database Partitioning Scheme* (see *Database Sandbox*).

The tests themselves can be the same as those used for a basic *Prebuilt Fixture*; likewise, the fixture setup is the same as that for a *Prebuilt Fixture*. What's different here are the kinds of problems we can encounter. Because the fixture is now shared among multiple users, each of whom is running a separate *Test Runner* (page 377) on a different CPU, we may experience all sorts of multiprocessing-related issues. The most common problem is a *Test Run War* (see *Erratic Test*) where we see seemingly random results. We can avoid this possibility by adopting some kind of *Database Partitioning Scheme* or by using *Distinct Generated Values* (see *Generated Value* on page 723) for any fields with unique key constraints.

Implementation Notes

The tests themselves look identical to a basic *Shared Fixture*. What's different is how the fixture is set up. The test reader won't be able to find any sign of it either within the *Testcase Class* (page 373) or in a *Setup Decorator* or *Suite Fixture Setup* method. Instead, the fixture setup is most probably performed manually via some kind of database copy operation, by using a *Data Loader* (see *Back Door Manipulation* on page 327) or by running a database population script. In these examples of *Back Door Setup* (see *Back Door Manipulation*), we bypass the SUT and interact with its database directly. (See the sidebar "Database as

SUT API?" on page 336 for an example of when the back door really is a front door.) Another option is to use a *Fixture Setup Testcase* (see *Chained Tests* on page 454) run from a *Test Runner* either manually or on a regular schedule.

Another difference is how the *Finder Methods* (see *Test Utility Method* on page 599) are implemented. We cannot just store the results of creating the objects in a class variable or an in-memory *Test Fixture Registry* (see *Test Helper* on page 643) because we aren't setting the fixture up in code within the test run. Two of the more commonly used options available to us are (1) to store the unique identifiers generated during fixture construction in a persistent *Test Fixture Registry* (such as a file) as we build the fixture so that the *Finder Methods* can retrieve them later and (2) to hard-code the identifiers in the *Finder Methods*. We *could* search for objects/records that meet the *Finder Methods'* criteria at runtime, but that approach might result in *Nondeterministic Tests* (see *Erratic Test*) because each test run could end up using a different object/record from the *Prebuilt Fixture*. This strategy may be a good idea if each test run modifies the objects such that they no longer satisfy the criteria. Nevertheless, it may make debugging a failing test rather difficult, especially if the failures occur intermittently because some other attribute of the selected object is different.

Prebuilt Fixture

Motivating Example

The following example shows the construction of a *Shared Fixture* using *Lazy Setup:*[1]

```
protected void setUp() throws Exception {
    if (sharedFixtureInitialized) {
        return;
    }
    facade = new FlightMgmtFacadeImpl();
    setupStandardAirportsAndFlights();
    sharedFixtureInitialized = true;
}

protected void tearDown() throws Exception {
    // Cannot delete any objects because we don't know
    // whether this is the last test
}
```

Note the call to setupStandardAirports in the setUp method. The tests use this fixture by calling *Finder Methods* that return objects from the fixture that match certain criteria:

---

[1] Of course, there are other ways to set up the *Shared Fixture,* such as *Setup Decorator* and *Suite Fixture Setup.*

```
public void testGetFlightsByFromAirport_OneOutboundFlight()
        throws Exception {
    FlightDto outboundFlight = findOneOutboundFlight();
    // Exercise System
    List flightsAtOrigin = facade.getFlightsByOriginAirport(
                        outboundFlight.getOriginAirportId());
    // Verify Outcome
    assertOnly1FlightInDtoList( "Flights at origin",
                                outboundFlight,
                                flightsAtOrigin);
}

public void testGetFlightsByFromAirport_TwoOutboundFlights()
        throws Exception {
    FlightDto[] outboundFlights =
        findTwoOutboundFlightsFromOneAirport();
    // Exercise System
    List flightsAtOrigin = facade.getFlightsByOriginAirport(
                        outboundFlights[0].getOriginAirportId());
    // Verify Outcome
    assertExactly2FlightsInDtoList( "Flights at origin",
                                    outboundFlights,
                                    flightsAtOrigin);
}
```

**Prebuilt
Fixture**

Refactoring Notes

One way to convert a *Testcase Class* from a *Standard Fixture* (page 305) to a
Prebuilt Fixture is to do an Extract Class [Fowler] refactoring so that the fixture
is set up in one class and the *Test Methods* (page 348) are located in another
class. Of course, we need to provide a way for the *Finder Methods* to determine which objects or records exist in the structure because we won't be able to
guarantee that any instance or class variables will bridge the time gap between
fixture construction and fixture usage.

Example: Prebuilt Fixture Test

Here is the resulting *Testcase Class* that contains the *Test Methods*. Note that it
looks almost identical to the basic *Shared Fixture* tests.

```
public void testGetFlightsByFromAirport_OneOutboundFlight()
        throws Exception {
    FlightDto outboundFlight = findOneOutboundFlight();
    // Exercise System
    List flightsAtOrigin = facade.getFlightsByOriginAirport(
                        outboundFlight.getOriginAirportId());
    // Verify Outcome
```

```
        assertOnly1FlightInDtoList( "Flights at origin",
                                    outboundFlight,
                                    flightsAtOrigin);
    }

    public void testGetFlightsByFromAirport_TwoOutboundFlights()
            throws Exception {
        FlightDto[] outboundFlights =
            findTwoOutboundFlightsFromOneAirport();
        // Exercise System
        List flightsAtOrigin = facade.getFlightsByOriginAirport(
                    outboundFlights[0].getOriginAirportId());
        // Verify Outcome
        assertExactly2FlightsInDtoList( "Flights at origin",
                                    outboundFlights,
                                    flightsAtOrigin);
    }
```

What's different is how the fixture is set up and how the *Finder Methods* are implemented.

Example: Fixture Setup Testcase

We may find it to be convenient to set up our *Prebuilt Fixture* using xUnit. This is simple to do if we already have the appropriate *Creation Methods* (page 415) or constructors already defined and we have a way to easily persist the objects into the *Database Sandbox*. In the following example, we call the same method as in the previous example from the setUp method, except that now the method lives in the setUp method of a *Fixture Setup Testcase* that can be run whenever we want to regenerate the *Prebuilt Fixture*:

```
public class FlightManagementFacadeSetupTestcase
        extends AbstractFlightManagementFacadeTestCase {
    public FlightManagementFacadeSetupTestcase(String name) {
        super(name);
    }

    protected void setUp() throws Exception {
        facade = new FlightMgmtFacadeImpl();
        helper = new FlightManagementTestHelper();
        setupStandardAirportsAndFlights();
        saveFixtureInformation();
    }

    protected void tearDown() throws Exception {
        // Leave the Prebuilt Fixture for later use
    }

}
```

Note that there are no *Test Methods* on this *Testcase Class* and the tearDown method is empty. Here we want to do *only* the setup—nothing else.

Once we created the objects, we saved the information to the database using the call to saveFixtureInformation; this method persists the objects and saves the various keys in a file so that we can reload them for use from the subsequent real test runs. This approach avoids the need to hard-code knowledge of the fixture into *Test Methods* or *Test Utility Methods*. In the interest of space, I'll spare you the details of how we find the "dirty" objects and save the key information; there is more than one way to handle this task and any of these tactics will suffice.

Example: Prebuilt Fixture Setup Using a Data Population Script

There are as many ways to build a *Prebuilt Fixture* in a *Database Sandbox* as there are programming languages—everything from SQL scripts to Pearl and Ruby programs. These scripts can contain the data or they can read the data from a collection of flat files. We can even copy the contents of a "golden" database into our *Database Sandbox*. I'll leave it as an exercise for you to figure out what's most appropriate in your particular circumstance.

Lazy Setup

*How do we cause the Shared Fixture to be built before the
first test method that needs it?*

We use Lazy Initialization of the fixture to create it in the first test that needs it.

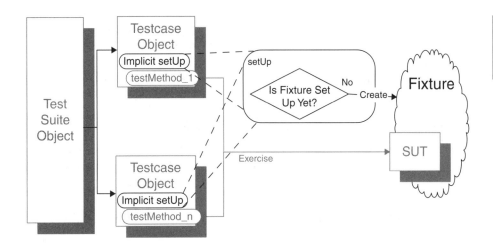

Shared Fixtures (page 317) are often used to speed up test execution by reducing the number of times a complex fixture needs to be created. Unfortunately, a test that depends on other tests to set up the fixture cannot be run by itself; it is a *Lonely Test* (see *Erratic Test* on page 228)

We can avoid this problem by having each test use *Lazy Setup* to set up the fixture if it is not already set up.

How It Works

We use Lazy Initialization [SBPP] to construct the fixture in the first test that needs it and then store a reference to the fixture in a class variable that every test can access. All subsequently run tests will discover that the fixture is already created and that they can reuse it, thereby avoiding the effort of constructing the fixture anew.

When to Use It

We can use *Lazy Setup* whenever we need to create a *Shared Fixture* yet still want to be able to run each test by itself. We can also use *Lazy Setup* instead of other techniques such as *Setup Decorator* (page 447) and *Suite Fixture Setup* (page 441) if it is not crucial that the fixture be torn down. For example, we could use *Lazy Setup* when we are using a fixture that can be torn down by *Garbage-Collected Teardown* (page 500). We might also use *Lazy Setup* when we are using *Distinct Generated Values* (see *Generated Value* on page 723) for all database keys and aren't worried about leaving extra records lying around after each test; *Delta Assertions* (page 485) make this approach possible.

The major disadvantage of *Lazy Setup* is the fact that while it is easy to discover that we are running the first test and need to construct the fixture, it is difficult to determine that we are running the last test and the fixture should be destroyed. Most members of the xUnit family of *Test Automation Frameworks* (page 298) do not provide any way to determine this fact other than by using a *Setup Decorator* for the entire test suite. A few members of the xUnit family support *Suite Fixture Setup* (NUnit, VbUnit, and JUnit 4.0 and newer, to name a few), which provides setUp/tearDown "bookends" for a *Testcase Class* (page 373). Unfortunately, this ability won't help us if we are writing our tests in Ruby, Python, or PLSQL!

Some IDEs and *Test Runners* (page 377) automatically reload our classes every time the test suite is run. This causes the original class variable to go out of scope, and the fixture *will* be garbage-collected before the new version of the class is run. In these cases there may be no negative consequence of using *Lazy Setup*.

A *Prebuilt Fixture* (page 429) is another alternative to setting up the *Shared Fixture* for each test run. Its use can lead to *Unrepeatable Tests* (see *Erratic Test*) if the fixture is corrupted by some of the tests.

Implementation Notes

Because *Lazy Setup* makes sense only with *Shared Fixtures*, *Lazy Setup* carries all the same baggage that comes with *Shared Fixtures*.

Normally, *Lazy Setup* is used to build a *Shared Fixture* to be used by a single *Testcase Class*. The reference to the fixture is held in a class variable. Things get a bit trickier if we want to share the fixture across several *Testcase Classes*. We could move both the Lazy Initialization logic and the class variable to a *Testcase Superclass* (page 638) but only if our language supports inheritance of class variables. The other alternative is to move the logic and variables to a *Test Helper* (page 643).

Of course, we *could* use an approach such as reference counting as a way to know whether all *Test Methods* (page 348) have run. The challenge would be to know how many *Testcase Objects* (page 382) are in the *Test Suite Object* (page 387) so that we can compare this number with the number of times the tearDown method has been called. I have never seen anyone do this so I won't call it a pattern! Adding logic to the *Test Runner* to invoke a tearDown method at the *Test Suite Object* level would amount to implementing *Suite Fixture Setup*.

Motivating Example

In this example, we have been building a new fixture for each *Testcase Object*:

```
public void testGetFlightsByFromAirport_OneOutboundFlight()
        throws Exception {
   setupStandardAirportsAndFlights();
   FlightDto outboundFlight = findOneOutboundFlight();
   // Exercise System
   List flightsAtOrigin = facade.getFlightsByOriginAirport(
            outboundFlight.getOriginAirportId());
   // Verify Outcome
   assertOnly1FlightInDtoList( "Flights at origin",
                        outboundFlight,
                        flightsAtOrigin);
}

public void testGetFlightsByFromAirport_TwoOutboundFlights()
        throws Exception {
   setupStandardAirportsAndFlights();
   FlightDto[] outboundFlights =
            findTwoOutboundFlightsFromOneAirport();
   // Exercise System
   List flightsAtOrigin = facade.getFlightsByOriginAirport(
            outboundFlights[0].getOriginAirportId());
   // Verify Outcome
   assertExactly2FlightsInDtoList( "Flights at origin",
                        outboundFlights,
                        flightsAtOrigin);
}
```

Not surprisingly, these tests are slow because creating the airports and flights involves a database. We can try refactoring these tests to set up the fixture in the setUp method (*Implicit Setup;* see page 424):

```
protected void setUp() throws Exception {
   facade = new FlightMgmtFacadeImpl();
   helper = new FlightManagementTestHelper();
   setupStandardAirportsAndFlights();
   oneOutboundFlight = findOneOutboundFlight();
}
```

```
protected void tearDown() throws Exception {
   removeStandardAirportsAndFlights();
}

public void testGetFlightsByOriginAirport_NoFlights_td()
       throws Exception {
   // Fixture Setup
   BigDecimal outboundAirport = createTestAirport("1OF");
   try {
      // Exercise System
      List flightsAtDestination1 =
            facade.getFlightsByOriginAirport(outboundAirport);
      // Verify Outcome
      assertEquals(0,flightsAtDestination1.size());
   } finally {
      facade.removeAirport(outboundAirport);
   }
}

public void testGetFlightsByFromAirport_OneOutboundFlight()
       throws Exception {
   // Exercise System
   List flightsAtOrigin = facade.getFlightsByOriginAirport(
               oneOutboundFlight.getOriginAirportId());
   // Verify Outcome
   assertOnly1FlightInDtoList( "Flights at origin",
                               oneOutboundFlight,
                               flightsAtOrigin);
}

public void testGetFlightsByFromAirport_TwoOutboundFlights()
       throws Exception {
   FlightDto[] outboundFlights =
            findTwoOutboundFlightsFromOneAirport();
   // Exercise System
   List flightsAtOrigin = facade.getFlightsByOriginAirport(
            outboundFlights[0].getOriginAirportId());
   // Verify Outcome
   assertExactly2FlightsInDtoList( "Flights at origin",
                                   outboundFlights,
                                   flightsAtOrigin);
}
```

Lazy Setup

This doesn't speed up our tests one bit because the *Test Automation Framework* calls the setUp and tearDown methods for each *Testcase Object*. All we have done is moved the code. We need to find a way to set up the fixture only once per test run.

Refactoring Notes

We can reduce the number of times we set up the fixture by converting this test to *Lazy Setup*. Because the fixture setup is already handled by the setUp method, we need simply insert the Lazy Initialization logic into the setUp method so that only the first test will cause it to be run. We must not forget to remove the tearDown logic, because it will render the Lazy Initialization logic useless if it removes the fixture after each *Test Method* has run! Sorry, but there is nowhere that we can move this logic to so that it will be run after the *last Test Method* has completed if our xUnit family member doesn't support *Suite Fixture Setup*.

Example: Lazy Setup

Here is the same test refactored to use *Lazy Setup*:

```
protected void setUp() throws Exception {
    if (sharedFixtureInitialized) {
        return;
    }
    facade = new FlightMgmtFacadeImpl();
    setupStandardAirportsAndFlights();
    sharedFixtureInitialized = true;
}

protected void tearDown() throws Exception {
    // Cannot delete any objects because we don't know
    // whether this is the last test
}
```

While there is a tearDown method on AirportFixture, there is no way to know when to call it! That's the main consequence of using *Lazy Setup*. Because the variables are static, they will not go out of scope; hence the fixture will not be garbage collected until the class is unloaded or reloaded.

The tests are unchanged from the *Implicit Setup* version:

```
public void testGetFlightsByFromAirport_OneOutboundFlight()
        throws Exception {
    FlightDto outboundFlight = findOneOutboundFlight();
    // Exercise System
    List flightsAtOrigin = facade.getFlightsByOriginAirport(
                        outboundFlight.getOriginAirportId());
    // Verify Outcome
    assertOnly1FlightInDtoList( "Flights at origin",
                                outboundFlight,
                                flightsAtOrigin);
}
```

```
public void testGetFlightsByFromAirport_TwoOutboundFlights()
        throws Exception {
    FlightDto[] outboundFlights =
        findTwoOutboundFlightsFromOneAirport();
    // Exercise System
    List flightsAtOrigin = facade.getFlightsByOriginAirport(
                    outboundFlights[0].getOriginAirportId());
    // Verify Outcome
    assertExactly2FlightsInDtoList( "Flights at origin",
                                    outboundFlights,
                                    flightsAtOrigin);
}
```

Lazy Setup

Suite Fixture Setup

*How do we cause the Shared Fixture to be built before the
first test method that needs it?*

**We build/destroy the shared fixture in special methods called by the Test
Automation Framework before/after the first/last Test Method is called.**

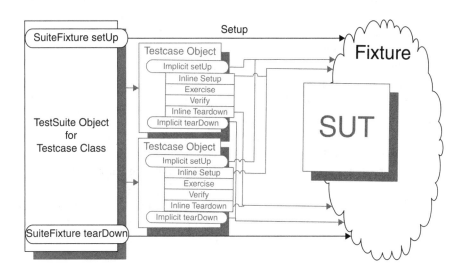

Shared Fixtures (page 317) are commonly used to reduce the amount of per-test
overhead required to set up the fixture. Sharing a fixture involves extra test programming effort because we must create the fixture and have a way of discovering the
fixture in each test. Regardless of how the fixture is accessed, it must be initialized
(constructed) before it is used.

   Suite Fixture Setup is one way to initialize the fixture if all the *Test Methods* (page 348) that need it are defined on the same *Testcase Class* (page 373).

How It Works

We implement or override a pair of methods that the *Test Automation Framework* (page 298) calls automatically. The name or annotation of these methods
varies between members of the xUnit family but all work the same way: The
framework calls the *Suite Fixture Setup* method before it calls the setUp method
for the first *Test Method*; it calls the *Suite Fixture Teardown* method after it
calls the tearDown method for the final *Test Method*. (I would have preferred to

say, "method on the first/final *Testcase Object*" but that isn't true: NUnit, unlike other members of the xUnit family, creates only a single *Testcase Object*. See the sidebar "There's Always an Exception" on page 384 for details.)

When to Use It

We can use *Suite Fixture Setup* when we have a test fixture we wish to share between all *Test Methods* of a single *Testcase Class* and our variant of xUnit supports this feature. This pattern is particularly useful if we need to tear down the fixture after the last test is run. At the time of writing this book, only VbUnit, NUnit, and JUnit 4.0 supported *Suite Fixture Setup* "out of the box." Nevertheless, it is not difficult to add this capability in most variants of xUnit.

If we need to share the fixture more widely, we must use either a *Prebuilt Fixture* (page 429), a *Setup Decorator* (page 447), or *Lazy Setup* (page 435). If we don't want to share the actual instance of the fixture but we do want to share the code to set up the fixture, we can use *Implicit Setup* (page 424) or *Delegated Setup* (page 411).

The main reason for using a *Shared Fixture*, and hence *Suite Fixture Setup*, is to overcome the problem of *Slow Tests* (page 253) caused by too many test fixture objects being created each time every test is run. Of course, a *Shared Fixture* can lead to *Interacting Tests* (see *Erratic Test* on page 228) or even a *Test Run War* (see *Erratic Test*); the sidebar "Faster Tests Without Shared Fixtures" (page 319) describes other ways to solve this problem.

Implementation Notes

For *Suite Fixture Setup* to work properly, we must ensure that the fixture is remembered between calls to the *Test Methods*. This criterion implies we need to use a class variable, Registry [PEAA], or Singleton [GOF] to hold the references to the fixture (except in NUnit; see the sidebar "There's Always an Exception" on page 384). The exact implementation varies from one member of the xUnit family to the next. Here are a few highlights:

- In VbUnit, we implement the interface IFixtureFrame in the *Testcase Class*, thereby causing the *Test Automation Framework* (1) to call the IFixture Frame_Create method before the first *Test Method* is called and (2) to call the IFixtureFrame_Destroy method after the last *Test Method* is called.

- In NUnit, the attributes [TestFixtureSetUp] and [TestFixtureTearDown] are used inside a test fixture to designate the methods to be called (1) once prior to executing any of the tests in the fixture and (2) once after all tests are completed.

- In JUnit 4.0 and later, the attribute @BeforeClass is used to indicate that a method should be run once before the first *Test Method* is executed. The method with the attribute @AfterClass is run after the last *Test Method* is run. JUnit allows these methods to be inherited and overridden; the subclass's methods are run between the superclass's methods.

Just because we use a form of *Implicit Setup* to invoke the construction and destruction of the test fixture, it doesn't mean that we should dump all the fixture setup logic into the *Suite Fixture Setup*. We can call *Creation Methods* (page 415) from the *Suite Fixture Setup method* to move complex construction logic into places where it can be tested and reused more easily, such as a *Testcase Superclass* (page 638) or a *Test Helper* (page 643).

Suite Fixture Setup

Motivating Example

Suppose we have the following test:

```
[SetUp]
protected void setUp() {
    helper.setupStandardAirportsAndFlights();
}

[TearDown]
protected void tearDown()  {
    helper.removeStandardAirportsAndFlights();
}

[Test]
public void testGetFlightsByOriginAirport_2OutboundFlights(){
    FlightDto[] expectedFlights =
        helper.findTwoOutboundFlightsFromOneAirport();
    long originAirportId = expectedFlights[0].OriginAirportId;
    // Exercise System
    IList flightsAtOrigin =
        facade.GetFlightsByOriginAirport(originAirportId);
    // Verify Outcome
    AssertExactly2FlightsInDtoList(
        expectedFlights[0], expectedFlights[1],
        flightsAtOrigin,    "Flights at origin");
}

[Test]
public void testGetFlightsByOriginAirport_OneOutboundFlight(){
    FlightDto expectedFlight = helper.findOneOutboundFlight();
    // Exercise System
```

```
ILIist flightsAtOrigin = facade.GetFlightsByOriginAirport(
    expectedFlight.OriginAirportId);
// Verify Outcome
AssertOnly1FlightInDtoList( expectedFlight,
        flightsAtOrigin, "Outbound flight at origin");
}
```

Figure 20.1 is the console generated by an instrumented version of these tests.

```
--------------------
 setUp
  setupStandardAirportsAndFlights
 testGetFlightsByOriginAirport_OneOutboundFlight
 tearDown
  removeStandardAirportsAndFlights
--------------------
 setUp
  setupStandardAirportsAndFlights
 testGetFlightsByOriginAirport_TwoOutboundFlights
 tearDown
  removeStandardAirportsAndFlights
--------------------
```

Figure 20.1 *The calling sequence of Implicit Setup and Test Methods. The* setupStandardAirportsAndFlights *method is called before each Test Method. The horizontal lines delineate the Test Method boundaries.*

Refactoring Notes

Suppose we want to refactor this example to a *Shared Fixture*. If we don't care about destroying the fixture when the test run is finished, we could use *Lazy Setup*. Otherwise, we can convert this example to a Suite Fixture Setup strategy by simply moving our code from the setUp and tearDown methods to the suiteFixtureSetUp and suiteFixtureTearDown methods, respectively.

In NUnit, we use the attributes [TestFixtureSetUp] and [TestFixtureTearDown] to indicate these methods to the *Test Automation Framework*. If we don't want to leave anything in our setUp/tearDown methods, we can simply change the attributes from [Setup] and TearDown to [TestFixtureSetUp] and [TestFixtureTearDown], respectively.

Example: Suite Fixture Setup

Here's the result of our refactoring to *Suite Fixture* Setup:

```
[TestFixtureSetUp]
protected void suiteFixtureSetUp()
{
```

```
      helper.setupStandardAirportsAndFlights();
   }

   [TestFixtureTearDown]
   protected void suiteFixtureTearDown()  {
      helper.removeStandardAirportsAndFlights();
   }

   [SetUp]
   protected void setUp() {
   }

   [TearDown]
   protected void tearDown()  {
   }

   [Test]
   public void testGetFlightsByOrigin_TwoOutboundFlights(){
      FlightDto[] expectedFlights =
            helper.findTwoOutboundFlightsFromOneAirport();
      long originAirportId = expectedFlights[0].OriginAirportId;
      // Exercise System
      IList flightsAtOrigin =
            facade.GetFlightsByOriginAirport(originAirportId);
      // Verify Outcome
      AssertExactly2FlightsInDtoList(
            expectedFlights[0], expectedFlights[1],
            flightsAtOrigin,     "Flights at origin");
   }

   [Test]
   public void testGetFlightsByOrigin_OneOutboundFlight() {
      FlightDto expectedFlight = helper.findOneOutboundFlight();
      // Exercise System
      IList flightsAtOrigin = facade.GetFlightsByOriginAirport(
         expectedFlight.OriginAirportId);
      // Verify Outcome
      AssertOnly1FlightInDtoList( expectedFlight,
               flightsAtOrigin, "Outbound flight at origin");
   }
```

Now when various methods of the *Testcase Class* are called, the console looks like Figure 20.2.

```
suiteFixtureSetUp
    setupStandardAirportsAndFlights
--------------------
   setUp
   testGetFlightsByOriginAirport_OneOutboundFlight
   tearDown
--------------------
   setUp
   testGetFlightsByOriginAirport_TwoOutboundFlights
   tearDown
--------------------
suiteFixtureTearDown
    removeStandardAirportsAndFlights
```

Figure 20.2 *The calling sequence of Suite Fixture Setup and Test Methods.
The* setupStandardAndAirportsAndFlights *method is called once only for the Testcase
Class rather than before each Test Method. The horizontal lines delineate the
Test Method boundaries.*

The setUp method is still called before each *Test Method,* along with the suite
FixtureSetUp method where we are now calling setupStandardAirportsAndFlights to
set up our fixture. So far, this is no different than *Lazy Setup;* the difference
arises in that removeStandardAirportsAndFlights is called after the last of our *Test
Methods.*

About the Name

Naming this pattern was tough because each variant of xUnit that implements
it has a different name for it. Complicating matters is the fact that the Microsoft
camp uses "test fixture" to mean more than what the Java/Pearl/Ruby/etc. camp
means. I landed on *Suite Fixture Setup* by focusing on the scope of the *Shared
Fixture;* it is shared across the test suite for one *Testcase Class* that spawns a
single *Test Suite Object* (page 387). The fixture that is built for the *Test Suite
Object* could be called a "SuiteFixture."

Further Reading

See http://www.vbunit.com/doc/Advanced.htm for more information on *Suite
Fixture Setup* as implemented in VbUnit. See http://nunit.org for more information on *Suite Fixture Setup* as implemented in NUnit.

Setup Decorator

*How do we cause the Shared Fixture to be built before the
first test method that needs it?*

**We wrap the test suite with a Decorator that sets up the shared test fixture
before running the tests and tears it down after all tests are done.**

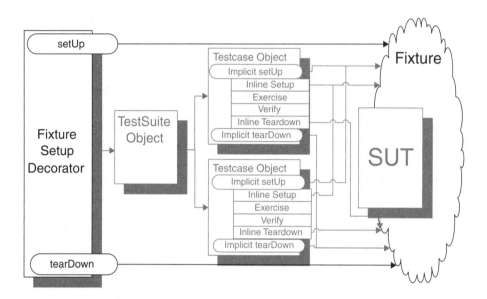

If we have chosen to use a *Shared Fixture* (page 317), whether for reasons of
convenience or out of necessity, and we have chosen not to use a *Prebuilt Fixture* (page 429), we will need to ensure that the fixture is built before each test
run. *Lazy Setup* (page 435) is one strategy we could employ to create the test
fixture "just in time" for the first test. But if it is critical to tear down the fixture
after the last test, how do we know that all tests have been completed?

How It Works

A *Setup Decorator* works by "bracketing" the execution of the entire test suite
with a set of matching setUp and tearDown "bookends." The pattern Decorator
[GOF] is just what we need to make this happen. We construct a *Setup Decorator* that holds a reference to the *Test Suite Object* (page 387) we wish to decorate
and then pass our Decorator to the *Test Runner* (page 377). When it is time to

run the test, the *Test Runner* calls the run method on our *Setup Decorator* rather than the run method on the actual *Test Suite Object*. The *Setup Decorator* performs the fixture setup before calling the run method on the *Test Suite Object* and tears down the fixture after it returns.

When to Use It

We can use a *Setup Decorator* when it is critical that a *Shared Fixture* be set up before every test run and that the fixture is torn down after the run is complete. This behavior may be critical because tests are using *Hard-Coded Values* (see *Literal Value* on page 714) that would cause the tests to fail if they are run again without cleaning up after each run (*Unrepeatable Tests; see Erratic Test on page* 228). Alternatively, this behavior may be necessary to avoid the incremental consumption of some limited resource, such as our database slowly filling up with data from repeated test runs.

We might also use a *Setup Decorator* when the tests need to change some global parameter before exercising the SUT and then need to change this parameter back when they are finished. Replacing the database with a *Fake Database* (see *Fake Object* on page 551) in an effort to avoid *Slow Tests* (page 253) is one common reason for taking this approach; setting global switches to a particular configuration is another. *Setup Decorators* are installed at runtime, so nothing stops us from using several different decorators on the same test suite at different times (or even the same time).

As an alternative to a *Setup Decorator,* we can use *Suite Fixture Setup* (page 441) if we only want to share the fixture across the tests in a single *Testcase Class* (page 373) and our member of the xUnit family supports this behavior. If it is not essential that the fixture be torn down after every test run, we could use *Lazy Setup* instead.

Implementation Notes

A *Setup Decorator* consists of an object that sets up the fixture, delegates test execution to the test suite to be run, and then executes the code to tear down the fixture. To better line up with the normal xUnit calling conventions, we typically put the code that constructs the test fixture into a method called setUp and the code that tears down the fixture into a method called tearDown. Then our *Setup Decorator's* run logic consists of three lines of code:

```
void run() {
    setup();
    decoratedSuite.run();
    teardown();
}
```

There are several ways to build the *Setup Decorator*.

Variation: Abstract Setup Decorator

Many members of the xUnit family of *Test Automation Frameworks* (page 298) provide a reusable superclass that implements a *Setup Decorator*. This class usually implements the setUp/run/tearDown sequence as a Template Method [GOF]. All we have to do is to subclass this class and implement the setUp and tearDown methods as we would in a normal *Testcase Class*. When instantiating our *Setup Decorator* class, we pass the *Test Suite Object* we are decorating as the constructor argument.

Variation: Hard-Coded Setup Decorator

If we need to build our *Setup Decorator* from scratch, the "simplest thing that could possibly work" is to hard-code the name of the decorated class in the suite method of the *Setup Decorator*. This allows the *Setup Decorator* class to act as the *Test Suite Factory* (see *Test Enumeration* on page 399) for the decorated suite.

Variation: Parameterized Setup Decorator

If we want to reuse the *Setup Decorator* for different test suites, we can parameterize its constructor method with the *Test Suite Object* to be run. This means that the setup and teardown logic can be coded within the *Setup Decorator,* thereby eliminating the need for a separate *Test Helper* (page 643) class just to reuse the setup logic across tests.

Variation: Decorated Lazy Setup

One of the main drawbacks of using a *Setup Decorator* is that tests cannot be run by themselves because they depend on the *Setup Decorator* to set up the fixture. We can work around this requirement by augmenting the *Setup Decorator* with *Lazy Setup* in the setUp method so that an undecorated *Testcase Object* (page 382) can construct its own fixture. The *Testcase Object* can also remember that it built its own fixture and destroy it in the tearDown method. This functionality could be implemented on a generic *Testcase Superclass* (page 638) so that it has to be built and tested just once.

The only other alternative is to use a *Pushdown Decorator.* That would negate any test speedup the *Shared Fixture* bought us, however, so this approach can be used only in those cases when we use the *Setup Decorator* for reasons other than setting up a *Shared Fixture.*

Variation: Pushdown Decorator

Setup Decorator

One of the main drawbacks of using a *Setup Decorator* is that tests cannot be run by themselves because they depend on the *Setup Decorator* to set up the fixture. One way we can circumvent this obstacle is to provide a means to push the decorator down to the level of the individual tests rather than the whole test suite. This step requires a few modifications to the TestSuite class to allow the *Setup Decorator* to be passed down to where the individual *Testcase Objects* are constructed during the *Test Discovery* (page 393) process. As each object is created from the *Test Method* (page 348), it is wrapped in the *Setup Decorator* before it is added to the *Test Suite Object's* collection of tests.

Of course, this negates one of the major sources of the speed advantage created by using a *Setup Decorator* by forcing a new test fixture to be built for each test. See the sidebar "Faster Tests Without Shared Fixtures" on page 319 for other ways to address the test execution speed issue.

Motivating Example

In this example, we have a set of tests that use *Lazy Setup* to build the *Shared Fixture* and *Finder Methods* (see *Test Utility Method* on page 599) to find the objects in the fixture. We have discovered that the leftover fixture is causing *Unrepeatable Tests,* so we want to clean up properly after the last test has finished running.

```
protected void setUp() throws Exception {
    if (sharedFixtureInitialized) {
        return;
    }
    facade = new FlightMgmtFacadeImpl();
    setupStandardAirportsAndFlights();
    sharedFixtureInitialized = true;
}

protected void tearDown() throws Exception {
    // Cannot delete any objects because we don't know
    // whether this is the last test
}
```

Because there is no easy way to accomplish this goal with *Lazy Setup*, we must change our fixture setup strategy. One option is to use a *Setup Decorator* instead.

Refactoring Notes

When creating a *Setup Decorator*, we can reuse the exact same fixture setup logic; we just need to call it at a different time. Thus this refactoring consists mostly of moving the call to the fixture setup logic from the setUp method on the *Testcase Class* to the setUp method of a *Setup Decorator* class. Assuming we have an *Abstract Setup Decorator* available to subclass, we can create our new subclass and provide concrete implementations of the setUp and tearDown methods.

If our instance of xUnit does not support *Setup Decorator* directly, we can create our own *Setup Decorator* superclass by building a single-purpose *Setup Decorator* and then introducing a constructor parameter and instance variable to hold the test suite to be run. Finally, we do an Extract Superclass [Fowler] refactoring to create our reusable superclass.

Example: Hard-Coded Setup Decorator

In this example, we have moved all of the setup logic to the setUp method of a *Setup Decorator* that inherits its basic functionality from an *Abstract Setup Decorator*. We have also written some fixture teardown logic in the tearDown method so that we clean up the fixture after the entire test suite has been run.

```
public class FlightManagementTestSetup extends TestSetup {
    private FlightManagementTestHelper helper;

    public FlightManagementTestSetup() {
        // Construct the Test Suite Object to be decorated and
        // pass it to our Abstract Setup Decorator superclass
        super( SafeFlightManagementFacadeTest.suite() );
        helper = new FlightManagementTestHelper();
    }

    public void setUp() throws Exception {
        helper.setupStandardAirportsAndFlights();
    }

    public void tearDown() throws Exception {
        helper.removeStandardAirportsAndFlights();
    }
```

```
public static Test suite() {
    // Return an instance of this decorator class
    return new FlightManagementTestSetup();
}
}
```

Because this is a *Hard-Coded Setup Decorator,* the call to the *Test Suite Factory* that builds the actual *Test Suite Object* is hard-coded inside the constructor. The suite method just calls the constructor.

Example: Parameterized Setup Decorator

To make our *Setup Decorator* reusable with several different test suites, we need to do an Introduce Parameter [JBrains] refactoring on the name of the *Test Suite Factory* inside the constructor:

```
public class ParameterizedFlightManagementTestSetup extends TestSetup {

    private FlightManagementTestHelper helper =
        new FlightManagementTestHelper();

    public ParameterizedFlightManagementTestSetup(
                            Test testSuiteToDecorate) {
        super(testSuiteToDecorate);
    }

    public void setUp() throws Exception {
        helper.setupStandardAirportsAndFlights();
    }

    public void tearDown() throws Exception {
        helper.removeStandardAirportsAndFlights();
    }
}
```

To make it easy for the *Test Runner* to create our test suite, we also need to create a *Test Suite Factory* that calls the *Setup Decorator's* constructor with the *Test Suite Object* to be decorated:

```
public class DecoratedFlightManagementFacadeTestFactory {
    public static Test suite() {
        // Return a new Test Suite Object suitably decorated
        return new ParameterizedFlightManagementTestSetup(
                        SafeFlightManagementFacadeTest.suite());
    }
}
```

We will need one of these *Test Suite Factories* for each test suite we want to be able to run by itself. Even so, this is a small price to pay for reusing the actual *Setup Decorator*.

Example: Abstract Decorator Class

Here's what the *Abstract Decorator Class* looks like:

```java
public class TestSetup extends TestCase {
   Test decoratedSuite;

   AbstractSetupDecorator(Test testSuiteToDecorate) {
      decoratedSuite = testSuiteToDecorate;
   }

   public void setUp() throws Exception {
      // subclass responsibility
   }
   public void tearDown() throws Exception {
      // subclass responsibility
   }

   void run() {
      setup();
      decoratedSuite.run();
      teardown();
   }
}
```

Setup Decorator

Chained Tests

*How do we cause the Shared Fixture to be built before the
first test method that needs it?*

We let the other tests in a test suite set up the test fixture.

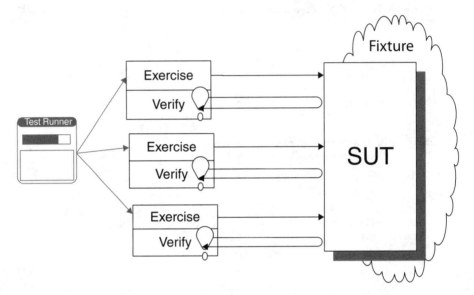

Shared Fixtures (page 317) are commonly used to reduce the amount of per-test overhead required to set up the fixture. Sharing a fixture involves extra test programming effort because we need to create the fixture and have a way of discovering the fixture in each test. Regardless of how the fixture is accessed, it must be initialized (constructed) before it is used.

Chained Tests offer a way to reuse the test fixture left over from one test and the *Shared Fixture* of a subsequent test.

How It Works

Chained Tests take advantage of the objects created by the tests that run before our current test in the test suite. This approach is very similar to how a human tester tests a large number of test conditions in a single test—by building up a complex test fixture through a series of actions, with the outcome of each action first being verified. We can achieve a similar result with automated tests by building a set of *Self-Checking Tests* (see page 26) that do not perform any fixture setup but instead rely on the "leftovers" of the test(s) that run before them. Unlike with the *Reuse Test for Fixture Setup* pattern (see *Creation Method* on page 415), we don't actually call another *Test Method* (page 348) from within out test; we just *assume* that it has been run and has left behind something we can use as a test fixture.

When to Use It

Chained Tests is a fixture strategy that people either love or hate. Those who hate it do so because this approach is simply the test smell *Interacting Tests* (see *Erratic Test* on page 228) recast as a pattern. Those who love it typically do so because it solves a nasty problem introduced by using *Shared Fixtures* to deal with *Slow Tests* (page 253). Either way, it is a valid strategy for refactoring existing tests that are overly long and contain many steps that build on one another. Such tests will stop executing when the first assertion fails. We can refactor such tests into a set of *Chained Tests* fairly quickly because this strategy doesn't require determining exactly which test fixture we need to build for each test. This may be the first step in evolving the tests into a set of *Independent Tests* (see page 42).

 Chained Tests help prevent *Fragile Tests* (page 239) because they are a crude form of *SUT API Encapsulation* (see *Test Utility Method* on page 599). Our test doesn't need to interact with the SUT to set up the fixture because we let another test that was already using the same API set up the fixture for us. *Fragile Fixtures* (see *Fragile Test*) may be a problem, however; if one of the preceding tests is modified to create a different fixture, the depending test will probably fail. This is also true if some of the earlier tests fail or have errors; they may leave the *Shared Fixture* in a different state from what the current test expects.

 One of the key problems with *Chained Tests* is the nondeterminism of the order in which xUnit executes tests in a test suite. Most members of the family make no guarantees about this order (TestNG is an exception). Thus tests could start to fail when a new version of xUnit is installed or even when one of the *Test Methods* is renamed [if the xUnit implementation happens to sort the *Testcase Objects* (page 382) by method name].

 Another problem is that *Chained Tests* are *Lonely Tests* (see *Erratic Test*) because the current test depends on the tests that precede it to set up the test fixture. If we run the test by itself, it will likely fail because the test fixture it assumes is not set up for it. As a consequence, we cannot run just the one test when we are debugging failures it exposes.

 Depending on other tests to set up the test fixture invariably results in tests that are more difficult to understand because the test fixture is invisible to the test reader—a classic case of a *Mystery Guest* (see *Obscure Test* on page 186). This problem can be at least partially mitigated through the use of appropriately named *Finder Methods* (see *Test Utility Method*) to access the objects in the *Shared Fixture*. It is less of an issue if all the *Test Methods* are on the same *Testcase Class* (page 373) and are listed in the same order as they are executed.

Variation: Fixture Setup Testcase

Chained Tests

If we need to set up a *Shared Fixture* and we cannot use any of the other techniques to set it up [e.g., *Lazy Setup* (page 435), *Suite Fixture Setup* (page 441), or *Setup Decorator* (page 447)], we can arrange to have a *Fixture Setup Testcase* run as the first test in the test suite. This is simple to do if we are using *Test Enumeration* (page 399); we just include the appropriate addTest method call in our *Test Suite Factory* (see *Test Enumeration*). This variation is a degenerate form of the *Chained Tests* pattern in that we are chaining a test suite behind a single *Fixture Setup Testcase*.

Implementation Notes

There are two key challenges in implementing *Chained Tests*:

- Getting tests in the test suite to run in the desired order
- Accessing the fixture leftover by the previous test(s)

While a few members of the xUnit family provide an explicit mechanism for defining the order of tests, most members make no such guarantees about this order. We can probably figure out what order the xUnit member uses by performing a few experiments. Most commonly, we will discover that it is either the order in which the *Test Methods* appear in the file or alphabetical order by *Test Method* name (in which case, the easiest solution is to include a test sequence number in the test name). In the worst-case scenario, we could always revert to *Test Method Enumeration* (see *Test Enumeration*) to ensure that *Testcase Objects* are added to the test suite in the correct order.

To refer to the objects created by the previous tests, we need to use one of the fixture object access patterns. If the preceding tests are *Test Methods* on the same *Testcase Class*, it is sufficient for each test to store any object references that subsequent tests will use to access the fixture in a **fixture holding class variable. (Fixture holding instance variables** typically won't work here because each test runs on a separate *Testcase Object* and, therefore, the tests don't share instance variables. See the sidebar "There's Always an Exception" on page 384 for a description of when instance variations do not behave this way.)

If our test depends on a *Test Method* on a different *Testcase Class* being run as a part of a *Suite of Suites* (see *Test Suite Object* on page 387), neither of these solutions will work. Our best bet will be to use a *Test Fixture Registry* (see *Test Helper* on page 643) as the means to store references to the objects used by the tests. A test database is a good example.

Obviously, we don't want the test we are depending on to clean up after itself—that would leave nothing for us to reuse as our test fixture. That requirement makes *Chained Tests* incompatible with the *Fresh Fixture* (page 311) approach.

Motivating Example

Here's an example of an incremental *Tabular Test* (see *Parameterized Test* on page 607) provided by Clint Shank on his blog:

```
public class TabularTest extends TestCase {
   private Order order = new Order();
   private static final double tolerance = 0.001;

   public void testGetTotal() {
      assertEquals("initial", 0.00, order.getTotal(), tolerance);
      testAddItemAndGetTotal("first", 1, 3.00, 3.00);
      testAddItemAndGetTotal("second",3, 5.00, 18.00);
      // etc.
   }

   private void testAddItemAndGetTotal( String msg,
                                        int lineItemQuantity,
                                        double lineItemPrice,
                                        double expectedTotal) {
      // setup
      LineItem item = new LineItem(   lineItemQuantity, lineItemPrice);
      // exercise SUT
      order.addItem(item);
      // verify total
      assertEquals(msg,expectedTotal,order.getTotal(),tolerance);
   }
}
```

This test begins by building an empty order, verifies the total is zero, and then proceeds to add several items verifying the total after each item (Figure 20.3). The main issue with this test is that if one of the subtests fails, all subsequent subtests don't get run. For example, suppose a rounding error makes the total after the second item incorrect: Wouldn't we like to see whether the fourth, fifth, and six items are still correct?

**Chained
Tests**

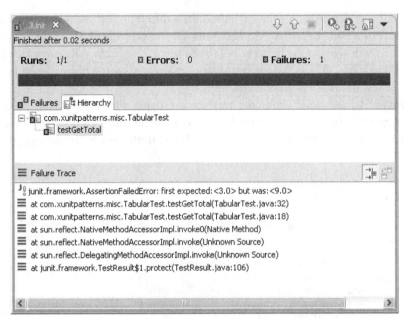

Figure 20.3 *Tabular Test results. The lower pane shows the details of the first failure inside the single Tabular Test method listed in the upper pane. Because of the failure, the rest of the test method is not executed.*

Refactoring Notes

We can convert this *Tabular Test* to a set of *Chained Tests* simply by breaking up the single *Test Method* into one *Test Method* per subtest. One way to do so is to use a series of Extract Method [Fowler] refactorings to create the *Test Methods*. This will force us to use an Introduce Field [JetBrains] refactoring for any local variables before the first Extract Method refactoring operation. Once we have defined all of the new *Test Methods*, we simply delete the original *Test Method* and let the *Test Automation Framework* (page 298) call our new methods directly.[2]

We need to ensure the tests run in the same order. Because JUnit seems to sort the *Testcase Objects* by method name, we can force them into the right order by including a sequence number in the Test Method name.

Finally, we need to convert our *Fresh Fixture* into a *Shared Fixture*. We do so by changing our order field (instance variable) into a class variable (a static variable in Java) so that all of the *Testcase Objects* use the same Order.

---

[2] If we don't have a refactoring tool handy, no worries. Just end the *Test Method* after each subtest and type in the signature of the next *Test Method* before the next subtest. We then move any *Shared Fixture* variables out of the first *Test Method*.

Example: Chained Tests

Here's the simple example turned into three separate tests:

```
private static Order order = new Order();
private static final double tolerance = 0.001;

public void test_01_initialTotalShouldBeZero() {
    assertEquals("initial", 0.00, order.getTotal(), tolerance);
}
public void test_02_totalAfter1stItemShouldBeOnlyItemAmount(){
    testAddItemAndGetTotal( "first", 1, 3.00, 3.00);
}
public void test_03_totalAfter2ndItemShouldBeSumOfAmounts() {
    testAddItemAndGetTotal( "second",3, 5.00, 18.00);
}
private void testAddItemAndGetTotal( String msg,
                                     int lineItemQuantity,
                                     double lineItemPrice,
                                     double expectedTotal) {
    // create a line item
    LineItem item =
        new LineItem(lineItemQuantity, lineItemPrice);
    // add line item to order
    order.addItem(item);
    // verify total
    assertEquals(msg,expectedTotal,order.getTotal(),tolerance);
}
```

The *Test Runner* (page 377) gives us a better overview of what is wrong and what is working (Figure 20.4).

Unfortunately, we will not be able to run any of the tests by themselves while we debug this problem (except for the very first test) because of the interdependencies between the tests; they are *Lonely Tests*.

Chained Tests

**Chained
Tests**

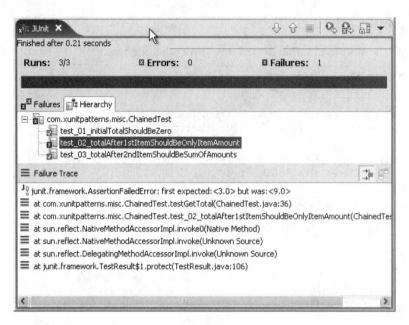

Figure 20.4   *Chained Tests result. The upper pane shows the three test methods
with two tests passing. The lower pane shows the details of the one failing Test
Method.*

Chapter 21

Result Verification Patterns

Patterns in This Chapter

State Verification

How do we make tests self-checking when there is state to be verified?

Also known as:
*State-Based
Testing*

We inspect the state of the system under test after it has been exercised and compare it to the expected state.

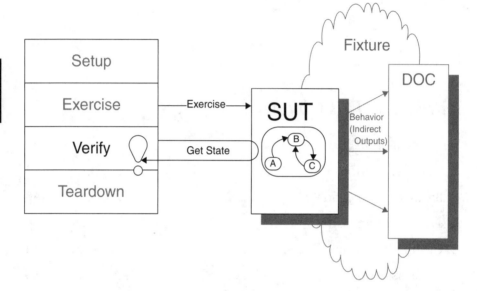

A *Self-Checking Test* (see page 26) must verify that the expected outcome has occurred without manual intervention by whoever is running the test. But what do we mean by "expected outcome"? The SUT may or may not be "stateful"; if it is stateful, it may or may not have a different state after it has been exercised. As test automaters, it is our job to determine whether our expected outcome is a change of final state or whether we need to be more specific about what occurs *while* the SUT is being exercised.

State Verification involves inspecting the state of the SUT after it has been exercised.

How It Works

We exercise the SUT by invoking the methods of interest. Then, as a separate step, we interact with the SUT to retrieve its post-exercise state and compare it with the expected end state by calling *Assertion Methods* (page 362).

Normally, we can access the state of the SUT simply by calling methods or functions that return its state. This is especially true when we are doing test-driven development because the tests will have ensured that the state is easily accessible. When we are retrofitting tests, however, we may find it more challenging to access the relevant state information. In these cases, we may need to use a *Test-Specific Subclass* (page 579) or some other technique to expose the state without introducing *Test Logic in Production* (page 217).

A related question is "Where is the state of the SUT stored?" Sometimes, the state is stored within the actual SUT; in other cases, the state may be stored in another component such as a database. In the latter case, *State Verification* may involve accessing the state within the other component (essentially a layer-crossing test). By contrast, *Behavior Verification* (page 468) would involve verifying the interactions between the SUT and the other component.

State
Verification

When to Use It

We should use *State Verification* when we care about only the end state of the SUT—not how the SUT got there. Taking such a limited view helps us maintain encapsulation of the implementation of the SUT.

State Verification comes naturally when we are building the software inside out. That is, we build the innermost objects first and then build the next layer of objects on top of them. Of course, we may need to use *Test Stubs* (page 529) to control the indirect inputs of the SUT to avoid *Production Bugs* (page 268) caused by untested code paths. Even then, we are choosing not to verify the indirect outputs of the SUT.

When we *do* care about the side effects of exercising the SUT that are not visible in its end state (its indirect outputs), we can use *Behavior Verification* to observe the behavior directly. We must be careful, however, not to create *Fragile Tests* (page 239) by overspecifying the software.

Implementation Notes

There are two basic styles of implementing *State Verification*.

Variation: Procedural State Verification

When doing *Procedural State Verification*, we simply write a series of calls to *Assertion Methods* that pick apart the state information into pieces and compare those bits of information to individual expected values. Most people who are new to automating tests take such a "path of least resistance." The major disadvantage of this approach is that it can result in *Obscure Tests* (page 186) owing to the number of assertions it may take to specify the expected outcome. When the same sequence of assertions must be carried out in many tests or many times within a single *Test Method* (page 348), we also have *Test Code Duplication* (page 213).

Variation: Expected State Specification

When doing *Expected State Specification*, we construct a specification for the post-exercise state of the SUT in the form of one or more objects populated with the expected attributes. We then compare the actual state directly with these objects using a single call to an *Equality Assertion* (see *Assertion Method*). This tends to result in more concise and readable tests. We can use an *Expected State Specification* whenever we need to verify several attributes and it is possible to construct an object that looks like the object we expect the SUT to return. The more attributes we have that need to be compared and the more tests that need to compare them, the more compelling the argument for using an *Expected State Specification*. In the most extreme cases, when we have a lot of data to verify, we can construct an "expected table" and verify that the SUT contains it. Fit's "row fixtures" offer a good way to do this in customer tests; tools such as DbUnit are a good way to use *Back Door Manipulation* (page 327) for this purpose.

When constructing the *Expected State Specification*, we may prefer to use a *Parameterized Creation Method* (see *Creation Method* on page 415) so that the reader is not distracted by all the necessary but unimportant attributes of the *Expected State Specification*. The *Expected State Specification* is most often an instance of the same class that we expect to get back from the SUT. We may have difficulty using an *Expected State Specification* if the object doesn't implement equality in a way that involves comparing the values of attributes (e.g., by comparing the object references with each other) or if our test-specific definition of equality differs from that implemented by the equals method.

In these cases, we can still use an *Expected State Specification* if we create a *Custom Assertion* (page 474) that implements test-specific equality. Alternatively, we can build the *Expected State Specification* from a class that implements our test-specific equality. This class can either be a *Test-Specific Subclass* that overrides the equals method or a simple Data Transfer Object [CJ2EEP] that implements equals(TheRealObjectClass other). Both of these measures are preferable to modifying (or introducing) the equals method on the production class, as that would be a form of *Equality Pollution* (see *Test Logic in Production*). When the class is difficult to instantiate, we can define a *Fake Object* (page 551) that has the necessary attributes plus an equals method that implements test-specific equality. These last few "tricks" are made possible by the fact that *Equality*

Assertions usually ask the *Expected State Specification* to compare itself to the actual result, rather than the reverse.

We can build the *Expected State Specification* either during the result verification phase of the test immediately before it is used in the *Equality Assertion* or during the fixture setup phase of the test. The latter strategy allows us to use attributes of the *Expected State Specification* as parameters passed to the SUT or as the base for *Derived Values* (page 718) when building other objects in the test fixture. This makes it easier to see the cause–effect relationship between the fixture and the *Expected State Specification,* which in turn helps us achieve *Tests as Documentation* (see page 23). It is particularly useful when the *Expected State Specification* is created out of sight of the test reader such as when using *Creation Methods* to do the construction.

State Verification

Motivating Example

This simple[1] example features a test that exercises the code that adds a line item to an invoice. Because it contains no assertions, it is not a *Self-Checking Test.*

```
public void testInvoice_addOneLineItem_quantity1() {
   // Exercise
   inv.addItemQuantity(product, QUANTITY);
}
```

We have chosen to create the `invoice` and `product` in the `setUp` method, an approach called *Implicit Setup* (page 424).

```
public void setUp() {
   product = createAnonProduct();
   anotherProduct = createAnonProduct();
   inv = createAnonInvoice();
}
```

Refactoring Notes

The first refactoring we can do is not really a refactoring at all, because we are changing the behavior of the tests (for the better): We introduce some assertions that specify the expected outcome. This results in an example of *Procedural State Verification* because we make this change within the *Test Method* as a series of calls to built-in *Assertion Methods.*

---

[1] The natural example for this pattern is not very good at illustrating the difference between *State Verification* and *Behavior Verification*. For this purpose, refer to *Behavior Verification,* which provides a second example of *State Verification* that is more directly comparable.

We can further simplify the *Test Method* by refactoring it to use an *Expected Object*. First, we build an *Expected Object* by constructing an object of the expected class, or a suitable *Test Double* (page 522), and initializing it with the values that were previously specified in the assertions. Then we replace the series of assertions with a single *Equality Assertion* that compares the actual result with an *Expected Object*. We may have to use a *Custom Assertion* if we need test-specific equality.

Example: Procedural State Verification

State Verification

Here we have added the assertions to the *Test Method* to turn it into a *Self-Checking Test*. Because several steps must be carried out to verify the expected outcome, this test suffers from a mild case of *Obscure Test*.

```
public void testInvoice_addOneLineItem_quantity1() {
    // Exercise
    inv.addItemQuantity(product, QUANTITY);
    // Verify
    List lineItems = inv.getLineItems();
    assertEquals("number of items", lineItems.size(), 1);
    // Verify only item
    LineItem actual = (LineItem) lineItems.get(0);
    assertEquals(inv, actual.getInv());
    assertEquals(product, actual.getProd());
    assertEquals(QUANTITY, actual.getQuantity());
}
```

Example: Expected Object

In this simplified version of the test, we use the *Expected Object* with a single *Equality Assertion* instead of a series of assertions on individual attributes:

```
public void testInvoice_addLineItem1() {
    LineItem expItem = new LineItem(inv, product, QUANTITY);
    // Exercise
    inv.addItemQuantity( expItem.getProd(), expItem.getQuantity());
    // Verify
    List lineItems = inv.getLineItems();
    assertEquals("number of items", lineItems.size(), 1);
    LineItem actual = (LineItem) lineItems.get(0);
    assertEquals("Item", expItem, actual);
}
```

Because we are also using some of the attributes as arguments of the SUT, we have chosen to build the *Expected Object* during the fixture setup phase of the test and to use the attributes of the *Expected Object* as the SUT arguments.

State
Verification

Behavior Verification

Also known as:
*Interaction
Testing*

How do we make tests self-checking when there is no state to verify?

We capture the indirect outputs of the SUT as they occur and compare them to the expected behavior.

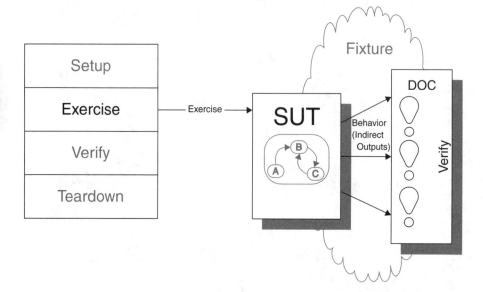

A *Self-Checking Test* (see page 26) must verify that the expected outcome has occurred without manual intervention by whoever is running the test. But what do we mean by "expected outcome"? The SUT may or may not be "stateful"; if it is stateful, it may or may not be expected to end up in a different state after it has been exercised. The SUT may also be expected to invoke methods on other objects or components.

Behavior Verification involves verifying the indirect outputs of the SUT as it is being exercised.

How It Works

Each test specifies not only how the client of the SUT interacts with it during the exercise SUT phase of the test, but also how the SUT interacts with the components on which it should depend. This ensures that the SUT really is *behaving* as specified rather than just ending up in the correct post-exercise state.

Behavior Verification almost always involves interacting with or replacing a depended-on component (DOC) with which the SUT interacts at runtime. The line between *Behavior Verification* and *State Verification* (page 462) can get a bit blurry when the SUT stores its state in the DOC because both forms of verification involve layer-crossing tests. We can distinguish between the two cases based on whether we are verifying the post-test state in the DOC (*State Verification*) or whether we are verifying the method calls made by the SUT on the DOC (*Behavior Verification*).

When to Use It

Behavior Verification

Behavior Verification is primarily a technique for unit tests and component tests. We can use *Behavior Verification* whenever the SUT calls methods on other objects or components. We *must* use *Behavior Verification* whenever the expected outputs of the SUT are transient and cannot be determined simply by looking at the post-exercise state of the SUT or the DOC. This forces us to monitor these indirect outputs as they occur.

A common application of *Behavior Verification* is when we are writing our code in an "outside-in" manner. This approach, which is often called **need-driven development,** involves writing the client code *before* we write the DOC. It is a good way to find out exactly what the interface provided by the DOC needs to be based on real, concrete examples rather than on speculation. The main objection to this approach is that we need to use a lot of *Test Doubles* (page 522) to write these tests. That *could* result in *Fragile Tests* (page 239) because each test knows so much about how the SUT is implemented. Because the tests specify the behavior of the SUT in terms of its interactions with the DOC, a change in the implementation of the SUT could break a lot of tests. This kind of *Overspecified Software* (see *Fragile Test*) could lead to *High Test Maintenance Cost* (page 265).

The jury is still out on whether *Behavior Verification* is a better approach than *State Verification*. In most cases, *State Verification* is clearly necessary; in some cases, *Behavior Verification* is clearly necessary. What has yet to be determined is whether *Behavior Verification* should be used in *all* cases or whether we should use *State Verification* most of the time and resort to *Behavior Verification* only when *State Verification* falls short of full test coverage.

Implementation Notes

Before we exercise the SUT by invoking the methods of interest, we must ensure that we have a way of observing its behavior. Sometimes the mechanisms that the

SUT uses to interact with the components surrounding it make such observation possible; when this is not the case, we must install some sort of *Test Double* to monitor the SUT's indirect outputs. We can use a *Test Double* as long as we have a way to replace the DOC with the *Test Double*. This could be via *Dependency Injection* (page 678) or by *Dependency Lookup* (page 686).

There are two fundamentally different ways to implement *Behavior Verification*, each with its own proponents. The *Mock Object* (page 544) community has been very vocal about the use of "mocks" as an *Expected Behavior Specification*, so it is the more commonly used approach. Nevertheless, *Mock Objects* are not the only way of doing *Behavior Verification*.

Behavior Verification

Also known as:
Expected Behavior

Variation: Procedural Behavior Verification

In *Procedural Behavior Verification*, we capture the method calls made by the SUT as it executes and later get access to them from within the *Test Method* (page 348). Then we use *Equality Assertions* (see *Assertion Method* on page 362) to compare them with the expected results.

The most common way of trapping the indirect outputs of the SUT is to install a *Test Spy* (page 538) in place of the DOC during the fixture setup phase of the *Four-Phase Test* (page 358). During the result verification phase of the test, we ask the *Test Spy* how it was used by the SUT during the exercise SUT phase. Use of a *Test Spy* does not require any advance knowledge of how the methods of the DOC will be called.

The alternative is to ask the real DOC how it was used. Although this scheme is not always feasible, when it is, it avoids the need to use a *Test Double* and minimizes the degree to which we have *Overspecified Software*.

We can reduce the amount of code in the *Test Method* (and avoid *Test Code Duplication;* see page 213) by defining *Expected Objects* (see *State Verification*) for the arguments of method calls or by delegating the verification of them to *Custom Assertions* (page 474).

Variation: Expected Behavior Specification

Expected Behavior Specification is a different way of doing *Behavior Verification*. Instead of waiting until after the fact to verify the indirect outputs of the SUT by using a sequence of assertions, we load the *Expected Behavior Specification* into a *Mock Object* and let it verify that the method calls are correct as they are received.

We can use an *Expected Behavior Specification* when we know exactly what should happen ahead of time and we want to remove all *Procedural Behavior Verification* from the *Test Method*. This pattern variation tends to make the test shorter (assuming we are using a compact representation of the expected behavior) and can be used to cause the test to fail on the first deviation from the expected behavior if we so choose.

One distinct advantage of using *Mock Objects* is that *Test Double* generation tools are available for many members of the xUnit family. They make implementing *Expected Behavior Specification* very easy because we don't need to manually build a *Test Double* for each set of tests. One drawback of using a *Mock Object* is that it requires that we can predict how the methods of the DOC will be called and what arguments will be passed to it in the method calls.

Motivating Example

The following test is not a *Self-Checking Test* because it does not verify that the expected outcome has actually occurred; it contains no calls to *Assertion Methods,* nor does it set up any expectations on a *Mock Object.* Because we are testing the logging functionality of the SUT, the state that interests us is actually stored in the `logger` rather than within the SUT itself. The writer of this test hasn't found a way to access the state we are trying to verify.

Behavior Verification

```
public void testRemoveFlightLogging_NSC() throws Exception {
    // setup
    FlightDto expectedFlightDto = createARegisteredFlight();
    FlightManagementFacade facade =
            new FlightManagementFacadeImpl();
    // exercise
    facade.removeFlight(expectedFlightDto.getFlightNumber());
    // verify
    // have not found a way to verify the outcome yet
    //  Log contains record of Flight removal
}
```

To verify the outcome, whoever is running the tests must access the database and the log console and compare what was actually output to what should have been output.

One way to make the test *Self-Checking* is to enhance the test with *Expected State Specification* (see *State Verification*) of the SUT as follows:

```
public void testRemoveFlightLogging_ESS() throws Exception {
    // fixture setup
    FlightDto expectedFlightDto = createAnUnregFlight();
    FlightManagementFacadeImplTI facade =
            new FlightManagementFacadeImplTI();
    // exercise
    facade.removeFlight(expectedFlightDto.getFlightNumber());
    // verify
```

```
        assertFalse("flight still exists after being removed",
                facade.flightExists( expectedFlightDto.
                                        getFlightNumber())));
    }
```

Unfortunately, this test does not verify the logging function of the SUT in any way. It also illustrates one reason why *Behavior Verification* came about: Some functionality of the SUT is not visible within the end state of the SUT itself, but can be seen only if we intercept the behavior at an internal observation point between the SUT and the DOC or if we express the behavior in terms of state changes for the objects with which the SUT interacts.

Refactoring Notes

When we made the changes in the second code sample in the "Motivating Example," we weren't really refactoring; instead, we added verification logic to make the tests behave differently. There are, however, several refactoring cases that *are* worth discussing.

To refactor from *State Verification* to *Behavior Verification,* we must do a Replace Dependency with Test Double (page 522) refactoring to gain visibility of the indirect outputs of the SUT via a *Test Spy* or *Mock Object.*

To refactor from an *Expected Behavior Specification* to *Procedural Behavior Verification*, we install a *Test Spy* instead of the *Mock Object.* After exercising the SUT, we make assertions on values returned by the *Test Spy* and compare them with the expected values that were originally used as arguments when we initially configured the *Mock Object* (the one that we just converted into a *Test Spy*).

To refactor from *Procedural Behavior Verification* to an *Expected Behavior Specification,* we configure a *Mock Object* with the expected values from the assertions made on values returned by the *Test Spy* and install the *Mock Object* instead of the *Test Spy.*

Example: Procedural Behavior Verification

The following test verifies the basic functionality of creating a flight but uses *Procedural Behavior Verification* to verify the indirect outputs of the SUT. That is, it uses a *Test Spy* to capture the indirect outputs and then verifies those outputs are correct by making in-line calls to the *Assertion Methods.*

```
public void testRemoveFlightLogging_recordingTestStub()
        throws Exception {
    // fixture setup
    FlightDto expectedFlightDto = createAnUnregFlight();
    FlightManagementFacade facade =
        new FlightManagementFacadeImpl();
```

```
// Test Double setup
AuditLogSpy logSpy = new AuditLogSpy();
facade.setAuditLog(logSpy);
// exercise
facade.removeFlight(expectedFlightDto.getFlightNumber());
// verify
assertEquals("number of calls", 1,
            logSpy.getNumberOfCalls());
assertEquals("action code",
            Helper.REMOVE_FLIGHT_ACTION_CODE,
            logSpy.getActionCode());
assertEquals("date", helper.getTodaysDateWithoutTime(),
            logSpy.getDate());
assertEquals("user", Helper.TEST_USER_NAME,
            logSpy.getUser());
assertEquals("detail",
            expectedFlightDto.getFlightNumber(),
            logSpy.getDetail());
}
```

Example: Expected Behavior Specification

In this version of the test, we use the JMock framework to define the expected behavior of the SUT. The method expects on mockLog configures the *Mock Object* with the *Expected Behavior Specification* (specifically, the expected log message).

```
public void testRemoveFlight_JMock() throws Exception {
    // fixture setup
    FlightDto expectedFlightDto = createAnonRegFlight();
    FlightManagementFacade facade =
        new FlightManagementFacadeImpl();
    // mock configuration
    Mock mockLog = mock(AuditLog.class);
    mockLog.expects(once()).method("logMessage")
            .with(eq(helper.getTodaysDateWithoutTime()),
                eq(Helper.TEST_USER_NAME),
                eq(Helper.REMOVE_FLIGHT_ACTION_CODE),
                eq(expectedFlightDto.getFlightNumber())));
    // mock installation
    facade.setAuditLog((AuditLog) mockLog.proxy());
    // exercise
    facade.removeFlight(expectedFlightDto.getFlightNumber());
    // verify
    // verify() method called automatically by JMock
}
```

Custom Assertion

How do we make tests self-checking when we have test-specific equality logic?
How do we reduce Test Code Duplication when the same assertion
logic appears in many tests?
How do we avoid Conditional Test Logic?

Also known as:
Bespoke
Assertion

Custom
Assertion

We create a purpose-built Assertion Method that compares only those attributes of the object that define test-specific equality.

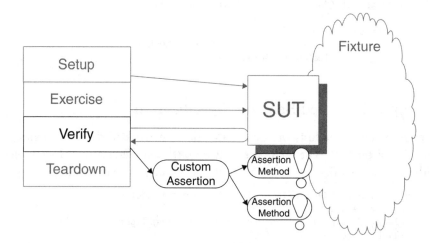

Most members of the xUnit family provide a reasonably rich set of *Assertion Methods* (page 362). But sooner or later, we inevitably find ourselves saying, "This test would be so much easier to write if I just had an assertion that did . . . ." So why not write it ourselves?

The reasons for writing a *Custom Assertion* are many, but the technique is pretty much the same regardless of our goal. We hide the complexity of whatever it takes to prove the system is behaving correctly behind an *Assertion Method* with an Intent-Revealing Name [SBPP].

How It Works

We encapsulate the mechanics of verifying that something is true (an assertion) behind an Intent-Revealing Name. To do so, we factor out all the common assertion code within the tests into a *Custom Assertion* that implements the verification logic. A *Custom Equality Assertion* takes two parameters: an *Expected Object* (see *State Verification* on page 462) and the actual object.

A key characteristic of *Custom Assertions* is that they receive everything they need to pass or fail the test as parameters. Other than causing the test to fail, they have no side effects.

Typically, we create *Custom Assertions* through refactoring by identifying common patterns of assertions in our tests. When test driving, we might just go ahead and call a nonexistent *Custom Assertion* because it makes writing our test easier; this tactic lets us focus on the part of the SUT that needs to be tested rather than the mechanics of how the test would be carried out.

When to Use It

We should consider creating a *Custom Assertion* whenever *any* of the following statements are true:

- We find ourselves writing (or cloning) the same assertion logic in test after test (*Test Code Duplication*; see page 213).

- We find ourselves writing *Conditional Test Logic* (page 200) in the result verification part of our tests. That is, our calls to *Assertion Methods* are embedded in if statements or loops.

- The result verification parts of our tests suffer from *Obscure Test* (page 186) because we use procedural rather than declarative result verification in the tests.

- We find ourselves doing *Frequent Debugging* (page 248) whenever assertions fail because they do not provide enough information.

A key reason for moving the assertion logic out of the tests and into *Custom Assertions* is to *Minimize Untestable Code* (see page 44). Once the verification logic has been moved into a *Custom Assertion*, we can write *Custom Assertion Tests* (see *Custom Assertion* on page 474) to prove the verification logic is working properly. Another important benefit of using *Custom Assertions* is that they help avoid *Obscure Tests* and make tests *Communicate Intent* (see page 41). That, in turn, will help produce robust, easily maintained tests.

If the verification logic must interact with the SUT to determine the actual outcome, we can use a *Verification Method* (see *Custom Assertion*) instead of a *Custom Assertion*. If the setup and exercise parts of the tests are also the same except for the values of the actual/expected objects, we should consider using a *Parameterized Test* (page 607). The primary advantage of *Custom Assertions* over both of these techniques is reusability; the same *Custom Assertion* can be reused in many different circumstances because it is independent of its context (its only contact with the outside world occurs through its parameter list).

We most commonly write *Custom Assertions* that are *Equality Assertions* (see *Assertion Method*), but there is no reason why we cannot write other kinds as well.

Variation: Custom Equality Assertion

For custom equality assertions, the *Custom Assertion* must be passed an *Expected Object* and the actual object to be verified. It should also take an *Assertion Message* (page 370) to avoid playing *Assertion Roulette* (page 224). Such an assertion is essentially an `equals` method implemented as a Foreign Method [Fowler].

Variation: Object Attribute Equality Assertion

We often run across *Custom Assertions* that take one actual object and several different *Expected Objects* that need to be compared with specific attributes of the actual object. (The set of attributes to be compared is implied by the name of the *Custom Assertion*.) The key difference between these *Custom Assertions* and a *Verification Method* is that the latter interacts with the SUT while the *Object Attribute Equality Assertion* looks only at the objects passed in as parameters.

Variation: Domain Assertion

All of the built-in *Assertion Methods* are domain independent. *Custom Equality Assertions* implement test-specific equality but still compare only two objects. Another style of *Custom Assertion* helps contribute to the definition of a "domain-specific" *Higher-Level Language* (see page 41)—namely, the *Domain Assertion*.

A *Domain Assertion* is a *Stated Outcome Assertion* (see *Assertion Method*) that states something that should be true in domain-specific terms. It helps elevate the test into "business-speak."

Variation: Diagnostic Assertion

Sometimes we find ourselves doing *Frequent Debugging* whenever a test fails because the assertions tell us only that something is wrong but do not identify the specific problem (e.g., the assertions indicate these two objects are not equal but it isn't clear *what* isn't equal about the object). We can write a special kind of *Custom Assertion* that may look just like one of the built-in assertions but provide more information about what is different between the expected and actual values than a built-in assertion because it is specific to our types. (For example, it might tell us which attributes are different or where long strings differ.)

On one project, we were comparing string variables containing XML. Whenever a test failed, we had to bring up two string inspectors and scroll through them looking for the difference. Finally, we got smart and included the logic in a *Custom Assertion* that told us where the first difference between the two XML strings occurred. The small amount of time we spent writing the diagnostic custom assertion was paid back many times over as we ran our tests.

Variation: Verification Method

In customer tests, a lot of the complexity of verifying the outcome is related to interacting with the SUT. *Verification Methods* are a form of *Custom Assertions* that interact directly with the SUT, thereby relieving their callers from this task. This simplifies the tests significantly and leads to a more "declarative" style of outcome specification. After the *Custom Assertion* has been written, we can write subsequent tests that result in the same outcome much more quickly. In some cases, it may be advantageous to incorporate even the exercise SUT phase of the test into the *Verification Method*. This is one step short of a full *Parameterized Test* that incorporates all the test logic in a reusable *Test Utility Method* (page 599).

Custom
Assertion

Implementation Notes

The *Custom Assertion* is typically implemented as a set of calls to the various built-in *Assertion Methods*. Depending on how we plan to use it in our tests, we may also want to include the standard *Equality Assertion* template to ensure correct behavior with null parameters. Because the *Custom Assertion* is itself an *Assertion Method*, it should not have any side effects, nor should it call the SUT. (If it needs to do so, it would be a *Verification Method*.)

Variation: Custom Assertion Test

Testing zealots would also write a *Custom Assertion Test* (a *Self-Checking Test*— see page 26—for *Custom Assertions*) to verify the *Custom Assertion*. The benefit from doing so is obvious: increased confidence in our tests. In most cases, writing *Custom Assertion* Tests isn't particularly difficult because *Assertion Methods* take all their arguments as parameters.

We can treat the *Custom Assertion* as the SUT simply by calling it with various arguments and verifying that it fails in the right cases. *Single-Outcome Assertions* (see *Assertion Method*) need only a single test because they don't take any parameters (other than possibly an *Assertion Message*). *Stated Outcome Assertions* need one test for each possible value (or boundary value). *Equality Assertions* need one test that compares two objects deemed to be equivalent, one test that compares an object with itself, and one test for each attribute whose inequality should cause the assertion to fail. Attributes that don't affect equality can be verified in one additional test because the *Equality Assertion* should not raise an error for any of them.

The *Custom Assertions* follow the normal *Simple Success Test* (see *Test Method* on page 348) and *Expected Exception Test* (see *Test Method*) templates with one minor difference: Because the *Assertion Method* is the SUT, the exercise SUT and verify outcome phases of the *Four-Phase Test* (page 358) are combined into a single phase.

Each test consists of setting up the *Expected Object* and the actual object and then calling the *Custom Assertion*. If the objects should be equivalent, that's all there is to it. (The *Test Automation Framework* described on page 298 would catch any assertion failures and fail the test.) For the tests where we expect the *Custom Assertion* to fail, we can write the test as an *Expected Exception Test* (except that the exercise SUT and verify outcome phases of the *Four-Phase Test* are combined into the single call to the *Custom Assertion*).

The simplest way to build the objects to be compared for a specific test is to do something similar to *One Bad Attribute* (see *Derived Value* on page 718)—that is, build the first object and make a deep copy of it. For successful tests, modify any of the attributes that should *not* be compared. For each test failure, modify one attribute that *should* be grounds for failing the assertion.

A brief warning about a possible complication in a few members of the xUnit family: If all of the test failure handling does not occur in the *Test Runner* (page 377), calls to fail or built-in assertions may add messages to the failure log even if we catch the error or exception in our *Custom Assertion Test*. The only way to circumvent this behavior is to use an "Encapsulated Test Runner" to run each test by itself and verify that the one test failed with the expected error message.

Motivating Example

In the following example, several test methods repeat the same series of assertions:

```
public void testInvoice_addOneLineItem_quantity1_b() {
    // Exercise
    inv.addItemQuantity(product, QUANTITY);
    // Verify
    List lineItems = inv.getLineItems();
    assertEquals("number of items", lineItems.size(), 1);
```

```
   // Verify only item
   LineItem expItem = new LineItem(inv, product, QUANTITY);
   LineItem actual = (LineItem)lineItems.get(0);
   assertEquals(expItem.getInv(), actual.getInv());
   assertEquals(expItem.getProd(), actual.getProd());
   assertEquals(expItem.getQuantity(), actual.getQuantity());
}


public void testRemoveLineItemsForProduct_oneOfTwo() {
   // Setup
   Invoice inv = createAnonInvoice();
   inv.addItemQuantity(product, QUANTITY);
   inv.addItemQuantity(anotherProduct, QUANTITY);
   LineItem expItem = new LineItem(inv, product, QUANTITY);
   // Exercise
   inv.removeLineItemForProduct(anotherProduct);
   // Verify
   List lineItems = inv.getLineItems();
   assertEquals("number of items", lineItems.size(), 1);
   LineItem actual = (LineItem)lineItems.get(0);
   assertEquals(expItem.getInv(), actual.getInv());
   assertEquals(expItem.getProd(), actual.getProd());
   assertEquals(expItem.getQuantity(), actual.getQuantity());
}

//
//   Adding TWO line items
//

public void testInvoice_addTwoLineItems_sameProduct() {
   Invoice inv = createAnonInvoice();
   LineItem expItem1 = new LineItem(inv, product, QUANTITY1);
   LineItem expItem2 = new LineItem(inv, product, QUANTITY2);
   // Exercise
   inv.addItemQuantity(product, QUANTITY1);
   inv.addItemQuantity(product, QUANTITY2);
   // Verify
   List lineItems = inv.getLineItems();
   assertEquals("number of items", lineItems.size(), 2);
   //   Verify first item
   LineItem actual = (LineItem)lineItems.get(0);
   assertEquals(expItem1.getInv(), actual.getInv());
   assertEquals(expItem1.getProd(), actual.getProd());
   assertEquals(expItem1.getQuantity(), actual.getQuantity());
   //   Verify second item
   actual = (LineItem)lineItems.get(1);
   assertEquals(expItem2.getInv(), actual.getInv());
   assertEquals(expItem2.getProd(), actual.getProd());
   assertEquals(expItem2.getQuantity(), actual.getQuantity());
}
```

Custom
Assertion

Note that the first test ends with a series of three assertions and the second test repeats the series of three assertions twice, once for each line item. This is clearly a bad case of *Test Code Duplication*.

Refactoring Notes

Refactoring zealots can probably see that the solution is to do an Extract Method [Fowler] refactoring on these tests. If we pull out all the common calls to *Assertion Methods,* we will be left with only the differences in each test. The extracted method is our *Custom Assertion.* We may also need to introduce an *Expected Object* to hold all the values that were being passed to the individual *Assertion Methods* on a single object to be passed to the *Custom Assertion.*

Custom Assertion

Example: Custom Assertion

In this test, we use a *Custom Assertion* to verify that LineItem matches the expected LineItem(s). For one reason or another, we have chosen to implement a test-specific equality rather than using a standard *Equality Assertion.*

```
public void testInvoice_addOneLineItem_quantity1_() {
    Invoice inv = createAnonInvoice();
    LineItem expItem = new LineItem(inv, product, QUANTITY);
    // Exercise
    inv.addItemQuantity(product, QUANTITY);
    // Verify
    List lineItems = inv.getLineItems();
    assertEquals("number of items", lineItems.size(), 1);
    // Verify only item
    LineItem actual = (LineItem)lineItems.get(0);
    assertLineItemsEqual("LineItem", expItem, actual);
}

public void testAddItemQuantity_sameProduct_() {
    Invoice inv = createAnonInvoice();
    LineItem expItem1 = new LineItem(inv, product, QUANTITY1);
    LineItem expItem2 = new LineItem(inv, product, QUANTITY2);
    // Exercise
    inv.addItemQuantity(product, QUANTITY1);
    inv.addItemQuantity(product, QUANTITY2);
    // Verify
    List lineItems = inv.getLineItems();
    assertEquals("number of items", lineItems.size(), 2);
    // Verify first item
    LineItem actual = (LineItem)lineItems.get(0);
    assertLineItemsEqual("Item 1",expItem1,actual);
    // Verify second item
```

```
    actual = (LineItem)lineItems.get(1);
    assertLineItemsEqual("Item 2",expItem2, actual);
}
```

The tests have become significantly smaller and more intent-revealing. We have also chosen to pass a string indicating which item we are examining as an argument to the *Custom Assertion* to avoid playing *Assertion Roulette* when a test fails.

This simplified test was made possible by having the following *Custom Assertion* available to us:

```
static void assertLineItemsEqual(
            String  msg, LineItem exp, LineItem act) {
    assertEquals(msg+" Inv",  exp.getInv(),act.getInv());
    assertEquals(msg+" Prod", exp.getProd(), act.getProd());
    assertEquals(msg+" Quan", exp.getQuantity(), act.getQuantity());
}
```

**Custom
Assertion**

This *Custom Assertion* compares the same attributes of the object as we were comparing on an in-line basis in the previous version of the test; thus the semantics of the test haven't changed. We also concatenate the name of the attribute being compared with the message parameter to get a unique failure message, which allows us to avoid playing *Assertion Roulette* when a test fails.

Example: Domain Assertion

In this next version of the test, we have further elevated the level of the assertions to better communicate the expected outcome of the test scenarios:

```
public void testAddOneLineItem_quantity1() {
    Invoice inv = createAnonInvoice();
    LineItem expItem = new LineItem(inv, product, QUANTITY);
    // Exercise
    inv.addItemQuantity( product, QUANTITY);
    // Verify
    assertInvoiceContainsOnlyThisLineItem( inv, expItem);
}

public void testRemoveLineItemsForProduct_oneOfTwo_() {
    Invoice inv = createAnonInvoice();
    inv.addItemQuantity( product, QUANTITY);
    inv.addItemQuantity( anotherProduct, QUANTITY);
    LineItem expItem = new LineItem( inv, product, QUANTITY);
    // Exercise
    inv.removeLineItemForProduct( anotherProduct );
    // Verify
    assertInvoiceContainsOnlyThisLineItem( inv, expItem);
}
```

This simplified version of the test was made possible by extracting the following *Domain Assertion* method:

```
void assertInvoiceContainsOnlyThisLineItem(
                               Invoice inv,
                               LineItem expItem) {
   List lineItems = inv.getLineItems();
   assertEquals("number of items", lineItems.size(), 1);
   LineItem actual = (LineItem)lineItems.get(0);
   assertLineItemsEqual("item",expItem, actual);
}
```

This example chose to forgo passing a message to the *Domain Assertion* to save a bit of space. In real life, we would typically include a message string in the parameter list and concatenate the messages of the individual assertions to one passed in. See *Assertion Message* (page 370) for more details.

**Custom
Assertion**

Example: Verification Method

If the exercise SUT and result verification phases of several tests are pretty much identical, we can incorporate both phases into our reusable *Custom Assertion*. Because this approach changes the semantics of the *Custom Assertion* from being just a function free of side effects to an operation that changes the state of the SUT, we usually give it a more distinctive name starting with "verify".

This version of the test merely sets up the test fixture before calling a *Verification Method* that incorporates both the exercise SUT and verify outcome phases of the test. It is most easily recognized by the lack of a distinct "exercise" phase in the calling test and the presence of calls to methods that modify the state of one of the objects passed as a parameter of the *Verification Method*.

```
public void testAddOneLineItem_quantity2() {
   Invoice inv = createAnonInvoice();
   LineItem expItem = new LineItem(inv, product, QUANTITY);
   // Exercise & Verify
   verifyOneLineItemCanBeAdded(inv, product, QUANTITY, expItem);
}
```

The *Verification Method* for this example looks like this:

```
public void verifyOneLineItemCanBeAdded(
               Invoice inv, Product product,
               int QUANTITY, LineItem expItem) {
   // Exercise
   inv.addItemQuantity(product, QUANTITY);
   // Verify
   assertInvoiceContainsOnlyThisLineItem(inv, expItem);
}
```

This *Verification Method* calls the "pure" *Custom Assertion*, although it could just as easily have included all the assertion logic if we didn't have the other *Custom Assertion* to call. Note the call to addItemQuantity on the parameter inv; this is what changes if from a *Custom Assertion* to a *Verification Method*.

Example: Custom Assertion Test

This *Custom Assertion* isn't particularly complicated, so we may feel comfortable without having any automated tests for it. If there is anything complex about it, however, we may find it worthwhile to write tests like these:

```
public void testassertLineItemsEqual_equivalent() {
   Invoice inv = createAnonInvoice();
   LineItem item1 = new LineItem(inv, product, QUANTITY1);
   LineItem item2 = new LineItem(inv, product, QUANTITY1);
   // exercise/verify
   assertLineItemsEqual("This should not fail",item1, item2);
}

public void testassertLineItemsEqual_differentInvoice() {
   Invoice inv1 = createAnonInvoice();
   Invoice inv2 = createAnonInvoice();
   LineItem item1 = new LineItem(inv1, product, QUANTITY1);
   LineItem item2 = new LineItem(inv2, product, QUANTITY1);
   // exercise/verify
   try {
      assertLineItemsEqual("Msg",item1, item2);
   } catch (AssertionFailedError e) {
      assertEquals("e.getMsg",
                   "Invoice-expected: <123> but was <124>",
                   e.getMessage());
      return;
   }
   fail("Should have thrown exception");
}

public void testassertLineItemsEqual_differentQuantity() {
   Invoice inv = createAnonInvoice();
   LineItem item1 = new LineItem(inv, product, QUANTITY1);
   LineItem item2 = new LineItem(inv, product, QUANTITY2);
   // exercise/verify
   try {
      assertLineItemsEqual("Msg",item1, item2);
   } catch (AssertionFailedError e) {
      pass();  // to indicate that no assertion is needed
      return;
   }
   fail("Should have thrown exception");
}
```

Custom Assertion

This example includes a few of the *Custom Assertion Tests* needed for this *Custom Assertion*. Note that the code includes one "equivalent" and several "different" tests (one for each attribute whose difference should cause the test to fail). We have to use the second form of the *Expected Exception Test* template in those cases where the assertion was expected to fail, because fail throws the same exception as our assertion method. In one of the "different" tests, we have included sample logic for asserting on the exception message. (Although I've abridged it to save space, the example here should give you an idea of where to assert on the message.)

Custom
Assertion

Delta Assertion

How do we make tests self-checking when we cannot control the initial contents of the fixture?

We specify assertions based on differences between the pre- and post-exercise state of the SUT.

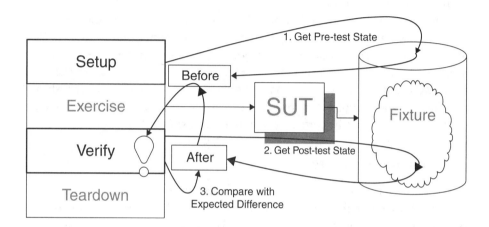

Delta
Assertion

When we are using a *Shared Fixture* (page 317) such as a test database, it can be challenging to code the assertions that state what the content of the fixture should be after the SUT has been exercised. This is because other tests may have created objects in the fixture that our assertions may detect and that may cause our assertions to fail. One solution is to isolate the current test from all other tests by using a *Database Partitioning Scheme* (see *Database Sandbox* on page 650). But what can we do if this option is not available to us?

Using *Delta Assertions* allows us to be less dependent on which data already exist in the *Shared Fixture*.

How It Works

Before exercising the SUT, we take a snapshot of relevant parts of the *Shared Fixture*. After exercising the SUT, we specify our assertions relative to the saved snapshot. The *Delta Assertions* typically verify that the number of objects has changed by the right number and that the contents of collections of objects returned by the SUT in response to our queries have been augmented by the expected objects.

When to Use It

We can use a *Delta Assertion* whenever we don't have full control over the test fixture and we want to avoid *Interacting Tests* (see *Erratic Test* on page 228). Using *Delta Assertions* will help make our tests more resilient to changes in the fixture. We can also use *Delta Assertions* in concert with *Implicit Teardown* (page 516) to detect memory or data leaks in the code that we are testing. See the sidebar "Using Delta Assertions to Detect Data Leakage" on page 487 for a more detailed description.

Delta Assertions work well when tests are run one after another from the same *Test Runner* (page 377). Unfortunately, they cannot prevent a *Test Run War* (see *Erratic Test*) because such a problem arises when tests are run at the same time from different processes. *Delta Assertions* work whenever the state of the SUT and the fixture are modified only by our own test. If other tests are running in parallel (not before or after the current test, but *at the same time*), a *Delta Assertion* won't be sufficient to avoid the *Test Run War* problem.

Delta Assertion (sidebar label)

Implementation Notes

When saving the pre-test state of the *Shared Fixture* or SUT, we must make sure that the SUT cannot change our snapshot. For example, if our snapshot consists of a collection of objects returned by the SUT in response to a query, we must perform a deep copy; a shallow copy copies only the `Collection` object and not the objects to which it refers. Shallow copying would allow the SUT to modify the very objects it returned to us as we exercise it; as a consequence, we would lose the reference snapshot with which we are comparing the post-test state.

We can ensure that we have the correct post-test state in several different ways. Assuming that our test adds any new objects it plans to modify, one approach is to first check that the result collection (1) has the right number of items, (2) contains all the pre-test items, and (3) contains the new *Expected Objects* (see *State Verification* on page 462). Another approach is to remove all the saved items from the result collection and then compare what remains with the collection of new expected objects. Both of these approaches can be hidden behind a *Custom Assertion* (page 474) or a *Verification Method* (see *Custom Assertion*).

Using Delta Assertions to Detect Data Leakage

A long time ago, on a project far away, we were experimenting with different ways to clean up our test fixtures after the customer tests. Our tests were accessing a database and leaving objects behind. This behavior caused all sorts of problems with *Unrepeatable Tests* (see *Erratic Test* on page 228) and *Interacting Tests* (see *Erratic Test*). We were also suffering from *Slow Tests* (page 253).

Eventually we hit upon the idea of keeping track of all the objects we were creating in our tests by registering them with an *Automated Teardown* (page 503) mechanism. Then we found a way to stub out the database with a *Fake Database* (see *Fake Object* on page 551). Next we made it possible to run the same test against either the fake database or the real one. This solved many of the interaction problems when running against the fake database, although those problems still occurred when we ran the tests against the real database—tests still left objects behind, and we wanted to know why. But first we had to determine precisely which tests were at fault.

The solution turned out to be pretty simple. In our *Fake Database*—which was implemented using simple hash tables—we added a method to count the total number of objects. We simply saved this value in an instance variable in the setUp method and used it as the expected value passed to an *Equality Assertion* (see *Assertion Method* on page 362) called in the tearDown method to verify that we had cleaned up all objects properly. [This is an example of using *Delta Assertions* (page 485).] Once we implemented this little trick, we quickly found out which tests were suffering from the *Data Leak* (see *Erratic Test*). We could then focus our efforts on a much smaller number of tests.

Even today, we find it useful to be able to run the same test against the database and in memory. Similarly, we still occasionally see a test fail when the tearDown method inherited from our company-specific *Testcase Superclass* (page 638) has a *Delta Assertion* failure. Perhaps the same idea could be applied to checking for memory leaks in programming languages with manual memory management (such as C++).

Motivating Example

The following test retrieves some objects from the SUT. It then compares the objects it actually found with the objects it expected to find.

```
public void testGetFlightsByOriginAirport_OneOutboundFlight()
        throws Exception {
    FlightDto expectedFlightDto =
        createNewFlightBetweenExistingAirports();
    // Exercise System
    facade.createFlight(
            expectedFlightDto.getOriginAirportId(),
            expectedFlightDto.getDestinationAirportId());
    // Verify Outcome
    List flightsAtOrigin = facade.getFlightsByOriginAirport(
                    expectedFlightDto.getOriginAirportId());
    assertOnly1FlightInDtoList( "Outbound flight at origin",
                                expectedFlightDto,
                                flightsAtOrigin);
}
```

Delta
Assertion

Unfortunately, because this test used a *Shared Fixture*, other tests that ran before it may have added objects as well. That behavior could cause the current test to fail if we encounter additional, unexpected objects.

Refactoring Notes

To convert the test to use a *Delta Assertion*, we must first take a snapshot of the data (or collection of objects) we will later be asserting on. Next, we need to modify our assertions to focus on the difference between the pre-test data/objects and the post-test data/objects. To avoid introducing *Conditional Test Logic* (page 200) into the *Test Method* (page 348), we may want to introduce a new *Custom Assertion*. Although we may be able to use existing assertions (custom or otherwise) as a starting point, we'll probably have to modify them to take the pre-test data into account.

Example: Delta Assertion

In this version of the test, we use a *Delta Assertion* to verify the objects added when we exercised the SUT. Here we are verifying that we have one more object than before and that the collection of objects returned by the SUT includes the new *Expected Object* and all objects that it previously contained.

```
public void testCreateFlight_Delta()
        throws Exception {
    FlightDto expectedFlightDto =
        createNewFlightBetweenExistingAirports();
```

```
            // Remember prior state
            List flightsBeforeCreate =
                facade.getFlightsByOriginAirport(
                            expectedFlightDto.getOriginAirportId());
            // Exercise system
            facade.createFlight(
                        expectedFlightDto.getOriginAirportId(),
                        expectedFlightDto.getDestinationAirportId());
            // Verify outcome relative to prior state
            List flightsAfterCreate =
                facade.getFlightsByOriginAirport(
                            expectedFlightDto.getOriginAirportId());
            assertFlightIncludedInDtoList( "new flight ",
                                            expectedFlightDto,
                                            flightsAfterCreate);
            assertAllFlightsIncludedInDtoList( "previous flights",
                                                flightsBeforeCreate,
                                                flightsAfterCreate);
            assertEquals( "Number of flights after create",
                        flightsBeforeCreate.size()+1,
                        flightsAfterCreate.size());
    }
```

**Delta
Assertion**

Because the SUT returns Data Transfer Objects [CJ2EEP], we can be assured that the objects we saved before exercising the SUT cannot possibly change. We have modified our *Custom Assertions* to ignore the pre-test objects (by not insisting that the *Expected Object* is the only one) and have written a new *Custom Assertion* that ensures all pre-test objects are also present. Another way to accomplish this task is to remove the pre-test objects from the result collection and then verify that only the new *Expected Objects* are left.

I've omitted the implementation of the *Custom Assertions,* as it is purely an exercise in comparing objects and is not salient to understanding the *Delta Assertion* pattern. The "test infected" among us would, of course, write the *Custom Assertions* driven by some *Custom Assertion Tests* (see *Custom Assertion*).

Guard Assertion

How do we avoid Conditional Test Logic?

**We replace an if statement in a test with an assertion that fails the test
if not satisfied.**

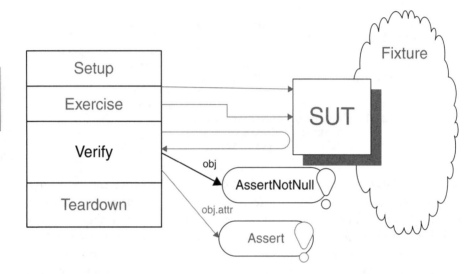

Some verification logic may fail because information returned by the SUT is not
initialized as expected. When a test encounters an unexpected problem, it may
produce a test error rather than a test failure. While the *Test Runner* (page 377)
does its best to provide useful diagnostic information, the test automater can often do better by checking for the particular condition and reporting it explicitly.

A *Guard Assertion* is a good way to do so without introducing *Conditional
Test Logic* (page 200).

How It Works

Tests either pass or fail. We fail tests by calling *Assertion Methods* (page 362)
that stop the test from executing further if the assertion's condition is not met.
Alternatively, we can replace *Conditional Test Logic* that is used to avoid executing assertions when they would cause test errors with assertions that fail the
test instead. This pattern also documents the fact that we expect the condition of
the *Guard Assertion* to be true. A failure of the *Guard Assertion* makes it very

clear that some condition we expected to be true was not; it eliminates the effort needed to infer the test result from the conditional logic.

When to Use It

We should use a *Guard Assertion* whenever we want to avoid executing statements in our *Test Method* (page 348) because they would cause an error if they were executed when some condition related to values returned by the SUT is not true. We take this step instead of putting an if then else fail code construct around the sensitive statements. Normally, a *Guard Assertion* is placed between the exercise SUT and the verify outcome phases of a *Four-Phase Test* (page 358).

Variation: Shared Fixture State Assertion

When the test uses a *Shared Fixture* (page 317), a *Guard Assertion* can also be useful at the beginning of the test (before the exercise SUT phase) to verify that the *Shared Fixture* satisfies the test's needs. It also makes it clearer to the test reader which parts of the *Shared Fixture* this test actually uses; the greater clarity improves the likelihood of achieving *Tests as Documentation* (see page 23).

Implementation Notes

We can use *Stated Outcome Assertions* (see *Assertion Method*) like assertNotNil and *Equality Assertions* (see *Assertion Method*) like assertEquals as *Guard Assertions* that fail the test and prevent execution of other statements that would cause test errors.

Motivating Example

Consider the following example:

```
public void testWithConditionals() throws Exception {
    String expectedLastname = "smith";
    List foundPeople = PeopleFinder.
        findPeopleWithLastname(expectedLastname);
    if (foundPeople != null) {
        if (foundPeople.size() == 1) {
            Person solePerson = (Person) foundPeople.get(0);
            assertEquals( expectedLastname,solePerson.getName());
        } else {
            fail("list should have exactly one element");
        }
    } else {
        fail("list is null");
    }
}
```

This example includes plenty of conditional statements that the author might get wrong—things like writing (foundPeople == null) instead of (foundPeople != null). In C-based languages, one might mistakenly use = instead of ==, which would result in the test always passing!

Refactoring Notes

We can use a Replace Nested Conditional with Guard Clauses [Fowler] refactoring to transform this spider web of *Conditional Test Logic* into a nice linear sequence of statements. (In a test, even a single conditional statement is considered too much and hence "nested"!) We can use *Stated Outcome Assertions* to check for null object references and *Equality Assertions* to verify the number of objects in the collection. If each assertion is satisfied, the test proceeds. If they are not satisfied, the test ends in failure before it reaches the next statement.

Example: Simple Guard Assertion

This simplified version of the test replaces all conditional statements with assertions. It is shorter than the original test and much easier to read.

```
public void testWithoutConditionals() throws Exception {
    String expectedLastname = "smith";
    List foundPeople = PeopleFinder.
        findPeopleWithLastname(expectedLastname);
    assertNotNull("found people list", foundPeople);
    assertEquals( "number of people", 1, foundPeople.size() );
    Person solePerson = (Person) foundPeople.get(0);
    assertEquals( "last name",
                    expectedLastname,
                    solePerson.getName() );
}
```

We now have a single linear execution path through this *Test Method* (page 348); it should improve our confidence in the correctness of this test immensely!

Example: Shared Fixture Guard Assertion

Here's an example of a test that depends on a *Shared Fixture*. If a previous test (or even this test in a previous test run) modifies the state of the fixture, our SUT could return unexpected results. It might take a fair bit of effort to determine that the problem lies in the test's pre-conditions rather than being a bug in the SUT. We can avoid all of this trouble by making the assumptions of this test explicit through the use of a *Guard Assertion* during the fixture lookup phase of the test.

```
public void testAddFlightsByFromAirport_OneOutboundFlight_GA()
        throws Exception {
    // Fixture Lookup
    List flights = facade.getFlightsByOriginAirport(
                        ONE_OUTBOUND_FLIGHT_AIRPORT_ID );
    //    Guard Assertion on Fixture Contents
    assertEquals( "# flights precondition", 1, flights.size());
    FlightDto firstFlight = (FlightDto) flights.get(0);
    // Exercise System
    BigDecimal flightNum = facade.createFlight(
                        firstFlight.getOriginAirportId(),
                        firstFlight.getDestAirportId());
    // Verify Outcome
    FlightDto expFlight = (FlightDto) firstFlight.clone();
    expFlight.setFlightNumber( flightNum );
    List actual = facade.getFlightsByOriginAirport(
                        firstFlight.getOriginAirportId());
    assertExactly2FlightsInDtoList( "Flights at origin",
                                firstFlight,
                                expFlight,
                                actual);
}
```

Guard
Assertion

We now have a way to determine that the assumptions were violated without extensive debugging! This is another way we achieve *Defect Localization* (see page 22). This time the defect is in the tests' assumptions on the previously run tests' behavior.

Unfinished Test Assertion

How do we structure our test logic to avoid leaving tests unfinished?

We ensure that incomplete tests fail by executing an assertion that is guaranteed to fail.

```
void testSomething() {
    // Outline:
        // create a flight in ... state
        // call the ... method
        // verify flight is in ... state
    fail("Unfinished Test!");
}
```

**Unfinished
Test
Assertion**

When we start defining the tests for a particular piece of code, it is useful to "rough in" the tests by defining *Test Methods* (page 348) on the appropriate *Testcase Class* (page 373) as we think of the test conditions. We do, however, want to ensure that we don't accidentally forget to fill in the bodies of these tests if we get distracted. We want the tests to fail until we finish coding them.

Including an *Unfinished Test Assertion* is a good way to make sure we don't forget.

How It Works

We put a single call to fail in each *Test Method* as we define it. The fail method is a *Single-Outcome Assertion* (see *Assertion Method* on page 362) that always fails. We include the *Assertion Message* (page 370) "Unfinished Test" as a reminder of why the test fails when we do run the tests.

When to Use It

We should not deliberately write any tests that might accidentally pass. A failing test makes a good reminder that we still have work to do. We can remind ourselves of this work by putting an *Unfinished Test Assertion* at the end of every test we write and by removing it only when we are satisfied that the test is coded properly. There is no real cost to doing so, but a lot of benefit. It is just a matter of getting into the habit. Some IDEs even help us out by letting us put the *Unfinished Test Assertion* into the code generation template for a *Test Method*

If we need to check in the tests before all code is working, we shouldn't remove the tests or the *Unfinished Test Assertions* just to get a green bar, as this could result in *Lost Tests* (see *Production Bugs* on page 268). Instead, we can add an [Ignore] attribute to the test if our member of the xUnit family supports it, rename the test method if xUnit uses name-based *Test Discovery* (page 393), or exclude the entire *Testcase Class* from the *AllTests Suite* (see *Named Test Suite* on page 592) if we are using *Test Enumeration* (page 399) at the suite level.

Implementation Notes

Most members of the xUnit family have a fail method already defined. If the member that we are using doesn't include it, we should avoid the temptation to sprinkle assertTrue(false) throughout our code. This kind of code is obtuse and easy to get wrong because it is counter-intuitive. Instead, we should take a minute to write this method ourselves as a *Custom Assertion* (page 474) and write the *Custom Assertion Test* (see *Custom Assertion*) for it first to make sure we got it right.

Unfinished Test Assertion

Some IDEs include the ability to customize code generation templates. Some even include a template for a *Test Method* that includes an *Unfinished Test Assertion*.

Motivating Example

Consider the following *Testcase Class* that we are roughing in:

```
public void testPull_emptyStack() {

}

public void testPull_oneItemOnStack () {

}

public void testPull_twoItemsOnStack () {
   //To do: Write this test
}

public void testPull_oneItemsRemainingOnStack () {
   //To do: Write this test
}
```

Including the // To do: ... comments may remind us that the test still needs work if our IDE supports that feature—but it won't remind us of the unfinished work when we run the tests. Running this *Testcase Class* will result in a green bar even though we may not have implemented our stack at all!

Refactoring Notes

To implement *Unfinished Test Assertion* all we need to do is add the following line to each test as we rough it in:

```
fail("Unfinished Test!");
```

The exclamation mark is optional. It might be even better to create a *Custom Assertion* such as this one:

```
private void unfinishedTest() {
    fail("Test not implemented!");
}
```

**Unfinished
Test
Assertion**

This would allow us to find all the *Unfinished Test Assertions* easily by using the "search for references" feature of our IDE.

Example: Unfinished Test Assertion

Here are the tests with an *Unfinished Test Assertion* added to each one:

```
    public void testPull_emptyStack() {
        unfinishedTest();
    }

    public void testPull_oneItemOnStack () {
        unfinishedTest();
    }

    public void testPull_twoItemsOnStack() {
        unfinishedTest();
    }

    public void testPull_oneItemsRemainingOnStack () {
        unfinishedTest();
    }
```

Now we have a *Testcase Class* that is guaranteed to fail until we finish writing the code. The failing tests act as a "to do" list for writing the tests.

Example: Unfinished Test Method Generation from Template

Eclipse (version 3.0) is an example of an IDE that includes the ability to customize templates. Its testmethod template inserts the following code into our *Testcase Class*:

```
public void testname() throws Exception {
    fail("ClassName::testname not implemented");
}
```

The strings "ClassName" and "testname" are placeholders for the names of the *Testcase Class* and *Test Method*, respectively; they are filled in automatically by the IDE. As we modify the test name in the signature, the test name in the `fail` statement is adjusted automatically. All we have to do to insert a new *Test Method* into a class is to type "testmethod" and then press CTRL-SPACEBAR.

Unfinished
Test
Assertion

Chapter 22

Fixture Teardown Patterns

Fixture
Teardown
Patterns

499

Garbage-Collected Teardown

How do we tear down the Test Fixture?

We let the garbage collection mechanism provided by the programming language clean up after our test.

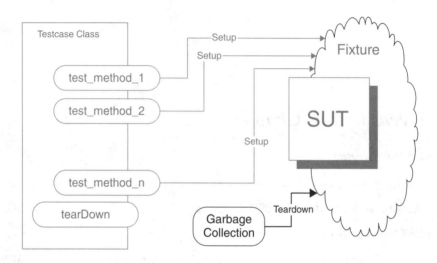

A large part of making tests repeatable and robust is ensuring that the test fixture is torn down after each test and a new one created for the next test run. This strategy is known as a *Fresh Fixture* (page 311). In languages that provide **garbage collection,** much of the teardown can happen automatically if we refer to resources via local and instance variables.

How It Works

Many of the objects created during the course of our test (including both fixture setup and exercising the SUT) are transient objects that are kept alive only as long as there is a reference to them somewhere in the program that created them. The garbage collection mechanisms of modern languages use various algorithms to detect "garbage." What is most important, though, is how they determine that something is *not* garbage: Any object that is reachable from any other live object or from global (i.e., static) variables will not be garbage collected.

When running our tests, the *Test Automation Framework* (page 298) creates a *Testcase Object* (page 382) for each *Test Method* (page 348) in our *Testcase*

Class (page 373) and adds those objects to a *Test Suite Object* (page 387). Whenever a new test run is started, the framework typically throws away the existing test suite and builds a new one (to be sure everything is fresh). When the old test suite is discarded, any objects referenced only by instance variables in those tests become candidates for garbage collection.

When to Use It

We should use *Garbage-Collected Teardown* whenever we possibly can because it will save us a lot of effort!

If our programming takes place in an environment that doesn't support garbage collection, or if we have resources that aren't garbage collected automatically (e.g., files, sockets, records in a database), we'll need to destroy or free those resources explicitly. If we are using a *Shared Fixture* (page 317), we won't be able to use *Garbage-Collected Teardown* unless we do something fancy to hold the reference to the fixture in such a way that it will go out of scope when our test suite has finished running.

We can use *In-line Teardown* (page 509), *Implicit Teardown* (page 516), or *Automated Teardown* (page 503) to ensure that they are released properly.

Garbage-Collected Teardown

Implementation Notes

Some members of the xUnit family and some IDEs go so far as to replace the classes each time the test suite is run. We may see this behavior show up as an option called "Reload Classes" or it may be forced upon us. We must be careful if we decide to take advantage of this feature to perform *Garbage-Collected Teardown* with **fixture holding class variables,** as our tests may stop running if we change IDEs or try running our tests from the command line (e.g., from "Cruise Control" or a build script.)

Motivating Example

The following test creates some in-memory objects during fixture setup and explicitly destroys them using *In-line Teardown*. (We could have used *Implicit Teardown* in this example but that just makes it harder for readers to see what is going on.)

```
public void testCancel_proposed_UIT() {
    // fixture setup
    Flight proposedFlight = createAnonymousProposedFlight();
    // exercise SUT
    proposedFlight.cancel();
```

```
    // verify outcome
    try{
        assertEquals( FlightState.CANCELLED,
                        proposedFlight.getStatus());
    } finally {
        // teardown
        proposedFlight.delete();
        proposedFlight = null;
    }
}
```

Because these objects are not persistent, the code to delete the proposedFlight is unnecessary and just makes the test more complicated and harder to understand.

Refactoring Notes

To convert to *Garbage-Collected Teardown,* we need only remove the unnecessary cleanup code. If we had been using a class variable to hold the reference to the object, we would have had to convert it to either an instance variable or a local variable, both of which would have moved us from a *Shared Fixture* to a *Fresh Fixture.*

Garbage-Collected Teardown

Example: Garbage-Collected Teardown

In this reworked test, we let *Garbage-Collected Teardown* do the job for us.

```
public void testCancel_proposed_GCT() {
    // fixture setup
    Flight proposedFlight = createAnonymousProposedFlight();
    // exercise SUT
    proposedFlight.cancel();
    // verify outcome
    assertEquals( FlightState.CANCELLED,
                    proposedFlight.getStatus());
    // teardown
    //   Garbage collected when proposedFlight goes out of scope
}
```

Note how much simpler the test has become!

Automated Teardown

How do we tear down the Test Fixture?

We keep track of all resources that are created in a test and automatically destroy/free them during teardown.

Also known as:
Test Object Registry

Automated Teardown

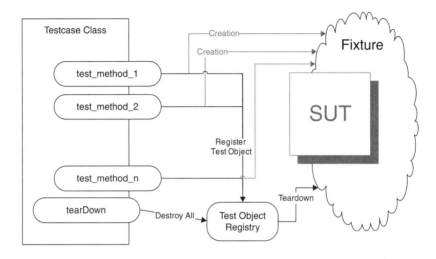

A large part of making tests repeatable and robust is ensuring that the test fixture is torn down after each test and a new one created for the next test run. This strategy is known as a *Fresh Fixture* (page 311). Leftover objects and database records, as well as open files and connections, can at best cause performance degradations and at worst cause tests to fail or systems to crash. While some of these resources may be cleaned up automatically by garbage collection, others may be left hanging if they are not torn down explicitly.

Writing teardown code that can be relied upon to clean up properly in all possible circumstances is challenging and time-consuming. It involves understanding what could be left over for each possible outcome of the test and writing code to deal with that scenario. This *Complex Teardown* (see *Obscure Test* on page 186) introduces a fair bit of *Conditional Test Logic* (page 200) and—worst of all—*Untestable Test Code* (see *Hard-to-Test Code* on page 209).

A better solution is to let the test infrastructure track the objects created and clean them up auto-magically when the test is complete.

How It Works

The core of the solution is a mechanism to register each persistent item (i.e., object, record, connection, and so on) we create in the test. We maintain a list (or lists) of registered objects that need some action to be taken to destroy them. This can be as simple as tossing each object into a collection. At the end of the test, we traverse the collection and destroy each object. We will want to catch any errors that we encounter so that one object's cleanup error will not cause the rest of the cleanup to be aborted.

When to Use It

We can use *Automated Teardown* whenever we have persistent resources that need to be cleaned up to keep the test environment functioning. (This happens more often in customer tests than in unit tests.) This pattern addresses both *Unrepeatable Tests* (see *Erratic Test* on page 228) and *Interacting Tests* (see *Erratic Test*) by keeping the objects created in one test from lingering into the execution of a subsequent test.

Automated Teardown isn't very difficult to build, and it will save us a large amount of grief and effort. Once we have built it for one project, we should be able to reuse the teardown logic on subsequent projects for very little effort.

Implementation Notes

Automated Teardown comes in two flavors. The basic flavor tears down only objects that were created as part of fixture setup. The more advanced version also destroys any objects that were created by the SUT while it was being exercised.

Variation: Automated Fixture Teardown

The simplest solution is to register the objects we create in our *Creation Methods* (page 415). Although this pattern will not tear down the objects created by the SUT, by dealing with our fixture it reduces the effort and likelihood of errors significantly.

There are two key challenges with this variation:

- Finding a generic way to clean up the registered objects

- Ensuring that our *Automated Teardown* code is run for each registered object

Given that the latter challenge is the easier problem, let us deal with it first. When we are tearing down a *Persistent Fresh Fixture* (see *Fresh Fixture*), the

Automated
Teardown

simplest solution is to put the call to the *Automated Teardown* mechanism into the tearDown method on our *Testcase Class* (page 373). This method is called regardless of whether the test passes or fails as long as the setUp method succeeds. When we are tearing down a *Shared Fixture* (page 317), we want the tearDown method to run only after all the *Test Methods* (page 348) have been run. In this case, we can use either *Suite Fixture Setup* (page 441), if our member of the xUnit family supports it, or a *Setup Decorator* (page 447).

Now let's go back to the harder problem: the generic mechanism for cleaning up the resources. We have at least two options here. First, we can ensure that all persistent (non-garbage-collected) objects implement a generic cleanup mechanism that we can call from within the *Automated Teardown* mechanism. Alternatively, we can wrap each object in another object that knows how to clean up the object in question. The latter strategy is an example of the Command [GOF] pattern.

If we build our *Automated Teardown* mechanism in a completely generic way, we can include it in the *Testcase Superclass* (page 638) on which we can base all our *Testcase Classes*. Otherwise, we may need to put it onto a *Test Helper* (page 643) that is visible from all *Testcase Classes* that need it. A *Test Helper* that both creates fixture objects and tears them down automatically is sometimes called an *Object Mother* (see *Test Helper*).

Being a nontrivial (and very critical) piece of code, the *Automated Teardown* mechanism deserves its own unit tests. Because it is now outside the *Test Method*, we can write *Self-Checking Tests* (see page 26) for it! If we want to be really careful (some might say paranoid), we can use *Delta Assertions* (page 485) to verify that any objects that persist after the teardown operation really existed before the test was performed.

Variation: Automated Exercise Teardown

We can make the tests even more "self-cleaning" by also cleaning up the objects created by the SUT. This effort involves designing the SUT using an observable *Object Factory* (see *Dependency Lookup* on page 686) so that we can automatically register any objects created by the SUT while it is being exercised. During the teardown phase we can delete these objects, too.

Motivating Example

In this example, we create several objects using *Creation Methods* and need to tear them down when the test in complete. To do so, we introduce a try/finally block to ensure that our *In-line Teardown* (page 509) code executes even when the assertions fail.

```
public void testGetFlightsByOrigin_NoInboundFlight_SMRTD()
        throws Exception {
  // Fixture Setup
  BigDecimal outboundAirport = createTestAirport("1OF");
  BigDecimal inboundAirport = null;
  FlightDto expFlightDto = null;
  try {
     inboundAirport = createTestAirport("1IF");
     expFlightDto = createTestFlight(outboundAirport, inboundAirport);
     // Exercise System
     List flightsAtDestination1 =
           facade.getFlightsByOriginAirport(inboundAirport);
     // Verify Outcome
     assertEquals(0,flightsAtDestination1.size());
  } finally {
     try {
        facade.removeFlight(expFlightDto.getFlightNumber());
     } finally {
        try {
           facade.removeAirport(inboundAirport);
        } finally {
           facade.removeAirport(outboundAirport);
        }
     }
  }
}
```

Automated Teardown

Note that we must use nested try/finally constructs within the finally block to ensure that any errors in the teardown don't keep us from finishing the job.

Refactoring Notes

Introducing *Automated Teardown* involves two steps. First, we add the *Automated Teardown* mechanism to our *Testcase Class*. Second, we remove any *In-line Teardown* code from our tests.

Automated Teardown can be implemented on a specific *Testcase Class* or it can be inherited (or mixed in) via a generic class. Either way, we need to make sure we register all of our newly created objects so that the mechanism knows to delete them when the test is finished. This is most easily done inside *Creation Methods* that already exist. Alternatively, we can use an Extract Method [Fowler] refactoring to move the direct constructor calls into newly created *Creation Methods* and add the registration.

The generic *Automated Teardown* mechanism should be invoked from the tearDown method. Although this can be done on our own *Testcase Class,* it is almost always better to put this method on a *Testcase Superclass* that all our *Testcase Classes* inherit from. If we don't already have a *Testcase Superclass,* we can easily create one by doing an Extract Class [Fowler] refactoring and then doing a Pull Up Method [Fowler] refactoring on any methods (and fields) associated with the *Automated Teardown* mechanism.

Example: Automated Teardown

There is not much to see in this refactored test because all of the teardown code has been removed.

```
public void testGetFlightsByOriginAirport_OneOutboundFlight()
throws Exception {
   // Fixture Setup
   BigDecimal outboundAirport = createTestAirport("1OF");
   BigDecimal inboundAirport = createTestAirport("1IF");
   FlightDto expectedFlightDto =
         createTestFlight( outboundAirport, inboundAirport);
   // Exercise System
   List flightsAtOrigin =
         facade.getFlightsByOriginAirport(outboundAirport);
   // Verify Outcome
   assertOnly1FlightInDtoList( "Flights at origin",
                              expectedFlightDto,
                              flightsAtOrigin);
}
```

Here is where all the work gets done! The *Creation Method* has been modified to register the object it just created.

```
private List allAirportIds;
private List allFlights;

protected void setUp() throws Exception {
   allAirportIds = new ArrayList();
   allFlights = new ArrayList();
}

private BigDecimal createTestAirport(String airportName)
throws FlightBookingException {
   BigDecimal newAirportId = facade.createAirport(
                  airportName, " Airport" + airportName,
                  "City" + airportName);
   allAirportIds.add(newAirportId);
   return newAirportId;
}
```

Next comes the actual *Automated Teardown* logic. In this example, it lives on our *Testcase Class* and is called from the tearDown method. To keep this example very simple, this logic has been written specifically to handle airports and flights. More typically, it would live in the *Testcase Superclass*, where it could be used by all *Testcase Classes*, and would use a generic object destruction mechanism so that it would not have to care what types of objects it was deleting.

```
protected void tearDown() throws Exception {
    removeObjects(allAirportIds, "Airport");
    removeObjects(allFlights, "Flight");
}

public void removeObjects(List objectsToDelete, String type) {
    Iterator i = objectsToDelete.iterator();
    while (i.hasNext()) {
        try {
            BigDecimal id = (BigDecimal) i.next();
            if ("Airport"==type) {
                facade.removeAirport(id);
            } else {
                facade.removeFlight(id);
            }
        } catch (Exception e) {
            // do nothing if the remove failed
        }
    }
}
```

**Automated
Teardown**

If we were tearing down a *Shared Fixture*, we would annotate our tearDown method with the suitable annotation or attribute (e.g., @afterClass or [TestFixtureTearDown]) or move it to a *Setup Decorator*.

Example: Automated Exercise Teardown

If we wanted to take the next step and automatically tear down any objects created within the SUT, we could modify the SUT to use an observable *Object Factory*. In our test, we would add the following code:

```
ResourceTracker tracker;

public void setUp() {
    tracker = new ResourceTracker();
    ObjectFactory.addObserver(tracker);
}

public void tearDown() {
    tracker.cleanup();
    ObjectFactory.removeObserver(tracker);
}
```

This last example assumes that the *Automated Teardown* logic has been moved into the cleanup method on the ResourceTracker.

In-line Teardown

How do we tear down the Test Fixture?

We include teardown logic at the end of the Test Method immediately after the result verification.

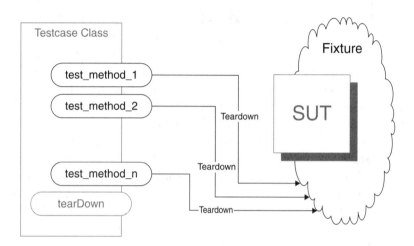

A large part of making tests repeatable and robust is ensuring that the test fixture is torn down after each test and a new one created for the next test run. This strategy is known as a *Fresh Fixture* (page 311). Leftover objects and database records, as well as open files and connections, can at best cause performance degradations and at worst cause tests to fail or systems to crash. While some of these resources may be cleaned up automatically by garbage collection, others may be left hanging if they are not torn down explicitly.

At a minimum, we should write *In-line Teardown* code that cleans up resources left over after our test.

How It Works

As we write a test, we mentally keep track of all objects the test creates that will not be cleaned up automatically. After writing the code to exercise the SUT and verify the outcome, we add logic to the end of the *Test Method* (page 348) to destroy any objects that will not be cleaned up automatically by the garbage collector. We use the relevant language feature to ensure that the teardown code is run regardless of the outcome of the test.

When to Use It

We should use some form of teardown logic whenever we have resources that will not be freed automatically after the *Test Method* is run; we can use *In-line Teardown* when each test has different objects to clean up. We may discover that objects need to be cleaned up because we have *Unrepeatable Tests* (see *Erratic Test* on page 228) or *Slow Tests* (page 253) caused by the accumulation of detritus from many test runs.

Unlike fixture setup, the teardown logic is not important from the perspective of *Tests as Documentation* (see page 23). Use of any form of teardown logic may potentially contribute to *High Test Maintenance Cost* (page 265) and should be avoided if at all possible. Thus the only real benefit of including the teardown logic on an in-line basis is that it may make it easier to maintain the teardown logic—a pretty slim benefit, indeed. It is almost always better to strive for *Automated Teardown* (page 503) or to use *Implicit Teardown* (page 516) if we are using *Testcase Class per Fixture* (page 631), where all tests in a *Testcase Class* (page 373) have the same test fixture.

In-line Teardown

We can also use *In-line Teardown* as a steppingstone to *Implicit Teardown*, thereby following the principle of "the simplest thing that could possibly work." First, we learn how to do *In-line Teardown* for each *Test Method*; next, we extract the common logic from those tests into the tearDown method. We should *not* use *In-line Teardown* if the objects created by the test are subject to automated memory management. In such a case, we should use *Garbage-Collected Teardown* (page 500) instead because it is much less error-prone and keeps the tests easier to understand and maintain.

Implementation Notes

The primary consideration in *In-line Teardown* is ensuring that the teardown code actually runs even when the test is failed by an *Assertion Method* (page 362) or ends in an error in either the SUT or the *Test Method*. A secondary consideration is ensuring that the teardown code does not introduce additional errors.

The key to doing *In-line Teardown* correctly is to use language-level constructs to ensure that the teardown code is run. Most modern languages include some sort of error/exception-handling construct that will attempt the execution of a block of code with the guarantee that a second block of code will be run regardless of how the first block terminates. In Java, this construct takes the form of a try block with an associated finally block.

Variation: Teardown Guard Clause

To protect against a failure caused by trying to tear down a resource that doesn't exist, we can put a "guard clause" around the logic. Its inclusion reduces the likelihood of a test error caused by the teardown logic.

Variation: Delegated Teardown

We can move much of the teardown logic out of the *Test Method* by calling a *Test Utility Method* (page 599). Although this strategy reduces the amount of teardown logic cluttering the test, we still need to place an error-handling construct around at least the assertions and the exercising of the SUT to ensure that it gets called. Using *Implicit Teardown* is almost always a better solution.

Variation: Naive In-line Teardown

Naive In-line Teardown is what we have when we forget to put the equivalent of a try/finally block around our test logic to ensure that our teardown logic always executes. It leads to *Resource Leakage* (see *Erratic Test*), which in turn may lead to *Erratic Tests*.

In-line
Teardown

Motivating Example

The following test creates a persistent object (airport) as part of the fixture. Because the object is stored in a database, it is not subject to *Garbage-Collected Teardown* and must be explicitly destroyed. If we do not include teardown logic in the test, each time the test is run it will create another object in the database. This may lead to *Unrepeatable Tests* unless the test uses *Distinct Generated Values* (see *Generated Value* on page 723) to ensure that the created objects do not violate any unique key constraints.

```
public void testGetFlightsByOriginAirport_NoFlights_ntd()
        throws Exception {
    // Fixture Setup
    BigDecimal outboundAirport = createTestAirport("1OF");
    // Exercise System
    List flightsAtDestination1 =
        facade.getFlightsByOriginAirport(outboundAirport);
    // Verify Outcome
    assertEquals(0,flightsAtDestination1.size());
}
```

Example: Naive In-line Teardown

In this naive solution to this problem, we added a line after the assertion to destroy the airport created in the fixture setup.

```
public void testGetFlightsByOriginAirport_NoFlights()
        throws Exception {
   // Fixture Setup
   BigDecimal outboundAirport = createTestAirport("1OF");
   // Exercise System
   List flightsAtDestination1 =
         facade.getFlightsByOriginAirport(outboundAirport);
   // Verify Outcome
   assertEquals(0,flightsAtDestination1.size());
   facade.removeAirport(outboundAirport);
}
```

Unfortunately, this solution isn't really adequate because the teardown logic won't be exercised if the SUT encounters an error or if the assertions fail. We could try moving the fixture cleanup before the assertions but this still wouldn't address the issue with errors occurring inside the SUT. Clearly, we need a more general solution.

Refactoring Notes

We need either to place an error-handling construct around the exercising of the SUT and the assertions or to move the teardown code into the tearDown method. Either way, we need to ensure that *all* the teardown code runs, even if some parts of it fail. This usually involves the judicious use of try/finally control structures around each step of the teardown process.

Example: In-line Teardown

In this Java example, we have introduced a try/finally block around the exercise SUT and result verification phases of the test to ensure that our teardown code is run.

```
public void testGetFlightsByOriginAirport_NoFlights_td()
        throws Exception {
   // Fixture Setup
   BigDecimal outboundAirport = createTestAirport("1OF");
   try {
      // Exercise System
      List flightsAtDestination1 =
            facade.getFlightsByOriginAirport(outboundAirport);
      // Verify Outcome
      assertEquals(0,flightsAtDestination1.size());
```

```
    } finally {
        facade.removeAirport(outboundAirport);
    }
}
```

Now the exercising of the SUT and the assertions both appear in the try block
and the teardown logic is found in the `finally` block. This separation is crucial to
making *In-line Teardown* work properly. We should *not* include a catch block
unless we are writing an *Expected Exception Test* (see *Test Method*).

Example: Teardown Guard Clause

Here, we've added a *Teardown Guard Clause* to the teardown code to ensure it
isn't run if the airport doesn't exist:

```
public void testGetFlightsByOriginAirport_NoFlights_TDGC()
        throws Exception {
    // Fixture Setup
    BigDecimal outboundAirport = createTestAirport("1OF");
    try {
        // Exercise System
        List flightsAtDestination1 =
            facade.getFlightsByOriginAirport(outboundAirport);
        // Verify Outcome
        assertEquals(0,flightsAtDestination1.size());
    } finally {
        if (outboundAirport!=null) {
            facade.removeAirport(outboundAirport);
        }
    }
}
```

**In-line
Teardown**

Example: Multiresource In-line Teardown (Java)

If multiple resources need to be cleaned up in the same test, we must ensure that
all the teardown code runs even if some of the teardown statements contain
errors. This goal can be accomplished by nesting each subsequent teardown step
inside another block of guaranteed code, as in this Java example:

```
public void testGetFlightsByOrigin_NoInboundFlight_SMRTD()
        throws Exception {
    // Fixture Setup
    BigDecimal outboundAirport = createTestAirport("1OF");
    BigDecimal inboundAirport = null;
    FlightDto expFlightDto = null;
    try {
        inboundAirport = createTestAirport("1IF");
        expFlightDto = createTestFlight(outboundAirport, inboundAirport);
```

```
    // Exercise System
    List flightsAtDestination1 =
            facade.getFlightsByOriginAirport(inboundAirport);
    // Verify Outcome
    assertEquals(0,flightsAtDestination1.size());
} finally {
    try {
        facade.removeFlight(expFlightDto.getFlightNumber());
    } finally {
        try {
            facade.removeAirport(inboundAirport);
        } finally {
            facade.removeAirport(outboundAirport);
        }
    }
}
}
```

In-line Teardown

This scheme gets very messy in a hurry if we must clean up more than a few resources. In such a situation, it makes more sense to organize the resources into an array or list and then to iterate over that array or list. At that point we are halfway to implementing *Automated Teardown*.

Example: Delegated Teardown

We can also delegate the teardown from within the *Test Method* if we don't believe we can come up with a completely generic way cleanup strategy that will work for all tests.

```
public void testGetFlightsByOrigin_NoInboundFlight_DTD()
        throws Exception {
    // Fixture Setup
    BigDecimal outboundAirport = createTestAirport("1OF");
    BigDecimal inboundAirport = null;
    FlightDto expectedFlightDto = null;
    try {
        inboundAirport = createTestAirport("1IF");
        expectedFlightDto =
            createTestFlight( outboundAirport, inboundAirport);
        // Exercise System
        List flightsAtDestination1 =
            facade.getFlightsByOriginAirport(inboundAirport);
        // Verify Outcome
        assertEquals(0,flightsAtDestination1.size());
    } finally {
        teardownFlightAndAirports( outboundAirport,
                                   inboundAirport,
                                   expectedFlightDto);
    }
}
```

```
      private void teardownFlightAndAirports(
                                    BigDecimal firstAirport,
                                    BigDecimal secondAirport,
                                    FlightDto flightDto)
            throws FlightBookingException {
    try {
      facade.removeFlight( flightDto.getFlightNumber() );
    } finally {
      try {
          facade.removeAirport(secondAirport);
      } finally {
          facade.removeAirport(firstAirport);
      }
    }
  }
```

The optimizers among us will notice that the two flight numbers are actually available as attributes of the flightDto. The paranoid will counter that because the teardownFlightAndAirports method could be called before the flightDto is constructed, we cannot count on using it to access the Airports. Hence we must pass the Airports in individually. The need to think this way is why a generic *Automated Teardown* is so attractive; it avoids having to think at all!

In-line Teardown

Implicit Teardown

How do we tear down the Test Fixture?

The Test Automation Framework calls our cleanup logic in the tearDown method after every Test Method.

Also known as:
Hooked Teardown, Framework-Invoked Teardown, Teardown Method

Implicit Teardown

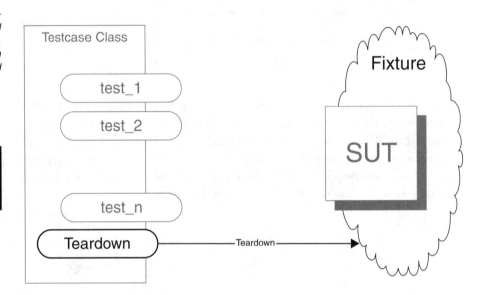

A large part of making tests repeatable and robust is ensuring that the test fixture is torn down after each test and a new one created for the next test run. This strategy is known as a *Fresh Fixture* (page 311). Leftover objects and database records, as well as open files and connections, can at best cause performance degradation and at worst cause tests to fail or systems to crash.

When we can't take advantage of *Garbage-Collected Teardown* (page 500) and we have several tests with the same objects to tear down, we can put the teardown logic into a special tearDown method that the *Test Automation Framework* (page 298) calls after each *Test Method* (page 348) is run.

How It Works

Anything that needs to be cleaned up can be freed or destroyed in the final phase of the *Four-Phase Test* (page 358)—namely, the fixture teardown phase. Most members of the xUnit family of *Test Automation Frameworks* support the concept of *Implicit Teardown*, wherein they call the tearDown method of each *Testcase Object* (page 382) after the *Test Method* has been run.

The tearDown method is called regardless of whether the test passes or fails. This scheme ensures that we have the opportunity to clean up, undisturbed by any failed assertions. Be aware, however, that many members of the xUnit family do not call tearDown if the setUp method raises an error.

When to Use It

We can use *Implicit Teardown* whenever several tests with the same resources need to be destroyed or freed explicitly after the test has been completed and those resources will not be destroyed or freed automatically. We may discover this requirement because we have *Unrepeatable Tests* (see *Erratic Test* on page 228) or *Slow Tests* (page 253) caused by the accumulation of detritus from many test runs.

If the objects created by the test are internal resources and subject to automated memory management, then *Garbage-Collected Teardown* may eliminate a lot of work for us. If each test has a completely different set of objects to tear down, then *In-line Teardown* (page 509) may be more appropriate. In many cases, we can completely avoid manually written teardown logic by using *Automated Teardown* (page 503).

Implementation Notes

The teardown logic in the tearDown method is most often created by refactoring from tests that had *In-line Teardown*. The tearDown method may need to be "flexible" or "accommodating" for several reasons:

- When a test fails or when a test error occurs, the *Test Method* may not have created all the fixture objects.

- If all the *Test Methods* in the *Testcase Class* (page 373) don't use identical fixtures,[1] there may be different sets of objects to clean up for different tests.

Variation: Teardown Guard Clause

We can avoid arbitrarily *Conditional Test Logic* (page 200) if we deal with the case where only a subset of the objects to be torn down are actually present by putting a guard clause (a simple if statement) around each teardown operation

---

[1] That is, they augment the *Implicit Teardown* with some additional *In-line Setup* (page 408) or *Delegated Setup* (page 411).

to guard against the resource not being present. With this technique, a suitably coded tearDown method can tear down various fixture configurations. Contrast this with the setUp method, which can set up only the lowest common denominator fixture for the *Test Methods* that share it.

Motivating Example

The following test creates several standard objects during fixture setup. Because the objects are persisted in a database, they must be cleaned up explicitly after every test. Each test (only one of several is shown here) contains the same in-line teardown logic to delete the objects.

```
public void testGetFlightsByOrigin_NoInboundFlight_SMRTD()
        throws Exception {
  // Fixture Setup
  BigDecimal outboundAirport = createTestAirport("1OF");
  BigDecimal inboundAirport = null;
  FlightDto expFlightDto = null;
  try {
     inboundAirport = createTestAirport("1IF");
     expFlightDto = createTestFlight(outboundAirport, inboundAirport);
     // Exercise System
     List flightsAtDestination1 =
           facade.getFlightsByOriginAirport(inboundAirport);
     // Verify Outcome
     assertEquals(0,flightsAtDestination1.size());
  } finally {
     try {
        facade.removeFlight(expFlightDto.getFlightNumber());
     } finally {
        try {
           facade.removeAirport(inboundAirport);
        } finally  {
           facade.removeAirport(outboundAirport);
        }
     }
  }
}
```

There is enough *Test Code Duplication* (page 213) here to warrant converting these tests to *Implicit Teardown*.

Refactoring Notes

First, we find the most representative example of teardown in all the tests. Next, we do an Extract Method [Fowler] refactoring on that code and call the resulting method tearDown. Finally, we delete the teardown logic in each of the other tests.

We may need to introduce *Teardown Guard Clauses* around any teardown logic that may not be needed in every test. We should also surround each teardown attempt with a try/finally block to ensure that the remaining teardown logic executes even if an earlier attempt fails.

Example: Implicit Teardown

This example shows the same tests with the teardown logic removed to the tearDown method. Note how much smaller the tests have become.

```
BigDecimal outboundAirport;
BigDecimal inboundAirport;
FlightDto expFlightDto;

public void testGetFlightsByAirport_NoInboundFlights_NIT()
        throws Exception {
   // Fixture Setup
   outboundAirport = createTestAirport("1OF");
   inboundAirport = createTestAirport("1IF");
   expFlightDto = createTestFlight( outboundAirport, inboundAirport);
   // Exercise System
   List flightsAtDestination1 =
        facade.getFlightsByOriginAirport(inboundAirport);
   // Verify Outcome
   assertEquals(0,flightsAtDestination1.size());
}

protected void tearDown() throws Exception {
   try {
      facade.removeFlight( expFlightDto.getFlightNumber() );
   } finally {
      try {
         facade.removeAirport(inboundAirport);
      } finally {
         facade.removeAirport(outboundAirport);
      }
   }
}
```

Implicit
Teardown

Note that there is no try/finally block around the exercising of the SUT and the assertions. This structure helps the test reader understand that this is not an *Expected Exception Test* (see *Test Method*). Also, we didn't need to put a Guard Clause [SBPP] in front of each operation because the try/finally block ensures that a failure is noncatastrophic; thus there is no real harm in trying to perform the operation. We did have to convert our fixture holding local variables into instance variables to allow the tearDown method to access the fixture.

Chapter 23

Test Double Patterns

Patterns in This Chapter

Test Double
Patterns

521

Test Double

How can we verify logic independently when code it depends on is unusable?
How can we avoid Slow Tests?

We replace a component on which the SUT depends with a "test-specific equivalent."

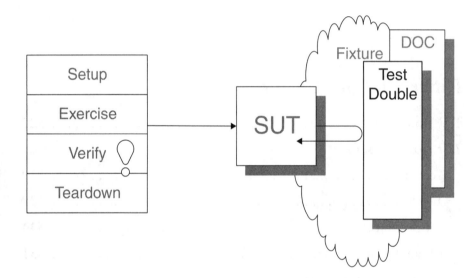

Test Double

Sometimes it is just plain hard to test the SUT because it depends on other components that cannot be used in the test environment. Such a situation may arise because those components aren't available, because they will not return the results needed for the test, or because executing them would have undesirable side effects. In other cases, our test strategy requires us to have more control over or visibility of the internal behavior of the SUT.

When we are writing a test in which we cannot (or choose not to) use a real depended-on component (DOC), we can replace it with a *Test Double*. The *Test Double* doesn't have to behave exactly like the real DOC; it merely has to provide the same API as the real DOC so that the SUT *thinks* it is the real one!

How It Works

When the producers of a movie want to film something that is potentially risky or dangerous for the leading actor to carry out, they hire a "stunt double" to take the place of the actor in the scene. The stunt double is a highly trained individual who is capable of meeting the specific requirements of the scene. The stunt double may not be able to act, but he or she knows how to fall from great heights, crash a car, or do whatever the scene calls for. How closely the stunt double needs to resemble the actor depends on the nature of the scene. Usually, things can be arranged such that someone who vaguely resembles the actor in stature can take the actor's place.

For testing purposes, we can replace the real DOC (not the SUT!) with *our* equivalent of the "stunt double": the *Test Double*. During the fixture setup phase of our *Four-Phase Test* (page 358), we replace the real DOC with our *Test Double*. Depending on the kind of test we are executing, we may hard-code the behavior of the *Test Double* or we may configure it during the setup phase. When the SUT interacts with the *Test Double*, it won't be aware that it isn't talking to the real McCoy, but we will have achieved our goal of making impossible tests possible.

Regardless of which variation of *Test Double* we choose to use, we must keep in mind that we don't need to implement the entire interface of the DOC. Instead, we provide only the functionality needed for our particular test. We can even build different *Test Doubles* for different tests that involve the same DOC.

Test Double

When to Use It

We might want to use some sort of *Test Double* during our tests in the following circumstances:

- If we have an *Untested Requirement* (see *Production Bugs* on page 268) because neither the SUT nor its DOCs provide an observation point for the SUT's indirect output that we need to verify using *Behavior Verification* (page 468)

- If we have *Untested Code* (see *Production Bugs*) and a DOC does not provide the control point to allow us to exercise the SUT with the necessary indirect inputs

- If we have *Slow Tests* (page 253) and we want to be able to run our tests more quickly and hence more often

Each of these scenarios can be addressed in some way by using a *Test Double*. Of course, we have to be careful when using *Test Doubles* because we are testing the SUT in a different configuration from the one that will be used in production. For this reason, we really should have at least one test that verifies the SUT works without a *Test Double*. We need to be careful that we don't replace the parts of the SUT that we are trying to verify because that practice can result in tests that test the wrong software! Also, excessive use of *Test Doubles* can result in *Fragile Tests* (page 239) as a result of *Overspecified Software*.

Test Doubles come in several major flavors, as summarized in Figure 23.1. The implementation variations of these patterns are described in more detail in the corresponding pattern write-ups.

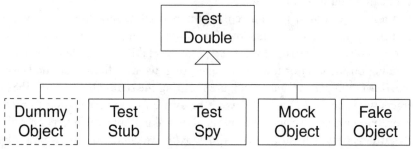

Test Double

Figure 23.1 *Types of Test Doubles. Dummy Objects are really an alternative to the value patterns. Test Stubs are used to verify indirect inputs; Test Spies and Mock Objects are used to verify indirect outputs. Fake objects provide an alternative implementation.*

These variations are classified based on how/why we *use* the *Test Double*. We will deal with variations around how we *build* the *Test Doubles* in the "Implementation" section.

Variation: Test Stub

We use a *Test Stub* (page 529) to replace a real component on which the SUT depends so that the test has a control point for the indirect inputs of the SUT. Its inclusion allows the test to force the SUT down paths it might not otherwise execute. We can further classify *Test Stubs* by the kind of indirect inputs they are used to inject into the SUT. A *Responder* (see *Test Stub*) injects valid values, while a *Saboteur* (see *Test Stub*) injects errors or exceptions.

Some people use the term "test stub" to mean a temporary implementation that is used only until the real object or procedure becomes available. I prefer to call this usage a *Temporary Test Stub* (see *Test Stub*) to avoid confusion.

Variation: Test Spy

We can use a more capable version of a *Test Stub*, the *Test Spy* (page 538), as an observation point for the indirect outputs of the SUT. Like a *Test Stub*, a *Test Spy* may need to provide values to the SUT in response to method calls. The *Test Spy*, however, also captures the indirect outputs of the SUT as it is exercised and saves them for *later* verification by the test. Thus, in many ways, the *Test Spy* is "just a" *Test Stub* with some recording capability. While a *Test Spy* is used for the same fundamental purpose as a *Mock Object* (page 544), the style of test we write using a *Test Spy* looks much more like a test written with a *Test Stub*.

Variation: Mock Object

We can use a *Mock Object* as an observation point to verify the indirect outputs of the SUT *as* it is exercised. Typically, the *Mock Object* also includes the functionality of a *Test Stub* in that it must return values to the SUT if it hasn't already failed the tests but the em*pha*sis[1] is on the verification of the indirect outputs. Therefore, a *Mock Object* is a lot more than just a *Test Stub* plus assertions: It is used in a fundamentally different way.

Variation: Fake Object

We use a *Fake Object* (page 551) to replace the functionality of a real DOC in a test for reasons other than verification of indirect inputs and outputs of the SUT. Typically, a *Fake Object* implements the same functionality as the real DOC but in a much simpler way. While a *Fake Object* is typically built specifically for testing, the test does not use it as either a control point or an observation point.

The most common reason for using a *Fake Object* is that the real DOC is not available yet, is too slow, or cannot be used in the test environment because of deleterious side effects. The sidebar "Faster Tests Without Shared Fixtures" (page 319) describes how we encapsulated all database access behind a persistence layer interface and then replaced the database with in-memory hash tables and made our tests run 50 times faster. Chapter 6, *Test Automation Strategy*, and Chapter 11, *Using Test Doubles*, provide an overview of the various techniques available for making our SUT easier to test.

Test
Double

---

[1] My mother grew up in Hungary and has retained a part of her Hungarian accent—think Zsa Zsa Gabor—all her life. She says, "It is important to put the em*pha*sis on the right syl*la*ble."

Variation: Dummy Object

Some method signatures of the SUT may require objects as parameters. If neither the test nor the SUT cares about these objects, we may choose to pass in a *Dummy Object* (page 728), which may be as simple as a null object reference, an instance of the Object class, or an instance of a *Pseudo-Object* (see *Hard-Coded Test Double* on page 568). In this sense, a *Dummy Object* isn't really a *Test Double* per se but rather an alternative to the value patterns *Literal Value* (page 714), *Derived Value* (page 718), and *Generated Value* (page 723).

Variation: Procedural Test Stub

A *Test Double* implemented in a procedural programming language is often called a "test stub," but I prefer to call it a *Procedural Test Stub* (see *Test Stub*) to distinguish this usage from the modern *Test Stub* variation of *Test Doubles*. Typically, we use a *Procedural Test Stub* to allow testing/debugging to proceed while waiting for other code to become available. It is rare for these objects to be "swapped in" at runtime but sometimes we make the code conditional on a "Debugging" flag—a form of *Test Logic in Production* (page 217).

Test Double

Implementation Notes

Several considerations must be taken into account when we are building the *Test Double* (Figure 23.2):

- Whether the *Test Double* should be specific to a single test or reusable across many tests
- Whether the *Test Double* should exist in code or be generated on-the-fly
- How we tell the SUT to use the *Test Double* (installation)

The first and last points are addressed here. The discussion of *Test Double* generation is left to the section on *Configurable Test Doubles*.

Because the techniques for building *Test Doubles* are pretty much independent of their behavior (e.g., they apply to both *Test Stubs* and *Mock Objects*), I've chosen to split out the descriptions of the various ways we can build *Hard-Coded Test Doubles* and *Configurable Test Doubles* (page 558) into separate patterns.

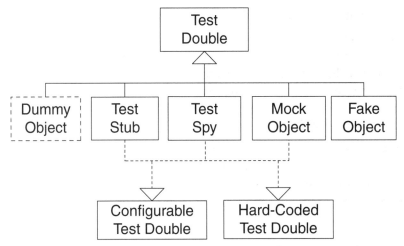

Figure 23.2 *Types of Test Doubles with implementation choices. Only Test Stubs, Test Spies, and Mock Objects need to be hard-coded or configured by the test. Dummy Objects have no implementation; Fake Objects are installed but not controlled by the test.*

Variation: Unconfigurable Test Doubles

Neither *Dummy Objects* nor *Fake Objects* need to be configured, each for their own reason. Dummies should never be used by the receiver so they need no "real" implementation. *Fake Objects*, by contrast, need a "real" implementation but one that is much simpler or "lighter" than the object that they replace. Therefore, neither the test nor the test automater will need to configure "canned" responses or expectations; we just install the *Test Double* and let the SUT use it as if it were real.

Variation: Hard-Coded Test Double

When we plan to use a specific *Test Double* in only a single test, it is often simplest to just hard-code the *Test Double* to return specific values (for *Test Stubs*) or expect specific method calls (*Mock Objects*). *Hard-Coded Test Doubles* are typically hand-built by the test automater. They come in several forms, including the *Self Shunt* (see *Hard-Coded Test Double*), where the *Testcase Class* (page 373) acts as the *Test Double*; the *Anonymous Inner Test Double* (see *Hard-Coded Test Double*), where language features are used to create the *Test Double* inside the *Test Method* (page 348); and the *Test Double* implemented as separate *Test Double Class* (see *Hard-Coded Test Double*). Each of these options is discussed in more detail in *Hard-Coded Test Double*.

Variation: Configurable Test Double

When we want to use the same *Test Double* implementation in many tests, we will typically prefer to use a *Configurable Test Double*. Although the test automater can manually build these objects, many members of the xUnit family have reusable toolkits available for generating *Configurable Test Doubles*.

Installing the Test Double

Before we can exercise the SUT, we must tell it to use the *Test Double* instead of the object that the *Test Double* replaces. We can use any of the **substitutable dependency** patterns to install the *Test Double* during the fixture setup phase of our *Four-Phase Test*. *Configurable Test Doubles* need to be configured before we exercise the SUT, and we typically perform this configuration before we install them.

Example: Test Double

Test Double

Because there are a wide variety of reasons for using the variations of *Test Doubles*, it is difficult to provide a single example that characterizes the motivation behind each style. Please refer to the examples in each of the more detailed patterns referenced earlier.

Test Stub

How can we verify logic independently when it depends on indirect inputs from other software components?

We replace a real object with a test-specific object that feeds the desired indirect inputs into the system under test.

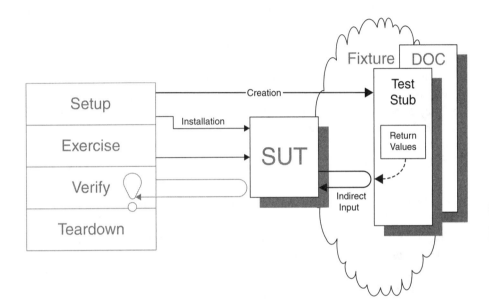

Test
Stub

In many circumstances, the environment or context in which the SUT operates very much influences the behavior of the SUT. To get adequate control over the indirect inputs of the SUT, we may have to replace some of the context with something we can control—namely, a *Test Stub*.

How It Works

First, we define a test-specific implementation of an interface on which the SUT depends. This implementation is configured to respond to calls from the SUT with the values (or exceptions) that will exercise the *Untested Code* (see *Production Bugs* on page 268) within the SUT. Before exercising the SUT, we install the *Test Stub* so that the SUT uses it *instead of* the real implementation. When called by the SUT during test execution, the *Test Stub* returns the previously defined values. The test can then verify the expected outcome in the normal way.

When to Use It

A key indication for using a *Test Stub* is having *Untested Code* caused by our inability to control the indirect inputs of the SUT. We can use a *Test Stub* as a control point that allows us to control the behavior of the SUT with various indirect inputs and we have no need to verify the indirect outputs. We can also use a *Test Stub* to inject values that allow us to get past a particular point in the software where the SUT calls software that is unavailable in our test environment.

If we do need an observation point that allows us to verify the indirect outputs of the SUT, we should consider using a *Mock Object* (page 544) or a *Test Spy* (page 538). Of course, we must have a way of installing a *Test Double* (page 522) into the SUT to be able to use any form of *Test Double*.

Variation: Responder

Test Stub

A *Test Stub* that is used to inject valid indirect inputs into the SUT so that it can go about its business is called a *Responder. Responders* are commonly used in "happy path" testing when the real component is uncontrollable, is not yet available, or is unusable in the development environment. The tests will invariably be *Simple Success Tests* (see *Test Method* on page 348).

Variation: Saboteur

A *Test Stub* that is used to inject invalid indirect inputs into the SUT is often called a *Saboteur* because its purpose is to derail whatever the SUT is trying to do so that we can see how the SUT copes under these circumstances. The "derailment" might be caused by returning unexpected values or objects, or it might result from raising an exception or causing a runtime error. Each test may be either a *Simple Success Test* or an *Expected Exception Test* (see *Test Method*), depending on how the SUT is expected to behave in response to the indirect input.

Variation: Temporary Test Stub

A *Temporary Test Stub* stands in for a DOC that is not yet available. This kind of *Test Stub* typically consists of an empty shell of a real class with hard-coded return statements. As soon as the real DOC is available, it replaces the *Temporary Test Stub*. Test-driven development often requires us to create *Temporary*

Test Stubs as we write code from the outside in; these shells evolve into the real classes as we add code to them. In need-driven development, we tend to use *Mock Objects* because we want to verify that the SUT calls the right methods on the *Temporary Test Stub*; in addition, we typically continue using the *Mock Object* even after the real DOC becomes available.

Variation: Procedural Test Stub

A *Procedural Test Stub* is a *Test Stub* written in a procedural programming language. It is particularly challenging to create in procedural programming languages that do not support procedure variables (also known as **function pointers**). In most cases, we must put if testing then hooks into the production code (a form of *Test Logic in Production*; see page 217).

Variation: Entity Chain Snipping

Entity Chain Snipping (see *Test Stub* on page 529) is a special case of a *Responder* that is used to replace a complex network of objects with a single *Test Stub* that pretends to be the network of objects. Its inclusion can make fixture setup go much more quickly (especially when the objects would normally have to be persisted into a database) and can make the tests much easier to understand.

Implementation Notes

We must be careful when using *Test Stubs* because we are testing the SUT in a different configuration from the one that will be used in production. We really should have at least one test that verifies the SUT works without a *Test Stub*. A common mistake made by test automaters who are new to stubs is to replace a part of the SUT that they are trying to test. For this reason, it is important to be really clear about what is playing the role of SUT and what is playing the role of test fixture. Also, note that excessive use of *Test Stubs* can result in *Overspecified Software* (see *Fragile Test* on page 239).

   Test Stubs may be built in several different ways depending on our specific needs and the tools we have on hand.

Variation: Hard-Coded Test Stub

A *Hard-Coded Test Stub* has its responses hard-coded within its program logic. These *Test Stubs* tend to be purpose-built for a single test or a very small number of tests. See *Hard-Coded Test Double* (page 568) for more information.

Test
Stub

Variation: Configurable Test Stub

When we want to avoid building a different *Hard-Coded Test Stub* for each test, we can use a *Configurable Test Stub* (see *Configurable Test Double* on page 558). A test configures the *Configurable Test Stub* as part of its fixture setup phase. Many members of the xUnit family offer tools with which to generate *Configurable Test Doubles* (page 558), including *Configurable Test Stubs*.

Motivating Example

The following test verifies the basic functionality of a component that formats an HTML string containing the current time. Unfortunately, it depends on the real system clock so it rarely ever passes!

```
public void testDisplayCurrentTime_AtMidnight() {
   // fixture setup
   TimeDisplay sut = new TimeDisplay();
   // exercise SUT
   String result = sut.getCurrentTimeAsHtmlFragment();
   // verify direct output
   String expectedTimeString =
        "<span class=\"tinyBoldText\">Midnight</span>";
   assertEquals( expectedTimeString, result);
}
```

Test Stub

We could try to address this problem by making the test calculate the expected results based on the current system time as follows:

```
public void testDisplayCurrentTime_whenever() {
   // fixture setup
   TimeDisplay sut = new TimeDisplay();
   // exercise SUT
   String result = sut.getCurrentTimeAsHtmlFragment();
   // verify outcome
   Calendar time = new DefaultTimeProvider().getTime();
   StringBuffer expectedTime = new StringBuffer();
   expectedTime.append("<span class=\"tinyBoldText\">");

   if ((time.get(Calendar.HOUR_OF_DAY) == 0)
        && (time.get(Calendar.MINUTE) <= 1)) {
     expectedTime.append( "Midnight");
   } else if ((time.get(Calendar.HOUR_OF_DAY) == 12)
             && (time.get(Calendar.MINUTE) == 0)) { // noon
     expectedTime.append("N3oon");
   } else {
     SimpleDateFormat fr = new SimpleDateFormat("h:mm a");
     expectedTime.append(fr.format(time.getTime()));
   }
```

```
    expectedTime.append("</span>");

    assertEquals( expectedTime, result);
}
```

This *Flexible Test* (see *Conditional Test Logic* on page 200) introduces two problems. First, some test conditions are never exercised. (Do *you* want to come in to work to run the tests at midnight to prove the software works at midnight?) Second, the test needs to duplicate much of the logic in the SUT to calculate the expected results. How do we prove the logic is actually correct?

Refactoring Notes

We can achieve proper verification of the indirect inputs by getting control of the time. To do so, we use the Replace Dependency with Test Double (page 522) refactoring to replace the real system clock (represented here by TimeProvider) with a Virtual Clock [VCTP]. We then implement it as a *Test Stub* that is configured by the test with the time we want to use as the indirect input to the SUT.

Example: Responder (as Hand-Coded Test Stub)

The following test verifies one of the happy path test conditions using a *Responder* to get control over the indirect inputs of the SUT. Based on the time injected into the SUT, the expected result can be hard-coded safely.

```
public void testDisplayCurrentTime_AtMidnight()
        throws Exception {
  // Fixture setup
  //      Test Double configuration
  TimeProviderTestStub tpStub = new TimeProviderTestStub();
  tpStub.setHours(0);
  tpStub.setMinutes(0);
  //    Instantiate SUT
  TimeDisplay sut = new TimeDisplay();
  //      Test Double installation
  sut.setTimeProvider(tpStub);
  // Exercise SUT
  String result = sut.getCurrentTimeAsHtmlFragment();
  // Verify outcome
  String expectedTimeString =
        "<span class=\"tinyBoldText\">Midnight</span>";
  assertEquals("Midnight", expectedTimeString, result);
}
```

This test makes use of the following hand-coded configurable *Test Stub* implementation:

```
private Calendar myTime = new GregorianCalendar();
/**
 * The complete constructor for the TimeProviderTestStub
 * @param hours specifies the hours using a 24-hour clock
 *    (e.g., 10 = 10 AM, 12 = noon, 22 = 10 PM, 0 = midnight)
 * @param minutes specifies the minutes after the hour
 *    (e.g., 0 = exactly on the hour, 1 = 1 min after the hour)
 */
public TimeProviderTestStub(int hours, int minutes) {
   setTime(hours, minutes);
}

public void setTime(int hours, int minutes) {
   setHours(hours);
   setMinutes(minutes);
}

// Configuration interface
public void setHours(int hours) {
   // 0 is midnight; 12 is noon
   myTime.set(Calendar.HOUR_OF_DAY, hours);
}

public void setMinutes(int minutes) {
   myTime.set(Calendar.MINUTE, minutes);
}
// Interface used by SUT
public Calendar getTime() {
   // @return the last time that was set
   return myTime;
}
```

Test Stub

Example: Responder (Dynamically Generated)

Here's the same test coded using the JMock *Configurable Test Double* framework:

```
public void testDisplayCurrentTime_AtMidnight_JM()
      throws Exception {
   // Fixture setup
   TimeDisplay sut = new TimeDisplay();
   //  Test Double configuration
   Mock tpStub = mock(TimeProvider.class);
   Calendar midnight = makeTime(0,0);
   tpStub.stubs().method("getTime").
                   withNoArguments().
                   will(returnValue(midnight));
```

```
    // Test Double installation
    sut.setTimeProvider((TimeProvider) tpStub);
    // Exercise SUT
    String result = sut.getCurrentTimeAsHtmlFragment();
    // Verify outcome
    String expectedTimeString =
            "<span class=\"tinyBoldText\">Midnight</span>";
    assertEquals("Midnight", expectedTimeString, result);
}
```

There is no *Test Stub* implementation to examine for this test because the JMock framework implements the *Test Stub* using reflection. Thus we had to write a *Test Utility Method* (page 599) called makeTime that contains the logic to construct the Calendar object to be returned. In the hand-coded *Test Stub*, this logic appeared inside the getTime method.

Example: Saboteur (as Anonymous Inner Class)

The following test uses a *Saboteur* to inject invalid indirect inputs into the SUT so we can see how the SUT copes under these circumstances.

```
public void testDisplayCurrentTime_exception()
        throws Exception {
    // Fixture setup
    //    Define and instantiate Test Stub
    TimeProvider testStub = new TimeProvider()
        { // Anonymous inner Test Stub
          public Calendar getTime() throws TimeProviderEx {
              throw new TimeProviderEx("Sample");
          }
    };
    //    Instantiate SUT
    TimeDisplay sut = new TimeDisplay();
    sut.setTimeProvider(testStub);
    // Exercise SUT
    String result = sut.getCurrentTimeAsHtmlFragment();
    // Verify direct output
    String expectedTimeString =
            "<span class=\"error\">Invalid Time</span>";
    assertEquals("Exception", expectedTimeString, result);
}
```

Test Stub

In this case, we used an *Inner Test Double* (see *Hard-Coded Test Double*) to throw an exception that we expect the SUT to handle gracefully. One interesting thing about this test is that it uses the *Simple Success Test* method template rather than the *Expected Exception Test* template, even though we are injecting an exception as the indirect input. The rationale behind this choice is that we are expecting the SUT to catch the exception and change the string formatting; we are not expecting the SUT to throw an exception.

Example: Entity Chain Snipping

In this example, we are testing the Invoice but require a Customer to instantiate the Invoice. The Customer requires an Address, which in turn requires a City. Thus we find ourselves creating numerous additional objects just to set up the fixture. Suppose the behavior of the invoice depends on some attribute of the Customer that is calculated from the Address by calling the method get_zone on the Customer.

```
public void testInvoice_addLineItem_noECS() {
    final int QUANTITY = 1;
    Product product = new Product(getUniqueNumberAsString(),
                                  getUniqueNumber());
    State state = new State("West Dakota", "WD");
    City city = new City("Centreville", state);
    Address address = new Address("123 Blake St.", city, "12345");
    Customer customer= new Customer(getUniqueNumberAsString(),
                                    getUniqueNumberAsString(),
                                    address);
    Invoice inv = new Invoice(customer);
    // Exercise
    inv.addItemQuantity(product, QUANTITY);
    // Verify
    List lineItems = inv.getLineItems();
    assertEquals("number of items", lineItems.size(), 1);
    LineItem actual = (LineItem)lineItems.get(0);
    LineItem expItem = new LineItem(inv, product, QUANTITY);
    assertLineItemsEqual("",expItem, actual);
}
```

In this test, we want to verify only the behavior of the invoice logic that depends on this zone attribute—not the way this attribute is calculated from the Customer's address. (There are separate Customer unit tests to verify the zone is calculated correctly.) All of the setup of the address, city, and other information merely distracts the reader.

Here's the same test using a *Test Stub* instead of the Customer. Note how much simpler the fixture setup has become as a result of *Entity Chain Snipping*!

```
public void testInvoice_addLineItem_ECS() {
    final int QUANTITY = 1;
    Product product = new Product(getUniqueNumberAsString(),
                                  getUniqueNumber());
    Mock customerStub = mock(ICustomer.class);
    customerStub.stubs().method("getZone").will(returnValue(ZONE_3));
    Invoice inv = new Invoice((ICustomer)customerStub.proxy());
    // Exercise
    inv.addItemQuantity(product, QUANTITY);
    // Verify
```

Test Stub

```
    List lineItems = inv.getLineItems();
    assertEquals("number of items", lineItems.size(), 1);
    LineItem actual = (LineItem)lineItems.get(0);
    LineItem expItem = new LineItem(inv, product, QUANTITY);
    assertLineItemsEqual("", expItem, actual);
}
```

We have used JMock to stub out the Customer with a customerStub that returns
ZONE_3 when getZone is called. This is all we need to verify the Invoice behavior, and
we have managed to get rid of all that distracting extra object construction. It
is also much clearer from reading this test that invoicing behavior depends only
on the value returned by get_zone and not any other attributes of the Customer or
Address.

Further Reading

Almost every book on automated testing using xUnit has something to say about
Test Stubs, so I won't list those resources here. As you are reading other books,
however, keep in mind that the term *Test Stub* is often used to refer to a *Mock
Object*. *Mocks, Fakes, Stubs, and Dummies* (in Appendix B) contains a more
thorough comparison of the terminology used in various books and articles.

Sven Gorts describes a number of different ways we can use a *Test Stub*
[UTwHCM]. I have adopted many of his names and adapted a few to better
fit into this pattern language. Paolo Perrotta wrote a pattern describing a common example of a *Responder* called Virtual Clock. He uses a *Test Stub* as a
Decorator [GOF] for the real system clock that allows the time to be "frozen"
or resumed. Of course, we could use a *Hard-Coded Test Stub* or a *Configurable Test Stub* just as easily for most tests.

**Test
Stub**

Test Spy

How do we implement Behavior Verification?
How can we verify logic independently when it has indirect outputs
to other software components?

Also known as:
Spy, Recording
Test Stub

We use a Test Double to capture the indirect output calls made to another component by the SUT for later verification by the test.

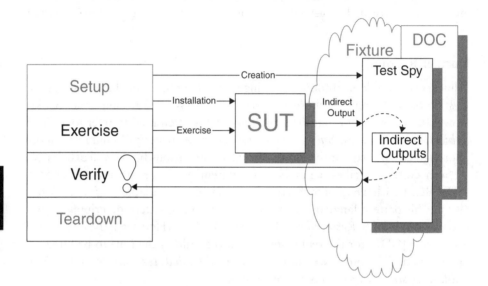

Test Spy

In many circumstances, the environment or context in which the SUT operates very much influences the behavior of the SUT. To get adequate visibility of the indirect outputs of the SUT, we may have to replace some of the context with something we can use to capture these outputs of the SUT.

Use of a *Test Spy* is a simple and intuitive way to implement *Behavior Verification* (page 468) via an observation point that exposes the indirect outputs of the SUT so they can be verified.

How It Works

Before we exercise the SUT, we install a *Test Spy* as a stand-in for a DOC used by the SUT. The *Test Spy* is designed to act as an observation point by recording the method calls made to it by the SUT as it is exercised. During the result verification phase, the test compares the actual values passed to the *Test Spy* by the SUT with the values expected by the test.

When to Use It

A key indication for using a *Test Spy* is having an *Untested Requirement* (see *Production Bugs* on page 268) caused by an inability to observe the side effects of invoking methods on the SUT. *Test Spies* are a natural and intuitive way to extend the existing tests to cover these indirect outputs because the calls to the *Assertion Methods* (page 362) are invoked by the test after the SUT has been exercised just like in "normal" tests. The *Test Spy* merely acts as the observation point that gives the *Test Method* (page 348) access to the values recorded during the SUT execution.

We should use a *Test Spy* in the following circumstances:

- We are verifying the indirect outputs of the SUT and we *cannot* predict the values of all attributes of the interactions with the SUT ahead of time.

- We want the assertions to be visible in the test and we don't think the way in which the *Mock Object* (page 544) expectations are established is sufficiently intent-revealing.

- Our test requires test-specific equality (so we cannot use the standard definition of equality as implemented in the SUT) *and* we are using tools that generate the *Mock Object* but do not give us control over the *Assertion Methods* being called.

- A failed assertion cannot be reported effectively back to the *Test Runner* (page 377). This might occur if the SUT is running inside a container that catches all exceptions and makes it difficult to report the results or if the logic of the SUT runs in a different thread or process from the test that invokes it. (Both of these cases really beg refactoring to allow us to test the SUT logic directly, but that is the subject of another chapter.)

- We would like to have access to all the outgoing calls of the SUT before making any assertions on them.

If none of these criteria apply, we may want to consider using a *Mock Object*. If we are trying to address *Untested Code* (see *Production Bugs*) by controlling the indirect inputs of the SUT, a simple *Test Stub* (page 529) may be all we need.

Unlike a *Mock Object,* a *Test Spy* does not fail the test at the first deviation from the expected behavior. Thus our tests will be able to include more detailed diagnostic information in the *Assertion Message* (page 370) based on information gathered after a *Mock Object* would have failed the test. At the point of test failure, however, only the information within the *Test Method* itself is available to be used in the calls to the *Assertion Methods.* If we need to include information that is accessible only while the SUT is being exercised, either we must explicitly capture it within our *Test Spy* or we must use a *Mock Object.*

Of course, we won't be able to use any *Test Doubles* (page 522) unless the SUT implements some form of substitutable dependency.

Implementation Notes

The *Test Spy* itself can be built as a *Hard-Coded Test Double* (page 568) or as a *Configurable Test Double* (page 558). Because detailed examples appear in the discussion of those patterns, only a quick summary is provided here. Likewise, we can use any of the substitutable dependency patterns to install the *Test Spy* *before* we exercise the SUT.

The key characteristic in how a test uses a *Test Spy* relates to the fact that assertions are made from within the *Test Method.* Therefore, the test must recover the indirect outputs captured by the *Test Spy* before it can make its assertions, which can be done in several ways.

Variation: Retrieval Interface

We can define the *Test Spy* as a separate class with a *Retrieval Interface* that exposes the recorded information. The *Test Method* installs the *Test Spy* instead of the normal DOC as part of the fixture setup phase of the test. After the test has exercised the SUT, it uses the *Retrieval Interface* to retrieve the actual indirect outputs of the SUT from the *Test Spy* and then calls *Assertion Methods* with those outputs as arguments.

Variation: Self Shunt

We can collapse the *Test Spy* and the *Testcase Class* (page 373) into a single object called a *Self Shunt.* The *Test Method* installs itself, the *Testcase Object* (page 382), as the DOC into the SUT. Whenever the SUT delegates to the DOC, it is actually calling methods on the *Testcase Object,* which implements the methods by saving the actual values into instance variables that can be accessed by the *Test Method.* The methods could also make assertions in the *Test Spy* methods, in which case the *Self Shunt* is a variation on a *Mock Object* rather than a *Test Spy.* In statically typed languages, the *Testcase Class* must implement the outgoing interface

Test Spy

Also known as:
Loopback

(the observation point) on which the SUT depends so that the *Testcase Class is* type-compatible with the variables that are used to hold the DOC.

Variation: Inner Test Double

A popular way to implement the *Test Spy* as a *Hard-Coded Test Double* is to code it as an **anonymous inner class** or **block closure** within the *Test Method* and to have this class or **block** save the actual values into instance or local variables that are accessible by the *Test Method*. This variation is really another way to implement a *Self Shunt* (see *Hard-Coded Test Double*).

Variation: Indirect Output Registry

Yet another possibility is to have the *Test Spy* store the actual parameters in a well-known place where the *Test Method* can access them. For example, the *Test Spy* could save those values in a file or in a Registry [PEAA] object.

Motivating Example

The following test verifies the basic functionality of removing a flight but does not verify the indirect outputs of the SUT—namely, the fact that the SUT is expected to log each time a flight is removed along with the date/time and username of the requester.

```
public void testRemoveFlight() throws Exception {
    // setup
    FlightDto expectedFlightDto = createARegisteredFlight();
    FlightManagementFacade facade = new FlightManagementFacadeImpl();
    // exercise
    facade.removeFlight(expectedFlightDto.getFlightNumber());
    // verify
    assertFalse("flight should not exist after being removed",
            facade.flightExists( expectedFlightDto.
                                    getFlightNumber()));
}
```

Refactoring Notes

We can add verification of indirect outputs to existing tests using a Replace Dependency with Test Double (page 522) refactoring. It involves adding code to the fixture setup logic of the tests to create the *Test Spy*, configuring the *Test Spy* with any values it needs to return, and installing it. At the end of the test, we add assertions comparing the expected method names and arguments of the indirect outputs with the actual values retrieved from the *Test Spy* using the *Retrieval Interface*.

Example: Test Spy

In this improved version of the test, logSpy is our *Test Spy*. The statement facade.setAuditLog(logSpy) installs the *Test Spy* using the *Setter Injection* pattern (see *Dependency Injection* on page 678). The methods getDate, getActionCode, and so on are the *Retrieval Interface* used to access the actual arguments of the call to the logger.

```
public void testRemoveFlightLogging_recordingTestStub()
        throws Exception {
    // fixture setup
    FlightDto expectedFlightDto = createAnUnregFlight();
    FlightManagementFacade facade = new FlightManagementFacadeImpl();
    //    Test Double setup
    AuditLogSpy logSpy = new AuditLogSpy();
    facade.setAuditLog(logSpy);
    // exercise
    facade.removeFlight(expectedFlightDto.getFlightNumber());
    // verify
    assertFalse("flight still exists after being removed",
                facade.flightExists( expectedFlightDto.
                                        getFlightNumber()));
    assertEquals("number of calls", 1,
                logSpy.getNumberOfCalls());
    assertEquals("action code",
                Helper.REMOVE_FLIGHT_ACTION_CODE,
                logSpy.getActionCode());
    assertEquals("date", helper.getTodaysDateWithoutTime(),
                logSpy.getDate());
    assertEquals("user", Helper.TEST_USER_NAME,
                logSpy.getUser());
    assertEquals("detail",
                expectedFlightDto.getFlightNumber(),
                logSpy.getDetail());
}
```

This test depends on the following definition of the *Test Spy*:

```
public class AuditLogSpy implements AuditLog {
    // Fields into which we record actual usage information
    private Date date;
    private String user;
    private String actionCode;
    private Object detail;
    private int numberOfCalls = 0;
```

Test Spy

```
    // Recording implementation of real AuditLog interface
    public void logMessage(Date date,
                           String user,
                           String actionCode,
                           Object detail) {
       this.date = date;
       this.user = user;
       this.actionCode = actionCode;
       this.detail = detail;

       numberOfCalls++;
    }

    // Retrieval Interface
    public int getNumberOfCalls() {
       return numberOfCalls;
    }
    public Date getDate() {
       return date;
    }
    public String getUser() {
       return user;
    }
    public String getActionCode() {
       return actionCode;
    }
    public Object getDetail() {
       return detail;
    }
}
```

Test Spy

Of course, we could have implemented the *Retrieval Interface* by making the various fields of our spy public and thereby avoided the need for accessor methods. Please refer to the examples in *Hard-Coded Test Double* for other implementation options.

Mock Object

How do we implement Behavior Verification for indirect
outputs of the SUT?
How can we verify logic independently when it depends on indirect inputs
from other software components?

We replace an object on which the SUT depends on with a test-specific object
that verifies it is being used correctly by the SUT.

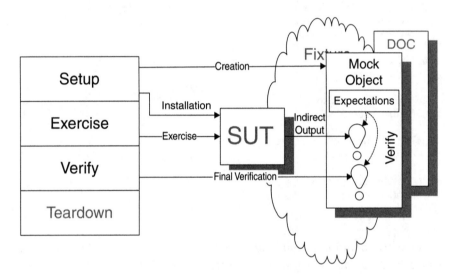

Mock
Object

In many circumstances, the environment or context in which the SUT operates very much influences the behavior of the SUT. In other cases, we must peer "inside"[2] the SUT to determine whether the expected behavior has occurred.

A *Mock Object* is a powerful way to implement *Behavior Verification* (page 468) while avoiding *Test Code Duplication* (page 213) between similar tests. It works by delegating the job of verifying the indirect outputs of the SUT entirely to a *Test Double* (page 522).

---

[2] Technically, the SUT is whatever software we are testing and doesn't include anything it depends on; thus "inside" is somewhat of a misnomer. It is better to think of the DOC that is the destination of the indirect outputs as being "behind" the SUT and part of the fixture.

How It Works

First, we define a *Mock Object* that implements the same interface as an object on which the SUT depends. Then, during the test, we configure the *Mock Object* with the values with which it should respond to the SUT *and* the method calls (complete with expected arguments) it should expect from the SUT. Before exercising the SUT, we install the *Mock Object* so that the SUT uses it *instead of* the real implementation. When called during SUT execution, the *Mock Object* compares the actual arguments received with the expected arguments using *Equality Assertions* (see *Assertion Method* on page 362) and fails the test if they don't match. The test need not make any assertions at all!

When to Use It

We can use a *Mock Object* as an observation point when we need to do *Behavior Verification* to avoid having an *Untested Requirement* (see *Production Bugs* on page 268) caused by our inability to observe the side effects of invoking methods on the SUT. This pattern is commonly used during endoscopic testing [ET] or need-driven development [MRNO]. Although we don't need to use a *Mock Object* when we are doing *State Verification* (page 462), we might use a *Test Stub* (page 529) or *Fake Object* (page 551). Note that test drivers have found other uses for the *Mock Object toolkits,* but many of these are actually examples of using a *Test Stub* rather than a *Mock Object*.

Mock
Object

To use a *Mock Object*, we must be able to predict the values of most or all arguments of the method calls *before* we exercise the SUT. We should not use a *Mock Object* if a failed assertion cannot be reported back to the *Test Runner* (page 377) effectively. This may be the case if the SUT runs inside a container that catches and eats all exceptions. In these circumstances, we may be better off using a *Test Spy* (page 538) instead.

Mock Objects (especially those created using dynamic mocking tools) often use the equals methods of the various objects being compared. If our test-specific equality differs from how the SUT would interpret equals, we may not be able to use a *Mock Object* or we may be forced to add an equals method where we didn't need one. This smell is called *Equality Pollution* (see *Test Logic in Production* on page 217). Some implementations of *Mock Objects* avoid this problem by allowing us to specify the "comparator" to be used in the *Equality Assertions*.

Mock Objects can be either "strict" or "lenient" (sometimes called "nice"). A "strict" *Mock Object* fails the test if the calls are received in a different order than was specified when the *Mock Object* was programmed. A "lenient" *Mock Object* tolerates out-of-order calls.

Implementation Notes

Tests written using *Mock Objects* look different from more traditional tests because all the expected behavior must be specified *before* the SUT is exercised. This makes the tests harder to write and to understand for test automation neophytes. This factor may be enough to cause us to prefer writing our tests using *Test Spies*.

The standard *Four-Phase Test* (page 358) is altered somewhat when we use *Mock Objects*. In particular, the fixture setup phase of the test is broken down into three specific activities and the result verification phase more or less disappears, except for the possible presence of a call to the "final verification" method at the end of the test.

Fixture setup:

- Test constructs *Mock Object*.

- Test configures *Mock Object*. This step is omitted for *Hard-Coded Test Doubles* (page 568).

- Test installs *Mock Object* into SUT.

Exercise SUT:

- SUT calls *Mock Object; Mock Object* does assertions.

Result verification:

- Test calls "final verification" method.

Fixture teardown:

- No impact.

Let's examine these differences a bit more closely:

Construction

As part of the fixture setup phase of our *Four-Phase Test*, we must construct the *Mock Object* that we will use to replace the substitutable dependency. Depending on which tools are available in our programming language, we can either build the *Mock Object* class manually, use a code generator to create a *Mock Object* class, or use a dynamically generated *Mock Object*.

Configuration with Expected Values

Because the *Mock Object* toolkits available in many members of the xUnit family typically create *Configurable Mock Objects* (page 544), we need to configure the *Mock Object* with the expected method calls (and their parameters) as well as the values to be returned by any functions. (Some *Mock Object* frameworks allow us to disable verification of the method calls or just their parameters.) We typically perform this configuration before we install the *Test Double*.

This step is not needed when we are using a *Hard-Coded Test Double* such as an *Inner Test Double* (see *Hard-Coded Test Double*).

Installation

Of course, we must have a way of installing a *Test Double* into the SUT to be able to use a *Mock Object*. We can use whichever substitutable dependency pattern the SUT supports. A common approach in the test-driven development community is *Dependency Injection* (page 678); more traditional developers may favor *Dependency Lookup* (page 686).

Usage

When the SUT calls the methods of the *Mock Object*, these methods compare the method call (method name plus arguments) with the expectations. If the method call is unexpected or the arguments are incorrect, the assertion fails the test immediately. If the call is expected but came out of sequence, a strict *Mock Object* fails the test immediately; by contrast, a lenient *Mock Object* notes that the call was received and carries on. Missed calls are detected when the final verification method is called.

If the method call has any outgoing parameters or return values, the *Mock Object* needs to return or update something to allow the SUT to continue executing the test scenario. This behavior may be either hard-coded or configured at the same time as the expectations. This behavior is the same as for *Test Stubs*, except that we typically return happy path values.

Final Verification

Most of the result verification occurs inside the *Mock Object* as it is called by the SUT. The *Mock Object* will fail the test if the methods are called with the wrong arguments or if methods are called unexpectedly. But what happens if the expected method calls are never received by the *Mock Object*? The *Mock Object* may have trouble detecting that the test is over and it is time to check for unfulfilled expectations. Therefore, we need to ensure that the final verification method is called. Some *Mock Object* toolkits have found a way to invoke this

Mock
Object

method automatically by including the call in the tearDown method.[3] Many other toolkits require us to remember to call the final verification method ourselves.

Motivating Example

The following test verifies the basic functionality of creating a flight. But it does not verify the indirect outputs of the SUT—namely, the SUT is expected to log each time a flight is created along with the date/time and username of the requester.

```
public void testRemoveFlight() throws Exception {
    // setup
    FlightDto expectedFlightDto = createARegisteredFlight();
    FlightManagementFacade facade = new FlightManagementFacadeImpl();
    // exercise
    facade.removeFlight(expectedFlightDto.getFlightNumber());
    // verify
    assertFalse("flight should not exist after being removed",
            facade.flightExists( expectedFlightDto.
                                          getFlightNumber()));
}
```

Mock Object

Refactoring Notes

Verification of indirect outputs can be added to existing tests by using a Replace Dependency with Test Double (page 522) refactoring. This involves adding code to the fixture setup logic of our test to create the *Mock Object*; configuring the *Mock Object* with the expected method calls, arguments, and values to be returned; and installing it using whatever substitutable dependency mechanism is provided by the SUT. At the end of the test, we add a call to the final verification method if our *Mock Object* framework requires one.

Example: Mock Object (Hand-Coded)

In this improved version of the test, mockLog is our *Mock Object*. The method setExpectedLogMessage is used to program it with the expected log message. The statement facade.setAuditLog(mockLog) installs the *Mock Object* using the *Setter Injection* (see *Dependency Injection*) test double-installation pattern. Finally, the verify() method ensures that the call to logMessage() was actually made.

---

[3] This usually requires that we subclass our testcase from a special MockObjectTestCase class.

```
public void testRemoveFlight_Mock() throws Exception {
    // fixture setup
    FlightDto expectedFlightDto = createAnonRegFlight();
    // mock configuration
    ConfigurableMockAuditLog mockLog =
        new ConfigurableMockAuditLog();
    mockLog.setExpectedLogMessage(
                        helper.getTodaysDateWithoutTime(),
                        Helper.TEST_USER_NAME,
                        Helper.REMOVE_FLIGHT_ACTION_CODE,
                        expectedFlightDto.getFlightNumber());
    mockLog.setExpectedNumberCalls(1);
    // mock installation
    FlightManagementFacade facade = new FlightManagementFacadeImpl();
    facade.setAuditLog(mockLog);
    // exercise
    facade.removeFlight(expectedFlightDto.getFlightNumber());
    // verify
    assertFalse("flight still exists after being removed",
            facade.flightExists( expectedFlightDto.
                                        getFlightNumber()));
    mockLog.verify();
}
```

This approach was made possible by use of the following *Mock Object*. Here we have chosen to use a hand-built *Mock Object*. In the interest of space, just the logMessage method is shown:

Mock
Object

```
public void logMessage( Date actualDate,
                        String actualUser,
                        String actualActionCode,
                        Object actualDetail) {
    actualNumberCalls++;

    Assert.assertEquals("date", expectedDate, actualDate);
    Assert.assertEquals("user", expectedUser, actualUser);
    Assert.assertEquals("action code",
                        expectedActionCode,
                        actualActionCode);
    Assert.assertEquals("detail", expectedDetail,actualDetail);
}
```

The *Assertion Methods* are called as static methods. In JUnit, this approach is required because the *Mock Object* is not a subclass of TestCase; thus it does not inherit the assertion methods from Assert. Other members of the xUnit family may provide different mechanisms to access the *Assertion Methods*. For example, NUnit provides them *only* as static methods on the Assert class, so even *Test Methods* (page 348) need to access the *Assertion Methods* this way. Test::Unit, the xUnit family member for the Ruby programming language, provides them as **mixins**; as a consequence, they can be called in the normal fashion.

Example: Mock Object (Dynamically Generated)

The last example used a hand-coded *Mock Object*. Most members of the xUnit family, however, have dynamic *Mock Object* frameworks available. Here's the same test rewritten using JMock:

```
public void testRemoveFlight_JMock() throws Exception {
    // fixture setup
    FlightDto expectedFlightDto = createAnonRegFlight();
    FlightManagementFacade facade = new FlightManagementFacadeImpl();
    // mock configuration
    Mock mockLog = mock(AuditLog.class);
    mockLog.expects(once()).method("logMessage")
            .with(eq(helper.getTodaysDateWithoutTime()),
                  eq(Helper.TEST_USER_NAME),
                  eq(Helper.REMOVE_FLIGHT_ACTION_CODE),
                  eq(expectedFlightDto.getFlightNumber()));
    // mock installation
    facade.setAuditLog((AuditLog) mockLog.proxy());
    // exercise
    facade.removeFlight(expectedFlightDto.getFlightNumber());
    // verify
    assertFalse("flight still exists after being removed",
                facade.flightExists( expectedFlightDto.
                                            getFlightNumber()));
    // verify() method called automatically by JMock
}
```

Mock
Object

Note how JMock provides a "fluent" *Configuration Interface* (see *Configurable Test Double*) that allows us to specify the expected method calls in a fairly readable fashion. JMock also allows us to specify the comparator to be used by the assertions; in this case, the calls to eq cause the default equals method to be called.

Further Reading

Almost every book on automated testing using xUnit has something to say about *Mock Objects*, so I won't list those resources here. As you are reading other books, keep in mind that the term *Mock Object* is often used to refer to a *Test Stub* and sometimes even to *Fake Objects*. *Mocks, Fakes, Stubs, and Dummies* (in Appendix B) contains a more thorough comparison of the terminology used in various books and articles.

Fake Object

How can we verify logic independently when depended-on objects
cannot be used?
How can we avoid Slow Tests?

We replace a component that the SUT depends on with a much
lighter-weight implementation.

Also known as:
Dummy

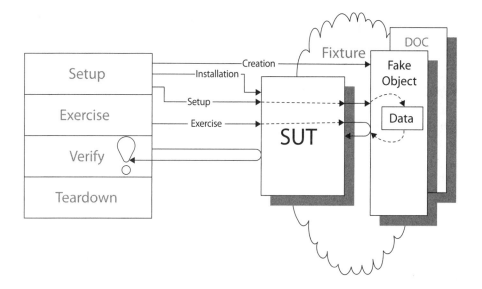

Fake
Object

The SUT often depends on other components or systems. Although the inter-actions with these other components may be necessary, the side effects of these interactions *as implemented by the real DOC* may be unnecessary or even detrimental.

A *Fake Object* is a much simpler and lighter-weight implementation of the functionality provided by the DOC without the side effects we choose to do without.

How It Works

We acquire or build a very lightweight implementation of the same functionality as provided by a component on which the SUT depends and instruct the SUT to use it instead of the real DOC. This implementation need not have any of the

"-ilities" that the real DOC needs to have (such as scalability); it need provide only the equivalent services to the SUT so that the SUT remains unaware it isn't using the real DOC.

A *Fake Object* is a kind of *Test Double* (page 522) that is similar to a *Test Stub* (page 529) in many ways, including the need to install into the SUT a substitutable dependency. Whereas a *Test Stub* acts as a control point to inject indirect inputs into the SUT, however, the *Fake Object* does not: It merely provides a way for the interactions to occur in a self-consistent manner. These interactions (i.e., between the SUT and the *Fake Object*) will typically be many, and the values passed in as arguments of earlier method calls will often be returned as results of later method calls. Contrast this behavior with that of *Test Stubs* and *Mock Objects* (page 544), where the responses are either hard-coded or configured by the test.

While the test does not normally configure a *Fake Object*, complex fixture setup that would typically involve initializing the state of the DOC may also be done with the *Fake Object* directly using *Back Door Manipulation* (page 327). Techniques such as *Data Loader* (see *Back Door Manipulation*) and *Back Door Setup* (see *Back Door Manipulation*) can be used quite successfully with less fear of *Overspecified Software* (see *Fragile Test* on page 239) because they simply bind us to the interface between the SUT and the *Fake Object*; the interface used to configure the *Fake Object* is a test-only concern.

Fake Object

When to Use It

We should use a *Fake Object* whenever the SUT depends on other components that are unavailable or that make testing difficult or slow (e.g., *Slow Tests;* see page 253) and the tests need more complex sequences of behavior than are worth implementing in a *Test Stub* or *Mock Object*. It must also be easier to create a lightweight implementation than to build and program suitable *Mock Objects*, at least in the long run, if building a *Fake Object* is to be worthwhile.

Using a *Fake Object* helps us avoid *Overspecified Software* because we do not encode the exact calling sequences expected of the DOC within the test. The SUT can vary how many times the methods of the DOC are called without causing tests to fail.

If we need to control the indirect inputs or verify the indirect outputs of the SUT, we should probably use a *Mock Object* or *Test Stub* instead.

Some specific situations where we replace the real component with a *Fake Object* are described next.

Variation: Fake Database

With the *Fake Database* pattern, the real database or persistence layer is replaced by a *Fake Object* that is functionally equivalent but that has much better performance characteristics. An approach we have often used involves replacing the database with a set of in-memory HashTables that act as a very lightweight way of retrieving objects that have been "persisted" earlier in the test.

Variation: In-Memory Database

Another example of a *Fake Object* is the use of a small-footprint, diskless database instead of a full-featured disk-based database. This kind of *In-Memory Database* will improve the speed of tests by at least an order of magnitude while giving up less functionality than a *Fake Database*.

Variation: Fake Web Service

When testing software that depends on other components that are accessed as Web services, we can build a small hard-coded or data-driven implementation that can be used instead of the real Web service to make our tests more robust and to avoid having to create a test instance of the real Web service in our development environment.

Variation: Fake Service Layer

When testing user interfaces, we can avoid *Data Sensitivity* (see *Fragile Test*) and *Behavior Sensitivity* (see *Fragile Test*) of the tests by replacing the component that implements the Service Layer [PEAA] (including the domain layer) of our application with a Fake Object that returns remembered or data-driven results. This approach allows us to focus on testing the user interface without having to worry about the data being returned changing over time.

Implementation Notes

Introducing a *Fake Object* involves two basic concerns:

- Building the *Fake Object* implementation
- Installing the *Fake Object*

Building the Fake Object

Most *Fake Objects* are hand-built. Often, the *Fake Object* is used to replace a real implementation that suffers from latency issues owing to real messaging or disk I/O with a much lighter *in-memory* implementation. With the rich class libraries available in most object-oriented programming languages, it is usually possible to build a fake implementation that is sufficient to satisfy the needs of the SUT, at least for the purposes of specific tests, with relatively little effort.

A popular strategy is to start by building a *Fake Object* to support a specific set of tests where the SUT requires only a subset of the DOC's services. If this proves successful, we may consider expanding the *Fake Object* to handle additional tests. Over time, we may find that we can run all of our tests using the *Fake Object*. (See the sidebar "Faster Tests Without Shared Fixtures" on page 319 for a description of how we faked out the entire database with hash tables and made our tests run 50 times faster.)

Installing the Fake Object

Of course, we must have a way of installing the *Fake Object* into the SUT to be able to take advantage of it. We can use whichever substitutable dependency pattern the SUT supports. A common approach in the test-driven development community is *Dependency Injection* (page 678); more traditional developers may favor *Dependency Lookup* (page 686). The latter technique is also more appropriate when we introduce a *Fake Database* (see *Fake Object* on page 551) in an effort to speed up execution of the customer tests; *Dependency Injection* doesn't work so well with these kinds of tests.

Fake Object

Motivating Example

In this example, the SUT needs to read and write records from a database. The test must set up the fixture in the database (several writes), the SUT interacts (reads and writes) with the database several more times, and then the test removes the records from the database (several deletes). All of this work takes time—several seconds per test. This very quickly adds up to minutes, and soon we find that our developers aren't running the tests quite so frequently. Here is an example of one of these tests:

```
public void testReadWrite() throws Exception{
    // Setup
    FlightMngtFacade facade = new FlightMgmtFacadeImpl();
    BigDecimal yyc = facade.createAirport("YYC", "Calgary", "Calgary");
    BigDecimal lax = facade.createAirport("LAX", "LAX Intl", "LA");
    facade.createFlight(yyc, lax);
    // Exercise
    List flights = facade.getFlightsByOriginAirport(yyc);
```

```
// Verify
assertEquals( "# of flights", 1, flights.size());
Flight flight = (Flight) flights.get(0);
assertEquals( "origin",
              yyc, flight.getOrigin().getCode());
}
```

The test calls createAirport on our *Service Facade* [CJ2EEP], which calls, among other things, our data access layer. Here is the actual implementation of several of the methods we are calling:

```
public BigDecimal createAirport( String airportCode,
                                 String name,
                                 String nearbyCity)
throws FlightBookingException{
   TransactionManager.beginTransaction();
   Airport airport = dataAccess.
       createAirport(airportCode, name, nearbyCity);
   logMessage("Wrong Action Code", airport.getCode());//bug
   TransactionManager.commitTransaction();
   return airport.getId();
}

public List getFlightsByOriginAirport(
               BigDecimal originAirportId)
    throws FlightBookingException {

   if (originAirportId == null)
      throw new InvalidArgumentException(
            "Origin Airport Id has not been provided",
            "originAirportId", null);
   Airport origin = dataAccess.getAirportByPrimaryKey(originAirportId);
   List flights = dataAccess.getFlightsByOriginAirport(origin);

   return flights;
}
```

The calls to dataAccess.createAirport, dataAccess.createFlight, and TransactionManager. commitTransaction cause our test to slow down the most. The calls to dataAccess. getAirportByPrimaryKey and dataAccess.getFlightsByOriginAirport are a lesser factor but still contribute to the slow test.

Refactoring Notes

The steps for introducing a *Fake Object* are very similar to those for adding a *Mock Object*. If one doesn't already exist, we use a Replace Dependency with Test Double (page 522) refactoring to introduce a way to substitute the *Fake Object* for the DOC—usually a field (attribute) to hold the reference to it. In statically typed languages, we may have to do an Extract Interface [Fowler] refactoring before we can introduce the fake implementation. Then, we use this interface as the type of variable that holds the reference to the substitutable dependency.

One notable difference is that we *do not* need to configure the *Fake Object* with expectations or return values; we merely set up the fixture in the normal way.

Example: Fake Database

In this example, we've created a *Fake Object* that replaces the database—that is, a *Fake Database* implemented entirely in memory using hash tables. The test doesn't change a lot, but the test execution occurs much, much faster.

```
public void testReadWrite_inMemory() throws Exception{
    // Setup
    FlightMgmtFacadeImpl facade = new FlightMgmtFacadeImpl();
    facade.setDao(new InMemoryDatabase());
    BigDecimal yyc = facade.createAirport("YYC", "Calgary", "Calgary");
    BigDecimal lax = facade.createAirport("LAX", "LAX Intl", "LA");
    facade.createFlight(yyc, lax);
    // Exercise
    List flights = facade.getFlightsByOriginAirport(yyc);
    // Verify
    assertEquals( "# of flights", 1, flights.size());
    Flight flight = (Flight) flights.get(0);
    assertEquals( "origin",
                     yyc, flight.getOrigin().getCode());
}
```

Fake Object

Here's the implementation of the *Fake Database:*

```
public class InMemoryDatabase implements FlightDao{
    private List airports = new Vector();
    public Airport createAirport(String airportCode,
                                  String name, String nearbyCity)
            throws DataException, InvalidArgumentException {
        assertParamtersAreValid( airportCode, name, nearbyCity);
        assertAirportDoesntExist( airportCode);
        Airport result = new Airport(getNextAirportId(),
                airportCode, name, createCity(nearbyCity));
        airports.add(result);
        return result;
    }
    public Airport getAirportByPrimaryKey(BigDecimal airportId)
            throws DataException, InvalidArgumentException {
        assertAirportNotNull(airportId);

        Airport result = null;
        Iterator i = airports.iterator();
        while (i.hasNext()) {
```

```
      Airport airport = (Airport) i.next();
      if (airport.getId().equals(airportId)) {
         return airport;
      }
   }
   throw new DataException("Airport not found:"+airportId);
}
```

Now all we need is the implementation of the method that installs the *Fake Database* into the facade to make our developers more than happy to run all the tests after every code change.

```
public void setDao(FlightDao) {
   dataAccess = dao;
}
```

Further Reading

The sidebar "Faster Tests Without Shared Fixtures" on page 319 provides a more in-depth description of how we faked out the entire database with hash tables and made our tests run 50 times faster. *Mocks, Fakes, Stubs, and Dummies* (in Appendix B) contains a more thorough comparison of the terminology used in various books and articles.

Fake
Object

Configurable Test Double

How do we tell a Test Double what to return or expect?

Also known as:
*Configurable
Mock Object,
Configurable
Test Spy,
Configurable
Test Stub*

**We configure a reusable Test Double with the values to be returned
or verified during the fixture setup phase of a test.**

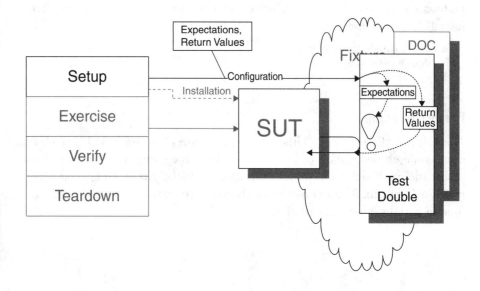

**Configurable
Test Double**

Some tests require unique values to be fed into the SUT as indirect inputs or to be
verified as indirect outputs of the SUT. This approach typically requires the use of
Test Doubles (page 522) as the conduit between the test and the SUT; at the same
time, the *Test Double* somehow needs to be told which values to return or verify.

A *Configurable Test Double* is a way to reduce *Test Code Duplication* (page 213)
by reusing a *Test Double* in many tests. The key to its use is to configure the *Test
Double's* values to be returned or expected at runtime.

How It Works

The *Test Double* is built with instance variables that hold the values to be returned
to the SUT or to serve as the expected values of arguments to method calls. The test
initializes these variables during the setup phase of the test by calling the appropriate methods on the *Test Double's* interface. When the SUT calls the methods on the
Test Double, the *Test Double* uses the contents of the appropriate variable as the
value to return or as the expected value in assertions.

When to Use It

We can use a *Configurable Test Double* whenever we need similar but slightly different behavior in several tests that depend on *Test Doubles* and we want to avoid *Test Code Duplication* or *Obscure Tests* (page 186)—in the latter case, we need to see what values the *Test Double* is using as we read the test. If we expect only a single usage of a *Test Double*, we can consider using a *Hard-Coded Test Double* (page 568) if the extra effort and complexity of building a *Configurable Test Double* are not warranted.

Implementation Notes

A *Test Double* is a *Configurable Test Double* because it needs to provide a way for the tests to configure it with values to return and/or method arguments to expect. Configurable *Test Stubs* (page 529) and *Test Spies* (page 538) simply require a way to configure the responses to calls on their methods; configurable *Mock Objects* (page 544) also require a way to configure their expectations (which methods *should* be called and with which arguments).

Configurable *Test Doubles* may be built in many ways. Deciding on a particular implementation involves making two relatively independent decisions: (1) how the *Configurable Test Double* will be configured and (2) how the *Configurable Test Double* will be coded.

Configurable
Test Double

There are two common ways to configure a *Configurable Test Double*. The most popular approach is to provide a *Configuration Interface* that is used only by the test to configure the values to be returned as indirect inputs and the expected values of the indirect outputs. Alternatively, we may build the *Configurable Test Double* with two modes. The *Configuration Mode* is used during fixture setup to install the indirect inputs and expected indirect outputs by calling the methods of the *Configurable Test Double* with the expected arguments. Before the *Configurable Test Double* is installed, it is put into the normal ("usage" or "playback") mode.

The obvious way to build a *Configurable Test Double* is to create a *Hand-Built Test Double*. If we are lucky, however, someone will have already built a tool to generate a *Configurable Test Double* for us. *Test Double* generators come in two flavors: code generators and tools that fabricate the object at runtime. Developers have built several generations of "mocking" tools, and several of these have been ported to other programming languages; check out http://xprogramming.com to see what is available in your programming language of choice. If the answer is "nothing," you can hand-code the *Test Double* yourself, although this does take somewhat more effort.

Variation: Configuration Interface

A *Configuration Interface* comprises a separate set of methods that the *Configurable Test Double* provides specifically for use by the test to set each value that the *Configurable Test Double* returns or expects to receive. The test simply calls these methods during the fixture setup phase of the *Four-Phase Test* (page 358). The SUT uses the "other" methods on the *Configurable Test Double* (the "normal" interface). It isn't aware that the *Configuration Interface* exists on the object to which it is delegating.

Configuration Interfaces come in two flavors. Early toolkits, such as Mock-Maker, generated a distinct method for each value we needed to configure. The collection of these setter methods made up the *Configuration Interface*. More recently introduced toolkits, such as JMock, provide a generic interface that is used to build an *Expected Behavior Specification* (see *Behavior Verification* on page 468) that the *Configurable Test Double* interprets at runtime. A well-designed **fluent interface** can make the test much easier to read and understand.

Variation: Configuration Mode

We can avoid defining a separate set of methods to configure the *Test Double* by providing a *Configuration Mode* that the test uses to "teach" the *Configurable Test Double* what to expect. At first glance, this means of configuring the *Test Double* can be confusing: Why does the *Test Method* (page 348) call the methods of this other object before it calls the methods it is exercising on the SUT? When we come to grips with the fact that we are doing a form of "record and play-back," this technique makes a bit more sense.

The main advantage of using a *Configuration Mode* is that it avoids creating a separate set of methods for configuring the *Configurable Test Double* because we reuse the same methods that the SUT will be calling. (We do have to provide a way to set the values to be returned by the methods, so we have at least one additional method to add.) On the flip side, each method that the SUT is expected to call now has two code paths through it: one for the *Configuration Mode* and another for the "usage mode."

Variation: Hand-Built Test Double

A *Hand-Built Test Double* is one that was defined by the test automater for one or more specific tests. A *Hard-Coded Test Double* is inherently a *Hand-Built Test Double*, while a *Configurable Test Double* can be either hand-built or generated. This book uses *Hand-Built Test Doubles* in a lot of the examples because it is easier to see what is going on when we have actual, simple, concrete code to look at. This is the main advantage of using a *Hand-Built Test Double*; indeed,

Configurable Test Double

some people consider this benefit to be so important that they use *Hand-Built Test Doubles* exclusively. We may also use a *Hand-Built Test Double* when no third-party toolkits are available or if we are prevented from using those tools by project or corporate policy.

Variation: Statically Generated Test Double

The early third-party toolkits used code generators to create the code for *Statically Generated Test Doubles*. The code is then compiled and linked with our handwritten test code. Typically, we will store the code in a source code repository [SCM]. Whenever the interface of the target class changes, of course, we must regenerate the code for our *Statically Generated Test Doubles*. It may be advantageous to include this step as part of the automated build script to ensure that it really does happen whenever the interface changes.

Instantiating a *Statically Generated Test Double* is the same as instantiating a *Hand-Built Test Double*. That is, we use the name of the generated class to construct the *Configurable Test Double*.

An interesting problem arises during refactoring. Suppose we change the interface of the class we are replacing by adding an argument to one of the methods. Should we then refactor the generated code? Or should we regenerate the *Statically Generated Test Double* after the code it replaces has been refactored? With modern refactoring tools, it may seem easier to refactor the generated code and the tests that use it in a single step; this strategy, however, may leave the *Statically Generated Test Double* without argument verification logic or variables for the new parameter. Therefore, we should regenerate the *Statically Generated Test Double* after the refactoring is finished to ensure that the refactored *Statically Generated Test Double* works properly and can be recreated by the code generator.

Variation: Dynamically Generated Test Double

Newer third-party toolkits generate *Configurable Test Doubles* at runtime by using the reflection capabilities of the programming language to examine a class or interface and build an object that is capable of understanding all calls to its methods. These *Configurable Test Doubles* may interpret the behavior specification at runtime or they may generate executable code; nevertheless, there is no source code for us to generate and maintain or regenerate. The down side is simply that there is no code to look at—but that really isn't a disadvantage unless we are particularly suspicious or paranoid.

Most of today's tools generate *Mock Objects* because they are the most fashionable and widely used options. We can still use these objects as *Test Stubs*, however, because they do provide a way of setting the value to be returned when a particular method is called. If we aren't particularly interested in verifying the methods being called or the arguments passed to them, most toolkits provide a way to specify "don't care" arguments. Given that most toolkits generate *Mock Objects*, they typically don't provide a *Retrieval Interface* (see *Test Spy*).

Motivating Example

Here's a test that uses a *Hard-Coded Test Double* to give it control over the time:

```
public void testDisplayCurrentTime_AtMidnight_HCM()
        throws Exception {
   // Fixture Setup
   //    Instantiate hard-code Test Stub:
   TimeProvider testStub = new MidnightTimeProvider();
   //    Instantiate SUT
   TimeDisplay sut = new TimeDisplay();
   //    Inject Stub into SUT
   sut.setTimeProvider(testStub);
   // Exercise SUT
   String result = sut.getCurrentTimeAsHtmlFragment();
   // Verify Direct Output
   String expectedTimeString =
      "<span class=\"tinyBoldText\">Midnight</span>";
   assertEquals("Midnight", expectedTimeString, result);
}
```

This test is hard to understand without seeing the definition of the *Hard-Coded Test Double*. It is easy to see how this lack of clarity can lead to a *Mystery Guest* (see *Obscure Test*) if the definition is not close at hand.

```
class MidnightTimeProvider implements TimeProvider {
    public Calendar getTime() {
       Calendar myTime = new GregorianCalendar();
       myTime.set(Calendar.HOUR_OF_DAY, 0);
       myTime.set(Calendar.MINUTE, 0);
       return myTime;
    }
}
```

We can solve the *Obscure Test* problem by using a *Self Shunt* (see *Hard-Coded Test Double*) to make the *Hard-Coded Test Double* visible within the test:

```
public class SelfShuntExample extends TestCase
implements TimeProvider {
   public void testDisplayCurrentTime_AtMidnight() throws Exception {
      // Fixture Setup
```

```
        TimeDisplay sut = new TimeDisplay();
        // Mock Setup
        sut.setTimeProvider(this); // self shunt installation
        // Exercise SUT
        String result = sut.getCurrentTimeAsHtmlFragment();
        // Verify Direct Output
        String expectedTimeString =
            "<span class=\"tinyBoldText\">Midnight</span>";
        assertEquals("Midnight", expectedTimeString, result);
    }

    public Calendar getTime() {
        Calendar myTime = new GregorianCalendar();
        myTime.set(Calendar.MINUTE, 0);
        myTime.set(Calendar.HOUR_OF_DAY, 0);
        return myTime;
    }
}
```

Unfortunately, we will need to build the *Test Double* behavior into each *Testcase Class* (page 373) that requires it, which results in *Test Code Duplication*.

Refactoring Notes

Refactoring a test that uses a *Hard-Coded Test Double* to become a test that uses a third-party *Configurable Test Double* is relatively straightforward. We simply follow the directions provided with the toolkit to instantiate the *Configurable Test Double* and configure it with the same values as we used in the *Hard-Coded Test Double*. We may also have to move some of the logic that was originally hard-coded within the *Test Double* into the *Test Method* and pass it in to the *Test Double* as part of the configuration step.

Converting the actual *Hard-Coded Test Double* into a *Configurable Test Double* is a bit more complicated, but not overly so if we need to capture only simple behavior. (For more complex behavior, we're probably better off examining one of the existing toolkits and porting it to our environment if it is not yet available.) First we need to introduce a way to set the values to be returned or expected. The best choice is to start by modifying the test to see how we want to interact with the *Configurable Test Double*. After instantiating it during the fixture setup part of the test, we then pass the test-specific values to the *Configurable Test Double* using the emerging *Configuration Interface* or *Configuration Mode*. Once we've seen how we want to use the *Configurable Test Double*, we can use an Introduce Field [JetBrains] refactoring to create the instance variables of the *Configurable Test Double* to hold each of the previously hard-coded values.

Example: Configuration Interface Using Setters

The following example shows how a test would use a simple hand-built *Configuration Interface* using *Setter Injection*:

```
public void testDisplayCurrentTime_AtMidnight()
            throws Exception {
  // Fixture setup
  //      Test Double configuration
  TimeProviderTestStub tpStub = new TimeProviderTestStub();
  tpStub.setHours(0);
  tpStub.setMinutes(0);
  //   Instantiate SUT
  TimeDisplay sut = new TimeDisplay();
  //      Test Double installation
  sut.setTimeProvider(tpStub);
  // Exercise SUT
  String result = sut.getCurrentTimeAsHtmlFragment();
  // Verify Outcome
  String expectedTimeString =
          "<span class=\"tinyBoldText\">Midnight</span>";
  assertEquals("Midnight", expectedTimeString, result);
}
```

Configurable Test Double

The *Configurable Test Double* is implemented as follows:

```
class TimeProviderTestStub implements TimeProvider {
  // Configuration Interface
  public void setHours(int hours) {
    // 0 is midnight; 12 is noon
    myTime.set(Calendar.HOUR_OF_DAY, hours);
  }

  public void setMinutes(int minutes) {
    myTime.set(Calendar.MINUTE, minutes);
  }
  // Interface Used by SUT
  public Calendar getTime() {
    // @return the last time that was set
    return myTime;
  }
}
```

Example: Configuration Interface Using Expression Builder

Now let's contrast the *Configuration Interface* we defined in the previous example with the one provided by the JMock framework. JMock generates *Mock Objects* dynamically and provides a generic fluent interface for configuring the *Mock Object* in an intent-revealing style. Here's the same test converted to use JMock:

```
public void testDisplayCurrentTime_AtMidnight_JM()
      throws Exception {
   // Fixture setup
   TimeDisplay sut = new TimeDisplay();
   //  Test Double configuration
   Mock tpStub = mock(TimeProvider.class);
   Calendar midnight = makeTime(0,0);
   tpStub.stubs().method("getTime").
                  withNoArguments().
                  will(returnValue(midnight));
   //  Test Double installation
   sut.setTimeProvider((TimeProvider) tpStub);
   // Exercise SUT
   String result = sut.getCurrentTimeAsHtmlFragment();
   // Verify Outcome
   String expectedTimeString =
         "<span class=\"tinyBoldText\">Midnight</span>";
   assertEquals("Midnight", expectedTimeString, result);
}
```

Here we have moved some of the logic to construct the time to be returned into the *Testcase Class* because there is no way to do it in the generic mocking framework; we've used a *Test Utility Method* (page 599) to construct the time to be returned. This next example shows a configurable *Mock Object* complete with multiple expected parameters:

```
public void testRemoveFlight_JMock() throws Exception {
   // fixture setup
   FlightDto expectedFlightDto = createAnonRegFlight();
   FlightManagementFacade facade = new FlightManagementFacadeImpl();
   // mock configuration
   Mock mockLog = mock(AuditLog.class);
   mockLog.expects(once()).method("logMessage")
          .with(eq(helper.getTodaysDateWithoutTime()),
               eq(Helper.TEST_USER_NAME),
               eq(Helper.REMOVE_FLIGHT_ACTION_CODE),
               eq(expectedFlightDto.getFlightNumber())));
   // mock installation
   facade.setAuditLog((AuditLog) mockLog.proxy());
   // exercise
   facade.removeFlight(expectedFlightDto.getFlightNumber());
   // verify
   assertFalse("flight still exists after being removed",
            facade.flightExists( expectedFlightDto.
                                     getFlightNumber()));
   // verify() method called automatically by JMock
}
```

The *Expected Behavior Specification* is built by calling expression-building methods such as expects, once, and method to describe how the *Configurable*

Test Double should be used and what it should return. JMock supports the specification of much more sophisticated behavior (such as multiple calls to the same method with different arguments and return values) than does our hand-built *Configurable Test Double*.

Example: Configuration Mode

In the next example, the test has been converted to use a *Mock Object* with a *Configuration Mode*:

```
public void testRemoveFlight_ModalMock() throws Exception {
    // fixture setup
    FlightDto expectedFlightDto = createAnonRegFlight();
    // mock configuration (in Configuration Mode)
    ModalMockAuditLog mockLog = new ModalMockAuditLog();
    mockLog.logMessage(Helper.getTodaysDateWithoutTime(),
                       Helper.TEST_USER_NAME,
                       Helper.REMOVE_FLIGHT_ACTION_CODE,
                       expectedFlightDto.getFlightNumber());
    mockLog.enterPlaybackMode();
    // mock installation
    FlightManagementFacade facade = new FlightManagementFacadeImpl();
    facade.setAuditLog(mockLog);
    // exercise
    facade.removeFlight(expectedFlightDto.getFlightNumber());
    // verify
    assertFalse("flight still exists after being removed",
                facade.flightExists( expectedFlightDto.
                                            getFlightNumber()));
    mockLog.verify();
}
```

Here the test calls the methods on the *Configurable Test Double* during the fixture setup phase. If we weren't aware that this test uses a *Configurable Test Double* mock, we might find this structure confusing at first glance. The most obvious clue to its intent is the call to the method enterPlaybackMode, which tells the *Configurable Test Double* to stop saving expected values and to start asserting on them.

The *Configurable Test Double* used by this test is implemented like this:

```
private int mode = record;

public void enterPlaybackMode() {
    mode = playback;
}

public void logMessage( Date date,
                        String user,
                        String action,
                        Object detail) {
```

Configurable Test Double

```
    if (mode == record) {
       Assert.assertEquals("Only supports 1 expected call",
                              0, expectedNumberCalls);
       expectedNumberCalls = 1;
       expectedDate = date;
       expectedUser = user;
       expectedCode = action;
       expectedDetail = detail;
    } else {
       Assert.assertEquals("Date", expectedDate, date);
       Assert.assertEquals("User", expectedUser, user);
       Assert.assertEquals("Action", expectedCode, action);
       Assert.assertEquals("Detail", expectedDetail, detail);
    }
 }
```

The if statement checks whether we are in record or playback mode. Because
this simple hand-built *Configurable Test Double* allows only a single value to
be stored, a *Guard Assertion* (page 490) fails the test if it tries to record more
than one call to this method. The rest of the then clause saves the parameters
into variables that it uses as the expected values of the *Equality Assertions* (see
Assertion Method on page 362) in the else clause.

Configurable
Test Double

Hard-Coded Test Double

How do we tell a Test Double what to return or expect?

Also known as:
*Hard-Coded
Mock Object,
Hard-Coded
Test Stub,
Hard-Coded
Test Spy*

**We build the Test Double by hard-coding the return values and/or
expected calls.**

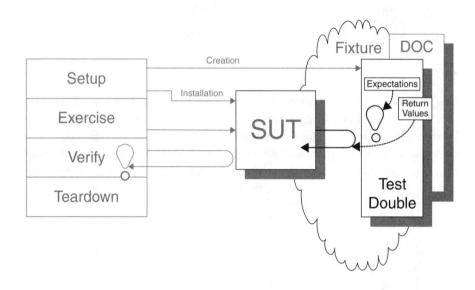

**Hard-Coded
Test Double**

Test Doubles (page 522) are used for many reasons during the development of
Fully Automated Tests (see page 26). The behavior of the *Test Double* may vary
from test to test, and there are many ways to define this behavior.

When the *Test Double* is very simple or very specific to a single test, the simplest solution is often to hard-code the behavior into the *Test Double*.

How It Works

The test automater hard-codes all of the *Test Double's* behavior into the *Test
Double*. For example, if the *Test Double* needs to return a value for a method
call, the value is hard-coded into the return statement. If it needs to verify that a
certain parameter had a specific value, the assertion is hard-coded with the value
that is expected.

When to Use It

We typically use a *Hard-Coded Test Double* when the behavior of the *Test Double* is very simple or is very specific to a single test or *Testcase Class* (page 373). The *Hard-Coded Test Double* can be either a *Test Stub* (page 529), a *Test Spy* (page 538), or a *Mock Object* (page 544), depending on what we encode in the method(s) called by the SUT.

Because each *Hard-Coded Test Double* is purpose-built by hand, its construction may take more effort than using a third-party *Configurable Test Double* (page 558). It can also result in more test code to maintain and refactor as the SUT changes. If different tests require that the *Test Double* behave in different ways and the use of *Hard-Coded Test Doubles* results in too much *Test Code Duplication* (page 213), we should consider using a *Configurable Test Double* instead.

Implementation Notes

Hard-Coded Test Doubles are inherently *Hand-Built Test Doubles* (see *Configurable Test Double*) because there tends to be no point in generating *Hard-Coded Test Doubles* automatically. *Hard-Coded Test Doubles* can be implemented with dedicated classes, but they are most commonly used when the programming language supports blocks, **closures,** or **inner classes.** All of these language features help to avoid the file/class overhead associated with creating a *Hard-Coded Test Double*; they also keep the *Hard-Coded Test Double's* behavior visible within the test that uses it. In some languages, this can make the tests a bit more difficult to read. This is especially true when we use anonymous inner classes, which require a lot of syntactic overhead to define the class in-line. In languages that support blocks directly, and in which developers are very familiar with their usage idioms, using *Hard-Coded Test Doubles* can actually make the tests easier to read.

There are many different ways to implement a *Hard-Coded Test Double,* each of which has its own advantages and disadvantages.

Hard-Coded Test Double

Variation: Test Double Class

We can implement the *Hard-Coded Test Double* as a class distinct from either the *Testcase Class* or the SUT. This allows the *Hard-Coded Test Double* to be reused by several *Testcase Classes* but may result in an *Obscure Test* (page 186; caused by a *Mystery Guest*) because it moves important indirect inputs or indirect outputs of the SUT out of the test to somewhere else, possibly out of sight of the test reader. Depending on how we implement the *Test Double Class*, it may also result in code proliferation and additional *Test Double* classes to maintain.

One way to ensure that the *Test Double Class* is type-compatible with the component it will replace is to make the *Test Double Class* a subclass of that component. We then override any methods whose behavior we want to change.

Variation: Test Double Subclass

We can also implement the *Hard-Coded Test Double* by subclassing the real DOC and overriding the behavior of the methods we expect the SUT to call as we exercise it. Unfortunately, this approach can have unpredictable consequences if the SUT calls other DOC methods that we have not overridden. It also ties our test code very closely to the implementation of the DOC and can result in *Over-specified Software* (see *Fragile Test* on page 239). Using a *Test Double Subclass* may be a reasonable option in very specific circumstances (e.g., while doing a spike or when it is the only option available to us), but this strategy isn't recommended on a routine basis.

Variation: Self Shunt

We can implement the methods that we want the SUT to call on the *Testcase Class* and install the *Testcase Object* (page 382) into the SUT as the *Test Double* to be used. This approach is called a *Self Shunt*.

The *Self Shunt* can be either a *Test Stub*, a *Test Spy*, or a *Mock Object*, depending on what the method called by the SUT does. In each case, it will need to access instance variables of the *Testcase Class* to know what to do or expect. In statically typed languages, the *Testcase Class* must also implement the interface on which the SUT depends.

We typically use a *Self Shunt* when we need a *Hard-Coded Test Double* that is very specific to a single *Testcase Class*. If only a single *Test Method* (page 348) requires the *Hard-Coded Test Double*, using an *Inner Test Double* may result in greater clarity if our language supports it.

Variation: Inner Test Double

A popular way to implement a *Hard-Coded Test Double* is to code it as an anonymous inner class or block closure within the *Test Method*. This strategy gives the *Test Double* access to instance variables and constants of the *Testcase Class* and even the local variables of the *Test Method*, which can eliminate the need to configure the *Test Double*.

While the name of this variation is based on the name of the Java language construct of which it takes advantage, many programming languages have an equivalent mechanism for defining code to be run later using blocks or closures.

**Hard-Coded
Test Double**

Also known as:
*Loopback,
Testcase Class
as Test Double*

We typically use an *Inner Test Double* when we are building a *Hard-Coded Test Double* that is relatively simple and is used only within a single *Test Method*. Many people find the use of a *Hard-Coded Test Double* more intuitive than using a *Self Shunt* because they can see exactly what is going on within the *Test Method*. Readers who are unfamiliar with the syntax of anonymous inner classes or blocks may find the test difficult to understand, however.

Variation: Pseudo-Object

One challenge facing writers of *Hard-Coded Test Doubles* is that we must implement all the methods in the interface that the SUT *might* call. In statically typed languages such as Java and C#, we must at least implement all methods declared in the interface implied by the class or type associated with however we access the DOC. This often "forces" us to subclass from the real DOC to avoid providing dummy implementations for these methods.

One way of reducing the programming effort is to provide a default class that implements all the interface methods and throws a unique error. We can then implement a *Hard-Coded Test Double* by subclassing this concrete class and overriding just the one method we expect the SUT to call while we are exercising it. If the SUT calls any other methods, the *Pseudo-Object* throws an error, thereby failing the test.

**Hard-Coded
Test Double**

Motivating Example

The following test verifies the basic functionality of the component that formats an HTML string containing the current time. Unfortunately, it depends on the real system clock, so it rarely passes!

```
public void testDisplayCurrentTime_AtMidnight() {
    // fixture setup
    TimeDisplay sut = new TimeDisplay();
    // exercise SUT
    String result = sut.getCurrentTimeAsHtmlFragment();
    // verify direct output
    String expectedTimeString =
        "<span class=\"tinyBoldText\">Midnight</span>";
    assertEquals( expectedTimeString, result);
}
```

Refactoring Notes

The most common transition is from using the real component to using a *Hard-Coded Test Double*.[4] To make this transition, we need to build the *Test Double* itself and install it from within our *Test Method*. We may also need to introduce a way to install the *Test Double* using one of the *Dependency Injection* patterns (page 678) if the SUT does not already support this installation. The process for doing so is described in the Replace Dependency with Test Double (page 522) refactoring.

Example: Test Double Class

Here's the same test modified to use a *Hard-Coded Test Double* class to allow control over the time:

```
public void testDisplayCurrentTime_AtMidnight_HCM()
        throws Exception {
   // Fixture setup
   //   Instantiate hard-coded Test Stub
   TimeProvider testStub = new MidnightTimeProvider();
   //   Instantiate SUT
   TimeDisplay sut = new TimeDisplay();
   //   Inject Test Stub into SUT
   sut.setTimeProvider(testStub);
   // Exercise SUT
   String result = sut.getCurrentTimeAsHtmlFragment();
   // Verify direct output
   String expectedTimeString =
      "<span class=\"tinyBoldText\">Midnight</span>";
   assertEquals("Midnight", expectedTimeString, result);
}
```

This test is hard to understand without seeing the definition of the *Hard-Coded Test Double*. We can readily see how this approach might lead to an *Obscure Test* caused by a *Mystery Guest* if the *Hard-Coded Test Double* is not close at hand.

```
class MidnightTimeProvider implements TimeProvider {
   public Calendar getTime() {
      Calendar myTime = new GregorianCalendar();
      myTime.set(Calendar.HOUR_OF_DAY, 0);
      myTime.set(Calendar.MINUTE, 0);
      return myTime;
   }
}
```

---

[4] We rarely move from a *Configurable Test Double* to a *Hard-Coded Test Double* because we generally seek to make the *Test Double* more—not less—reusable.

Hard-Coded Test Double

Depending on the programming language, this *Test Double Class* can be defined in a number of different places, including within the body of the *Testcase Class* (an inner class) and as a separate free-standing class either in the same file as the test or in its own file. Of course, the farther away the *Test Double Class* resides from the *Test Method*, the more of a *Mystery Guest* it becomes.

Example: Self Shunt/Loopback

Here's a test that uses a *Self Shunt* to allow control over the time:

```
public class SelfShuntExample extends TestCase
implements TimeProvider {
   public void testDisplayCurrentTime_AtMidnight() throws Exception {
      // fixture setup
      TimeDisplay sut = new TimeDisplay();
      // mock setup
      sut.setTimeProvider(this); // self shunt installation
      // exercise SUT
      String result = sut.getCurrentTimeAsHtmlFragment();
      // verify direct output
      String expectedTimeString =
         "<span class=\"tinyBoldText\">Midnight</span>";
      assertEquals("Midnight", expectedTimeString, result);
   }

   public Calendar getTime() {
      Calendar myTime = new GregorianCalendar();
      myTime.set(Calendar.MINUTE, 0);
      myTime.set(Calendar.HOUR_OF_DAY, 0);
      return myTime;
   }
}
```

Note how both the *Test Method* that installs the *Hard-Coded Test Double* and the implementation of the getTime method called by the SUT are members of the same class. We used the *Setter Injection* pattern (see *Dependency Injection*) to install the *Hard-Coded Test Double*. Because this example is written in a statically typed language, we had to add the clause implements TimeProvider to the *Testcase Class* declaration so that the sut.setTimeProvider(this) statement will compile. In a dynamically typed language, this step is unnecessary.

**Hard-Coded
Test Double**

Example: Subclassed Inner Test Double

Here's a JUnit test that uses a *Subclassed Inner Test Double* using Java's "Anonymous Inner Class" syntax:

```
public void testDisplayCurrentTime_AtMidnight_AIM() throws Exception {
   // Fixture setup
   //    Define and instantiate Test Stub
   TimeProvider testStub = new TimeProvider() {
   // Anonymous inner stub
      public Calendar getTime() {
         Calendar myTime = new GregorianCalendar();
         myTime.set(Calendar.MINUTE, 0);
         myTime.set(Calendar.HOUR_OF_DAY, 0);
         return myTime;
      }
   };
   //    Instantiate SUT
   TimeDisplay sut = new TimeDisplay();
   //    Inject Test Stub into SUT
   sut.setTimeProvider(testStub);
   // Exercise SUT
   String result = sut.getCurrentTimeAsHtmlFragment();
   // Verify direct output
   String expectedTimeString =
         "<span class=\"tinyBoldText\">Midnight</span>";
   assertEquals("Midnight", expectedTimeString, result);
}
```

Hard-Coded Test Double

Here we used the name of the real depended-on class (TimeProvider) in the call to new for the definition of the *Hard-Coded Test Double*. By including a definition of the method getTime within curly braces after the classname, we are actually creating an anonymous *Subclassed Test Double* inside the *Test Method*.

Example: Inner Test Double Subclassed from Pseudo-Class

Suppose we have replaced one implementation of a method with another implementation that we need to leave around for backward-compatibility purposes, but want to write tests to ensure that the old method is no longer called. This is easy to do if we already have the following *Pseudo-Object* definition:

```
/**
 * Base class for hand-coded Test Stubs and Mock Objects
 */
public class PseudoTimeProvider implements ComplexTimeProvider {

   public Calendar getTime() throws TimeProviderEx {
      throw new PseudoClassException();
   }

   public Calendar getTimeDifference(Calendar baseTime,
                                     Calendar otherTime)
          throws TimeProviderEx {
      throw new PseudoClassException();
```

```
      }

   public Calendar getTime( String timeZone ) throws TimeProviderEx {
      throw new PseudoClassException();
   }
}
```

We can now write a test that ensures the old version of the getTime method is *not* called by subclassing and overriding the newer version of the method (the one we *expect* to be called by the SUT):

```
public void testDisplayCurrentTime_AtMidnight_PS() throws Exception {
   // Fixture setup
   //    Define and instantiate Test Stub
   TimeProvider testStub = new PseudoTimeProvider()
   { // Anonymous inner stub
      public Calendar getTime(String timeZone) {
         Calendar myTime = new GregorianCalendar();
         myTime.set(Calendar.MINUTE, 0);
         myTime.set(Calendar.HOUR_OF_DAY, 0);
         return myTime;
      }
   };
   //    Instantiate SUT
   TimeDisplay sut = new TimeDisplay();
   //    Inject Test Stub into SUT:
   sut.setTimeProvider(testStub);
   // Exercise SUT
   String result = sut.getCurrentTimeAsHtmlFragment();
   // Verify direct output
   String expectedTimeString =
         "<span class=\"tinyBoldText\">Midnight</span>";
   assertEquals("Midnight", expectedTimeString, result);
}
```

Hard-Coded
Test Double

If any of the other methods are called, the base class methods are invoked and throw an exception. Therefore, if we run this test and one of the methods we didn't override is called, we will see the following output as the first line of the JUnit stack trace for this test error:

```
com..PseudoClassEx: Unexpected call to unsupported method.
at com..PseudoTimeProvider.getTime(PseudoTimeProvider.java:22)
at com..TimeDisplay.getCurrentTimeAsHtmlFragment(TimeDisplay.java:64)
at com..TimeDisplayTestSolution.
   testDisplayCurrentTime_AtMidnight_PS(
      TimeDisplayTestSolution.java:247)
```

What's in a (Pattern) Name?

The Importance of Good Names

Names are important because they are a key part of how we communicate. Names are labels we attach to concepts. Good names help us communicate those concepts. This is true when we are communicating with people who already know the names, but especially when we are communicating with people who don't. Consider the following example.

Early in my pattern-writing days, I attended the very first Pattern Languages of Programs (PLoP) conference (http://www.hillside.net/conferences/plop). At the conference, the well-known author Jim Coplien ("Cope," to his friends) had a pattern language of organizational patterns being workshopped. One of the patterns was called "Buffalo Mountain"; another was called "Architect Also Implements." These two pattern names are at opposite ends of the spectrum as far as pattern names are concerned.

The gist of "Architect Also Implements" can be gleaned from the pattern name even if a person has not read the actual pattern. The name is both a placeholder for the pattern and meaningful in its own right.

The name "Buffalo Mountain," by contrast, does not readily communicate its underlying meaning. To this day I can still remember the story behind the name—but I cannot remember the actual focus of the pattern. The name was based on a graph that plotted some data related to the pattern. An early reviewer thought it resembled the profile of a nearby mountain called Buffalo Mountain. Thus, while the pattern name is memorable, it is not very evocative.

Closer to home, *Self Shunt* (see *Hard-Coded Test Double* on page 568) is an example of a name that is less than evocative because the term "shunt" is not widely used except in a few specialized fields. Michael Feathers does a good job explaining the background of the name in his description of the pattern. Unless you've read that description, however, the name is "just a name." A more evocative name might be something like "Testcase Class as Test Double" or "Loopback" but even the latter suffers from ambiguity because it isn't clear what is being looped back. So the name *Self Shunt* survives because it is in common use.

Hard-Coded Test Double

Other Naming Considerations

People might ask why I sometimes propose alternative names for some patterns. The preceding story highlights one of the reasons. Another reason is that in a larger collection of patterns (such as this book), it is important that there exists a "system of names."

Let me illustrate this second reason with an example. Many people advocate the use of a setUp method to create the test fixture. This approach moves the fixture setup logic out of each individual *Test Method* (page 348) and into a single place where it can be reused. Many people might refer to this pattern as "Shared Setup Method." But in this **pattern language**, I've chosen to call it *Implicit Setup* (page 424). Why?

It comes down to the names of other patterns in the language. On the one hand, "Shared Setup Method" could easily be confused with the existing pattern *Shared Fixture* (page 317). (The former pattern deals with sharing code, whereas the latter pattern focuses on sharing the runtime objects in the fixture.) On the other hand, the two major alternatives to *Implicit Setup* are called *In-line Setup* (page 408) and *Delegated Setup* (page 411). Wouldn't you agree that "In-line Setup, Delegated Setup, Implicit Setup" forms a better "system of names" than "In-line Setup, Delegated Setup, Shared Setup Method"? The connection between the pattern names is much more obvious when we consider all the major alternative patterns when choosing the system of names.

Why Standardize Testing Patterns?

The last part of this soapbox highlights why I think it is important for us to standardize the names of the test automation patterns, especially those related to *Test Stubs* (page 529) and *Mock Objects* (page 544). The key issue here relates to succinctness of communication.

When someone tells you, "Put a mock in it" (pun intended!), what advice is that person giving you? Depending on what the person means by a "mock," he or she could be suggesting that you control the indirect inputs of your SUT using a *Test Stub* or that you replace your database with a *Fake Database* (see *Fake Object* on page 551) that will reduce test interactions and speed up your tests by a factor of 50. (Yes, 50! See the sidebar "Faster Tests Without Shared Fixtures" on page 319.) Or perhaps the person is suggesting that you verify that your SUT calls the correct methods by installing an *Eager Mock Object* (see *Mock Object*) preconfigured

Continued...

Hard-Coded
Test Double

with the *Expected Behavior* (see *Behavior Verification* on page 468). If everyone used "mock" to mean a *Mock Object*—no more or less—then the advice would be pretty clear. As I write this, the advice is very murky because we have taken to calling just about any *Test Double* (page 522) a "mock object" (despite the objections of the authors of the original paper on *Mock Objects* [ET]).

Further Reading

If you want to find out what "Buffalo Mountain" is really about, go to http://www1.bell-labs.com/user/cope/Patterns/Process/section29.html.

You can find "Architect Also Implements" at http://www1.bell-labs.com/user/cope/Patterns/Process/section16.html.

Interestingly, Alistair Cockburn wrote a similar comparison of pattern names in an article on his Web site (http://alistair.cockburn.us) and chose exactly the same two pattern names in his comparison. Coincidence or pattern?

**Hard-Coded
Test Double**

In addition to failing the test, this scheme makes it very easy to see exactly which method *was* called. The bonus is that it works for calls to all unexpected methods with no additional effort.

Further Reading

Many of the "how to" books on test-driven development provide examples of *Self Shunt*, including [TDD-APG], [TDD-BE], [UTwJ], [PUT], and [JuPG]. The original write-up was by Michael Feathers and is accessible at http://www.objectmentor.com/resources/articles/SelfShunPtrn.pdf

The original "Shunt" pattern is written up at http://http://c2.com/cgi/wiki?ShuntPattern, along with a list of alternative names including "Loopback." See the sidebar "What's in a (Pattern) Name?" on page 576 for a discussion of how to select meaningful and evocative pattern names.

The *Pseudo-Object* pattern is described in the paper "Pseudo-Classes: Very Simple and Lightweight Mock Object-like Classes for Unit-Testing" available at http://www.devx.com/Java/Article/22599/1954?pf=true.

Test-Specific Subclass

*How can we make code testable when we need to access
private state of the SUT?*

**We add methods that expose the state or behavior needed by the test
to a subclass of the SUT.**

Also known as:
*Test-Specific
Extension*

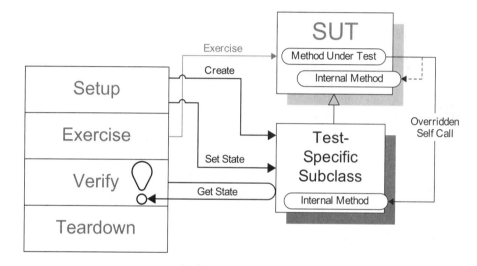

**Test-Specific
Subclass**

If the SUT was not designed specifically to be testable, we may find that the
test cannot gain access to a state that it must initialize or verify at some point
in the test.

A *Test-Specific Subclass* is a simple yet very powerful way to open up the
SUT for testing purposes without modifying the code of the SUT itself.

How It Works

We define a subclass of the SUT and add methods that modify the behavior of
the SUT just enough to make it testable by implementing control points and
observation points. This effort typically involves exposing instance variables
using setters and getters or perhaps adding a method to put the SUT into a
specific state without moving through its entire life cycle.

Because the *Test-Specific Subclass* would be packaged together with the tests that use it, the use of a *Test-Specific Subclass* does not change how the SUT is seen by the rest of the application.

When to Use It

We should use a *Test-Specific Subclass* whenever we need to modify the SUT to improve its testability but doing so directly would result in *Test Logic in Production* (page 217). Although we can use a *Test-Specific Subclass* for a number of purposes, all of those scenarios share a common goal: They improve testability by letting us get at the insides of the SUT more easily. A *Test-Specific Subclass* can be a double-edged sword, however. By breaking encapsulation, it allows us to tie our tests even more closely to the implementation, which can in turn result in *Fragile Tests* (page 239).

Variation: State-Exposing Subclass

If we are doing *State Verification* (page 462), we can subclass the SUT (or some component of it) so that we can see the internal state of the SUT for use in *Assertion Methods* (page 362). Usually, this effort involves adding **accessor** methods for private instance variables. We may also allow the test to set the state as a way to avoid *Obscure Tests* (page 186) caused by *Obscure Setup* (see *Obscure Test*) logic.

Variation: Behavior-Exposing Subclass

If we want to test the individual steps of a complex algorithm individually, we can subclass the SUT to expose the private methods that implement the Self-Calls [WWW]. Because most languages do not allow for relaxing the visibility of a method, we often have to use a different name in the *Test-Specific Subclass* and make a call to the superclass's method.

Variation: Behavior-Modifying Subclass

If the SUT contains some behavior that we do not want to occur when testing, we can override whatever method implements the behavior with an empty method body. This technique works best when the SUT uses Self-Calls (or a Template Method [GOF]) to delegate the steps of an algorithm to methods on itself or subclasses.

Also known as:
Subclassed Test Double

Variation: Test Double Subclass

To ensure that a *Test Double* (page 522) is type-compatible with a DOC we wish to replace, we can make the *Test Double* a subclass of that component. This may be the only way we can build a *Test Double* that the compiler will accept when variables are statically typed using concrete classes.[5] (We should not have to take this step with dynamically typed languages such as Ruby, Python, Perl, and JavaScript.) We then override any methods whose behavior we want to change and add any methods we require to transform the *Test Double* into a *Configurable Test Double* (page 558) if we so desire.

Unlike the *Behavior-Modifying Subclass*, the *Test Double Subclass* does not just "tweak" the behavior of the SUT (or a part thereof) but replaces it entirely with canned behavior.

Variation: Substituted Singleton

Also known as:
*Subclassed
Singleton,
Substitutable
Singleton*

The Substituted Singleton is a special case of *Test Double Subclass*. We use it when we want to replace a DOC with a *Test Double* and the SUT does not support *Dependency Injection* (page 678) or *Dependency Lookup* (page 686).

Implementation Notes

The use of a *Test-Specific Subclass* brings some challenges:

- Feature granularity: ensuring that any behavior we want to override or expose is in its own single-purpose method. It is enabled through copious use of small methods and Self-Calls.

Test-Specific Subclass

- Feature visibility: ensuring that subclasses can access attributes and behavior of the SUT class. It is primarily an issue in statically typed languages such as Java, C#, and C++; dynamically typed languages typically do not enforce visibility.

As with *Test Doubles*, we must be careful to ensure that we do not replace any of the behavior we are actually trying to test.

In languages that support class extensions without the need for subclassing (e.g., Smalltalk, Ruby, JavaScript, and other dynamic languages), a *Test-Specific Subclass* can be implemented as a class extension in the test package. We need to be aware, however, whether the extensions will make it into production; doing so would introduce *Test Logic in Production*.

---

[5] That is, by using a concrete class as the type of the variable rather than an abstract class or interface.

Visibility of Features

In languages that enforce scope (visibility) of variables and methods, we may
need to change the visibility of the variables to allow subclasses to access them.
While such a change affects the actual SUT code, it would typically be considered much less intrusive or misleading than changing the visibility to public
(thereby allowing any code in the application to access the variables) or adding
the test-specific methods directly to the SUT.

   For example, in Java, we might change the visibility of instance variables
from private to protected to allow the *Test-Specific Subclass* to access them.
Similarly, we might change the visibility of methods to allow the *Test-Specific
Subclass* to call them.

Granularity of Features

Long methods are difficult to test because they often bring too many dependencies into play. By comparison, short methods tend to be much simpler to test
because they do only one thing. Self-Call offers an easy way to reduce the size
of methods. We delegate parts of an algorithm to other methods implemented
on the same class. This strategy allows us to test these methods independently.
We can also confirm that the calling method calls these methods in the right
sequence by overriding them in a *Test Double Subclass* (see *Test-Specific Subclass*
on page 579).

   Self-Call is a part of good object-oriented code design in that it keeps methods
small and focused on implementing a single responsibility of the SUT. We can use
this pattern whenever we are doing test-driven development and have control
over the design of the SUT. We may find that we need to introduce Self-Call when
we encounter long methods where some parts of the algorithm depend on things
we do not want to exercise (e.g., database calls). This likelihood is especially
high, for example, when the SUT is built using a *Transaction Script* [PEAA]
architecture. Self-Call can be retrofitted easily using the Extract Method [Fowler]
refactoring supported by most modern IDEs.

(sidebar:) **Test-Specific Subclass**

Motivating Example

The test in the following example is nondeterministic because it depends on the
time. Our SUT is an object that formats the time for display as part of a Web
page. It gets the time by asking a Singleton called TimeProvider to retrieve the time
from a calendar object that it gets from the container.

```
public void testDisplayCurrentTime_AtMidnight() throws Exception {
    // Set up SUT
```

```
    TimeDisplay theTimeDisplay = new TimeDisplay();
    // Exercise SUT
    String actualTimeString =
        theTimeDisplay.getCurrentTimeAsHtmlFragment();
    // Verify outcome
    String expectedTimeString =
        "<span class=\"tinyBoldText\">Midnight</span>";
    assertEquals( "Midnight",
                 expectedTimeString,
                 actualTimeString);
}

public void testDisplayCurrentTime_AtOneMinuteAfterMidnight()
        throws Exception {
    // Set up SUT
    TimeDisplay actualTimeDisplay = new TimeDisplay();
    // Exercise SUT
    String actualTimeString =
        actualTimeDisplay.getCurrentTimeAsHtmlFragment();
    // Verify outcome
    String expectedTimeString =
        "<span class=\"tinyBoldText\">12:01 AM</span>";
    assertEquals( "12:01 AM",
                 expectedTimeString,
                 actualTimeString);
}
```

Test-Specific Subclass

These tests rarely pass, and they never pass in the same test run! The code within the SUT looks like this:

```
public String getCurrentTimeAsHtmlFragment() {
    Calendar timeProvider;
    try {
        timeProvider = getTime();
    } catch (Exception e) {
        return e.getMessage();
    }
        // etc.
}

protected Calendar getTime() {
    return TimeProvider.getInstance().getTime();
}
```

The code for the Singleton follows:

```
public class TimeProvider {
    protected static TimeProvider soleInstance = null;

    protected TimeProvider() {};

    public static TimeProvider getInstance() {
```

```
        if (soleInstance==null) soleInstance = new TimeProvider();
        return soleInstance;
    }

    public Calendar getTime() {
        return Calendar.getInstance();
    }
}
```

Refactoring Notes

The precise nature of the refactoring employed to introduce a *Test-Specific Subclass* depends on why we are using one. When we are using a *Test-Specific Subclass* to expose "private parts" of the SUT or override undesirable parts of its behavior, we merely define the *Test-Specific Subclass* as a subclass of the SUT and create an instance of the *Test-Specific Subclass* to exercise in the setup fixture phase of our *Four-Phase Test* (page 358).

When we are using the *Test-Specific Subclass* to replace a DOC of the SUT, however, we need to use a Replace Dependency with Test Double (page 522) refactoring to tell the SUT to use our *Test-Specific Subclass* instead of the real DOC.

In either case, we either override existing methods or add new methods to the *Test-Specific Subclass* using our language-specific capabilities (e.g., subclassing or mixins) as required by our tests.

Example: Behavior-Modifying Subclass (Test Stub)

Because the SUT uses a Self-Call to the getTime method to ask the TimeProvider for the time, we have an opportunity to use a *Subclassed Test Double* to control the time.[6] Based on this idea we can take a stab at writing our tests as follows (I have shown only one test here):

```
public void testDisplayCurrentTime_AtMidnight() {
    // Fixture setup
    TimeDisplayTestStubSubclass tss = new TimeDisplayTestStubSubclass();
    TimeDisplay sut = tss;
    //   Test Double configuration
    tss.setHours(0);
    tss.setMinutes(0);
    // Exercise SUT
    String result = sut.getCurrentTimeAsHtmlFragment();
```

---

[6] This decision is enabled by the fact that getTime was defined to be protected; we would not be able to do this if it was private.

```
        // Verify outcome
        String expectedTimeString =
                "<span class=\"tinyBoldText\">Midnight</span>";
        assertEquals( expectedTimeString, result );
    }
```

Note that we have used the *Test-Specific Subclass* class for the variable that receives the instance of the SUT; this approach ensures that the methods of the *Configuration Interface* (see *Configurable Test Double*) defined on the *Test-Specific Subclass* are visible to the test.[7] For documentation purposes, we have then assigned the *Test-Specific Subclass* to the variable sut; this is a safe cast because the *Test-Specific Subclass* class is a subclass of the SUT class. This technique also helps us avoid the *Mystery Guest* (see *Obscure Test*) problem caused by hard-coding an important indirect input of our SUT inside the *Test Stub* (page 529).

Now that we have seen how it will be used, it is a simple matter to implement the *Test-Specific Subclass*:

```
public class TimeDisplayTestStubSubclass extends TimeDisplay {

    private int hours;
    private int minutes;

    // Overridden method
    protected Calendar getTime() {
        Calendar myTime = new GregorianCalendar();
        myTime.set(Calendar.HOUR_OF_DAY, this.hours);
        myTime.set(Calendar.MINUTE, this.minutes);
        return myTime;
    }
    /*
     * Configuration Interface
     */
    public void setHours(int hours) {
        this.hours = hours;
    }

    public void setMinutes(int minutes) {
        this.minutes = minutes;
    }
}
```

Test-Specific Subclass

There's no rocket science here—we just had to implement the methods used by the test.

---

[7] We could have used a *Hard-Coded Test Double* (page 568) subclass instead, but that tactic would have required a different *Test-Specific Subclass* for each time we want to test with. Each subclass would simply hard-code the return value of the getTime method.

Example: Behavior-Modifying Subclass (Substituted Singleton)

Suppose our getTime method was declared to be private[8] or static, final or sealed, and so on.[9] Such a declaration would prevent us from overriding the method's behavior in our *Test-Specific Subclass*. What could we do to address our *Nondeterministic Tests* (see *Erratic Test* on page 228)?

Because the design uses a Singleton [GOF] to provide the time, a simple solution is to replace the Singleton during test execution with a *Test Double Subclass*. We can do so as long as it is possible for a subclass to access its soleInstance variable. We use the Introduce Local Extension [Fowler] refactoring (specifically, the subclass variant of it) to create the *Test-Specific Subclass*. Writing the tests first helps us understand the interface we want to implement.

```
public void testDisplayCurrentTime_AtMidnight() {
   TimeDisplay sut = new TimeDisplay();
   //   Install test Singleton
   TimeProviderTestSingleton timeProvideSingleton =
       TimeProviderTestSingleton.overrideSoleInstance();
   timeProvideSingleton.setTime(0,0);
   //   Exercise SUT
   String actualTimeString = sut.getCurrentTimeAsHtmlFragment();
   // Verify outcome
   String expectedTimeString =
       "<span class=\"tinyBoldText\">Midnight</span>";
   assertEquals( expectedTimeString, actualTimeString );
}
```

Test-Specific Subclass

Now that we have a test that uses the *Substituted Singleton*, we can proceed to implement it by subclassing the Singleton and defining the methods the tests will use.

```
public class TimeProviderTestSingleton extends TimeProvider {
   private Calendar myTime = new GregorianCalendar();
   private TimeProviderTestSingleton() {};

   // Installation Interface
   static TimeProviderTestSingleton overrideSoleInstance() {
      // We could save the real instance first, but we won't!
      soleInstance = new TimeProviderTestSingleton();
      return (TimeProviderTestSingleton) soleInstance;
   }

   // Configuration Interface used by the test
```

---

[8] A private method cannot be seen or overridden by a subclass.

[9] This choice prevents a subclass from overriding the method's behavior.

```
public void setTime(int hours, int minutes) {
    myTime.set(Calendar.HOUR_OF_DAY, hours);
    myTime.set(Calendar.MINUTE, minutes);
}

// Usage Interface used by the client
public Calendar getTime() {
    return myTime;
    }
}
```

Here the *Test Double* is a subclass of the real component and has overridden the instance method called by the clients of the Singleton.

Example: Behavior-Exposing Subclass

Suppose we wanted to test the getTime method directly. Because getTime is protected and our test is in a different package from the TimeDisplay class, our test cannot call this method. We could try making our test a subclass of TimeDisplay or we could put it into the same package as TimeDisplay. Unfortunately, both of these solutions come with baggage and may not always be possible.

A more general solution is to expose the behavior using a *Behavior-Exposing Subclass*. We can do so by defining a *Test-Specific Subclass* and adding a public method that calls this method.

Test-Specific Subclass

```
public class TimeDisplayBehaviorExposingTss extends TimeDisplay {

    public Calendar callGetTime() {
        return super.getTime();
    }
}
```

We can now write the test using the *Behavior-Exposing Subclass* as follows:

```
public void testGetTime_default() {
    // create SUT
    TimeDisplayBehaviorExposingTss tsSut =
            new TimeDisplayBehaviorExposingTss();
    // exercise SUT
    //   want to do
    //     Calendar time = sut.getTime();
    //   have to do
    Calendar time = tsSut.callGetTime();
    // verify outcome
    assertEquals( defaultTime, time );
}
```

Example: Defining Test-Specific Equality (Behavior-Modifying Subclass)

Here is an example of a very simple test that fails because the object we pass to assertEquals does not implement test-specific equality. That is, the default equals method returns false even though our test considers the two objects to be equals.

```
protected void setUp() throws Exception {
    oneOutboundFlight = findOneOutboundFlightDto();
}

public void testGetFlights_OneFlight() throws Exception {
    // Exercise System
    List flights = facade.getFlightsByOriginAirport(
                    oneOutboundFlight.getOriginAirportId());
    // Verify Outcome
    assertEquals("Flights at origin - number of flights: ",
                1,
                flights.size());
    FlightDto actualFlightDto = (FlightDto)flights.get(0);
    assertEquals("Flight DTOs at origin",
                oneOutboundFlight,
                actualFlightDto);
}
```

One option is to write a *Custom Assertion* (page 474). Another option is to use a *Test-Specific Subclass* to add a more appropriate definition of equality for our test purposes alone. We can change our fixture setup code slightly to create the *Test-Specific Subclass* as our *Expected Object* (see *State Verification*).

```
private FlightDtoTss oneOutboundFlight;

private FlightDtoTss findOneOutboundFlightDto() {
    FlightDto realDto = helper.findOneOutboundFlightDto();
    return new FlightDtoTss(realDto) ;
}
```

Finally, we implement the *Test-Specific Subclass* by copying and comparing only those fields that we want to use for our test-specific equality.

```
public class FlightDtoTss extends FlightDto {
    public FlightDtoTss(FlightDto realDto) {
        this.destAirportId = realDto.getDestinationAirportId();
        this.equipmentType = realDto.getEquipmentType();
        this.flightNumber = realDto.getFlightNumber();
        this.originAirportId = realDto.getOriginAirportId();
    }
```

```
public boolean equals(Object obj) {
    FlightDto otherDto = (FlightDto) obj;
    if (otherDto == null) return false;
    if (otherDto.getDestAirportId()!= this.destAirportId)
        return false;
    if (otherDto.getOriginAirportId()!= this.originAirportId)
        return false;
    if (otherDto.getFlightNumber()!= this.flightNumber)
        return false;
    if (otherDto.getEquipmentType() != this.equipmentType )
        return false;
    return true;
    }
}
```

In this case we copied the fields from the real DTO into our *Test-Specific Subclass*, but we could just as easily have used the *Test-Specific Subclass* as a wrapper for the real DTO. There are other ways we could have created the *Test-Specific Subclass*; the only real limit is our imagination.

This example also assumes that we have a reasonable toString implementation on our base class that prints out the values of the fields being compared. It is needed because assertEquals will use that implementation when the equals method returns false. Otherwise, we will have no idea of why the objects are considered unequal.

Test-Specific Subclass

Example: State-Exposing Subclass

Suppose we have the following test, which requires a Flight to be in a particular state:

```
protected void setUp() throws Exception {
    super.setUp();
    scheduledFlight = createScheduledFlight();
}

Flight createScheduledFlight() throws InvalidRequestException{
    Flight newFlight = new Flight();
    newFlight.schedule();
    return newFlight;
}

public void testDeschedule_shouldEndUpInUnscheduleState()
                    throws Exception {
    scheduledFlight.deschedule();
    assertTrue("isUnsched", scheduledFlight.isUnscheduled());
}
```

Setting up the fixture for this test requires us to call the method schedule on the flight:

```
public class Flight{
    protected FlightState currentState = new UnscheduledState();

    /**
     * Transitions the Flight from the <code>unscheduled</code>
     * state to the <code>scheduled</code> state.
     * @throws InvalidRequestException when an invalid state
     *              transition is requested
     */
    public void schedule() throws InvalidRequestException{
        currentState.schedule();
    }
}
```

The Flight class uses the State [GOF] pattern and delegates handling of the schedule method to whatever State object is currently referenced by currentState. This test will fail during fixture setup if schedule does not work yet on the default content of currentState. We can avoid this problem by using a *State-Exposing Subclass* that provides a method to move directly into the state, thereby making this an *Independent Test* (see page 42).

Test-Specific Subclass

```
public class FlightTss extends Flight {

    public void becomeScheduled() {
        currentState = new ScheduledState();
    }
}
```

By introducing a new method becomeScheduled on the *Test-Specific Subclass*, we ensure that we will not accidentally override any existing behavior of the SUT. Now all we have to do is instantiate the *Test-Specific Subclass* in our test instead of the base class by modifying our *Creation Method* (page 415).

```
Flight createScheduledFlight() throws InvalidRequestException{
    FlightTss newFlight = new FlightTss();
    newFlight.becomeScheduled();
    return newFlight;
}
```

Note how we still declare that we are returning an instance of the Flight class when we are, in fact, returning an instance of the *Test-Specific Subclass* that has the additional method.

Chapter 24

Test Organization Patterns

Patterns in This Chapter

Test
Organization
Patterns

Named Test Suite

How do we run the tests when we have arbitrary groups of tests to run?

We define a test suite, suitably named, that contains a set of tests that we wish to be able to run as a group.

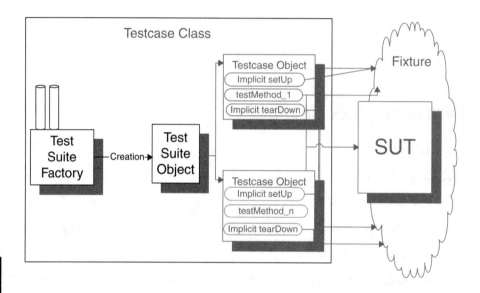

When we have a large number of tests, we need to organize them in a systematic way. A test suite allows us to group tests that have related functionality close to each other. Although we want to be able to run all the tests for the entire application or component easily, we also want to be able to run only those tests applicable to specific subsets of the functionality or subcomponents of the system. In other situations, we want to run only a subset of all the tests we have defined.

Named Test Suites give us a way to choose which predefined subset of the tests we want to run.

How It Works

For each group of related tests that we would like to be able to run as a group, we can define a special *Test Suite Factory* (see *Test Enumeration* on page 399) with an Intent-Revealing Name. The Factory Method [GOF] can use any of several test suite construction techniques to return a *Test Suite Object* (page 387) containing only the specific *Testcase Objects* (page 382) we wish to execute.

When to Use It

Although we often want to run all the tests with a single command, sometimes we want to run only a subset of the tests. The most common reason for doing so is time; for this purpose, running the *AllTests Suite* for a specific context is probably our best bet. When our member of xUnit doesn't support *Test Selection* and the tests we want to run are scattered across multiple contexts and some contexts contain tests we definitely don't want run, we can use a *Subset Suite*.

Variation: AllTests Suite

We often want to run all the tests we have available. With smaller systems, it may be standard practice to run the *AllTests Suite* after checking out a new code base (to ensure we start at a known point) and before every check-in (to ensure all our code works). We typically have an *AllTests Suite* for each package or namespace of software so that we can run subsets of the tests after each code change as part of the "red–green–refactor" cycle.

Variation: Subset Suite

Developers often do not want to run tests because they are *Slow Tests* (page 253). Tests that exercise components that access a database will inevitably run much more slowly than tests that run entirely in memory. By defining one *Named Test Suite* for the database tests and another *Named Test Suite* for the in-memory tests, we can choose not to run the database tests simply by choosing to run the in-memory *Subset Suite*.

Named Test Suite

Another common reason given for not running tests is because the context they need to run is not available. For example, if we don't have a Web server running on our development desktop, or if deploying our software to the Web server takes too long, we won't want to run the tests of components that require the Web server to be running (they would just take extra time to run, and we know they will fail and spoil our chances of achieving a green bar).

Variation: Single Test Suite

The degenerate form of a *Subset Suite* is the *Single Test Suite*, in which we instantiate a single *Testcase Object* so that we can run a single *Test Method* (page 348). This variation is particularly useful when we don't have a *Test Tree Explorer* (see *Test Runner* on page 377) available or when the *Test Method* requires some form of *Setup Decorator* (page 447) to run properly. Some test automaters keep a "MyTest" *Testcase Class* (page 373) open in their workspace at all times specifically for this purpose.

Implementation Notes

The concept of running named sets of tests is independent of how we build the *Named Test Suites*. For example, we can use *Test Enumeration* to build up our suites of tests explicitly or we can use *Test Discovery* (page 393) to find all tests in a particular place (e.g., a namespace or assembly). We can also do *Test Selection* (page 403) from within a suite of tests to create a smaller suite dynamically. Some members of the xUnit family require us to define the *AllTests Suites* for each test package or subsystem manually; others, such as NUnit, automatically create a *Test Suite Object* for each namespace.

When we are using *Test Enumeration* and have *Named Test Suites* for various subsets of the tests, it is better to define our *AllTests Suite* in terms of these subsets. When we implement the *AllTests Suite* as a *Suite of Suites* (see *Test Suite Object*), we need to add a new *Testcase Class* to only a single *Named Test Suite*; this collection of tests is then rolled up into the *AllTests Suite* for the local context as well as the *Named Test Suite* and the next higher context.

Refactoring Notes

Named Test
Suite

The steps to refactor existing code to a *Named Test Suite* are highly dependent on the variant of *Named Test Suite* we are using. For this reason, I'll dispense with the motivating example and skip directly to examples of *Named Test Suites*.

Example: AllTests Suite

An *AllTests Suite* helps us run all the tests for different subsets of the functionality of our choosing. For each subcomponent or context (e.g., a Java package), we define a special test suite (and its corresponding *Test Suite Factory*) called AllTests. In the suite Factory Method on the *Test Suite Factory*, we add all the tests in the current context and all the *Named Test Suites* from any nested contexts (such as nested Java packages). That way, when the top-level *Named Test Suite* is run, all *Named Test Suites* for the nested contexts will be run as well.

The following example illustrates the kind of code that would be required to run all the tests in most members of the xUnit family:

```
public class AllTests {

    public static Test suite() {
```

```
        TestSuite suite = new TestSuite("Test for allJunitTests");
        //$JUnit-BEGIN$
        suite.addTestSuite(
                com.clrstream.camug.example.test.InvoiceTest.class);
        suite.addTest(com.clrstream.ex7.test.AllTests.suite());
        suite.addTest(com.clrstream.ex8.test.AllTests.suite());
        suite.addTestSuite(
                com.xunitpatterns.guardassertion.Example.class);
        //$JUnit-END$
        return suite;
    }
}
```

We had to use a mix of methods in this case because we are adding other *Named Test Suites* as well as *Test Suite Objects* representing a single *Testcase Class*. In JUnit, we use different methods to do this. Other members of the xUnit family, however, may use the same method signature.

The other notable aspect of this example is the JUnit-start and JUnit-end comments. The IDE (in this case, Eclipse) helps us out by automatically regenerating the list between these two comments—a semi-automated form of *Test Discovery*.

Example: Special-Purpose Suite

Suppose we have three major packages (A, B, and C) containing business logic. Each package contains both in-memory objects and database access classes. We would then have corresponding test packages for each of the three packages. Some tests in each package would require the database, while others could run purely in memory.

We want to be able to run the following sets of tests for the entire system, and for each package (A, B, and C):

- All tests

- All database tests

- All in-memory tests

This implies a total of 12 named sets of tests (three named sets for each of four contexts).

In each of the three packages (A, B, and C), we should define the following *Named Test Suites*:

Named Test
Suite

- AllDbTests, by adding all the *Testcase Classes* containing database tests

- AllInMemoryTests, by adding all the *Testcase Classes* containing in-memory tests

- AllTests, by combining AllDbTests and AllInMemoryTests

Then, at the top-level testing context, we define *Named Test Suites* by the same names as follows:

- AllDbTests, by composing all the AllDbTests *Testcase Classes* from packages A, B, and C

- AllInMemoryTests, by composing all the AllInMemoryTests *Testcase Classes* from packages A, B, and C

- AllTests, by composing all the AllTests *Testcase Classes* from packages A, B, and C (This is just the normal *AllTests Suite*.)

If we find ourselves needing to include some tests from a single *Testcase Class* in both *Named Test Suites*, we should split the class into one class for each context (e.g., database tests and in-memory tests).

Example: Single Test Suite

In some circumstances—especially when we are using a debugger—it is highly desirable to not run all the tests in a *Testcase Class*. One way to run only a subset of these tests is to use the *Test Tree Explorer* provided by some *Graphical Test Runners* (see *Test Runner*). When this capability isn't available, a common practice is to disable the tests we don't want run by either commenting them out, copying the entire *Testcase Class* and deleting most of the tests, or changing the names or attributes of the test that cause them to be included by the *Test Discovery* algorithm.

```
public class LostTests extends TestCase {
    public LostTests(String name) {
        super(name);
    }

    public void xtestOne() throws Exception {
        fail("test not implemented");
    }

    /*
    public void testTwo() throws Exception {
        fail("test not implemented");
    }
    */
```

```
    public void testSeventeen() throws Exception {
        assertTrue(true);
    }
}
```

All of these approaches suffer from the potential for *Lost Tests* (see *Production Bugs* on page 268) if the means of running a single test is not reversed properly when the situation requiring this testing strategy has passed. A *Single Test Suite* makes it possible to run the specific test(s) without making *any* changes to the *Testcase Class* in question. This technique takes advantage of the fact that most implementations of xUnit require a one-argument constructor on our *Testcase Class;* this argument consists of the name of the method that this instance of the class will invoke using reflection. The one-argument constructor is called once for each *Test Method* on the class, and the resulting *Testcase Object* is added to the *Test Suite Object*. (This is an example of the Pluggable Behavior [SBPP] pattern.)

We can run a single test by implementing a *Test Suite Factory* class with a single method suite that creates an instance of the desired *Testcase Class* by calling the one-argument constructor with the name of the one *Test Method* to be run. By returning a *Test Suite Object* containing only this one *Testcase Object* from suite, we achieve the desired result (running a single test) without touching the target *Testcase Class*.

```
public class MyTest extends TestCase {

    public  static Test suite() {
        return new LostTests("testSeventeen");
    }
}
```

Named Test Suite

I like to keep a *Single Test Suite* class around all the time and just plug in whatever test I want to run by changing the import statements and the suite method. Often, I maintain several *Single Test Suite* classes so I can flip back and forth between different tests very quickly. I find this technique easier to do than drilling down in the *Test Tree Explorer* and picking the specific test to run manually. (Your mileage may vary!)

Example: Smoke Test Suite

We can take the idea of a *Special-Purpose Suite* and combine it with the implementation technique of a *Single Test Suite* to create a Smoke Test [SCM] suite. This strategy involves picking a representative test or two from each of the major areas of the system and including those tests in a single *Test Suite Object*.

```
public class SmokeTestSuite extends TestCase {
   public static Test suite() {
      TestSuite mySuite = new TestSuite("Smoke Tests");

      mySuite.addTest( new LostTests("testSeventeen") );
      mySuite.addTest( new SampleTests("testOne")      );
      mySuite.addTest( new FlightManagementFacadeTest(
         "testGetFlightsByOriginAirports_TwoOutboundFlights"));
      // add additional tests here as needed...
      return mySuite;
   }
}
```

This scheme won't test our system thoroughly, but it is a quick way to find out whether some part of the core functionality is broken.

Named Test Suite

Test Utility Method

How do we reduce Test Code Duplication?

We encapsulate the test logic we want to reuse behind a suitably named utility method.

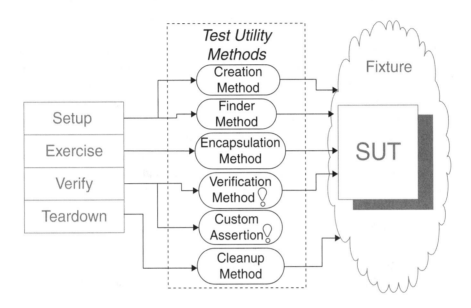

As we write tests, we will invariably find ourselves needing to repeat the same logic in many, many tests. Initially, we will just "clone and twiddle" as we write additional tests that need the same logic. Sooner or later, however, we will come to the realization that this *Test Code Duplication* (page 213) is starting to cause problems. This point is a good time to think about introducing a *Test Utility Method*.

How It Works

The subroutine and the function were two of the earliest ways devised to reuse logic in several places within a program. A *Test Utility Method* is just the same principle applied to object-oriented test code. We move any logic that appears in more than one test into a *Test Utility Method*; we can then call this method from various tests or even several times from within a single test. Of course, we will want to pass in anything that varies from usage to usage as arguments to the *Test Utility Method*.

When to Use It

We should use a *Test Utility Method* whenever test logic appears in several tests and we want to be able to reuse that logic. We might also use a *Test Utility Method* because we want to be very sure that the logic works as expected. The best way to achieve that kind of certainty is to write *Self-Checking Tests* (unit tests—see page 26) for the reusable test logic. Because the *Test Methods* (page 348) cannot easily be tested, it is best to do this by moving the logic out of the test methods and into *Test Utility Methods*, where it can be more easily tested.

The main drawback of using the *Test Utility Method* pattern is that it creates another API that the test automaters must build and understand. This extra effort can be largely mitigated through the use of Intent-Revealing Names [SBPP] for the *Test Utility Methods* and through the use of refactoring as the means for defining the *Test Utility Methods*.

There are as many different kinds of *Test Utility Methods* as there are kinds of logic in a *Test Method*. Next, we briefly summarize some of the most popular kinds. Some of these variations are important enough to warrant their own pattern write-ups in the corresponding section of this book.

Variation: Creation Method

Creation Methods (page 415) are used to create ready-to-use objects as part of fixture setup. They hide the complexity of object creation and interdependencies from the test. *Creation Method* has enough variants to warrant addressing this pattern in its own section.

Variation: Attachment Method

An *Attachment Method* (see *Creation Method*) is a special form of *Creation Method* used to amend already-created objects as part of fixture setup.

Variation: Finder Method

We can encapsulate any logic required to retrieve objects from a *Shared Fixture* (page 317) within a function that returns the object(s). We then give this function an Intent-Revealing Name so that anyone reading the test can easily understand the fixture we are using in this test.

We should use a *Finder Method* whenever we need to find an existing *Shared Fixture* object that meets some criteria and we want to avoid a *Fragile Fixture* (see *Fragile Test* on page 239) and *High Test Maintenance Cost* (page 265). *Finder Methods* can be used in either a pure *Shared Fixture* strategy or a hybrid strategy such as *Immutable Shared Fixture* (see *Shared Fixture*). *Finder*

Methods also help prevent *Obscure Tests* (page 186) by encapsulating the mechanism of how the required objects are found and exactly which objects to use, thereby enabling the reader to focus on understanding *why* a particular object is being used and how it relates to the expected outcome described in the assertions. This helps us move toward *Tests as Documentation* (see page 23).

Although most *Finder Methods* return a single object reference, that object may be the root of a tree of objects (e.g., an invoice might refer to the customer and various addresses as well as containing a list of line items). In some circumstances, we may choose to define a *Finder Method* that returns a collection (Array or Hash) of objects, but the use of this type of *Finder Method* is less common. *Finder Methods* may also update parameters to pass additional objects back to the test that called them, although this approach is not as intent-revealing as use of a function. I do not recommend initialization of instance variables as a way of passing back objects because it is obscure and keeps us from moving the *Finder Method* to a *Test Helper* (page 643) later.

The *Finder Method* can find objects in the *Shared Fixture* in several ways: by using direct references (instance variables or class variables initialized in the fixture setup logic), by looking the objects up using known keys, or by searching for the objects using specific criteria. Using direct references or known keys has the advantage of always returning exactly the same object each time the test is run. The main drawback is that some other test may have modified the object such that it may no longer match the criteria implied by the *Finder Method's* name. Searching by criteria can avoid this problem, though the resulting tests may take longer to run and might be less deterministic if they use different objects each time they are run. Either way, we must modify the code in fewer places whenever the *Shared Fixture* is modified (compared to when the objects are used directly within the *Test Method*).

Test Utility Method

Variation: SUT Encapsulation Method

Also known as:
SUT API Encapsulation

Another reason for using a *Test Utility Method* is to encapsulate *unnecessary* knowledge of the API of the SUT. What constitutes unnecessary? Any method we call on the SUT that is not the method being tested creates additional coupling between the test and the SUT. *Creation Methods* and *Custom Assertions* (page 474) are common enough examples of *SUT Encapsulation Methods* to warrant their own write-ups as separate patterns. This section focuses on the less common uses of *SUT Encapsulation Methods*. For example, if the method that we are exercising (or that we use for verifying the outcome) has a complicated signature, we increase the amount of work involved to write and maintain the test code and may make it harder to understand the tests (*Obscure Test*). We can avoid this problem by wrapping these calls in *SUT Encapsulation Methods* that are intent-revealing and may have simpler signatures.

Variation: Custom Assertion

Custom Assertions are used to specify test-specific equality in a way that is reusable across many tests. They hide the complexity of comparing the expected outcome with the actual outcome. *Custom Assertions* are typically free of side effects in that they do not interact with the SUT to retrieve the outcome; that task is left to the caller.

Variation: Verification Method

Verification Methods (see *Custom Assertion*) are used to verify that the expected outcome has occurred. They hide the complexity of verifying the outcome from the test. Unlike *Custom Assertions*, *Verification Methods* interact with the SUT.

Variation: Parameterized Test

The most complete form of the *Test Utility Method* pattern is the *Parameterized Test* (page 607). It is, in essence, an almost complete test that can be reused in many circumstances. We simply provide the data that varies from test to test as a parameter and let the *Parameterized Test* execute all the stages of the *Four-Phase Test* (page 358) for us.

Variation: Cleanup Method

Cleanup Methods[1] are used during the fixture teardown phase of the test to clean up any resources that might still be allocated after the test ends. Refer to the pattern *Automated Teardown* (page 503) for a more detailed discussion and examples.

Implementation Notes

The main objection some people have to using *Test Utility Methods* is that this pattern removes some of the logic from the test, which *may* make the test harder to read. One way we can avoid this problem when using *Test Utility Methods* is to give Intent-Revealing Names to the *Test Utility Methods*. In fact, well-chosen names can make the tests even easier to understand because they

---

[1] One could call this pattern a "Teardown Method," but that name might be confused with the method used in *Implicit Teardown* (page 516).

help prevent *Obscure Tests* by defining a *Higher Level Language* (see page 41) for defining tests. It is also helpful to keep the *Test Utility Methods* relatively small and self-contained. We can achieve this goal by passing all arguments to these methods explicitly as parameters (rather than using instance variables) and by returning any objects that the tests will require as explicit return values or updated parameters.

To ensure that the *Test Utility Methods* have Intent-Revealing Names, we should let the tests pull the *Test Utility Methods* into existence rather than just inventing *Test Utility Methods* that we think *may* be needed later. This "outside-in" approach to writing code avoids "borrowing tomorrow's trouble" and helps us find the minimal solution.

Writing the reusable *Test Utility Method* is relatively straightforward. The trickier question is where we would put this method. If the *Test Utility Method* is needed only in *Test Methods* in a single *Testcase Class* (page 373), then we can put it onto that class. If we need the *Test Utility Method* in several classes, however, the solution becomes a bit more complicated. The key issue relates to *type visibility*. The client classes need to be able to see the *Test Utility Method,* and the *Test Utility Method* needs to be able to see all the types and classes on which it depends. When it doesn't depend on many types/classes or when everything it depends on is visible from a single place, we can put the *Test Utility Method* into a common *Testcase Superclass* (page 638) that we define for our project or company. If it depends on types/classes that cannot be seen from a single place that all the clients can see, then we may need to put the *Test Utility Method* on a *Test Helper* in the appropriate test package or subsystem. In larger systems with many groups of domain objects, it is common practice to have one *Test Helper* for each group (package) of related domain objects.

Test Utility Method

Variation: Test Utility Test

One major advantage of using *Test Utility Methods* is that otherwise *Untestable Test Code* (see *Hard-to-Test Code* on page 209) can now be tested with *Self-Checking Tests*. The exact nature of such tests varies based on the kind of *Test Utility Method* being tested but a good example is a *Custom Assertion Test* (see *Custom Assertion*).

Motivating Example

The following example shows a test as many novice test automaters would first write it:

```
public void testAddItemQuantity_severalQuantity_v1(){
    Address billingAddress = null;
```

```
        Address shippingAddress = null;
        Customer customer = null;
        Product product = null;
        Invoice invoice = null;
        try {
            //    Fixture Setup
            billingAddress = new Address("1222 1st St SW",
                                    "Calgary", "Alberta",
                                    "T2N 2V2", "Canada");
            shippingAddress = new Address("1333 1st St SW",
                                    "Calgary", "Alberta",
                                    "T2N 2V2", "Canada");
            customer = new Customer( 99, "John", "Doe",
                                    new BigDecimal("30"),
                                    billingAddress,
                                    shippingAddress);
            product = new Product( 88, "SomeWidget",
                                    new BigDecimal("19.99"));
            invoice = new Invoice( customer );
            // Exercise SUT
            invoice.addItemQuantity( product, 5 );
            // Verify Outcome
            List lineItems = invoice.getLineItems();
            if (lineItems.size() == 1) {
                LineItem actItem = (LineItem) lineItems.get(0);
                assertEquals("inv", invoice, actItem.getInv());
                assertEquals("prod", product, actItem.getProd());
                assertEquals("quant", 5, actItem.getQuantity());
                assertEquals("discount",
                            new BigDecimal("30"),
                            actItem.getPercentDiscount());
                assertEquals("unit price",
                            new BigDecimal("19.99"),
                            actItem.getUnitPrice());
                assertEquals("extended",
                            new BigDecimal("69.96"),
                            actItem.getExtendedPrice());
            } else {
                assertTrue("Invoice should have 1 item", false);
            }
        } finally {
            // Teardown
            deleteObject(invoice);
            deleteObject(product);
            deleteObject(customer);
            deleteObject(billingAddress);
            deleteObject(shippingAddress);
        }
    }
```

**Test Utility
Method**

This test is difficult to understand because it exhibits many code smells, including *Obscure Test* and *Hard-Coded Test Data* (see *Obscure Test*).

Refactoring Notes

We often create *Test Utility Methods* by mining existing tests for reusable logic when we are writing new tests. We can use an Extract Method [Fowler] refactoring to pull the code for the *Test Utility Method* out of one *Test Method* and put it onto the *Testcase Class* as a *Test Utility Method*. From there, we may choose to move the *Test Utility Method* to a superclass by using a Pull Up Method [Fowler] refactoring or to another class by using a Move Method [Fowler] refactoring.

Example: Test Utility Method

Here's the refactored version of the earlier test. Note how much simpler this test is to understand than the original version. And this is just one example of what we can achieve by using *Test Utility Methods*!

```
public void testAddItemQuantity_severalQuantity_v13(){
    final int QUANTITY = 5;
    final BigDecimal CUSTOMER_DISCOUNT = new BigDecimal("30");
    //   Fixture Setup
    Customer customer =
        findActiveCustomerWithDiscount(CUSTOMER_DISCOUNT);
    Product product = findCurrentProductWith3DigitPrice( );
    Invoice invoice = createInvoice(customer);
    // Exercise SUT
    invoice.addItemQuantity(product, QUANTITY);
    // Verify Outcome
    final BigDecimal BASE_PRICE = product.getUnitPrice().
    multiply(new BigDecimal(QUANTITY));
    final BigDecimal EXTENDED_PRICE =
        BASE_PRICE.subtract(BASE_PRICE.multiply(
                        CUSTOMER_DISCOUNT.movePointLeft(2)));
    LineItem expected =
            createLineItem( QUANTITY, CUSTOMER_DISCOUNT,
                        EXTENDED_PRICE, product, invoice);
    assertContainsExactlyOneLineItem(invoice, expected);
}
```

**Test Utility
Method**

Let's go through the changes step by step. First, we replaced the code to create the Customer and the Product with calls to *Finder Methods* that retrieve those objects from an *Immutable Shared Fixture*. We altered the code in this way because we don't plan to change these objects.

```
protected Customer findActiveCustomerWithDiscount(
                        BigDecimal percentDiscount) {
    return CustomerHome.findCustomerById(
                ACTIVE_CUSTOMER_WITH_30PC_DISCOUNT_ID);
}
```

Next, we introduced a *Creation Method* for the Invoice to which we plan to add the LineItem.

```
protected Invoice createInvoice(Customer customer) {
    Invoice newInvoice = new Invoice(customer);
    registerTestObject(newInvoice);
    return newInvoice;
}

List testObjects;
protected void registerTestObject(Object testObject) {
    testObjects.add(testObject);
}
```

To avoid the need for *In-line Teardown* (page 509), we registered each of the objects we created with our *Automated Teardown* mechanism, which we call from the tearDown method.

```
private void deleteTestObjects() {
    Iterator i = testObjects.iterator();
    while (i.hasNext()) {
        try {
            deleteObject(i.next());
        } catch (RuntimeException e) {
            // Nothing to do; we just want to make sure
            // we continue on to the next object in the list.
        }
    }
}
```

**Test Utility
Method**

```
public void tearDown() {
    deleteTestObjects();
}
```

Finally, we extracted a *Custom Assertion* to verify that the correct LineItem has been added to the Invoice.

```
void assertContainsExactlyOneLineItem( Invoice invoice,
                                       LineItem expected) {
    List lineItems = invoice.getLineItems();
    assertEquals("number of items", lineItems.size(), 1);
    LineItem actItem = (LineItem)lineItems.get(0);
    assertLineItemsEqual("",expected, actItem);
}
```

Parameterized Test

How do we reduce Test Code Duplication when the same test logic appears in many tests?

We pass the information needed to do fixture setup and result verification to a utility method that implements the entire test life cycle.

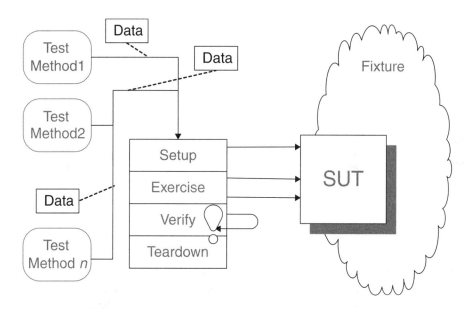

Testing can be very repetitious not only because we must run the same test over and over again, but also because many of the tests differ only slightly from one another. For example, we might want to run essentially the same test with slightly different system inputs and verify that the actual output varies accordingly. Each of these tests would consist of the exact same steps. While having a large number of tests is an excellent way to ensure good code coverage, it is not so attractive from a test maintainability standpoint because any change made to the algorithm of one of the tests must be propagated to all similar tests.

A *Parameterized Test* offers a way to reuse the same test logic in many *Test Methods* (page 348).

How It Works

The solution, of course, is to factor out the common logic into a utility method. When this logic includes all four parts of the entire *Four-Phase Test* (page 358) life cycle—that is, fixture setup, exercise SUT, result verification, and fixture teardown—we call the resulting utility method a *Parameterized Test*. This kind of test gives us the best coverage with the least code to maintain and makes it very easy to add more tests as they are needed.

If the right utility method is available to us, we can reduce a test that would otherwise require a series of complex steps to a single line of code. As we detect similarities between our tests, we can factor out the commonalities into a *Test Utility Method* (page 599) that takes only the information that differs from test to test as its arguments. The *Test Methods* pass in as parameters any information that the *Parameterized Test* requires to run and that varies from test to test.

When to Use It

We can use a *Parameterized Test* whenever *Test Code Duplication* (page 213) results from several tests implementing the same test algorithm but with slightly different data. The data that differs becomes the arguments passed to the *Parameterized Test*, and the logic is encapsulated by the utility method. A *Parameterized Test* also helps us avoid *Obscure Tests* (page 186); by reducing the number of times the same logic is repeated, it can make the *Testcase Class* (page 373) much more compact. A *Parameterized Test* is also a good steppingstone to a *Data-Driven Test* (page 288); the name of the *Parameterized Test* maps to the verb or "action word" of the *Data-Driven Test*, and the parameters are the attributes.

If our extracted utility method doesn't do any fixture setup, it is called a *Verification Method* (see *Custom Assertion* on page 474). If it also doesn't exercise the SUT, it is called a *Custom Assertion*.

Implementation Notes

We need to ensure that the *Parameterized Test* has an Intent-Revealing Name [SBPP] so that readers of the test will understand what it is doing. This name should imply that the test encompasses the whole life cycle to avoid any confusion. One convention is to start or end the name in "test"; the presence of parameters conveys the fact that the test is parameterized. Most members of the xUnit family that implement *Test Discovery* (page 393) will create only *Testcase Objects* (page 382) for "no arg" methods that start with "test," so this restriction shouldn't prevent us from starting our *Parameterized Test* names with "test." At least one member of the xUnit family—MbUnit—implements

Parameterized Tests at the *Test Automation Framework* (page 298) level. Extensions are becoming available for other members of the xUnit family, with **DDSteps** for JUnit being one of the first to appear.

Testing zealots would advocate writing a *Self-Checking Test* (see page 26) to verify the *Parameterized Test*. The benefits of doing so are obvious—including increased confidence in our tests—and in most cases it isn't that hard to do. It *is* a bit harder than writing unit tests for a *Custom Assertion* because of the interaction with the SUT. We will likely need to replace the SUT[2] with a *Test Double* so that we can observe how it is called and control what it returns.

Variation: Tabular Test

Also known as: *Row Test*

Several early reviewers of this book wrote to me about a variation of *Parameterized Test* that they use regularly: the *Tabular Test*. The essence of this test is the same as that for a *Parameterized Test*, except that the entire table of values resides in a single *Test Method*. Unfortunately, this approach makes the test an *Eager Test* (see *Assertion Roulette* on page 224) because it verifies many test conditions. This issue isn't a problem when all of the tests pass, but it does lead to a lack of *Defect Localization* (see page 22) when one of the "rows" fails.

Another potential problem is that "row tests" may depend on one another either on purpose or by accident because they are running on the same *Testcase Object*; see *Incremental Tabular Test* for an example of this behavior.

Despite these potential issues, *Tabular Tests* can be a very effective way to test. At least one member of the xUnit family implements *Tabular Tests* at the framework level: MbUnit provides an attribute [RowTest] to indicate that a test is a *Parameterized Test* and another attribute [Row(x,y,...)] to specify the parameters to be passed to it. Perhaps it will be ported to other members of the xUnit family? (Hint, hint!)

Parameterized Test

Variation: Incremental Tabular Test

An *Incremental Tabular Test* is a variant of the *Tabular Test* pattern in which we deliberately build on the fixture left over by the previous rows of the test. It is identical to a deliberate form of *Interacting Tests* (see *Erratic Test* on page 228)

---

[2] The terminology of SUT becomes very confusing in this case because we cannot replace the SUT with a *Test Double* if it truly is the SUT. Strictly speaking, we are replacing the object that would normally be the SUT with respect to this test. Because we are actually verifying the behavior of the *Parameterized Test*, whatever normally plays the role of SUT for this test now becomes a DOC. (My head is starting to hurt just describing this; fortunately, it really isn't very complicated and will make a lot more sense when you actually try it out.)

called *Chained Tests* (page 454), except that all the tests reside within the same *Test Method*. The steps within the *Test Method* act somewhat like the steps of a "DoFixture" in Fit but without individual reporting of failed steps.[3]

Variation: Loop-Driven Test

When we want to test the SUT with all the values in a particular list or range, we can call the *Parameterized Test* from within a loop that iterates over the values in the list or range. By nesting loops within loops, we can verify the behavior of the SUT with combinations of input values. The main requirement for doing this type of testing is that we must either enumerate the expected result for each input value (or combination) or use a *Calculated Value* (see *Derived Value* on page 718) without introducing *Production Logic in Test* (see *Conditional Test Logic* on page 200). A *Loop-Driven Test* suffers from many of the same issues associated with a *Tabular Test*, however, because we are hiding many tests inside a single *Test Method* (and, therefore, *Testcase Object*).

Motivating Example

The following example includes some of the runit (Ruby Unit) tests from the Web site publishing infrastructure I built in Ruby while writing this book. All of the *Simple Success Tests* (see *Test Method*) for my cross-referencing tags went through the same sequence of steps: defining the input XML, defining the expected HTML, stubbing out the output file, setting up the handler for the XML, extracting the resulting HTML, and comparing it with the expected HTML.

Parame-
terized Test

```
def test_extref
    # setup
    sourceXml = "<extref id='abc'/>"
    expectedHtml = "<a href='abc.html'>abc</a>"
    mockFile = MockFile.new
    @handler = setupHandler(sourceXml, mockFile)
    # execute
    @handler.printBodyContents
    # verify
    assert_equals_html( expectedHtml, mockFile.output,
                        "extref: html output")
end

def testTestterm_normal
    sourceXml = "<testterm id='abc'/>"
    expectedHtml = "<a href='abc.html'>abc</a>"
```

---

[3] This is because most members of the xUnit terminate the *Test Method* on the first failed assertion.

```
      mockFile = MockFile.new
      @handler = setupHandler(sourceXml, mockFile)
      @handler.printBodyContents
      assert_equals_html( expectedHtml, mockFile.output,
                          "testterm: html output")
   end

   def testTestterm_plural
      sourceXml ="<testterms id='abc'/>"
      expectedHtml = "<a href='abc.html'>abcs</a>"
      mockFile = MockFile.new
      @handler = setupHandler(sourceXml, mockFile)
      @handler.printBodyContents
      assert_equals_html( expectedHtml, mockFile.output,
                          "testterms: html output")
   end
```

Even though we have already factored out much of the common logic into the setupHandler method, some *Test Code Duplication* remains. In my case, I had at least 20 tests that followed this same pattern (with lots more on the way), so I felt it was worthwhile to make these tests *really easy* to write.

Refactoring Notes

Refactoring to a *Parameterized Test* is a lot like refactoring to a *Custom Assertion*. The main difference is that we include the calls to the SUT made as part of the exercise SUT phase of the test within the code to which we apply the Extract Method [Fowler] refactoring. Because these tests are virtually identical once we have defined our fixture and expected results, the rest can be extracted into the *Parameterized Test*.

Parame-
terized Test

Example: Parameterized Test

In the following tests, we have reduced each test to two steps: initializing two variables and calling a utility method that does all the real work. This utility method is a *Parameterized Test*.

```
   def test_extref
      sourceXml = "<extref id='abc' />"
      expectedHtml = "<a href='abc.html'>abc</a>"
      generateAndVerifyHtml(sourceXml,expectedHtml,"<extref>")
   end

   def test_testterm_normal
      sourceXml = "<testterm id='abc'/>"
      expectedHtml = "<a href='abc.html'>abc</a>"
      generateAndVerifyHtml(sourceXml,expectedHtml,"<testterm>")
```

```
    end

    def test_testterm_plural
       sourceXml = "<testterms id='abc'/>"
       expectedHtml = "<a href='abc.html'>abcs</a>"
       generateAndVerifyHtml(sourceXml,expectedHtml,"<plural>")
    end
```

The succinctness of these tests is made possible by defining the *Parameterized Test* as follows:

```
    def generateAndVerifyHtml( sourceXml, expectedHtml,
                                 message, &block)
       mockFile = MockFile.new
       sourceXml.delete!("\t")
       @handler = setupHandler(sourceXml, mockFile )
       block.call unless block == nil
       @handler.printBodyContents
       actual_html = mockFile.output
       assert_equal_html( expectedHtml,
                            actual_html,
                            message + "html output")
       actual_html
    end
```

What distinguishes this *Parameterized Test* from a *Verification Method* is that it contains the first three phases of the *Four-Phase Test* (from setup to verify), whereas the *Verification Method* performs only the exercise SUT and verify result phases. Note that our tests did not need the teardown phase because we are using *Garbage-Collected Teardown* (page 500).

Parameterized Test

Example: Independent Tabular Test

Here's an example of the same tests coded as a single *Independent Tabular Test*:

```
    def test_a_href_Generation
       row( "extref"   ,"abc","abc.html","abc" )
       row( "testterm" ,'abc','abc.html',"abc" )
       row( "testterms",'abc','abc.html',"abcs")
    end

    def row( tag, id, expected_href_id, expected_a_contents)
       sourceXml = "<" + tag + " id='" + id + "'/>"
       expectedHtml = "<a href='" + expected_href_id + "'>"
                                    + expected_a_contents + "</a>"
       msg = "<" + tag + "> "
       generateAndVerifyHtml( sourceXml, expectedHtml, msg)
    end
```

Isn't this a nice, compact representation of the various test conditions? I simply did an In-line Temp [Fowler] refactoring on the local variables sourceXml and expectedHtml in the argument list of generateAndVerify and "munged" the various *Test Methods* together into one. Most of the work involved something we won't have to do in real life: squeeze the table down to fit within the page-width limit for this book. That constraint forced me to abridge the text in each row and rebuild the HTML and the expected XML within the row method. I chose the name row to better align this example with the MbUnit example provided later in this section but I could have called it something else like test_element.

Unfortunately, from the *Test Runner's* (page 377) perspective, this is a single test, unlike the earlier examples. Because the tests all reside within the same *Test Method*, a failure in any row other than the last will cause a loss of information. In this example, we need not worry about *Interacting Tests* because generateAndVerify builds a new test fixture each time it is called. In the real world, however, we have to be aware of that possibility.

Example: Incremental Tabular Test

Because a *Tabular Test* is defined in a single *Test Method*, it will run on a single *Testcase Object*. This opens up the possibility of building up series of actions. Here's an example provided by Clint Shank on his blog:

```
public class TabularTest extends TestCase {
   private Order order = new Order();
   private static final double tolerance = 0.001;

   public void testGetTotal() {
      assertEquals("initial", 0.00, order.getTotal(), tolerance);
      testAddItemAndGetTotal("first", 1, 3.00, 3.00);
      testAddItemAndGetTotal("second",3, 5.00, 18.00);
      // etc.
   }

   private void testAddItemAndGetTotal( String msg,
                                        int lineItemQuantity,
                                        double lineItemPrice,
                                        double expectedTotal) {
      // setup
      LineItem item = new LineItem( lineItemQuantity,
                                    lineItemPrice);
      // exercise SUT
      order.addItem(item);
      // verify total
      assertEquals(msg,expectedTotal,order.getTotal(),tolerance);
   }
}
```

Parame-
terized Test

Note how each row of the *Incremental Tabular Test* builds on what was already done by the previous row.

Example: Tabular Test with Framework Support (MbUnit)

Here's an example from the MbUnit documentation that shows how to use the [RowTest] attribute to indicate that a test is a *Parameterized Test* and another attribute [Row(x,y,...)] to specify the parameters to be passed to it.

```
[RowTest()]
[Row(1,2,3)]
[Row(2,3,5)]
[Row(3,4,8)]
[Row(4,5,9)]
public void tAdd(Int32 x, Int32 y, Int32 expectedSum)
{
   Int32 Sum;
   Sum = this.Subject.Add(x,y);
   Assert.AreEqual(expectedSum, Sum);
}
```

Except for the syntactic sugar of the [Row(x,y,...)] attributes, this code sure looks similar to the previous example. It doesn't suffer from the loss of *Defect Localization,* however, because each row is considered a separate test. It would be a simple matter to convert the previous example to this format using the "find and replace" feature in a text editor.

**Parame-
terized Test**

Example: Loop-Driven Test (Enumerated Values)

The following test uses a loop to exercise the SUT with various sets of input values:

```
public void testMultipleValueSets() {
   // Set up fixture
   Calculator sut = new Calculator();
   TestValues[] testValues = {
                  new TestValues(1,2,3),
                  new TestValues(2,3,5),
                  new TestValues(3,4,8), // special case!
                  new TestValues(4,5,9)
                              };

   for (int i = 0; i < testValues.length; i++) {
      TestValues values = testValues[i];
      // Exercise SUT
      int actual = sut.calculate( values.a, values.b);
      // Verify result
```

```
        assertEquals(message(i), values.expectedSum, actual);
      }
   }

   private String message(int i) {
      return "Row "+ String.valueOf(i);
   }
```

In this case we enumerated the expected value for each set of test inputs. This strategy avoids *Production Logic in Test*.

Example: Loop-Driven Test (Calculated Values)

This next example is a bit more complex:

```
   public void testCombinationsOfInputValues() {
      // Set up fixture
      Calculator sut = new Calculator();
      int expected;   // TBD inside loops

      for (int i = 0; i < 10; i++) {
         for (int j = 0; j < 10; j++) {
            // Exercise SUT
            int actual = sut.calculate( i, j );

            // Verify result
            if (i==3 & j==4)   // Special case
               expected = 8;
            else
               expected = i+j;

            assertEquals(message(i,j), expected, actual);
         }
      }
   }

   private String message(int i, int j) {
      return "Cell( " + String.valueOf(i)+ ","
                      + String.valueOf(j) + ")";
}
```

Unfortunately, it suffers from *Production Logic in Test* because of the need to deal with the special case.

Further Reading

See the documentation for MbUnit for more information on the [RowTest] and [Row()] attributes. Likewise, see http://www.ddsteps.org for a description of the DDSteps extension for JUnit; while its name suggests a tool that supports

Parame-terized Test

Data-Driven Testing, the examples given are *Parameterized Tests*. More arguments for *Tabular Test* can be found on Clint Shank's blog at http://clintshank. javadevelopersjournal.com/tabulartests.htm.

Parameterized Test

Testcase Class per Class

How do we organize our Test Methods onto Testcase Classes?

We put all the Test Methods for one SUT class onto a single Testcase Class.

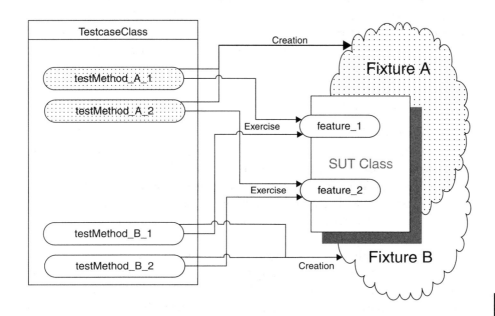

As the number of *Test Methods* (page 348) grows, we need to decide on which *Testcase Class* (page 373) to put each *Test Method*. Our choice of a test organization strategy affects how easily we can get a "big picture" view of our tests. It also affects our choice of a fixture setup strategy.

Using a *Testcase Class per Class* is a simple way to start off organizing our tests.

How It Works

We create a separate *Testcase Class* for each class we wish to test. Each *Testcase Class* acts as a home to all the *Test Methods* that are used to verify the behavior of the SUT class.

When to Use It

Using a *Testcase Class per Class* is a good starting point when we don't have very many *Test Methods* or we are just starting to write tests for our SUT. As the number of tests increases and we gain a better understanding of our test fixture requirements, we may want to split the *Testcase Class* into multiple classes. This choice will result in either *Testcase Class per Fixture* (page 631; if we have a small number of frequently used starting points for our tests) or *Testcase Class per Feature* (page 624; if we have several distinct features to test). As Kent Beck would say, "Let the code tell you what to do!"

Implementation Notes

Choosing a name for the *Testcase Class* is pretty simple: Just use the SUT classname, possibly prefixed or suffixed with "Test." The method names should try to capture at least the starting state (fixture) and the feature (method) being exercised, along with a summary of the parameters to be passed to the SUT. Given these requirements, we likely won't have "room" for the expected outcome in the method name, so the test reader must look at the *Test Method* body to determine the expected outcome.

The creation of the fixture is the primary implementation concern when using a *Testcase Class per Class*. Conflicting fixture requirements will inevitably arise among the various *Test Methods*, which makes use of *Implicit Setup* (page 424) difficult and forces us to use either *In-line Setup* (page 408) or *Delegated Setup* (page 411). A second consideration is how to make the nature of the fixture visible within each test method so as to avoid *Obscure Tests* (page 186). *Delegated Setup* (using *Creation Methods*; see *page* 415) tends to lead to more readable tests unless the *In-line Setup* is very simple.

Example: Testcase Class per Class

Here's an example of using the *Testcase Class per Class* pattern to structure the *Test Methods* for a `Flight` class that has three states (`Unscheduled`, `Scheduled`, and `AwaitingApproval`) and four methods (`schedule`, `requestApproval`, `deSchedule`, and `approve`). Because the class is stateful, we need *at least* one test for each state for each method.

```
public class FlightStateTest extends TestCase {

    public void testRequestApproval_FromScheduledState() throws Exception {
        Flight flight = FlightTestHelper.getAnonymousFlightInScheduledState();
```

```
      try {
         flight.requestApproval();
         fail("not allowed in scheduled state");
      } catch (InvalidRequestException e) {
         assertEquals("InvalidRequestException.getRequest()",
                      "requestApproval",
                      e.getRequest());
         assertTrue("isScheduled()", flight.isScheduled());
      }
   }

   public void testRequestApproval_FromUnsheduledState()
                  throws Exception {
      Flight flight = FlightTestHelper.
                  getAnonymousFlightInUnscheduledState();
      flight.requestApproval();
      assertTrue("isAwaitingApproval()",
               flight.isAwaitingApproval());
   }

   public void testRequestApproval_FromAwaitingApprovalState()
               throws Exception {
      Flight flight = FlightTestHelper.
               getAnonymousFlightInAwaitingApprovalState();
      try {
         flight.requestApproval();
         fail("not allowed in awaitingApproval state");
      } catch (InvalidRequestException e) {
         assertEquals("InvalidRequestException.getRequest()",
                      "requestApproval",
                      e.getRequest());
         assertTrue("isAwaitingApproval()",
                  flight.isAwaitingApproval());
      }
   }

   public void testSchedule_FromUnscheduledState()
                  throws Exception {
      Flight flight = FlightTestHelper.
                     getAnonymousFlightInUnscheduledState();
      flight.schedule();
      assertTrue( "isScheduled()", flight.isScheduled());
   }

   public void testSchedule_FromScheduledState()
                  throws Exception {
      Flight flight = FlightTestHelper.
      getAnonymousFlightInScheduledState();
      try {
         flight.schedule();
         fail("not allowed in scheduled state");
```

Testcase
Class per
Class

```
    } catch (InvalidRequestException e) {
       assertEquals("InvalidRequestException.getRequest()",
                    "schedule",
                    e.getRequest());
       assertTrue("isScheduled()", flight.isScheduled());
    }
}

public void testSchedule_FromAwaitingApprovalState()
                throws Exception {
   Flight flight = FlightTestHelper.
                    getAnonymousFlightInAwaitingApprovalState();
   try {
      flight.schedule();
      fail("not allowed in scheduled state");
   } catch (InvalidRequestException e) {
      assertEquals("InvalidRequestException.getRequest()",
                   "schedule",
                   e.getRequest());
       assertTrue( "isAwaitingApproval()",
                   flight.isAwaitingApproval());
   }
}

public void testDeschedule_FromScheduledState()
                throws Exception {
   Flight flight = FlightTestHelper.
                   getAnonymousFlightInScheduledState();
   flight.deschedule();
   assertTrue("isUnscheduled()", flight.isUnscheduled());
}

public void testDeschedule_FromUnscheduledState()
                throws Exception {
   Flight flight = FlightTestHelper.
                   getAnonymousFlightInUnscheduledState();
   try {
      flight.deschedule();
      fail("not allowed in unscheduled state");
   } catch (InvalidRequestException e) {
      assertEquals("InvalidRequestException.getRequest()",
                   "deschedule",
                   e.getRequest());
      assertTrue("isUnscheduled()", flight.isUnscheduled());
   }
}

public void testDeschedule_FromAwaitingApprovalState()
                throws Exception {
   Flight flight = FlightTestHelper.
                    getAnonymousFlightInAwaitingApprovalState();
   try {
```

Testcase Class per Class

```
      flight.deschedule();
      fail("not allowed in awaitingApproval state");
   } catch (InvalidRequestException e) {
      assertEquals("InvalidRequestException.getRequest()",
                   "deschedule",
                   e.getRequest());
      assertTrue( "isAwaitingApproval()",
                   flight.isAwaitingApproval());
   }
}

public void testApprove_FromScheduledState()
                throws Exception {
   Flight flight = FlightTestHelper.
                   getAnonymousFlightInScheduledState();
   try {
      flight.approve("Fred");
      fail("not allowed in scheduled state");
   } catch (InvalidRequestException e) {
      assertEquals("InvalidRequestException.getRequest()",
                   "approve",
                   e.getRequest());
      assertTrue("isScheduled()", flight.isScheduled());
   }
}

public void testApprove_FromUnsheduledState()
                throws Exception {
   Flight flight = FlightTestHelper.
                   getAnonymousFlightInUnscheduledState();
   try {
      flight.approve("Fred");
      fail("not allowed in unscheduled state");
   } catch (InvalidRequestException e) {
      assertEquals("InvalidRequestException.getRequest()",
                   "approve",
                   e.getRequest());
      assertTrue( "isUnscheduled()", flight.isUnscheduled());
   }
}

public void testApprove_FromAwaitingApprovalState()
                throws Exception {
   Flight flight = FlightTestHelper.
                   getAnonymousFlightInAwaitingApprovalState();
   flight.approve("Fred");
   assertTrue("isScheduled()", flight.isScheduled());
}

public void testApprove_NullArgument() throws Exception {
   Flight flight = FlightTestHelper.
                   getAnonymousFlightInAwaitingApprovalState();
```

```
        try {
          flight.approve(null);
          fail("Failed to catch no approver");
        } catch (InvalidArgumentException e) {
          assertEquals("e.getArgumentName()",
                         "approverName", e.getArgumentName());
          assertNull(  "e.getArgumentValue()",
                         e.getArgumentValue());
          assertTrue(  "isAwaitingApproval()",
                         flight.isAwaitingApproval());
        }
      }

      public void testApprove_InvalidApprover() throws Exception {
        Flight flight = FlightTestHelper.
                          getAnonymousFlightInAwaitingApprovalState();
        try {
          flight.approve("John");
          fail("Failed to validate approver");
        } catch (InvalidArgumentException e) {
          assertEquals("e.getArgumentName()",
                        "approverName",
                        e.getArgumentName());
          assertEquals("e.getArgumentValue()",
                         "John",
                         e.getArgumentValue());
          assertTrue(  "isAwaitingApproval()",
                         flight.isAwaitingApproval());
        }
      }
    }
```

Testcase Class per Class

This example uses *Delegated Setup* of a *Fresh Fixture* (page 311) to achieve a more declarative style of fixture construction. Even so, this class is getting rather large and keeping track of the *Test Methods* is becoming a bit of a chore. Even the "big picture" provided by our IDE is not that illuminating; we can see the test conditions being exercised but cannot tell what the expected outcome should be without looking at the method bodies (Figure 24.1).

Figure 24.1 *Testcase Class per Class example as seen in the Package Explorer of the Eclipse IDE. Note how both the starting state and event are included in the Test Method names.*

Testcase
Class per
Class

Testcase Class per Feature

How do we organize our Test Methods onto Testcase Classes?

We group the Test Methods onto Testcase Classes based on which testable feature of the SUT they exercise.

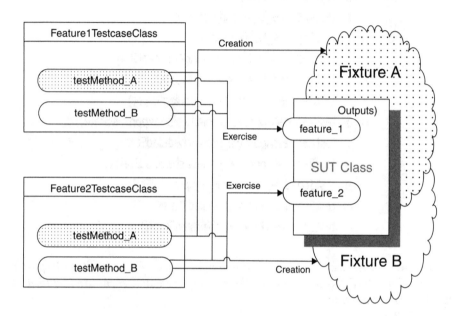

Testcase Class per Feature

As the number of *Test Methods* (page 348) grows, we need to decide on which *Testcase Class* (page 373) to put each *Test Method*. Our choice of a test organization strategy affects how easily we can get a "big picture" view of our tests. It also affects our choice of a fixture setup strategy.

Using a *Testcase Class per Feature* gives us a systematic way to break up a large *Testcase Class* into several smaller ones without having to change our *Test Methods*.

How It Works

We group our *Test Methods* onto *Testcase Classes* based on which feature of the *Testcase Class* they verify. This organizational scheme allows us to have smaller *Testcase Classes* and to see at a glance all the test conditions for a particular feature of the class.

When to Use It

We can use a *Testcase Class per Feature* when we have a significant number of *Test Methods* and we want to make the specification of each feature of the SUT more obvious. Unfortunately, *Testcase Class per Feature* does not make each individual *Test Method* any simpler or easier to understand; only *Testcase Class per Fixture* (page 631) helps on that front. Likewise, it doesn't make much sense to use *Testcase Class per Feature* when each feature of the SUT requires only one or two tests; in that case, we can stick with a single *Testcase Class per Class* (page 617).

Note that having a large number of features on a class is a "smell" indicating the possibility that the class might have too many responsibilities. We typically use *Testcase Class per Feature* when we are writing customer tests for methods on a service Facade [GOF].

Variation: Testcase Class per Method

When a class has methods that take a lot of different parameters, we may have many tests for the one method. We can group all of these *Test Methods* onto a single *Testcase Class per Method* and put the rest of the *Test Methods* onto one or more other *Testcase Classes*.

Variation: Testcase Class per Feature

Although a "feature" of a class is typically a single operation or function, it may also be a set of related methods that operate on the same instance variable of the object. For example, the set and get methods of a Java Bean would be considered a single (and trivial) "feature" of the class that contains those methods. Similarly, a Data Access Object [CJ2EEP] would provide methods to both read and write objects. It is difficult to test these methods in isolation, so we can treat the reading and writing of one kind of object as a feature.

Testcase Class per Feature

Variation: Testcase Class per User Story

If we are doing highly incremental development (such as we might do with eXtreme Programming), it can be useful to put the new *Test Methods* for each story into a different *Testcase Class*. This practice prevents commit-related conflicts when different people are working on different stories that affect the same SUT class. The *Testcase Class per User Story* pattern may or may not end up being the same as *Testcase Class per Feature* or *Testcase Class per Method*, depending on how we partition our user stories.

Implementation Notes

Because each *Testcase Class* represents the requirements for a single feature of the SUT, it makes sense to name the *Testcase Class* based on the feature it verifies. Similarly, we can name each test method based on which test condition of the SUT is being verified. This nomenclature allows us to see all the test conditions at a glance by merely looking at the names of the *Test Methods* of the *Testcase Class*.

One consequence of using *Testcase Class per Feature* is that we end up with a larger number of *Testcase Classes* for a single production class. Because we still want to run all the tests for this class, we should put these *Testcase Classes* into a single nested folder, package, or namespace. We can use an *AllTests Suite* (see *Named Test Suite* on page 592) to aggregate all of the *Testcase Classes* into a single test suite if we are using *Test Enumeration* (page 399).

Motivating Example

This example uses the *Testcase Class per Class* pattern to structure the *Test Methods* for a Flight class that has three states (Unscheduled, Scheduled, and AwaitingApproval) and four methods (schedule, requestApproval, deSchedule, and approve. Because the class is stateful, we need *at least* one test for each state for each method. (In the interest of saving trees, I've omitted many of the method bodies; please refer to *Testcase Class per Class* for the full listing.)

Testcase Class per Feature

```
public class FlightStateTest extends TestCase {

    public void testRequestApproval_FromScheduledState()
                        throws Exception {
        Flight flight = FlightTestHelper.
                        getAnonymousFlightInScheduledState();
        try {
            flight.requestApproval();
            fail("not allowed in scheduled state");
        } catch (InvalidRequestException e) {
            assertEquals("InvalidRequestException.getRequest()",
                        "requestApproval",
                        e.getRequest());
            assertTrue("isScheduled()", flight.isScheduled());
        }
    }

    public void testRequestApproval_FromUnsheduledState()
                        throws Exception {
        Flight flight = FlightTestHelper.
                        getAnonymousFlightInUnscheduledState();
```

```
      flight.requestApproval();
      assertTrue("isAwaitingApproval()",
                 flight.isAwaitingApproval());
   }

   public void testRequestApproval_FromAwaitingApprovalState()
                  throws Exception {
      Flight flight = FlightTestHelper.
                      getAnonymousFlightInAwaitingApprovalState();
      try {
         flight.requestApproval();
         fail("not allowed in awaitingApproval state");
      } catch (InvalidRequestException e) {
         assertEquals("InvalidRequestException.getRequest()",
                      "requestApproval",
                      e.getRequest());
         assertTrue("isAwaitingApproval()",
                    flight.isAwaitingApproval());
      }
   }

   public void testSchedule_FromUnscheduledState()
                  throws Exception {
      Flight flight = FlightTestHelper.
                      getAnonymousFlightInUnscheduledState();
      flight.schedule();
      assertTrue( "isScheduled()", flight.isScheduled());
   }

   public void testSchedule_FromScheduledState()
                  throws Exception {
   // I've omitted the bodies of the rest of the tests to
   // save a few trees
   }
}
```

Testcase
Class per
Feature

This example uses *Delegated Setup* (page 411) of a *Fresh Fixture* (page 311) to achieve a more declarative style of fixture construction. Even so, this class is getting rather large and keeping track of the *Test Methods* is becoming a bit of a chore. Because the *Test Methods* on this *Testcase Class* require four distinct methods, it is a good example of a test that can be improved through refactoring to *Testcase Class per Feature*.

Refactoring Notes

We can reduce the size of each *Testcase Class* and make the names of the *Test Methods* more meaningful by converting them to follow the *Testcase Class per Feature* pattern. First, we determine how many classes we want to create and which *Test Methods* should go into each one. If some *Testcase Classes* will end up being smaller than others, it makes the job easier if we start by building the smaller classes. Next, we do an Extract Class [Fowler] refactoring to create one of the new *Testcase Classes* and give it a name that describes the *feature it exercises*. Then, we do a Move Method [Fowler] refactoring (or a simple "cut and paste") on each *Test Method* that belongs in this new class along with any instance variables it uses.

We repeat this process until we are down to just one feature in the original *Testcase Class;* we then rename that class based on the *feature it exercises*. At this point, each of the *Testcase Classes* should compile and run—but we still aren't completely done. To get the full benefit of the *Testcase Class per Feature* pattern, we have one final step to carry out. We should do a Rename Method [Fowler] refactoring on each of the *Test Methods* to better reflect what the *Test Method* is verifying. As part of this refactoring, we can remove any mention of the feature being exercised from each *Test Method* name—that information should be captured in the name of the *Testcase Class*. This leaves us with "room" to include both the starting state (the fixture) and the expected result in the method name. If we have multiple tests for each feature with different method arguments, we'll need to find a way to include those aspects of the test conditions in the method name, too.

Another way to perform this refactoring is simply to make copies of the original *Testcase Class* and rename them as described above. Then we simply delete the *Test Methods* that aren't relevant for each class. We do need to be careful that we don't delete all copies of a *Test Method*; a less critical oversight is to leave a copy of the same method in several *Testcase Classes*. We can avoid both of the potential errors by making one copy of the original *Testcase Class* for *each* of the features and rename them as described above. Then we simply delete the *Test Methods* that aren't relevant for each class. When we are done, we simply delete the original *Testcase Class*.

Testcase Class per Feature

Example: Testcase Class per Feature

In this example, we have converted the previously mentioned set of tests to use *Testcase Class per Feature*.

```
public class TestScheduleFlight extends TestCase {

    public void testUnscheduled_shouldEndUpInScheduled()
            throws Exception {
        Flight flight = FlightTestHelper.
                        getAnonymousFlightInUnscheduledState();
        flight.schedule();
        assertTrue( "isScheduled()", flight.isScheduled());
```

```
   }

   public void testScheduledState_shouldThrowInvalidRequestEx()
            throws Exception {
      Flight flight = FlightTestHelper.
                          getAnonymousFlightInScheduledState();
      try {
         flight.schedule();
         fail("not allowed in scheduled state");
      } catch (InvalidRequestException e) {
         assertEquals("InvalidRequestException.getRequest()",
                       "schedule",
                       e.getRequest());
         assertTrue( "isScheduled()", flight.isScheduled());
      }
   }

   public void testAwaitingApproval_shouldThrowInvalidRequestEx()
            throws Exception {
      Flight flight = FlightTestHelper.
                          getAnonymousFlightInAwaitingApprovalState();
      try {
         flight.schedule();
         fail("not allowed in scheduled state");
      } catch (InvalidRequestException e) {
         assertEquals("InvalidRequestException.getRequest()",
                       "schedule",
                       e.getRequest());
         assertTrue( "isAwaitingApproval()",
                       flight.isAwaitingApproval());
      }
   }
}
```

**Testcase
Class per
Feature**

Except for their names, the *Test Methods* really haven't changed here. Because the names include the pre-conditions (fixture), the feature being exercised, and the expected outcome, they help us see the big picture when we look at the list of tests in our IDE's "outline view" (see Figure 24.2). This satisfies our need for *Tests as Documentation* (see page 23).

Testcase Class per Feature

Figure 24.2 *Testcase Class per Feature example as seen in the Package Explorer of the Eclipse IDE. Note how we do not need to include the starting state in the Test Method names, leaving room for the name of the method being called and the expected end state.*

Testcase Class per Fixture

How do we organize our Test Methods onto Testcase Classes?

We organize Test Methods into Testcase Classes based on commonality of the test fixture.

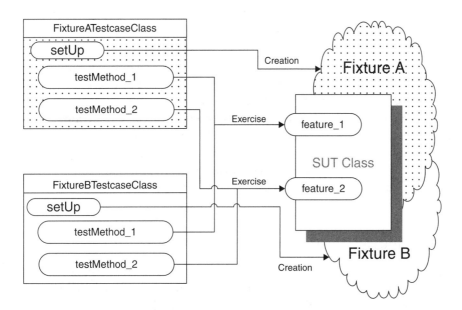

Testcase
Class per
Fixture

As the number of *Test Methods* (page 348) grows, we need to decide on which *Testcase Class* (page 373) to put each *Test Method*. Our choice of a test organization strategy affects how easily we can get a "big picture" view of our tests. It also affects our choice of a fixture setup strategy.

Using a *Testcase Class per Fixture* lets us take advantage of the *Implicit Setup* (page 424) mechanism provided by the *Test Automation Framework* (page 298).

How It Works

We group our *Test Methods* onto *Testcase Classes* based on which test fixture they require as a starting point. This organization allows us to use *Implicit Setup* to move the entire fixture setup logic into the setUp method, thereby allowing each test method to focus on the exercise SUT and verify outcome phases of the *Four-Phase Test* (page 358).

When to Use It

We can use the *Testcase Class per Fixture* pattern whenever we have a group of *Test Methods* that need an identical fixture and we want to make each test method as simple as possible. If each test needs a unique fixture, using *Testcase Class per Fixture* doesn't make a lot of sense because we will end up with a large number of single-test classes; in such a case, it would be better to use either *Testcase Class per Feature* (page 624) or simply *Testcase Class per Class* (page 617).

One benefit of *Testcase Class per Fixture* is that we can easily see whether we are testing all the operations from each starting state. We should end up with the same lineup of test methods on each *Testcase Class,* which is very easy to see in an "outline view" or "method browser" of an IDE. This attribute makes the *Testcase Class per Fixture* pattern particularly useful for discovering *Missing Unit Tests* (see *Production Bugs* on page 268) long before we go into production.

Testcase Class per Fixture is a key part of the **behavior-driven development** style of testing/specification. It leads to very short test methods, often featuring only a single assertion per test method. When combined with a test method naming convention that summarizes the expected outcome of the test, this pattern leads to *Tests as Documentation* (see page 23).

Implementation Notes

Because we set up the fixture in a method called by the *Test Automation Framework* (the setUp method), we must use an instance variable to hold a reference to the fixture we created. In such a case, we must be careful not to use a class variable, as it can lead to a *Shared Fixture* (page 317) and the *Erratic Tests* (page 228) that often accompany this kind of fixture. [The sidebar "There's Always an Exception" on page 384 lists xUnit members that don't guarantee *Independent Tests* (see page 42) when we use instance variables.]

Because each *Testcase Class* represents a single test fixture configuration, it makes sense to name the *Testcase Class* based on the fixture it creates. Similarly, we can name each test method based on the method of the SUT being exercised, the characteristics of any arguments passed to the SUT method, and the expected outcome of that method call.

One side effect of using *Testcase Class per Fixture* is that we end up with a larger number of *Testcase Classes.* We may want to find a way to group the various *Testcase Classes* that verify a single SUT class. One way to do so is to create a nested folder, package, or namespace to hold just these test classes. If we are using *Test Enumeration* (page 399), we'll also want to create an *AllTests*

Suite (see *Named Test Suite* on page 592) to aggregate all the *Testcase Class per Fixtures* into a single suite.

Another side effect is that the tests for a single feature of the SUT are spread across several *Testcase Classes*. This distribution may be a good thing if the features are closely related to one another because it highlights their interdependency. Conversely, if the features are somewhat unrelated, their dispersal may be disconcerting. In such a case, we can either refactor to use *Testcase Class per Feature* or apply an Extract Class [Fowler] refactoring on the SUT if we decide that this symptom indicates that the class has too many responsibilities.

Motivating Example

The following example uses *Testcase Class per Class* to structure the *Test Methods* for a Flight class that has three states (Unscheduled, Scheduled, and AwaitingApproval) and four methods (schedule, requestApproval, deSchedule, and approve). Because the class is stateful, we need *at least* one test for each state for each method. (In the interest of saving trees, I've omitted many of the method bodies; please refer to *Testcase Class per Class* for the full listing.)

```
public class FlightStateTest extends TestCase {

  public void testRequestApproval_FromScheduledState()
                throws Exception {
    Flight flight = FlightTestHelper.
                    getAnonymousFlightInScheduledState();
    try {
      flight.requestApproval();
      fail("not allowed in scheduled state");
    } catch (InvalidRequestException e) {
      assertEquals("InvalidRequestException.getRequest()",
                   "requestApproval",
                   e.getRequest());
      assertTrue("isScheduled()", flight.isScheduled());
    }
  }

  public void testRequestApproval_FromUnsheduledState()
                throws Exception {
    Flight flight = FlightTestHelper.
                    getAnonymousFlightInUnscheduledState();
    flight.requestApproval();
    assertTrue("isAwaitingApproval()",
               flight.isAwaitingApproval());
  }

  public void testRequestApproval_FromAwaitingApprovalState()
                throws Exception {
```

Testcase Class per Fixture

```
    Flight flight = FlightTestHelper.
                        getAnonymousFlightInAwaitingApprovalState();
    try {
      flight.requestApproval();
      fail("not allowed in awaitingApproval state");
    } catch (InvalidRequestException e) {
      assertEquals("InvalidRequestException.getRequest()",
                    "requestApproval",
                    e.getRequest());
      assertTrue("isAwaitingApproval()",
                  flight.isAwaitingApproval());
    }
  }

  public void testSchedule_FromUnscheduledState()
                  throws Exception {
    Flight flight = FlightTestHelper.
                        getAnonymousFlightInUnscheduledState();
    flight.schedule();
    assertTrue( "isScheduled()", flight.isScheduled());
  }

  public void testSchedule_FromScheduledState()
                  throws Exception {
   // I've omitted the bodies of the rest of the tests to
   // save a few trees
  }
}
```

Testcase Class per Fixture

This example uses *Delegated Setup* (page 411) of a *Fresh Fixture* (page 311) to achieve a more declarative style of fixture construction. Even so, this class is getting rather large and keeping track of the *Test Methods* is becoming a bit of a chore. Because the *Test Methods* on this *Testcase Class* require three distinct test fixtures (one for each state the flight can be in), it is a good example of a test that can be improved through refactoring to *Testcase Class per Fixture*.

Refactoring Notes

We can remove *Test Code Duplication* (page 213) in the fixture setup and make the *Test Methods* easier to understand by converting them to use the *Testcase Class per Fixture* pattern. First, we determine how many classes we want to create and which *Test Methods* should go into each one. If some *Testcase Classes* will end up being smaller than others, it will reduce our work if we start with the smaller ones. Next, we do an Extract Class refactoring to create one of the *Testcase Classes* and give it a name that describes the fixture it requires. Then, we do a Move Method [Fowler] refactoring on each *Test Method* that belongs in this new class, along with any instance variables it uses.

We repeat this process until we are down to just one fixture in the original class; we can then rename that class based on the *fixture* it creates. At this point, each of the *Testcase Classes* should compile and run—but we still aren't completely done. To get the full benefit of the *Testcase Class per Fixture* pattern, we have two more steps to complete. First, we should factor out any common fixture setup logic from each of the *Test Methods* into the setUp method, resulting in an *Implicit Setup*. This type of setup is made possible because the *Test Methods* on each class have the same fixture requirements. Second, we should do a Rename Method [Fowler] refactoring on each of the *Test Methods* to better reflect what the *Test Method* is verifying. We can remove any mention of the starting state from each *Test Method* name, because that information should be captured in the name of the *Testcase Class*. This refactoring leaves us with "room" to include both the action (the method being called plus the nature of the arguments) and the expected result in the method name.

As described in *Testcase Class per Fixture,* we can also refactor to this pattern by making one copy of the *Testcase Class* (suitably named) for each fixture, deleting the unnecessary *Test Methods* from each one, and finally deleting the old *Testcase Class.*

Example: Testcase Class per Fixture

In this example, the earlier set of tests has been converted to use the *Testcase Class per Fixture* pattern. (In the interest of saving trees, I've shown only one of the resulting *Testcase Classes;* the others look pretty similar.)

```
public class TestScheduledFlight extends TestCase {

    Flight scheduledFlight;

    protected void setUp() throws Exception {
        super.setUp();
        scheduledFlight = createScheduledFlight();
    }

    Flight createScheduledFlight() throws InvalidRequestException{
        Flight newFlight = new Flight();
        newFlight.schedule();
        return newFlight;
    }

    public void testDeschedule_shouldEndUpInUnscheduleState()
                    throws Exception {
        scheduledFlight.deschedule();
        assertTrue("isUnsched", scheduledFlight.isUnscheduled());
    }
```

```java
    public void testRequestApproval_shouldThrowInvalidRequestEx(){
        try {
            scheduledFlight.requestApproval();
            fail("not allowed in scheduled state");
        } catch (InvalidRequestException e) {
            assertEquals("InvalidRequestException.getRequest()",
                    "requestApproval", e.getRequest());
            assertTrue("isScheduled()",
                        scheduledFlight.isScheduled());
        }
    }

    public void testSchedule_shouldThrowInvalidRequestEx() {
        try {
            scheduledFlight.schedule();
            fail("not allowed in scheduled state");
        } catch (InvalidRequestException e) {
            assertEquals("InvalidRequestException.getRequest()",
                        "schedule", e.getRequest());
            assertTrue("isScheduled()",
                        scheduledFlight.isScheduled());
        }
    }

    public void testApprove_shouldThrowInvalidRequestEx()
            throws Exception {
        try {
            scheduledFlight.approve("Fred");
            fail("not allowed in scheduled state");
        } catch (InvalidRequestException e) {
            assertEquals("InvalidRequestException.getRequest()",
                        "approve", e.getRequest());
            assertTrue("isScheduled()",
                        scheduledFlight.isScheduled());
        }
    }
}
```

Testcase
Class per
Fixture

Note how much simpler each *Test Method* has become! Because we have used Intent-Revealing Names [SBPP] for each of the *Test Methods,* we can use the *Tests as Documentation.* By looking at the list of methods in the "outline view" of our IDE, we can see the starting state (fixture), the action (method being called), and the expected outcome (what it returns or the post-test state)—all without even opening up the method body (Figure 24.3).

Figure 24.3 *The tests for our Testcase Class per Fixture as seen in the Package Explorer of the Eclipse IDE. Note how we do not need to include the name of the method being called in the Test Method names, leaving room for the starting state and the expected end state.*

This "big picture" view of our tests makes it clear that we are only testing the approve method arguments when the Flight is in the awaitingApproval state. We can now decide whether that limitation is a shortcoming of the tests or part of the specification (i.e., the result of calling approve is "undefined" for some states of the Flight).

Testcase Superclass

Where do we put our test code when it is in reusable Test Utility Methods?

We inherit reusable test-specific logic from an abstract Testcase Super class.

Also known as:
*Abstract Testcase,
Abstract Test Fixture,
Testcase Baseclass*

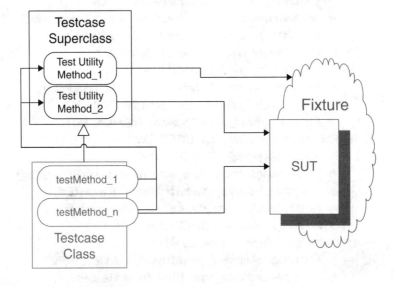

Testcase Superclass

As we write tests, we will invariably find ourselves needing to repeat the same logic in many, many tests. Initially, we may just "clone and twiddle" as we write additional tests that need the same logic. Ultimately, we may introduce *Test Utility Methods* (page 599) to hold this logic—but where do we put the *Test Utility Methods*?

A *Testcase Superclass* is one option as a home for our *Test Utility Methods*.

How It Works

We define an abstract superclass to hold the reusable *Test Utility Method* that should be available to several *Testcase Classes* (page 373). We make the methods that will be reused visible to subclasses (e.g., protected in Java). We then use this abstract class as the superclass (base class) for any tests that wish to reuse the logic. The logic can be accessed simply by calling the method as though it were defined on the *Testcase Class* itself.

When to Use It

We can use a *Testcase Superclass* if we wish to reuse *Test Utility Methods* between several *Testcase Classes* and can find or define a *Testcase Superclass* from which we can subclass all tests that require the logic.

This pattern assumes that our programming language supports inheritance, we are not already using inheritance for some other conflicting purpose, and the *Test Utility Method* doesn't need access to specific types that are not visible from the *Testcase Superclass*.

The decision between a *Testcase Superclass* and a *Test Helper* (page 643) comes down to *type visibility*. The client classes need to see the *Test Utility Method,* and the *Test Utility Method* needs to see the types and classes it depends on. When it doesn't depend on many types/classes or when everything it depends on is visible from a single place, we can put the *Test Utility Method* into a common *Testcase Superclass* we define for our project or company. If the *Test Utility Method* depends on types/classes that cannot be seen from a single place that all clients can access, it may be necessary to put it on a *Test Helper* in the appropriate test package or subsystem.

Variation: Test Helper Mixin

In languages that support mixins, *Test Helper Mixins* give us the best of both worlds. As with a *Test Helper*, we can choose which *Test Helper Mixins* to include without being constrained by a single-inheritance hierarchy. As with a *Test Helper Object* (see *Test Helper*), we can hold a test-specific state in the mixin but we don't have to instantiate and delegate that task to a separate object. As with a *Testcase Superclass*, we can access everything as methods and attributes on self.

Testcase Superclass

Implementation Notes

In variants of xUnit that require all *Testcase Classes* to be subclasses of a *Testcase Superclass* provided by the *Test Automation Framework* (page 298), we define that class as the superclass of our *Testcase Superclass*. In variants that use annotations or method attributes to identify the *Test Method* (page 348), we can subclass any class that we find useful.

We can implement the methods on the *Testcase Superclass* either as class methods or as instance methods. For any stateless *Test Utility Methods,* it is perfectly reasonable to use class methods. If it isn't possible to use class methods for some reason, we can work with instance methods. Either way, because the methods are inherited, we can access them as though they were defined on the *Testcase Class* itself. If our language supports managing the visibility of methods, we must ensure that we make the methods visible enough (e.g., protected in Java).

Motivating Example

The following example shows a *Test Utility Method* that is on the *Testcase Class*:

```java
public class TestRefactoringExample extends TestCase {
  public void testAddOneLineItem_quantity1() {
    Invoice inv = createAnonInvoice();
    LineItem expItem = new LineItem(inv, product, QUANTITY);
    // Exercise
    inv.addItemQuantity(product, QUANTITY);
    // Verify
    assertInvoiceContainsOnlyThisLineItem(inv, expItem);
  }

  void assertInvoiceContainsOnlyThisLineItem(
                               Invoice inv,
                               LineItem expItem) {
    List lineItems = inv.getLineItems();
    assertEquals("number of items", lineItems.size(), 1);
    LineItem actual = (LineItem)lineItems.get(0);
    assertLineItemsEqual("",expItem, actual);
  }
}
```

**Testcase
Superclass**

This *Test Utility Method* is not reusable outside this particular class or its subclasses.

Refactoring Notes

We can make the *Test Utility Method* more reusable by moving it to a *Testcase Superclass* by using a Pull Up Method [Fowler] refactoring. Because the method is inherited by our *Testcase Class*, we can access it as if the method were defined locally. If the *Test Utility Method* accesses any instance variables, we must perform a Pull Up Field [Fowler] refactoring to move those variables to a place where the *Test Utility Method* can see them. In languages that have visibility restrictions, we may need to make the fields visible to subclasses (e.g., default or protected in Java) if *Test Methods* on the *Testcase Class* need to access the fields as well.

Example: Testcase Superclass

Because the method is inherited by our *Testcase Class*, we can access it as if it were defined locally. Thus the usage looks identical.

```
public class TestRefactoringExample extends OurTestCase {
   public void testAddItemQuantity_severalQuantity_v12(){
      // Fixture Setup
      Customer cust = createACustomer(new BigDecimal("30"));
      Product prod = createAProduct(new BigDecimal("19.99"));
      Invoice invoice = createInvoice(cust);
      // Exercise SUT
      invoice.addItemQuantity(prod, 5);
      // Verify Outcome
      LineItem expected = new LineItem(invoice, prod, 5,
            new BigDecimal("30"), new BigDecimal("69.96"));
      assertContainsExactlyOneLineItem(invoice, expected);
   }
}
```

The only difference is the class in which the method is defined and its visibility:

```
public class OurTestCase extends TestCase {
   void assertContainsExactlyOneLineItem(Invoice invoice,
                                         LineItem expected) {
      List lineItems = invoice.getLineItems();
      assertEquals("number of items", lineItems.size(), 1);
      LineItem actItem = (LineItem)lineItems.get(0);
      assertLineItemsEqual("",expected, actItem);
   }
}
```

**Testcase
Superclass**

Example: Test Helper Mixin

Here are some tests written in Ruby using Test::Unit:

```
def test_extref
   # setup
   sourceXml = "<extref id='abc'/>"
   expectedHtml = "<a href='abc.html'>abc</a>"
   mockFile = MockFile.new
   @handler = setupHandler(sourceXml, mockFile)
   # execute
   @handler.printBodyContents
   # verify
   assert_equals_html( expectedHtml, mockFile.output,
                       "extref: html output")
end

def testTestterm_normal
   sourceXml = "<testterm id='abc'/>"
```

```
      expectedHtml = "<a href='abc.html'>abc</a>"
      mockFile = MockFile.new
      @handler = setupHandler(sourceXml, mockFile)
      @handler.printBodyContents
      assert_equals_html( expectedHtml, mockFile.output,
                          "testterm: html output")
   end

   def testTestterm_plural
      sourceXml ="<testterms id='abc'/>"
      expectedHtml = "<a href='abc.html'>abcs</a>"
      mockFile = MockFile.new
      @handler = setupHandler(sourceXml, mockFile)
      @handler.printBodyContents
      assert_equals_html( expectedHtml, mockFile.output,
                          "testterms: html output")
   end
```

These tests contain a fair bit of *Test Code Duplication* (page 213). We can address this issue by using an Extract Method [Fowler] refactoring to create a *Test Utility Method*. We can then make the *Test Utility Method* more reusable by moving it to a *Test Helper Mixin* using a Pull Up Method refactoring. Because the mixed-in functionality is considered part of our *Testcase Class*, we can access it as if it were defined locally. Thus the usage looks identical.

```
class CrossrefHandlerTest  <  Test::Unit::TestCase
    include HandlerTest

    def test_extref
        sourceXml = "<extref id='abc' />"
        expectedHtml = "<a href='abc.html'>abc</a>"
        generateAndVerifyHtml(sourceXml,expectedHtml,"<extref>")
    end
```

Testcase Superclass

The only difference is the location where the method is defined and its visibility. In particular, Ruby requires mixins to be defined in a module rather than a class.

```
module HandlerTest
   def generateAndVerifyHtml( sourceXml, expectedHtml,
                              message, &block)
      mockFile = MockFile.new
      sourceXml.delete!("\t")
      @handler = setupHandler(sourceXml, mockFile )
      block.call unless block == nil
      @handler.printBodyContents
      actual_html = mockFile.output
      assert_equal_html( expectedHtml,
                         actual_html,
                         message + "html output")
      actual_html
   end
```

Test Helper

Where do we put our test code when it is in reusable Test Utility Methods?

We define a helper class to hold any Test Utility Methods we want to reuse in several tests.

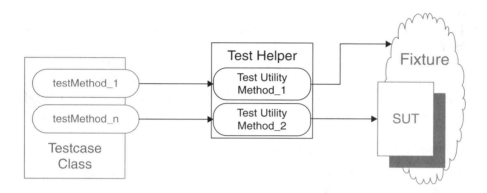

As we write tests, we will invariably find ourselves needing to repeat the same logic in many, many tests. Initially, we may just "clone and twiddle" as we write additional tests that need the same logic. Ultimately, we may introduce *Test Utility Methods* (page 599) to hold this logic—but where should we put such reusable logic?

A *Test Helper* is one possible choice of home for reusable test logic.

Test Helper

How It Works

We define a separate class to hold the reusable *Test Utility Methods* that should be available to several *Testcase Classes* (page 373). In each test that wishes to use this logic, we access the logic either using static method calls or via an instance created specifically for the purpose.

When to Use It

We can use a *Test Helper* if we wish to share logic or variables between several *Testcase Classes* and cannot (or choose not to) find or define a *Testcase Superclass* (page 638) from which we might otherwise subclass all tests that require this logic. We might pursue this course in several circumstances: Perhaps our programming language doesn't support inheritance (e.g., Visual Basic 5 or 6), perhaps we are already using inheritance for some other conflicting purpose, or perhaps the *Test Utility Method* needs access to specific types that are not visible from the *Testcase Superclass*.

The decision between a *Test Helper* and a *Testcase Superclass* comes down to *type visibility*. The client classes need to see the *Test Utility Method*, and the *Test Utility Method* needs to see all the types and classes it depends on. When it doesn't depend on many types/classes or when everything it depends on is visible from a single place, we can put the *Test Utility Method* into a common *Testcase Superclass* we define for our project or company. If the *Test Utility Method* depends on types/classes that cannot be seen from a single place that all clients can access, it may be necessary to put it on a *Test Helper* in the appropriate test package or subsystem. In larger systems with many groups of domain objects, it is common practice to have one *Test Helper* for each group (package) of related domain objects.

Variation: Test Fixture Registry

A Registry [PEAA] is a well-known object that can be accessed from anywhere in a program. We can use the Registry to store and retrieve objects from different parts of our program or tests. (Registry objects are often confused with Singletons [GOF], which are also well known but have only a single instance. With a Registry object, there may be one or more instances—we don't really care.) A *Test Fixture Registry* gives the tests the ability to access the same fixture as other tests in the same test run. Depending on how we implement our *Test Helper*, we may choose to provide a different instance of the *Test Fixture Registry* for each *Test Runner* (page 377) in an effort to prevent a *Test Run War* (see *Erratic Test* on page 228). A common example of a *Test Fixture Registry* is the *Database Sandbox* (page 650).

A *Test Fixture Registry* is typically used with a *Setup Decorator* (page 447) or with *Lazy Setup* (page 435); it isn't needed with *Suite Fixture Setup* (page 441) because only tests on the same *Testcase Class* need to share the fixture. In such a case, using a fixture holding class variable works well for this purpose.

Variation: Object Mother

The *Object Mother* pattern is simply an aggregate of several other patterns, each of which makes a small but significant contribution to making the test fixture easier to manage. The *Object Mother* consists of one or more *Test Helpers* that provide *Creation Methods* (page 415) and *Attachment Methods* (see *Creation Method*), which our tests then use to create ready-to-use test fixture objects. *Object Mothers*

Test Helper

often provide several *Creation Methods* that create instances of the same class, where each method results in a test object in a different starting state (a *Named State Reaching Method; see Creation Method*). The *Object Mother* may also have the ability to delete the objects it creates automatically—an example of *Automated Teardown* (page 503).

Because there is no single, crisp definition of what someone means by "Object Mother," it is advisable to refer to the individual patterns (such as *Automated Teardown*) when referring to specific capabilities of the *Object Mother*.

Implementation Notes

The methods on the *Test Helper* can be implemented as either class methods or instance methods depending on the degree to which we want to keep the tests from interacting.

Variation: Test Helper Class

If all of the *Test Utility Methods* are stateless, the simplest approach is to implement the functionality of the *Test Helper* as class methods and then to have the tests access those methods using the ClassName.methodName (or equivalent) notation. If we need to hold references to fixture objects, we *could* place them in class variables. We need to be careful to avoid inadvertently creating a *Shared Fixture* (page 317), however—unless, of course, that is exactly what we are trying to do. In such a case, we are actually building a *Test Fixture Registry*.

Test Helper

Variation: Test Helper Object

If we can't use class methods for some reason, we can work with instance methods instead. In this case, the client test will need to create an instance of the *Test Helper* class and store it in an instance variable; the methods can then be accessed via this variable. This pattern is a good approach when the *Test Helper* holds references to fixture or SUT objects and we want to make sure that we don't creep into a *Shared Fixture* situation. It is also useful when the *Test Helper* stores expectations for a set of *Mock Objects* (page 544), because this pattern ensures that we can verify the calls are interleaved between the *Mock Objects* correctly.

Motivating Example

The following example shows a *Test Utility Method* that is on the *Testcase Class:*

```
public class TestUtilityExample extends TestCase {

    public void testAddOneLineItem_quantity1() {
```

```
      Invoice inv = createAnonInvoice();
      LineItem expItem = new LineItem(inv, product, QUANTITY);
      // Exercise
      inv.addItemQuantity(product, QUANTITY);
      // Verify
      assertInvoiceContainsOnlyThisLineItem(inv, expItem);
   }

   void assertInvoiceContainsOnlyThisLineItem(
                                  Invoice inv,
                                  LineItem expItem) {
      List lineItems = inv.getLineItems();
      assertEquals("number of items", lineItems.size(), 1);
      LineItem actual = (LineItem)lineItems.get(0);
      assertLineItemsEqual("",expItem, actual);
   }
}
```

This *Test Utility Method* is not reusable outside this particular class.

Refactoring Notes

We can make a *Test Utility Method* more reusable by moving it to a *Test Helper* class. This transformation is often as simple as doing a Move Method [Fowler] refactoring to our *Test Helper* class. One potential problem arises when we have used instance variables to pass arguments to or return data from the *Test Utility Method*. These "global data" need to be converted to explicit arguments and return values before we can perform the Move Method refactoring.

Test Helper

Example: Test Helper with Class Methods

In this modified version of the preceding test, we have turned the *Test Utility Method* into a class method on a *Test Helper Class* so we can access it via the classname without creating an instance:

```
public class TestUtilityExample extends TestCase {
   public void testAddOneLineItem_quantity1_staticHelper() {
      Invoice inv = createAnonInvoice();
      LineItem expItem = new LineItem(inv, product, QUANTITY);
      // Exercise
      inv.addItemQuantity(product, QUANTITY);
      // Verify
      TestHelper.assertContainsExactlyOneLineItem(inv, expItem);
   }
}
```

Example: Test Helper with Instance Methods

In this example, we have moved the *Test Utility Method* to a *Test Helper* as an instance method. Note that we must now access the method via an object reference (a variable that holds an instance of the *Test Helper*).

```
public class TestUtilityExample extends TestCase {
   public void testAddOneLineItem_quantity1_instanceHelper() {
      Invoice inv = createAnonInvoice();
      LineItem expItem = new LineItem(inv, product, QUANTITY);
      // Exercise
      inv.addItemQuantity(product, QUANTITY);
      // Verify
      TestHelper helper = new TestHelper();
      helper.assertInvContainsExactlyOneLineItem(inv, expItem);
   }
}
```

Test Helper

CHAPTER 25

Database Patterns

Patterns in This Chapter

Database
Patterns

Database Sandbox

How do we develop and test software that depends on a database?

We provide a separate test database for each developer or tester.

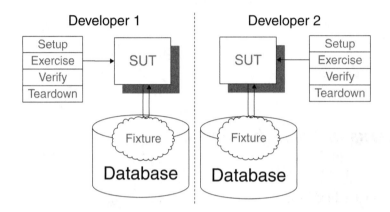

Many applications use a database to store the persistent state of the application. At least some of the tests for such an application will require accessing the database. Unfortunately, a database is a primary cause of *Erratic Tests* (page 228) due to the fact that data may persist between tests. A major goal in keeping tests from interacting is ensuring that the test fixtures used by each test do not overlap. This is especially difficult when the development environment contains only a single test database and all tests run by all developers run against the same database.

A *Database Sandbox* is one way to keep the tests from interacting by accidentally accessing the same records in the database.

Database Sandbox

How It Works

We provide each user with a separate, self-consistent sandbox in which to work. This sandbox includes the user's own copy of any code plus—most importantly—the user's own copy of the database. Such an arrangement allows each user to modify the database in any way he or she sees fit and to exercise the application with tests without worrying about any interactions between the user's own tests and the tests conducted by other users.

When to Use It

We should use a *Database Sandbox* whenever we are building or modifying an application that depends on a database for a significant portion of its functionality.

This need is especially evident if we have chosen to use a *Shared Fixture* (page 317). Using a *Database Sandbox* will help us avoid *Test Run Wars* (see *Erratic Test*) between different users of the database. Depending on how we have chosen to implement the *Database Sandbox*, it may or may not allow different users to modify the structure of the database. A *Database Sandbox* will not prevent *Unrepeatable Tests* (see *Erratic Test*) or *Interacting Tests* (see *Erratic Test*), however, because it merely separates different users (and their test runs) from one another; tests within a single test run may continue to share a test fixture.

Implementation Notes

The application needs to be made configurable so that the database to be used in testing can be changed without modifying the code. Typically, this goal is accomplished by reading the database configuration information from a properties file that is customized in each user's environment.

A *Database Sandbox* can be implemented in many different ways. Fundamentally, the choice comes down to whether we give each user a separate database instance or just simulate one. In general, giving each user a real separate database instance is the preferred choice. This scheme may not always be feasible, however—especially if the database vendor's licensing structure makes it cost prohibitive.

Variation: Dedicated Database Sandbox

We give each developer, tester, or test user a separate database instance. This is typically accomplished by installing a lightweight database technology in each user's test environment. Examples of lightweight database technologies include MySql and Personal Oracle. The database instance can be installed on the user's own machine, on a shared test server, or on a dedicated "virtual server" running on shared server hardware.

A *Dedicated Database Sandbox* is the preferred solution because it provides the greatest flexibility. It allows a developer to modify the database schema, load his or her own test data, and so on.

Variation: DB Schema per Test Runner

With *DB Schema per Test Runner*, we give each developer, tester, or test user what appears to be a separate database instance by using built-in database support for multiple schemas.

One considerable advantage that the *DB Schema per Test Runner* pattern enjoys relative to the *Dedicated Database Sandbox* pattern is that we can share an *Immutable Shared Fixture* (see *Shared Fixture*) defined in a common schema and put each user's mutable fixture in his or her own private schema. Note that this scheme does not allow the user to modify the structure of the database (at least not to the same degree as is possible with a *Dedicated Database Sandbox*). It also forces all users, including both developers and testers, to use the same database structure. This can create logistical issues when database structure upgrades need to be rolled out.

Variation: Database Partitioning Scheme

We give each developer, tester, or test user a separate set of data within a single *Database Sandbox*. Each user can modify that data as he or she sees fit but is not allowed to modify the data assigned to other users.

   This approach requires less database administration overhead but more data administration overhead than with the other ways to implement a *Database Sandbox*. Because it does not allow developers to modify the database schema, a *Database Partitioning Scheme* is not appropriate for evolutionary database development. It is, however, appropriate for preventing *Interacting Tests* when applied to different tests run from the *same Test Runner*. That is, we give each test a unique key such as a CustomerNumber that it uses for all data. As a consequence, other tests within the same test run use different data. This pattern can be combined with many of the other variations of *Database Sandbox* to prevent *Interacting Tests* when using a *Shared Fixture*. Note that this pattern does not prevent *Unrepeatable Tests* unless we also use *Distinct Generated Values* (see *Generated Value* on page 723).

Motivating Example

The following test uses *Literal Values* for the arguments to a constructor of a Product that is persisted into a database instance shared among several developers. The name of the Product must be unique:

```
public void testProductPrice_HCV() {
   //    Setup
   Product product =
      new Product( 88,                    // ID
                   "Widget",              // Name
                   new BigDecimal("19.99")); // Price
   // Exercise SUT
   //   ...
}
```

Unfortunately, we may end up with a *Test Run War* when we run this test against a shared database instance regardless of how effectively we tear down the Product after each test. This is because we are trying to create the same Product that the same test run from another *Test Runner* might be in the process of using *at the same time*.

Refactoring Notes

There are no code changes required of our test when we create a *Dedicated Database Sandbox* for each developer and tester. Therefore, tests should not have to do anything special to run completely independently of tests being run from other *Test Runners* (page 377). There is a small change required of the SUT, however, to allow the SUT to connect to different database instances based on configuration data. How we make this change varies with the technology we use and is beyond the scope of this book.

We can convert the test to use a *Database Partitioning Scheme* by replacing the *Literal Values* with calls to the appropriate getUnique method passing an ID specific to the *Test Runner* as a seed.

Example: Database Partitioning Scheme

Here is the same test using a *Database Partitioning Scheme* to ensure that each test uses a different set of products. For the getUniqueString method, we pass a string based on the MAC address of our computer.

```java
public void testProductPrice_DPS() {
    // Setup
    Product product =
        new Product( getUniqueInt(),                      // ID
                     getUniqueString(getMacAddress()),    // Name
                     new BigDecimal("19.99"));            // Price
    // Exercise SUT
    //   ...
}

static int counter = 0;

int getUniqueInt() {
    counter++;
    return counter;
}

BigDecimal getUniqueBigDecimal() {
    return new BigDecimal(getUniqueInt());
}

String getUniqueString(String baseName) {
    return baseName.concat(String.valueOf( getUniqueInt()));
}
```

Database
Sandbox

This test can now be run from several different computers against the same shared database instance without fear of a *Test Run War.*

Stored Procedure Test

How can we verify logic independently when we have stored procedures?

We write Fully Automated Tests for each stored procedure.

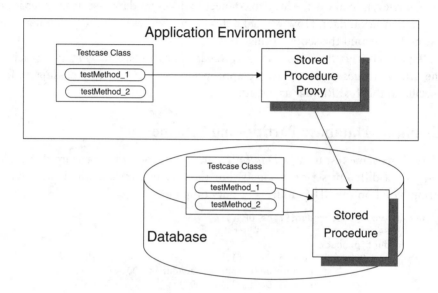

Many applications that use a database to store the persistent state of the application also use stored procedures and triggers to improve performance and do common processing on updates.

A *Stored Procedure Test* is a way to apply automated testing practices to this code that lives inside the database.

Stored
Procedure
Test

How It Works

We write unit tests for the stored procedures independent of the client application software. These tests may be layer-crossing tests or round-trip tests, depending on the nature of the store procedure(s) being tested.

When to Use It

We should write *Stored Procedure Tests* whenever we have nontrivial logic in stored procedures. This pattern will help us verify that the stored procedures—our

SUT for the purposes of these tests—are working properly independently of the client application. This consideration is particularly important when more than one application will use the stored procedures or when the stored procedures are being developed by a different development team. *Stored Procedure Tests* are particularly important when we cannot ensure the procedures are tested adequately simply by exercising the application software (a form of *Indirect Testing; see Obscure Test* on page 186). Using *Stored Procedure Tests* also helps us to enumerate all the conditions under which the stored procedure *could* be called and what should happen in each circumstance. The very act of thinking about these circumstances is likely to improve the design—a common result of doing test-first development.

Implementation Notes

There are two fundamentally different ways to implement *Stored Procedure Tests*: (1) We can write the tests in the same programming language as the stored procedure and run them in the database or (2) we can write the tests in our application programming language and access the stored procedure via a Remote Proxy [GOF]. We might even write tests both ways. For example, the stored-procedure developers might write unit tests in the database programming language, whereas the application developers might prepare some acceptance tests in the application programming language to run as part of the application build.

Either way, we need to decide how the test will set up the fixture (the "before" state of the database) and verify the expected outcome (the "after" state of the database as well as any expected actions such as cascading deletes). The test may interact directly with the database to insert/verify the data (a form of *Back Door Manipulation;* see page 327) or it could use another stored procedure (a form of round-trip test).

Stored Procedure Test

Variation: In-Database Stored Procedure Test

One advantage of the xUnit approach to automated testing is that the tests are written in the same language as the code we are testing. This makes it easier for the developers to learn how to automate the tests without learning a new programming language, debugger, and so on. Extending this idea to its logical conclusion, it makes sense to test stored procedures using tests that are written in the stored-procedure programming language. Naturally, we will need to run these tests inside the database. Unfortunately, that requirement may make it hard to run them as part of the Integration Build [SCM].

This variation on the *Stored Procedure Test* pattern is appropriate when we have more experience writing code in the stored-procedure language and/or environment than in the application environment and it is not essential that all tests be run from a single place. For example, a database or data services team that is writing stored procedures for use by other teams would find this approach attractive. Another circumstance in which it would be appropriate to use *In-Database Stored Procedure Tests* arises when the procedures are stored in a different source code repository than the application logic. Using *In-Database Stored Procedure Test* allows us to store the tests in the same repository as the SUT (in this case, the stored procedures).

In-Database Stored Procedure Tests may allow somewhat more thorough unit testing (and test-driven development) of the stored procedures because we may have better access to implementation details of the stored procedure from our tests. Of course, this violation of encapsulation could result in *Overspecified Software* (see *Fragile Test* on page 239). If the client code uses a data access layer, we must still write unit tests for that software in the application programming language to ensure that we handle errors correctly (e.g., failure to connect).

Some databases support several programming languages. In such a case, we can choose to use the more test-friendly programming language for our tests but write the stored procedures in the more traditional stored-procedure programming language. For example, Oracle databases support both PLSQL and Java, so we could use JUnit tests to verify our PLSQL stored procedures. Likewise, Microsoft's SQL Server supports C#, so we could use NUnit tests written in C# to verify the stored procedures written in Transact-SQL.

Variation: Remote Stored Procedure Test

The purpose of *Remoted Stored Procedure Tests* is to allow us to write the tests in the same language as the unit tests for the client application logic. We must access the stored procedure via a Remote Proxy [GOF] that hides the mechanics of interacting with that procedure. This proxy can be structured as either a Service Facade [CJ2EEP] or a *Command* [GOF] (such as Java's JdbcOdbcCallableStatement).

Remoted Stored Procedure Tests are, in effect, component tests in that they treat the stored procedure as a "black box" component. Because *Remoted Stored Procedure Tests* do not run inside the database, we are more likely to write them as round-trip tests (calling other stored procedures to set up the fixture, verify the outcome, and perform other necessary tasks) unless we have an easy way to insert or verify data. Some members of the xUnit family have extensions that are specifically intended to facilitate this behavior (e.g., DbUnit for Java and NDbUnit for .NET languages).

This solution is more appropriate if we want to keep all our tests in a single programming language. The *Remoted Stored Procedure Test* pattern makes it easier to run all the tests every time we check in changes to the application code.

Stored
Procedure
Test

Testing Stored Procedures with JUnit

On an early XP project, our application was mandated to use stored procedures being developed by another group. It seemed that every time we integrated our Java with those developers' PLSQL code, we found serious bugs in the fundamental behavior of their stored procedures. We were writing automated tests using JUnit for our code. Although we were sure that writing unit tests for the stored procedures would clarify the interface contract and improve the quality of the other group's code, we couldn't force the other team to write unit tests. Nor had **utPLSQL** even been invented at that point.

We decided to try writing unit tests for the stored procedures in the xUnit family member we were comfortable with: JUnit. Because we had to write JDBC code to access the stored procedures anyway, we defined JUnit tests for each stored procedure via the JDBC PreparedStatement classes that we had built. The tests exercised the basic behavior of the stored behaviors and a few of the more obvious failure cases. Whenever we received a new version of the stored procedures, we would run the JUnit tests before we even tried to exercise the procedures from our application code. Needless to say, many of the tests failed.

We sat down with the developers who were building the stored procedures and showed them our tests—including how they were failing left, right, and center. Needless to say, the developers were a bit embarrassed but they agreed that our tests were correct. They went off to fix the stored procedures and gave us a new version to test. The revision fared somewhat better but still produced some failures. Then a very important thing happened: The members of the other group asked for a copy of the tests we had written and instructions on how to run them for themselves. Before long, these developers were writing their own PLSQL unit tests in JUnit!

Stored Procedure Test

This capability is particularly useful if the stored procedures are being written and/or modified by the same team that is developing the client code. We can also use *Remoted Stored Procedure Tests* when another team is providing the stored procedures and we are not confident in those developers' ability to write defect-free code (probably because they are not writing *In-Database Stored Procedure Tests* for their code). In this situation, we can use the *Remoted Stored Procedure Tests* as a form of acceptance test for their code. See the sidebar "Testing Stored Procedures with JUnit" for an illustration of how this setup worked on one project.

One disadvantage of using *Remoted Stored Procedure Tests* is that they will likely cause the test suite to run more slowly because the tests require the database to be available and populated with data. The tests for the stored procedures can be put into a separate *Subset Suite (see Named Test Suite on page 592)* so that they need not be run with all the in-memory tests. This can significantly speed up test execution, thereby avoiding *Slow Tests* (page 253).

Remoted Stored Procedure Tests also come in handy when logic written in our programming language of choice already has unit tests and we need to move that logic into the database. By using a *Remoted Stored Procedure Test*, we can avoid rewriting the tests in a different programming language and *Test Automation Framework* (page 298), which can in turn save time and money. This pattern also enables us to avoid any translation errors when recoding the logic, so we can be sure the recoded logic really does produce the same results.

Motivating Example

Here is an example of a stored procedure written in PLSQL:

```
CREATE OR REPLACE PROCEDURE calc_secs_between (
    date1 IN DATE,
    date2 IN DATE,
    secs OUT NUMBER
)
IS
BEGIN
    secs := (date2 - date1) * 24 * 60 * 60;
END;
/
```

This sample was taken from the examples that come with the utPLSQL tool. In real life we might not bother testing this code because it is so simple (but then again, maybe not?) but it will work just fine to illustrate how we *could* go about testing it.

Stored Procedure Test

Refactoring Notes

This example doesn't deal so much with refactoring as with adding a missing test. Let's find a way to write one. We will see what is involved by using the two main variants: *In-Database Stored Procedure Test* and *Remote Stored Procedure Test*.

Example: In-Database Stored Procedure Test

This example uses utPLSQL, the xUnit family member for PLSQL, to automate tests that run inside the database:

```
CREATE OR REPLACE PACKAGE BODY ut_calc_secs_between
IS
   PROCEDURE ut_setup
   IS
   BEGIN
      NULL;
   END;

   PROCEDURE ut_teardown
   IS
   BEGIN
      NULL;
   END;

   -- For each program to test...
   PROCEDURE ut_CALC_SECS_BETWEEN
   IS
      secs PLS_INTEGER;
   BEGIN
      CALC_SECS_BETWEEN (
            DATE1 => SYSDATE
            '
            DATE2 => SYSDATE
            '
            SECS => secs
      );

      utAssert.eq (
         'Same dates',
         secs,
         0
         );
   END ut_CALC_SECS_BETWEEN;

END ut_calc_secs_between;
/
```

This test uses many of the familiar xUnit patterns. It is one of several tests we would normally write for this stored procedure—one test for each possible scenario. (This sample was taken from the examples that come with the utPLSQL tool. Not being a PLSQL programmer, I did not want to mess with the formatting in case it mattered!)

Example: Remoted Stored Procedure Test

To test this stored procedure in our normal programming and test execution environment, we must first find or create a Remote Proxy for it in our unit-testing environment of choice. Then we can write our unit tests in the usual manner.

The following test uses JUnit to automate tests that run outside the database and call our PLSQL stored procedure remotely:

```
public class StoredProcedureTest extends TestCase {
    public void testCalcSecsBetween_SameTime() {
        // Setup
        TimeCalculatorProxy SUT = new TimeCalculatorProxy();
        Calendar cal = new GregorianCalendar();
        long now = cal.getTimeInMillis();
        // Exercise
        long timeDifference = SUT.calc_secs_between(now,now);
        // Verify
        assertEquals( 0, timeDifference );
    }
}
```

We have reduced the complexity of the original test to a simple test of a function by hiding the JdbcOdbcCallableStatement behind a Service Facade. Looking at this example, it is difficult to tell that we are not testing a Java method. We would probably have additional *Expected Exception Tests* (see *Test Method* on page 348) to verify failed connections and other problems.

Stored
Procedure
Test

Table Truncation Teardown

How do we tear down the Test Fixture when it is in a relational database?

We truncate the tables modified during the test to tear down the fixture.

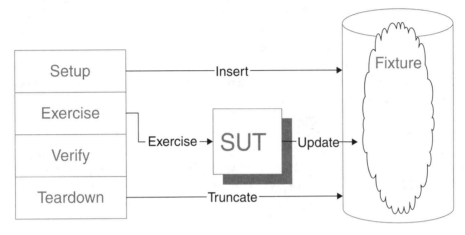

A large part of making tests repeatable and robust is ensuring that the test fixture is torn down after each test. Leftover objects and database records, as well as open files and connections, can at best cause performance degradation and at worst cause tests to fail or systems to crash. While some of these resources may be cleaned up automatically by garbage collection, others may be left hanging if they are not torn down explicitly.

Writing teardown code that can be relied upon to clean up properly in all possible circumstances is challenging and time-consuming. It involves understanding what could be left over for each possible outcome of the test and writing code to deal with that possibility. This *Complex Teardown* (see *Obscure Test* on page 186) introduces a fair bit of *Conditional Test Logic* (page 200) and—worst of all—*Untestable Test Code* (see *Hard-to-Test Code* on page 209).

When testing a system that uses a relational database, we can take advantage of the database's capabilities by using the TRUNCATE command to remove all data from a table we have modified.

How It Works

When we no longer need a persistent fixture, we issue a TRUNCATE command for each table in the fixture. It blasts all data out of the tables very efficiently with no side effects (e.g., triggers).

Table Truncation Teardown

When to Use It

We often turn to *Table Truncation Teardown* when we are using a *Persistent Fresh Fixture* (see *Fresh Fixture* on page 311) strategy with an SUT that includes a database. It is rarely our first choice, however. That distinction goes to *Transaction Rollback Teardown* (page 668). Nevertheless, *Table Truncation Teardown* is a better choice for use with a *Shared Fixture* (page 317), as this type of fixture, by definition, outlives any one test. By contrast, using *Transaction Rollback Teardown* with a *Shared Fixture* would require a very long-running transaction. While not impossible, such a long-lived transaction is troublesome.

Before we can use *Table Truncation Teardown,* we must satisfy a couple of criteria. The first requirement is that we really want *all* data in the affected tables removed. The second requirement is that each *Test Runner* (page 377) has its own *Database Sandbox* (page 650). *Table Truncation Teardown* will not work if we are using a *Database Partitioning Scheme* (see *Database Sandbox*) to isolate users or tests from one another. It *is* ideally suited for use with a *DB Schema per Test Runner* (see *Database Sandbox*), especially when we are implementing an *Immutable Shared Fixture* (see *Shared Fixture*) as a separate shared schema in the database. This allows us to blast away all the *Fresh Fixture* data in our own *Database Sandbox* without affecting the *Immutable Shared Fixture*.

If we are not using a transactional database, the closest approximation is *Automated Teardown* (page 503), which deletes only those records that were created by the test. *Automated Teardown* does not depend on the database transactions to do the work for it, but it does involve more development work on our part. We can also avoid the need to do teardown entirely by using *Delta Assertions* (page 485).

Implementation Notes

Besides the usual "Where do we put the teardown code?" decision, implementation of *Table Truncation Teardown* needs to deal with the following questions:

- How do we actually delete the data—that is, which database commands do we use?

- How do we deal with foreign key constraints and triggers?

- How do we ensure consistency when we are using an **object-relational mapping (ORM)**?

Some databases support the TRUNCATE command directly. Where this is the case, the obvious choice is to use this command. Oracle, for example, supports TRUNCATE.

Otherwise, we may have to use a DELETE * FROM table-name command instead. The TRUN-CATE or DELETE commands can be issued using *In-line Teardown* (page 509—called from within each *Test Method*; see page 348) or *Implicit Teardown* (page 516—called from the tearDown method). Some people prefer to use this command with *Lazy Teardown* because it ensures that the tables are empty at the *beginning* of the test in cases where those tables would be affected by extraneous data.

Database foreign key constraints can be a problem for *Table Truncation Teardown* if our database does not offer something similar to Oracle's ON DELETE CASCADE option. In Oracle, if the command to truncate a table includes the ON DELETE CASCADE option, then rows dependent on the truncated table rows are deleted as well. If our database does not cascade deletes, we must ensure that the tables are truncated in the order required by the schema. Schema changes can invalidate this order, resulting in failures in the teardown code. Fortunately, such failures are easy to detect: A test error tells us that our teardown needs adjusting. Correction is fairly straightforward—typically, we just need to reorder the TRUNCATE commands. We could, of course, come up with a way to issue the TRUNCATE commands in the correct order dynamically based on the dependencies between the tables. Usually, however, it is enough to encapsulate this truncation logic behind a *Test Utility Method* (page 599).

If we want to avoid the side effects of triggers and other complications for databases where TRUNCATE is not supported, we can disable the constraints and/or triggers for the duration of the test. We should take this step only if other tests exercise the SUT with the constraints and triggers in place.

If we are using an ORM layer such as Toplink, (N)Hibernate, or EJB 3.0, we may need to force the ORM to clear its cache of objects already read from the database so that subsequent object lookups do not find the recently deleted objects. For example, NHibernate provides the ClearAllCaches method on the TransactionManager for this purpose.

Table Truncation Teardown

Variation: Lazy Teardown

A teardown technique that works with only a few styles of *Shared Fixtures* is *Lazy Teardown*. With this pattern, the fixture must be destroyable at an arbitrary point in time. Thus we cannot depend on "remembering" what needs to be torn down; it must be obvious without any "memory." *Table Truncation Teardown* fits the bill because how we perform teardown is exactly the same whenever we choose to do it. We simply issue the table truncation commands during fixture setup *before* setting up the new fixture.

Motivating Example

The following test attempts to use *Guaranteed In-line Teardown* (see *In-line Teardown*) to remove all the records it created:

```
[Test]
public void TestGetFlightsByOrigin_NoInboundFlights()
{
    // Fixture Setup
    long OutboundAirport = CreateTestAirport("1OF");
    long InboundAirport = CreateTestAirport("1IF");
    FlightDto ExpFlightDto = null;
    try
    {
        ExpFlightDto =
            CreateTestFlight(OutboundAirport, InboundAirport);
        // Exercise System
        IList FlightsAtDestination1 =
            Facade.GetFlightsByOriginAirport( InboundAirport);
        // Verify Outcome
        Assert.AreEqual( 0, FlightsAtDestination1.Count );
    }
    finally
    {
        Facade.RemoveFlight( ExpFlightDto.FlightNumber );
        Facade.RemoveAirport( OutboundAirport );
        Facade.RemoveAirport( InboundAirport );
    }
}
```

This code is neither easy to write nor correct![1] Trying to keep track of the many objects the SUT has created and then tear them down one by one in a safe manner is very tricky.

Refactoring Notes

We can avoid most of the issues with coordinating *In-line Teardown* of multiple resources in a safe way by using *Table Truncation Teardown* and blasting away all the airports in one fell swoop.[2] Most of the refactoring work involves deleting the existing teardown code from the finally clause and inserting a call to cleanDatabase. We then implement this method using the truncation commands.

---

[1] See *In-line Teardown* for an explanation of what is wrong here.

[2] This assumes that we start with no airports and want to end with no airports. If we want to delete just these specific airports, we cannot use *Table Truncation Teardown*.

Example: Table Truncation (Delegated) Teardown Test

This is what the test looks like when we are done:

```
public void TestGetFlightsByOrigin_NoInboundFlight_TTTD()
{
    // Fixture Setup
    long OutboundAirport = CreateTestAirport("1OF");
    long InboundAirport = 0;
    FlightDto ExpectedFlightDto = null;
    try
    {
        InboundAirport = CreateTestAirport("1IF");
        ExpectedFlightDto =
            CreateTestFlight( OutboundAirport,InboundAirport);
        // Exercise System
        IList FlightsAtDestination1 =
            Facade.GetFlightsByOriginAirport(InboundAirport);
        // Verify Outcome
        Assert.AreEqual(0,FlightsAtDestination1.Count);
    }
    finally
    {
        CleanDatabase();
    }
}
```

This example uses *Delegated Teardown* (see *In-line Teardown*) to keep the
teardown code visible. Normally, however, we would use *Implicit Teardown*
by putting this logic into the tearDown method. The try/catch ensures that clean-
Database is run but it does not ensure that a failure inside cleanDatabase will not
prevent the teardown from completing.

Example: Lazy Teardown Test

Here is the same example converted to use *Lazy Teardown*:

```
[Test]
public void TestGetFlightsByOrigin_NoInboundFlight_LTD()
{
    // Lazy Teardown
    CleanDatabase();
    // Fixture Setup
    long OutboundAirport = CreateTestAirport("1OF");
    long InboundAirport = 0;
    FlightDto ExpectedFlightDto = null;
    InboundAirport = CreateTestAirport("1IF");
    ExpectedFlightDto =
        CreateTestFlight( OutboundAirport, InboundAirport);
    // Exercise System
```

Table
Truncation
Teardown

```
    IList FlightsAtDestination1 =
        Facade.GetFlightsByOriginAirport(InboundAirport);
    // Verify Outcome
    Assert.AreEqual(0,FlightsAtDestination1.Count);
}
```

By moving the call to cleanDatabase to the front of the *Test Method,* we ensure that the database is in the state we expect it. This code cleans up whatever the last test did, regardless of whether that test provided proper teardown. It also takes care of anything added to the relevant tables since the last test was run. It has the added benefit of eliminating the need for the try/finally construct, thereby making the test simpler and easier to understand.

Example: Table Truncation Teardown Using SQL

This implementation of the cleanDatabase method uses SQL statements constructed within the code:

```
public static void CleanDatabase() {
    string[] tablesToTruncate =
        new string[] {"Airport","City","Airline_Cd","Flight"};
        IDbConnection conn = getCurrentConnection();
    IDbTransaction txn = conn.BeginTransaction();
    try {
        foreach (string eachTableToTruncate in tablesToTruncate)
        {
            TruncateTable(txn, eachTableToTruncate);
        }
        txn.Commit();
        conn.Close();
    } catch (Exception e) {
        txn.Rollback();
    } finally {
        conn.Close();
    }
}

private static void TruncateTable( IDbTransaction txn,
                                   string tableName)
{
    const string C_DELETE_SQL = "DELETE FROM {0}";

    IDbCommand cmd = txn.Connection.CreateCommand();
    cmd.Transaction = txn;
    cmd.CommandText = string.Format(C_DELETE_SQL, tableName);

    cmd.ExecuteNonQuery();
}
```

Table
Truncation
Teardown

Because we are using SQL Server as the database, we had to implement our own TruncateTable method that issues a Delete * from ... SQL command. We would not have to take this step if our database implemented TRUNCATE directly.

Example: Table Truncation Teardown Using ORM

Here is the implementation of the cleanDatabase method using NHibernate, an ORM layer:

```
public static void CleanDatabase() {
    ISession session =
            TransactionManager.Instance.CurrentSession;
    TransactionManager.Instance.BeginTransaction();
    try {
        // We need to delete only the root classes because
        // cascade rules will delete all related child entities
        session.Delete("from Airport");
        session.Delete("from City");
        session.Flush();
        TransactionManager.Instance.Commit();
    } catch (Exception e) {
        Console.Write(e);
        throw e;
    } finally {
        TransactionManager.Instance.CloseSession();
    }
}
```

When using an ORM, we read, write, and delete domain objects; the tool determines which underlying tables they map to and takes the appropriate actions. Because we have chosen to make City and Airport "root" (parent) objects, any subordinate (child) objects such as the Flights are deleted automatically when the root is deleted. This approach further decouples us from the details of the table implementations.

Table Truncation Teardown

Transaction Rollback Teardown

How do we tear down the Test Fixture when it is in a relational database?

We roll back the uncommitted test transaction as part of the teardown.

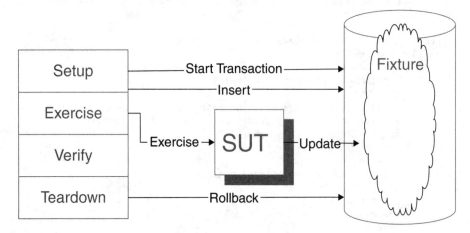

A large part of making tests repeatable and robust is ensuring that the test fixture is torn down after each test. Leftover objects and database records, as well as open files and connections, can at best cause performance degradation and at worst cause tests to fail or systems to crash. While some of these resources may be cleaned up automatically by garbage collection, others may be left hanging if they are not torn down explicitly.

Transaction
Rollback
Teardown

Writing teardown code that can be relied upon to clean up properly in all possible circumstances is challenging and time-consuming. It involves understanding what could be left over for each possible outcome of the test and writing code to deal with this case. This *Complex Teardown* (see *Obscure Test* on page 186) introduces a fair bit of *Conditional Test Logic* (page 200) and—worst of all—*Untestable Test Code* (see *Hard-to-Test Code* on page 209).

We can avoid making any lasting changes to the database contents by not committing the transaction and taking advantage of the rollback capabilities of the database.

How It Works

Our test starts a new test transaction, sets up the fixture, exercises the SUT, and verifies the outcome of the test. Each of these steps may involve interacting with the database. At the end of the test, the test rolls back the test transaction, which prevents any of the changes from becoming persistent.

When to Use It

We can use *Transaction Rollback Teardown* when we are using a *Fresh Fixture* (page 311) approach with an SUT that includes a database that supports rolling back a transaction. There are, however, some prerequisites for using *Transaction Rollback Teardown*.

In particular, the SUT must expose methods that are normally called in the context of an existing transaction by a *Humble Transaction Controller* (see *Humble Object* on page 695). That is, the methods should not start their own transaction and must *never* commit a transaction. If we are doing test-driven development, this design will come about as a *result* of applying the *Transaction Rollback Teardown* pattern as we write our code. If we are retrofitting the tests to existing software, we may need to refactor the code to use a *Humble Transaction Controller* before we can use *Transaction Rollback Teardown*.

The nice thing about *Transaction Rollback Teardown* is that it leaves the database in *exactly* the same state as it was when we started the test, regardless of what changes we made to the database contents during the test. As a result, we do not need to determine what needs to be cleaned up and what does not. Changes to the database schema or contents do not affect our teardown logic. Clearly, this pattern is much simpler to apply than *Table Truncation Teardown* (page 661).

The usual caveats apply to any tests that run against a real database; such tests will take approximately 50 (yes, 50!) times as long to run as tests that do not access the database. This testing approach will almost surely result in *Slow Tests* (page 253) unless we replace the real database with an *In-Memory Database* (see *Fake Object* on page 551) for most of our tests. Because we are depending on the transactional properties of the database, a simple *Fake Database* (see *Fake Object*) will probably not be sufficient unless it supports **ACID**.

Another prerequisite with *Transaction Rollback Teardown* is that we cannot do *anything* that results in a commit anywhere in the tests or the code they exercise. The sidebar "Transaction Rollback Pain" on page 670 describes examples of where commits can sneak in and cause havoc.

Transaction Rollback Pain

John Hurst sent me an e-mail in which he described some of the issues his team had encountered using *Transaction Rollback Teardown*. He writes:

We used Transaction Rollback Teardown for our database integration tests for a while, after a discussion on TheServerSide during which Rod Johnson advocated the approach. I gathered his main motivation for using it was for performance; a rollback is usually a lot faster than repriming the database in a new transaction for the next test. Indeed, we did find it somewhat faster than our previous approach. We used Spring's excellent AbstractTransactionalDataSourceSpringContextTests base class, which supports most of what you need to do for this pattern out of the box.

However, I chose to abandon this pattern after a few months. Here are the drawbacks I came across with this approach:

1. *You lose some test isolation. In the way we implemented this pattern, anyway, each test assumed the database was in a certain base starting condition, and the rollback would revert it to that condition. In our current model, each test is responsible—usually via a base class's setUp()—for priming the database into a known state.*

2. *You can't see what's in the database when something goes wrong. If your test fails, you usually want to examine the database to see what happened. If you've rolled back all the changes, it makes it harder to find the bug.*

3. *You have to be very careful not to inadvertently commit during your test. Yes, the code under test has declarative transaction management, and does nothing surprising. But we occasionally would need to do things in the test setup like drop and recreate a sequence to reset its value. This, being DDL, commits any outstanding transaction—and confused programmers.*

4. *You can't easily mix in tests that do need to commit changes. Lately I have added some PLSQL stored procedures and tests. Some of the stored procedures do explicit commits. I cannot mix these in the same JUnit suite with tests that assume the database always remains in a certain state.*

I apologize if my terminology isn't consistent with what's in your book. Also, my experience is probably a little limited; I've only

Transaction Rollback Teardown

> tried this approach in a Spring environment and I prefer to do most
> things in a "Spring" way. Finally, I am sure these limitations can be
> and are worked around in various ways. It's just that, for our team,
> this pattern turned out to be more trouble than it was worth.
>
> Don't get me wrong—I DO think the pattern should be included.
> I just think the consequences should be noted, and maybe it isn't
> for everyone.

Implementation Notes

A few members of the xUnit family support *Transaction Rollback Teardown*
directly; open-source extensions may be available for other members. If nothing
is available, coding this teardown logic is not very complicated. The more significant implementation consideration is giving the tests access to nontransactional
methods on the SUT. Most domain model objects are nontransactional, so this
requirement should not be a problem for unit tests of domain objects. We are
more likely to experience a problem when we are writing *Subcutaneous Tests*
(see *Layer Test* on page 337) against a Service Facade [CJ2EEP] because these
methods often perform transaction control. If this is the case, we will need to
expose a nontransactional version of the methods by refactoring to the *Humble
Transaction Controller* pattern. We could either use a transactional Decorator
[GOF] as a separate object or simply have the transactional methods delegate to
the nontransactional versions of the methods on self. This approach is called a
Poor Man's Humble Object (see *Humble Object*).

If the methods exist but are not visible to the client, we will need to expose
them to the test. We can do so either by making the methods to be tested public or by exposing them indirectly via a *Test-Specific Subclass* (page 579). We
could also do an Extract Testable Component (page 735) refactoring to move
the nontransactional versions of the methods to a different class and make them
visible to the test from there.

Any reading of the updated data in the database must occur within the
context of the same transaction. This normally is not a problem except when
we are trying to simulate or test concurrency. If we are using an ORM layer
such as Toplink, (N)Hibernate, or EJB 3.0, we may need to force the ORM
to write the changes made to the objects to the database so that methods that
read the database directly (from within the same transactional context) can
see them. For example, EJB 3.0 provides the `EntityManager.flush` static method
for exactly this purpose.

**Transaction
Rollback
Teardown**

Motivating Example

The following test attempts to use *Guaranteed In-line Teardown* (see *In-line Teardown* on page 509) to remove all the records it created:

```
public void testGetFlightsByOriginAirport_NoInboundFlights()
        throws Exception {
  // Fixture Setup
  BigDecimal outboundAirport = createTestAirport("1OF");
  BigDecimal inboundAirport = createTestAirport("1IF");
  FlightDto expFlightDto = null;
  try {
     expFlightDto = createTestFlight(outboundAirport, inboundAirport);
     // Exercise System
     List flightsAtDestination1 =
             facade.getFlightsByOriginAirport( inboundAirport);
     // Verify Outcome
     assertEquals( 0, flightsAtDestination1.size() );
  } finally {
      facade.removeFlight( expFlightDto.getFlightNumber() );
      facade.removeAirport( outboundAirport );
      facade.removeAirport( inboundAirport );
  }
}
```

This code is neither easy to write nor correct![3] Trying to keep track of all objects the SUT has created and then tear them down one by one in a safe manner is very tricky.

Refactoring Notes

Transaction Rollback Teardown

We can avoid most of the issues related to coordinating *In-line Teardown* of multiple resources in a safe way by using *Transaction Rollback Teardown* and blasting away all changes to the objects in one fell swoop. Most of the refactoring work consists of deleting the existing teardown code from the finally clause and inserting a call to the abortTransaction method. We also need to make the call to beginTransaction before we do any fixture setup, and we have to modify the *Creation Methods* (page 415) to ensure that they do not commit a transaction. To do so, we have them call a nontransactional version of the methods on the Service Facade.

---

[3] See *In-line Teardown* for an explanation of what is wrong here.

Example: Object Transaction Rollback Teardown

Here is what the test looks like when we are done:

```
public void testGetFlightsByOrigin_NoInboundFlight_TRBTD()
        throws Exception {
    // Fixture Setup
    TransactionManager.beginTransaction();
    BigDecimal outboundAirport = createTestAirport("1OF");
    BigDecimal inboundAirport = null;
    FlightDto expectedFlightDto = null;
    try {
        inboundAirport = createTestAirport("1IF");
        expectedFlightDto =
            createTestFlight( outboundAirport, inboundAirport);
        // Exercise System
        List flightsAtDestination1 =
            facade.getFlightsByOriginAirport(inboundAirport);
        // Verify Outcome
        assertEquals(0,flightsAtDestination1.size());
    } finally {
        TransactionManager.abortTransaction();
    }
}
```

In this refactored test, we have replaced the multiple lines of teardown code in the finally clause with a single call to abortTransaction. We still need the finally clause because this example is using *In-line Teardown*; we could easily move this call to the TransactionManager to the tearDown method because it is so generic.

In this example, *Transaction Rollback Teardown* undoes the fixture setup performed by the various *Creation Methods* we called earlier in the test. The fixture objects have not yet been committed to the database. Because getFlightsFromAirport is being called within the context of the transaction, however, it returns the newly added but not yet committed flights. (That is the "C" for "consistent" in ACID working on our behalf!)

Transaction Rollback Teardown

```
private BigDecimal createTestAirport(String airportName)
        throws FlightBookingException {
    BigDecimal newAirportId =
        facade._createAirport( airportName,
                                " Airport" + airportName,
                                "City" + airportName);
    return newAirportId;
}
```

The creation method calls the nontransactional version of the facade method (an example of a *Poor Man's Humble Object*):

```
public BigDecimal createAirport( String airportCode,
                                  String name,
                                  String nearbyCity)
       throws FlightBookingException{
   TransactionManager.beginTransaction();
   BigDecimal airportId = _createAirport(airportCode, name, nearbyCity);
   TransactionManager.commitTransaction();
   return airportId;
}

// private, nontransactional version for use by tests
BigDecimal _createAirport( String airportCode,
                           String name,
                           String nearbyCity)
       throws DataException, InvalidArgumentException {
   Airport airport =
       dataAccess.createAirport(airportCode,name,nearbyCity);
   logMessage("CreateFlight", airport.getCode());
   return airport.getId();
}
```

If the method we were exercising (e.g., getFlightsFromAirport) *did* modify the state of the SUT and *did* begin and end its own transaction, we would have to do a similar refactoring on it as well.

Example: Database Transaction Rollback Teardown

The first example hid the database from the code behind a data access layer that returned or accepted objects. This is common practice when using the Domain Model [PEAA] pattern for organizing the business logic. *Transaction Rollback Teardown* is typically used when manipulating the database directly in our application logic (a style known as a Transaction Script [PEAA]). The following example illustrates this approach using .NET row sets (or something similar):

```
[TestFixture]
public class TransactionRollbackTearDownTest
{
   private SqlConnection _Connection;
   private SqlTransaction _Transaction;

   public TransactionRollbackTearDownTest()
   {
   }

   [SetUp]
```

```
    public void Setup()
    {
        string dbConnectionString = ConfigurationSettings.
                        AppSettings.Get("DbConnectionString");
        _Connection = new SqlConnection(dbConnectionString);
        _Connection.Open();
        _Transaction = _Connection.BeginTransaction();
    }

    [TearDown]
    public void TearDown()
    {
        _Transaction.Rollback();
        _Connection.Close();
        // Avoid NUnit "instance behavior" bug
        _Transaction = null;
        _Connection = null;
    }

    [Test]
    public void AnNUnitTest()
    {
        const string C_INSERT_SQL =
            "INSERT INTO Invoice(Amount, Tax, CustomerId)" +
            " VALUES({0}, {1}, {2})";
        SqlCommand cmd = _Connection.CreateCommand();
        cmd.Transaction = _Transaction;
        cmd.CommandText = string.Format(
                    C_INSERT_SQL,
                    new object[] {"100.00", "7.00", 2001});
        // Exercise SUT
        cmd.ExecuteNonQuery();
        // Verify result
        //    etc.
    }
  }
}
```

This example uses *Implicit Setup* (page 424) to establish the connection and start the transaction. After the *Test Method* (page 348) has run, it uses *Implicit Teardown* (page 516) to roll back the transaction and close the connection. We assign null to the instance variables because NUnit does not create a separate *Testcase Object* (page 382) for each *Test Method*, unlike most other members of xUnit. See the sidebar "There's Always an Exception" on page 384 for details.

Chapter 26

Design-for-Testability
Patterns

Patterns in This Chapter

Design-for-
Testability
Patterns

Dependency Injection

*How do we design the SUT so that we can replace its
dependencies at runtime?*

The client provides the depended-on object to the SUT.

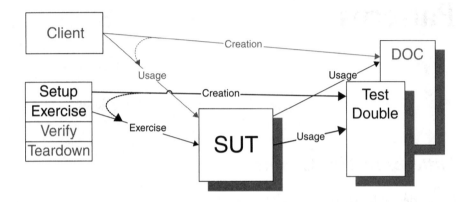

Almost every piece of code depends on some other classes, objects, modules, or procedures. To unit-test a piece of code properly, we would like to isolate the code from its dependencies. This isolation is difficult to achieve if those dependencies are hard-coded in the form of literal classnames.

Dependency Injection is a way to allow the normal coupling between a SUT and its dependencies to be broken during automated testing.

How It Works

We avoid hard-coding the names of classes on which we depend into our code by providing some other means for the client or system configuration to tell the SUT which objects to use for each dependency as it is executed. As part of the design of the SUT, we arrange to pass the dependency in to the SUT through the "front door." That is, the means to specify the dependency becomes part of the API of the SUT. We can include it as an argument with each method call, include it on the constructor, or make it a settable attribute (property).

When to Use It

We need to provide a means to substitute a depended-on component (DOC) to make it easy to use a *Test Double* (page 522) while testing our code. **Static** binding—that is, specifying exact types or classes at compile time—severely limits our options regarding how the software is configured as it runs. **Dynamic binding** creates much more flexible software by deferring the decision of exactly which type or class to use until runtime. *Dependency Injection* is a good choice for communicating which class to use when we are designing the software from scratch. It offers a natural way to design the code when we are doing test-driven development (TDD) because many of the tests we write for dependent objects seek to replace a DOC with a *Test Double*.

When we don't have complete control over the code we are testing, such as when we are retrofitting tests to existing code,[1] we may need to use some other means to introduce the *Test Doubles*. If the SUT uses *Dependency Lookup* (page 686) to find the DOC, we can override the lookup mechanism to return the *Test Double*. We can also use a *Test-Specific Subclass* (page 579) of the SUT to return a *Test Double* as long as access to the DOC remains encapsulated behind a method call.

Implementation Notes

Introducing *Dependency Injection* requires solving two problems. First, we must be able to use a *Test Double* wherever the real DOC is used. This constraint is primarily an issue in statically typed languages because we must convince the compiler to allow us to pass off a *Test Double* as the real thing. Second, we must provide a way to tell the SUT to use the *Test Double*.

Type Compatibility

Whichever way we choose to install the dependency into the SUT, we must also ensure that the *Test Double* we want to replace it with is "type compatible" with the code that uses the *Test Double*. This is most easily accomplished if both the real component and the *Test Double* implement the same interface (in statically typed languages) or have the same signature (in dynamically typed languages). A quick way to introduce a *Test Double* into existing code is to do an Extract Interface [Fowler] refactoring on the real DOC and then have the *Test Double* implement the new interface.

Dependency Injection

Installing the Test Double

There are a number of different ways to tell the SUT to use the *Test Double,* but they all involve replacing a hard-coded name with a mechanism that determines the type of object to use at execution time. The three basic options are as follows:

---

[1] "If it ain't broke, don't change it (even to improve the testability)" is a common, albeit somewhat misguided, constraint in these circumstances.

- *Parameter Injection:* We pass the dependency directly to the SUT as we invoke it.

- *Constructor Injection:* We tell the SUT which DOC to use when we construct it.

- *Setter Injection:* We tell the SUT about the DOC sometime between when we construct it and when we exercise it.

Each of these three variations of *Dependency Injection* can be hand-coded. Another option is to use an "Inversion of Control" (IoC) framework to link the various components together at runtime. This scheme avoids superfluous diversity in how *Dependency Injection* is implemented across the application and can simplify the process of reconfiguring the application for different deployment models.

Variation: Parameter Injection

Parameter Injection is a form of *Dependency Injection* in which the SUT does not keep or initialize a reference to the DOC; instead, it is passed in as an argument of the method being called on the SUT. All clients of the SUT—whether they are tests or production code—supply the DOC. As a consequence, the SUT is more independent of the context because it makes no assumptions about the dependency other than its usage interface. The main drawback is that *Parameter Injection* forces the client to know about the dependency, which is more appropriate in some circumstances than in others. Most of the other variants of *Dependency Injection* move this knowledge somewhere other than the client or at least make it optional.

   Parameter Injection is advocated by the original paper on *Mock Objects* (page 544) [ET]. It is especially effective when we are doing true TDD because that's when we have the greatest control over the design. It is possible to introduce *Parameter Injection* in an optional fashion by providing an alternative signature for the method in question with the extra parameter; we can then have the more traditional style method create the instance of the dependency and call the method that takes the dependency as a parameter.

**Dependency
Injection**

Variation: Constructor Injection

Both *Constructor Injection* and *Setter Injection* involve storing a reference to the DOC as an attribute (field or instance variable) of the SUT. With *Dependency Injection,* the field is initialized from a constructor argument. The SUT may optionally provide a simpler constructor that calls this constructor with the value normally used in production. When a test wants to replace the real DOC with a *Test Double,* it passes in the *Test Double* to the constructor when it builds the SUT.

This approach to introducing *Dependency Injection* works well when the code includes only one or two constructors and they have small argument lists. *Constructor Injection* is the *only* approach that works if the DOC is an active object that creates its own thread of execution during construction; such behavior would make for *Hard-to-Test Code* (page 209), and we should probably consider turning it into a *Humble Executable* (see *Humble Object* on page 695). If we have a large number of dependencies as constructor arguments, we probably need to refactor the code to remove this code smell.

Variation: Setter Injection

As with *Constructor Injection*, the SUT holds a reference to the DOC as an attribute (field) that is initialized in the constructor. Where it differs is that the attribute is exposed to the client either as a public attribute or via a "setter" method. When a test wants to replace the real DOC with a *Test Double*, it assigns to the exposed attribute (or calls the setter with) an instance of the *Test Double*. This approach works well when constructing the real DOC has no unpleasant side effects and assuming that nothing can happen automatically between the constructor call and the point at which the test calls the setter for the property. *Setter Injection* cannot be used if the SUT performs any significant processing in the constructor that relies on the dependency. In that case, we must use *Constructor Injection*. If constructing the real DOC has deleterious side effects, we can avoid creating it via the constructor by modifying the SUT to use Lazy Initialization [SBPP] to instantiate the DOC the first time the SUT needs to use it.

Retrofitting Dependency Injection

When the SUT does not support any of these options "out of the box," we may be able to retrofit this capability via a *Test-Specific Subclass*. If the actual class to be used is normally retrieved from configuration data, this retrieval should be done by some component other than the SUT and the class then passed to the SUT using *Dependency Injection*. Such a use of the *Humble Object* pattern for the client or configuration decouples the SUT from the environment and ensures that tests do not need to set up some external dependency (the configuration file) to introduce the *Test Double*.

Dependency Injection

Another possibility is to use **aspect-oriented programming** (AOP) to insert the *Dependency Injection* mechanism into the development environment. For example, we might inject the decision to use the *Test Double* or inject the test-specific logic—the *Test Double*—directly into the SUT. I don't think we have enough experience with using AOP to call this a pattern just yet.

Motivating Example

The following test cannot be made to pass "as is":

```
public void testDisplayCurrentTime_AtMidnight() {
    // fixture setup
    TimeDisplay sut = new TimeDisplay();
    // exercise SUT
    String result = sut.getCurrentTimeAsHtmlFragment();
    // verify direct output
    String expectedTimeString =
        "<span class=\"tinyBoldText\">Midnight</span>";
    assertEquals( expectedTimeString, result);
}
```

This test almost always fails because it depends on the current time being returned to the SUT by a DOC. The test cannot control the values being returned by that component, the DefaultTimeProvider. Therefore, this test will pass only when the system time is exactly midnight.

```
public String getCurrentTimeAsHtmlFragment() {
    Calendar currentTime;
    try {
        currentTime = new DefaultTimeProvider().getTime();
    } catch (Exception e) {
        return e.getMessage();
    }
    // etc.
}
```

Because the SUT is hard-coded to use a particular class to retrieve the time, we cannot replace the DOC with a *Test Double*. That constraint makes this test nondeterministic and pretty much useless. We need to find a way to gain control over the indirect inputs of the SUT.

Refactoring Notes

Dependency
Injection

We can use a Replace Dependency with Test Double (page 522) refactoring to gain control over the time. *Setter Injection* can be introduced into existing code if we have control over the code and the method in question is not widely used or if we have refactoring tools that support the Introduce Parameter [JBrains] refactoring. Failing that, we can use an Extract Method [Fowler] refactoring to create the new method signature that takes the *Dependency Injection* as an argument and leave the old method as an Adapter [GOF] that calls the new method.

Example: Parameter Injection

Here's the test rewritten to use *Parameter Injection:*

```
public void testDisplayCurrentTime_AtMidnight_PI() {
   // Fixture setup
   //      Test Double instantiation
   TimeProvider tpStub = new MidnightTimeProvider();
   //      Instantiate SUT
   TimeDisplay sut = new TimeDisplay();
   // Exercise SUT using Test Double
   String result = sut.getCurrentTimeAsHtmlFragment(tpStub);
   // Verify outcome
   String expectedTimeString =
        "<span class=\"tinyBoldText\">Midnight</span>";
   assertEquals("Midnight", expectedTimeString, result);
}
```

In this case, only the test will use the new signature. The existing code can use the old signature and the method adapter instantiates the real dependency object before passing it in.

```
public String getCurrentTimeAsHtmlFragment(
                  TimeProvider timeProviderArg) {
   Calendar currentTime;
   try {
      currentTime = timeProviderArg.getTime();
   } catch (Exception e) {
      return e.getMessage();
   }
   // etc.
}
```

Example: Constructor Injection

Here's the same test rewritten to use *Constructor Injection:*

```
public void testDisplayCurrentTime_AtMidnight_CI()
            throws Exception {
   // Fixture setup
   //      Test Double instantiation
   TimeProvider tpStub = new MidnightTimeProvider();
   //   Instantiate SUT injecting Test Double
   TimeDisplay sut = new TimeDisplay(tpStub);
   // Exercise SUT
   String expectedTimeString =
        "<span class=\"tinyBoldText\">12:01 AM</span>";
   // Verify outcome
```

Dependency
Injection

```
assertEquals("12:01 AM",
                expectedTimeString,
                sut.getCurrentTimeAsHtmlFragment());
}
```

To convert the SUT to use *Constructor Injection,* we can do an Introduce Field
[JetBrains] refactoring to hold the DOC in a field that is initialized in the existing
constructor. We can then do an Introduce Parameter refactoring to modify all
callers of the existing constructor so that they pass the real DOC as a parameter
of the constructor. If we cannot or do not want to modify all existing callers of the
constructor, we can define a new constructor that takes the DOC as a parameter
and modify the existing constructor to instantiate the real DOC and pass it in to
our new constructor.

```
public class TimeDisplay {

    private TimeProvider timeProvider;

    public TimeDisplay() {      // backwards compatible constructor
        timeProvider = new DefaultTimeProvider();
    }
    public TimeDisplay(TimeProvider timeProvider) { // new constructor
        this.timeProvider = timeProvider;
    }
```

Another approach is to do an Extract Method refactoring on the call to the constructor and then use Move Method [Fowler] refactoring to move it to an *Object
Factory* (see *Dependency Lookup*). That would result in *Dependency Lookup*.

Example: Setter Injection

Here is the same test refactored to use *Setter Injection*:

Dependency
Injection

```
public void testDisplayCurrentTime_AtMidnight_SI()
            throws Exception {
    // Fixture setup
    //      Test Double instantiation
    TimeProvider tpStub = new MidnightTimeProvider();
    //    Instantiate SUT
    TimeDisplay sut = new TimeDisplay();
    //      Test Double installation
    sut.setTimeProvider(tpStub);
    // Exercise SUT
    String result = sut.getCurrentTimeAsHtmlFragment();
    // Verify outcome
    String expectedTimeString =
            "<span class=\"tinyBoldText\">Midnight</span>";
    assertEquals("Midnight", expectedTimeString, result);
}
```

Note the call to setTimeProvider to install the *Hard-Coded Test Double* (page 568). If we had used a *Configurable Test Double* (page 558), its configuration would occur immediately before the call to setTimeProvider.

To refactor the SUT to support *Setter Injection*, we can do an Introduce Field refactoring to hold the DOC in a variable that is initialized in the existing constructor and call the DOC via this field. We can then expose the field either directly or via a setter so that the test can override its value. Here is the refactored version of the SUT:

```
public class TimeDisplay {

    private TimeProvider timeProvider;

    public TimeDisplay() {
        timeProvider = new DefaultTimeProvider();
    }
    public void setTimeProvider(TimeProvider provider) {
        this.timeProvider = provider;
    }
    public String getCurrentTimeAsHtmlFragment()
            throws TimeProviderEx {
        Calendar currentTime;
        try {
            currentTime = getTimeProvider().getTime();
        } catch (Exception e) {
            return e.getMessage();
        }
        // etc.
```

Here we chose to use a getter to retrieve the DOC. We could just as easily have used the timeProvider field directly.

Dependency Lookup

How do we design the SUT so that we can replace its
dependencies at runtime?

Also known as:
Service Locator,
Object Factory,
Component
Broker,
Component
Registry

The SUT asks another object to return the depended-on object before it uses it.

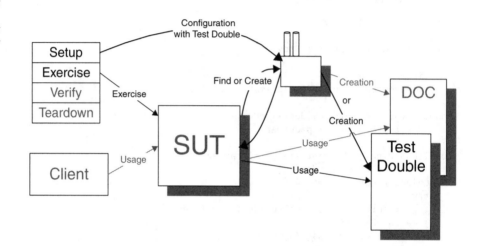

Almost every piece of code depends on some other classes, objects, modules, or procedures. To unit-test a piece of code properly, we would like to isolate it from its dependencies. Such isolation is difficult to achieve, however, if those dependencies are hard-coded within the code in the form of literal classnames.

Dependency Lookup is a way to allow the normal coupling between a SUT and its dependencies to be broken during automated testing.

Dependency
Lookup

How It Works

We avoid hard-coding the names of classes on which the SUT depends into our code because static binding severely limits our options regarding how the software is configured as it runs. Instead, we hard-code that name of a "component broker" that returns a ready-to-use object. The component broker provides some means for the client software or perhaps a system configuration manager to tell the SUT in question which objects to use for each component request.

When to Use It

Dependency Lookup is most appropriate when we need to retrieve DOCs from deep inside the system and it would be too messy to pass the *Test Double* (page 522) in from the client. A good example of such a situation is when we want to replace the data access layer of the system with a *Fake Database* (see *Fake Object* on page 551) or *In-Memory Database* (see *Fake Object*) to speed up execution of the automated customer tests. It would be too complex for each *Subcutaneous Test* (see *Layer Test* on page 337) to pass the *Fake Database* in through the Service Facade [CJ2EEP] and all the way down to the data access layer. Using *Dependency Lookup* allows the test or even a *Setup Decorator* (page 447) to use a "configuration facade" to install the *Fake Database,* which the SUT can magically use without any further ado. Jeremy Miller writes:

> *You cannot understate the value of using a Service Locator for automated testing. We routinely use alternative dependencies in testing, both to deal with difficult dependencies and for test performance. For example, in a functional test we'll collapse a Web site and a backing application server into a single process for better performance.*

Dependency Lookup tends to be a lot simpler to retrofit onto existing legacy software because it affects only those places where object construction actually occurs; we do not need to modify every intermediate object or method, as we might have to do with *Dependency Injection* (page 678). It is also much simpler to retrofit existing round-trip tests so that they use a *Fake Object* to speed them up by wrapping them in a *Setup Decorator.* With this scheme, we do not have to change each test; instead, we can create new instances of the SUT in each test and still have the test use the same *Fake Object* because the *Service Locator* remembers it across tests.[2]

The main alternative to *Dependency Lookup* is to provide a substitution mechanism within the SUT using *Dependency Injection.* This approach is generally preferable for unit tests because it makes the replacement of the DOC more obvious and directly connected to exercising the SUT. Another option is to use AOP to install test-specific logic using the development tools rather than modifying the design of the software. The least preferred solution is to use a *Test Hook* (page 709) within the SUT to avoid calling the DOC or within the DOC so that it behaves in a test-specific way.

Dependency Lookup

---

[2] We call these tests "bimodal" or "multimodal" because they can be run with both real and fake DOCs.

The well-known intermediary may be called a "Service Locator," "Object Factory," "Component Broker," or "Component Registry." While these names imply different semantics (new versus existing objects), this need not be the case. For performance reasons, we may choose to return new objects from a "Service Locator" or "previously enjoyed" objects from an *Object Factory*. To simplify this discussion, the term "Component Broker" is used here.

Implementation Notes

A desire to use a *Test Double* when testing our code implies a need to make DOCs substitutable. This constraint rules out hard-coding the names of classes on which we depend into our code because static binding severely limits our options regarding how the software is configured as it runs. One way to avoid this issue is to have the SUT delegate DOC fabrication to another object. Of course, this scheme implies we need a way to get a reference to *that* object. We solve this recursive problem by having a well-known object act as an intermediary between the test and the DOC. This well-known object is referenced by a hard-coded classname. To be useful for installing *Test Doubles,* this well-known object must supply a mechanism by which the test can specify the object to be returned.

Dependency Lookup has the following characteristics:

- Either a Singleton [GOF], a Registry [PEAA], or some kind of Thread-Specific Storage [POSA2]

- An interface that fully encapsulates which implementation we are using

- A built-in substitution mechanism for replacing the returned object with a *Test Double*

- Access via well-known global name

Dependency Lookup

The *Dependency Lookup* mechanism returns an object that can be used directly by the client. The nature of the actual object returned determines whether it is more appropriate to call it a "Service Locator" or an "Object Factory." Once the object is retrieved, the SUT uses it directly. During testing, the test arranges for the *Dependency Lookup* mechanism to return a test-specific object.

Encapsulated Implementation

A major requirement of *Dependency Lookup* is the existence of a well-known object to which we can delegate our requests for DOCs. This well-known object could be a Singleton, a Registry, or some kind of Thread-Specific Storage mechanism.[3]

The "Component Broker" should encapsulate its implementation from the client (our SUT). That is, the interface provided by the "Component Broker" should not expose whether it is a Singleton or a Registry or whether some type of Thread-Specific Storage mechanism is in use under the covers. In fact, the test environment may want to provide a different implementation specifically to avoid issues caused by Singletons in tests, such as a *Substitutable Singleton* (see *Test-Specific Subclass* on page 579).

Substitution Mechanism

When a test wants to replace the real DOC with a *Test Double*, it needs a way to tell the "Component Broker" that a *Test Double* should be returned instead of the real component. The "Component Broker" may provide a configuration interface to configure it with the object to be returned or the test can replace the component Registry with a suitable *Test-Specific Subclass*. It may also need to provide a way to restore the original or default configuration of the broker so that the configuration used in one test does not "leak" into another test, effectively changing the "Component Broker" into a *Shared Fixture* (page 317).

A less desirable configuration alternative is to have the "Component Broker" read the classnames to be constructed for each request from a configuration file. This approach poses several problems, however. First, the test must write the file as part of fixture setup unless the test offers a way to replace the file access mechanism. This is sure to result in *Slow Tests* (page 253). Second, this scheme will not work with *Configurable Test Doubles* (page 558) unless the configuration file can also provide initialization data for the object. Finally, the need to write a file opens the door to *Interacting Tests* (see *Erratic Test* on page 228) because different tests may need different configuration information.

If the "Component Broker" must return objects based on configuration data, a better solution is to have a separate *Humble Object* (page 695) read the file and call a configuration interface on the "Component Broker." The test can then use this same interface to configure the broker on a per-test basis.

Dependency Lookup

---

[3] The main difference is that a Singleton has only a single instance, whereas a Registry makes no such promise. Thread-Specific Storage allows objects to access "global" data via a well-known object, where the data accessed is specific to a particular thread; the same object might retrieve different data depending on which thread is being run.

Motivating Example

The following test cannot be made to pass "as is":

```
public void testDisplayCurrentTime_AtMidnight() {
   // fixture setup
   TimeDisplay sut = new TimeDisplay();
   // exercise SUT
   String result = sut.getCurrentTimeAsHtmlFragment();
   // verify direct output
   String expectedTimeString =
         "<span class=\"tinyBoldText\">Midnight</span>";
   assertEquals( expectedTimeString, result);
}
```

This test almost always fails because it assumes that the current time will be returned to the SUT by a DOC. The test cannot control which values are returned by that component (the DefaultTimeProvider), however, so this test will pass only when the system time is exactly midnight.

```
public String getCurrentTimeAsHtmlFragment() {
   Calendar currentTime;
   try {
      currentTime = new DefaultTimeProvider().getTime();
   } catch (Exception e) {
      return e.getMessage();
   }
   // etc.
}
```

Because the SUT is hard-coded to use a particular class to retrieve the time, we cannot replace the DOC with a *Test Double*. That makes this test nondeterministic and pretty much useless. We need to find a way to gain control over the indirect inputs of the SUT.

Refactoring Notes

Dependency Lookup

The first step to making this behavior testable is to replace the hard-coded classname with a call to a "Service Locator":

```
public String getCurrentTimeAsHtmlFragment() {
   Calendar currentTime;
   try {
      TimeProvider timeProvider =
            (TimeProvider) ServiceLocator.getInstance().
                                    findService("Time");
      currentTime = timeProvider.getTime();
   } catch (Exception e) {
      return e.getMessage();
   }
   // etc.
```

Although we could have provided a class method to avoid the chained method calls, that step would just move the getInstance into the class method. The next refactoring step depends on whether we have a configuration interface on our "Service Locator." If it makes sense to configure the production version of the "Service Locator," we can introduce the configuration mechanism directly into it (as illustrated in the next example). Otherwise, we can simply override what the Service Locator returns in a *Test-Specific Subclass* (as illustrated in the second example).

Example: Configurable Registry

This version of the test has been modified to use the configuration interface on the "Service Locator" to install a *Test Double:*

```
public void testDisplayCurrentTime_AtMidnight_CSL() {
   // Fixture setup
   //      Test Double configuration
   MidnightTimeProvider tpStub = new MidnightTimeProvider();
   //    Instantiate SUT
   TimeDisplay sut = new TimeDisplay();
   //      Test Double installation
   ServiceLocator.getInstance().registerServiceForName(tpStub, "Time");
   // Exercise SUT
   String result = sut.getCurrentTimeAsHtmlFragment();
   // Verify outcome
   String expectedTimeString =
           "<span class=\"tinyBoldText\">Midnight</span>";
   assertEquals("Midnight", expectedTimeString, result);
}
```

The code in the SUT was described previously. The code for the *Configuration Interface* (see *Configurable Test Double*) of the *Configurable Registry* follows:

```
public class ServiceLocator {
   protected ServiceLocator() {};

   protected static ServiceLocator soleInstance = null;

   public static ServiceLocator getInstance() {
      if (soleInstance==null)
         soleInstance = new ServiceLocator();
      return soleInstance;
   }

   private HashMap providers = new HashMap();

   public ServiceProvider findService(String serviceName) {
      return (ServiceProvider) providers.get(serviceName);
```

```
        }

        // configuration interface
        public void registerServiceForName( ServiceProvider provider,
                                            String serviceName) {
            providers.put( serviceName, provider);
        }
    }
```

The interesting thing about this example is our use of a *Configuration Interface* on a production class rather than a *Test Double*. In fact, the *Configurable Registry* avoids the need to use a *Test Double* by providing the test with a mechanism to alter the service component the *Configurable Registry* returns.

Example: Substituted Singleton

This version of the test deals with a nonconfigurable *Dependency Lookup* mechanism by replacing the soleInstance of the "Service Locator" with a *Substituted Singleton* (see *Test-Specific Subclass*). To ensure the reusability of the configuration interface of the *Substituted Singleton*, we pass the TimeProvider *Test Stub* (page 529) as an argument to overrideSoleInstance.

```
    public void testDisplayCurrentTime_AtMidnight_TSS() {
        // Fixture setup
        //      Test Double configuration
        MidnightTimeProvider tpStub = new MidnightTimeProvider();

        //    Instantiate SUT
        TimeDisplay sut = new TimeDisplay();
        //      Test Double installation
        //       Replaces the entire Service Locator with one that
        //        always returns our Test Stub
        ServiceLocatorTestSingleton.overrideSoleInstance(tpStub);
        // Exercise SUT
        String result = sut.getCurrentTimeAsHtmlFragment();
        // Verify outcome
        String expectedTimeString =
               "<span class=\"tinyBoldText\">Midnight</span>";
        assertEquals("Midnight", expectedTimeString, result);
    }
```

Dependency Lookup

Note how the test overrides the object normally returned by getInstance with an instance of a *Test-Specific Subclass*. The code for the Singleton follows:

```
public class ServiceLocator {
    protected ServiceLocator() {};

    protected static ServiceLocator soleInstance = null;
```

```
    public static ServiceLocator getInstance() {
        if (soleInstance==null)
            soleInstance = new ServiceLocator();
        return soleInstance;
    }

    private HashMap providers = new HashMap();

    public ServiceProvider findService(String serviceName) {
        return (ServiceProvider) providers.get(serviceName);
    }
}
```

Note that we had to make the constructor and soleInstance protected rather than private to allow them to be overridden by the subclass. Finally, here is the code for the *Substituted Singleton*:

```
public class ServiceLocatorTestSingleton extends ServiceLocator {
    private ServiceProvider tpStub;

    private ServiceLocatorTestSingleton(TimeProvider newTpStub) {
        this.tpStub = newTpStub;
    };

    // Installation interface
    static ServiceLocatorTestSingleton
                        overrideSoleInstance(TimeProvider tpStub) {
        // We could save the real instance before reassigning
        // soleInstance so we could restore it later, but we'll
        // forego that complexity for this example
        soleInstance = new ServiceLocatorTestSingleton( tpStub);
        return (ServiceLocatorTestSingleton) soleInstance;
    }

    // Overridden superclass method
    public ServiceProvider findService(String serviceName) {
        return tpStub;  // Hard-coded; ignores serviceName
    }
}
```

Dependency Lookup

Because it cannot see the private HashMap of providers, this code simply returns the contents of the tpStub field that it initialized in the constructor.

About the Name

Choosing a name for this pattern was tough. *Service Locator* and *Component Broker* were already in widespread use. Both are good names for use in their particular circumstance. Unfortunately, neither name can encompass the other, so I had to come up with another name that unified the two major variants.

The name *Dependency Injection* was already in widespread use for the alternate pattern; a desire for consistency with that name led to using *Dependency Lookup*. See the sidebar "What's in a (Pattern) Name?" on page 576 for more on this decision-making process.

Dependency
Lookup

Humble Object

*How can we make code testable when it is too closely coupled
to its environment?*

**We extract the logic into a separate, easy-to-test component that is decoupled
from its environment.**

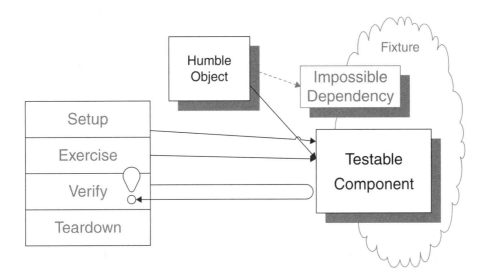

We are often faced with trying to test software that is closely coupled to
some kind of framework. Examples include visual components (e.g., widgets,
dialogs) and transactional component plug-ins. Testing these objects is difficult
because constructing all the objects with which our SUT needs to interact may
be expensive—or even impossible. In other cases, objects may be hard to test
because they run asynchronously; examples include active objects (e.g., threads,
processes, Web servers) and user interfaces. These objects' asynchronicity introduces uncertainty, a requirement for interprocess coordination, and the need
for delays into tests. Faced with these thorny issues, developers often just give
up on testing this kind of code. The result: *Production Bugs* (page 268) caused
by *Untested Code* and *Untested Requirements*.

   Humble Object is a way to bring the logic of these hard-to-instantiate objects
under test in a cost-effective manner.

How It Works

We extract all the logic from the hard-to-test component into a component that is testable via **synchronous tests**. This component implements a service interface consisting of methods that expose the logic of the untestable component; the only difference is that these methods are accessible via synchronous method calls. As a result, the *Humble Object* component becomes a very thin adapter layer that contains very little code. Each time the framework calls the *Humble Object*, this object delegates its responsibilities to the testable component. If the testable component needs any information from the context, the *Humble Object* is responsible for retrieving it and passing it to the testable component. The *Humble Object* code is typically so simple that we often don't bother writing tests for it because it can be quite difficult to set up the environment needed to run those tests.

When to Use It

We can and should introduce a *Humble Object* whenever we have nontrivial logic in a component that is problematic to instantiate because it depends on a framework or can be accessed only asynchronously. There are lots of reasons for objects being hard to test; consequently, there are lots of variations in how we break the dependencies that are required. The following variations are the most common examples of *Humble Object*—but we shouldn't be surprised if we sometimes need to invent our own variation.

Variation: Humble Dialog

Graphical user interface (GUI) frameworks require us to provide objects to represent our pages and controls. These objects provide logic to translate user actions into the underlying system actions and to translate the system responses back into user recognizable behavior. This logic may involve invoking the application behind the user interface and/or modifying the state of this or other visual objects.

Visual objects are very difficult to test efficiently because they are tightly coupled to the presentation framework that invokes them. To be effective, a test would need to simulate that environment to provide the visual object with all the information and facilities it requires. Further complicating the issue is the fact that these frameworks often run in their own thread of control, which means that we must use **asynchronous tests**. These tests are challenging to write, and they often result in *Slow Tests* (page 253) and *Nondeterministic Tests* (see *Erratic Test* on page 228). Under these circumstances, we may benefit by using

Humble Object

a *Humble Object* to move all of the controller and view-updating logic out of the framework-dependent object and into a testable object.

Variation: Humble Executable

Many programs contain active objects. Active objects have their own thread of execution so they can do things in parallel with other activities of the system. Examples of active objects include anything that runs in a separate process (e.g., Windows applications in .exe files) or thread (in Java, any object that implements Runnable). These objects may be launched directly by the client, or they may be started automatically, process requests from a queue, and send replies via a return message. Either way, we must write asynchronous tests (complete with interprocess coordination and/or explicit delays and *Neverfail Tests; see Production Bugs*) to verify their behavior.

The *Humble Executable* pattern provides a way to bring the logic of the executable under test without incurring the delays that might otherwise lead to *Slow Tests* and *Nondeterministic Tests*. We extract all the logic from the executable into a component that is testable via synchronous tests. This component implements a service interface consisting of methods that expose all logic of the executable; the only difference is that these methods are accessible via synchronous method calls. The testable component may be a Windows DLL, a Java JAR containing a Service Facade [CJ2EEP] class, or some other language component or class that exposes the services of the executable in a testable way.

The *Humble Executable* component itself contains very little code. All it does in its thread of control is to load the testable component (if a *True Humble Object*) and delegate to it. As a result, the *Humble Executable* requires only one or two tests to verify that it performs this load/delegate function correctly. Although these tests still take seconds to execute, they have a much smaller impact on the overall test suite execution time because so few of them exist. Given that this code will not change very often, these tests can even be omitted from the suite of tests that developers execute before check-in to speed up test suite execution times. Of course, we would still prefer to run the *Humble Executable* tests as part of the automated build process.

Variation: Humble Transaction Controller

Many applications use databases to persist their state. Fixture setup with databases can be slow and complex, and leftover fixtures can wreak havoc with subsequent tests and test runs. If we are using a *Shared Fixture* (page 317), the fixture's persistence may lead to *Erratic Tests*. *Humble Transaction Controller* facilitates testing of the logic that runs within the transaction by making it possible for the test to control the transaction. As a consequence, we can exercise the logic, verify the outcome, and then abort the transaction, leaving no trace of our activity in the database.

To implement *Humble Transaction Controller,* we use an Extract Method [Fowler] refactoring to move all the logic we want to test out of the code that controls the transaction and into a separate method that knows nothing about transaction control and that can be called by the test. Because the caller controls the transaction, the test can start, commit (if it so chooses), and (most commonly) roll back the transaction. In this case, the behavior—not the dependencies—causes us to bypass the *Humble Object* when we are testing the business logic. As a result, we are more likely to be able to get away with a *Poor Man's Humble Object*.

As for the *Humble Object*, it contains no business logic. Thus the only behavior that needs to be tested is whether the *Humble Object* commits and rolls back the transaction properly based on the outcome of the methods it calls. We can write a test that replaces the testable component with a *Test Stub* (page 529) that throws an exception and then verify that this activity results in a rollback of the transaction. If we are using a *Poor Man's Humble Object*, the stub would be implemented as a *Subclassed Test Double* (see *Test-Specific Subclass* on page 579) that overrides the "real" methods with methods that throw exceptions.

Many of the major application server technologies support this pattern either directly or indirectly by taking transaction control away from the business objects that we write. If we are building our software without using a transaction control framework, we may need to implement our own *Humble Transaction Controller.* See the "Implementation Notes" section for some ideas on how we can enforce the separation.

Variation: Humble Container Adapter

Speaking of "containers," we often have to implement specific interfaces to allow our objects to run inside an application server (e.g., the "EJB session bean" interface). Another variation on the *Humble Object* pattern is to design our objects to be container-independent and then have a *Humble Container Adapter* adapt them to the interface required by container. This strategy makes our logic components easy to test outside the container, which dramatically reduces the time required for an "edit–compile–test" cycle.

Implementation Notes

We can make the logic that normally runs inside the *Humble Object* testable in several different ways. All of these techniques share one commonality: They involve exposing the logic so that it can be verified using synchronous tests. They vary, however, in terms of how the logic is exposed. Regardless of how logic exposure occurs, test-driven purists would prefer that tests verify that the *Humble Object* is calling the extracted logic properly. This can be done by replacing the real logic methods with some kind of *Test Double* (page 522) implementation.

Variation: Poor Man's Humble Object

The simplest way to isolate and expose each piece of logic we want to verify is to place it into a separate method. We can do so by using an Extract Method refactoring on in-line logic and then making the resulting method visible from the test. Of course, this method cannot require anything from the context. Ideally everything the method needs to do its work will be passed in as arguments but this information could also be placed in fields. Problems may arise if the testable component needs to call methods to access information it needs and those methods are dependent on the (nonexistent/faked) context, as this dependency makes writing the tests more complex.

This approach, which constitutes the "poor man's" *Humble Object,* works well if no obstacles prevent the instantiation of the *Humble Object* (e.g., automatically starting its thread, no public constructor, unsatisfiable dependencies). Use of a *Test-Specific Subclass* can also help break these dependencies by providing a test-friendly constructor and exposing private methods to the test.

When testing a *Subclassed Humble Object* or a *Poor Man's Humble Object,* we can build the *Test Spy* (page 538) as a *Subclassed Test Double* of the *Humble Object* to record when the methods in question were called. We can then use assertions within the *Test Method* (page 348) to verify that the values recorded match the values expected.

Variation: True Humble Object

At the other extreme, we can put the logic we want to test into a separate class and have the *Humble Object* delegate to an instance of it. This approach, which was implied in the introduction to this pattern, will work in almost any circumstance where we have complete control over the code.

Sometimes the host framework requires that its objects hold certain responsibilities that we cannot move elsewhere. For example, a GUI framework expects its view objects to contain data for the controls of the GUI and the data that those controls display on the screen. In these cases we must either give the testable object a reference to the *Humble Object* and have it manipulate the data for that object or put some minimal update logic in the *Humble Object* and accept that it won't be covered by automated tests. The former approach is almost always possible and is always preferable.

Humble Object

To refactor to a *True Humble Object*, we normally do a series of Extract Method refactorings to decouple the public interface of the *Humble Object* from the implementation logic we plan to delegate. Then we do an Extract Class [Fowler] refactoring to move all the methods—except the ones that define the public interface of the *Humble Object*—to the new "testable" class. We introduce an attribute (a field) to hold a reference to an instance of the new class and initialize it to an instance of the new class either as part of the constructor or using Lazy Initialization [SBPP] in each interface method.

When testing a *True Humble Object* (where the *Humble Object* delegates to a separate class), we typically use a *Lazy Mock Object* (see *Mock Object* on page 544) or *Test Spy* to verify that the extracted class is called correctly. By contrast, using the more common *Active Mock Object* (see *Mock Object*) is problematic in this situation because the assertions are made on a different thread from the *Testcase Object* (page 382) and failures won't be detected unless we find a way to channel them back to the test thread.

To ensure that the extracted testable component is instantiated properly, we can use an observable *Object Factory* (see *Dependency Lookup* on page 686) to construct the extracted component. The test can register as a listener to verify the correct method is called on the factory. We can also use a regular **factory** object and replace it during the test with a *Mock Object* or *Test Stub* to monitor which factory method was called.

Variation: Subclassed Humble Object

In between the extremes of the *Poor Man's Humble Object* and the *True Humble Object* are approaches that involve clever use of subclassing to put the logic into separate classes while still allowing them to be on a single object. A number of different ways to do this are possible, depending on whether the *Humble Object* class needs to subclass a specific framework class. I won't go into a lot of detail here as this technique is very specific to the language and runtime environment. Nevertheless, you should recognize that the basic options are either having the framework-dependent class inherit the logic to be tested from a superclass or having the class delegate to an abstract method that is implemented by a subclass.

Motivating Example (Humble Executable)

In this example, we are testing some logic that runs in its own thread and processes each request as it arrives. In each test, we start up the thread, send it some messages, and wait long enough so that our assertions pass. Unfortunately, it takes several seconds for the thread to start up, become initialized,

Humble Object

and process the first request. Thus the test fails sporadically unless we include a two-second delay after starting the thread.

```
public class RequestHandlerThreadTest extends TestCase {
   private static final int TWO_SECONDS = 3000;

   public void testWasInitialized_Async()
            throws InterruptedException {
     // Setup
     RequestHandlerThread sut = new RequestHandlerThread();
     // Exercise
     sut.start();
     //    Verify
     Thread.sleep(TWO_SECONDS);
     assertTrue(sut.initializedSuccessfully());
   }

   public void testHandleOneRequest_Async()
            throws InterruptedException {
     // Setup
     RequestHandlerThread sut = new RequestHandlerThread();
     sut.start();
     // Exercise
     enqueRequest(makeSimpleRequest());
     // Verify
     Thread.sleep(TWO_SECONDS);
     assertEquals(1, sut.getNumberOfRequestsCompleted());
     assertResponseEquals(makeSimpleResponse(), getResponse());
   }
}
```

Ideally, we would like to test the thread with each kind of transaction individually to achieve better *Defect Localization* (see page 22). Unfortunately, if we did so our test suite would take many minutes to run because each test includes a delay of several seconds. Another problem is that the tests won't result in an error if our active object has an exception in its own thread.

A two-second delay may not seem like a big deal, but consider what happens when we have a dozen such tests. It would take us almost half a minute to run these tests. Contrast this performance with that of normal tests—we can run several hundred of those tests each second. Testing via the executable is affecting our productivity negatively. For the record, here's the code for the executable:

```
public class RequestHandlerThread extends Thread {
   private boolean _initializationCompleted = false;
   private int _numberOfRequests = 0;

   public void run()  {
      initializeThread();
      processRequestsForever();
   }
```

Humble Object

```
    public boolean initializedSuccessfully() {
        return _initializationCompleted;
    }

    void processRequestsForever() {
        Request request = nextMessage();
        do {
            Response response = processOneRequest(request);
            if (response != null) {
                putMsgOntoOutputQueue(response);
            }
            request = nextMessage();
        } while (request != null);
    }
}
```

To avoid the distraction of the business logic, I have already used an Extract Method refactoring to move the real logic into the method processOneRequest. Likewise, the actual initialization logic is not shown here; suffice it to say that this logic sets the variable _initializationCompleted when it finishes successfully.

Refactoring Notes

To create a *Poor Man's Humble Object*, we expose the methods to make them visible from the test. (If the code used in-line logic, we would do an Extract Method refactoring first.) If there were any dependencies on the context, we would need to do an Introduce Parameter [JBrains] refactoring or an Introduce Field [JetBrains] refactoring so that the processOneRequest method need not access anything from the context.

To create a true *Humble Object*, we can do an Extract Class refactoring on the executable to create the testable component, leaving behind just the *Humble Object* as an empty shell. This step typically involves doing the Extract Method refactoring described above to separate the logic we want to test (e.g., the initializeThread method and the processOneRequest method) from the logic that interacts with the context of the executable. We then do an Extract Class refactoring to introduce the testable component class (essentially a single Strategy [GOF] object) and move all methods except the public interface methods over to it. The Extract Class refactoring includes introducing a field to hold a reference to the new object and creating an instance. It also includes fixing all of the public methods so that they call the methods that were moved to the new testable class.

Humble Object

Example: Poor Man's Humble Executable

Here is the same set of tests rewritten as a *Poor Man's Humble Object*:

```
public void testWasInitialized_Sync()
        throws InterruptedException {
   // Setup
   RequestHandlerThread sut = new RequestHandlerThread();
   // Exercise
   sut.initializeThread();
   // Verify
   assertTrue(sut.initializedSuccessfully());
}

public void testHandleOneRequest_Sync()
        throws InterruptedException {
   // Setup
   RequestHandlerThread sut = new RequestHandlerThread();
   // Exercise
   Response response = sut.processOneRequest(makeSimpleRequest());
   // Verify
   assertEquals(1, sut.getNumberOfRequestsCompleted());
   assertResponseEquals(makeSimpleResponse(), response);
}
```

Here, we have made the methods initializeThread and processOneRequest public so that we can call them synchronously from the test. Note the absence of a delay in this test. This approach works well as long as we can instantiate the executable component easily.

Example: True Humble Executable

Here is the code for our SUT refactored to use a *True Humble Executable*:

```
public class HumbleRequestHandlerThread extends Thread
implements Runnable {
   public RequestHandler requestHandler;

   public HumbleRequestHandlerThread() {
      super();
      requestHandler = new RequestHandlerImpl();
   }

   public void run() {
      requestHandler.initializeThread();
      processRequestsForever();
   }

   public boolean initializedSuccessfully() {
```

Humble
Object

```
      return requestHandler.initializedSuccessfully();
   }

   public void processRequestsForever() {
      Request request = nextMessage();
      do {
         Response response =
            requestHandler.processOneRequest(request);
         if (response != null) {
            putMsgOntoOutputQueue(response);
         }
         request = nextMessage();
      } while (request != null);
   }
```

Here, we have moved the method processOneRequest to a separate class that we can instantiate easily. Below is the same test rewritten to take advantage of the extracted component. Note the absence of a delay in this test.

```
   public void testNotInitialized_Sync()
           throws InterruptedException {
      // Setup/Exercise
      RequestHandler sut = new RequestHandlerImpl();
      // Verify
      assertFalse("init", sut.initializedSuccessfully());
   }

   public void testWasInitialized_Sync()
           throws InterruptedException {
      //    Setup
      RequestHandler sut = new RequestHandlerImpl();
      //    Exercise
      sut.initializeThread();
      // Verify
      assertTrue("init", sut.initializedSuccessfully());
   }

   public void testHandleOneRequest_Sync()
           throws InterruptedException {
      // Setup
      RequestHandler sut = new RequestHandlerImpl();
      // Exercise
      Response response = sut.processOneRequest( makeSimpleRequest() );
      // Verify
      assertEquals( 1, sut.getNumberOfRequestsDone());
      assertResponseEquals( makeSimpleResponse(), response);
   }
```

Because we have introduced delegation to another object, we should probably verify that the delegation occurs properly. The next test verifies that the *Humble*

Object calls the `initializeThread` method and the `processOneRequest` method on the newly created testable component:

```
public void testLogicCalled_Sync()
        throws InterruptedException {
   // Setup
   RequestHandlerRecordingStub mockHandler =
        new RequestHandlerRecordingStub();
   HumbleRequestHandlerThread sut = new HumbleRequestHandlerThread();
   //    Mock Installation
   sut.setHandler( mockHandler );
   sut.start();
   // Exercise
   enqueRequest(makeSimpleRequest());
   // Verify
   Thread.sleep(TWO_SECONDS);
   assertTrue("init", mockHandler.initializedSuccessfully() );
   assertEquals( 1, mockHandler.getNumberOfRequestsDone() );
}
```

Note that this test *does* require at least a small delay to allow the thread to start up. The delay is shorter, however, because we have replaced the real logic component with a *Test Double* that responds instantly and only one test now requires the delay. We could even move this test to a separate test suite that is run less frequently (e.g., only during the automated build process) to ensure that all tests performed before each check-in run quickly.

The other significant thing to note is that we are using a *Test Spy* rather than a *Mock Object*. Because the assertions done by the *Mock Object* would be raised in a different thread from the *Test Method*, the *Test Automation Framework* (page 298)—in this example, JUnit—won't catch them. As a consequence, the test might indicate "pass" even though assertions in the *Mock Object* are failing. By making the assertions in the *Test Method*, we avoid having to do something special to relay the exceptions thrown by the *Mock Object* back to the thread in which the *Test Method* is executing.

The preceding test verified that our *Humble Object* actually delegates to the *Test Spy* that we have installed. It would also be a good idea to verify that our *Humble Object* actually initializes the variable holding the delegate to the appropriate class. Here's a simple way to do so:

Humble Object

```
public void testConstructor() {
   // Exercise
   HumbleRequestHandlerThread sut = new HumbleRequestHandlerThread();
   // Verify
   String actualDelegateClass = sut.requestHandler.getClass().getName();
   assertEquals( RequestHandlerImpl.class.getName(),
                actualDelegateClass);
}
```

This *Constructor Test* (see *Test Method*) verifies that a specific attribute has been initialized.

Example: Humble Dialog

Many development environments let us build the user interface visually by dragging and dropping various objects ("widgets") onto a canvas. They let us add behavior to these visual objects by selecting one of several possible actions or events specific to that visual object and typing logic into the code window presented by the IDE. This logic may involve invoking the application behind the user interface or it may involve modifying the state of this or some other visual object.

Visual objects are very difficult to test efficiently because they are tightly coupled to the presentation framework that invokes them. To provide the visual object with all the information and facilities it requires, the test would need to simulate that environment—quite a challenge. This makes testing very complicated, so much so that many development teams don't bother testing the presentation logic at all. This lack of testing, not surprisingly, often leads to *Production Bugs* caused by untested code and *Untested Requirements*.

To create the *Humble Dialog*, we extract all the logic from the view component into a nonvisual component that is testable via synchronous tests. If this component needs to update the view object's (*Humble Dialog's*) state, the *Humble Dialog* is passed in as an argument. When testing the nonvisual component, we typically replace the *Humble Dialog* with a *Mock Object* that is configured with the indirect input values and the expected behavior (indirect outputs). In GUI frameworks that require the *Humble Dialog* to register itself with the framework for each event it wishes to see, the nonvisual component can register itself instead of the *Humble Dialog* (as long as that doesn't introduce unmanageable dependencies on the context). This flexibility makes the *Humble Dialog* even simpler because the events go directly to the nonvisual component and require no delegation logic.

The following code sample is taken from a VB view component (.ctl) that includes some nontrivial logic. It is part of a custom plug-in we built for Mercury Interactive's TestDirector tool.

```
' Interface method, TestDirector will call this method
' to display the results.
Public Sub ShowResultEx(TestSetKey As TdTestSetKey, _
                        TSTestKey As TdTestKey, _
                        ResultKey As TdResultKey)
```

Humble Object

```
    Dim RpbFiles As OcsRpbFiles
    Set RpbFiles = getTestResultFileNames(ResultKey)
    ResultsFileName = RpbFiles.ActualResultFileName
    ShowFileInBrowser ResultsFileName
End Sub

Function getTestResultFileNames(ResultKey As Variant) As OcsRpbFiles
    On Error GoTo Error
    Dim Attachments As Collection
    Dim thisTest As Run
    Dim RpbFiles As New OcsRpbFiles

    Call EnsureConnectedToTd

    Set Attachments = testManager.GetAllAttachmentsOfRunTest(ResultKey)
    Call RpbFiles.LoadFromCollection(Attachments, "RunTest")
    Set getTestResultFileNames = RpbFiles
    Exit Function
Error:
    ' do something ...
End Function
```

Ideally, we would like to test the logic. Unfortunately, we cannot construct the objects passed in as parameters because they don't have public constructors. Passing in objects of some other type isn't possible either, because the types of the function parameters are hard-coded to be specific concrete classes.

We can do an Extract Testable Component (page 735) refactoring on the executable to create the testable component, leaving behind just the *Humble Dialog* as an empty shell. This approach typically involves doing several Extract Method refactorings (already done in the original example to make the refactoring easier to understand), one for each chunk of logic that we want to move. We then do an Extract Class refactoring to create our new testable component class. The Extract Class refactoring may include both Move Method [Fowler] and Move Field [Fowler] refactorings to move the logic and the data it requires out of the *Humble Dialog* and into the new testable component.

Here's the same view converted to a *Humble Dialog*:

Humble Object

```
' Interface method, TestDirector will call this method
' to display the results.
Public Sub ShowResultEx(TestSetKey As TdTestSetKey, _
                        TSTestKey As TdTestKey, _
                        ResultKey As TdResultKey)
    Dim RpbFiles As OcsRpbFiles
    Call EnsureImplExists
    Set RpbFiles = Implementation.getTestResultFileNames(ResultKey)
```

```
        ResultsFileName = RpbFiles.ActualResultFileName
        ShowFileInBrowser ResultsFileName
End Sub

Private Sub EnsureImplExists()
    If Implementation Is Nothing Then
        Set Implementation = New OcsScriptViewerImpl
    End If
End Sub
```

Here's the testable component OcsScriptViewerImpl that the *Humble Object* calls:

```
'   ResultViewer Implementation:
Public Function getTestResultFileNames(ResultKey As Variant) As OcsRpbFiles
    On Error GoTo Error

    Dim Attachments As Collection
    Dim thisTest As Run
    Dim RpbFiles As New OcsRpbFiles

    Call EnsureConnectedToTd

    Set Attachments = testManager.GetAllAttachmentsOfRunTest(ResultKey)
    Call RpbFiles.LoadFromCollection(Attachments, "RunTest")
    Set getTestResultFileNames = RpbFiles
    Exit Function
Error:
    ' do something ...
End Function
```

We could now instantiate this OcsScriptViewerImpl class easily and write VbUnit tests for it. I've omitted the tests for space reasons because they don't really show anything particularly interesting.

Example: Humble Transaction Controller

Transaction Rollback Teardown (page 668) contains an example of writing tests that bypass the *Humble Transaction Controller*.

Further Reading

See http://www.objectmentor.com/resources/articles/TheHumbleDialogBox.pdf for Michael Feathers' original write-up of the *Humble Dialog* pattern.

Humble Object

Test Hook

How do we design the SUT so that we can replace its dependencies at runtime?

We modify the SUT to behave differently during the test.

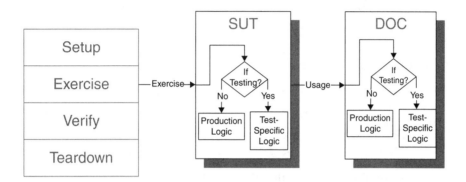

Almost every piece of code depends on some other classes, objects, modules, or procedures. To unit-test a piece of code properly, we would like to isolate it from its dependencies. Such isolation is difficult to achieve if those dependencies are hard-coded within the code in the form of literal classnames.

Test Hook is a "method of last resort" for introducing test-specific behavior during automated testing.

How It Works

We modify the behavior of the SUT to support testing by putting a hook directly into the SUT or into a DOC. This approach implies that we use some kind of testing flag that can be checked in the appropriate place.

When to Use It

Sometimes it is appropriate to use this "pattern of last resort" when we cannot use either *Dependency Injection* (page 678) or *Dependency Lookup* (page 686). In this situation, we use a *Test Hook* because we have no other way to address the *Untested Code* (see *Production Bugs* on page 268) caused by a *Hard-Coded Dependency* (see *Hard-to-Test Code* on page 209).

Test Hook

A *Test Hook* may be the only way to introduce *Test Double* (page 522) behavior when we are programming in a procedural language that does not support objects, **function pointers,** or any other form of dynamic binding.

Test Hooks can be used as a transition strategy to bring legacy code under the testing umbrella. We can introduce testability using the *Test Hooks* and then use those *Tests as Safety Net* (see page 24) while we refactor for even more testability. At some point we should be able to discard the initial round of tests that required the *Test Hooks* because we have enough "modern" tests to protect us.

Implementation Notes

The essence of the *Test Hook* pattern is that we insert some code into the SUT that lets us test it. Regardless of how we insert this code into the SUT, the code itself can either

- Divert control to a *Test Double* instead of the real object, or

- Be the *Test Double* within the real object, or

- Be a test-specific Decorator [GOF] that delegates to the real object when in production.

The flag that indicates testing is in progress can be a compile-time constant, which may, for example, cause the compiler to optimize out all the testing logic. In languages that support preprocessors or compiler macros, such constructs may also be used to remove the *Test Hook* before the code enters the production phase. The value of the flag can also be read in from configuration data or stored in a global variable that the test sets directly.

Motivating Example

The following test cannot be made to pass "as is":

```
public void testDisplayCurrentTime_AtMidnight() {
    // fixture setup
    TimeDisplay sut = new TimeDisplay();
    // exercise SUT
    String result = sut.getCurrentTimeAsHtmlFragment();
    // verify direct output
    String expectedTimeString =
        "<span class=\"tinyBoldText\">Midnight</span>";
    assertEquals( expectedTimeString, result);
}
```

This test almost always fails because it depends on a DOC to return the current time to the SUT. The test cannot control the values returned by that component,

Test Hook

the DefaultTimeProvider. As a consequence, this test will pass only when the system time is exactly midnight.

```
public String getCurrentTimeAsHtmlFragment() {
   Calendar currentTime;
   try {
      currentTime = new DefaultTimeProvider().getTime();
   } catch (Exception e) {
      return e.getMessage();
   }
   // etc.
}
```

Because the SUT is hard-coded to use a particular class to retrieve the time, we cannot replace the DOC with a *Test Double*. As a result, this test is nondeterministic and pretty much useless. We need to find a way to gain control over the indirect inputs of the SUT.

Refactoring Notes

We can introduce a *Test Hook* by creating a flag that can be checked into the SUT. We then wrap the production code with an if/then/else control structure and put the test-specific logic into the then clause.

Example: Test Hook in System Under Test

Here's the production code modified to accommodate testing via a *Test Hook:*

```
public String getCurrentTimeAsHtmlFragment() {
   Calendar theTime;
   try {
      if (TESTING) {
         theTime = new GregorianCalendar();
         theTime.set(Calendar.HOUR_OF_DAY, 0);
         theTime.set(Calendar.MINUTE, 0);}
      else {
         theTime = new DefaultTimeProvider().getTime();
      }
   } catch (Exception e) {
      return e.getMessage();
   }
   // etc.
```

Test Hook

Here we have implemented the testing flag as global constant, which we can edit as necessary. This flexibility implies a separate build step is necessary for versions of the system to be tested. Such a strategy is somewhat safer than using a dynamic configuration parameter or member variable because many compilers will optimize this hook right out of the object code.

Example: Test Hook in Depended-on Component

We can also introduce a *Test Hook* by putting the hook into a DOC rather than into the SUT:

```
public Calendar getTime() throws TimeProviderEx {
   Calendar theTime = new GregorianCalendar();
   if (TESTING) {
      theTime.set(Calendar.HOUR_OF_DAY, 0);
      theTime.set(Calendar.MINUTE, 0);}
   else {
      // just return the calendar
   }
   return theTime;
};
```

This approach is somewhat better because we are not modifying the SUT as we test it.

Test Hook

Chapter 27

Value Patterns

Patterns in This Chapter

Value
Patterns

713

Literal Value

Also known as:
*Hard-Coded
Value, Constant
Value*

How do we specify the values to be used in tests?

We use literal constants for object attributes and assertions.

```
BigDecimal expectedTotal = new BigDecimal("99.95");
```

The values we use for the attributes of objects in our test fixture and the expected outcome of our test are often related to one another in a way that is defined in the requirements. Getting these values—and, in particular, the relationship between the pre-conditions and the post-conditions—right is crucial because it drives the correct behavior into the SUT.

Literal Values are a popular way to specify the values of attributes of objects in a test.

How It Works

We use a literal constant of the appropriate type for each attribute of an object or for use as an argument of a method call to the SUT or an *Assertion Method* (page 362). The expected values are calculated by hand, calculator, or spreadsheet and hard-coded within the test as *Literal Values*.

When to Use It

Using a *Literal Value* in-line makes it very clear which value is being used; there is no doubt about the value's identity because it is right in front of our face. Unfortunately, using *Literal Values* can make it difficult to see the relationships between the values used in various places in the test, which may in turn lead to *Obscure Tests* (page 186). It certainly makes sense to use *Literal Values* if the testing requirements specify which values are to be used and we want to make it clear that we are, in fact, using those values. [We might sometimes consider using a *Data-Driven Test* (page 288) instead to avoid the effort and transcription errors associated with copying the data into test methods.]

One downside of using a *Literal Value* is that we might use the same value for two unrelated attributes; if the SUT happens to use the wrong one, tests may pass even though they should not. If the *Literal Value* is a filename or a key used to access a database, the meaning of the value is lost—the content of the file or record actually drives the behavior of the SUT. Using a *Literal Value* as the key does nothing to help the reader understand the test in such a case, and we are likely to suffer from *Obscure Tests*.

Literal Value

If the values in the expected outcome can be derived from the values in the fixture setup logic, we will be more likely to use the *Tests as Documentation* (see page 23) if we use *Derived Values* (page 718). Conversely, if the values are not important to the specification of the logic being tested, we should consider using *Generated Values* (page 723).

Implementation Notes

The most common way to use a *Literal Value* is with literal constants within the code. When the same value needs to be used in several places in the test (typically during fixture setup and result verification), this approach can obscure the relationship between the test pre-conditions and post-conditions. Introducing an evocatively named symbolic constant can make this relationship much clearer. Likewise, if we cannot use a self-describing value, we can still make the code easier to use by defining a suitably named symbolic constant and using it wherever we would have used the *Literal Value*.

Variation: Symbolic Constant

When we need to use the same *Literal Value* in several places in a single *Test Method* (page 348) or within several distinct tests, it is a good practice to use a *Symbolic Constant* instead of a *Literal Value*. A *Symbolic Constant* is functionally equivalent to a *Literal Value* but reduces the likelihood of *High Test Maintenance Cost* (page 265).

Variation: Self-Describing Value

When several attributes of an object need the same kind of value, using different values provides advantages by helping us to prove that the SUT is working with the correct attribute. When an attribute or argument is an unconstrained string, it can be useful to choose a value that describes the role of the value in the test (a *Self-Describing Value*). For example, using "Not an existing customer" for the name of a customer might be more helpful to the reader than using "Joe Blow," especially when we are debugging or when the attributes are included in the test failure output.

Example: Literal Value

Because *Literal Value* is usually the starting point when writing tests, I'll dispense with a motivating example and cut straight to the chase. Here's an example of the *Literal Value* pattern in action. Note the use of *Literal Values* in both the fixture setup logic and the assertion.

Literal Value

```
public void testAddItemQuantity_1() throws Exception {
    Product product = new Product("Widget", 19.95);
    Invoice invoice = new Invoice();
    // Exercise
    invoice.addItemQuantity(product, 1);
    // Verify
    List lineItems = invoice.getLineItems();
    LineItem actualItem = (LineItem)lineItems.get(0);
    assertEquals(new BigDecimal("19.95"),
                    actualItem.getExtendedPrice());
}
```

The Product constructor requires both a name and a cost. The assertion on the extendedCost of the lineItem requires a value for the total cost of the product for that line item. In this example, we included these values as hard-coded literal constants. In the next example, we'll use symbolic constants instead.

Refactoring Notes

We can reduce the *Test Code Duplication* (page 213) in the form of the hard-coded *Literal Value* of 19.95 by doing a Replace Magic Number with Symbolic Constant [Fowler] refactoring.

Example: Symbolic Constant

This refactored version of the original test replaces the duplicated *Literal Value* of the widget's price (19.95) with a suitably named *Symbolic Constant* that is used during fixture setup as well as result verification:

```
public void testAddItemQuantity_1s() throws Exception {
    BigDecimal widgetPrice = new BigDecimal("19.95");
    Product product = new Product("Widget", widgetPrice);
    Invoice invoice = new Invoice();
    // Exercise
    invoice.addItemQuantity(product, 1);
    // Verify
    List lineItems = invoice.getLineItems();
    LineItem actualItem = (LineItem)lineItems.get(0);
    assertEquals(widgetPrice, actualItem.getExtendedPrice());
}
```

Literal Value

Example: Self-Describing Value

This refactored version of the test provides a *Self-Describing Value* for the mandatory name argument passed to the Product constructor. This value is not used by the method we are testing; it is merely stored for later access by another method we are not testing here.

```
public void testAddItemQuantity_1b() throws Exception {
    BigDecimal widgetPrice = new BigDecimal("19.95");
    Product product = new Product("Irrelevant product name",
                                   widgetPrice);
    Invoice invoice = new Invoice();
    // Exercise
    invoice.addItemQuantity(product, 1);
    // Verify
    List lineItems = invoice.getLineItems();
    LineItem actualItem = (LineItem)lineItems.get(0);
    assertEquals(widgetPrice, actualItem.getExtendedPrice());
}
```

Example: Distinct Value

This test needs to verify that the item's name is taken from the product's name. We'll use a *Distinct Value* for the name and the SKU so we can tell them apart.

```
public void testAddItemQuantity_1c() throws Exception {
    BigDecimal widgetPrice = new BigDecimal("19.95");
    String name = "Product name";
    String sku = "Product SKU";
    Product product = new Product(name, sku, widgetPrice);
    Invoice invoice = new Invoice();
    // Exercise
    invoice.addItemQuantity(product, 1);
    // Verify
    List lineItems = invoice.getLineItems();
    LineItem actualItem = (LineItem)lineItems.get(0);
    assertEquals(name, actualItem.getName());
}
```

This also happens to be an example of a self-describing value.

Literal Value

Derived Value

How do we specify the values to be used in tests?

Also known as:
*Calculated
Value*

**We use expressions to calculate values that can be derived from
other values.**

```
BigDecimal expectedTotal = itemPrice.multiply(QUANTITY);
```

The values we use for the attributes of objects in our test fixtures and the result verification parts of our tests are often related to one another in a way that is defined in the requirements. Getting these values—and, in particular, the relationship between the pre-conditions and the post-conditions—right is crucial because it drives the correct behavior into the SUT and helps the tests act as documentation of our software.

Often, some of these values can be derived from other values in the same test. In these cases the benefits from using our *Tests as Documentation* (see page 23) are improved if we show the derivation by calculating the values using the appropriate expression.

How It Works

Computers are really good at math and string concatenation. We can avoid doing the math in our head (or with a calculator) by coding the math for expected results as arguments of the *Assertion Method* (page 362) calls directly into the tests. We can also use *Derived Values* as arguments for fixture object creation and as method arguments when exercising the SUT.

Derived Values, by their very nature, encourage us to use variables or symbolic constants to hold the values. These variables/constants can be initialized at compile time (constants), during class or *Testcase Object* (page 382) initialization, during fixture setup, or within the body of the *Test Method* (page 348).

When to Use It

We should use a *Derived Value* whenever we have values that can be derived in some deterministic way from other values in our tests. The main drawback of using *Derived Values* is that the same math error (e.g., rounding errors) *could* appear in both the SUT and the tests. To be safe, we might want to code a few of the pathological test cases using *Literal Values* (page 714) just in case such a problem might be present. If the values we are using must be unique or don't affect the logic in the SUT, we may be better off using *Generated Values* (page 723) instead.

We can use a *Derived Value* either as part of fixture setup (*Derived Input* or *One Bad Attribute*) or when determining the expected values to be compared with those generated by the SUT (*Derived Expectation*). These uses are described in a bit more detail later in this section.

Variation: Derived Input

Sometimes our test fixture contains similar values that the SUT might compare or use to base its logic on the difference between them. For example, a *Derived Input* might be calculated in the fixture setup portion of the test by adding the difference to a base value. This operation makes the relationship between the two values explicit. We can even put the value to be added in a symbolic constant with an Intent-Revealing Name [SBPP] such as MAXIMUM_ALLOWABLE_TIME_DIFFERENCE.

Variation: One Bad Attribute

A *Derived Input* is often employed when we need to test a method that takes a complex object as an argument. For example, thorough "input validation" testing requires that we exercise the method with each of the attributes of the object set to one or more possible invalid values to ensure that it handles all of these cases correctly. Because the first rejected value could cause termination of the method, we must verify each bad attribute in a separate call to the SUT; each of these calls, in turn, should be done in a separate test method (each should be a *Single-Condition Test;* see page 45). We can instantiate the invalid object easily by first creating a valid object and then replacing one of its attributes with an invalid value. It is best to create the valid object using a *Creation Method* (page 415) so as to avoid *Test Code Duplication* (page 213).

Variation: Derived Expectation

When some value produced by the SUT should be related to one or more of the values we passed in to the SUT as arguments or as values in the fixture, we can often derive the expected value from the input values as the test executes rather than using precalculated *Literal Values*. We then use the result as the expected value in an *Equality Assertion* (see *Assertion Method*).

Motivating Example

The following test doesn't use *Derived Values*. Note the use of *Literal Values* in both the fixture setup logic and the assertion.

```
public void testAddItemQuantity_2a() throws Exception {
    BigDecimal widgetPrice = new BigDecimal("19.99");
```

Derived
Value

```
    Product product = new Product("Widget", widgetPrice);
    Invoice invoice = new Invoice();
    // Exercise
    invoice.addItemQuantity(product, 5);
    // Verify
    List lineItems = invoice.getLineItems();
    LineItem actualItem = (LineItem)lineItems.get(0);
    assertEquals(new BigDecimal("99.95"),
                 actualItem.getExtendedPrice());
}
```

Test readers may have to do some math in their heads to fully appreciate the relationship between the values in the fixture setup and the value in the result verification part of the test.

Refactoring Notes

To make this test more readable, we can replace any *Literal Values* that are actually derived from other values with formulas that calculate these values.

Example: Derived Expectation

The original example contained only one line item for five instances of the product. We therefore calculated the expected value of the extended price attribute by multiplying the unit price by the quantity, which makes the relationship between the values explicit.

```
    public void testAddItemQuantity_2b() throws Exception {
        BigDecimal widgetPrice = new BigDecimal("19.99");
        BigDecimal numberOfUnits = new BigDecimal("5");
        Product product = new Product("Widget", widgetPrice);
        Invoice invoice = new Invoice();
        // Exercise
        invoice.addItemQuantity(product, numberOfUnits);
        // Verify
        List lineItems = invoice.getLineItems();
        LineItem actualItem = (LineItem)lineItems.get(0);
        BigDecimal totalPrice = widgetPrice.multiply(numberOfUnits);
        assertEquals(totalPrice, actualItem.getExtendedPrice());
    }
```

Derived Value

Note that we have also introduced symbolic constants for the unit price and quantity to make the expression even more obvious and to reduce the effort of changing the values later.

Example: One Bad Attribute

Suppose we have the following Customer Factory Method [GOF], which takes a CustomerDto object as an argument. We want to write tests to verify what occurs when we pass in invalid values for each of the attributes in the CustomerDto. We could create the CustomerDto in-line in each *Test Method* with the appropriate attribute initialized to some invalid value.

```
public void testCreateCustomerFromDto_BadCredit() {
   // fixture setup
   CustomerDto customerDto = new CustomerDto();
   customerDto.firstName = "xxx";
   customerDto.lastName = "yyy";
   // etc.
   customerDto.address = createValidAddress();
   customerDto.creditRating = CreditRating.JUNK;
   // exercise the SUT
   try {
      sut.createCustomerFromDto(customerDto);
      fail("Expected an exception");
   } catch (InvalidInputException e) {
      assertEquals( "Field", "Credit", e.field );
   }
}

public void testCreateCustomerFromDto_NullAddress() {
   // fixture setup
   CustomerDto customerDto = new CustomerDto();
   customerDto.firstName = "xxx";
   customerDto.lastName = "yyy";
   // etc.
   customerDto.address = null;
   customerDto.creditRating = CreditRating.AAA;
   // exercise the SUT
   try {
      sut.createCustomerFromDto(customerDto);
      fail("Expected an exception");
   } catch (InvalidInputException e) {
      assertEquals( "Field", "Address", e.field );
   }
}
```

The obvious problem with this code is that we end up with a lot of *Test Code Duplication* because we need at least one test per attribute. The problem becomes even worse if we are doing incremental development: We will require more tests for each newly added attribute, and we will have to revisit all existing tests to add the new attribute to the Factory Method signature.

Derived Value

The solution is to define a *Creation Method* that produces a valid instance of the CustomerDto (by doing an Extract Method [Fowler] refactoring on one of the tests) and uses it in each test to create a valid **DTO.** Then we simply replace one of the attributes with an invalid value in each of the tests. Each test now has an object with *One Bad Attribute*, with each one invalid in a slightly different way.

```java
public void testCreateCustomerFromDto_BadCredit_OBA() {
   CustomerDto customerDto = createValidCustomerDto();
   customerDto.creditRating = CreditRating.JUNK;
   try {
      sut.createCustomerFromDto(customerDto);
      fail("Expected an exception");
   } catch (InvalidInputException e) {
      assertEquals( "Field", "Credit", e.field );
   }
}

public void testCreateCustomerFromDto_NullAddress_OBA() {
   CustomerDto customerDto = createValidCustomerDto();
   customerDto.address = null;
   try {
      sut.createCustomerFromDto(customerDto);
      fail("Expected an exception");
   } catch (InvalidInputException e) {
      assertEquals( "Field", "Address", e.field );
   }
}
```

Derived
Value

Generated Value

How do we specify the values to be used in tests?

We generate a suitable value each time the test is run.

```
BigDecimal uniqueCustomerNumber = getUniqueNumber();
```

When initializing the objects in the test fixture, one issue that must be dealt with is the fact that most objects have various attributes (fields) that need to be supplied as arguments to the constructor. Sometimes the exact values to be used affect the outcome of the test. More often than not, however, it is important only that each object use a different value. When the precise values of these attributes are not important to the test, it is important not to have them visible within the test!

Generated Values are used in conjunction with *Creation Methods* (page 415) to help us remove this potentially distracting information from the test.

How It Works

Instead of deciding which values to use in our tests while we are coding the tests, we generate the values when we actually execute the tests. We can then pick values to satisfy specific criteria such as "must be unique in the database" that can be determined only as the test run unfolds.

When to Use It

We use a *Generated Value* whenever we cannot or do not want to specify the test values until the test is executing. Perhaps the value of an attribute is not expected to affect the outcome of the test and we don't want to be bothered to define *Literal Values* (page 714), or perhaps we need to ensure some quality of the attribute that can be determined only at runtime. In some cases, the SUT requires the value of an attribute to be unique; using a *Generated Value* can ensure that this criterion is satisfied and thereby prevent *Unrepeatable Tests* (see *Erratic Test* on page 228) and *Test Run Wars* (see *Erratic Test*) by reducing the likelihood of a test conflicting with its parallel incarnation in another test run. Optionally, we can use this distinct value for all attributes of the object; object recognition then becomes very easy when we inspect the object in a debugger.

One thing to be wary of is that different values could expose different bugs. For example, a single-digit number may be formatted correctly, whereas a multidigit number might not (or vice versa). *Generated Values* can result

Generated Value

in *Nondeterministic Tests* (see *Erratic Test*); if we encounter nondeterminism (sometimes the test passes and then fails during the very next run), we must check the SUT code to see whether differences in value could be the root cause.

In general, we shouldn't use a *Generated Value* unless the value *must* be unique because of the nondeterminism such a value may introduce. The obvious alternative is to use a *Literal Value*. A less obvious alternative is to use a *Derived Value* (page 718), especially when we must determine the expected results of a test.

Implementation Notes

We can generate values in a number of ways. The appropriateness of each technique depends on the circumstance.

Variation: Distinct Generated Value

When we need to ensure that each test or object uses a different value, we can take advantage of *Distinct Generated Values*. In such a case, we can create a set of utility functions that will return unique values of various types (e.g., integers, strings, floating-point numbers). The various getUnique methods can all be built upon an integer sequence number generator. For numbers that must be unique within the scope of a shared database, we can use database sequences or a sequence table. For numbers that must be unique within the scope of a particular test run, we can use an in-memory sequence number generator (e.g., use a Java static variable that is incremented before usage). In-memory sequence numbers that start from the number 1 each time a test suite is run offer a useful quality: The values generated in each test are the same for each run and can simplify debugging.

Variation: Random Generated Value

One way to obtain good test coverage without spending a lot of time analyzing the behavior and generating test conditions is to use different values each time we run the tests. Using a *Random Generated Value* is one way to accomplish this goal. While use of such values may seem like a good idea, it makes the tests nondeterministic (*Nondeterministic Tests*) and can make debugging failed tests very difficult. Ideally, when a test fails, we want to be able to repeat that test failure on demand. To do so, we can log the *Random Generated Value* as the test is run and show it as part of the test failure. We then need to find a way to force the test to use that value again while we are troubleshooting the failed test. In most cases, the effort required outweighs the potential benefit. Of course, when we need this technique, we *really* need it.

Variation: Related Generated Value

An optional enhancement is to combine a *Generated Value* with a *Derived Value* by using the same generated integer as the root for all attributes of a single object. This result can be accomplished by calling getUniqueInt once and then using that value to build unique strings, floating-point numbers, and other values. With a *Related Generated Value*, all fields of the object contain "related" data, which makes the object easier to recognize when debugging. Another option is to separate the generation of the root from the generation of the values by calling generateNewUniqueRoot explicitly before calling getUniqueInt, getUniqueString, and so on.

Another nice touch for strings is to pass a *role-describing argument* to the function that is combined with the unique integer key to make the code more intent-revealing. Although we could also pass such arguments to the other functions, of course we wouldn't be able to build them into an integer value.

Motivating Example

The following test uses *Literal Values* for the arguments to a constructor:

```
public void testProductPrice_HCV() {
    //    Setup
    Product product =
        new Product( 88,                       // ID
                     "Widget",                 // Name
                     new BigDecimal("19.99")); // Price
    // Exercise
    //   ...
}
```

Refactoring Notes

We can convert the test to use *Distinct Generated Values* by replacing the *Literal Values* with calls to the appropriate getUnique method. These methods simply increment a counter each time they are called and use that counter value as the root for construction of an appropriately typed value.

Example: Distinct Generated Value

Here is the same test using a *Distinct Generated Value*. For the getUniqueString method, we'll pass a string describing the role ("Widget Name").

```
public void testProductPrice_DVG() {
    // Setup
    Product product =
```

Generated
Value

```
        new Product( getUniqueInt(),                      // ID
                     getUniqueString("Widget"), // Name
                     getUniqueBigDecimal());    // Price
   // Exercise
   //   ...
}

static int counter = 0;

int getUniqueInt() {
   counter++;
   return counter;
}

BigDecimal getUniqueBigDecimal() {
   return new BigDecimal(getUniqueInt());
}

String getUniqueString(String baseName) {
   return baseName.concat(String.valueOf( getUniqueInt()));
}
```

This test uses a different generated value for each argument of the constructor call. The numbers generated in this way are consecutive but the test reader still needs to look at a specific attribute when debugging to get a consistent view. We probably should not generate the price value if the logic we were testing was related to price calculation because that would force our verification logic to accommodate different total costs.

Example: Related Generated Value

We can ensure that all values used by the test are obviously related by separating the generation of the root value from the construction of the individual values. In the following example, we've moved the generation of the root to the setUp method so each test method gets a new value only once. The methods that retrieve the various values (e.g., getUniqueString) simply use the previously generated root when deriving the *Generated Values*.

**Generated
Value**

```
public void testProductPrice_DRVG() {
   //     Setup
   Product product =
       new Product( getUniqueInt(),                      // ID
                    getUniqueString("Widget"), // Name
                    getUniqueBigDecimal());    // Price
   // Exercise
   //   ...
}
```

```
static int counter = 0;

public void setUp() {
    counter++;
}

int getUniqueInt() {
    return counter;
}

String getUniqueString(String baseName) {
    return baseName.concat(String.valueOf( getUniqueInt()));
}

BigDecimal getUniqueBigDecimal() {
    return new BigDecimal(getUniqueInt());
}
```

If we looked at this object in an object inspector or database or if we dumped part of it to a log, we could readily tell which object we were looking at regardless of which field we happened to see.

Generated Value

Dummy Object

How do we specify the values to be used in tests when the only usage is as irrelevant arguments of SUT method calls?

We pass an object that has no implementation as an argument of a method called on the SUT.

```
Invoice inv = new Invoice( new DummyCustomer() );
```

Getting the SUT into the right state to start a test often requires calling other methods of the SUT. These methods commonly take as arguments objects that are stored in instance variables for later use. Often, these objects (or at least some attributes of these objects) are never used in the code that we are actually testing. Instead, we create them solely to conform to the signature of some method we must call to get the SUT into the right state. Constructing these objects can be nontrivial and adds unnecessary complexity to the test.

In these cases, a *Dummy Object* can be passed as an argument, eliminating the need to build a real object.

How It Works

We create an instance of some object that can be instantiated easily and with no dependencies; we then pass that instance as the argument of the method of the SUT. Because it won't actually be used within the SUT, we don't need any implementation for this object. If any of the methods of the *Dummy Object are* invoked, the test really should throw an error. Trying to invoke a nonexistent method will typically produce that result.

When to Use It

We can use *Dummy Objects* whenever we need to use objects as attributes of other objects or arguments of methods on the SUT or other fixture objects. Using *Dummy Objects* helps us avoid *Obscure Tests* (page 186) by leaving out the irrelevant code that would be necessary to build real objects and by making it clear which objects and values are not used by the SUT.

If we need to control the indirect inputs or verify the indirect outputs of the SUT, we should probably use a *Test Stub* (page 529) or a *Mock Object* (page 544) instead. If the object will be used by the SUT but we cannot provide the real object, we should consider providing a *Fake Object* (page 551) that provides just enough behavior for the test to execute.

We can use one of the value patterns when the SUT really does need to use the object in some way. Either a *Literal Value* (page 714), a *Generated Value* (page 723), or a *Derived Value* (page 718) may be appropriate, depending on the circumstance.

Variation: Dummy Argument

We can use a *Dummy Argument* whenever methods of the SUT take objects as arguments[1] and those objects are not relevant to the test.

Variation: Dummy Attribute

We can use a *Dummy Attribute* whenever we are creating objects that will be used as part of the fixture or as arguments of SUT methods, and some of the attributes of those objects are not relevant to the test.

Implementation Notes

The simplest implementation of a *Dummy Object* is to pass a null value as the argument. This approach works even in a statically typed language such as Java, albeit only if the method being called doesn't check for null arguments. If the method complains when we pass it null, we'll need to employ a slightly more sophisticated implementation. The biggest disadvantage to using null is that it is not very descriptive.

In dynamically typed languages such as Ruby, Perl, and Python, the actual type of the object will never be checked (because it will never be used), so we can use any class such as String or Object. In such a case, it is useful to give the object a *Self-Describing Value* (see *Literal Value*) such as "Dummy Customer."

In statically typed languages (such as Java, C#, and C++), we must ensure that the *Dummy Object* is type compatible with the parameter it is to match. Type compatibility is much easier to achieve if the parameter has an abstract type (e.g., an Interface in Java) because we can create our own trivial implementation of the type or pass a suitable *Pseudo-Object* (see *Hard-Coded Test Double* on page 568). If the parameter type is a concrete class, we may be able to create

---

[1] From *Wikipedia:* Parameters are also commonly referred to as arguments, although arguments are more properly thought of as the actual values or references assigned to the parameter variables when the subroutine is called at runtime. When discussing code that is calling into a subroutine, any values or references passed into the subroutine are the arguments, and the place in the code where these values or references are given is the parameter list. When discussing the code inside the subroutine definition, the variables in the subroutine's parameter list are the parameters, while the values of the parameters at runtime are the arguments.

a trivial instance of it or we may need to create an instance of a *Test-Specific Subclass* (page 579) within our test.

Some *Mock Object* frameworks have *Test Utility Methods* (page 599) that will generate a *Dummy Object* for a specified class that takes a String argument for a *Self-Describing Value*.

While the *Dummy Object* may, in fact, be null, it is not the same as a Null Object [PLOPD3]. A *Dummy Object* is *not* used by the SUT, so its behavior is either irrelevant or it should throw an exception when executed. In contrast, a Null Object is used by the SUT but is designed to do nothing. That's a small but very important distinction!

Motivating Example

In this example, we are testing the Invoice but we require a Customer to instantiate the invoice. The Customer requires an Address, which in turn requires a City. Thus we find ourselves creating several additional objects just to set up the fixture. But if we know that the behavior we are testing should not access the Customer at all, why do we need to create it and all the objects on which it depends?

```
public void testInvoice_addLineItem_noECS() {
    final int QUANTITY = 1;
    Product product = new Product(getUniqueNumberAsString(),
                                  getUniqueNumber());
    State state = new State("West Dakota", "WD");
    City city = new City("Centreville", state);
    Address address = new Address("123 Blake St.", city, "12345");
    Customer customer= new Customer(getUniqueNumberAsString(),
                                    getUniqueNumberAsString(),
                                    address);
    Invoice inv = new Invoice(customer);
    // Exercise
    inv.addItemQuantity(product, QUANTITY);
    // Verify
    List lineItems = inv.getLineItems();
    assertEquals("number of items", lineItems.size(), 1);
    LineItem actual = (LineItem)lineItems.get(0);
    LineItem expItem = new LineItem(inv, product, QUANTITY);
    assertLineItemsEqual("",expItem, actual);
}
```

Dummy Object

This test is quite cluttered as a result of the extra object creation. How is the behavior we are testing related to the Address and City? From this test, we can only assume that there is some relation. But this misleads the test reader!

Refactoring Notes

If the objects in the fixture are not relevant to the test, they should not be visible in the test. Therefore, we should try to eliminate the need to create all these objects. We could try passing in null for the Customer. In this case, the constructor checks for null and rejects it, so we have to find another way.

The solution is to replace the object that is not important to our test with a *Dummy Object*. In dynamically typed languages, we could just pass in a string. In statically typed languages such as Java and C#, however, we must pass in a type-compatible object. In this case, we have chosen to do an Extract Interface [Fowler] refactoring on Customer to create a new interface and then create a new implementation class called DummyCustomer. Of course, as part of the Extract Interface refactoring, we must replace all references to Customer with the new interface name so that the DummyCustomer will be acceptable. A less intrusive option would be to use a *Test-Specific Subclass* of Customer that adds a test-friendly constructor.

Example: Dummy Values and Dummy Objects

Here's the same test using a *Dummy Object* instead of the Product name and the Customer. Note how much simpler the fixture setup has become!

```
public void testInvoice_addLineItem_DO() {
    final int QUANTITY = 1;
    Product product = new Product("Dummy Product Name",
                                  getUniqueNumber());
    Invoice inv = new Invoice( new DummyCustomer() );
    LineItem expItem = new LineItem(inv, product, QUANTITY);
    // Exercise
    inv.addItemQuantity(product, QUANTITY);
    // Verify
    List lineItems = inv.getLineItems();
    assertEquals("number of items", lineItems.size(), 1);
    LineItem actual = (LineItem)lineItems.get(0);
    assertLineItemsEqual("", expItem, actual);
}
```

Using a *Dummy Object* for the name of the Product was simple because it is a string and has no uniqueness requirement. Thus we were able to use a *Self-Describing Value*. We were not able to use a *Dummy Object* for the Product number because it must be unique, so we left it as a *Generated Value*. The Customer was a bit trickier because the LineItem's constructor expected a non-null object. Because this example is written in Java, the method parameter is strongly typed; for this reason, we needed to create an alternative implementation of the ICustomer interface with a no-argument constructor to simplify in-line construction. Because the DummyCustomer is never used, we have created

Dummy Object

it in-line rather than declaring a variable to hold it. This choice reduces the fixture setup code by one line, and the presence of the in-line constructor call within the call to the Invoice constructor reinforces the message that we need the *Dummy Object* only for the constructor call and not for the rest of the test. Here is the code for the DummyCustomer:

```
public class DummyCustomer implements ICustomer {

    public DummyCustomer() {
        // Real simple; nothing to initialize!
    }

    public int getZone() {
        throw new RuntimeException("This should never be called!");
    }
}
```

We have implemented the DummyCustomer class with just those methods declared in the interface; because each method throws an exception, we know when it is hit. We could also have used a *Pseudo-Object* for the DummyCustomer. In other circumstances we might have been able to simply pass in null or construct a dummy instance of the real class. The major problem with the latter technique is that we won't know for sure if the *Dummy Object* is actually used.

Further Reading

When [UTwJ] refers to a "dummy object," these authors are referring to what *this* book terms a *Test Stub*. See *Mocks, Fakes, Stubs, and Dummies* in Appendix B for a more thorough comparison of the terminology used in various books and articles. The JMock and NMock frameworks for testing with *Mock Objects* support auto-generation of *Dummy Objects*.

Dummy Object

PART IV

Appendixes

Appendix A

Test Refactorings

Extract Testable Component

You want to be able to test the logic easily but the component is too closely tied to its context to allow such testing.

Extract the logic you want to test into a separate component that is designed for testability and is independent of the context in which it is run.

Also known as:
Sprout Class
[WEwLC]

Implementation Notes

We extract the logic from the untestable component into a component that is testable via synchronous tests, leaving behind all the ties to the context. This usually means that anything required by the testable component logic from the context is retrieved by the untestable component and passed in to the testable component as arguments of the methods under test or constructor methods. The untestable component then contains very little code and is considered to be a *Humble Object* (page 695). It simply retrieves the information the testable component requires from the context, instantiates the testable component, and delegates to it. All interactions with the new testable component consist of synchronous method calls.

The testable component may be a Windows DLL, a Java JAR containing a Service Facade [CJ2EEP] class, or some other language component or class that exposes the services of the executable in a testable way. The untestable code may be an executable, a dialog box or some other presentation component, logic that is executed inside a transaction, or even a complex test method. Extraction of the testable component should leave behind a *Humble Object* that requires very little, if any, testing.

735

Depending on the nature of the untestable component, we may choose to write tests for the delegation logic or we may be unable to do so because the logic is so closely tied to the context. If we do write tests for it, we require only one or two tests to verify that the instantiation and delegation occur correctly. Because this code will not change very often, these tests are much less critical than other tests and can even be omitted from the suite of tests that developers execute before check-in if we want to speed up test suite execution times. Of course, we would still prefer to run them from the automated build process.

Further Reading

This refactoring is similar to an Extract Interface [Fowler] refactoring and an Extract Implementer [Fowler] refactoring, except that *Extract Testable Component* does not require keeping the same interface. It can also be viewed as a special case of the Extract Class [Fowler] refactoring.

In-line Resource

Tests that depend on an unseen external resource create a Mystery Guest problem.

Move the contents of an external resource into the fixture setup logic of the test.

From [RTC]:

> *To remove the dependency between a test method and some external resource, we incorporate that resource in the test code. This is done by setting up a fixture in the test code that holds the same contents as the resource. This fixture is then used instead of the resource to run the test. A simple example of this refactoring is putting the contents of a file that is used into some string in the test code.*

> *If the contents of the resource are large, chances are high that you are also suffering from Eager Tests (see Assertion Roulette on page 224). Consider applying an Extract Method [Fowler] refactoring or a Minimize Data (page 738) refactoring.*

Implementation Notes

The problem with tests that depend on an external resource is that we cannot see the pre-conditions of the test. The resource may be a file sitting in the file system, the contents of a database, or some other object created outside the test. None of these *Prebuilt Fixtures* (page 429) is visible to the test reader. The solution is to make them visible by including the resource in-line within the test. The simplest way to do so is to create the resource from within the test itself. For example, we could build the contents of a text file by writing to the file rather than just referring to a preexisting file. If we delete the file at the end of the test, this step also moves us from a *Prebuilt Fixture* approach to a *Persistent Fresh Fixture* (see *Fresh Fixture* on page 311) approach. As a result, our tests may execute somewhat more slowly.

A more innovative way to in-line the external resource is to replace the actual resource with a *Test Stub* (page 529) that is initialized within the test. The contents of the resource then become visible to the test reader. When the system under test (SUT) executes, it uses the *Test Stub* instead of the real resource.

Another option is to refactor the design of the SUT so as to improve its testability. We can apply the Extract Testable Component (page 735) refactoring to the part of the SUT that uses the *contents* of the resource so that it can be tested directly without actually accessing an external resource. That is, the test passes the contents of the resource to the logic that uses it. We can also test the *Humble Object* (page 695) that reads the resource independently by replacing the extracted component with a *Test Stub* or *Mock Object* (page 544).

Make Resource Unique

> *Several tests are accidentally creating or using the same resource in a Shared Fixture.*

Make the name of any resources used by a test unique.

From [RTC]:

> *A lot of problems originate from the use of overlapping resource names, either between different tests run by the same user or between simultaneous test runs done by different users.*
>
> *Such problems can easily be prevented (or repaired) by using unique identifiers for all resources that are allocated—for example, by including a time stamp. When you also include the name of the test responsible for*

allocating the resource in this identifier, you will have fewer problems finding tests that do not properly release their resources.

Implementation Notes

We make the name of any resources used by a test unique across all tests by using a *Distinct Generated Value* (see *Generated Value* on page 723) as part of the name. Ideally, the name should include the name of the test that "owns" the resource. To avoid *Interacting Tests* (see *Erratic Test* on page 228), we include a time stamp in the name of any resources created by the tests and use *Automated Teardown* (page 503) to delete those resources at the end of the test.

Minimize Data

The test fixture is too large, making the test hard to understand.

Also known as:
Reduce Data

We remove things from the fixture until we have a Minimal Fixture.

From [RTC]:

Minimize the data that is set up in fixtures to the bare essentials. This will have two advantages: (1) It makes them more suitable as documentation, and (2) your tests will be less sensitive to changes.

Implementation Notes

Reducing the data in our test fixture to the bare minimum results in a *Minimal Fixture* (page 302) that helps the tests achieve *Tests as Documentation* (see page 23). How we do this depends on how our *Test Methods* (page 348) are organized into *Testcase Classes* (page 373).

When our *Test Methods* are organized via the *Testcase Class per Fixture* pattern (page 631) and we believe we have a *General Fixture* (see *Obscure Test* on page 186), we can remove the fixture setup logic for any parts of the fixture that we suspect are not used by the tests. It is best to remove this logic incrementally so that if a test fails, we can undo our most recent change and try again.

When our *Test Methods* are organized as a *Testcase Class per Feature* (page 624) or a *Testcase Class per Class* (page 617), *Minimize Data* may also involve copying fixture setup logic from the setUp method of a *Testcase Class* or *Setup Decorator* (page 447) into each test that needs the fixture. Assuming the collection of objects in the *Shared Fixture* (page 317) is overkill for any one test, we can use a series of Extract Method [Fowler] refactorings to create a set of *Creation Methods* (page 415), which we then call from the tests. Next, we remove the calls to the *Creation Methods* from the setUp method and put them into only those *Test Methods* that require that part of the original fixture. The final step would be to convert any fixture-holding instance variables into local variables.

Replace Dependency with Test Double

The dependencies of an object being tested get in the way of running tests.

**Break the dependency by replacing a depended-on component
with a Test Double.**

Implementation Notes

The first step is to choose the form of dependency substitution. *Dependency Injection* (page 678) is the best option for unit tests, whereas *Dependency Lookup* (page 686) often works better for customer tests. We then refactor the SUT to support this choice or design the capability into the SUT as we do test-driven development. The next decision is whether to use a *Fake Object* (page 551), a *Test Stub* (page 529), a *Test Spy* (page 538), or a *Mock Object* (page 544) based on how the *Test Double* will be used by the test. This decision is described in Chapter 11, *Using Test Doubles.*

If we are using a *Test Stub* or *Mock Object*, we must decide whether we want to use a *Hard-Coded Test Double* (page 568) or a *Configurable Test Double* (page 558). The trade-offs are discussed in Chapter 11 and in the detailed descriptions of the patterns. That decision then dictates the shape of our test—for example, Tests that use *Mock Objects* are more "front-loaded" by the construction of the *Mock Object.*

Finally, we modify our test to construct, optionally configure, and then install the *Mock Object.* We may also have to add a call to the verification method for some kinds of *Mock Objects.* In statically typed languages, we may have to do an Extract Interface [Fowler] refactoring before we can introduce the fake implementation. We then use this interface as the type of the variable that holds the reference to the substitutable dependency.

Setup External Resource

The SUT depends on the contents of an external resource that is acting as a Mystery Guest in our test.

Create an external resource within the fixture setup logic of the test rather than using a predefined resource.

From [RTC]:

> *If it is necessary for a test to rely on external resources, such as directories, databases, or files, make sure the test that uses them explicitly creates or allocates these resources before testing, and releases them when done (take precautions to ensure the resource is also released when tests fail).*

Implementation Notes

When our SUT *must* use an external resource such as a file and we absolutely, positively cannot replace the access mechanism with a *Test Stub* (page 529) or *Fake Object* (page 551), we may need to live with the fact that we have to use an external resource. The problems with external resources are obvious: The test reader cannot tell what they contain; those resources may disappear unexpectedly, causing tests to fail because of *Resource Optimism* (see *Erratic Test* on page 228); and the resources may result in *Interacting Tests* (see *Erratic Test*) and *Test Run Wars* (see *Erratic Test*). Setup External Resource does not help us with the last problem but it does avoid the problems of a *Mystery Guest* (see *Obscure Test* on page 186) and *Resource Optimism*.

To implement the *Setup External Resource* refactoring, we simply pull the contents of the external resource into our *Test Method* (page 348), setUp method, or a *Test Utility Method* (page 599) called by them. Using the contents we construct the external resource within our test code, thereby making it evident to the test reader exactly what the test depends on. This approach also guarantees that the resource exists because we create it in every test run.

Appendix B

xUnit Terminology

Mocks,
Fakes, Stubs,
and
Dummies

Mocks, Fakes, Stubs, and Dummies

Are you confused about what someone means when that individual says "test stub" or "mock object"? Do you sometimes feel that the person you are talking to is using a very different definition? Well, you are not alone!

The terminology for the various kinds of *Test Doubles* (page 522) is confusing and inconsistent. Different authors use different terms to mean the same thing. And sometimes they mean different things even when they use the same term! Ouch! (See the sidebar "What's in a (Pattern) Name?" on page 576 for why I think names are important.)

Part of my reason for writing this book was to try to establish some consistency in the terminology, thereby giving people a set of names with clear definitions of what they mean. In this appendix, I provide a list of the current sources and cross-reference the terminology they use with the terminology used in this book.

Role Descriptions

The table on page 742 is a summary of what I mean by each of the major *Test Double* pattern names.

Role Descriptions

Pattern	Purpose	Has Behavior	Injects Indirect Inputs into SUT	Handles Indirect Outputs of SUT	Values Provided by Test(er)	Examples
Test Double (page 522)	Generic name for family					
Dummy Object (page 728)	Attribute or method parameter	No	No, never called	No, never called	No	Null, "Ignored String," new Object()
Test Stub (page 529)	Verify indirect inputs of SUT	Yes	Yes	Ignores them	Inputs	
Test Spy (page 538)	Verify indirect outputs of SUT	Yes	Optional	Captures them for later verification	Inputs (optional)	
Mock Object (page 544)	Verify indirect outputs of SUT	Yes	Optional	Verifies correctness against expectations	Inputs (optional) and expected outputs.	
Fake Object (page 551)	Run (unrunnable) tests (faster)	Yes	No	Uses them	None	In-memory database emulator
Temporary Test Stub (see Test Stub)	Stand in for procedural code not yet written	Yes	No	Uses them	None	In-memory database emulator

Terminology Cross-Reference

The following table lists some sources of conflicting definitions just to make it clear what the mapping is to the pattern names used in this book.

Pattern	Sources and Names Used in Them								
	Astels	Beck	Feathers	Fowler	jMock	UTWJ	OMG	Pragmatic	Recipes
Test Double								Double or stand-in	
Dummy Object	Stub				Dummy				Stub
Test Stub	Fake		Fake	Stub	Stub	Dummy		Mock	Fake
Test Spy						Dummy			Spy
Mock Object	Mock		Mock	Mock	Mock	Mock		Mock	Mock
Fake Object						Dummy			
Temporary Test Stub						Stub			
OMG's CORBA Stub								Stub	

- *Unit Testing with Java* [UTwJ] uses the term "Dummy Object" to refer to what this book calls a "Fake Object."

- *Pragmatic Unit Testing* [PUT] describes a "Stub" as an empty implementation of a method. This is a common interpretation in the procedural world; in the object world, however, it is typically called a Null Object [PLOPD3].

- Some of the early Mock Objects literature could be interpreted to equate a "Stub" with a "Mock Object." The distinction between the two has since been clarified in [MRNO] and [MAS].

- The CORBA standard[1] and other remote-procedure call specifications use the terms "stubs" and "skeletons" to refer to the automatically generated code for the near- and far-end implementations of a remote interface defined in IDL. (I've included this information here because it is another use of a term that is commonly used in the TDD and automated developer testing community.)

The sources quoted in the preceding table are provided here:

Source	Description	Citation	Publisher
Astels	Book: *Test-Driven Development*	[TDD-APG]	Prentice Hall
Beck	Book: *Test-Driven Development*	[TDD-BE]	Addison-Wesley
Feathers	Book: *Working Effectively with Legacy Code*	[WEwLC]	Prentice Hall
Fowler	Blog: Mocks Aren't Stubs	[MAS]	martinfowler.com
jMock	Paper: Mock Roles, Not Objects	[MRNO]	ACM (OOPSLA)
UTWJ	Book: *Unit Testing in Java*	[UTwJ]	Morgan Kaufmann
OMG	Object Management Group's CORBA specifications		OMG
Pragmatic	Book: *Pragmatic Unit Testing with NUnit*	[PUT]	Pragmatic Programmers
Recipes	Book: *JUnit Recipes*		Manning

xUnit Terminology Cross-Reference

The following table maps the terminology used in this book to the terminology used by specific members of the xUnit family. This list is not intended to be exhaustive but rather is meant to illustrate the adaptations of the standard xUnit terminology to the idioms and culture of each language and community.

---

[1] CORBA is an acronym for Common Object Request Broker Architecture. This standard is defined by the Object Management Group.

| Tool | | Book Term | | | | | | | |
Language	xUnit Member	Testcase Class	Test Suite Factory	Test Method	Fixture setup	Fixture teardown	Suite Fixture Setup	Suite Fixture Teardown	Expected Exception Test
Java 1.4	JUnit 3.8.2	Subclass of TestCase	static suite()	testXxx()	setUp()	tearDown()	Not applicable	Not applicable	Subclass of Expected Exception Test
Java 5	JUnit 4.0+	import org.junit.Test	static suite()	@Test	@Before	@After	@Before Class	@After Class	@Exception
.NET	CsUnit	[TestFixture]	[Suite]	[Test]	[SetUp]	[TearDown]	Not applicable	Not applicable	[Expected Exception()]
.NET	NUnit 2.0	[TestFixture]	[Suite]	[Test]	[SetUp]	[TearDown]	Not applicable	Not applicable	[Expected Exception()]
.NET	NUnit 2.1+	[TestFixture]	[Suite]	[Test]	[SetUp]	[TearDown]	[Test Fixture SetUp]	[TestFixture TearDown]	[Expected Exception()]
.NET	MbUnit 2.0+	[TestFixture]	[Suite]	[Test]	[SetUp]	[TearDown]	[Fixture Setup]	[Fixture Teardown]	[Expected Exception()]
.NET	MSTest	[TestClass]	Not applicable	[Test Method]	[Test Initialize]	[Test Cleanup]	[Class Initialize]	[Class Cleanup]	[Expected Exception()]
PHP	PHPUnit	Subclass of TestCase	static suite()	testXxx()	setUp()	tearDown()	Not applicable	Not applicable	Subclass of Expected Exception Test

Continued...

Tool		Book Term							
Language	xUnit Member	Testcase Class	Test Suite Factory	Test Method	Fixture Setup	Fixture Teardown	Suite Fixture Test	Suite Fixture	Expected Exception
Python	PyUnit	Subclass of unittest.TestCase	Test Loader()	testXxx	setUp	tearDown	Not applicable	Not applicable	assert raise
Ruby	Test::Unit	Subclass of Test::Unit::TestCase	Classname.suite()	testXxx()	setup()	teardown	Not applicable	Not applicable	assert_raise
Smalltalk	SUnit	Superclass: TestCase	TestSuite named:	testXxx	setUp	tearDown	To be determined	To be determined	should:raise:
VB 6	VbUnit	Implements IFixture	Implements ISuite	TestXxx()	IFixture_Setup()	IFixture_TearDown	IFixture Frame_Create()	IFixture Frame_Destroy	on error...
SAP ABAP	ABAP Unit	FOR TESTING	Automatic	Any	setup	teardown	class_setup	class_teardown	To be determined

Appendix C

xUnit Family Members

This (incomplete) list of members of the xUnit family of test automation frameworks is included here to illustrate the diversity of the family and the extent to which automated unit testing is supported in various programming languages. This appendix also includes comments about specific capabilities of some members of the family. A much more complete and up-to-date list can be found at http://xprogramming.com/software.htm.

ABAP Object Unit

The member of the xUnit family for SAP's ABAP programming language. *ABAP Object Unit* is more or less a direct port of JUnit to ABAP except for the fact that it cannot catch exceptions encountered within the system under test (SUT).

ABAP Object Unit is available for download at http://www.abapunittests. com, along with articles about unit testing in ABAP. See ABAP Unit for versions of SAP/ABAP starting with 6.40.

ABAP Unit

The member of the xUnit family for versions of SAP's ABAP programming language starting with Basis version 6.40 (NetWeaver 2004s). The most notable aspect of ABAP Unit is its special support that allows tests to be stripped from the code as the code is "transported" from the acceptance test environment to the production environment.

ABAP Unit is available directly from SAP AG as part of the NetWeaver 2004s development tools. More information on unit testing in ABAP is available in the SAP documentation and from http://www.abapunittests.com. See **ABAP Object Unit** for versions of SAP/ABAP prior to Basis version 6.40 (NetWeaver 2004s).

CppUnit

The member of the xUnit family for the C++ programming language. It is available for download from http://cppunit.sourceforge.net. Another option for some .NET programmers is NUnit.

CsUnit

The member of the xUnit family for the C# programming language. It is available from http://www.csunit.org. Another option for .NET programmers is NUnit.

CUnit

The member of the xUnit family for the C programming language. Details can be found at http://cunit.sourceforge.net/doc/index.html.

DbUnit

An extension of the JUnit framework intended to simplify testing of databases. It can be downloaded from http://www.dbunit.org/.

IeUnit

The member of the xUnit family for testing Web pages rendered in Microsoft's Internet Explorer browser using JavaScript and DHTML. It can be downloaded from http://ieunit.sourceforge.net/.

JBehave

One of the first of a new generation of xUnit members designed to make tests written as part of TDD more useful *Tests as Specification*. The main difference between *JBehave* and more traditional members of the xUnit family is that *JBehave* eschews the "test" terminology and replaces it with terms more appropriate for specification—that is, "fixture" becomes "context," "assert" becomes "should," and so on. *JBehave* is available at http://jbehave.codehaus.org. RSpec is the Ruby equivalent.

JUnit

The member of the xUnit family for the Java programming language. *JUnit* was rewritten in late 2005 to take advantage of the annotations introduced in Java 1.5. It can be downloaded from http://www.junit.org.

MbUnit

A member of the xUnit family for the .NET programming languages. *MbUnit's* main claim to fame is its direct support for *Parameterized Tests*. It is available from http://www.mbunit.com. Other options for .NET programmers include NUnit, CsUnit, and MSTest.

MSTest

Microsoft's member of xUnit family does not seem to have a formal name other than its namespace `Microsoft.VisualStudio.TestTools.UnitTesting` but most people refer to it as *MSTest*. Technically, it is just the name of the *Command-Line Test Runner* `mstest.exe`. *MSTest's* main claim to fame is that it ships with Visual Studio 2005 Team System. It does not appear to be available in the less expensive versions of Visual Studio or for free download. *MSTest* includes a number of innovative features, such as direct support for *Data-Driven Tests*. Information is available on MSDN at http://msdn.microsoft.com/en-us/library/ms182516.aspx. Other (and cheaper) options for .NET programmers include NUnit, CsUnit, and MbUnit.

NUnit

The member of the xUnit family for the .NET programming languages. It is available from http://www.nunit.org. Other options for C# programmers include CsUnit, MbUnit, and MSTest.

PHPUnit

The member of the xUnit family for the PHP programming language. According to Sebastian Bergmann, "*PHPUnit* is a complete port of JUnit 3.8. On top of this original feature set it adds out-of-the-box support for Mock Objects, Code Coverage, Agile Documentation, and Incomplete and Skipped Tests." More information about *PHPUnit* can be found at http://www.phpunit.de, including the free book on *PHPUnit*.

PyUnit

The member of the xUnit family written to support Python programmers. It is a full port of JUnit. More information can be found at http://pyunit.sourceforge.net/.

RSpec

One of the first of a new generation of xUnit members designed to make tests written as part of TDD more useful *Tests as Specification*. The main difference between *RSpec* and more traditional members of the xUnit family is that *RSpec* eschews the "test" terminology and replaces it with terms more appropriate for specification—for example, "fixture" becomes "context," *Test Methods* becomes "specify," "assert" becomes "should," and so on. *RSpec* is available at http://rspec.rubyforge.org. JBehave is the Java equivalent.

runit

One member of the xUnit family for the Ruby programming language. It is a wrapper on Test::Unit that adds additional functionality. It is available at www.rubypeople.org.

SUnit

The self-proclaimed "mother of all unit-testing frameworks." *SUnit* is the member of the xUnit family for the Smalltalk programming language. It is available for download at http://sunit.sourceforge.net.

Test::Unit

The member of the xUnit family for the Ruby programming language. It is available for download from http://www.rubypeople.org and comes as part of the "Ruby Development Tools" feature for the Eclipse IDE framework.

TestNG

A member of the xUnit family for Java that behaves a bit differently from JUnit. *TestNG* specifically supports dependencies between tests and the sharing of the test fixture between *Test Methods*. More information is available at http://testng.org.

utPLSQL

The member of the xUnit family for the PLSQL database programming language. You can get more information and download the source for this tool at http://utplsql.sourceforge.net/. A plug-in that integrates utPLSQL into the Oracle toolset is available at http://www.ounit.com.

VB Lite Unit

Another member of the xUnit family written to support Visual Basic and VBA (Visual Basic for Applications). "VB Lite Unit is a reliable, lightweight unit-testing tool for Visual Basic and VBA written by Steve Jorgensen. The driving principle behind VB Lite Unit was to create the simplest, most reliable unit-testing tool possible that would still do everything that usually matters for doing test-driven development in VB 6 or VBA. Things that don't work or don't work reliably in VB and VBA are avoided, such as attempts at introspection to identify the test methods." Another option for VB and VBA programmers is VbUnit. For VB.NET programmers, options include NUnit, CsUnit, and MbUnit.

VbUnit

The member of the xUnit family written to support Visual Basic 6.0. It was the first member of the xUnit family to support *Suite Fixture Setup* and introduced the concept of calling a *Testcase Class* "test fixture."

One major quirk of *VbUnit* is that when an *Assertion Method* fails the test, it writes the messages into the failure log immediately rather than just raising an error that is then caught by the *Test Runner*. The practical implication of this behavior is that it becomes difficult to test *Custom Assertions* because the messages in the logs are not prevented by the normal *Expected Exception Test* construct. The work-around is to run the *Custom Assertion Tests* inside an "Encapsulated Test Runner."

Another quirk is that *VbUnit* is one of the few members of the xUnit family that is not free (as in beer). It is available from http://www.vbunit.org. There used to be a free version available—who knows, it may reappear some day. Another option for VB and VBA programmers is VB Lite Unit. For VB.NET programmers, options include NUnit, CsUnit, and MbUnit.

xUnit

The generic name for any *Test Automation Framework* for unit testing that is patterned on JUnit or SUnit. The *xUnit* test framework for most languages can be found at http://xprogramming.com or http://en.wikipedia.org/wiki/XUnit. Another place to look for both unit test and customer test tools is http://www.opensourcetesting.org.

Appendix D

Tools

The following tools are mentioned at some point within this book. This section describes their purpose and how they relate to xUnit test automation in just a wee bit more detail.

Ant

A build automation tool used in the Java community. NAnt is the equivalent for .NET projects.

AntHill

A continuous integration tool used in the Java community.

BPT

A commercial *Scripted Test* tool that allows less technically advanced users to compose tests from reusable test components that are the result of *Refactored Recorded Tests*. It can also be used to specify reusable test components to be built by more technically oriented test automaters. More information can be found on Mercury Interactive's Web site. As this book went to press, Mercury Interactive was in the process of being acquired by Hewlett-Packard, so the URL may have changed.

Canoo WebTest

A framework for preparing *Scripted Tests* written in XML. Conceptually, *Canoo WebTest* is similar to Fit in that it allows us to define our own domain-specific testing language for defining customer tests. More information can be found at http://webtest.canoo.com and http://webtest-community.canoo.com.

Cruise Control

A continuous integration tool used in the Java community. *Cruise Control.net* is the equivalent for .NET projects.

DDSteps

A *Data-Driven Test* extension for JUnit. "*DDSteps* is a JUnit extension for building data driven test cases. In a nutshell, *DDSteps* lets you parameterize your test cases, and run them more than once using different data." See http://www.ddsteps.org for more information.

EasyMock

A static *Mock Object* generation toolkit for Java tests. Because *EasyMock* uses a *Configuration Mode* for specifying the expectations, the tests look a bit strange and may take a bit of getting used to. More information can be found at http://www.easymock.org.

eCATT

The *Recorded Test* tool that comes with SAP's development tools. More information can be found at http://www.sap.com and at http://www.sdn.sap.com.

Eclipse

A Java integrated development environment (IDE) and platform for rich client applications. *Eclipse* was originally created by IBM and is now managed by the Eclipse Foundation. Several of the language-specific plug-ins are integrated with the corresponding xUnit family member. For example, the Java IDE includes JUnit and the Ruby Development Tools IDE includes Test::Unit. *Eclipse* is available for download from http://www.eclipse.org.

Fit

The framework conceived by Ward Cunningham that made it possible for customers to write automated tests. *Fit* separates the work of defining the tests using tables in Web pages or spreadsheets from the programming work of exercising the SUT. While *Fit* was once a particular tool, it is now a specification for a family of tools implemented in a variety of languages, including Java, .NET, Ruby, and Python. Some members of the family are simply test execution frameworks; others, such as Fitnesse, include test authoring and versioning capabilities. All should implement the same set of standard fixtures. More information can be found at Ward's Web site (http://fit.c2.com) or in the book [FitB] he co-wrote with Rick Mudgridge.

FitNesse

A Fit test authoring tool conceived by (Uncle) Bob Martin of Object Mentor. *FitNesse* provides a wiki-like test authoring system with a set of predefined Fit fixtures that makes it possible for customers to write and run automated tests. More information can be found at http://www.fitnesse.org.

HttpUnit

A front end that layers on top of JUnit to allow tests to exercise a Web application via the HTTP protocol. *HttpUnit* bypasses the browser, so it is not suitable for use with applications that make extensive use of on-page scripting (e.g., AJAX). See http://httpunit.sourceforge.net for more information.

Idea

A Java IDE that offers rich support for refactoring. The *Idea* Web site [JBrains] contains fairly detailed descriptions of many of the refactorings. The same group also offers a very popular refactoring plug-in for Visual Studio, called ReSharper.

JFCUnit

A JUnit front end that layers on top of HttpUnit to allow tests to exercise a Web application via the HTTP protocol. *JFCUnit* provides a number of *Test Utility Methods* that form a *Higher-Level Language* for expressing tests of Web applications. Because it is a layer on top of HttpUnit, it bypasses the browser. Thus *JFCUnit* is not suitable for use with applications that make extensive use of on-page scripting (e.g., AJAX). See http://jfcunit.sourceforge.net for more information.

JMock

A widely used dynamic *Mock Object* framework for Java tests. The fluent *Configuration Interface* used for specifying the expectations makes the tests highly readable. More information can be found at http://www.jmock.org.

NMock

A widely used dynamic *Mock Object* framework for .NET tests. The fluent *Configuration Interface* used for specifying the expectations makes the tests highly readable. More information can be found at http://nmock.org.

QTP (QuickTest Professional)

A commercial *Recorded Test* tool that allows less technically advanced users to record tests as they use an application. In conjunction with the "Expert View" of the *Recorded Tests*, *QTP* can also be used to refactor the tests into reusable test components that are appropriate for use by less technically adept test automaters. More information can be found on Mercury Interactive's Web site. As this book went to press, Mercury Interactive was in the process of being acquired by Hewlett-Packard, so the URL has probably changed.

ReSharper

A refactoring plug-in for Visual Studio by JetBrains, the makers of the Idea IDE. Their Web site [JBrains] contains fairly detailed descriptions of many of the refactorings.

Visual Studio

Microsoft's integrated development environment intended for developing .NET applications software. *Visual Studio* comes in several versions (at various price points), some of which include MSTest and code/test refactoring support. Third-party plug-ins are also available for both refactoring (see [JBrains]) and xUnit (see CsUnit, MbUnit, and NUnit).

Watir

"Web Application Testing in Ruby." This set of components allows us to drive Internet Explorer from *Scripted Tests* written in the Ruby programming language. More information can be found at http://wtr.rubyforge.org/.

Appendix E

Goals and Principles

Name	Page	Relation	Base Name	Chapter
Bug Repellent	22		Bug Repellent	Chapter 3, *Goals of Test Automation*
Communicate Intent	41		Communicate Intent	Chapter 5, *Principles of Test Automation*
Defect Localization	22		Defect Localization	Chapter 3, *Goals of Test Automation*
Design for Testability	40		Design for Testability	Chapter 5, *Principles of Test Automation*
Do No Harm	24		Do No Harm	Chapter 3, *Goals of Test Automation*
Don't Modify the SUT	41		Don't Modify the SUT	Chapter 5, *Principles of Test Automation*
Ensure Commensurate Effort and Responsibility	47		Ensure Commensurate Effort and Responsibility	Chapter 5, *Principles of Test Automation*
Executable Specification	22	Alias	Tests as Specification	Chapter 3, *Goals of Test Automation*
Expressive Tests	28		Expressive Tests	Chapter 3, *Goals of Test Automation*
Front Door First	40	Alias	Use the Front Door First	Chapter 5, *Principles of Test Automation*
Fully Automated Test	26		Fully Automated Test	Chapter 3, *Goals of Test Automation*
Higher Level Language	41	Alias	Communicate Intent	Chapter 5, *Principles of Test Automation*

Continued...

Name	Page	Relation	Base Name	Chapter
Independent Test	42	Alias	Keep Tests Independent	Chapter 5, *Principles of Test Automation*
Isolate the SUT	43		Isolate the SUT	Chapter 5, *Principles of Test Automation*
Keep Test Logic Out of Production Code	45		Keep Test Logic Out of Production Code	Chapter 5, *Principles of Test Automation*
Keep Tests Independent	42		Keep Tests Independent	Chapter 5, *Principles of Test Automation*
Minimize Test Overlap	44		Minimize Test Overlap	Chapter 5, *Principles of Test Automation*
Minimize Untestable Code	44		Minimize Untestable Code	Chapter 5, *Principles of Test Automation*
No Test Logic in Production Code	45		Keep Test Logic Out of Production Code	Chapter 5, *Principles of Test Automation*
No Test Risk	21	Alias	Do No Harm	Chapter 5, *Principles of Test Automation*
Repeatable Test	26		Repeatable Test	Chapter 3, *Goals of Test Automation*
Robust Test	29		Robust Test	Chapter 3, *Goals of Test Automation*
Safety Net	24	Alias	Tests as Safety Net	Chapter 3, *Goals of Test Automation*
Self-Checking Test	26		Self-Checking Test	Chapter 3, *Goals of Test Automation*
Separation of Concerns	28		Separation of Concerns	Chapter 3, *Goals of Test Automation*
Simple Tests	28		Simple Tests	Chapter 3, *Goals of Test Automation*
Single Condition Test	45	Alias	Verify One Condition per Test	Chapter 5, *Principles of of Test Automation*
Single Glance Readable	41	Alias	Communicate Intent	Chapter 5, *Principles of Test Automation*
Test Concerns Separately	47		Test Concerns Separately	Chapter 5, *Principles of Test Automation*
Test-Driven Development	40	Alias	Write the Tests First	Chapter 5, *Principles of Test Automation*

Goals and Principles

Name	Page	Relation	Base Name	Chapter
Test First Development	40	Alias	Write the Tests First	Chapter 5, *Principles of Test Automation*
Tests as Documentation	23		Tests as Documentation	Chapter 3, *Goals of Test Automation*
Tests as Safety Net	24		Tests as Safety Net	Chapter 3, *Goals of Test Automation*
Tests as Specification	22		Tests as Specification	Chapter 3, *Goals of Test Automation*
Use the Front Door First	40		Use the Front Door First	Chapter 5, *Principles of Test Automation*
Verify One Condition per Test	45		Verify One Condition per Test	Chapter 5, *Principles of Test Automation*
Write the Tests First	40		Write the Tests First	Chapter 5, *Principles of Test Automation*

Appendix F

Smells, Aliases, and Causes

Name	Page	Relationship	Base Name	Chapter
Assertion Roulette	224		Assertion Roulette	Chapter 16, *Behavior Smells*
Asynchronous Code	210	Cause of	Hard-to-Test Code	Chapter 15, *Code Smells*
Asynchronous Test	255	Cause of	Slow Tests	Chapter 16, *Behavior Smells*
Behavior Sensitivity	242	Cause of	Fragile Test	Chapter 16, *Behavior Smells*
Buggy Tests	260		Buggy Tests	Chapter 17, *Project Smells*
Complex Teardown	206	Cause of	Conditional Test Logic	Chapter 15, *Code Smells*
Complex Test	186	Alias	Obscure Test	Chapter 15, *Code Smells*
Conditional Test Logic	200		Conditional Test Logic	Chapter 15, *Code Smells*
Conditional Verification Logic	203	Cause of	Conditional Test Logic	Chapter 15, *Code Smells*
Context Sensitivity	245	Cause of	Fragile Test	Chapter 16, *Behavior Smells*
Cut-and-Paste Code Reuse	214	Cause of	Test Code Duplication	Chapter 15, *Code Smells*
Data Sensitivity	243	Cause of	Fragile Test	Chapter 16, *Behavior Smells*
Developers Not Writing Tests	263		Developers Not Writing Tests	Chapter 17, *Project Smells*

Continued...

Name	Page	Relationship	Base Name	Chapter
Eager Test	224	Cause of	Assertion Roulette	Chapter 16, *Behavior Smells*
Equality Pollution	221	Cause of	Test Logic in Production	Chapter 15, *Code Smells*
Erratic Test	228		Erratic Test	Chapter 16, *Behavior Smells*
Flexible Test	202	Cause of	Conditional Test Logic	Chapter 15, *Code Smells*
For Tests Only	219	Cause of	Test Logic in Production	Chapter 15, *Code Smells*
Fragile Fixture	246	Cause of	Fragile Test	Chapter 16, *Behavior Smells*
Fragile Test	239		Fragile Test	Chapter 16, *Behavior Smells*
Frequent Debugging	248		Frequent Debugging	Chapter 16, *Behavior Smells*
General Fixture	190	Cause of	Obscure Test	Chapter 15, *Code Smells*
Hard-to-Test Code	209		Hard-to-Test Code	Chapter 15, *Code Smells*
Hard-Coded Dependency	210	Alias	Hard-to-Test Code	Chapter 15, *Code Smells*
Hard-Coded Test Data	194	Cause of	Obscure Test	Chapter 15, *Code Smells*
High Test Maintenance Cost	265		High Test Maintenance Cost	Chapter 17, *Project Smells*
Highly Coupled Code	210	Cause of	Hard-to-Test Code	Chapter 15, *Code Smells*
Indented Test Code	200	Alias	Conditional Test Logic	Chapter 15, *Code Smells*
Indirect Testing	196	Cause of	Obscure Test	Chapter 15, *Code Smells*
Infrequently Run Tests	268	Cause of	Production Bugs	Chapter 17, *Project Smells*

Name	Page	Relationship	Base Name	Chapter
Interacting Test Suites	231	Cause of	Erratic Test	Chapter 16, *Behavior Smells*
Interacting Tests	229	Cause of	Erratic Test	Chapter 16, *Behavior Smells*
Interface Sensitivity	241	Cause of	Fragile Test	Chapter 16, *Behavior Smells*
Irrelevant Information	192	Cause of	Obscure Test	Chapter 15, *Code Smells*
Lonely Test	232	Cause of	Erratic Test	Chapter 16, *Behavior Smells*
Long Test	186	Alias	Obscure Test	Chapter 15, *Code Smells*
Lost Test	269	Cause of	Production Bugs	Chapter 17, *Project Smells*
Manual Debugging	248	Alias	Frequent Debugging	Chapter 16, *Behavior Smells*
Manual Event Injection	281	Cause of	Manual Intervention	Chapter 16, *Behavior Smells*
Manual Fixture Setup	250	Cause of	Manual Intervention	Chapter 16, *Behavior Smells*
Manual Intervention	250		Manual Intervention	Chapter 16, *Behavior Smells*
Manual Result Verification	251	Cause of	Manual Intervention	Chapter 16, *Behavior Smells*
Missing Assertion Message	226	Cause of	Assertion Roulette	Chapter 16, *Behavior Smells*
Missing Unit Test	271	Cause of	Production Bugs	Chapter 17, *Project Smells*
Multiple Test Conditions	207	Cause of	Conditional Test Logic	Chapter 15, *Code Smells*
Mystery Guest	188	Cause of	Obscure Test	Chapter 15, *Code Smells*
Neverfail Test	274	Cause of	Production Bugs	Chapter 17, *Project Smells*
Nondeterministic Test	237	Cause of	Erratic Test	Chapter 16, *Behavior Smells*

Continued...

Name	Page	Relationship	Base Name	Chapter
Not Enough Time	263	Cause of	Developers Not Writing Tests	Chapter 17, *Project Smells*
Obscure Test	186		Obscure Test	Chapter 15, *Code Smells*
Overcoupled Test	246	Alias	Fragile Test	Chapter 16, *Behavior Smells*
Overspecified Software	246	Cause of	Fragile Test	Chapter 16, *Behavior Smells*
Production Bugs	268		Production Bugs	Chapter 17, *Project Smells*
Production Logic in Test	204	Cause of	Conditional Test Logic	Chapter 15, *Code Smells*
Reinventing the Wheel	215	Cause of	Test Code Duplication	Chapter 15, *Code Smells*
Resource Leakage	233	Cause of	Erratic Test	Chapter 16, *Behavior Smells*
Resource Optimism	233	Cause of	Erratic Test	Chapter 16, *Behavior Smells*
Sensitive Equality	246	Cause of	Fragile Test	Chapter 16, *Behavior Smells*
Slow Component Usage	254	Cause of	Slow Tests	Chapter 16, *Behavior Smells*
Slow Tests	253		Slow Tests	Chapter 16, *Behavior Smells*
Test Code Duplication	213		Test Code Duplication	Chapter 15, *Code Smells*
Test Dependency in Production	220	Cause of	Test Logic in Production	Chapter 15, *Code Smells*
Test Logic in Production	217		Test Logic in Production	Chapter 15, *Code Smells*
Test Run War	235	Cause of	Erratic Test	Chapter 16, *Behavior Smells*
Too Many Tests	256	Cause of	Slow Tests	Chapter 16, *Behavior Smells*
Unrepeatable Test	234	Cause of	Erratic Test	Chapter 16, *Behavior Smells*
Untestable Test Code	211	Cause of	Hard-to-Test Code	Chapter 15, *Code Smells*

Name	Page	Relationship	Base Name	Chapter
Untested Code	271	Cause of	Production Bugs	Chapter 17, *Project Smells*
Untested Requirement	272	Cause of	Production Bugs	Chapter 17, *Project Smells*
Verbose Test	186	Alias	Obscure Test	Chapter 15, *Code Smells*
Wrong Test Automation Strategy	264	Cause of	Developers Not Writing Tests	Chapter 17, *Project Smells*

Appendix G

Patterns, Aliases, and Variations

Name	Page	Relationship	Base Name	Chapter
Abstract Setup Decorator	449	Variation	Setup Decorator	Chapter 20, *Fixture Setup Patterns*
Abstract Test Fixture	638	Alias	Testcase Superclass	Chapter 24, *Test Organization Patterns*
Abstract Testcase	638	Alias	Testcase Superclass	Chapter 24, *Test Organization Patterns*
AllTests Suite	593	Variation	Named Test Suite	Chapter 24, *Test Organization Patterns*
Anonymous Creation Method	417	Variation	Creation Method	Chapter 20, *Fixture Setup Patterns*
Argument-Describing Message	371	Variation	Assertion Message	Chapter 19, *xUnit Basics Patterns*
Assertion-Identifying Message	371	Variation	Assertion Message	Chapter 19, *xUnit Basics Patterns*
Assertion Message	370		Assertion Message	Chapter 19, *xUnit Basics Patterns*
Assertion Method	362		Assertion Method	Chapter 19, *xUnit Basics Patterns*
Attachment Method	418	Variation	Creation Method	Chapter 20, *Fixture Setup Patterns*

Continued...

Name	Page	Relationship	Base Name	Chapter
Automated Exercise Teardown	505	Variation	Automated Teardown	Chapter 22, *Fixture Teardown Patterns*
Automated Fixture Teardown	504	Variation	Automated Teardown	Chapter 22, *Fixture Teardown Patterns*
Automated Teardown	503		Automated Teardown	Chapter 22, *Fixture Teardown Patterns*
Automated Unit Test	285	Alias	Scripted Test	Chapter 18, *Test Strategy Patterns*
Back Door Manipulation	327		Back Door Manipulation	Chapter 18, *Test Strategy Patterns*
Back Door Setup	329	Variation	Back Door Manipulation	Chapter 18, *Test Strategy Patterns*
Back Door Teardown	330	Variation	Back Door Manipulation	Chapter 18, *Test Strategy Patterns*
Back Door Verification	329	Variation	Back Door Manipulation	Chapter 18, *Test Strategy Patterns*
Behavior-Exposing Subclass	580	Variation	Test-Specific Subclass	Chapter 23, *Test Double Patterns*
Behavior-Modifying Subclass	580	Variation	Test-Specific Subclass	Chapter 23, *Test Double Patterns*
Behavior Verification	468		Behavior Verification	Chapter 21, *Result Verification Patterns*
Bespoke Assertion	474	Alias	Custom Assertion	Chapter 21, *Result Verification Patterns*
Built-in Test Recording	281	Variation	Recorded Test	Chapter 18, *Test Strategy Patterns*
Calculated Values	718	Alias	Derived Value	Chapter 27, *Value Patterns*
Capture/ Playback Test	278	Alias	Recorded Test	Chapter 18, *Test Strategy Patterns*
Chained Tests	454		Chained Tests	Chapter 20, *Fixture Setup Patterns*
Cleanup Method	602	Variation	Test Utility Method	Chapter 24, *Test Organization Patterns*

Name	Page	Relationship	Base Name	Chapter
Command-Line Test Runner	379	Variation	Test Runner	Chapter 19, *xUnit Basics Patterns*
Component Broker	686	Alias	Dependency Lookup	Chapter 26, *Design-for-Testability Patterns*
Component Registry	686	Alias	Dependency Lookup	Chapter 26, *Design-for-Testability Patterns*
Component Test	340	Variation	Layer Test	Chapter 18, *Test Strategy Patterns*
Configurable Mock Object	558	Alias	Configurable Test Double	Chapter 23, *Test Double Patterns*
Configurable Test Double	558		Configurable Test Double	Chapter 23, *Test Double Patterns*
Configurable Test Spy	558	Alias	Configurable Test Double	Chapter 23, *Test Double Patterns*
Configurable Test Stub	558	Alias	Configurable Test Double	Chapter 23, *Test Double Patterns*
Configuration Interface	560	Variation	Configurable Test Double	Chapter 23, *Test Double Patterns*
Configuration Mode	560	Variation	Configurable Test Double	Chapter 23, *Test Double Patterns*
Constant Value	714	Alias	Literal Value	Chapter 27, *Value Patterns*
Constructor Injection	680	Variation	Dependency Injection	Chapter 26, *Design-for-Testability Patterns*
Constructor Test	351	Variation	Test Method	Chapter 19, *xUnit Basics Patterns*
Creation Method	415		Creation Method	Chapter 20, *Fixture Setup Patterns*
Custom Assertion	474		Custom Assertion	Chapter 21, *Result Verification Patterns*
Custom Assertion Test	477	Variation	Custom Assertion	Chapter 21, *Result Verification Patterns*
Custom Equality Assertion	476	Variation	Custom Assertion	Chapter 21, *Result Verification Patterns*

Continued...

Patterns, Aliases, and Variations

Name	Page	Relationship	Base Name	Chapter
DB Schema per Test-Runner	651	Variation	Database Sandbox	Chapter 25, *Database Patterns*
Data Loader	330	Variation	Back Door Manipulation	Chapter 18, *Test Strategy Patterns*
Data Retriever	331	Variation	Back Door Manipulation	Chapter 18, *Test Strategy Patterns*
Data-Driven Test	288		Data-Driven Test	Chapter 18, *Test Strategy Patterns*
Data-Driven Test Framework (Fit)	290	Variation	Data-Driven Test	Chapter 18, *Test Strategy Patterns*
Data-Driven Test Frameworks	300	Variation	Test Automation Framework	Chapter 18, *Test Strategy Patterns*
Database Extraction Script	331	Variation	Back Door Manipulation	Chapter 18, *Test Strategy Patterns*
Database Partitioning Scheme	652	Variation	Database Sandbox	Chapter 25, *Database Patterns*
Database Population Script	330	Variation	Back Door Manipulation	Chapter 18, *Test Strategy Patterns*
Database Sandbox	650		Database Sandbox	Chapter 25, *Database Patterns*
Decorated Lazy Setup	449	Variation	Setup Decorator	Chapter 20, *Fixture Setup Patterns*
Dedicated Database Sandbox	651	Variation	Database Sandbox	Chapter 25, *Database Patterns*
Delegated Setup	411		Delegated Setup	Chapter 20, *Fixture Setup Patterns*
Delegated Teardown	511	Variation	In-line Teardown	Chapter 22, *Fixture Teardown Patterns*
Delta Assertion	485		Delta Assertion	Chapter 21, *Result Verification Patterns*
Dependency Initialization Test	352	Variation	Test Method	Chapter 19, *xUnit Basics Patterns*
Dependency Injection	678		Dependency Injection	Chapter 26, *Design-for-Testability Patterns*

Name	Page	Relationship	Base Name	Chapter
Dependency Lookup	686		Dependency Lookup	Chapter 26, *Design-for-Testability Patterns*
Derived Expectation	719	Variation	Derived Value	Chapter 27, *Value Patterns*
Derived Input	719	Variation	Derived Value	Chapter 27, *Value Patterns*
Derived Value	718		Derived Value	Chapter 27, *Value Patterns*
Diagnostic Assertion	476	Variation	Custom Assertion	Chapter 21, *Result Verification Patterns*
Direct Test Method Invocation	401	Variation	Test Enumeration	Chapter 19, *xUnit Basics Patterns*
Distinct Generated Value	724	Variation	Generated Value	Chapter 27, *Value Patterns*
Domain Assertion	476	Variation	Custom Assertion	Chapter 21, *Result Verification Patterns*
Dummy	728	Alias	Dummy Object	Chapter 27, *Value Patterns*
Dummy Argument	729	Variation	Dummy Object	Chapter 27, *Value Patterns*
Dummy Attribute	729	Variation	Dummy Object	Chapter 27, *Value Patterns*
Dummy Object	728		Dummy Object	Chapter 27, *Value Patterns*
Dummy Parameter	728	Alias	Dummy Object	Chapter 27, *Value Patterns*
Dummy Value	728	Alias	Dummy Object	Chapter 27, *Value Patterns*
Dynamically Generated Test Double	561	Variation	Configurable Test Double	Chapter 23, *Test Double Patterns*
Entity Chain Snipping	531	Variation	Test Stub	Chapter 23, *Test Double Patterns*
Equality Assertion	365	Variation	Assertion Method	Chapter 19, *xUnit Basics Patterns*

Patterns, Aliases, and Variations

Continued...

Name	Page	Relationship	Base Name	Chapter
Expectation-Describing Message	371	Variation	Assertion Message	Chapter 19, *xUnit Basics Patterns*
Expected Behavior	470	Alias	Behavior Verification	Chapter 21, *Result Verification Patterns*
Expected Behavior Specification	470	Variation	Behavior Verification	Chapter 21, *Result Verification Patterns*
Expected Exception Assertion	366	Variation	Assertion Method	Chapter 19, *xUnit Basics Patterns*
Expected Exception Test	350	Variation	Test Method	Chapter 19, *xUnit Basics Patterns*
Expected Object	464	Alias	State Verification	Chapter 21, *Result Verification Patterns*
Expected State Specification	464	Variation	State Verification	Chapter 21, *Result Verification Patterns*
External Test Recording	280	Variation	Recorded Test	Chapter 18, *Test Strategy Patterns*
Fake Database	553	Variation	Fake Object	Chapter 23, *Test Double Patterns*
Fake Object	551		Fake Object	Chapter 23, *Test Double Patterns*
Fake Service Layer	553	Variation	Fake Object	Chapter 23, *Test Double Patterns*
Fake Web Service	553	Variation	Fake Object	Chapter 23, *Test Double Patterns*
File System Test Runner	380	Variation	Test Runner	Chapter 19, *xUnit Basics Patterns*
Finder Method	600	Variation	Test Utility Method	Chapter 24, *Test Organization Patterns*
Fixture Setup Testcase	456	Variation	Chained Tests	Chapter 20, *Fixture Setup Patterns*
Four-Phase Test	358		Four-Phase Test	Chapter 19, *xUnit Basics Patterns*
Framework-Invoked Setup	424	Alias	Implicit Setup	Chapter 20, *Fixture Setup Patterns*

Patterns, Aliases, and Variations

Name	Page	Relationship	Base Name	Chapter
Framework-Invoked Teardown	516	Alias	Implicit Teardown	Chapter 22, *Fixture Teardown Patterns*
Fresh Context	311	Alias	Fresh Fixture	Chapter 18, *Test Strategy Patterns*
Fresh Fixture	311		Fresh Fixture	Chapter 18, *Test Strategy Patterns*
Fuzzy Equality Assertion	365	Variation	Assertion Method	Chapter 19, *xUnit Basics Patterns*
Garbage-Collected Teardown	500		Garbage-Collected Teardown	Chapter 22, *Fixture Teardown Patterns*
Generated Value	723		Generated Value	Chapter 27, *Value Patterns*
Global Fixture	430	Variation	Prebuilt Fixture	Chapter 20, *Fixture Setup Patterns*
Graphical Test Runner	378	Variation	Test Runner	Chapter 19, *xUnit Basics Patterns*
Guard Assertion	490		Guard Assertion	Chapter 21, *Result Verification Patterns*
Hand-Built Test Double	560	Variation	Configurable Test Double	Chapter 23, *Test Double Patterns*
Hand-Scripted Test	285	Alias	Scripted Test	Chapter 18, *Test Strategy Patterns*
Hand-Written Test	285	Alias	Scripted Test	Chapter 18, *Test Strategy Patterns*
Hard-Coded Mock Object	568	Alias	Hard-Coded Test Double	Chapter 23, *Test Double Patterns*
Hard-Coded Setup Decorator	449	Variation	Setup Decorator	Chapter 20, *Fixture Setup Patterns*
Hard-Coded Test Double	568		Hard-Coded Test Double	Chapter 23, *Test Double Patterns*
Hard-Coded Test Stub	568	Alias	Hard-Coded Test Double	Chapter 23, *Test Double Patterns*
Hard-Coded Value	714	Alias	Literal Value	Chapter 27, *Value Patterns*

Patterns, Aliases, and Variations

Continued...

Name	Page	Relationship	Base Name	Chapter
Hooked Setup	424	Alias	Implicit Setup	Chapter 20, *Fixture Setup Patterns*
Hooked Teardown	516	Alias	Implicit Teardown	Chapter 22, *Fixture Teardown Patterns*
Humble Container Adapter	698	Variation	Humble Object	Chapter 26, *Design-for-Testability Patterns*
Humble Dialog	696	Variation	Humble Object	Chapter 26, *Design-for-Testability Patterns*
Humble Executable	697	Variation	Humble Object	Chapter 26, *Design-for-Testability Patterns*
Humble Object	695		Humble Object	Chapter 26, *Design-for-Testability Patterns*
Humble Transaction Controller	697	Variation	Humble Object	Chapter 26, *Design-for-Testability Patterns*
Immutable Shared Fixture	323	Variation	Shared Fixture	Chapter 18, *Test Strategy Patterns*
Implicit Setup	424		Implicit Setup	Chapter 20, *Fixture Setup Patterns*
Implicit Teardown	516		Implicit Teardown	Chapter 22, *Fixture Teardown Patterns*
Imposter	522	Alias	Test Double	Chapter 23, *Test Double Patterns*
In-Database Stored Procedure Test	655	Variation	Stored Procedure Test	Chapter 25, *Database Patterns*
In-Memory Database	553	Variation	Fake Object	Chapter 23, *Test Double Patterns*
Incremental Tabular Test	609	Variation	Parameterized Test	Chapter 24, *Result Verification Patterns*
Incremental Tests	322	Variation	Shared Fixture	Chapter 18, *Test Strategy Patterns*
Indirect Output Registry	541	Variation	Test Spy	Chapter 23, *Test Double Patterns*

Name	Page	Relationship	Base Name	Chapter
In-line Setup	408		In-line Setup	Chapter 20, *Fixture Setup Patterns*
In-line Teardown	509		In-line Teardown	Chapter 22, *Fixture Teardown Patterns*
Inner Test Double	570	Variation	Hard-Coded Test Double	Chapter 23, *Test Double Patterns*
Interaction Testing	468	Alias	Behavior Verification	Chapter 21, *Result Verification Patterns*
Layer Test	337		Layer Test	Chapter 18, *Test Strategy Patterns*
Layer-Crossing Test	327	Alias	Back Door Manipulation	Chapter 18, *Test Strategy Patterns*
Layered Test	337	Alias	Layer Test	Chapter 18, *Test Strategy Patterns*
Lazy Setup	435		Lazy Setup	Chapter 20, *Fixture Setup Patterns*
Lazy Teardown	663	Variation	Table Truncation Teardown	Chapter 25, *Database Patterns*
Leftover Fixture	317	Alias	Shared Fixture	Chapter 18, *Test Strategy Patterns*
Literal Value	714		Literal Value	Chapter 27, *Value Patterns*
Loop-Driven Test	610	Variation	Parameterized Test	Chapter 24, *Result Verification Patterns*
Minimal Fixture	302		Minimal Fixture	Chapter 18, *Test Strategy Patterns*
Minimal Context	302	Alias	Minimal Fixture	Chapter 18, *Test Strategy Patterns*
Mock Object	544		Mock Object	Chapter 23, *Test Double Patterns*
Naive In-line Teardown	511	Variation	In-line Teardown	Chapter 22, *Fixture Teardown Patterns*
Naive xUnit Test Interpreter	292	Variation	Data-Driven Test	Chapter 18, *Test Strategy Patterns*
Named State Reaching Method	417	Variation	Creation Method	Chapter 20, *Fixture Setup Patterns*

Patterns, Aliases, and Variations

Continued...

Name	Page	Relationship	Base Name	Chapter
Named Test Suite	592		Named Test Suite	Chapter 24, *Test Organization Patterns*
Object Attribute Equality Assertion	476	Variation	Custom Assertion	Chapter 21, *Result Verification Patterns*
Object Factory	686	Alias	Dependency Lookup	Chapter 26, *Design-for-Testability Patterns*
Object Mother	644	Variation	Test Helper	Chapter 24, *Test Organization Patterns*
One Bad Attribute	719	Variation	Derived Value	Chapter 27, *Value Patterns*
Parameter Injection	680	Variation	Dependency Injection	Chapter 26, *Design-for-Testability Patterns*
Parameterized Anonymous Creation Method	417	Variation	Creation Method	Chapter 20, *Fixture Setup Patterns*
Parameterized Creation Method	417	Variation	Creation Method	Chapter 20, *Fixture Setup Patterns*
Parameterized Setup Decorator	449	Variation	Setup Decorator	Chapter 20, *Fixture Setup Patterns*
Parameterized Test	607		Parameterized Test	Chapter 21, *Result Verification Patterns*
Per-Run Fixture	323	Variation	Shared Fixture	Chapter 18, *Test Strategy Patterns*
Persistence Layer Test	339	Variation	Layer Test	Chapter 18, *Test Strategy Patterns*
Persistent Fresh Fixture	314	Variation	Fresh Fixture	Chapter 18, *Test Strategy Patterns*
Placeholder	728	Alias	Dummy Object	Chapter 27, *Value Patterns*
Poor Man's Humble Object	699	Variation	Humble Object	Chapter 26, *Design-for-Testability Patterns*

Patterns, Aliases, and Variations

Name	Page	Relationship	Base Name	Chapter
Prebuilt Context	429	Alias	Prebuilt Fixture	Chapter 20, *Fixture Setup Patterns*
Prebuilt Fixture	429		Prebuilt Fixture	Chapter 20, *Fixture Setup Patterns*
Presentation Layer Test	338	Variation	Layer Test	Chapter 18, *Test Strategy Patterns*
Private Fixture	311	Alias	Fresh Fixture	Chapter 18, *Test Strategy Patterns*
Procedural Behavior Verification	470	Variation	Behavior Verification	Chapter 21, *Result Verification Patterns*
Procedural State Verification	463	Variation	State Verification	Chapter 21, *Result Verification Patterns*
Procedural Test Stub	526	Variation	Test Stub	Chapter 23, *Test Double Patterns*
Programmatic Test	285	Alias	Scripted Test	Chapter 18, *Test Strategy Patterns*
Pseudo-Object	571	Variation	Hard-Coded Test Double	Chapter 23, *Test Double Patterns*
Pushdown Decorator	450	Variation	Setup Decorator	Chapter 20, *Fixture Setup Patterns*
Random Generated Value	724	Variation	Generated Value	Chapter 27, *Value Patterns*
Record and Playback Test	278	Alias	Recorded Test	Chapter 18, *Test Strategy Patterns*
Recorded Test	278		Recorded Test	Chapter 18, *Test Strategy Patterns*
Refactored Recorded Test	280	Variation	Recorded Test	Chapter 18, *Test Strategy Patterns*
Related Generated Value	725	Variation	Generated Value	Chapter 27, *Value Patterns*
Remoted Stored Procedure Test	656	Variation	Stored Procedure Test	Chapter 25, *Database Patterns*
Responder	530	Variation	Test Stub	Chapter 23, *Test Double Patterns*
Retrieval Interface	540	Variation	Test Spy	Chapter 23, *Test Double Patterns*

Patterns, Aliases, and Variations

Continued...

Name	Page	Relationship	Base Name	Chapter
Reuse Test for Fixture Setup	418	Variation	Creation Method	Chapter 20, *Fixture Setup Patterns*
Reused Fixture	317	Alias	Shared Fixture	Chapter 18, *Test Strategy Patterns*
Robot User Test	278	Alias	Recorded Test	Chapter 18, *Test Strategy Patterns*
Robot User Test Framework	299	Variation	Test Automation Framework	Chapter 18, *Test Strategy Patterns*
Row Test	609	Alias	Parameterized Test	Chapter 24, *Test Organization Patterns*
SUT API Encapsulation	601	Alias	Test Utility Method	Chapter 24, *Test Organization Patterns*
SUT Encapsulation Method	601	Variation	Test Utility Method	Chapter 24, *Test Organization Patterns*
Saboteur	530	Variation	Test Stub	Chapter 23, *Test Double Patterns*
Scripted Test	285		Scripted Test	Chapter 18, *Test Strategy Patterns*
Self Shunt	540	Variation	Hard-Coded Test Double	Chapter 23, *Test Double Patterns*
Self-Describing Value	715	Variation	Literal Value	Chapter 27, *Value Patterns*
Service Layer Test	339	Variation	Layer Test	Chapter 18, *Test Strategy Patterns*
Service Locator	686	Alias	Dependency Lookup	Chapter 26, *Design-for-Testability Patterns*
Setter Injection	681	Variation	Dependency Injection	Chapter 26, *Design-for-Testability Patterns*
Setup Decorator	447		Setup Decorator	Chapter 20, *Fixture Setup Patterns*
Shared Context	317	Alias	Shared Fixture	Chapter 18, *Test Strategy Patterns*
Shared Fixture	317		Shared Fixture	Chapter 18, *Test Strategy Patterns*

Name	Page	Relationship	Base Name	Chapter
Shared Fixture State Assertion	491	Variation	Guard Assertion	Chapter 21, *Result Verification Patterns*
Shared Setup Method	424	Alias	Implicit Setup	Chapter 20, *Fixture Setup Patterns*
Simple Success Test	349	Variation	Test Method	Chapter 19, *xUnit Basics Patterns*
Single-Layer Test	337	Alias	Layer Test	Chapter 18, *Test Strategy Patterns*
Single-Outcome Assertion	366	Variation	Assertion Method	Chapter 19, *xUnit Basics Patterns*
Single Test Suite	593	Variation	Named Test Suite	Chapter 24, *Test Organization Patterns*
Slow Tests	318	Variation	Shared Fixture	Chapter 18, *Test Strategy Patterns*
Spy	538	Alias	Test Spy	Chapter 23, *Test Double Patterns*
Stale Fixture	317	Alias	Shared Fixture	Chapter 18, *Test Strategy Patterns*
Standard Context	305	Alias	Standard Fixture	Chapter 18, *Test Strategy Patterns*
Standard Fixture	305		Standard Fixture	Chapter 18, *Test Strategy Patterns*
State-Exposing Subclass	580	Variation	Test-Specific Subclass	Chapter 23, *Test Double Patterns*
State Verification	462		State Verification	Chapter 21, *Result Verification Patterns*
State-Based Testing	462	Alias	State Verification	Chapter 21, *Result Verification Patterns*
Stated Outcome Assertion	366	Variation	Assertion Method	Chapter 19, *xUnit Basics Patterns*
Statically Generated Test Double	561	Variation	Configurable Test Double	Chapter 23, *Test Double Patterns*
Stored Procedure Test	654		Stored Procedure Test	Chapter 25, *Database Patterns*
Stub	529	Alias	Test Stub	Chapter 23, *Test Double Patterns*

Continued...

Name	Page	Relationship	Base Name	Chapter
Stub	728	Alias	Dummy Object	Chapter 27, *Value Patterns*
Subclassed Humble Object	700	Variation	Humble Object	Chapter 26, *Design-for-Testability Patterns*
Subclassed Singleton	581	Alias	Test-Specific Subclass	Chapter 23, *Test Double Patterns*
Subclassed Test Double	581	Alias	Test-Specific Subclass	Chapter 23, *Test Double Patterns*
Subcutaneous Test	340	Variation	Layer Test	Chapter 18, *Test Strategy Patterns*
Subset Suite	593	Variation	Named Test Suite	Chapter 24, *Test Organization Patterns*
Substitutable Singleton	581	Alias	Test-Specific Subclass	Chapter 23, *Test Double Patterns*
Substituted Singleton	581	Variation	Test-Specific Subclass	Chapter 23, *Test Double Patterns*
Suite of Suites	388	Variation	Test Suite Object	Chapter 19, *xUnit Basics Patterns*
Suite Fixture Setup	441		Suite Fixture Setup	Chapter 20, *Fixture Setup Patterns*
Symbolic Constant	715	Variation	Literal Value	Chapter 27, *Value Patterns*
Table Truncation Teardown	661		Table Truncation Teardown	Chapter 25, *Database Patterns*
Tabular Test	609	Variation	Parameterized Test	Chapter 24, *Test Organization Patterns*
Teardown Guard Clause	511	Variation	In-line Teardown	Chapter 22, *Fixture Teardown Patterns*
Temporary Test Stub	530	Variation	Test Stub	Chapter 23, *Test Double Patterns*
Test Automation Framework	298		Test Automation Framework	Chapter 18, *Test Strategy Patterns*
Test Bed	429	Alias	Prebuilt Fixture	Chapter 20, *Fixture Setup Patterns*

Name	Page	Relationship	Base Name	Chapter
Test Discovery	393		Test Discovery	Chapter 19, *xUnit Basics Patterns*
Test Double	522		Test Double	Chapter 23, *Test Double Patterns*
Test Double Class	569	Variation	Hard-Coded Test Double	Chapter 23, *Test Double Patterns*
Test Double Subclass	580	Variation	Test-Specific Subclass	Chapter 23, *Test Double Patterns*
Test Double as Back Door	332	Variation	Back Door Manipulation	Chapter 18, *Test Strategy Patterns*
Test Enumeration	399		Test Enumeration	Chapter 19, *xUnit Basics Patterns*
Test Fixture	373	Alias	Testcase Class	Chapter 19, *xUnit Basics Patterns*
Test Fixture Registry	644	Variation	Test Helper	Chapter 24, *Test Organization Patterns*
Test Helper	643		Test Helper	Chapter 24, *Test Organization Patterns*
Test Helper Class	645	Variation	Test Helper	Chapter 24, *Test Organization Patterns*
Test Helper Mixin	639	Variation	Testcase Superclass	Chapter 24, *Test Organization Patterns*
Test Helper Object	645	Variation	Test Helper	Chapter 24, *Test Organization Patterns*
Test Hook	709		Test Hook	Chapter 26, *Design-for-Testability Patterns*
Test Method	348		Test Method	Chapter 19, *xUnit Basics Patterns*
Test Method Discovery	394	Variation	Test Discovery	Chapter 19, *xUnit Basics Patterns*
Test Method Enumeration	401	Variation	Test Enumeration	Chapter 19, *xUnit Basics Patterns*

Continued...

Name	Page	Relationship	Base Name	Chapter
Test Method Selection	404	Variation	Test Selection	Chapter 19, *xUnit Basics Patterns*
Test Object Registry	503	Alias	Automated Teardown	Chapter 22, *Fixture Teardown Patterns*
Test Runner	377		Test Runner	Chapter 19, *xUnit Basics Patterns*
Test Selection	403		Test Selection	Chapter 19, *xUnit Basics Patterns*
Test Spy	538		Test Spy	Chapter 23, *Test Double Patterns*
Test Spy	568	Alias	Hard-Coded Test Double	Chapter 23, *Test Double Patterns*
Test Stub	529		Test Stub	Chapter 23, *Test Double Patterns*
Test Suite Enumeration	400	Variation	Test Enumeration	Chapter 19, *xUnit Basics Patterns*
Test Suite Factory	399	Alias	Test Enumeration	Chapter 19, *xUnit Basics Patterns*
Test Suite Object	387		Test Suite Object	Chapter 19, *xUnit Basics Patterns*
Test Suite Object Generator	293	Variation	Data-Driven Test	Chapter 18, *Test Strategy Patterns*
Test Suite Object Simulator	293	Variation	Data-Driven Test	Chapter 18, *Test Strategy Patterns*
Test Suite Procedure	388	Variation	Test Suite Object	Chapter 19, *xUnit Basics Patterns*
Test Tree Explorer	380	Variation	Test Runner	Chapter 19, *xUnit Basics Patterns*
Test Utility Method	599		Test Utility Method	Chapter 24, *Test Organization Patterns*
Test Utility Test	603	Variation	Test Utility Method	Chapter 24, *Test Organization Patterns*
Test-Specific Extension	579	Alias	Test-Specific Subclass	Chapter 23, *Test Double Patterns*
Test-Specific Subclass	579		Test-Specific Subclass	Chapter 23, *Test Double Patterns*

Name	Page	Relationship	Base Name	Chapter
Testcase Class	373		Testcase Class	Chapter 19, *xUnit Basics Patterns*
Testcase Class Discovery	394	Variation	Test Discovery	Chapter 19, *xUnit Basics Patterns*
Testcase Class per Method	625	Variation	Testcase Class per Feature	Chapter 24, *Test Organization Patterns*
Testcase Class per User Story	625	Variation	Testcase Class per Feature	Chapter 24, *Test Organization Patterns*
Testcase Class Selection	404	Variation	Test Selection	Chapter 19, *xUnit Basics Patterns*
Testcase Class Suite	388	Variation	Test Suite Object	Chapter 19, *xUnit Basics Patterns*
Testcase Class per Class	617		Testcase Class per Class	Chapter 24, *Test Organization Patterns*
Testcase Class per Feature	624		Testcase Class per Feature	Chapter 24, *Test Organization Patterns*
Testcase Class per Fixture	631		Testcase Class per Fixture	Chapter 24, *Test Organization Patterns*
Testcase Object	382		Testcase Object	Chapter 19, *xUnit Basics Patterns*
Testcase Superclass	638		Testcase Superclass	Chapter 24, *Test Organization Patterns*
Testing by Layers	337	Alias	Layer Test	Chapter 18, *Test Strategy Patterns*
The xUnit Family	300	Variation	Test Automation Framework	Chapter 18, *Test Strategy Patterns*
Transaction Rollback Teardown	668		Transaction Rollback Teardown	Chapter 25, *Database Patterns*
Transient Fresh Fixture	314	Variation	Fresh Fixture	Chapter 18, *Test Strategy Patterns*

Patterns, Aliases, and Variations

Continued...

Name	Page	Relationship	Base Name	Chapter
True Humble Object	699	Variation	Humble Object	Chapter 26, *Design-for-Testability Patterns*
Unfinished Test Assertion	494		Unfinished Test Assertion	Chapter 21, *Result Verification Patterns*
Verification Method	477	Variation	Custom Assertion	Chapter 21, *Result Verification Patterns*

Patterns,
Aliases, and
Variations

Glossary

This glossary contains the author's definitions of the terms used throughout this book.

acceptance test

A **customer test** that the customer of the software plans to run to help the customer decide whether he or she will accept the software system. Acceptance tests are usually run manually after all automated **customer tests** have passed. They exercise all layers of the system—from the user interface back to the database—and should include any integration with other systems on which the application depends.

Also known as:
user acceptance test (UAT)

accessor

A method that provides access to an **instance variable** of an object either by returning its value or by providing a way to set its value.

ACID

The four qualities of transactions that modern databases ensure:

- Atomic: A transaction is all or nothing.

- Consistent: All operations within a transaction see the same view of the world.

- Independent: Transactions are independent of one another (no cross-transaction leakage of changes).

- Durable: Once committed, the changes made within a transaction are permanent (they don't just vanish for no reason!).

agile method

A method of executing projects (typically, but not always, restricted to software) that reduces the cost of change and allows customers of the software to have more control over how much they spend and what they get for their money. Agile methods include **eXtreme Programming**, SCRUM, Feature-Driven Development (FDD), and Dynamic Systems Development Method (DSDM), among many others. A core practice of most agile methods is the use of automated **unit tests**.

annotation

A way of indicating something about something. **JUnit** version 4.0 uses annotations to indicate which classes are *Testcase Classes* and which methods are *Test Methods*; **NUnit** uses .NET attributes for this purpose.

anonymous inner class

An **inner class** in Java that is defined without a unique name. Anonymous inner classes are often used when defining *Hard-Coded Test Doubles*.

anti-pattern

A pattern that shouldn't be used because it is known to produce less than optimal results. **Code smells**, or their underlying causes, are a kind of anti-pattern.

application programming interface (API)

The means by which other software can invoke some piece of functionality. In object-oriented software, an API consists of the classes and their publicly accessible methods. In procedural software, it consists of the module or package name plus the publicly accessible procedures.

aspect-oriented programming

An advanced software modularization technique that allows improved separation of concerns by "weaving" cross-cutting concerns into code after the affected software has been built but before it is executed.

assertion

A statement that something should be true. In **xUnit**-style *Test Automation Frameworks*, an assertion takes the form of an *Assertion Method* that fails when the actual outcome passed to it does not match the expected outcome.

asynchronous test

A test that runs in a separate thread of control from the **system under test (SUT)** and interacts with it using asynchronous (i.e., "real") messages. An asynchronous test must coordinate its steps with those of the **SUT** because this interaction is not managed automatically by the runtime system. An asynchronous test may have to include delays to give the **SUT** enough time to finish execution before inspecting the outcome. Contrast this with a **synchronous test,** which interacts with the SUT via simple method calls.

attribute

A characteristic of something. The members of the xUnit family for the .NET languages use class and method attributes to indicate which classes are *Testcase Classes* and which methods are *Test Methods*. The term attribute is also a synonym for "**instance variable**" in some circles.

back door

An alternative interface to a **system under test (SUT)** that test software can use to inject **indirect inputs** into the SUT. A database is a common example of a back door, but it could also be any component that can be either manipulated to return test-specific values or replaced by a *Test Double*. Contrast this with the **front door:** the **application programming interface (API).**

BDUF

"Big design up front" is the classic "waterfall" approach to software design. In BDUF, all requirements must be understood early in the project, and the software is designed to support those requirements in a single design "phase." Contrast this with the **emergent design** favored by agile projects.

behavior-driven development

A variation on the **test-driven development** process wherein the focus of the tests is to clearly describe the expected behavior of the **system under test (SUT).** The emphasis is on *Tests as Documentation* rather than merely using tests for verification.

Behavior-driven development can be done using traditional members of the **xUnit** family. New "members" of the family, however, have been built specifically to emphasize the change in focus. They include changes in terminology (e.g., "test" becomes "spec"; "fixture" becomes "context") and more explicit framework support for clarity of the specification.

behavior smell

A test smell we encounter while compiling or running tests. We don't have to be particularly observant to notice behavior smells, as they will present themselves to us via compile errors or test failures. See also: **code smell**, **project smell**.

black box

A piece of software that we treat as an opaque object whose internal workings cannot be seen. Tests written for the black box can verify only externally visible behavior and are independent of the implementation inside the **system under test (SUT)**.

block

A block of code that can be run. Many programming languages (most notably, Smalltalk and Ruby) use blocks (also known as **"block closures"**) as a way of passing a chunk of code to a method, which can then run the code in its own context. Java's anonymous inner classes are a way to achieve the same thing without direct support for blocks. C# uses delegates for the same purpose.

block closure

See **block**.

boundary value

An input value for a **system under test (SUT)** that is immediately adjacent to the boundary between two **equivalence classes**. Tests using two adjacent boundary values help us verify that the behavior changes with exactly the right input and that we don't have "off by one" problems.

built-in self-test

A means of organizing test code in which the tests live inside the same module or class as the **production code** and are run automatically when the system is initialized.

business logic

The core logic related to the **domain model** of a business system. Because business logic usually reflects the results of many independent business decisions, it often seems anything *but* logical!

class attribute

An **attribute** that is placed on a class in the source code to tell the compiler or runtime system that this class is "special." In some variants of **xUnit**, class attributes are used to indicate that a class is a *Testcase Class*.

class method

A method that is associated with a class rather than an object. Class methods can be invoked using a classname.methodname notation [e.g., Assert.assertEquals(message, expected, actual);] and do not require an instance of the class to be invoked. Class methods cannot access **instance methods** or **instance variables** of objects; that is, they do not have access to self or this. In Java, a class method is called a **static method**. Other languages may use different names or keywords.

class variable

A variable that is associated with a class rather than an instance of the class and is typically used to access information that all instances need to share. In some languages, class variables can be accessed using the syntax classname.variablename (e.g., TestHelper.lineFeedCharacter;). That is, they do not need to be accessed via self or this. In Java, a class variable is called a **static variable**. Other languages may use different names or keywords.

closure

See **block**.

code smell

The "classic" bad smell, as first described by Martin Fowler in [Ref]. Test automaters must recognize code smells that arise as they maintain test code. Code smells typically affect maintenance cost of tests but may also be early warning signs of behavior smells to follow.

See also: **test smell**, **behavior smell**, **project smell**.

component

A larger part of the overall system that is often separately deployable. Component-based development involves decomposing the overall functionality into a series of individual components that can be built and deployed separately. This allows sharing of the components between applications that need the same functionality. Each component is a consequence of one or more design decisions, although its behavior may also be traced back to some aspect of the requirements.

Components can take many forms, depending on the technology being employed. The Windows platform uses dynamic linked libraries (DLLs) or assemblies as components. The Java platform uses Java Archives (JARs). A service-oriented architecture (SOA) uses Web Services as its large-grained *components*. The *components* may implement front-end logic (e.g., a "File Open Dialog") or back-end logic (e.g., a "Customer Persistence" *component*). A *component* can and should be verified using **component tests** before the overall application is tested using **customer tests**.

component test

A **test** that verifies the behavior of some **component** of the overall system. The **component** is a consequence of one or more design decisions, although its behavior may also be traced back to some aspect of the requirements. There is no need for component tests to be readable, recognizable, or verifiable by the customer or business domain expert. Contrast this with a **customer test,** which is derived almost entirely from the requirements and should be verifiable by the customer, and with a **unit test,** which verifies a much smaller component. A component test lies somewhere in between these two extremes.

During **test-driven development**, component tests are written after the **customer tests** are written and the overall design is solidified. They are written *as* the architectural decisions are made but before the individual units are designed or coded. They are usually automated using a member of the **xUnit** family.

constructor

A special method used in some object-oriented programming languages to construct a brand-new object. It often has the same name as the class and is typically called automatically by the runtime system whenever the special operation new is invoked. A Complete Constructor Method [SBPP] returns a ready-to-use object that requires no additional tweaking; this usually implies arguments must be passed to the constructor.

continuous integration

The agile software development practice of integrating software changes continuously. In practice, developers typically integrate their changes every few hours to days. Continuous integration often includes the practice of an automated build that is triggered by each check-in. The build process typically runs all automated tests and may even run tests that aren't run before check-in because they take too long. The build is considered to have "failed" if any tests fail. When the build fails, teams typically consider getting the build working again to be the top priority; only code changes aimed at fixing the build are allowed until a successful build has occurred.

control point

How the test asks the **system under test (SUT)** to do something for it. A control point could be created for the purpose of setting up or tearing down the fixture or it could be used during the **exercise SUT** phase of the test. It is a kind of **interaction point**. Some control points are provided strictly for testing purposes; they should not be used by the **production code** because they bypass input validation or short-circuit the normal life cycle of the **SUT** or some object on which it depends.

customer test

A **test** that verifies the behavior of a slice of the visible functionality of the overall system. The **system under test (SUT)** may consist of the entire system or a fully functional top-to-bottom slice ("module") of the system. A customer test should be independent of the design decisions made while building the **SUT**. That is, we should require the same set of customer tests regardless of how we choose to build the **SUT**. (Of course, how the customer tests interact with the **SUT** may be affected by high-level software architecture decisions.)

data access layer

A way of keeping data access logic from permeating the application code by putting it into a separate component that encapsulates the database.

Also known as: *data access object (DAO), data abstraction layer (DAL)*

depended-on component (DOC)

An individual class or a large-grained component on which the **system under test (SUT)** depends. The dependency is usually one of delegation via method calls. In test automation, the DOC is primarily of interest in that we need to be able to observe and control its interactions with the **SUT** to get complete test coverage.

design pattern

A **pattern** that we can use to solve a particular software design problem. Most design patterns are programming language independent; the language-specific ones are typically called "coding idioms." Design patterns were first popularized by the book *Design Patterns* [GOF].

design for testability

Also known as:
DfT

A way of ensuring that code is easily tested by making sure that testing requirements are considered as the code is designed. When doing **test-driven development,** design for testability occurs as a natural side effect of development

developer test

Another name for an automated **unit test** that is prepared by someone playing the developer role on an **eXtreme Programming** project.

DfT

See **design for testability**.

direct input

A test may interact with the **system under test (SUT)** directly via its "front door" or public application programming interface (API) or indirectly via its "back door." The stimuli injected by the test into the **SUT** via its front door are direct inputs of the **SUT**. Direct inputs may consist of method or function calls to another component or messages sent on a message channel (e.g., MQ or JMS) and the arguments or contents thereof.

direct output

A test may interact with the **system under test (SUT)** directly via its "front door" or public application programming interface (API) or indirectly via its "back door." The responses received by the test from the **SUT** via its front door are direct outputs of the **SUT**. Direct outputs may consist of the return values of method or function calls, updated arguments passed by reference, exceptions raised by the SUT, or messages received on a message channel (e.g., MQ or JMS) from the SUT.

document-driven development

A development process that focuses on producing documents that describe how the code will be structured and then coding from those documents. Document-driven development is normally associated with "big design up front" (BDUF, also known as "waterfall") software development. Contrast this with **test-driven development,** which focuses on producing working code one test at a time.

domain layer

The layer of a Layered Architecture [DDD, PEAA, WWW] that corresponds to the **domain model**. See Eric Evans' book, *Domain-Driven Design* [DDD].

domain model

A model of the problem domain that may form the basis of the object model in the business domain layer of a software application. See Eric Evans' book, *Domain-Driven Design* [DDD].

DTO

Short for the Data Transfer Object [CJ2EEP] design pattern.

dynamic binding

Deferring the decision about which piece of software to transfer control to until execution time. The same method name can be used to invoke different behavior (method bodies) based on the class of the object on which it is invoked; the latter class is determined only at execution time. Dynamic binding is the opposite of **static binding**; it is also called **polymorphism** (from the Latin, meaning "taking on many shapes").

EDD

See **example-driven development.**

emergent design

The opposite of **BDUF** (big design up front). Emergent design involves letting the right design be discovered as the software slowly evolves to pass one test at a time during **test-driven development**.

endoscopic testing

A testing technique pioneered by the authors of the original Mock Object paper [ET], which involves testing software from the inside.

entity object

Also known as:
domain object

An object that represents an entity concept from a domain. Entity objects typically have a life cycle that is represented as their state. Contrast this with a **service object,** which has no single state. EJB Entity Beans are one example of an entity object.

equivalence class

A **test condition** identification technique that reduces the number of tests required by grouping together inputs that should result in the same output or that should exercise the same logic in the system. This organization allows us to focus our tests on key **boundary values** at which the expected output changes.

example-driven development (EDD)

A reframing of the **test-driven development** process to focus on the "executable specification" aspect of the tests. The act of providing examples is more intuitive to many people; it doesn't carry the baggage of "testing" software that doesn't yet exist.

exercise SUT

After the **fixture setup** phase of testing, the test stimulates the **system under test (SUT)** logic that is to be tested. This phase of the testing process is called exercise SUT.

expectation

What a test expects the **system under test (SUT)** to have done. When we are using *Mock Objects* to verify the **indirect outputs** of the **SUT**, we load each *Mock Object* with the expected method calls (including the expected arguments); these are called the expectations.

expected outcome

The outcome that we verify after exercising the **system under test (SUT)**. A *Self-Checking Test* verifies the expected outcome using calls to *Assertion Methods*.

exploratory testing

Interactive testing of an application without a specific script in hand. The tester "explores" the system, making up theories about how it should behave based on what the application has already done and then testing those theories to see if they hold up. While there is no rigid plan, exploratory testing is a disciplined activity that is more likely to find real bugs than rigidly scripted tests.

eXtreme Programming

An agile software development methodology that showcases pair programming, automated unit testing, and short iterations.

factory

A method, object, or class that exists to build other objects.

false negative

A situation in which a test passes even though the **system under test (SUT)** is *not* working properly. Such a test is said to give a false-negative indication or a "false pass."
See also: **false positive**.

false positive

A situation in which a test fails even though the **system under test (SUT)** is working properly. Such a test is said to give a false-positive indication or a "false failure." The terminology comes from statistical science and relates to our attempt to calculate the probability of some observation error occurring. For example, in medicine we run tests to find out if a medical condition is present; if it is, the test is "positive." It is useful to know the probability that a test might indicate that a condition (such as diabetes) is present when it is not—that is, a *false* "positive." If we think of software tests as a way of determining whether a condition (a particular defect or bug) is present, a test that reports a defect (a test failure or error) when it is not, in fact, present is giving us a false positive.

See also: **false negative**. Wikipedia [Wp] has an extensive description under the topic "Type I and type II errors."

fault insertion test

A kind of test in which a deliberate fault is introduced in one part of the system to verify that another part reacts to the error appropriately. Initially, the faults were related to hardware but the same concept is now applied to software faults as well. Replacing a **depended-on component (DOC)** with a *Saboteur* that throws an exception is an example of a software fault insertion test.

feature

A testable unit of functionality that can be built onto the evolving software system. In **eXtreme Programming**, a **user story** corresponds roughly to a feature.

Fit test

A test that uses the **Fit** testing framework; most commonly a **customer test**.

fixture

See **test fixture (disambiguation)**.

fixture (Fit)

In **Fit**, the Adapter [GOF] that interprets the Fit table and invokes methods on the **system under test (SUT)**, thereby implementing a *Data-Driven Test*. For meanings in other contexts, see **test fixture (disambiguation)**, **test fixture (in xUnit)**, and **test fixture (in NUnit)**.

fixture holding class variable

A **class variable** of a *Testcase Class* that is used to hold a reference to the **test fixture**. It typically holds a reference to a *Shared Fixture*.

fixture holding instance variable

An **instance variable** of a *Testcase Object* that is used to hold a reference to the **test fixture**. It typically holds a reference to a *Fresh Fixture* that is set up using *Implicit Setup*.

fixture holding local variable

A **local variable** of a *Test Method* that is used to hold a reference to the **test fixture**. It typically holds a reference to a *Fresh Fixture* that is set up within the test method using *In-line Setup* or returned from *Delegated Setup*.

fixture setup

Before the desired logic of the **system under test (SUT)** can be exercised, the preconditions of the test need to be set up. Collectively, all objects (and their states) are called the **test fixture** (or **test context**), and the phase of the test that sets up the test fixture is called fixture setup.

fixture teardown

After a test is run, the **test fixture** that was built by the test should be destroyed. This phase of the test is called fixture teardown.

fluent interface

A style of object constructor **API** that results in easy-to-understand statements. The *Configuration Interface* provided by the *Mock Object* toolkit **JMock** is an example of a fluent interface.

front door

The public application programming interface (API) of a piece of software. Contrast this with the **back door**.

function pointer

From Wikipedia [Wp]: "A function pointer is a type of pointer in C, C++, D, and other C-like programming languages. When dereferenced, a function pointer invokes a function, passing it zero or more arguments like a normal function."

functional test (common usage)

A **black-box** test of the end-user functionality of an application. The agile community is trying to avoid this usage of "functional test" because of the potential for confusion when talking about verifying functional (as opposed to nonfunctional or extra-functional properties) properties of a **unit** or **component**. This book uses the terms "**customer test**" and "**acceptance test**" for a functional test of the entire application and "**unit test**" for a functional test of an individual unit of the application.

functional test (contrast with extra-functional test)

A **test** that verifies the functionality implemented by a piece of software. Depending on the scope of the software, a functional test may be a **customer test,** a **unit test,** or a **component test.**

In some circles a functional *test* is a **customer test.** This usage becomes confusing, however, when we talk about testing nonfunctional or extra-functional properties of the **system under test (SUT).** This book uses the terms "**customer test**" and "**acceptance test**" for a functional *test* of the entire application and "**unit test**" for a functional *test* of an individual unit of the application.

garbage collection

A mechanism that automatically recovers the memory used by any objects that are no longer accessible. Many modern object-oriented programming environments provide garbage collection.

global variable

A variable that is global to a whole program. A global variable is accessible from anywhere within the program and never goes out of scope, although the memory to which it refers can be deallocated explicitly.

green bar

Many *Graphical Test Runners* portray the progress of the **test run** using a progress bar. As long as all tests have passed, the bar stays green. When any tests fail, the indicator changes to a **red bar.**

GUI

Graphical user interface.

happy path

The "normal" path of execution through a use case or through the software that implements it; also known as the "sunny day" scenario. Nothing goes wrong, nothing out of the ordinary happens, and we swiftly and directly achieve the user's or caller's goal.

Hollywood principle

What directors in Hollywood tell aspiring actors at mass-casting calls: "Don't call us; we'll call you (if we want you)." In software, this concept is often called **inversion of control (IOC)**.

IDE

Integrated development environment. An environment that provides tools to edit, compile, execute, and (typically) test code within a single development tool.

incremental delivery

A method of building and deploying a software system in stages and releasing the software as each stage, called an "increment," is completed. This approach results in earlier delivery to the user of a working system, where the capabilities of the system increase over time. In **agile methods,** the increment of functionality is the **feature** or **user story**. Incremental delivery goes beyond **iterative development** and **incremental development, however,** by actually putting the functionality into **production** on a regular basis. This idea is summarized by the following mantra: "Deliver early, deliver often."

incremental development

A method of building a software system in stages such that the functionality built to date can be tested before the next stage is started. This approach allows for the earlier delivery to the user of a working system, where the capabilities of the system increase over time (see **incremental delivery**). In **agile methods,** the increment of functionality is the **feature** or **user story**. *Incremental* development goes beyond *iterative* **development,** however, in that it promises to produce working, testable, and *potentially* deployable software with every iteration. With *incremental* **delivery**, we also promise to "Deliver early, deliver often."

indirect input

When the behavior of the **system under test (SUT)** is affected by the values returned by another component whose services it uses, we call those values the indirect inputs of the **SUT**. Indirect inputs may consist of actual return values of functions, updated (out) parameters of procedures or subroutines, and any errors or exceptions raised by the **depended-on component (DOC)**. Testing of the **SUT** behavior with indirect inputs requires the appropriate **control point** on the "back side" of the **SUT**. We often use a *Test Stub* to inject the indirect inputs into the **SUT**.

indirect output

Also known as:
outgoing interface

When the behavior of the **system under test (SUT)** includes actions that cannot be observed through the public application programming interface (API) of the **SUT** but that are seen or experienced by other systems or application components, we call those actions the indirect outputs of the **SUT**. Indirect outputs may consist of method or function calls to another component, messages sent on a message channel (e.g., MQ or JMS), and records inserted into a database or written to a file. Verification of the indirect output behaviors of the **SUT** requires the use of appropriate **observation points** on the "back side" of the **SUT**. *Mock Objects* are often used to implement the **observation point** by intercepting the indirect outputs of the **SUT** and comparing them to the expected values.

See also: **outgoing interface**.

inner class

A class in Java that is defined inside another class. **Anonymous inner classes** are defined inside a method, whereas inner classes are defined outside a method. Inner classes are often used when defining *Hard-Coded Test Doubles*.

instance method

Also known as:
member variable

A method that is associated with an object rather than the class of the object. An instance method is accessible only from within or via an instance of the class. It is typically used to access information that is expected to differ from one instance to another.

The exact syntax used to access an *instance method* varies from language to language. The most common syntax is objectReference.methodName(). When referenced from within other methods on the object, some languages require an explicit reference to the object (e.g., this.methodName() or self methodName); other languages simply assume that any unqualified references to methods are references to *instance methods*.

instance variable

A variable that is associated with an object rather than the class of object. An instance variable is accessible only from within or via an instance of the class. It is typically used to access information that is expected to differ from one instance to another.

Also known as: member function

interaction point

A point at which a test interacts with the **system under test (SUT)**. An interaction point can be either a **control point** or an **observation point**.

interface

In general, a fully abstract class that defines only the public methods that all implementers of the interface must provide. In Java, an interface is a type definition that does not provide any implementation. In most single-inheritance languages, a class may implement any number of interfaces, even though it can extend (subclass) only one other class.

inversion of control (IOC)

A control paradigm that distinguishes software frameworks from "toolkits" or components. The framework calls the software plug-in (rather than the reverse). In the real world, inversion of control is often called the **Hollywood principle**. With the advent of automated **unit testing**, a class of framework known as an inversion of control framework has sprung up specifically to simplify the replacement of **depended-on components** (DOCs) with *Test Doubles*.

IOC

See **inversion of control**.

iterative development

A method of building a software system using time-boxed "iterations." Each iteration is planned and then executed. At the end of the "time box," the status of all the work is reviewed and the next iteration is planned. The strict time-boxing prevents "runaway development," where the state of the system is never assessed because nothing is ever finished. Unlike *incremental* **development**, *iterative* development does not *require* working software to be delivered at the end of each iteration.

layer-crossing test

A test that either sets up the fixture or verifies the outcome using *Back Door Manipulation,* which involves using a "back door" of the **system under test** (**SUT**) such as a database. Contrast this with a **round-trip test**.

legacy software

In the **test-driven development** community, any software that does not have a *Safety Net of Fully Automated Tests*.

liveware

Also known as:
wetware, mushware

The people who use our software. They are usually assumed to be much more intelligent than either the software or the hardware but they can also be rather unpredictable.

local variable

A variable that is associated with a block of code rather than an object or class. A local variable is accessible only from within the code block; it goes out of scope when the block of code returns to its caller.

manual test

A test that is executed by a person interacting with the **system under test** (**SUT**). The user may be following some sort of "test script" (not to be confused with a *Scripted Test*) or doing ad hoc or exploratory testing.

meta object

An object that holds data that controls the behavior of another object. A meta object protocol is the interface by which the meta object is constructed or configured.

metatest

A **test** that verifies the behavior of one or more tests. Such a test is mostly used during **test-driven development,** when we are writing tests as examples or course material and we want to ensure that tests are, indeed, failing to illustrate a particular problem.

method attribute

An **attribute** that is placed on a method in the source code to tell the compiler or runtime system that this method is "special." In some xUnit family members, method attributes are used to indicate that a method is a *Test Method.*

mixin

Functionality intended to be inherited by another class as part of that class's implementation without implying specialization ("kind of" relationship) of the providing class.

"The term *mixin* comes from an ice cream store in Somerville, Massachusetts, where candies and cakes were mixed into the basic ice cream flavors. This seemed like a good metaphor to some of the object-oriented programmers who used to take a summer break there, especially while working with the object-oriented programming language SCOOPS" (*SAMS Teach Yourself C++ in 21 Days,* 4th ed., p. 458).

module

In legacy programming environments (and probably a few current ones, too): An independently compilable unit of source code (e.g., the "file I/O module") that is later linked into the final executable. Unlike a **component**, this kind of module is typically not independently deployable. It may or may not have a corresponding set of **unit tests** or **component tests.**

When describing the functionality of a software system or application: A complete vertical chunk of the application that provides a particular piece of functionality (e.g., the "Customer Management Module") that can be used somewhat independently of the other *modules*. It would have a corresponding set of **acceptance tests** and may be the unit of **incremental delivery**.

need-driven development

A variation on the **test-driven development** process where code is written from the outside in and all depended-on code is replaced by *Mock Objects* that verify the expected **indirect outputs** of the code being written. This approach ensures that the responsibilities of each software unit are well understood before they are coded, by virtue of having **unit tests** inspired by examples of real usage. The outermost layer of software is written using **storytest-driven development**. It should have examples of usage by real clients (e.g., a user interface driving the Service Facade [CJ2EEP]) in addition to the **customer tests**.

object-relational mapping (ORM)

A middleware component that translates between the object-oriented **domain model** of an application and the table-oriented view presented by a relational database management system.

observation point

The means by which the test observes the behavior of the **system under test** (SUT). This kind of **interaction point** can be used to inspect the post-exercise state of the SUT or to monitor interactions between the SUT and its depended-on components. Some observation points are provided strictly for the tests; they should not be used by the **production code** because they may expose private implementation details of the SUT that cannot be depended on not to change.

ORM

See **object-relational mapping**.

outgoing interface

A component (e.g., a class or a collection of classes) often depends on other components to implement its behavior. The interfaces it uses to access these components are known as outgoing interfaces, and the inputs and outputs transmitted via test interfaces are called **indirect inputs** and **indirect outputs**. Outgoing interfaces may consist of method or function calls to another component, messages sent on a message channel (e.g., MQ or JMS), or records inserted into a database or written to a file. Testing the behavior of the **system under test (SUT)** with outgoing interfaces requires special techniques such as *Mock Objects* to intercept and verify the usage of outgoing interfaces.

pattern

A solution to a recurring problem. A pattern has a context in which it is typically applied and forces that help you choose one pattern over another based on that context. **Design patterns** are a particular kind of pattern. Organizational patterns are not discussed in this book.

pattern language

A collection of patterns that work together to lead the reader from a very high-level problem to a very detailed solution customized for his or her particular context. When a pattern language achieves this goal, it is said to be "generative"; this characteristic differentiates a pattern language from a simple collection of patterns. Refer to "A Pattern Language for Pattern Writing" [APLfPW] to learn more about how to write a pattern language.

polymorphism

Dynamic binding. The word is derived from the Latin, meaning "taking on many shapes."

presentation layer

The part of a Layered Architecture [DDD, PEAA, WWW] that contains the **presentation logic.**

presentation logic

The logic embedded in the **presentation layer** of a business system. It decides which screen to show, which items to put on menus, which items or buttons to enable or disable, and so on.

procedure variable

A variable that refers to a procedure or function rather than a piece of data. It allows the code to be called to be determined at runtime (dynamic binding) rather than at compile time. The actual procedure to be invoked is assigned to

Also known as:
*function pointer,
delegate
(in .NET
languages)*

the variable either during program initialization or during execution. Procedure variables were a precursor to true object-oriented programming languages (OOPLs). Early OOPLs such as C++ were built by using tables (arrays) of data structures containing procedure variables to implement the method (member function) dispatch tables for classes.

production

In IT shops, the environment in which applications being used by real users run. This environment is distinguished from the various testing environments, such as "acceptance," "integration," "development," and "qual" (short for "quality assessment or assurance").

production code

In IT shops, the environment in which applications run is often called **production**. Production code is the code that we are writing for eventual deployment to this environment, whether the code is to be shipped in a product or deployed into "**production**." Compare to "**test code**."

programmer test

A **developer test**.

project smell

A symptom that something has gone wrong on the project. Its underlying root cause is likely to be one or more **code smells** or **behavior smells**. Because project managers rarely run or write tests, project smells are likely the first hint they have that something may be less than perfect in test automation land.

pull

Also known as:
pull system

A concept from lean manufacturing that states that things should be produced only once a real demand for them exists. In a "pull system," upstream (i.e., subcomponent) assembly lines produce only enough products to replace the items withdrawn from the pool that buffers them from the downstream assembly lines. In software development, this idea can be translated as follows: "We should only write methods that have already been called by other software and only handle those cases that the other software actually needs." This approach avoids speculation and the writing of unnecessary software, which is one of software development's key forms of inventory (which is considered waste in lean systems).

red bar

Many *Graphical Test Runners* portray the progress of the **test run** using a progress bar that starts off green in color. When any tests fail, this indicator changes to a red bar.

refactoring

Changing the structure of existing code without changing its behavior. Refactoring is used to improve the design of existing code, often as a first step before adding new functionality. The authoritative source for information on refactoring is Martin Fowler's book [Ref].

reflection

The ability of a software program to examine its own structure as it is executing. Reflection is often used in software development tools to facilitate adding new capabilities.

regression test

A **test** that verifies that the behavior of a **system under test (SUT)** has not changed. Most regression tests are originally written as either **unit tests** or **acceptance tests,** but are subsequently included in the regression test suite to keep that functionality from being accidentally changed.

result verification

After the **exercise SUT** phase of the *Four-Phase Test*, the test verifies that the expected (correct) outcome has actually occurred. This phase of the test is called result verification.

retrospective

A process whereby a team reviews its processes and performance for the purpose of identifying better ways of working. Retrospectives are often conducted at the end of a project (called a project retrospective) to collect data and make recommendations for future projects. They have more impact if they are done

Also known as:
postmortem,
postpartum

regularly *during* a project. Agile projects tend to do retrospectives after at least every release (called a release retrospective) and often after every iteration (called an iteration retrospective.)

root cause analysis

A process wherein the cause of a failure or bug is traced back to all possible contributing factors. A root cause analysis helps us avoid treating symptoms by identifying the true sources of our problems. A number of techniques for doing root cause analysis exist, including Toyota's "five why's" [TPS].

round-trip test

A test that interacts only via the "front door" (public interface) of the **system under test (SUT)**. Compare with **layer-crossing test**.

service object

Also known as:
service component

An object that provides a service to other objects. Service objects typically do not have a life cycle of their own; any state they do contain tends to be an aggregate of the states of the **entity objects** that they vend. The interface of a service object is often defined via a Service Facade [CJ2EEP] class. EJB Session Beans are one example of a service object.

setter

A method provided by an object specifically to set the value of one of its attributes. By convention, it either has the same name as the attribute or its name includes the prefix "set" (e.g., setName).

smell

A symptom of a problem. A smell doesn't necessarily tell us what is wrong, because it may have several possible causes. A smell must pass the "sniffability test"—that is, it must grab us by the nose and say, "Something is wrong here." To figure out exactly what the smell means, we must perform **root cause analysis**.

We classify smells based on where we find them. The most common kinds are (production) **code smells**, **test smells**, and **project smells**. **Test smells** may be either (test) **code smells** or **behavior smells**.

spike

In **agile methods** such as **eXtreme Programming,** a time-boxed experiment used to obtain enough information to estimate the effort required to implement a new kind of functionality.

stateless

An object that does not maintain any state between invocations of its operations. That is, each request is self-contained and does not require that the same server object be used for a series of requests.

static binding

Resolving exactly which piece of software we will transfer control to at compile time. Static binding is the opposite of **dynamic binding.**

static method

In Java, a method that the compiler resolves at compile time (rather than at run-time using dynamic binding). This behavior is the opposite of dynamic (or virtual in C++). A static method is also a **class method** because only class methods can be resolved at compile time in Java. A static method is not necessarily a class method in all languages, however. For example:

```
Assert.assertEquals(message, expected, actual);
```

static variable

In Java, a variable (field) that the compiler resolves at compile time rather than at runtime using **dynamic binding.** A static variable is also a **class variable** because only class variables can be resolved at compile time in Java. Being static (i.e., not dynamic) does not necessarily imply that something is associated with a class (rather than an instance) in all languages.

STDD

See **storytest-driven development.**

story

See **user story.**

storytest

A **customer test** that is the "confirmation" part of the **user story** "trilogy": card, conversation, confirmation [XPC]. When the storytests are written before any software is developed, we call the process **storytest-driven development**.

storytest-driven development (STDD)

A variation of the **test-driven development** process that entails writing (and usually automating) **customer tests** before the development of the corresponding functionality begins. This approach ensures that integration of the various software units verified by the **unit tests** results in a usable whole. The term "storytest-driven development" was first coined by Joshua Kerievsky as part of his methodology "Industrial XP" [IXP].

STTCPW

"The simplest thing that could possibly work." This approach is commonly used on XP projects when someone is over-engineering the software by trying to anticipate future requirements.

substitutable dependency

A software component may depend on any number of other components. If we are to test this component by itself, we must be able to replace the other components with *Test Doubles*—that is, each component must be a substitutable dependency. We can turn something into a substitutable dependency in several ways, including *Dependency Injection, Dependency Lookup,* and *Test-Specific Subclass.*

synchronous test

A test that interacts with the **system under test (SUT)** using normal (synchronous) method calls that return the results that the test will make assertions against. A synchronous test does not need to coordinate its steps with those of the **SUT**; this activity is managed automatically by the runtime system. Contrast this with an **asynchronous test**, which runs in a separate thread of control from the SUT.

system under test (SUT)

Also known as:
AUT, CUT, MUT, OUT

Whatever thing we are testing. The SUT is always defined from the perspective of the test. When we are writing **unit tests,** the SUT is whatever class (also known as CUT), object (also known as OUT), or method (also known as MUT) we are testing; when we are writing **customer tests**, the **SUT** is probably the entire application (also known as AUT) or at least a major subsystem of it. The parts of the application that we are *not* verifying in this particular test may still be involved as a **depended-on component (DOC)**.

task

The unit of work assignment (or volunteering) in **eXtreme Programming**. One or more tasks may be involved in delivering a **user story** (a **feature**).

TDD

See **test-driven development**.

test

A procedure, whether manually executed or automated, that can be used to verify that the **system under test (SUT)** is behaving as expected. Often called a **test case**.

test automater

The person or project role that is responsible for building the **tests**. Sometimes a "subject matter expert" may be responsible for coming up with the **tests** to be automated by the test automater.

test case

Usually a synonym for "**test**." In xUnit, it may also refer to a *Testcase Class,* which is actually a *Test Suite Factory* as well as a place to put a set of related *Test Methods*.

test code

Code written specifically to test other code (either **production** or other test code).

test condition

A particular behavior of the **system under test (SUT)** that we need to verify. It can be described as the following collection of points:

- If the SUT is in some state S1, *and*

- We exercise the SUT in some way X, *then*

- The SUT should respond with R *and*

- The SUT should be in state S2.

test context

Everything a **system under test (SUT)** needs to have in place so that we can exercise the SUT for the purpose of verifying its behavior. For this reason, **RSpec** calls the **test fixture (as used in xUnit)** a "context."

```
Context: a set fruits with
    contents = {apple, orange, pear}
Exercise: remove orange from the fruits set
Verify: fruits set contents = {apple, pear}
```

In this example, the fixture consists of a single set and is created directly in the test. How we choose to construct the fixture has very far-reaching ramifications for all aspects of test writing and maintenance.

test database

A database instance that is used primarily for the execution of tests. It should not be the same database as is used in **production!**

test debt

I first became aware of the concept of various kinds of debts via the Industrial XP mailing list on the Internet. The concept of "debt" is a metaphor for "not doing enough of" something. To get out of debt, we must put extra effort into the something we were not doing enough of. Test debt arises when we do not write all of the necessary tests. As a result, we have "unprotected code" in that the code could break without causing any tests to fail.

test-driven bug fixing

A way of fixing bugs that entails writing and automating **unit tests** that reproduce each bug before we begin debugging the code and fixing the bug; the bug-fixing extension of **test-driven development**.

test-driven development (TDD)

A development process that entails writing and automating **unit tests** before the development of the corresponding units begins. TDD ensures that the responsibilities of each software unit are well understood before they are coded. Unlike **test-first development**, test-driven development is typically meant to imply that the **production code** is made to work one test at a time (a characteristic called **emergent design**).

See also: **storytest-driven development**.

test driver

A person doing **test-driven development**.

test driving

The act of doing **test-driven development**.

test error

When a **test** is run, an error that keeps the test from running to completion. The error may be explicitly raised or thrown by the system under test (**SUT**) or by the test itself, or it may be thrown by the runtime system (e.g., operating system, virtual machine). In general, it is much easier to debug a test error than a **test failure** because the cause of the problem tends to be much more local to where the test error occurs. Compare with **test failure** and **test success**.

test failure

When a **test** is run and the actual outcome does not match the expected outcome. Compare with **test error** and **test success**.

test-first development

A development process that entails writing and automating **unit tests** before the development of the corresponding units begins. Test-first development ensures that the responsibilities of each software unit are well understood before that unit is coded. Unlike **test-driven development**, test-first development merely says that the tests are written before the **production code**; it does not imply that the **production code** is made to work one test at a time (**emergent design**). Test-first development may be applied at the **unit test** or **customer test** level, depending on which tests we have chosen to automate.

test fixture (disambiguation)

In generic **xUnit:** All the things we need to have in place to run a test and expect a particular outcome. The test fixture comprises the pre-conditions of the test; that is, it is the "before" picture of the SUT and its context. See also: **test fixture (in xUnit) and test context.**

In NUnit and VbUnit: The *Testcase Class*. See also: **test fixture (in NUnit).**

In Fit: The adapter that interprets the Fit table and invokes methods on the **system under test (SUT)**, thereby implementing a *Data-Driven Test*.

See also: **fixture (Fit).**

test fixture (in NUnit)

Also known as:
Testcase Class

In **NUnit** (and in **VbUnit** and most .NET implementations of xUnit): The *Testcase Class* on which the *Test Methods* are implemented. We add the attribute [TestFixture] to the class that hosts the *Test Methods*.

Some members of the **xUnit** family assume that an instance of the *Testcase Class* "is a" **test context**; NUnit is a good example. This interpretation assumes we are using the *Testcase Class per Fixture* approach to organizing the tests. When we choose to use a different way of organizing the tests, such as *Testcase Class per Class* or *Testcase Class per Feature*, this merging of the concepts of **test context** and *Testcase Class* can be confusing. This book uses "**test fixture**" to mean "the pre-conditions of the test" (also known as the **test context**) and *Testcase Class* to mean "the class that contains the *Test Methods* and any code needed to set up the **test context**."

test fixture (in xUnit)

Also known as:
test context

In **xUnit:** All the things we need to have in place to run a test and expect a particular outcome (i.e., the **test context**). Some variants of **xUnit** keep the concept of the **test context** separate from the *Testcase Class* that creates it; **JUnit** and its direct ports fall into this camp. Setting up the test fixture is the first phase of the *Four-Phase Test*. For meanings of the term "test fixture" in other contexts, see **test fixture (disambiguation).**

test-last development

A development process that entails executing **unit tests** after the development of the corresponding units is finished. Unlike **test-first development**, test-last development merely says that testing should be done before the code goes into **production**; it does not imply that the tests are automated. Traditional QA (quality assurance) testing is inherently test-last development unless the tests are prepared as part of the requirements phase of the project and are shared with the development team.

test maintainer

The person or project role responsible for maintaining the **tests** as the system or application evolves. Most commonly, this person is enhancing the system with new functionality or fixing bugs. The test maintainer could also be whoever is called in when the automated tests fail for whatever reason. If the test maintainer is doing the enhancements by writing tests first, he or she is also a **test driver**.

test package

In languages that provide packages or namespaces, a package or name that exists for the purpose of hosting *Testcase Classes*.

test reader

Anyone who has reason to read **tests**, including a **test maintainer** or **test driver**. This individual may be reading the tests primarily for the purpose of understanding what the **system under test (SUT)** is supposed to do (*Tests as Documentation*) or as part of a test maintenance or software development activity.

test result

A **test** or **test suite** can be run many times, each time yielding a different test result.

test run

A **test** or **test suite** can be run many times, each time yielding a different **test result**. Some commercial test automation tools record the results of each test run for prosperity.

test smell

A symptom of a problem in **test code**. A smell doesn't necessarily tell us what is wrong because it may have several possible causes. Like all **smells**, a test smell must pass the "sniffability test"—that is, it must grab us by the nose and say, "Something is wrong here."

test-specific equality

Tests and the system under test (SUT) may have different ideas about what constitutes equality of two objects. In fact, this understanding may differ from one test to another. It is *not* advisable to modify the definition of equality within the **SUT** to match the tests' expectations, as this practice leads to *Equality Pollution*. Making individual *Equality Assertions* on many attributes of an object is not the answer either, as it can result in *Obscure Tests* and *Test Code Duplication*. Instead, build one or more *Custom Assertions* that meets your tests' needs.

test stripper

A step or program in the build process that removes all the test code from the compiled and linked executable.

test success

A situation in which a **test** is run and all actual outcomes match the expected outcomes. Compare with **test failure** and **test error**.

test suite

A way to name a collection of **tests** that we want to run together.

Unified Modeling Language (UML)

From Wikipedia [Wp]: "[A] nonproprietary specification language for object modeling. UML is a general-purpose modeling language that includes a standardized graphical notation used to create an abstract model of a system, referred to as a UML model."

unit test

A **test** that verifies the behavior of some small part of the overall system. What turns a test into a unit test is that the **system under test (SUT)** is a very small subset of the overall system and may be unrecognizable to someone who is not involved in building the software. The actual **SUT** may be as small as a single object or method that is a consequence of one or more design decisions, although its behavior may also be traced back to some aspect of the functional requirements. Unit tests need not be readable, recognizable, or verifiable by the customer or business domain expert. Contrast this with a **customer test,** which is derived almost entirely from the requirements and which should be verifiable by the customer. In **eXtreme Programming**, unit tests are also called **developer tests** or **programmer tests.**

use case

A way of describing the functionality of a system in terms of what its users are trying to achieve and what the system needs to do to achieve their goals. Unlike **user stories**, use cases may cover many different scenarios yet are often not testable independently.

user acceptance test (UAT)

See **acceptance test.**

user story

The unit of **incremental development** in eXtreme Programming. We must INVEST in good user stories—that is, each user story must be Independent, Negotiable, Valuable, Estimatable, Small, and Testable [XP123]. A user story corresponds roughly to a **"feature"** in non-**eXtreme Programming** terminology and is typically decomposed into one or more **tasks** to be carried out by project team members.

Also known as: *story, feature*

verify outcome

After the **exercise SUT** phase of the test, the test compares the actual outcome—including returned values, **indirect outputs,** and the post-test state of the **system under test (SUT)**—with the expected outcome. This phase of the test is called the verify outcome phase.

References

[AP]

AntiPatterns: Refactoring Software, Architectures, and Projects in Crisis
Published by: John Wiley (1998)
ISBN: 0-471-19713-0
By: William J. Brown et al.

> This book describes common problems on software projects and suggests how to eliminate them by changing the architecture or project organization.

[APLfPW]

A Pattern Language for Pattern Writing

In: *Pattern Languages of Program Design 3* [PLoPD3], pp. 529–574.
Published by: Addison-Wesley (1998)
By: Gerard Meszaros and James Doble

> As the patterns community has accumulated experience in writing and reviewing patterns and pattern languages, we have begun to develop insight into pattern-writing techniques and approaches that have been observed to be particularly effective at addressing certain recurring problems. This pattern language attempts to capture some of these "best practices" of pattern writing, both by describing them in pattern form and by demonstrating them in action. As such, this pattern language is its own running example.

Further Reading

> Full text of this paper is available online in PDF form at http://Pattern-WritingPatterns.gerardmeszaros.com and in HTML form, complete with a hyperlinked table of contents, at http://hillside.net/patterns/writing/pattern-writingpaper.htm.

[ARTRP]

Agile Regression Testing Using Record and Playback

http://AgileRegressionTestPaper.gerardmeszaros.com
By: Gerard Meszaros and Ralph Bohnet

> This paper was presented at XP/Agile Universe 2003. It describes how we built a "record and playback" test mechanism into a safety-critical application to make it easier to regression test it as it was ported from OS2 to Windows.

[CJ2EEP]

Core J2EE™ Patterns, Second Edition: Best Practices and Design Strategies

Published by: Prentice Hall (2003)
ISBN: 0-131-42246-4
By: Deepak Alur, Dan Malks, and John Crupi

> This book catalogs the core patterns of usage of Enterprise Java Beans (EJB), which are a key part of the Java 2 Enterprise Edition. Examples include Session Facade [CJ2EEP].

[DDD]

Domain-Driven Design: Tackling Complexity in the Heart of Software

Published by: Addison-Wesley (2004)
ISBN: 0-321-12521-5
By: Eric Evans

> This book is a good introduction to the process of using a domain model as the heart of a software system.

> *Readers learn how to use a domain model to make complex development effort more focused and dynamic. A core of best practices and standard patterns provides a common language for the development team.*

[ET]

Endo-Testing

http://www.connextra.com/aboutUs/mockobjects.pdf
By: Tim Mackinnon, Steve Freeman, and Philip Craig

This paper, which was presented at XP 2000 in Sardinia, describes the use of *Mock Objects* (page 544) to facilitate testing of the behavior of an object by monitoring its behavior while it is executing.

> *Unit testing is a fundamental practice in eXtreme Programming, but most nontrivial code is difficult to test in isolation. It is hard to avoid writing test suites that are complex, incomplete, and difficult to maintain and interpret. Using Mock Objects for unit testing improves both domain code and test suites. These objects allow unit tests to be written for everything, simplify test structure, and avoid polluting domain code with testing infrastructure.*

[FaT]

Frameworks and Testing

In: *Proceedings of XP2002*
http://www.agilealliance.org/articles/roockstefanframeworks/file
By: Stefan Roock

This paper is mandatory reading for framework builders. It describes four kinds of automated testing that should accompany a framework, including the ability to test a plug-in's compliance with the framework's protocol and a testing framework that makes it easier to test applications built on the framework.

[FitB]

Fit for Developing Software

Published by: Addison-Wesley (2005)
ISBN: 0-321-26934-9
By: Rick Mugridge and Ward Cunningham

> This book is a great introduction to the use of *Data-Driven Tests* (page 288) for preparing customer tests, whether as part of agile or traditional projects. This is what I wrote for inclusion as "advance praise":

> *Wow! This is the book I wish I had on my desk when I did my first storytest-driven development project. It explains the philosophy behind the Fit framework and a process for using it to interact with the customers to help define the requirements of the project. It makes Fit so easy and approachable that I wrote my first FitNesse tests before I even I finished the book.*

Further Reading

> More information on Fit can be found at Ward's Web site, http://fit.c2.com.

[GOF]

Design Patterns: Elements of Reusable Object-Oriented Software

Published by: Addison-Wesley (1995)
ISBN: 0-201-63361-2
By: Erich Gamma, Richard Helm, Ralph Johnson, and John M.Vlissides

> This book started the patterns movement. In it, the "Gang of Four" describe 23 recurring patterns in object-oriented software systems. Examples include Composite [GOF], Factory Method [GOF], and Facade [GOF].

[HoN]
Hierarchy of Needs

From Wikipedia [Wp]:

Maslow's hierarchy of needs is a theory in psychology that Abraham Maslow proposed in his 1943 paper "A Theory of Human Motivation," which he subsequently extended. His theory contends that as humans meet "basic needs," they seek to satisfy successively "higher needs" that occupy a set hierarchy. . . .

Maslow's hierarchy of needs is often depicted as a pyramid consisting of five levels: The four lower levels are grouped together as deficiency needs associated with physiological needs, while the top level is termed growth needs associated with psychological needs. While our deficiency needs must be met, our being needs are continually shaping our behavior. The basic concept is that the higher needs in this hierarchy only come into focus once all the needs that are lower down in the pyramid are mainly or entirely satisfied. Growth forces create upward movement in the hierarchy, whereas regressive forces push prepotent needs farther down the hierarchy.

[IEAT]
Improving the Effectiveness of Automated Tests

http://FasterTestsPaper.gerardmeszaros.com.
By: Gerard Meszaros, Shaun Smith, and Jennitta Andrea

This paper was presented at XP2001 in Sardinia, Italy. It describes a number of issues that reduce the speed and effectiveness of automated unit tests and suggests ways to address them.

[IXP]
Industrial XP

http://ixp.industriallogic.com.

Industrial XP is a "branded" variant of eXtreme Programming created by Joshua Kerievsky of Industrial Logic. It includes a number of practices required to scale eXtreme Programming to work in larger enterprises, such as "Project Chartering."

[JBrains]

JetBrains

http://www.jetbrains.com.

> *JetBrains* builds software development tools that automate (among other things) refactoring. Its Web site contains a list of all refactorings that the company's various tools support, including some that are not described in [Ref].

[JNI]

JUnit New Instance

http://www.martinfowler.com/bliki/JunitNewInstance.html

> This article by Martin Fowler provides the background for why it makes sense for JUnit and many of its ports to create a new instance of the *Testcase Class* (page 373) for each *Test Method* (page 348).

[JuPG]

JUnit Pocket Guide

Published by: O'Reilly
ISBN: 0-596-00743-4
By: Kent Beck

> This 80-page, small-format book is an excellent summary of key features of JUnit and best practices for writing tests. Being small enough to fit in a pocket, it doesn't go into much detail, but it does give us an idea of what is possible and where to look for details.

[LSD]

Lean Software Development : An Agile Toolkit

Published by: Addison-Wesley (2003)
ISBN: 0-321-15078-3
By: Mary Poppendieck and Tom Poppendieck

> This excellent book describes 22 "thinking tools" that are used to work quickly and effectively in many domains. The authors describe how to apply these tools to software development. If you want to understand *why* agile development methods work, this book is a *must read!*

[MAS]

Mocks Aren't Stubs

http://www.martinfowler.com/articles/mocksArentStubs.html

By: Martin Fowler

> This article clarifies the difference between *Mock Objects* (page 544) and *Test Stubs* (page 529). It goes on to describe the two fundamentally different approaches to test-driven development engendered by these differences: "classical TDD" versus "mockist TDD."

[MRNO]

Mock Roles, Not Objects

Paper presented at OOPSLA 2004 in Vancouver, British Columbia, Canada.

By: Steve Freeman, Tim Mackinnon, Nat Pryce, and Joe Walnes

> This paper describes the use of *Mock Objects* (page 544) to help the developer discover the signatures of the objects on which the class being designed and tested depends. This approach allows the design of the supporting classes to be deferred until after the client classes have been coded and tested. Members can obtain this paper at the ACM portal http://portal.acm.org/ft_gateway.cfm?id=1028765&type=pdf; nonmembers of the ACM can find it at http://joe.truemesh.com/MockRoles.pdf.

[PEAA]

Patterns of Enterprise Application Architecture

Published by: Addison-Wesley (2003)

ISBN: 0-321-12742-0

By: Martin Fowler

> This book is an indispensable handbook of architectural patterns that are applicable to any enterprise application platform. It is a great way to understand how the various approaches to developing large business systems differ.

[PiJV1]

Patterns in Java, Volume 1: A Catalog of Reusable Design Patterns Illustrated with UML

Published by: Wiley Publishing (2002)
ISBN: 0-471-22729-3
By: Mark Grand

A catalog of design patterns commonly used in Java.

Further Reading
http://www.markgrand.com/id1.html

[PLoPD3]

Pattern Languages of Program Design 3

Published by: Addison-Wesley (1998)
ISBN: 0-201-31011-2
Edited by: Robert C. Martin, Dirk Riehle, and Frank Buschmann

A collection of patterns originally workshopped at the Pattern Languages of Programs (PLoP) conferences.

[POSA2]

Pattern-Oriented Software Architecture, Volume 2: Patterns for Concurrent and Networked Objects

Published by: Wiley & Sons (2000)
ISBN: 0-471-60695-2
By: Douglas Schmidt, Michael Stal, Hans Robert, and Frank Buschmann

This book is the second volume in the highly acclaimed *Pattern-Oriented Software Architecture* (POSA) series. POSA1 was published in 1996; hence this book is referred to as POSA2. It presents 17 interrelated patterns that cover core elements of building concurrent and networked systems: service access and configuration, event handling, synchronization, and concurrency.

[PUT]

Pragmatic Unit Testing

Published by: Pragmatic Bookshelf
ISBN: 0-9745140-2-0 (*In C# with NUnit*)
ISBN: 0-9745140-1-2 (*In Java with JUnit*)
By: Andy Hunt and Dave Thomas

> This book by the "pragmatic programmers" introduces the concept of automated unit testing in a very approachable way. Both versions lower the entry barriers by focusing on the essentials without belaboring the finer points. They also include a very good section on how to determine which tests you need to write for a particular class or method.

[RDb]

Refactoring Databases: Evolutionary Database Design

Published by: Addison-Wesley (2006)
ISBN: 0-321-29353-3
By: Pramodkumar J. Sadalage and Scott W. Ambler

> This book is a good introduction to techniques for applying agile principles to development of database-dependent software. It describes techniques for eliminating the need to do "big design up front" on the database. It deserves to be on the bookshelf of every agile developer who needs to work with a database. A summary of the contents can be found at http://www.ambysoft.com/books/refactoringDatabases.html.

[Ref]

Refactoring: Improving the Design of Existing Code

Published by: Addison-Wesley (1999)
ISBN: 0-201-48567-2
By: Martin Fowler et al.

> This book offers a good introduction to the process of refactoring software. It introduces a number of "code smells" and suggests ways to refactor the code to eliminate those smells.

[RTC]

Refactoring Test Code

Paper presented at XP2001 in Sardinia, Italy

By: Arie van Deursen, Leon Moonen, Alex van den Bergh, and Gerard Kok

> This paper was the first to apply the concept of "code smells" to test code. It described a collection of 12 "test smells" and proposed a set of refactorings that could be used to improve the code. The original paper can be found at http://homepages.cwi.nl/~leon/papers/xp2001/xp2001.pdf.

[RtP]

Refactoring to Patterns

Published by: Addison-Wesley (2005)

ISBN: 0-321-21335-1

By: Joshua Kerievsky

> This book deals with the marriage of refactoring (the process of improving the design of existing code) with patterns (the classic solutions to recurring design problems). *Refactoring to Patterns* suggests that using patterns to improve an existing design is a better approach than using patterns early in a new design, whether the code is years old or minutes old. We can improve designs with patterns by applying sequences of low-level design transformations, known as refactorings.

[SBPP]

Smalltalk Best Practice Patterns

Published by: Prentice Hall (1997)

ISBN: 0-13-476904-X

By: Kent Beck

> This book describes low-level programming patterns that are used in good object-oriented software. On the back cover, Martin Fowler wrote:
>
> > *Kent's Smalltalk style is the standard I aim to emulate in my work. This book does not just set that standard, but also explains why it is the standard. Every Smalltalk developer should have it close at hand.*
>
> While Smalltalk is no longer the dominant object-oriented development language, many of the patterns established by Smalltalk programmers have been adopted as the standard way of doing things in the mainstream object-oriented development languages. The patterns in this book remain highly relevant even if the examples are in Smalltalk.

[SCMP]

Software Configuration Management Patterns: Effective Teamwork, Practical Integration

Published by: Addison-Wesley (2003)
ISBN: 0-201-74117-1
By: Steve Berczuk (with Brad Appleton)

> This book describes, in pattern form, the how's and why's of using a source code configuration management system to synchronize the activities of multiple developers on a project. The practices described here are equally applicable to agile and traditional projects.

Further Reading

> http://www.scmpatterns.com
>
> http://www.scmpatterns.com/book/pattern-summary.html

[SoC]

Secrets of Consulting: A Guide to Giving and Getting Advice Successfully

Published by: Dorset House (1985)
ISBN: 0-932633-01-3
By: Gerald M. Weinberg

> Full of Gerry's laws and rules, such as "The Law of Raspberry Jam: The farther you spread it, the thinner it gets."

[TAM]

Test Automation Manifesto

http://TestAutomationManifesto.gerardmeszaros.com
By: Shaun Smith and Gerard Meszaros

> This paper was presented at the August 2003 XP/Agile Universe meeting in New Orleans, Louisiana. It describes a number of principles that should be followed to make automated testing using xUnit cost-effective.

[TDD-APG]

Test-Driven Development: A Practical Guide

Published by: Prentice Hall (2004)
ISBN: 0-13-101649-0
By: David Astels

> This book provides a good introduction to the process of driving software development with unit tests. Part III of the book is an end-to-end example of using tests to drive a small Java project.

[TDD-BE]

Test-Driven Development: By Example

Published by: Addison-Wesley (2003)
ISBN: 0-321-14653-0
By: Kent Beck

> This book provides a good introduction to the process of driving software development with unit tests. In the second part of the book, Kent illustrates TDD by building a *Test Automation Framework* (page 298) in Python. In an approach he likens to "doing brain surgery on yourself," he uses the emerging framework to run the tests he writes for each new capability. It is a very good example of both TDD and bootstrapping.

[TDD.Net]

Test-Driven Development in Microsoft .NET

Published by: Microsoft Press (2004)
ISBN: 0-735-61948-4
By: James W. Newkirk and Alexei A. Vorontsov

> This book is a good introduction to the test-driven development process and the tools used to do it in Microsoft's. Net development environment.

[TI]

Test Infected

http://junit.sourceforge.net/doc/testinfected/testing.htm
By: Eric Gamma and Kent Beck

> This article was first published in the *Java Report* issue called "Test Infected—Programmers Love Writing Tests." It has been credited by some as being what led to the meteoric rise in JUnit's popularity. This article is an excellent introduction to the how's and why's of test automation using xUnit.

[TPS]

Toyota Production System: Beyond Large-Scale Production
Published by: Productivity Press (1995)
ISBN: 0-915-2991-4-3
By: Taiichi Ohno

> This book, which was written by the father of just-in-time manufacturing, describes how Toyota came up with the system driven by its need to produce a small number of cars while realizing economies of scale. Among the techniques described here are "kanban" and the "five why's."

[UTF]

Unit Test Frameworks: Tools for High-Quality Software Development
Published by: O'Reilly (2004)
ISBN: 0-596-00689-6
By: Paul Hamill

> This book is a brief introduction to the most popular implementations of xUnit.

[UTwHCM]

Unit Testing with Hand-Crafted Mocks
http://refactoring.be/articles/mocks/mocks.html
By: Sven Gorts

> This paper summarizes and names a number of idioms related to *Hand-Built Test Doubles* (see *Configurable Test Double* on page 522)—specifically, *Test Stubs* (page 529) and *Mock Objects* (page 544). Sven Gorts writes:

>> *Many of the unit tests I wrote over the last couple of years use mock objects in order to test the behavior of a component in isolation of the rest of the system. So far, despite the availability of various mocking frameworks, each of the mock classes I've used has been handwritten. In this article I do some retrospection and try to wrap up the mocking idioms I've found most useful.*

[UTwJ]

Unit Testing in Java: How Tests Drive the Code

Published by: Morgan Kaufmann
ISBN: 1-55860-868-0
By: Johannes Link, with contributions by Peter Fröhlich

> This book does a very nice job of introducing many of the concepts and techniques of unit testing. It uses intertwined narratives and examples to introduce a wide range of techniques. Unfortunately, due to the format, it can be difficult to find something at a later time.

[VCTP]

The Virtual Clock Test Pattern

http://www.nusco.org/docs/virtual_clock.pdf
By: Paolo Perrotta

> This paper describes a common example of a *Responder* called Virtual Clock [VCTP]. The author uses the *Virtual Clock Test Pattern* as a Decorator [GOF] for the real system clock, which allows the time to be "frozen" or resumed. One could use a *Hard-Coded Test Stub* or a *Configurable Test Stub* just as easily for most tests. Paolo Perrotta summarizes the thrust of his article:
>
> > *We can have a hard time unit-testing code that depends on the system clock. This paper describes both the problem and a common, reusable solution.*

[WEwLC]

Working Effectively with Legacy Code

Published by: Prentice Hall (2005)
ISBN: 0-13-117705-2
By: Michael Feathers

> This book describes how to get your legacy software system back under control by retrofitting automated unit tests. A key contribution is a set of "dependency-breaking techniques"—mostly refactorings—that can help you isolate the software for the purpose of automated testing.

[Wp]
Wikipedia

From Wikipedia [Wp]: "Wikipedia is a multilingual, Web-based free content encyclopedia project. The name Wikipedia is a blend of the words 'wiki' and 'encyclopedia.' Wikipedia is written collaboratively by volunteers, allowing most articles to be changed by almost anyone with access to the Web site."

[WWW]
World Wide Web

A reference annotation of [WWW] indicates that the information was found on the World Wide Web. You can use your favorite search engine to find a copy by searching for it by the title.

[XP123]
XP123

http://xp123.com
Web site hosted by: William Wake

A Web site hosting various resources for teams doing eXtreme Programming.

[XPC]
XProgramming.com

http://xprogramming.com
Web site hosted by: Ron Jeffries

A Web site hosting various resources for teams doing eXtreme Programming. One of the better places to look for links to software downloads for unit test automation tools including members of the xUnit family.

[XPE]

eXtreme Programming Explained, Second Edition: Embrace Change

Published by: Addison-Wesley (2005)

ISBN: 0-321-27865-8

By: Kent Beck

> This book kick-started the eXtreme Programming movement. The first edition (0-201-61641-6) described a recipe consisting of 12 practices backed by principles and values. The second edition focuses more on the values and principles. It breaks the practices into a primary set and a corollary set; the latter set should be attempted only after the primary practices are mastered. Among the practices both editions describe are pair programming and test-driven development.

Index

Q

QA (quality assurance), 22–23
QaRun, 244
QTP (QuickTest Professional)
    Data-Driven Tests, 290
    defined, 756
    record and playback tools, 282
    Test Automation
      Framework, 301
quality assurance (QA), 22–23
QuickTest Professional (QTP).
  See QTP (QuickTest Professional)

R

random values
    Nondeterministic Tests, 238
    Random Generated Values, 724
Record and Playback Test, 13
record and playback tools
    introduction, xxxi
    Recorded Tests, 282–283
    xUnit sweet spot, 58
Recorded Test
    built-in test recording,
      281–282
    commercial record and
      playback tool, 282–283
    customer testing, 5
    Data-Driven Tests and, 289
    implementation, 280–281
    Interface Sensitivity, 241
    overview, 278–279
    refactored commercial recorded
      tests, 283–284
    vs. Scripted Tests, 286
    smells, 10
    tools, 56
    tools for automating, 53–54
    when to use, 279–280
Recording Test Stub. *See* Test Spy

red bar, 807
Refactored Recorded Tests
    commercial, 283–284
    overview, 280
refactoring. *See also* test refactorings
    Assertion Message, 372
    Assertion Method, 368
    Automated Teardown,
      506–507
    Back Door Manipulation, 333
    Chained Test, 458
    Configurable Test Double, 463
    Creation Method, 420
    Custom Assertion, 480
    Database Sandbox, 653
    Data-Driven Test, 294
    defined, 807
    Delegated Setup, 413
    Delta Assertion, 488
    Dependency Injection, 682
    Dependency Lookup, 690–691
    Derived Value, 720
    Dummy Object, 731
    Fake Object, 555–556
    Fresh Fixture, 315–316
    Garbage-Collected
      Teardown, 502
    Generated Value, 725
    Guard Assertion, 492
    Hard-Coded Test Double, 572
    Humble Object, 702
    Implicit Setup, 427
    Implicit Teardown, 518–519
    In-line Setup, 410
    In-line Teardown, 512
    Layer Test, 342
    Lazy Setup, 439
    Literal Value, 716
    Mock Object, 548
    Named Test Suite, 594
    Parameterized Test, 611

U

UAT (user acceptance tests)
  defined, 817
  principles, 42
UI (User Interface) tests
  asynchronous tests, 70–71
  Hard-To-Test Code, 71–72
  tools, 55
UML (Unified Modeling
  Language), 816
Unconfigurable Test Doubles, 527
unexpected exceptions, 352
Unfinished Test Assertion, 494–497
Unfinished Test Method from
  Template, 496–497
Unified Modeling Language
  (UML), 816
unique resources, 737–738
Unit Testing with Java (Link), 743
unit tests
  defined, 817
  introduction, 6
  per-functionality, 51
  rules, 307
  Scripted Tests, 285–287
  xUnit vs. Fit, 290–292
unnecessary object elimination,
  303–304
Unrepeatable Test
  database testing, 169
  Erratic Test cause, 234–235
  introduction, 15, 64
  persistent fresh fixtures, 96
  vs. Repeatable Test, 26–27
Untestable Test Code
  avoiding Conditional Logic,
    119–121
  Hard-To-Test Code, 211–212

Untested Code
  alternative path verification,
    178–179
  indirect inputs and, 126
  Isolate the SUT, 43
  minimizing, 44–45
  preventing with Test Doubles,
    523
  Production Bugs, 271–272
  unit testing, 6
Untested Requirement
  Frequent Debugging cause,
    249
  indirect output testing, 127
  preventing with Test
    Doubles, 523
  Production Bugs cause,
    272–274
  reducing via Isolate the
    SUT, 43
usability tests, 53
use cases, 817
Use the Front Door First
  defined, 40–41
  Overspecified Software
    avoidance, 246
user acceptance tests (UAT)
  defined, 817
  principles, 42
User Interface (UI) tests
  asynchronous tests, 70–71
  Hard-To-Test Code, 71–72
  tools, 55
user story
  defined, 817
  Testcase Class per, 625
utility methods. *See* Test Utility
  Method
utPLSQL, 750

THIS BOOK IS SAFARI ENABLED

INCLUDES FREE 45-DAY ACCESS TO THE ONLINE EDITION

The Safari® Enabled icon on the cover of your favorite technology book means the book is available through Safari Bookshelf. When you buy this book, you get free access to the online edition for 45 days.

Safari Bookshelf is an electronic reference library that lets you easily search thousands of technical books, find code samples, download chapters, and access technical information whenever and wherever you need it.

TO GAIN 45-DAY SAFARI ENABLED ACCESS TO THIS BOOK:

- Go to **http://www.awprofessional.com/safarienabled**
- Complete the brief registration form
- Enter the coupon code found in the front of this book on the "Copyright" page

Addison
Wesley

If you have difficulty registering on Safari Bookshelf or accessing the online edition, please e-mail customer-service@safaribooksonline.com.

List of Smells

Assertion Roulette (224): It is hard to tell which of several assertions within the same test method caused a test failure. Includes **Eager Test, Missing Assertion Message.**

Buggy Tests (260): Bugs are regularly found in the automated tests. Includes **Fragile Test, Hard-to-Test Code, Obscure Test.**

Conditional Test Logic (200): A test contains code that may or may not be executed. Includes **Complex Teardown, Conditional Verification Logic, Flexible Test, Multiple Test Conditions, Production Logic in Test.**

Developers Not Writing Tests (263): Developers aren't writing automated tests. Includes **Hard-to-Test Code, Not Enough Time, Wrong Test Automation Strategy.**

Erratic Test (228): One or more tests are behaving erratically; sometimes they pass and sometimes they fail. Includes **Interacting Test Suites, Interacting Tests, Lonely Test, Nondeterministic Test, Resource Leakage, Resource Optimism, Test Run War, Unrepeatable Test.**

Fragile Test (239): A test fails to compile or run when the SUT is changed in ways that do not affect the part the test is exercising. Includes **Behavior Sensitivity, Context Sensitivity, Data Sensitivity, Fragile Fixture, Interface Sensitivity, Overspecified Software, Sensitive Equality.**

Frequent Debugging (248): Manual debugging is required to determine the cause of most test failures.

Hard-to-Test Code (209): Code is difficult to test. Includes **Asynchronous Code, Hard-Coded Dependency, Highly Coupled Code, Untestable Test Code.**

High Test Maintenance Cost (265): Too much effort is spent maintaining existing tests. Includes **Fragile Test, Hard-to-Test Code, Obscure Test.**

Manual Intervention (250): A test requires a person to perform some manual action each time it is run. Includes **Manual Event Injection, Manual Fixture Setup, Manual Result Verification.**

Obscure Test (186): It is difficult to understand the test at a glance. Includes **Eager Test, General Fixture, Hard-Coded Test Data, Indirect Testing, Irrelevant Information, Mystery Guest.**

Production Bugs (268): We find too many bugs during formal test or in production. Includes **Infrequently Run Tests, Lost Test, Missing Unit Test, Neverfail Test, Untested Code, Untested Requirement.**

Slow Tests (253): The tests take too long to run. Includes **Asynchronous Test, General Fixture, Slow Component Usage, Too Many Tests.**

Test Code Duplication (213): The same test code is repeated many times. Includes **Cut-and-Paste Code Reuse, Reinventing the Wheel.**

Test Logic in Production (217): The code that is put into production contains logic that should be exercised only during tests. Includes **Equality Pollution, For Tests Only, Test Dependency in Production, Test Hook.**